Britain and Victory
in the Great War

Britain and Victory in the Great War

Edited by

Peter Liddle

Pen & Sword
MILITARY

First published in Great Britain in 2018 by
PEN & SWORD MILITARY
an imprint of
Pen & Sword Books Ltd
47 Church Street
Barnsley
South Yorkshire
S70 2AS

ISBN: 978 1 47389 161 6

Typeset in Ehrhardt MT 10/12 by
Aura Technology and Software Services, India

Printed and bound in Great Britain by TJ International Ltd, Padstow, Cornwall

Pen & Sword Books Ltd incorporates the imprints of Pen & Sword Archaeology,
Atlas, Aviation, Battleground, Discovery, Family History, History, Maritime, Military,
Naval, Politics, Railways, Select, Social History, Transport, True Crime, and Claymore
Press, Frontline Books, Leo Cooper, Praetorian Press, Remember When, Seaforth
Publishing and Wharncliffe.

For a complete list of Pen & Sword titles please contact
PEN & SWORD BOOKS LIMITED
47 Church Street, Barnsley, South Yorkshire, S70 2AS, England
E-mail: enquiries@pen-and-sword.co.uk
Website: www.pen-and-sword.co.uk

Dedication

This book is dedicated to all the Great War men and women and their families who over more than two decades generously, in so many ways, helped the Editor's work in forming what became the First World War archive at the University of Leeds, the Liddle Collection. Inseparable from this memory is that of the teams of volunteers first in the Sunderland, Wearside, area, then around Leeds, who gave exceptional unstinting support in enhancing the collection and then finally those who achieved the archive's long-term security at Leeds.

Contents

List of Plates

List of Maps

Acknowledgements

As in the previous volumes of this trilogy on the Great War I have had the privilege of colleagues whose intellectual labour has been given generously amidst their many commitments. I am fully mindful of their kindness: the thinking, planning, research and then drawing it all together, and I do not forget their other commitments. Additionally, as I sincerely express my thanks and admiration, I have had help from a number of my colleagues by their introducing me to historians with whom I had no previous link. From such sources came scholarship further to enhance the book.

Next, on behalf of all the chapter authors, formally I thank the trustees of institutions and officers of agencies for all necessary permissions granted to reproduce illustrations and quotations. As Editor and on behalf of the contributors to this volume specifically I thank the authorities at the Australian War Memorial, Canberra, the Canadian War Museum, Ottawa, the National Library of Scotland, the Liddell Hart Centre for Military Archives, the Imperial War Museum, The Liddle Collection at the Brotherton Library, University of Leeds, the Museum of the Green Howards, Richmond, North Yorkshire, the Anne S.K. Brown Military Collection, Brown University Library, Providence, Rhode Island, USA, the Ivor Gurney Society, and Dr Daniele Serofini at the Museo Baracca, Lugo, Italy. I have reason to thank too, Martin Routledge of Sunderland Museum and Winter Gardens, Julian Harrop of Beamish Museum, Imogen Holmes-Roe of the National Coalmining Museum, Jack Inch, Wesley Gargett and colleagues at the Durham Mining Museum at Spennymoor, and Chris Baker of 'The Long Long Trail' for their readily given help in searching for suitable photographs and maps. David Newton's work in translation of the Italian chapter is also gratefully acknowledged.

It is then my pleasure to thank Rupert Harding of Pen and Sword for his vision and sustained support in commissioning and seeing this trilogy through to publication. It is with kindred pleasure that I thank Stephen Chumbley, the copy editor, who brought sharp-eyed, well-informed judgement to bear on this final volume, cover to cover.

At every stage of pre-publication formatting, and research for suitable illustrations and maps, my beloved wife, Louise, has been an essential, not just an invaluable, help. Altogether, I have been very fortunate.

Peter Liddle,
Mickley, North Yorkshire, June, 2017.

Preface

The publication of the final volume of a trilogy is a time for reflection as well as for relief. The Editor's vision for each volume was that it must include, according to the stage of the war it was covering, chapters on topics which the reader had every right to expect. For the first volume for example, why Britain entered the war, for the second, chapters on Gallipoli and the Somme, and for the third, how and why the war was won on the Western Front and worldwide. However, the aim was to offer more than this in each volume. There would also be consideration of fundamentally important topics which could not be circumscribed by a three-section chronological timescale and here for example, medical advances, the Indian Army, the use and treatment of animals, weaponry, religion, pacifism, or the creative arts. This concluding volume follows the original intention.

The British contribution to the achievement of victory is examined here first from a military perspective in an extended introduction arguing convincingly that in training, weaponry and tactics the British Expeditionary Force showed a capacity adaptively to learn from the 1916 experience. The argument advanced demonstrably demolishes what is left of any preconception of sustained, unimaginative, military incompetence. In this introduction, Edward Spiers identifies with the view expressed within Peter Simkins' book, *From the Somme to Victory*, that those studying the war know that constructive developments were taking place but there is still work to be done convincing sections of the media, and large-scale public assumption that castigation of senior levels of BEF command still needs reasoned rebuttal and on occasion summary dismissal as the prejudice of ignorance.

Niall Barr's masterly chapter on the dramatic 100 Days follows naturally from Edward Spiers' Introduction, stressing not merely the Allied nature of success won on the Western Front but the inappropriateness of seeking in this campaign, or indeed in any other area of the war effort, an exclusively defining factor to which victory may be attributed.

It is entirely in accord with Niall's verdict that the reader is not encouraged simply to focus on battlefield endeavour. Matthew Richardson lays out clearly that the essential base for maintaining a prolonged Great Power struggle was increasing development of industrial mass production. In Britain's case this was not always a story of worker/management/government unity. Matthew's locational focus is upon the East Midlands but achievements and industrial issues arising on Clydeside, the North East of England, Merseyside and Yorkshire are represented in a way which leaves no doubt about the fact that manpower – in a non-gender sense – industrial enterprise, adaptation and invention were at the heart of what was accomplished by 11 November 1918.

It is widely recognised that British propaganda proved a critically significant weapon from the opening of hostilities but how this 'weapon' was located and manned, and its 'fire' precisely aimed, are less well-known, a subject illuminatingly tackled by David Welch.

In a persuasively argued, challenging manner, the reader is next encouraged by an American historian, George Cassar, to question over-readily reached judgements on the comparative record of two of Britain's political leaders during the war, Lord Kitchener and David Lloyd George, in guiding the nation through its ordeal. In an emphasis on the soldiering wisdom of Kitchener, Cassar, with a wartime biography of Asquith as well as his books on Kitchener and Lloyd George, might have been tempted to turn on its head a celebrated quotation attributed to Clemenceau, leaving it as 'war is too serious a matter to be left to the politicians'.

Attention to the invaluable contribution of three Commonwealth nations is appropriately drawn by distinguished historians from their countries, Peter Burness from Australia, Tim Cook from Canada, and Chris Pugsley from New Zealand. The wider imperial military effort in campaigns to defeat the Ottoman Empire in Palestine and in Mesopotamia, the Bulgarians in Macedonia and the German-led force in East Africa, is a significant element in the strategic account by Rob Johnson of how the war was won beyond the Western Front.

In chapters necessarily balancing too Anglo-centric a view on the winning of the Great War, Bill Philpott vehemently asserts that the prime position on the victor's rostrum should be taken by France and to think otherwise is to parrot the self-promotion of the British Western Front Commander-in-Chief's post-war published reports and diary and the work of his advocates. How ironic it is to see Sir Douglas Haig, whom many see as disgracefully traduced by the memoirs and histories written by his political wartime 'colleagues', here similarly accused of shamefully belittling the French military performance in the final year of the war.

More revisionist thinking is put forward by Chris Bellamy who, with conviction to match that of Philpott, argues that to forget, by reason of revolutions and defeat, the Russian contribution to ultimate victory, is wilfully to distort the overall reality of what brought the Central Powers to their knees. Furthermore, the American, Ross Kennedy, corrects what is left of any British self-satisfaction in claiming the lion's share of honour in victory. He makes clear, first, that American neutrality was not balanced with regard to the western European antagonists but strikingly skewed in favour of Britain and France, massively assisting their war effort; second, President Wilson's hard-line diplomacy in dismissing German efforts to achieve the terms they sought in ending the war; and third, draws attention to the potential as well as the actual contribution of the United States in draining the spirit of any further worthwhile endeavour from Germany.

An international perspective is not limited to France, Russia and the United States, because from the Allied and associated powers, the way in which sectional interests in Italy viewed a war which had brought such suffering and for such disappointing reward, is comprehensively examined by Italian historians Irene Guerrini and Marco Pluviano. Reinforcing the international perspective, but self-evidently essential too, there are chapters which focus upon Germany, one by an acknowledged German army expert, Jack Sheldon, on the Western Front during the period of the Allied counter-attacks in 1918, and one by German historian Holger Afflerbach, on the German attempts and their failure to secure an armistice on terms avoiding humiliation.

Most of the chapters indicate the longer-term consequences of the topic upon which the author focuses, but this is soft-pedalled rather than stressed by the Israeli military historian Yigal Sheffy. His detailed examination of Allenby's campaign in

Palestine rather nicely traces the wartime transition of Britain's policy in the Middle East from that of collaborative concession towards France, in particular of her allies, to a far narrower concentration on British Imperial interests and then, Yigal, more provocatively, challenges the received wisdom of laudatory acclaim for the imaginative brilliance of Allenby's strategy.

National identity, together with, or separate from, national unity, has for some time now in the twenty-first century in the United Kingdom been a confrontationally debated issue. Much the same could be said of Britain in July 1914. Ian Whitehead draws from crises at the time and the judgements of numerous historians to illustrate how the 'propaganda gifts' of Germany early in the war forged out of disarray a British unity which survived the war but has in varying degree and for a range of reasons, remained intermittently under challenge during the century to follow. That is of course with the unsurprising exception of the years of the Second World War. In exploring his theme of British identity and the Great War, Ian looks at the verdict reached by politicians writing about the conduct of the war from their perspective and others verbally scourging 'guilty generals'. These lacerations, whether inflicted as self-defence by the politicians or from self-righteous wrath by critics in tune with different times and values, achieved their objective of lastingly influencing the public's perception of the war.

All these viewpoints came together at the centenary commemorations which themselves sometimes adjusted, or should have been adjusted, by the work of historians with argument and evidence to challenge prevailing misperceptions. However, as Ian convincingly explains, new influences on national identity and those dating from long ago, oxygenated by dissatisfaction with a continuing English-defined Britishness, continue to play a part in an issue far from being resolved.

The history of battlefield tourism, a topic handled by Clive Harris, has a time-span which dates quite extraordinarily from before the guns fell silent in France and Belgium, to today when it is 'big business'. Clive accounts for the falls and rises in this phenomenon; the veteran pilgrimage nature of the earliest venturers; and then the more recently varied but sometimes linked motivation for such tourism – school education, family pilgrimage, general interest and, for more scholarly understanding, on-site exploration by historians, biographers and those with a range of potential specialist interests.

Strictly more wartime-oriented is Kate Kennedy's work on musicians, composition and the link to contemporary poetry, a link demonstrably evident but deserving far more attention than commonly it receives. However, with regard to the focus of her research, Phylomena Badsey stresses the need to look back for historical context as she documents convincingly that those women campaigning for the vote who followed the wartime lead of Millicent Garrett Fawcett of the National Union of Women's Suffrage Societies, and of Emmeline Pankhurst and her daughter, Christabel, for the Women's Social and Political Union, were markedly influential in urging and organising a women's war effort. In due course they were to achieve the aim of the cause which had brought them together. Dr Badsey judges that there could be no question of the clock being turned back: women's war work and the logic of 'the cause' had permanently transformed the standing of women in British society.

The eyebrows of air-minded readers of this Preface may have been quizzically raised at there being no chapter dedicated to the part played by the RAF in winning the war.

Such a decision was made because with limitations upon the numbers of aircraft and again limitations upon their performance capability, to say nothing of the variable meteorological conditions, the British air arm, the RAF from April 1918, could only be a supportive rather than a major factor in the final year of the war. No matter the wisdom or otherwise of that decision, the contribution of the Royal Navy towards Allied victory has never been doubted. Duncan Redford had established this case so conclusively in the second volume of this series in a chapter on Jutland that in this volume, with the significance of Jutland and blockade re-stressed, his focus moves forward to the Armistice and beyond. The internment then scuttling of the High Seas Fleet, the issue of disarmament and then the Royal Navy's internal disputatious scrutiny of leadership at Jutland, all stimulatingly claim his attention.

Fully bearing in mind that this is the concluding volume of a trilogy on Britain and the Great War there could scarcely be a more appropriate topic upon which to reflect than the loss and devastation wrought by the war, something regularly brought to the editor's mind by recent television images of Syria and Iraq with regard to urban devastation, harrowing images of civilian death, wounds and suffering, and then, concerning Iraq perhaps more particularly, the world's loss of cultural heritage just as in France and Belgium in 1914–18. For the Great War, we lament the almost unimaginable loss of life, the mutilation and disablement, the displacement of peoples, the ruined landscape as well as the shell-pulverised villages and towns.

This overwhelmingly tragic topic is reflected on by Nick Bosanquet, but, in corrective balance, Nick counsels the reader not to miss shafts of sunlight illuminating the gloom of the British scene. He draws attention to creditable positive factors limiting the burden upon Britain, factors sadly soon forgotten in the aftermath of the war. While emphasising that we should be more mindful of the fact that the countries within which the war was waged suffered incomparably more severely than Britain, he speculates intriguingly on the longer-term impact upon the United Kingdom, wrong lessons from the war having been learned and the moral fibre of the nation having been worn thin.

And the diplomatic ending of the war – Alan Sharp looks at the constricting, sometimes conflicting framework of wartime promises within which Britain negotiated to achieve her aims – in one, wholly unrealised, the trial, conviction and execution of the Kaiser. We are reminded too of the overshadowing fear of the spread of communism and the more tangible issue of putting restraining limits upon the understandable but dangerously unrealistic French demand for both revenge and future ultra-security. Given the enormous problems to be tackled, Alan is more sympathetic than many in his judgement of the Treaty with Germany and draws different conclusions from those who see the November 1918 Armistice and the June 1919 Treaty of Versailles as marking the beginning of but two decades of truce before emergent ideological issues, progeny of those unresolved factors which had brought the Great Powers to conflict in 1914, unleashed a far greater second war. The latter is the received wisdom but Alan argues that to see the victors' Treaty of Versailles self-evidently condemning them to a renewal of the struggle is too simplistic.

So, a hundred years after the Great War, what soundly-based conclusions may British people draw from it? Well we should be aware first that in posing such a question it needs to be remembered that as a nation we have been transformed by the incoming movement of people whose forbears may well have had their own distinctive experience of the 1914–18 years and that this will influence the reflections of 'new' or more recent Britons. Then, second, the Editor must make it clear that no such question was put to the chapter authors of the three volumes concluded by *Britain and Victory in the Great War* though numerous chapters bear upon this wide-ranging issue. Hence, the Editor accepts sole responsibility for putting forward some thoughts for consideration by those who read this book.

Should the war be seen simply as a human tragedy on a scale so vast as to be scarcely comprehensible but the responsibility for which rests on the failure of diplomacy? To which must be added an hallucinatory mix of capitalist greed, imperial ambition, perceptions of insecurity, a naval arms race, French determination on revenge for 1870–1, Imperial Russia's grasp for a 'unifying cause', and the suicidal lunacy of Serbian complicit involvement in incendiary expansionist ideas. Along such lines might even be added a British readiness to evade, through European war, her own serious problem over Irish Home Rule?

For the human tragedy and the scale, the unequivocal answer is of course yes. For the fact that all the issues listed above were present or were factors in July 1914 in some degree is not to be denied but there really is not much mileage in the failed diplomacy which implies that war was by negotiation avoidable. Most, not all, but most, historians consider that the Central Powers, Germany and Austria-Hungary, bear the major share of blame for the outbreak of war and, as far as Britain was concerned, contentious issues with Germany had largely been settled or were quiescent no matter that there was governmental, armed services, industrialist and popular consciousness of rivalry. Then, could Britain have stayed out of the war?

She could not, and she should not, have stayed out. The Editor has no sympathy with Niall Fergusson's judgement that Britain's entry was an error on the greatest scale. On principle, her treaty obligation to Belgium and her practical and moral obligation to France through the secret military talks with their political implications, removed any justification for evading her responsibilities. Then in practical terms of Britain's national security, allowing France to be defeated would unquestionably imperil Britain with but the English Channel separating her from Germany's military power and appetite. Though there is an historian who sees Britain accepting war in Europe as a means of avoiding civil war in Ireland, or at least delaying having to implement Home Rule with its potentially serious consequences, the Editor is not persuaded in this matter either.

As far as the British conduct of the war in France is concerned, does the 'Lions led by Donkeys' school satisfy serious examination? As has been made clear above, it does not, and several chapter authors address this issue without whitewashing blame when it is due or missed opportunity when that may fairly be judged from evidence available at the time. A balanced case for measured defence of High Command, and in particular Douglas Haig, has been made most recently by Gary Sheffield in several books, most notably, *The Chief*, and the editor has no hesitation in recommending them and Peter Simkins' book cited above.

While by definition war brings death, disablement, devastation, despair and grief; does the Great War have no redeeming features beyond the courage and endurance of its servicemen and some servicewomen too and then the different but related human qualities required of those on the Home Front, something also documented in several chapters in this series? I venture to suggest that from the human spirit was required an unaccustomed selflessness and that this was a positive presence during the war years and that compassion beyond family was called for, another estimable quality which was widely evident. Yes certainly there were redeeming factors and, without any implication that they were 'balancing' factors against the dreadful consequences of war, we should remember medical research and advance, probably the most obvious positive outcome. However, in science, industry, telecommunications and technology for example, there were developments that while being war-directed in origin were markedly beneficial in society post-war. Indubitably these developments would have come in due time but they were precipitated by the conflict.

The advance in the status of women in British society, however limited in economic terms, was similarly a positive consequence of the war. Of course it was due recognition of the vital role they played in the national war effort but again it may be said that the cause for which the women's suffrage movement strove, was precipitated towards success by the war.

Social cohesion, a sense of unity beyond class division – was this improved or changed by the years of war? There is plenty of 1920s memoir and biographical evidence to deny this, some of it unattractive, as pleasure for the wealthy seemed heedlessly pursued while unemployment rose and soup-kitchen queues lengthened, but the overwhelming body of wartime trench documentation – letters, diaries, and indeed retrospective recall too, – testifies to admirable mutual respect and affection across social and income boundaries leaving the editor to conclude that, in respect of an 'unbridgeable class gulf', the war was one thing, post-war something different.

Still searching for positive outcomes from the nihilism of war, we might focus on the creative arts, a subject inviting debate along lines of inspiration by revulsion, by feelings or motives of patriotism, by the commitment to make an official or personal record, or, to paraphrase what the sculptor, Henry Moore, told the Editor: 'because the artist's world was as it was, and it was up to the artist to make something of it'. Painting, sculpture, poetry, prose, music, the theatre, offer countless examples of work of merit rooted in the challenging experience of the Great War.

For all these conclusions, the negative and the positive, it is likely that the Great War will continue to fascinate all those drawn to it as a formative period in our heritage. As for whether the Great War were to have lessons for statesmen and politicians today, this could well be the subject of a whole book. Certainly Woodrow Wilson thought at the time that it could, and despite American 'withdrawal' from Europe, the birth of Czechoslovakia, of Yugoslavia and of the League of Nations largely emerged from his vision.

It has to be asked however, what did the League achieve, what was the fate of Czechoslovakia and, much more recently, what happened to Yugoslavia? Given the indifferent record of the post-Second World War United Nations and now of another supra-national organisation, the European Union, the editor has to admit that searching for the Holy Grail of international amity in the years before, during and in the aftermath of the Great War does seem fruitless – but surely not so, the study of the war itself: its causes and consequences, the experience of leaders and those being led, the struggle being waged on its fields of battle and on the Home Front. It is a safe bet that the bicentenary of the Great War will see the 1914–18 years receiving in some form searching re-examination of that which holds the interest of so many today.

Preparing for Victory: British Military Innovation in Weaponry, Training and Tactics, 1916–1918

By Edward M. Spiers

As with the other belligerents, the British Expeditionary Force (BEF) grappled with unprecedented challenges following the battle of the Somme (1 July–20 November 1916). Just as the BEF had refined its tactics and used new technology during the Somme, it had also sustained its training where possible in rear areas, often by units recovering from 1 July.[1] Thereafter it reflected upon the legacy of the battle, innovated in the use of new technology, and adapted its tactics and training for more open and combined-arms warfare. These factors in themselves may not have transformed the operational capacity of the BEF by August 1918: undoubtedly changes in command and control from armies down to platoon contributed, as did an unprecedented mobilization of manpower and industry at home, supported by a modern communications, intelligence and logistics infrastructure.[2] Yet tactics, technology and training remain contentious issues; they reflect the unprecedented scale of the wartime commitment; the concentration of military effort in the densely-populated region of the Western Front, where local geography and meteorology periodically restricted forms of military action; and the implications of 'the scale and rapid change in weapons technology'.[3] This introduction to the chapters which follow will highlight some themes of the current historiographical debate, and then consider how these have developed in respect of tactics, technology and training from the legacy of the Somme over the ensuing eighteen months.

Sir James Edmonds memorably dismissed this entire approach in the final volume of the official history. In debunking the inter-war claims of J.F.C. Fuller and Basil Liddell Hart that the tank had proved decisive at the battle of Amiens,[4] he argued that 'In the end, however, it was not the weapons or the tactics but the superiority of the British soldier over the German on the ground, under the ground and in the air which won the day. . .'[5] Cyril Falls, a Great War veteran, agreed that his former comrades had displayed great spirit, courage and comradeship but dubbed it 'preposterous' to imply that 'the military art' had 'stood still in the greatest war up to date'.[6] Another two decades, though, would elapse before significant studies of the military art appeared, both in 1982, namely John Terraine's *White Heat* and Shelford Bidwell and Dominick

Graham's *Fire-Power*.[7] These pioneering works inspired 'a new era of scholarship'[8] that evolved over the next thirty years. Rooted in archival research and thematic analysis, this revisionist school eclipsed the 'butchers and bunglers' mode of writing[9] and focused upon the British Army as an evolving institution.

These authors claimed that the BEF responded to events on the Somme by steadily developing more sophisticated combined-arms methods, involving the inculcation of new tactics and the integrated use of new technologies, so contributing to the defeat of imperial Germany. Described as a 'learning curve', this concept drew attention to the improvement in the BEF's combat performance, albeit in a process that was fitful and disjointed at times. Attributed by some to Peter Simkins,[10] the 'learning curve' enjoyed the promotion of Brian Bond in the 1990s,[11] and its most complete synthesis by Gary Sheffield in *Forgotten Victory* (2001).[12]

The cycle of revisionism, nonetheless, kept turning and soon critics, perhaps taking the aphorism of a 'curve' too literally, argued that historians had to look beyond this model. In 2009 Bill Philpott asserted that the 'learning curve' had had its day, being 'too amorphous a concept, and too Anglo-centric . . .'. Learning, he argued, was only a facet of the BEF's transformation; the process was 'more up-and-down' than the curve implied, and the dynamic had to take account of operational and tactical changes by the French and Germans alike.[13] Subsequent studies have highlighted the degree of learning on the Western Front during 1915,[14] the deficiencies in the doctrinal manuals issued during 1917–18,[15] and the diversity of tactics employed by the British army in the 'Hundred Days' campaign of 1918.[16] Even so, the 'learning curve' had helped to move contemporary scholarship away from static perceptions of the BEF, and 'towards a more dynamic and progressive view' of the British army's development during the First World War.[17] Bolstered by the writings of Robin Prior and Trevor Wilson, it had also corrected the impression created by Tim Travers that victory in 1918 was somehow accidental, largely a consequence of overwhelming Allied artillery and collapsing German morale. It could not be otherwise, implied Travers, since the British officer corps was too hidebound to embrace the full potential of 'mechanical warfare'.[18] While there may be some truth in his critique of the traditional Edwardian officer, it was far from the whole truth, and modern scholarship demonstrates that the BEF was capable of embracing change in tactics, new technology and wartime training, and that these factors contributed to victory in 1918.

The Legacy of the Somme
However much the BEF learned from the battles of 1915, including the inability of chlorine gas dispersed from cylinders to achieve a breakthrough at the battle of Loos (25 September 1915),[19] the legacy of the Somme was much more important. This legacy has been the subject of ferocious debate, focusing upon the costly failure to achieve a breakthrough on 1 July and then the vast number of casualties incurred during a four-and-a-half month campaign. Although the casualty estimates, particularly on the German side, remain hotly contested, a scholarly consensus has settled around some 419,654 British casualties and 202,567 French, with at least 500,000, and possibly nearer 600,000 German.[20] Given the modest gains of territory by the British forces, about six miles in depth and the belated capture of some First Day objectives (Thiepval on 26 September,

Beaumont Hamel and Beaucourt on 14 November), the 'blood test' fuelled civil-military tensions at the time,[21] and interwar claims, not least by Winston Churchill and David Lloyd George, that this was simply a bloody and futile battle.[22]

Modern writing on the Somme, dominated as it is by the magisterial work of Bill Philpott, emphasizes that the battle had much more positive outcomes, whether described as a 'victory' in a strategy of attrition, 'an essential stepping stone to victory', or a strategic success.[23] Many of the outcomes were strategic and/or operational, including the fulfilment of a political commitment by Britain to a hard-pressed ally and the thwarting of Germany's strategic ambitions on the Western Front. Germany's heavy losses of men, including experienced officers and NCOs that could not be easily replaced, contributed to the dismissal of General Erich von Falkenhayn, although this was formally triggered by Romania's entry into the war. These losses also precipitated the subsequent withdrawal of German forces from the Somme battlefield to more defensible positions on the Hindenburg Line.[24]

If German morale was shaken by the Somme campaign, the effects were compounded by the enhanced morale among British officers and men in the fifty-three divisions (out of fifty-six) that took part. Doubtless this reflected the testing of the New Army soldier and the Territorial in battle, and their enduring beliefs in the righteousness of their cause, regimental pride, and small-group bonding: 'we have given the German Army some good hard knocks', wrote Charles Carrington (1/5th Royal Warwickshire Regiment),[25] while Christopher Stone (22nd Royal Fusiliers), writing on 24 October 1916, sympathized with:

> Those poor devils the Boches, they must be having an A1 rotten time, they get no peace at all from our guns and we devise all sorts of ways of keeping them on alert and wearing down their nerves.[26]

If the value of some of the later offensives were to have been debated, such as the storming of Beaumont Hamel and capture of Beaucourt, they had boosted the morale of surviving soldiers and enhanced the fighting reputations of units involved, notably the 63rd (Royal Naval) Division and the 51st (Highland) Division.[27] They had underlined, too, that artillery, if not yet the force it would become in 1918, had assumed an increasing importance after the largely ineffective seven-day preliminary bombardment that preceded the fateful infantry advance on 1 July. If the shortcomings evident in that bombardment, namely the shortage of guns and the excessive number of dud shells, were to have been only partly addressed, the creeping barrage, used by the French and a few divisions on 1 July, became standard by the offensive of 14 July. The field artillery fired shrapnel, air-bursted ahead of the infantry to screen infantry movements and kill enemy in front-line positions.[28]

In response, the Germans developed a more flexible defence-in-depth, employing front-line soldiers on narrower fronts, often in shell holes and not the pulverized trenches. Held further back were their support units and reserves, which were increasingly organized for counter-attacks, supported by machine-guns and artillery. The German expenditure of artillery ammunition rose from 3.5 million rounds in July to 5.4 million in September and 6.4 million in October.[29] Accordingly, British counter-battery fire, a low priority in the pre-1 July bombardment, became increasingly important. Although artillery units still pounded enemy positions, trying to cut barbed wire, interdict communications and support infantry advances, counter-battery fire now aimed at neutralization (killing enemy gunners and damaging guns) and not destruction. As the German 1st and 2nd Armies lost some 1,400 out of 2,000 guns from the beginning of the British bombardment to the end of August, they adopted evasive tactics and relocated their batteries.[30] Only improved reconnaissance, providing more precise and timely information, could counter these efforts, hence the artillery's ever-greater reliance on the Royal Flying Corps (RFC). Having gained aerial supremacy over the battlefield, the RFC registered 8,612 targets for the artillery and took over 19,000 photographs from which 420,000 prints were made. By the middle of November, 306 aircraft, equipped with wireless, were transmitting to 542 ground stations. In addition, the RFC supported the artillery directly by conducting 298 bombing raids, dropping 176,000 bombs (or 292 tons) upon tactical targets.[31]

Another 'accessory' to the normal modes of attack introduced on the Somme was the tank.[32] It made its debut on 15 September 1916, in the battle of Flers-Courcelette but the contribution was strictly limited. Of the thirty-two tanks making the start line, only nine spearheaded the infantry attack, another nine broke down, five ditched, and another nine never caught up with the infantry and undertook 'clearing up' work instead.[33] Brought up at night before the assault, with taped lanes laid out for them, the 30-ton rhomboidal machines were a surprise factor: one famously led British troops up the main street of Flers and another achieved the maximum depth of penetration on that day – some 3,500 yards. Although artillery, delivering fire of much greater density than on 1 July, achieved many of these gains,[34] Haig's chief of staff, Sir Launcelot E. Kiggell, declared that the utility of tanks had been 'proved', and that their employment had minimized the 'loss among the attacking troops'. The moral effects were deemed 'considerable', drawing hostile machine-gun and rifle fire away from the infantry and onto the tanks, while the machines had crushed barbed wire, and dealt with 'strong points' and enemy machine-guns.[35] Any problems encountered by the tank, Kiggell attributed to the nature of the terrain, its slopes, and mechanical failure.[36]

Although tank enthusiasts, including Churchill and Lloyd George, criticized the tank attack of 15 September as premature, wasting the surprise effect, Haig could hardly keep his tanks as a secret indefinitely and employed them in a manner that was perfectly consistent with contemporary thinking.[37] Moreover, in following up the first tank attack by requesting the provision of 1,000 tanks, and the requisite trained personnel,[38] he debunked the canard that he was a technophobic cavalryman. Haig consistently embraced the use of new technology – gas at Loos, tanks on the Somme – as well as new methods of delivery. When he learned that the French were employing lethal gas shell in 'large quantities' in counter-battery work and in attacks on fortified villages south of the Somme, he sought 'an immediate supply' as a matter of 'first importance'.[39] Not only were lethal gas shells used in preparation for the attacks on Ginchy (9 September) and Flers (13–14 and 14–15 September), but gas mortar bombs, delivering lachrymatory agent, and projectors delivering high concentrations of the lethal agent, phosgene, preceded the successful assaults upon Thiepval (25 September) and Beaumont Hamel (12 November).[40]

Finally, infantry profited from a far greater profusion of close support weapons: the Mills bomb, mass-produced in 1916, for clearing trenches; about twenty-four light (2-inch) and medium mortars per division; the 4-inch Stokes Mortar used in the screening of open flanks with smoke; and the portable Lewis gun.[41] These weapons facilitated the forward movement of infantry as it increasingly operated in attacking formations. 'Fighting platoons' led the assault, aiming to clear and cross enemy trenches. 'Mopping up platoons' followed, intending to crush residual strong points and consolidate captured positions. Thereafter, 'support platoons' and 'carrying platoons' moved forward, carrying the materials to build their own strong points within the newly-captured line, and thereby resist the expected counter-attack. The BEF had, in effect, reinvented fire and movement tactics, with the Lewis gun, rifle grenade and trench mortar supporting advances by riflemen and bombers, and enhancing confidence in the efficacy of creeping barrages, so bolstering belief in the attacking process.[42]

Post-Somme Tactics
Over the winter months of 1916–17, the BEF absorbed the lessons of the Somme. Accepting the platoon as the primary infantry tactical unit was fundamental but it was an evolving unit, increasingly well-armed and capable of manoeuvring towards the 'tactical point' of an attack. In February 1917, GHQ, which had issued doctrine publications since March 1916, produced S.S. 143: *Instructions for the Training of Platoons for Offensive Action* and S.S. 144: *The Normal Formation for the Attack*. The former, written by Major General Arthur Solly Flood, was particularly important as it drew on French tactics, but both were described as aides for platoon commanders in their training and fighting. Further documents codified artillery practice (the S.S. 139 series) and proffered guidance on how Royal Engineers should support the offensive (S.S. 148). By covering trench-to-trench attacks and open warfare, they stimulated debate within divisions. As Carrington recalled, at a time when 'good divisions' were working their tactics out 'after the Somme fighting', they benefited from these 'simple well-written pamphlets'.[43]

In essence each platoon had to possess sufficient weaponry to overcome the enemy's machine-gun strong points or major obstacles. An assault team led the advance, composed of sections of riflemen to project suppressive fire from the front while hand bombers attacked from the flank, followed by a Lewis gun section and rifle-grenadiers. If these platoons sometimes were to operate in diamond formations to maximize flexibility, and alter the point of attack or repel counter-attacks as necessary, units also advanced in 'a variety of lines and waves, "blobs", squares', and even extended order as the tactical situation required or their commanders preferred.[44] By 1918, when the 500-man battalions were only half the size of their 1916 predecessors, they each bristled with some thirty Lewis guns, eight light trench mortars and at least sixteen rifle-grenadiers. The heavily-armed platoon functioned as a combined-arms formation in itself, protected by the artillery's creeping barrages and, if in the vanguard of an advance, sometimes by the support of six tanks.[45]

Yet the emphasis upon platoon-based operations posed all manner of challenges. 'Truly the war', as A. M. McGilchrist observed, had become 'more than ever a platoon-commanders' war', with success largely dependent on 'their initiative and determination'.[46] Such a delegation of responsibility, argued James C. Dunn (2nd Royal Welch Fusiliers), was not only daunting in itself but also peculiarly demanding at a time when shattered divisions required large drafts of men to replace the losses on the Somme. 'Several men in my platoon', he wrote, 'seemed barely capable of carrying the weight of their equipment; and in one case "platoon training" began with the platoon commander teaching a man how to load his rifle.'[47] Training would have to adapt, too, as Captain James L. Jack (2nd West Yorkshires) entered in his diary for 18 March 1917: 'The prospect of mobile operations has introduced a new crop of lessons, since scarcely any in the Battalion has had proper training in mobile warfare.'[48]

Learning at local level, like experience in the field, was never uniform but in the winter fighting after the Somme, as the enemy retreated to the Hindenburg Line, the Rifle Brigade recorded 'men moving admirably in open formation' and a platoon using concentrated fire to capture a German strong point.[49] The flow of doctrinal publications persisted through the last two years of the war but from the spring of 1917 to the November armistice, three 'citizen soldiers' had oversight of the process: Lord Gorell, a former editor of the *Times Literary Supplement*, who was commissioned into the 7th Rifle Brigade in May 1915; Edward Grigg, a former colonial editor of *The Times*, who was commissioned into the Grenadier Guards in February 1915; and Cuthbert Headlam, a former clerk of the House of Lords and officer in the pre-war Bedfordshire Yeomanry. Their writing has incurred criticism for 'harking back to pre-war ideas', and, in Gorell's case, for failing to produce a manual on defensive operations, despite the widespread expectation of a major German offensive in the spring of 1918.[50] Even S.S.143 proved contentious, as Lieutenant General Sir Ivor Maxse, then commander of XVIII Corps, feared that it had been pitched beyond the practical implementation of platoon commanders, who were confronted with 'the human side of training'.[51] When the operations staff began to focus upon higher-level divisional doctrine from mid-1918 onwards, belatedly producing a divisional defensive doctrine in May and a divisional attack doctrine in November, the output was simply 'too little, too late'.[52]

Meanwhile organizational changes at the beginning of 1917 had underscored the tactical priorities of the Royal Artillery: counter-battery work with the appointment of a Counter-Battery Staff Officer at corps level,[53] and creeping barrages of HE and shrapnel to be delivered by field artillery brigades. Underpinning these changes was a prodigious increase in heavy artillery: by early 1917, the BEF possessed 1,157 guns and howitzers, a number that would double by the end of March 1917, compared with the 761 heavy guns and howitzers of the previous July. Complemented by a similar growth in the quantity and quality of ammunition, Third Army as well as the Canadian Corps and part of the I Corps Artillery prepared for the battle of Arras with a vast preponderance of guns: 2,817 pieces confronting the enemy's 1,014 pieces.[54] A few weeks later at Messines, where the preliminary bombardment ranged from 26 May to 6 June, the British possessed a threefold superiority in artillery (2,230 guns against 630), and delivered over 3.5 million shells across a front of 17,000 yards (compared with half as many shells delivered over 27,000 yards prior to 1 July).[55]

In the ensuing artillery duels, intelligence from aircraft, balloons, flash spotters, range finders and ground observers had to be interpreted, cross-checked with up-to-date maps, and distributed. By Messines, the RFC had 300 serviceable aircraft over the battle area, twice as many as the enemy, and so operated with little interference.[56]

Batteries benefited from communications secured by the burying of cables and duplicated circuits, meteorological information updated twice or three times a day, and the allocation of specific tasks, whether wire-cutting, bombardment of targets in depth or counter-battery work, with harassing fire at night. In the massive bombardment of Vimy Ridge, and across the Arras sector in depth, gunners sought to neutralize concentrations of enemy guns, targeting not only the batteries but also their headquarters, observation posts, supply dumps, communications and supply routes, with gas shelling added from ten hours before the attack. 'The artillery', wrote Sir Edmund Allenby, commanding Third Army, 'were brilliant, and the German guns smothered from the start.'[57] Similarly, at Messines, the German XIX Corps lost almost a quarter of its field artillery and nearly half of its heavy artillery during the preparatory barrage. Rates of fire from the surviving guns diminished, too, as gunners tried to operate wearing respirators during ten days of gas shelling.[58]

In both battles, infantry advanced under creeping barrages of shrapnel and high explosive, which moved at a uniform rate of a 100-yard lift every four minutes. Standing barrages were also laid upon selected areas and strong points up to 700 yards ahead of the creeping barrage, and then lifted onto successive pre-arranged targets when the assault was within 400 yards of its objective. At each objective, the creeping barrage became a protective barrage, 150 to 300 yards ahead of the infantry, sweeping and searching the area to check enemy movements or counter-attacks. A machine-gun barrage, using indirect overhead fire, lifted 400 yards ahead of the creeping barrage, providing a third belt in this protective barrage. A Leeds soldier wrote home at this time, commending 'our artillery' as 'frightfully effective, and we could see our men in the advanced platoons, walking forward, outlined in the blaze of light from our shells'.[59]

Both of these bombardments, aided at Messines by the detonation of nineteen mines, paved the way for the infantry, with fresh units 'leapfrogging' past each other once the latter reached their allotted targets. Sixty tanks, mainly Marks I, IIs and IIIs, were intended to support the infantry at Arras and sixty-eight new Mark IV models at Messines. On 9 April, the Canadians captured most of Vimy Ridge while the divisions of Third Army gained large tracts of territory and captured 5,600 prisoners, albeit without breaching the fourth line of trenches. They did so with little assistance from the tanks as a high proportion of them foundered on account of mechanical failure, ditching or sinking into the mud. On 7 June, General Herbert Plumer's Second Army seized Messines Ridge, and captured 7,354 prisoners, with support from only nineteen of the sixty-eight fighting tanks (most could not keep up with the infantry and forty-eight ditched or 'bellied' in this uphill battle).[60] These localised gains confirmed that the BEF, if given time to prepare, with sufficient guns, ammunition and an aggressive infantry, had become highly proficient in set-piece battles. Yet the lengthy bombardments forfeited any degree of surprise, with the timing only partially concealed by faked starts for the creeping barrage, and, at Arras, by the snowstorm. In both battles, commanders struggled to sustain the operational tempo and exploit their initial successes, while soldiers found the transition to semi-mobile operations after a breakthrough more demanding than anticipated.[61]

Surprise was also lost on the Ypres salient by the long delay between the battle of Messines (7–17 June) and the launching on 31 July of the battle of Third Ypres, later known as Passchendaele. In its preparatory barrage the Royal Artillery had to account for numerous pillboxes erected by the enemy, offset the geographical advantages of an enemy on the high ground, which overlooked and surrounded the salient on three sides, and counter the enemy's much more aggressive counter-battery tactics. German artillery, reinforced on several occasions, sought to disrupt and delay with harassing fire (often at night). It interdicted supplies, introduced mustard gas, and fired at general areas rather than specific targets. Ultimately British gunners, despite heavy losses, prevailed in the protracted counter-battery struggles, but the ensuing infantry advances encountered ferocious counter-attacks and made modest advances. As the battle continued, amidst worsening weather, the ensuing quagmire of mud thwarted the repositioning of guns, especially the heavy artillery. Forward movement of supplies and ammunition became extremely slow and arduous, every shell had to be cleaned before firing, and the men, wrapped in wet muddy blankets, could not get dry as 'sickness spread and numbers dwindled'.[62]

The infantry had the support of 136 tanks on the opening day but the latter struggled over the badly-cratered ground and only nineteen assisted in the assault of the German second line. J. F. C. Fuller, then a staff officer with the infant Tank Corps, described the Ypres battlefield as 'dead' for tanks.[63] On 7 September, his commander, Brigadier Hugh J. Elles, confirmed that unless the weather was 'exceptionally good', it would prevent 'the use of Tanks in large masses'.[64] That first mass use of tanks would follow across the firmer and less heavily cratered ground at Cambrai. The preparations for this battle were impressive: infantry trained with tanks from the beginning of November, fascines (stout bundles of brushwood weighing about a ton and a half) were mounted on tanks to provide trench crossing points upon release, and camouflage schemes kept the men, munitions and weapons secret. General Sir Julian Byng's Third Army fielded 476 tanks – 378 fighting tanks (Mark IVs) and 98 support vehicles – an unprecedented concentration of machines which launched a devastating assault on 20 November 1917. Described somewhat misleadingly as 'the first great tank battle', the assault of over 300 fighting tanks (fifty-four were held in reserve) and five divisions, achieved complete surprise, gaining penetration up to 4,000 yards on a six-mile front.[65]

Yet the surprise derived as much if not more from the artillery's first use of predicted fire. New sound-ranging systems, developed in mid-1917 by Lieutenant (later Professor) W. Lawrence Bragg, provided highly accurate information about the location of enemy guns, even in bad weather. This electrically-controlled sequence of microphones, placed behind the British front, recorded the low-frequency sound waves from the firing of guns and, by taking a cross bearing, located the position of enemy batteries. This complemented information from flash-spotting, aerial photography, and the use of more accurate maps and survey techniques. At the same time the accuracy of British gunnery was enhanced by adjusting each weapon before a major battle to compensate for any wearing of the gun barrels, and by requiring batches of shells to be sent from the factories in uniform weights. At the behest of Brigadier General H. H. Tudor, Commanding Royal Artillery, 9th (Scottish) Division, the gunners at Cambrai discarded a preparatory bombardment and employed a fully predicted fire plan. On the first day, they contributed to the massive surprise effect by firing only at the outset, with 75 per cent of their 1,003 guns concentrating upon the neutralization of the enemy's 34 guns.[66]

Cambrai's early successes, though, were never sustained as the offensive lost tempo and lacked exploitation without adequate reserves of infantry and tanks (179 of the tanks used on the first day were out of action by the second). The other great controversy of the first day concerned the failure of the 51st Highland Division to secure Flesquières, which Christopher Baker-Carr retrospectively attributed to the idiosyncratic tactics of Major General George M. Harper. Bryn Hammond confirms that this was not the view of contemporaries, that Harper, like Braithwaite of the 62nd Division, was at liberty to devise his own tactics, and that these reflected previous experience of infantry-tank co-operation.[67] The Germans, nonetheless, recovered from their rout to build up a firing line, and counter-attack successfully on 30 November, regaining much of the lost ground. Predicted fire had still proved itself, establishing a precedent that would be followed by the Royal Artillery in many of the engagements of 1918.

Technology

Throughout the war advances in weapon technology had held the prospect of refining tactics and facilitating breakthroughs on the Western Front. The Royal Artillery profited not only from a growing abundance of guns and ammunition, which would produce a four-to-one superiority by the battle of Amiens (8 August 1918),[68] but also from a range of technological improvements. Of particular importance was the introduction of the No. 106 instant percussion fuse for HE shells in the battle of Arras. It offered the prospect of friendly infantry crossing un-cratered ground by splintering on impact with the enemy's barbed wire. Another innovation at Arras was the first use of smoke shells, which could be used in support of creeping barrages. Gas shells, which had been used on the Somme, were also employed at Arras and in far larger quantities at Messines, where 120,000 rounds of gas shell and 60,000 rounds of smoke shell were made available.[69] Yet these stocks were not sufficient: on 17 September 1917, Haig informed Sir William Robertson, then Chief of the Imperial General Staff,

> An increased supply of 106 fuses and increased use of gas shell will reduce damage to the surface of the ground very considerably, the craters made by them being practically no obstacle to movement of tanks or infantry.[70]

Even worse was the response to the introduction of mustard gas in prodigious quantities at Third Ypres. For the Germans, who had a threefold superiority in gas shells and had integrated these weapons into their counter-battery doctrine, their first use of mustard gas (12/13 July 1917) heralded a new era in gas warfare. The persistence and casualty-causing qualities of mustard gas proved ideal as a defensive weapon since the Germans had no need to cross the contaminated ground, whereas the British, as the attackers, either had to do so or try to avoid the contamination. Mustard gas proved potent, too, during the offensives of spring and summer 1918, when the Germans wished to seal flanks or bombard fortified areas. Having seen 1,400 men gassed in the Villers-Bretonneux area, General Sir Henry Rawlinson wrote to Winston Churchill, then Minister of Munitions, on 22 April 1918:

> Can you give me any idea when we may expect to have available shells filled with mustard gas? I ask because we have had very severe casualties lately from this form of projectile . . . The men naturally feel that the enemy has a distinct advantage over us in possessing mustard gas and the contention of our chemists that our own

lethal shells are still more effective, a contention with which I do not agree, is no satisfactory answer. We feel that we are at a disadvantage in this respect and morale suffers in consequence.[71]

Production problems, however, persisted at the Avonmouth plant. Whereas the French were able to retaliate-in-kind from March 1918 onwards, another half year elapsed before British gunners could incorporate mustard-gas shells into their fire-plans. When the Fourth Army attacked the Hindenburg Line, it launched a preparatory four-day bombardment from 26 September 1918 onwards, firing 750,000 shells, including 32,000 mustard-gas shells.[72]

This preparatory bombardment emphasised that even in the age of predicted fire, commanders still adjusted their fire plans to local circumstances. When the Germans attacked the Fifth Army on 21 March 1918, they overwhelmed its counter-battery infrastructure; disrupted communications, flash-spotting and sound-ranging systems, and captured some 150 guns. Forced onto the defensive, British gunners had to attack observed German batteries directly. Apart from a few formations, most notably XV Corps, which still provided concentrated counter-battery fire, gunners and machine-gunners provided direct support for hard-pressed infantry divisions. During the German summer offensives, which petered out by mid-July, the Royal Artillery exploited all its technological assets in counter-battery barrages and in support of raids and small-scale attacks with predicted fire. At Hamel on 4 July, it maximized surprise and used two-thirds of its heavy artillery in counter-battery work.[73]

Hamel was the last major engagement before the Hundred Days' Campaign in which tanks were involved. As the Tank Corps history describes, 'sixty graceful Mark Vs slid forward after their infantry', escorted by two low-flying aircraft. They did so in two waves, 'the first of forty-eight, and the second of twelve machines', and, in a distinctly limited but highly successful operation, the tanks reportedly accounted for over 200 machine-guns and gained over 1,500 prisoners. Moreover, fifty-seven of the fighting tanks 'came through the day without a scratch'.[74] How far then had the technology of tanks overcome the shortcomings so evident on the Somme and in the battles of 1917?

All First World War tanks were slow, cumbersome, prone to breakdown, under-powered, and lightly armed (by comparison with their Second World War successors). The 30-ton Mark I moved at 2mph but it could crush barbed wire, cross trenches and supply the infantry with limited fire support. The eight-man tank crews operated in heat that could reach 125 degrees Fahrenheit, noise that required orders to be passed by hand signals, and an environment polluted by petrol, cordite and carbon-monoxide fumes. While the Mark IIs and IIIs were merely modifications of the Mark I, and never went into large-scale production, the Mark IV was a more reliable and less vulnerable machine (at least against 'K' machine-gun ammunition). With a considerably larger petrol supply, improved transmission, a limited silencer for the engine and better exhaust, it emitted less noise and fewer sparks to attract enemy fire. It remained, nonetheless, remarkably similar to the Mark I, with the same engine, armament, speed, difficulty of manoeuvre and high interior temperatures. Its deficiencies were evident before Cambrai: 'its mechanical improvements', wrote Fuller, 'have not kept pace with the change in the tactical conditions . . .'.[75] After the first day at Cambrai, where the Germans had used field guns and more penetrative armour-piercing bullets to disable tanks, Haig declared that tanks had 'great value' under suitable conditions but that these conditions 'cannot always or even often be found', and 'that our experience shows that methods of defeating tank attack have already been discovered'.[76]

The Tank Corps shared Haig's disappointment with the Mark IV. Handicapped by the delivery of only 700 machines by October 1917, it had had to deploy the Mark IVs in 'penny packets' prior to Cambrai. It now lobbied that some of the remaining 500 heavy tanks on order should be converted to Mark Vs. Equipped with the Ricardo engine and epicyclic gears, the Mark V was slightly faster than its predecessors (4.6mph), had better turning power, more endurance and reliability, and could be driven by one man instead of four. The tank had a better field of view (through an observer's turret) and its fuel tanks were removed from the cabin and attached with armour-protection to the outside of the vehicle. Its ventilation, nonetheless, would prove a serious drawback in protracted engagements, leaving tank crews suffering from heat exhaustion and carbon-monoxide poisoning.[77]

As early as 6 June 1917, Haig had endorsed the requirements for both the Mark V heavy tank, and the 14-ton Medium A ('Whippet') tank, which would have an average speed of 5mph. He maintained that tanks remained useful as a means of overcoming 'hostile resistance' and reducing casualties among 'attacking troops'.[78] However, neither Haig's orders nor the enthusiasm of the Tank Corps could accelerate the production process at home. Whereas some 'Whippets' arrived in time to fight in the rearguard actions of March and April 1918, the Mark Vs, despite their initial appearance in March, only appeared in significant numbers, about twenty per week, by the following May.[79] This facilitated intensive training in the Bermicourt area, the experimental attack at Hamel village, and the assembly of some 400 tanks, with retrained crews, by 1 August 1918. Throughout the war British tank production lagged far behind that of France and, more importantly, left the BEF only able to employ tanks en masse on a few occasions, and never with adequate tank reserves.

Meanwhile the technological limitations of the Mark IV tanks had again been exposed during Operation *Michael*, the German onslaught launched on 21 March 1918. In anticipating this battle, both Brigadier Elles and Fuller had pressed for the Mark IVs to be involved in counter-attack formations, fighting alongside aircraft and infantry in 'a new method of warfare . . . against which the enemy is at present impotent'.[80] In fact, the virtual collapse of command and control within Fifth Army undermined any effective combined-arms operations. Employed in 'penny packets', the Mark IVs sometimes caught the enemy by surprise but generally proved too slow and too cumbersome for open warfare. They often broke down, ran out of petrol, or had to be abandoned, whereupon their tank crews served in Lewis gun detachments. Small groups of 'Whippets' saw action for the first time with their Hotchkiss machine guns but, by mid-April, the Ministry of Munitions reckoned that 257 tanks had been lost. The 1st Tank Brigade (attached to First Army) had only fifty-nine Mark IV tanks remaining, the 2nd Tank Brigade (attached to Third Army) had lost seventy-one of its ninety-eight tanks, and the 4th Tank Brigade (with the Fifth Army) had lost all its tanks. The success of the Mark IV in the first tank-versus-tank engagement on 24 April was scant consolation since the Germans invested so little in the production of their A7V machines. British tank production remained a fundamental impediment, casting doubt upon Fuller's vision of 2,000 Medium Mark 'D' machines in service by March 1919, and leaving the BEF with models in 1918 which were far from war-winners.[81]

The same could be said about poison gas. Poison gas may not have broken the deadlock of trench warfare but this hardly excuses those critics, who simply disparaged chemical weaponry as 'unpredictable', or even a failure that achieved only 'limited tactical success'.[82] These criticisms followed commentary from the final volume of the official history, which was published in 1947. In this volume Edmonds asserted that 'Gas achieved but local success, nothing decisive: it made war uncomfortable to no purpose. It was not used in 1939-45.'[83] This contradicts commentary in earlier volumes,[84] and even where gas had a highly localised impact, the effects could be serious (as in Bourlon Wood, on 1 December 1917, when two infantry battalions and an artillery battery had to be relieved immediately on account of 'heavy gas casualties').[85]

Like other forms of new technology, chemical weaponry was under research and development throughout the First World War. At Porton Down, first acquired with 3,000 acres in January 1916, the experimental station more than doubled in size during the war, employing over 1,000 scientists and soldiers to develop and test new gases, or combinations of gases, their means of projection and effectiveness in light of the continuing improvements in chemical defences. By April 1916, the British had produced the Small Box Respirator (SBR), of which some sixteen million would be issued to British and American forces before the Armistice.[86] Having initially relied upon cloud-gas attacks emitted from cylinders at Loos, the British developed additional means of gas projection through the 4-inch Stokes Mortars (also introduced at Loos) and Livens projectors, first used en masse firing 2,340 drums at the battle of Arras, 4 April 1917. They followed the Germans and French in their use of gas shell and experimented with a variety of incapacitating and lethal chemical agents, primarily phosgene, and, in their cylinder discharges, 'white star' – a mixture of 50 per cent chlorine and 50 per cent phosgene.[87] Only in the last few months of the war did the British acquire mustard-gas shells.

Given the recurring shortage of gas shells, the British clung to other forms of chemical projection. The Special Brigade under the command of Brigadier General Charles H. Foulkes persisted with gas–cloud attacks from cylinders despite their weather dependence, and the infantry's dislike of installing cylinders at night in front-line trenches and their fear of accidental leakage. Of the 220 gas-cloud attacks launched between April 1915 and November 1918, the British launched 150, the Germans, fifty and the French, twenty.[88] For short-range gas attacks, the 4-inch Stokes Mortar could be brought into action quickly, and, on account of its calibre and rate of fire (about twenty rounds a minute) deliver 3 to 4kg of agent per round at ranges up to 1,094 yards. A highly versatile weapon system, it could also project barrages of smoke to screen an assault or bombard advanced enemy positions with thermit (globules of molten iron at 'white heat').[89] Captain William H. Livens designed the other technological innovation, a projector that fired canisters or drums, each holding 15kg of agent. This weapon was cheap, easily produced and not weather dependent. Installed at 45-degree angles behind the front lines, it delivered sudden, very high concentrations of agent that neither mortars nor gas shells could emulate. Less accurate than mortars or shells, projectors were also limited in range (about 1,300 yards), but the German 111th Division testified to their impact:

By this new procedure, the enemy has combined the advantages of gas cloud with those of gas shell, obtaining the density of the former with the surprise effect of the latter. Our losses have hitherto been heavy, because the enemy, in most cases, successfully took us unawares, and gas masks were put on too late.[90]

If the threat from short-range gas attacks were to have reinforced the German decision to deploy manpower thinly along their front-line, it confirmed that to achieve surprise in gas warfare would remain a struggle. Once the German respirator received a three-layer drum in June 1916, with additional fillings in April 1918, penetration was unlikely unless the masks were damaged or defective. Accordingly, Foulkes tried to catch the enemy unaware by attacking, usually at night, but at 'all hours of the day and night, and in all wind velocities', even dead calm, sometimes disguising the gas discharges by feints with smoke. Ultimately though he had hopes that a new arsenic compound, dispersed as a toxic smoke (the so-called 'M device'), would prove a mask-breaker but it was not available before 1919.[91]

In the final year of the war, the Special Brigade sought another form of surprise by mounting cylinder operations from 'retired' positions. Of the ten such attacks, nine of them involved thousands of cylinders transported on railway trucks, and discharged electrically from the trucks in 'retired' positions, once the infantry in front had been withdrawn. However spectacular the resulting 'beam', the attack was still weather dependent, and days could be 'wasted', as Captain Adrian E. Hodgkin, RE, recalled, 'on account of (the) wind'.[92]

No gas surprise, though, emulated the impact of mustard gas, the so-called 'king of the war gases'. Its persistence, particularly in low-lying areas, coupled with delayed effects of burning and blistering even through clothing, baffled army doctors initially and caused heavy casualties. These effects were not necessarily lethal but they caught soldiers unawares, incapacitated often by temporary blindness, and required protracted treatment from the medical support services. 'Some people', recalled C. Edgar Shelly (1/8 West Yorkshire), 'found that they were losing their sight and they had difficulty breathing. Rapidly men became casualties. One company was so badly affected that it lost all its officers while men lay about on the contaminated floor.'[93] In the first three weeks of mustard-gas shelling, the BEF suffered more casualties (14,276), and almost as many deaths (nearly 500), as they had from all previous gas engagements. From 12 July 1917 to 23 November 1918, British casualty clearing stations admitted 160,970 gas casualties, 77 per cent of whom were victims of mustard-gas, and 1,859 died.[94]

Like the German respirator, the SBR provided protection against all known war gases. Consequently during the Spring Offensive, the Germans aimed to break mask discipline, beginning with Blue Cross (lachrymatory) shells followed by Green Cross (phosgene) shells, with Yellow Cross (mustard gas) shells sealing the flanks or saturating specific areas, but the tactics never proved decisive. After a five-hour gas bombardment on 21 March 1918, the 7th Battalion Seaforth Highlanders reported 'no immediate casualties'.[95] A price, though, both physical and psychological, was paid for this protection, known in modern parlance as *operational degradation*. As Captain Arthur A. Hanbury-Sparrow (Royal Berkshires) recalled: 'The gas mask makes you feel only half a man. You can't think: the air you breathe has been filtered of all save a few filtered substances. A man doesn't live on what passes through a filter, he merely exists.'[96] Just as the Special Brigade sought to 'wear down' the enemy with their gas attacks, and disorganise his defence 'by causing constant reliefs', so British soldiers were ordered whenever they encountered mustard gas, to avoid contaminated areas if possible and move their batteries if practical.[97] At Arras, General Fritz von Below admitted that the 'fighting resistance' of his gunners had 'suffered considerably' from wearing gas masks 'for many hours', and that the severe effects on horses had caused the recurrent failure of the ammunition supply and the inability to withdraw batteries in a 'timely' manner.[98] Operational degradation meant that the effects of poison gas were not measurable purely in numbers of men and animals killed and injured. Despite the effective chemical defences, chemical weaponry remained a valuable means of harassment, degrading the operational efficiency of its victims and encumbering their medical and support services.

Training

Mask discipline was one of the many benefits of wartime training, a process that purportedly 'never ceased during the war'.[99] Although training continued while battles were in progress, it was particularly important towards the end of each fighting season, when heavily-depleted units were withdrawn from the front line, desperately in need of rest, reliefs and reinforcements. In the autumn of 1917, the 17th (Northern) Division was by no means alone in finding that all of its battalions were under strength. The replacements included 'fresh men', often with variable skills from basic training in the United Kingdom, men transferred from other units, and many men of 'middle age' combed from detachments undertaking line of communications duties, and given only perfunctory musketry instruction at the base area. 'They were keen enough', wrote A. Hilliard Atteridge, 'and their goodwill was worthy of all praise, but by no stretch of the imagination could they be classed as "trained soldiers".'[100] Compounding this recurrent problem was the extension of the British front from 95 to 123 miles in January 1918 at a time when the number of battalions in each British division fell from twelve to nine. As the depleted units spent a longer time defending an extended front, the BEF had a smaller reserve from which to draw working parties in the rear: 'It was by no means easy', as Hilliard Atteridge added, 'to give men any time for rest or training.'[101]

Just as demanding was the conflict, as Haig reportedly observed, between 'the desire for training and the necessity for work'.[102] The latter reduced the 'paper strength' of all battalions as hundreds of men undertook permanent or temporary fatigues. Among the former included the staffing of brigade and divisional headquarters; clerks, draughtsmen, orderlies, cooks, and men attached to the signal and tunnelling companies; and, at rest camp, clerks to the town majors, camp wardens, guardians of coal, straw, and ration dumps, and more cooks and servants. Any battalion of say 600 men might also incur additional losses: 'about forty on leave, and twenty sick not evacuated', with another twenty attending various schools. As Cyril Falls observed,

> There were infantry schools, artillery schools, and trench-mortar schools; machine-gun schools, Lewis gun schools, bombing schools, gas schools; schools which taught horse-mastership, shoe-making, brick-laying, carpentry, sanitation, butchery, cooking. For a weak Division, schools became a nightmare.[103]

These schools, though useful in up-dating officers and NCOs about their instructional and command responsibilities, added to the burdens of units leaving the front line (when specialist instructors were needed to lead the resumption of training) and then on returning to it (when the training instructors had to lead and command in action). Nor were the benefits of these schools always obvious beyond giving the officers, as Captain Cosmo Clark relished, 'a splendid rest': the gas lecturer, A. E. Hodgkin, complained that most of his audience fell asleep at the Infantry School in Domart, while Guy Chapman recalled a dire five-day course in which the 'only diversion' was a lecture by General Maxse, even if the audience greeted the event with 'sullen resignation'.[104] In addition, brigades had to provide 'anything between 1,200 and 1,500 men each night for fatigues'[105] – repairing roads, laying railway track, and rebuilding trenches and gun emplacements. As Captain Jack complained, 'while the "paper strength" of the Battalion yielded the attractively high figure of 37 officers and 680 other ranks, our "real or ration strength" was only 27 and 445 respectively . . .'.[106]

The demands for working parties undoubtedly vexed regimental officers like Jack, but they were not a waste of manpower. The work had to be done if the BEF were to restore its defences, build a logistics infrastructure and function efficiently. 'It was not inefficiency or carelessness', commented Falls, 'it was rather the Englishman's passion for organization, for orderliness and smoothness.'[107] In a similar vein, brigades tried to rotate the demands for working parties, so that other troops could 'carry out their training satisfactorily',[108] but useful training still suffered from a multitude of impediments. Until drafts arrived, battalions sometimes languished with severe shortages of officers and/or other ranks, and a mounting toll of sick. In March 1917, the 2nd Royal Welch Fusiliers found that its 'strongest platoon, before we filled up with drafts, numbered 22 when the specialists were withdrawn; one platoon numbered 4'.[109] Periodically too, the prospect of effective training suffered from adverse weather conditions and the exhaustion of men after months at the front, little rest, or particularly gruesome working parties amid abandoned, derelict or blown-in trenches, where 'bodies were turned up at almost every yard'.[110]

In a review of the winter training of 1917–18, Brevet Colonel Charles Bonham-Carter identified two main difficulties that bedevilled unit training: keeping divisions out of the line for long enough to undergo 'thorough training' (that is, 'six weeks' undisturbed training) and the provision of adequate training grounds, which was becoming increasingly difficult to find without damaging crops. He calculated that only one-third of the divisions in France had been 'in reserve during the winter months', and that only the 55th Division, almost 'entirely reformed' after suffering heavy casualties at Cambrai, had six weeks of undisturbed training. By 21 March 1918, concluded Bonham-Carter, 'we had less than half our divisions who had done even a month's training in a back area undisturbed and there were a certain number who had had practically no training at all'.[111]

Even worse followed as active service took its toll throughout the spring and summer of 1918. Of the fifty infantry divisions which would serve in the Hundred Days' campaign, Peter Simkins has calculated that forty-three had been heavily engaged in the *Michael* offensive or the *Georgette* attack upon the Lys in April; seventeen served in both of these; and five of the seventeen resisted the *Blücher-Yorck* offensive on the Aisne. Another four divisions fought in the second battle of the Marne in July 1918. Apart from two incoming divisions from Palestine, Simkins reckoned that only five divisions had not been seriously involved in the fighting from 21 March to 8 August 1918.[112]

In these circumstances the training of the BEF was far from perfect but it was generally progressive for units that were out of line for several weeks. After a few days of cleaning-up, drill and organization, there followed a honing of individual and specialist skills in musketry, bayonet fighting, signalling, grenade throwing and Lewis gunnery; route-marching; lectures on tactics, discipline, sanitation and gas warfare (particularly for units new to the Western Front);[113] platoon training for semi-open and open warfare, often on a competitive basis; and ultimately, if time and space were to permit, exercises at battalion, brigade and, on rare occasions, divisional levels. Efficient training sought to inculcate realism into musketry practice, patrolling and raiding, and it accepted the risk of accidents with live ammunition and bombs. Infantry tested their training in raids upon weakened German defences, honed their combined-arms skills with artillery and tanks, and, in the case of the Scots Guards, learned from the training practices of the 2nd Canadian Division.[114]

Assessing the quality of this training has always proved problematic, especially as contemporary critics differed among themselves. Major General Guy Dawnay, writing as late as 18 October 1918, asserted that:

> there is no doubt whatever that our training is neither perfectly co-ordinated nor altogether evenly distributed throughout the armies in France. I am constantly being told by divisions moving from corps to corps and army to army that they are taught differently – different doctrine and different methods – as they move from one command to another.[115]

Dawnay felt that some of the attempts to inculcate more uniformity in training, like the introduction of corps schools, had failed, and that too much had been expected of the new Inspector-General of Training, Sir Ivor Maxse, appointed in June 1918.[116] Other critics disagreed: Major General Aylmer Haldane, who had deprecated the quality of instruction at junior officer level, claimed that corps schools had proved productive. Lieutenant-Colonel William Fraser, who had disparaged Haldane as 'sticky' and complained about shortcomings at command level, including a lack of system 'in higher formations' with 'divisions doing as little or as much work as they please', saw improvements in the last year before the Hundred Days' Campaign.[117] Maxse, freed from his duties as a corps commander, exploited the potential of his new appointment. Described as 'a man of imagination, originality and drive with a wealth of battlefield experience', he visited formations, schools and units throughout the BEF, infusing the 'Army and Divisional Schools' with 'a new spirit'.[118] His inspectorate also produced 202,287 pamphlets and leaflets before it was dissolved in December 1918, including 41,496 copies of *Attack Formations for Small Units*. Yet Maxse's biographer accepts that there were limits upon what he could achieve by August 1918. Had the war dragged on into 1919, as many except Haig, anticipated, the IGT might have had a greater impact.[119]

Conclusion

Striving for perfection in training was commendable, and revealed areas where further improvements could be made, but it obscured how far the BEF had improved and become more formidable as a fighting machine by the autumn of 1918. Like other combatants, the BEF had adapted its tactics, integrated new weapons technology and trained as best it could within the limits of time and space available (and in accordance with the preferences of the respective commanding officers). Learning, bolstered by battlefield experience, had occurred but limits remained on how far the shortcomings at divisional level and above could be addressed. If platoons and battalions were to have struggled at times to find appropriate training facilities, exercises at divisional level were an understandable rarity.

The huge variations in front-line experience, training opportunities and unit strength meant that divisions were bound to vary as operational bodies. As late as 20 May 1918, Haig accepted that a unit like the 59th Division, even if it were to have received 'a month or more training', would only produce men who were 'suitable, but not for a marching Division'.[120] In the following month, after inspecting the 40th Division, Haig surmised that such divisions might be best deployed in the '"Support" lines, and if the front becomes quiet can relieve a division (for training) in the line . . .'.[121] By 21 July 1918, Haldane affirmed that 'the policy of having 2nd Class divisions' had been 'introduced. I advocated it months ago. If the authorities now give assault divisions more time out of the line we shall be more successful in future attacks.'[122]

As a pragmatic response to the vagaries of battlefield experience, unit cohesion and limited training, this was eminently sensible. These distinctions could hardly be made public, as divisional rivalry was already widespread with regimental and staff officers claiming that certain divisions (usually their own) had performed exceptionally 'in contrast to others'.[123] These distinctions were always a matter of opinion, as evidenced by the continuing debates among scholars about which line divisions should rank alongside the Guards Division and elite Dominion units.[124] All units, though, had vital tasks to perform not simply in undertaking assault or support roles but also in harassing the enemy on the flanks through bombardments, patrols, raids and small-scale attacks. The demarcation of duties, if by no means absolute, was at least based upon perceived operational capacity and wartime reputation. It was no longer between regular, Territorial and service battalions, still less between volunteers and conscripts.

If the limitations of the wartime learning process were evident in the implicit categorization of divisional readiness, equally significant was the widespread expectation that the war would continue into 1919. Few senior or junior officers agreed with Haig that the Allied and Dominion forces, coupled with the morale-boosting presence of the American Expeditionary Force, were on the cusp of securing victory in 1918. Haig may have been correct in asserting that 'None of us are . . . anxious about the result'[125] but some officers still looked forward to the introduction of new tanks or new gases in 1919, further improvements in doctrinal understanding, and enhanced operational training. In so doing, they reflected uncertainty about how far the strategic balance had tilted in respect of the Allied and Associated Powers. They knew that the Germans had lost heavily in manpower and equipment through their failed offensives, but it was not until the Hundred Days' Campaign began that it became more apparent that their weakened opponent had proved unable to replace its huge losses of men and matériel and restore the battered morale of its Western Army.[126]

The BEF, fighting alongside French, Dominion and American forces, was able to exploit these weaknesses because it had become a battle-hardened army. It had reflected upon the Somme, and the experience of fighting the Germans over the following twenty months, experimenting with its combined-arms tactics, introducing new weapons technologies, and employing training, where possible, to spread the benefits of battle experience among cohorts that were absorbing incoming men on a regular basis. In the shifting panorama of the Western Front, where all belligerents were seeking how to achieve a breakthrough, and exploit it effectively, the BEF had built on the fundamentals. It had replaced most of the guns, tanks and manpower (if not the horses) lost in the spring and summer, and secured extraordinary support from the 'mechanical and horsed' services of the Army Service Corps.[127] It may not have built a perfect military machine but it had built one that could make a leading contribution to the success of the Hundred Days' Campaign.

Notes

1. John Terraine (ed.), *General Jack's Diary 1914-18; The Trench Diary of Brigadier-General J. L. Jack, D.S.O.* (London: Cassell, 1964), pp. 162, 172 and 179.

2. Andrew Simpson, *Directing Operations: British Corps Command on the Western Front* (Staplehurst: Spellmount, 2006); Gary D. Sheffield and Dan Todman (eds), *Command and Control on the Western Front: The British Army's Experience 1914-18* (Staplehurst: Spellmount, 2004); Keith Grieves, *The Politics of Manpower, 1914-1918* (Manchester: Manchester University Press, 1988); David Stevenson, *With Our Backs to the Wall: Victory and Defeat in 1918* (London: Allen Lane, 2011), pp. 370-87; Guy Hartcup, *The War of Invention: Scientific Developments, 1914-18* (London: Brassey's Defence Publishers, 1988), pp. 74-7; Jim Beach, *Haig's Intelligence: GHQ and the German Army, 1916-1918* (Cambridge: Cambridge University Press, 2013); Ian Malcolm Brown, *British Logistics on the Western Front 1914-1919* (Westport Ct.: Praeger, 1998).

3. Dan Todman and Gary Sheffield, 'Command and Control in the British Army on the Western Front' in Sheffield and Todman (eds), *Command and Control*, pp. 1-11, at p. 7 see also Jonathan Bailey, *The First World War and the Birth of the Modern Style of Warfare*, Occasional Paper 22 (Camberley: Strategic & Combat Studies Institute, 1996).

4. Basil Liddell Hart, *The Remaking of Modern Armies* (Edinburgh: John Murray, 1927), pp. 38-60; J. F. C. Fuller, *Memoirs of an Unconventional Soldier* (London: Ivor Nicholson and Watson, 1936), pp. 316-17.

5. Brigadier-General Sir James E. Edmonds and Lieutenant-Colonel R. Maxwell-Hyslop, *Military Operations France and Belgium 1918*, vol. 5 (London: H.M.S.O., 1948), p. 609.

6. Cyril Falls, *The First World War* (London: Longmans, 1960), pp. xv-xvi.

7. John Terraine, *White Heat: The New Warfare 1914-18* (London: Sidgwick & Jackson, 1982) and Shelford Bidwell and Dominick Graham, *Fire-Power: British Army Weapons and Theories of War 1904-1945* (London: Allen & Unwin, 1982).

8. Gary Sheffield and John Bourne (eds), *Douglas Haig: War Diaries and Letters 1914-1918* (London: Weidenfeld & Nicolson, 2005), p. 1.

9. John Laffin, *British Butchers and Bunglers of World War One* (Stroud: A. Sutton, 1988) and Alan Clark, *The Donkeys* (London: Mayflower Books, 1967).

10. Stephen Badsey, review of *Douglas Haig and the First World War* in *War in History*, vol. 17, no. 4 (2010), pp. 362-9, at p. 367.

11. Brian Bond, 'Passchendaele: Verdicts, Past and Present' in Peter Liddle (ed.), *Passchendaele in Perspective: The Third Battle of Ypres* (London: Leo Cooper, 1997), pp. 479-88, at p. 485; see also Brian Bond, *A victory worse than defeat? British interpretations of the First World War* (King's College London: Liddell Hart Centre for Military Archives *Annual Lecture*, 20 November 1997), p. 3, 'Foreword', *'Look to Your Front': Studies in the First World War* (Staplehurst: Spellmount, 1999), p. vii and Brian Bond and Nigel Cave (eds), 'Editors' Foreword', *Haig: A Reappraisal 70 Years On* (London: Leo Cooper, 1999), p. xiv.

12. Gary Sheffield, *Forgotten Victory: The First World War: Myths and Realities* (London: Headline, 2001), pp. xvii, 140-1, 259.

13. William Philpott, 'Beyond the "Learning Curve": The British Army's Military Transformation in the First World War', 10 November 2009, https://rusi.org/commentary/beyond-learning-curve-british-armys-military-transformation-first-world-war (accessed 23 March 2016); see also David Stevenson, *1914-1918: The History of the First World War* (London: Penguin Books, 2004), p. 193.

14. Spencer Jones, 'Introduction: The Forgotten Year' in Spencer Jones (ed.), *Courage Without Glory: The British Front on the Western Front 1915* (Solihull: Helion & Co., 2015), pp. xxiv-xxx, at pp. xxv-xxvi.

15. Jim Beach, 'Issued by the General Staff: Doctrine Writing at British GHQ, 1917-18', *War in History*, vol. 19, no. 4 (2012), pp. 464-91.

16. Jonathan Boff, 'Combined Arms during the Hundred Days Campaign, August-November 1918', *War in History*, vol. 17, no. 4 (2010), pp. 459-78 and Jonathan Boff, *Winning and Losing on the Western Front: The British Army and the Defeat of Germany in 1918* (Cambridge: Cambridge University Press, 2012).

17. Boff, *Winning and Losing*, p. 248.

18. Tim Travers, *How The War Was Won: Command and Technology in the British Army on the Western Front, 1917-1918* (London: Routledge, 1992), pp. 42-3, 146-8, 168-9, 175, 179; Sheffield and Bourne (eds), *Douglas Haig*, p. 39; Robin Prior and Trevor Wilson, *Command on the Western Front: The Military Career of Sir Henry Rawlinson* (Oxford: Blackwell, 1992), pp. 289, 298 and 309. For excellent accounts of these debates, see Boff, *Winning and Losing*, pp. 7-15 and Peter Simkins, *From the Somme to Victory: The British Army's experience on the Western Front, 1916-1918* (Barnsley: Praetorian Press, 2014), Ch. 2.

19. Edward M. Spiers, *Chemical Warfare* (Basingstoke: Macmillan Press, 1986), pp. 19-21; Donald Richter, *Chemical Soldiers: British Gas Warfare in World War One* (London: Leo Cooper, 1992), Ch. 6; Albert Palazzo, *Seeking Victory on the Western Front: The British Army and Chemical Warfare in World War I* (Lincoln: University of Nebraska Press, 2000), pp. 62-77.

20. Estimates of British and French casualties are generally agreed but German losses are disputed: William Philpott, *Bloody Victory: The Sacrifice on the Somme and the Making of the Twentieth Century* (London: Little Brown, 2009), pp. 600-03; Gary Sheffield, *The Chief: Douglas Haig and the British Army* (London: Aurum, 2011), pp. 194, 197 and Gary Sheffield, *The Somme* (London: Cassell, 2003), p. 151; J. P. Harris, *Douglas Haig and the First World War* (Cambridge: Cambridge University Press, 2008), p. 271; Christopher Duffy, *Through German Eyes: The British and the Somme 1916* (London: Weidenfeld and Nicolson, 2006), p. 324.

21. Harris, *Douglas Haig*, pp. 265, 270-1 and 274-9; Sheffield and Bourne (eds), *Douglas Haig*, p. 33; David R. Woodward, *Lloyd George and the Generals* (London: Associated University Presses, 1983), Ch. 6.

22. Winston Churchill, *The World Crisis, 1911-1918*, 5 vols. (London: Thornton Butterworth, 1923-31), vol. 3, pp. 39, 42 and 59 and David Lloyd George, *War Memoirs*, 6 vols. (London: Ivor Nicholson and Watson, 1933-6), vol. 1, preface, pp. viii-ix; for critiques of this writing, see Philpott, *Bloody Victory*, pp. 5, 598-99, 603-5; Simkins, *From the Somme*, pp. 21-4; and Hew Strachan, '"The Real War": Liddell Hart, Crutwell and Falls', in B. Bond (ed.), *The First World War and British Military History* (Oxford: Clarendon Press, 1991), pp. 41-67.

23. Philpott, *Bloody Victory*, pp. 600-3, 624-5; Harris, *Douglas Haig*, p. 271; Sheffield, *Chief*, pp. 197-8 and *Somme*, p. 151.

24. Sheffield, *Forgotten Victory*, pp. 184-5; see also Captain G. H. F. Nichols, *The 18th Division in the Great War* (Edinburgh: Blackwood, 1922), p. 130.

25. Charles Carrington, *Soldier from the War Returning* (London: Hutchinson, 1965), p. 140; see also Sheffield, *Somme*, p. 157 and, on the sustaining of British morale, Peter Liddle, *The 1916 Battle of the Somme Reconsidered* (Barnsley: Pen & Sword, 2016), pp. 141-53.

26. Gary D. Sheffield and G. I. S. Inglis (eds), *From Vimy Ridge to the Rhine: The Great War Letters of Christopher Stone DSO, MC* (London: Crowood Press, 1989), p. 71.

27. Liddle, *1916 Battle of the Somme*, pp. 116-19, 140; Major F. W. Bewsher, *The History of the 51ˢᵗ (Highland) Division 1914-1918* (Edinburgh: Blackwood, 1921), pp. 85, 120.

28. Bidwell and Graham, *Fire-Power*, pp. 84-5; Sanders Marble, *British Artillery on the Western Front in the First World War: 'The Infantry cannot do with a gun less'* (Farnham: Ashgate, 2013), pp. 142-3, 159; Lt.-Colonel J. H. Boraston and Captain Cyril E. O. Bax, *The Eighth Division in War, 1914-1918* (London: Medici Society, 1926), p. 86.

29. Robert T. Foley, 'Learning War's Lessons: The German Army and the Battle of the Somme', *Journal of Military History*, vol. 75, no. 2 (2011), pp. 471-504; Stevenson, *1914-1918*, pp. 193-4.

30. Foley, 'Learning War's Lessons', pp. 495-6 and Marble, *British Artillery*, pp. 145-7.

31. Captain Wilfrid Miles, *Military Operations, 1916*, vol. 2, p. 576.

32. TNA, WO 158/832, Lieutenant-General Sir Launcelot E. Kiggell, 'Note on Use of Tanks', 5 October 1916 and WO 158/835, General Staff, General Headquarters, 'Preliminary Notes on Tactical Employment of Tanks', August 1916.

33. Major Clough Williams-Ellis and A. Williams-Ellis, *The Tank Corps* (London: Country Life, 1919), p. 29.

34. Philpott, *Bloody Victory*, pp. 362-4; see also TNA, WO 158/832, Kiggell, 'Note on Use of Tanks'; Sheffield, *Forgotten Victory*, pp. 175-77; Prior and Wilson, *Command*, pp. 234-5.
35. Liddell Hart Centre for Military Archives (LHCMA), Robertson Mss., 4/4/44, Lieutenant-General Sir L. E. Kiggell to General Sir William Robertson, 17 September 1916.
36. TNA, WO 158/832, Kiggell, 'Note on use of Tanks'.
37. TNA, WO 32/5754, 'Digest of Decisions at a Conference on the 26th June 1916' and WO 158/835, General Staff, 'Preliminary Notes on Tactical Employment of Tanks'; see also J. P. Harris, *Men, Ideas and Tanks: British military thought and armoured forces, 1903-1939* (Manchester: Manchester University Press, 1995), p. 61; J. P. Harris, 'Haig and The Tank' in Bond and Cave (eds), *Haig*, pp. 145-54, at p. 145 and Churchill, *World Crisis*, vol. 3, pp. 185-6.
38. LHCMA, Robertson Mss., 7/6/86, Robertson to Haig, 1 November 1916.
39. TNA, WO 158/21, Haig to Secretary, War Office, 17 July 1916.
40. TNA, WO 142/266, 'Special Brigade Operations' and WO 188/143, W. H. Livens, 'The Liven's Gas Projector – Its Use & Development', n.d.; Palazzo, *Seeking Victory*, pp. 104-5.
41. Hartcup, *War of Invention*, pp. 64-7; Stevenson, *1914-1918*, p. 186; Sheffield, *Somme*, p. 69.
42. John Lee, 'Some Lessons of the Somme: The British Infantry in 1917' in Bond, *'Look To Your Front'*, pp. 79-88 at p. 80; see also Paddy Griffith, *Battle Tactics of the Western Front: The British Army's Art of Attack, 1916-18* (New Haven: Yale University Press, 1994), pp. 57-8, 76.
43. Carrington, *Soldier*, p. 198; see also Beach, 'Issued by the General Staff', pp. 469-70 and Griffith, *Battle Tactics*, p. 95.
44. Boff, 'Combined Arms', p. 467.
45. Ibid; Prior and Wilson, *Command*, p. 311; Griffith, *Battle Tactics*, pp. 78-9, 96-7.
46. A. M. McGilchrist, *The Liverpool Scottish 1900-1919* (Liverpool: Henry Young & Sons, 1930), p. 131.
47. James C. Dunn, *The War the Infantry Knew 1914-1919: A Chronicle of Service in France and Belgium with the Second Battalion His Majesty's Twenty-Third Foot, The Royal Welch Fusiliers: founded on personal records, recollections and reflections, assembled, edited and partly written by One of their Medical Officers*, 2nd edition (New York: Jane's, 1987), pp. 303 and 306.
48. Terraine (ed), *General Jack's Diary*, p. 201.
49. William W. Seymour, *The History of The Rifle Brigade in The War of 1914-1918*, 2 vols. (London: The Rifle Brigade Club, 1927-36), vol. 2, pp. 20-1.
50. Beach, 'Issued by the General Staff', pp. 467-91.
51. Imperial War Museum (IWM), Maxse Mss., 69/53/11, file 42, Sir F. Ivor Maxse to Sir C. Bonham Carter, 9 December 1917.
52. LHCMA, Montgomery-Massingberd Mss., 7/33, General Staff, 'The Division in Attack', November 1918 and Beach, 'Issued by the General Staff', p. 491.
53. Albert P. Palazzo, 'The British Army's Counter-Battery Staff Office and Control of the Enemy in World War 1', *Journal of Military History*, vol. 63, no. 1 (1999), pp. 55-74.
54. Captain Cyril Falls, *Military Operations, 1917*, vol. 1, pp. 11-12, 182n1; Marble, *British Artillery*, p. 167.
55. Edmonds, *Military Operations, 1917*, vol. 2, pp. 42n1 and 49.
56. Ibid. p. 42.
57. LHCMA, Allenby Mss., 1/8/2, Sir Edmund Allenby to Lady Allenby, 10 April 1917; see also Sir Martin Farndale, *History of the Royal Regiment of Artillery, 1914-18* (London: The Royal Artillery Institution, 1986), pp. 164-66; Prior and Wilson, *Command*, pp. 293-5; Marble, *British Artillery*, pp. 178-81; Falls, *Military Operations, 1917*, vol. 1, pp. 14, 184-5.
58. Edmonds, *Military Operations, 1917*, vol. 2, pp. 49ns1-3.
59. 'An Attack in the West', *Yorkshire Evening Post*, 12 May 1917, p. 5.
60. TNA, WO 158/858, 'Messines: Detail of assistance rendered by Tanks', n.d.; 'How a Tank was held up by the Mud. Thrilling Adventure in the Messines Battle', *Yorkshire Evening Post*, 27 June 1917, p. 3; Harris, *Men, ideas and Tanks*, pp. 96, 99-100.
61. Trevor Wilson, *The Myriad Faces of War: Britain and the Great War, 1914-1918* (Oxford: Polity Press, 1986), pp. 449-53; Sheffield, *Forgotten Victory*, pp. 190-7 and 200-03; Harris, *Douglas Haig*, pp. 312-15 and 343-7; and Griffith, *Battle Tactics*, p. 145.
62. Farndale, *History*, pp. 204-05 and 211; Marble, *British Artillery*, pp. 190-1; Palazzo, 'British Army's Counter-Battery', p. 69.

63. LHCMA, Fuller Mss., 1/2/1, J. F. C. Fuller, 'Project for the capture of ST QUENTIN by a coup de main', 3 August 1917; see also Harris, *Men, Ideas and Tanks*, p. 102.

64. TNA, WO 158/835, Brigadier-General H. J. Elles to General Staff, 7 September 1917.

65. IWM, Docs 3354, Brigadier Richard C. Foot, 'Once a Gunner', p. 70; see also Williams-Ellis, *Tank Corps*, pp. 103-4; Bryn Hammond, *Cambrai 1917. The Myth of the First Great Tank Battle* (London: Weidenfeld & Nicolson, 2008), pp. 80, 430-2; A. J. Smithers, *Cambrai: The First Great Tank Battle* (London: Leo Cooper, 1992), p.123; Harris, *Men, Ideas and Tanks*, pp. 124-5; John Terraine, *The Smoke and the Fire: Myths and Anti-Myths of War 1861-1945* (London: Sidgwick & Jackson, 1980), p. 153.

66. Farndale, *History*, p. 217; Palazzo, 'British Army's Counter-Battery Staff', p. 70; Prior and Wilson, *Command*, pp. 292-5; Marble, *British Artillery*, pp. 200-1; Hew Strachan, *The First World War: A New Illustrated History* (London: Simon & Schuster, 2001), p. 306.

67. Hammond, *Cambrai*, pp. 62, 81, 83, 431; Miles, *Military Operations, 1917*, vol. 3, p. 90n1.

68. Prior and Wilson, *Command*, pp. 314-15.

69. Farndale, *History*, p. 185.

70. LHCMA, Robertson Mss., 7/7/52, Haig to Robertson, 17 September 1917; see also Terraine, *White Heat*, p. 216.

71. National Army Museum (NAM), Rawlinson Mss., Add. No. 1952-01-33-21, General Henry Rawlinson to Winston Churchill, 22 April 1918; see also Paddy Griffith, 'The Tactical Problem: Infantry, Artillery and the Salient' in Liddle, *Passchendaele in Perspective*, pp. 61-72, at p. 69.

72. Nick Lloyd, *Hundred Days: The Campaign that ended World War 1* (New York: Basic Books, 2014), p. 181; see also Marble, *British Artillery*, p. 238.

73. Marble, *British Artillery*, pp. 216-23; Harris, *Douglas Haig*, p. 448.

74. Williams-Ellis, *Tank Corps*, pp. 181-3.

75. LHCMA, Fuller Mss., 1/2/2b, 'The Tactical Employment of Tanks in 1918', 8 August 1917; see also Terraine, *White Heat*, p. 242; Harris, *Men, Ideas and Tanks*, p. 96; Frank Mitchell, *Tank Warfare: The Story of the Tanks in the Great War* (London: T. Nelson & Sons, 1933), pp. 18-20; Brian Holden Reid, *J. F. C. Fuller: Military Thinker* (Basingstoke: MacMillan Press, 1987), p. 43.

76. LHCMA, Robertson Mss., I/3/44a, Haig to Robertson, 21 November 2017; see also Bidwell and Graham, *Fire-Power*, p. 92.

77. Williams-Ellis, *Tank Corps*, pp. 123-4, 211; Prior and Wilson, *Command*, p. 295; Hartcup, *War of Invention*, p. 87.

78. TNA, MUN 4/2791, Haig to the War Office, 5 June 1917; see also Mitchell, *Tank Warfare*, p. 166.

79. National Library of Scotland (NLS), Acc. 3155/97, Haig diaries, vol. 11, 16 May 1918. Haig's 20 per week contradicts the 60 per week in Williams-Ellis, *Tank Corps*, p. 177, but as Haig reckoned that he had only 129 Mark Vs by 16 May, his concerns about tank production seem more reasonable.

80. TNA, WO 158/835, Brigadier-General H. J. Elles to General Staff G.H.Q., 3 January 1918, enclosing J. F. C. Fuller, 'Defensive and Offensive Use of Tanks 1918'.

81. LHCMA, Fuller Mss., 1/50/1, Fuller, 'The Tactics of the Attack as Affected by the Speed and Circuit of the Medium 'D' Tank', June 1918; Edmonds, *Military Operations, 1918*, vol. 1, pp. 118, 294, 419, 428, 526 and 526n4 and *Military Operations, 1918*, vol. 2, pp. 36, 134, 261n2; see also Harris, *Men, Ideas and Tanks*, pp. 148-51.

82. Ludwig Haber, *Poisonous Cloud: Chemical Warfare in the First World War* (Oxford: Clarendon Press, 1986), pp. 264, 270 and Julian Perry Robinson in Stockholm Institute for Peace Research, *The Problem of Chemical and Biological Warfare*, 6 vols. (Stockholm: Almqvist & Wiksell, 1971-5), vol.1, pp. 51-2, 59.

83. Edmonds, *Military Operations, 1918*, vol. 5, p. 606n2 but the Japanese used poison gas extensively in China, Spiers, *Chemical Warfare*, pp. 97-104.

84. Edmonds, *Military Operations, 1917*, vol. 2, p. 49n1 and *Military Operations, 1918*, vol. 2, pp. 163-4, 383, 390, 412.

85. Miles, *Military Operations, 1917*, vol. 3, p. 246n4.

86. TNA, WO 32/5783, 'Diary of Development of British Respirator', p. 4; Victor Lefebure, *The Riddle of the Rhine: Chemical Strategy in Peace and War* (London: Collins, 1921), p. 122.

87. Major-General Charles H. Foulkes, *"GAS !" The Story of the Special Brigade* (Edinburgh: Blackwood, 1934), pp. 112 and 114.

88. Augustin M. Prentiss, *Chemicals in War: A Treatise on Chemical Warfare* (New York: McGraw-Hill, 1937), pp. 52 and 348; TNA, WO 158/270, General George de S. Barrow, 'Report, First Army No. 852(G)', 18 August 1916.

89. LHCMA, Foulkes Mss., 6/13, Foulkes, 'Notes on the Offensive Use of Gas and Methods of Gas Discharge', a lecture delivered to commanders and staffs of the Second Army at Helfaut, 28 April 1917; see also Prentiss, *Chemicals*, pp. 362-4.

90. TNA, WO 158/294, 'Effect of British Gas Projectors', 8 July 1917.

91. TNA, SUPP 10/292, Brigadier-General C. H. Foulkes, 'Report on the Activity of the Special Brigade during the War', 19 December 1918, pp. 2-3; *The History of the Corps of Royal Engineers*, vol. 5 (Chatham: The Institution of Royal Engineers, 1952), p. 523.

92. IWM, P.399, Captain Adrian E. Hodgkin, diary, 9 July 1918; *History of the Corps*, vol. 5, p. 524. On the skepticism about this mode of attack, see NLS, Acc. 3155/97, Haig diaries, vol. 11, 13 May 1918.

93. University of Leeds, Liddle Collection (LC), LIDDLE/WW1/GS/1452, C. Edgar Shelly, memoir, p. 21; see also LIDDLE/WW1/GS/0140, Private William H. Bink, diary 21 July 1917; LC, LIDDLE/WW1/GS/1025, Captain Joseph MacLean Mss., Maclean to Alex, 15 August 1917; and Terraine, *General Jack's Diary*, 27 July 1917, p. 233.

94. W. G. Macpherson et al, *History of the Great War: Medical Services Diseases of War*, 2 vols (London: HMSO, 1922-3), vol. 2, pp. 294 and 306; TNA, WO 142/99, 'Report on the Gas Shell Bombardment at Nieuport on Night of 21/22nd July 1917'.

95. TNA, WO 95/1765, War Diary of 7th Battalion, Seaforth Highlanders, 21 March 1918; WO 158/70, General Staff, 'Notes on Recent Fighting – No. 16. Use of Gas by the enemy prior to his attack on the British on the Aisne, the 27th of May 1918', 11 June 1918.

96. Lieutenant-Colonel Arthur A. Hanbury-Sparrow, *The Land-Locked Lake: Impressions of Active Service in the European War* (London: Arthur Barker, 1932), p. 309.

97. Royal Engineers Museum, R/15, Special Brigade regarding Gas in World War 1, 1915-18, 'Report on Operations of the Special Companies, R. E., attached Canadian Corps, July 15th 1917 to August 15th 1917' and TNA, WO 95/62, Major-General G. P. Dawnay to First Army, Third Army, Fourth Army, Fifth Army', 16 March 1918.

98. TNA, WO 158/294, 'Experiences Derived From The Arras Battle', 11 April 1917.

99. Major C. H. Dudley Ward, *History of the Welsh Guards* (London: John Murray, 1920), p. 18.

100. A. Hilliard Atteridge, *History of the 17th (Northern) Division* (Glasgow: Robert MacLehose, 1929), pp. 249, 268 and 278; see also John Ewing, *The History of the 9th (Scottish) Division 1914-1919* (London: John Murray, 1921), p. 175.

101. Hilliard Atteridge, *History of the 17th*, p. 269; see also Harris, *Douglas Haig*, pp. 432-3.

102. Seymour, *History of the Rifle Brigade*, vol. 2, p. 214.

103. Cyril Falls, *The History of the 36th (Ulster) Division* (London: Constable, 1998, originally Belfast: McCaw, Stevenson & Orr, 1922), p. 138.

104. IWM, Docs. 7460 Captain Cosmo Clark Mss., Clark to mother and father, 4 June 1916 and IWM, P.399, Hodgkin diary, 8 February 1917; Guy Chapman, *A Passionate Prodigality: Fragments of Autobiography* (London: MacGibbon & Kee, 1965), p. 153; Boff, *Winning and Losing*, p. 63.

105. Major C. H. Dudley Ward, *The 56th Division – 1st London Territorial Division* (London: John Murray, 1921), p. 247.

106. Terraine, *General Jack's Diary*, pp. 218, 233-4, 250, 252; see also LHCMA, 7/32, Montgomery-Massingberd Mss., Major-General Guy Dawnay to Major-General A. A. Montgomery, 31 October 1918.

107. Falls, *History of the 36th*, p. 139.

108. Everard Wyrall, *The History of the 62nd (West Riding) Division 1914-1919*, 2 vols. (London: John Lane, 1925), vol. 1, p. 59.

109. Dunn, *War the Infantry Knew*, p. 304.

110. Boraston and Bax, *Eighth Division*, p. 80; see also NLS, MS 20249, f.375, Major-General J. Aylmer L. Haldane, war diary, 26 December 1917; Dudley Ward, *56th Division*, p. 214; Terraine, *General Jack's Diary*, p. 194.

111. IWM, 69/53/13, file 54, Maxse Mss., Col. Charles Bonham-Carter to Gen. F. Ivor Maxse, 25 June 1918.

112. Peter Simkins, 'Co-Stars or Supporting Cast? British Divisions in the "Hundred Days", 1918' in Paddy Griffith (ed), *British Fighting Methods in the Great War* (London: Frank Cass, 1996), pp. 50-69 at pp. 55-6.

113. Lt.-Col. R. R. Thompson, *The Fifty-Second (Lowland) Division 1914-1918* (Glasgow: MacLehose, Jackson & Co., 1923), p. 512. Despite such training, incoming units could suffer severely from poison gas, Colonel J. M. Findlay, *With the 8th Scottish Rifles 1914-1919* (London: Blackie & Son, 1926), pp. 153, 171-2.

114. F. Loraine Petre: Wilfrid Ewart and Major-General Sir Cecil Lowther, *The Scots Guards in the Great War 1914-1918* (London: John Murray, 1925), p. 263; Lt.-Colonel W. D. Croft, *Three Years with the 9th (Scottish) Division* (London: John Murray, 1919), pp. 72; Wyrall, *History of the 62nd*, vol. 1, pp. 48, 52, 59, 68; Sheffield and Inglis, *From Vimy Ridge to the Rhine*, pp. 89-90; Boff, *Winning and Losing*, p. 64; McGilchrist, *Liverpool Scottish*, p. 131; Cyril Falls, *The Life of A Regiment: The Gordon Highlanders in the First World War 1914-1919* (Aberdeen: The University Press, 1958), vol. 4, pp. 119 and 167; Frederick P. Gibbon, *42nd (East Lancashire) Division 1914-1918* (London: Country Life, 1920), pp. 110, 122; Marble, *British Artillery*, p. 227.

115. LHCMA, 7/32, Montgomery-Massingberd Mss., Maj.-Gen. G. Dawnay to Maj.-Gen. Sir A. A. Montgomery, 31 October 1918.

116. Ibid.

117. NLS, MS 20249, ff. 269, 295 and 298, Haldane war diary, 18 April 1917, 25 May 1917 and 4 June 1917, and MS 20250, ff. 90, 103 and 119, 28 May 1918, 5 July 1918 and 10 August 1918; David Fraser (ed), *In Good Company: The First World War Letters and Diaries of The Hon. William Fraser Gordon Highlanders* (London: Michael Russell, 1990), pp. 109, 147, 160, 190, 214, but he was still critical of training at battalion level, pp. 215, 218; see also Lt.-Col. L. B. Oatts, *Proud Heritage: The Story of the Highland Light Infantry*, 3 vols. (Glasgow: The House of Grant, 1961), vol. 3, p. 345 and Terraine, *General Jack's Diary*, pp. 209, 252-3, 258.

118. Major-General Hugh H. Essame, *The Battle for Europe, 1918* (London: Batsford, 1972), p. 102.

119. John Baynes, *Far From A Donkey: The Life of General Sir Ivor Maxse* (London: Brassey's, 1995), pp. 211-14.

120. NLS, Acc 3155/97, Haig diaries, vol. 11, 20 May 1918.

121. NLS, Acc 3155/97, Haig diaries, vol. 11, 24 June 1918.

122. NLS, MS 20250, f. 110, Haldane war diary, 21 July 1918.

123. Sheffield and Inglis, *From Vimy Ridge*, p. 111; see also Fraser, *In Good Company*, pp. 161, 173 and 229.

124. Compare Boff, *Winning and Losing*, p. 64 with Peter Simkins, 'Co-Stars or Supporting Cast?', pp. 56-8 and Gary D. Sheffield, 'The Indispensable Factor: The Performance of British Troops in 1918' in Peter Dennis and `Jeffrey Grey (eds.), *1918 Defining Victory: Proceedings of the Chief of Army's History Conference held at the National Convention Centre, Canberra 29 September 1998* (Canberra: Army History Unit, Department of Defence, 1999), pp. 72-95, at pp. 78-9.

125. NLS, Acc 3155/97, Haig diaries, vol. 11, 7 May 1918.

126. Wilhelm Deist, 'The Military Collapse of the German Empire: The Reality Behind the Stab-in-the-Back Myth', *War in History*, vol. 3, no. 2 (1996), pp. 186-207.

127. Falls, *History of the 36th*, p. 279.

Suggested Further Reading

Bidwell, Shelford and Dominick Graham, *Fire-Power: British Army Weapons and Theories of War 1904-1945* (London: George Allen & Unwin, 1982)

Boff, Jonathan, *Winning and Losing on the Western Front: The British Third Army and the Defeat of Germany in 1918* (Cambridge: Cambridge University Press, 2012)

Griffith, Paddy, *Battle Tactics of the Western Front: The British Army's Art of Attack, 1916-18* (New Haven: Yale University Press, 1994)

Harris, J.P., *Men, Ideas and Tanks: British military thought and armoured forces, 1903-1939* (Manchester: Manchester University Press, 1995)

Marble, Sanders, *British Artillery on the Western Front in the First World War* (Farnham: Ashgate, 2013)

Philpott, William, *Bloody Victory: The Sacrifice on the Somme and the Making of the Twentieth Century* (London: Abacus, 2009)

Prior, Robin and Trevor Wilson, *Command on the Western Front: The Military Career of Sir Henry Rawlinson* (Oxford: Blackwell, 1992)

Sheffield, Gary D., *Forgotten Victory: The First World War: Myths and Realities* (London: Headline, 2001)

Simkins, Peter, *From the Somme to Victory: the British Army's experience on the Western Front, 1916-1918* (Barnsley: Praetorian Press, 2014)

Stevenson, David, *With Our Backs to the Wall: Victory and Defeat in 1918* (London: Allen Lane, 2011)

PART ONE

PART ONE

Chapter 1

The BEF and the Hundred Days

By Niall Barr

General Sir Frederick Maurice, of 'Maurice case' fame, wrote one of the first books which considered the British Expeditionary Force's victories in 1918.[1] His early assessment emphasised the contribution of the BEF to final victory:

> I am convinced that the achievement of the National Army of Great Britain transcends even that of her old Regular Army . . . starting on August 8, it fought uninterruptedly and victoriously for three months, driving the enemy back 120 miles, taking more than twice as many prisoners and more than three times as many guns as it had lost, and completely routing the German armies by which it was opposed. This is . . . an achievement to which no words can do justice.[2]

This was a fine tribute to the armies of the BEF and its British and Commonwealth soldiers. Yet while the nature and achievement of that victory might have seemed clear in 1919 when Maurice wrote this paean of praise, it has to be said that the lustre, and even the memory, of these victories seems to have faded quickly. Today, the great battles fought by the BEF in the summer and autumn, not to mention those fought in the spring, of 1918, have almost no register in the British public consciousness next to the battles of the Somme and Passchendaele. Perhaps it is because the battles of 1918 which represent dogged defence against considerable odds and then a rolling series of hard-won victories simply do not chime with the popular image of the war that 1918 remains the 'forgotten year' of the Great War.[3] Even in historical scholarship there has tended, until recently, to be less emphasis upon the battles of 1918.[4] Gary Sheffield has argued powerfully that the achievements of the BEF in 1918 remain a 'forgotten victory'.[5] Yet it is in the last, dramatic phases of the war that we can divine just how much the BEF had learnt from its long years of struggle and understand the changing character of the Great War in its final year.

This chapter aims to provide an outline of the BEF during the last hundred days of the war and as such can only offer a glimpse of the vast range of the BEF's activities during that period. However, it is possible to examine the changing balance and the altered strategic situation on the Western Front, and the manner in which the BEF met and overcame the diverse operational and tactical challenges which it faced during one of the most dramatic years of the Great War. In doing so, the chapter will focus on a number of the most important events which illuminate significant issues for, and developments in, the BEF during the last days of the war.

At the same time, it is important to remember that whatever the BEF was in 1918, it could not be described as the National Army of Great Britain. It was very much an Imperial force with soldiers and airmen drawn from all over the British Empire. Central to this Imperial effort were the military contributions of the Dominions in which the Canadian Corps and Australian Corps were two distinct formations, while New Zealand contributed its own division. These were powerful combat formations and in essence, the Canadian, Australian and New Zealand formations were now the national forces of junior, but sovereign allies. British official failure properly to recognise this changed status of the Dominion contribution created tension and irritation even during the war.

However, Maurice's title of a 'National Army' was in one sense correct. By 1918, the distinctions between the Regular Army, the Territorial Army and the New Armies of Kitchener's volunteers were less obvious than they had been in previous years of the war. During the emergency of the spring battles, units and formations had been drawn from many other fighting fronts to reinforce the BEF. Most notable amongst these was the 74th 'Broken Spur' Division, formed from Yeomanry regiments which had served in Palestine in 1917 and 1918 and was now serving as infantry on the Western Front. Its baptism of fire there came as quite a shock to soldiers used to operating in the lower density, more open terrain of Palestine and now found themselves in the cauldron of the Western Front. Some battalions which had been fought out during the spring battles were now filled with young conscripts. These men were noticeably younger than their Territorial or volunteer counterparts. In this sense, at least, the BEF resembled a national army with the distinctions of previous years blurred if not absent.

Some scholars have questioned whether there is much to be learned from considering the evolution of the BEF over the course of the war. John Keegan once described any such attempt as 'a pointless waste'.[6] However, many historians have considered this 'learning curve' as an important dimension to understanding how the British Army eventually overcame the tactical deadlock of the Western Front.[7] There is no doubt that much changed in tactics, technology and technique between 1914 and 1918 and that this had a profound impact upon the outcome of the war. Whether we were to consider infantry tactics and equipment, the profound changes in artillery techniques or the innovations in the use of the tank or airpower, the British Army's methods had changed beyond all recognition over four years of fighting. The importance of all these technological improvements and tactical developments was that the BEF had learned to work and fight together. It was the combination of all these developments in the use of combined arms warfare which made the BEF such a formidable instrument in the autumn of 1918.

But an emphasis on the complex and seemingly bewildering range of change in tactics and technology of all the armies on the Western Front can sometimes obscure the less obvious but no less profound accretion of hard-won experience by the BEF. Whether we were to consider Battalion commanders and their subordinates who by 1918 had often fought in many of the bitter battles of previous years or the commanders and their staffs at all levels from Brigade, Division to Corps and Army, they now all had valuable experience and in-depth knowledge of their roles and functions. The movement, feeding and supply of the vast machine that the BEF had become was now practised and effective. It was thus this complex evolution – both off and on the battlefield – which enabled the BEF to cope with the challenges of 1918.[8]

It is also important to remember that the BEF came very close to defeat during the spring of 1918. With the war against Russia concluded in Germany's favour, Hindenburg and Ludendorff took the opportunity to transfer large numbers of soldiers to the Western Front. With this overall superiority in manpower, Ludendorff planned to break the British Army and force Britain and France to sue for peace before the United States could properly weigh into the fight. Operation *Michael*, launched on 21 March 1918, battered the British Fifth Army with a vast artillery bombardment before unleashing storm troops to infiltrate and break through the British lines. By 30 March, Gough's Army had effectively been destroyed and its remnants forced into a disorderly retreat. However, when the Germans expanded the offensive around Arras, their forces met with a resolute defence which gave ground but remained unbroken. The Germans had inflicted roughly 350,000 casualties on the Allies, taking 90,000 prisoners and 1,000 guns while advancing over 40 miles into the Allied rear.

Nevertheless, British and French powers of resilience were still far beyond Ludendorff's expectations. He had anticipated that the surprise, speed and ferocity of the German attack mounted on the junction between the two allies would effectively force them apart, allowing the Germans to defeat each in detail. This situation very nearly arose when Pétain suffered a critical loss of nerve on 25 March. He informed Haig that if the Germans were to advance any further he would be forced to break contact with the British and cover Paris. In justice to Pétain, he had been shocked and disconcerted by the breakup of the British Fifth Army which was now threatening to unhinge his line, but if Pétain were to have acted on his instincts, it would have heralded disaster and defeat for the Allies. This was the supreme crisis of the war for the Allies, and their response was both cool and creditable – quite unlike Ludendorff's handling of the August 1918 crisis for the Germans. Haig – not without self-interest – now pushed through the proposal for a co-ordinating Commander-in-Chief – something which he had been stubbornly opposing for the past four months. The Doullens agreement of 26 March set the framework for an Allied Supreme Commander which was firmed up by subsequent conferences. After discussion, General Ferdinand Foch became the Allied Generalissimo with the power to co-ordinate the activity of all the armies on the Western Front. Finally, the Allies had adopted a policy of co-ordination, albeit imperfect, which had a great influence on the conduct of the war in its last hundred days.

After the crisis of Operation *Michael*, each successive German offensive, planned without any guiding strategic concept other than ultimate victory, was impressive in its sound and fury but suffered from steadily diminishing returns. *Georgette*, the offensive mounted from 9–21 April against the British Third Army in Flanders, made little progress, though *Blücher*, the attack on the Chemin des Dames from 27 May to 3 June, again shocked the Allies with its scale, ferocity and success. Within three days the Germans forced three river lines, advanced 40 miles and took 65,000 prisoners. *Gneisenau*, fought around Metz, was less successful, and the limited French counter-attack mounted on 12 June showed that Allied powers of resistance remained undiminished. In mounting successive diversionary offensives to draw Allied strength away from the north and Flanders, Ludendorff had diverted his own troops as well as the Allies.

Left without any other strategy than offensive, Ludendorff believed that one more assault mounted around the Rheims salient would draw Allied reserves from the north and enable him to fight *Hagen*, the supposedly decisive battle to be fought in Flanders. Ludendorff gave the Rheims offensive the unfortunate name of *Friedensturm*, or Peace Offensive, which raised the German people's hopes of victory. Having been asked to suffer so much in order to achieve victory, the German people were willing to mount one last effort. However, the hopes raised by *Friedensturm* were to be cruelly shattered. The offensive was halted on the first day and, two days later on 18 July, was vigorously counter-attacked by Mangin's Sixth Army in the first major Allied offensive since March.

This French and American counter-attack on 18 July was an event of the greatest importance even though its impetus petered out two days later. It might, indeed, be considered the critical turning point of the war. For Ludendorff, this counter-attack meant the proven failure of his offensive strategy. German strength was at an end and the final projected offensive to attack the British in Flanders would remain still-born. The British and French armies had managed to survive the greatest onslaught of the war and while both had taken terrific batterings, they were still in the field and capable of offensive action. Their governments had not fallen apart nor sued for peace. Ludendorff's 'gambler's throw' had failed.

While the Allies by July 1918 could look forward to a steadily improving rifle strength on the Western Front, the Germans were facing a serious shortage of replacements – and most important of all, a sharp decline in the morale of their men. Much of this crisis was of Ludendorff's own making. It had been his decision to attack in the West with the last available strength of the German army. His division of the army into two elements, the *Sturmtruppen* or Storm Troops, and the *Stellungtruppen* or Trench Troops, had an unfortunate effect on morale. By combing out the best men and officers for the elite storm troop divisions, Ludendorff had indeed maximised the offensive potential of the army, but at the same time had reduced the effectiveness and motivation of the rest of the army. In attack, the army had proved a formidable instrument, as the results of the *Michael* and *Blücher* offensives showed. However, by July, with the ultimate failure of Ludendorff's offensives, the army was left in a lamentable state. The advances of the storm troop divisions had been impressive, but had not inflicted a major strategic defeat on the Allies. Once the momentum of the advance petered out, the ground gained actually became a liability because the Germans were now holding large salients without prepared defences which both increased the front to occupy and made it difficult, if not impossible, to hold it securely.

Worst of all were the huge German losses sustained. From January until July 1918, their forces suffered one million casualties of which the vast majority came from the storm troop divisions. Ludendorff's opportunistic strategy, which kept feeding reserves into the attack long after any hope of meaningful progress, had drained the army of its best men and officers. This left a weakened force composed of less capable and motivated soldiers in the *Stellung* divisions, holding a longer front line. At the same time, the losses sustained could not possibly be made good. Ludendorff had gambled away the final reserves of manpower. For the whole of 1918, the Germans could only expect another 600,000 replacements.

Increasingly, drafts sent up to the front were composed of wounded veterans, factory workers, young boys and other less capable and often disaffected members of German society. They could not be of the same quality as the tough, well-motivated soldiers who had begun the offensive in March. Indeed, many of the men being sent up to the front had been deeply affected by the inequality in Germany and had become influenced by socialist ideas. These men were reluctant soldiers at best, unreliable deserters at worst. Rates of desertion and combat refusal grew dramatically from July onwards, and new drafts of soldiers were often greeted with shouts of 'blackleg' by their disillusioned comrades. It is this situation which accounts for the patchy performance of the German army from July onwards. Some units were still composed of hardened veterans and they generally fought with toughness and determination. However, many German units did not have the experience or the inclination to fight well and did not possess the stamina or fighting spirit of the previous years. Divisions composed of such men were thus a much easier proposition for Allied troops than the German army of 1916 or 1917.

All of these problems were compounded by the leadership of Germany, where Hindenburg and Ludendorff were virtually military dictators. As with almost every major combatant, 1916 and 1917 had seen a distinct move towards a thorough prosecution of the war and total war aims. Hindenburg and Ludendorff had become an almost physical embodiment of this idea in Germany. Ludendorff's spring offensives had been a final all out attempt to win the war but the German duo was now left with total aims but no means of achieving them. Having viewed the war solely from a military perspective and with no real knowledge of the wider implications of diplomacy, political aims or the importance of home front morale and support, neither Ludendorff nor Hindenburg possessed the answer to their dilemma. As far as they were concerned, the evident discontent and disturbance at home simply required more discipline and repression in order to bring about eventual victory. What they failed to realise was that too much had been asked of the German people already.

By July, with his offensive strategy in ruins, Ludendorff could find no alternative. He was not willing to surrender his total aims – the occupation of Northern France, Belgium and large areas of Russia were not negotiable, just at the time when it was no longer within Germay's power to maintain her conquests. His desire to hold onto these territories meant that he was unwilling to consider a phased and orderly withdrawal to a shorter front which would have been easier to defend. His refusal to countenance this committed his army to a defensive battle on long frontages with tired, weakened divisions – a battle it could not win. He argued that such a withdrawal would have severe political consequences at home and amongst Germany's allies. This was quite correct, but the alternative – neither offence nor defence – was no strategy at all. The German army was effectively in limbo without an offensive or defensive posture and left vulnerable to any Allied counter-stroke.

Ludendorff was not able to admit to himself – let alone the German Chancellor and people – that Germany had lost the war. Nevertheless, it is not surprising that Allied leaders did not realise that the war was won. The German army remained a formidable instrument and in possession of large tracts of France and Belgium. The French army, although still capable of offensive action, was largely exhausted, with unreliable morale and limited fighting spirit. The American army, now finally growing in formidable numbers, was becoming a force to be reckoned with in terms of size, but was almost entirely without an experienced staff, artillery train, aircraft or logistic support.

The British army was a fully effective fighting force but was also a wasting asset. After two years of full-scale continental land warfare, the British Empire's reserves of manpower had been more or less exhausted. Thus, while the British Army of 1918 was undoubtedly a well-trained, experienced and highly professional force, many worried that it might not survive another year of intense fighting. While the balance of the war had irrevocably shifted, this change was almost invisible to the protagonists. Until the Allies could actually impose their will on the German army, thus proving the extent of the German defeat, the situation remained in the balance.

The battle of Le Hamel, fought on 4 July 1918, proved to be a miniature harbinger of the future and a precursor to the series of British offensives which followed. This minor assault by the Australian Corps, with two companies of American infantry in support, encompassed all the new techniques of warfare developed and practised by the BEF in 1918. Taking advantage of the weakness of the German position in front of Le Hamel, the Australian Corps used deception and surprise in its assault and a sophisticated artillery fireplan, along with tank and aircraft support, to overwhelm the shocked German defenders. This all-arms assault achieved complete surprise and the combination of assaulting tanks and infantry proved too much for the German defence. Within twenty minutes, the Australian and American infantry had reached their objectives and suffered what were, for the Western Front at least, very light casualties. Le Hamel proved that the combined use of all arms could indeed compensate for the lack of infantry. The British army had moved increasingly towards a mechanised form of methodical warfare which emphasised firepower at the expense of manpower. The exploitation of this model operation was strictly limited but in yet another innovation, machine-gun ammunition was dropped to the consolidating troops by parachute. Le Hamel was a very small tactical action, designed to straighten out the line, but it was both operationally and strategically significant. The Australian Corps had utilised all of the methods which would characterise British assaults during the rest of the war and the German defenders had found it difficult to respond to the nature of the assault. German forces, now at the end of long supply lines, badly weakened by the losses of the spring offensives, were vulnerable to Allied counter-attack.[9]

Le Hamel had proved the weakness of the extended German positions and Haig decided to exploit this situation with an attack on an altogether larger scale. On 8 August 1918, after considerable preparations which had been masked by sophisticated camouflage and deception techniques, the British Fourth Army mounted a major attack astride the River Somme which became known as the battle of Amiens. Making full use of surprise, along with 450 tanks, which proved to be the largest single use of tanks during the war, and under an extremely heavy but well-timed bombardment, the Fourth Army managed to penetrate up to eight miles into the German defences and capture over 400 guns and 20,000 prisoners at the cost of 4,000 casualties.[10] Such results were unprecedented for the BEF which was more used to counting gains in yards and casualties in tens of thousands. Although German resistance began to stiffen on 10 and 11 August, and this slowed the advance, the battle of Amiens had resulted in a major British success. Ludendorff later remarked that: 'August 8th was the black day for Germany in the history of the war'.[11] The battle of Amiens had demoralised the German army and demonstrated

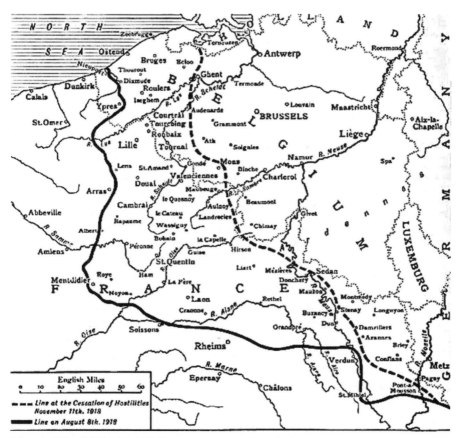

Map 1. The BEF, the 100 Days, start to finish, 8 August to 11 November 1918. (Chris Baker, www.longlongtrail.co.uk)

the bankruptcy of Ludendorff's strategy. Ludendorff tendered his resignation to the Kaiser who refused it but both agreed that the war must be brought to an end. However, pessimism and optimism would continue to wax and wane amongst Germany's leaders for the rest of the war.

While in previous years Haig might have persisted with an offensive on the Fourth Army front, by 1918 he had learnt from experience that once an offensive was begun, and German reserves had flowed to the threatened sector, any continuation was beset by the law of diminishing returns. Accordingly, in August 1918, Haig did not persist with the same attack but instead began a separate but related offensive. The British Third Army began its attack to the north around Albert on the old Somme battlefields on 23 August which increased the pressure on the German forces still further.

Just before this offensive, under the command of General Byng, began, Haig issued his Army Commanders with an important set of orders. He wrote on 22 August 1918 that:

> The methods which we have followed, hitherto, in our battles with limited objectives when the enemy was strong, are no longer suited to his present condition.

. . .To turn the present situation to account the most resolute offensive is everywhere desireable. Risks which a month ago would have been criminal to incur, ought now to be incurred as a duty.

The situation is most favourable; let each one of us act energetically, and without hesitation push forward to our objective.[12]

Haig had made optimistic assessments of the military situation before, both in 1916 and 1917, and, as the events of late August and early September 1918 were to show, he was premature in ordering the abandonment of methodical progress for all-out pursuit. German defence, although it now approximated to a rearguard, remained tough and difficult to overcome. The rearguards were composed of the most reliable troops and generally consisted of a web of machine-gun posts sited for all-round defence backed up by field guns and mortars. It was still perilous to incur risks against such a determined foe. However, although Third Army was unable to meet the ambitious objectives which Byng set for it, it nonetheless was able to push through the old Somme battlefields in a matter of days. In 1916 such progress had been measured in months, not days, and at the cost of thousands of casualties.

The reason for such progress was that the German army, with its reserves exhausted, had mounted a phased withdrawal to the 'Winter Line'; a series of defences stretching from the River Somme at Peronne to the Drocourt-Quéant Line in the north. It was hoped that an orderly withdrawal to these strong defensive positions would gain time in which to rest and re-organise its battered divisions. Yet even the naming of the 'Winter Line' as the position which the German army would hold throughout the winter months until the spring campaign of 1919, was simply another example of misguided propaganda. Haig and his staff set to work on plans to breach this line long before the winter came.

Having brought both the Fourth and Third Armies into action, Haig now planned to activate General Sir Henry Horne's First Army around Arras. German reserves had been drawn into action to the south and Haig now hoped that Horne's attack would have an even greater impact. On 24 August, First Army's objective was to 'pierce the DROCOURT-QUEANT line and subsequently to operate in a south-easterly direction against the right flank of the enemy's troops opposed to the Third Army'.[13] This attack was meant to breach the 'Winter Line' and throw the German troops out of their positions with the possibility of rolling up the troops opposite the Third Army.

On 26 August, the 2nd and 3rd Divisions of the Canadian Corps attacked along a four-mile frontage aligned along the main Arras-Cambrai road and, after heavy fighting, broke into the Monchy Le Preux defences which had cost so many British casualties in 1917. With this attack First Army had successfully extended the scope of the British offensive. Once again, the British had managed to wrong-foot the German defence with the use of deception and camouflage measures. Considerable effort, in the form of heavy artillery bombardments, dummy ammunition dumps, casualty clearing stations and false radio traffic, had been expended to suggest that an attack would be made to the north of Arras and to draw German attention away from the Arras-Cambrai road.[14]

Now three armies were attacking along a 40-mile front, exerting increasing pressure upon the German defences. Third and Fourth Army continued to make ground against the German rearguards and on 27 and 28 August the Australian Corps, operating south of the Somme, was able to advance over four miles, pushing through numerous abandoned villages.[15] Over the last days of August, First Army, with considerable artillery and air support, kept up its offensive and by dint of hard fighting managed to close up towards the Drocourt-Quéant Line. One measure of how hard the fighting had been was demonstrated by the experience of the 2nd and 3rd Canadian Divisions. Over three days of fighting they had advanced nearly five miles and captured 3,380 prisoners, but in the process they had lost 254 officers and 5,547 men as casualties. On 27 August, both formations were relieved by the 1st and 4th Canadian Divisions who took on the advance towards the 'Winter Line'.[16]

As the German withdrawal continued further south, Rawlinson and his commanders began to chafe at their now less-active role. John Monash, the commander of the Australian Corps, persuaded Rawlinson to allow him to mount an attack to seize Mont St Quentin, an eminence which commanded the line of the Somme and Peronne, even though Rawlinson 'considered it over-bold to attempt with so weak a force'.[17] On 31 August, the Australian Corps stormed Mont St Quentin in one of the great feats of arms in the war. The Australian charge up the hill had caught the defenders by surprise but heavy fighting continued throughout the day. Monash ordered up more troops to exploit the success and the next day, the Australian Corps was able to secure Mont St Quentin and seize the town of Peronne.[18] The daring Australian assault had broken the German defensive line along the Somme just days before the First Army's assault further north.

First Army's assault on the Drocourt-Quéant Line was conceived as the centerpiece to Haig's series of offensives. Yet, with the preparations for this assault nearly complete, Haig was understandably rattled by a telegram from Henry Wilson, the Chief of the Imperial General Staff (CIGS), which expressed concern about the coming attack. Wilson warned Haig that the War Cabinet would become worried if the attack were to result in heavy losses without success. Wilson's expression of such concerns made Haig understandably angry:

> It is impossible for a C.I.G.S. to send a telegram of this nature to a C-in-C in the Field as a 'personal' one. The Cabinet are ready to meddle and interfere in my plans in an underhand way, but do not dare openly say that they mean me to take the responsibility for any failure though ready to take credit for every success.[19]

It is hard not to feel at least some sympathy for Haig over this exhange. Haig could hardly have changed his plans or postponed this major attack just a few hours before it began. The plan had been discussed in great detail and already modified many times: it was far too late to change it further. Like any Great War commander, with the plan fixed and all preparations made, Haig could only wait for the outcome. On the other hand, British attacks had all too often resulted in heavy losses without success: Wilson was in effect reminding Haig to be careful with the lives of the BEF

At 05.00 on 2 September 1918, just as dawn broke, First Army began its assault on the Drocourt–Quéant Line. The 1st and 4th Canadian Divisions attacked on a narrow frontage and punched through the German front lines. While the 1st Canadian Division met with considerable success and found that large numbers of the German defenders simply surrendered, the 4th Canadian Division was able to wrest control of its objectives only after bitter fighting. By the end of 2 September, First Army had smashed clean through the very strong defences of the Drocourt-Quéant Line over a frontage of 7,000 yards, and taken over 8,000 prisoners. Full exploitation of these gains, however, proved difficult in the face of increasingly determined German opposition. Nevertheless, positions which had worried British planners for years had crumbled in just a day. Haig commented in his diary that: 'Discipline in the German Army seemed to have gone – if this is true, then the end cannot now be far off, I think. To-day's battle has truly been a great and glorious success'.[20] The Canadian official history claimed that the breaching of the Drocourt-Quéant Line was felt 'along the whole front from Ypres to the Oise'.[21] The success of the Canadian Corps in breaking the Drocourt-Quéant Line, considered at the time to be a greater achievement even than the battle of Amiens, has quite extraordinarily faded from public memory.

Since 24 August, the British armies had, with hard fighting, pushed through the old Somme battlefields and had then come up against the prepared positions of the 'Winter Line'. But these fortifications, meant to hold the British for months until 1919, had only held for a matter of days. By midday on 2 September, the German High Command was forced to order the abandonment of the 'Winter Line', and begin a fifteen-mile withdrawal to the *Hindenburg* Line proper – the line they had held before the start of their March offensive. Little was left to them but continued retreat and the German army had no strategic answer now to the problems facing it.

The length and extent of the retreat caught the British by surprise and their armies followed up the withdrawal with relative caution. It was clear that the next major offensive would be against the formidable defences of the *Hindenburg* Line. But this assault would only be one part of a 'general offensive', conceived by Ferdinand Foch, which aimed to engage the German army on the Western Front to such an extent that the allies could achieve an all-out victory. This 'general offensive' would open with a combined Franco-American attack in the Meuse-Argonne sector on 26 September. The next day, the British First and Third Armies would attack the Canal du Nord near Cambrai, and the following day, the Belgian army, the British Second Army and some French forces would mount an offensive in Flanders. The British Fourth Army would then assault the main *Hindenburg* Line and cross the St Quentin Canal.[22] This then, was a combined and co-ordinated offensive across the entire front which would exhaust German reserves and put intolerable pressure upon their army.

Ultimately, this series of attacks met with success but it was, perhaps, the Fourth Army's assault on the *Hindenburg* Line which proved the most impressive. Constructed during 1916 and 1917, the *Hindenburg* Line, known as the *Siegfried* Line to the Germans, was comprised of two main defence lines and had been considered impregnable in 1917. Fourth Army had to fight a series of bitter battles to close up to these defences but, by 27 September, was ready to launch its assault the next morning. The Australian Corps, in its last major engagement, was supported by the 27th and 30th US Divisions but made little progress in the face of stiff resistance and at the cost of heavy casualties. Further south, the troops of the 46th North Midland Division experienced greater success. Using a mixture of rafts, ferries and floats, and even by swimming, its troops were able to cross the St Quentin Canal and breach the line by nightfall. In a particularly fine feat of arms, men of the 1/6th North Staffords were able to capture the Riequeval Bridge over the St Quentin Canal intact.[23] This major success, involving British, Australian and American troops, can almost be seen as a microcosm of the 'general offensive'. It was the combined Allied effort of troops drawn from many nations which was now overwhelming German defence.

After this major sequence of Allied offensives, however, the pattern of events again repeated itself. The Germans withdrew, leaving the British unable to exploit their success. This highlights the difficulties inherent in the BEF's attempt to restore mobile warfare and seek a 'decisive battle'. The problems in getting this huge and complex machine to move fast enough and far enough in order to achieve a breakout were too great. In essence, the BEF was straining against the limits of technology as they existed in 1918. The BEF's operations, in the use of its armies in co-operation, in its use of surprise and deception to deceive the Germans of the location of the main blow, in its use of aircraft, tanks, artillery and infantry in combined arms attacks, and indeed in the sophisticated and professional planning of offensives, all pointed towards the future. The BEF could now force the Germans back through its skilled use of combined arms and improved technology but no matter how many tactical battles the BEF could win, given the existing technology and with no reliable mechanised force which could penetrate deeply behind German lines, the British were incapable of winning an operational victory. However, despite all these wider frustrations, these last offensives clearly show Haig and his army at the height of their powers.

During September 1918, the Allies had managed to put the German forces under enormous pressure. The Germans, however, rather than see their front crack open, which would restore mobile warfare but on distinctly unfavourable terms, quite naturally preferred to withdraw to new defences, shorten their line, and allow the entire process to begin again. The Allied armies could only follow up yet another retreat. Just as the fighting troops became weary from constant activity, so the engineers and supply troops had to struggle to keep up with a constantly-moving front. Meanwhile, the artillery found it very difficult to bring up sufficient guns and ammunition to support the advance. British success depended not just on the increasingly evident confidence and skill of the fighting troops, but on the ability of their logistic chain to match the rate of forward progress. Ultimately, all these factors operated as brakes on the advance so that its pace was never as rapid as the Germans in the spring but it was more sustainable. Furthermore, the limitations of technology and supply stressed above meant that the BEF was unable to break through the German lines and turn defeat into rout.

October saw the BEF fight major battles at Cambrai and on the Selle river, as the Belgians, French and Americans also continued their offensives. Ludendorff, on the verge of a nervous breakdown, had insisted on 3 October that negotiations for an armistice were opened but, by the end of the month, there was no real agreement on what terms Germany should seek. Ludendorff now argued that Germany should fight on, but, with his position now fatally compromised, he was forced to resign on 27 October. He was replaced by General Groener as First Quartermaster-General.

With all of Germany's allies on the point of collapse, Germany's situation was grim, yet Hindenburg later wrote that: 'by the end of October the collapse was complete at all points. It was only on the Western Front that we still thought we could avert it.'[24]

Groener hoped that an immediate withdrawal to the River Meuse might prevent complete disaster. However, the German forces would need to hold the Allied armies back for some time in order to remove the vast quantities of supplies behind their current lines. It was in this context that, as First and Third British Armies fought the battle of Valenciennes, the Fourth Army slowly closed up to the Sambre-Oise Canal and the forest of Mormal. Haig was not willing to give the Germans any respite and issued orders on 29 October for another major attack. Third and Fourth Armies, in conjunction with the French First Army, would mount a major attack along the front from Le Quesnoy to Oisy in the south. Fourth Army was to mount an attack across the Sambre-Oise Canal and through the forest of Mormal further north. The total frontage of this combined attack was 30 miles. Designed as a massive blow which would puncture the last major German defence line, Haig clearly hoped finally to bring about the disintegration of the German army.

On 4 November 1918, both Third and Fourth Armies went into the assault. In the Third Army sector, the New Zealand Division had the unusual task of assaulting the fortified town of Le Quesnoy which fell rapidly even with its Vauban-designed ravelins and bastions.[25] Fourth Army, facing the formidable twin barriers of the forest and the canal, was able to push through the forest, cross the canal and breach the German defences at many points along its course. It was only in the 32nd Division sector that the crossings failed and casualties were heavy. Among the many casualties suffered by the 2nd Manchesters, was Lieutenant Wilfrid Owen, who became known posthumously as one of the outstanding poets of the war.[26] By the end of the day, the main objectives had all been achieved, and Fourth Army, along with the other British Armies, had fought its last major battle. The German rearguard position had been comprehensively breached and there was little or nothing the Germans could do to halt the advance of the British armies.

The action of the British Third and Fourth Armies in breaking through the last possible German defence line before the Meuse was thus of critical importance. The German High Command had no option but to confront the reality that the war was lost. Groener realised, after touring the front on 5 November, that his armies were no longer capable of sustained resistance and might well be broken up in the field. He now believed that an armistice had to be negotiated immediately. On 6 November, he told the Chancellor: 'We shall have to cross the lines with a white flag. Even a week is too long to wait. It must be Saturday [9 November] at the latest'.[27] On 11 November 1918, the armistice finally came into effect.

There is no question that the BEF had played a major part in finally bringing the war to an end. From 18 July until 11 November, it had captured 188,700 prisoners and 2,840 guns[28] in an almost unbroken series of battles and pursuit. The BEF, as it fought these battles, had emerged as a confident and capable military machine able to tackle whatever challenge it was confronted with. However, its operations during 1918 came at a heavy price. The dogged and sometimes desperate defence against the German spring and summer offensives had been very costly. While the BEF prevailed against a weakening German army in the summer and autumn of 1918, each attack, every advance, was still costly in mens' lives. The difference, in the autumn of 1918 was that the BEF was an army on the move and at last prevailing against its opponent.

This chapter began with Frederick's Maurice's praise for the invididual efforts of the BEF in 1918. However, Maurice was well aware of the wider complexities of the war. He understood that:

Germany could not have been beaten in the field, as she was beaten, without the intimate co-operation of all the Allied armies on the Western Front directed by a great leader, nor without the co-ordination for a common purpose of all the resources of the Allies, naval, military industrial and economic. If victory is to be attributed to any one cause, then that cause is not to be found in the wisdom of any one statesman, the valour of any one army, the prowess of any one navy, or the skill of any one general.[29]

Historians, politicians and commentators have been arguing about the nature of the Allied victory over Germany in 1918 ever since. Maurice's belief, shared by all the Allies at the time, that the German was beaten in the field, remains controversial to this day and, of course, the 'alternative fact' of the 'stab-in-the-back', that the German army had remained undefeated and that Germany had been brought down by political revolution at home, became a powerful factor in the rise of the National Socialists in Germany after the war.

At the same time, far too many historians and commentators have searched and argued fruitlessly for the one factor which finally decided the outcome of the Great War. With a war so vast in scope, so complex and deep in its course and consequences, it was and is impossible to identify any one factor which led to the collapse of the Central Powers. As Maurice argued, the victory of the Allies cannot be ascribed to any one factor, let alone any one army. However, there is also little doubt that the BEF played a major part in the military defeat of the German army in the last 'Hundred Days' of the war. Ultimately, the weakening strength of the German army on the Western Front was only one factor amongst many which determined the collapse of the Central powers. Her efforts to prop up her failing allies, most notably Austria-Hungary, the growing impact of the naval blockade, and not least the myopic, narrow and sometimes self-defeating domestic policies of the German military government, all have to be considered, amongst many other factors too.

What can be said with certainty is that the BEF remained an effective and capable fighting formation even after having narrowly survived the hammer blows of the German spring offensives. That this was the case resulted from much wider factors than simply battlefield tactics or operational command. Britain still had access to manpower reserves, although these were diminishing, still had access to finance, most notably in the form of war loans from the United States, still had access to raw materials and had developed the industrial capacity to build armaments on a scale undreamt-of even three years before. That such a scale of effort had produced real fissures and tensions within Britain's polity, armed forces and society, was not surprising; what was remarkable was that Britain had managed to hold these competing pressures together towards the common goal of victory for four years. Britain's prodigious war effort was thus still running at full capacity in the summer and autumn of 1918, while Germany's was visibly fraying under the enormous pressure. Britain's war effort was also one amongst many. France was still putting forth vast effort while the United States, even after putting one million men in the field by November 1918, was yet to mobilise fully. Meanwhile, the German army was in the process of being comprehensively defeated on the Western Front, at the same time as the country faced unrest and revolution at home and the ruination of all her allies. It was thus the knowledge that this grand coalition would be able to put forth even greater strength in the spring of 1919 which made any thought of continuing the war impossible for the German authorities, army and people in November 1918.

It is in this much wider context that we have to judge the performance of the BEF on the Western Front in the 'Hundred Days'. The BEF, with its Commonwealth components, achieved a series of stunning military victories in the autumn of 1918, in combination with the French, American and Belgian armies. Viewing these achievements within its essential wider framework ensures that we do not view the performance as an isolated spectacle at the end of a war but rather the final, logical consequence of a total national and alliance effort for victory. It is for the very reason that these offensives – and their results – do not fit neatly with the received opinion of the Great War that we should consider and remember them today.

Notes

1. Maurice, when serving as Director of Military Operations at the War Office in 1918 had publicly challenged Lloyd George's veracity over the number of men sent to Haig's armies in the winter of 1918. See John Gooch, 'The Maurice Debate 1918', *Journal of Contemporary History* 3/4 (1968), pp. 211–28.
2. Major General Sir F. Maurice, *The Last Four Months: The End of the War in the West* (Cassell and Company, 1919), pp. 249–50.
3. John Terraine certainly attempted to raise awareness of the importance of 1918 in his *To Win a War: 1918, the Year of Victory* (Sidgwick & Jackson, 1978).
4. This has begun to be rectified, see: J.P. Harris with Niall Barr, *Amiens to the Armistice: The BEF in the Hundred Days Campaign 8 August–11 November 1918* (Brassey's, 1999); David Stevenson, *With Our Backs to the Wall: Victory and Defeat in the Great War* (Allen Lane, 2011); Nick Lloyd, *Hundred Days: The End of the Great War* (Viking, 2013); Jonathan Boff, *Winning and Losing on the Western Front: The British Third Army and the Defeat of Germany in 1918*(Cambridge University Press, 2014).
5. See Gary Sheffield, *Forgotten Victory: The First World War, Myths and Realities* (Review, 2002).
6. John Keegan, *The First World War* (Hutchinson, 1998), p. 315
7. Such works include, Tim Travers, *The Killing Ground: The British Army, the Western Front and the Emergence of Modern Warfare 1900-1918* (Allen and Unwin, 1987), Robin Prior and Trevor Wilson, *Command on the Western Front: The Military Career of Sir Henry Rawlinson 1914-18* (Blackwell, 1992), and Paddy Griffith, *Battle Tactics of the Western Front: The British Army's Art of Attack 1916-18* (Yale University Press, 1996).
8. Harris with Barr, *Amiens to the Armistice*, pp. 23–57.
9. C.W. Bean, *The Official History of Australia in the War of 1914-1918, Vol.VI: The Australian Imperial Force in France during the Allied Offensive, 1918* (Angus & Robertson, 1929), pp. 276–9.
10. Maurice, *The Last Four Months*, pp. 103–4.
11. Erich Ludendorff, *My War Memoirs*, Vol. II (Hutchinson, 1919), p. 679.
12. Douglas Haig to Army Commanders, OAD 911, 22 August 1918, WO158/2415225, The National Archives, Kew [TNA].
13. 24 August 1918, Lawrence to Horne, OAD907/13, WO158/241, TNA.
14. First Army Report to all Corps Commanders, 31 August 1918 from a summary of information on 30 August, WO158/191, TNA.
15. A.A. Montgomery, *The Story of the Fourth Army in the Battles of the Hundred Days August 8th to November 1918* (Hodder and Stoughton, 1919), p. 86.
16. Ibid., p. 432.
17. Quoted in Prior and Wilson, *Command on the Western Front*, p. 342.
18. Montgomery, *The Story of the Fourth Army*, pp. 99–103.
19. Haig's Diary, 1 September 1918, WO256/36, TNA.
20. Haig's Diary, 2 September 1918, WO256/36, TNA.
21. G.W.L. Nicholson, *Canadian Expeditionary Force 1914-19* (Queen's Printer, 1962), p. 440.
22. GHQ to Army commanders, OAD 926/4, 25 September 1918, WO 158/242, TNA.
23. R. E. Priestley, *Breaking the Hindenburg Line: The Story of the 46th North Midland Division* (Fisher Unwin, 1919), p. 143.

24. Charles Messenger (ed.), Field Marshal von Hindenburg, *The Great War* (Greenhill, 2006), p. 222.
25. J.E. Edmonds and R. Maxwell-Hyslop, *Military Operations France and Belgium 1918*, Vol. V (HMSO, 1947), pp. 480–3.
26. Helen McPhail, *Portrait of Wilfrid Owen: Poet and Soldier, 1893-1918* (Gliddon Books, 1993), p. 61.
27. John W. Wheeler-Bennett, *Hindenburg: The Wooden Titan* (Macmillan, 1936), p. 186.
28. Edmonds and Maxwell-Hyslop, *Military Operations 1918*, Vol. V, p. 557.
29. Maurice, *The Last Four Months*, p. 251.

Suggested Further Reading

Boff, Jonathan, *Winning and Losing on the Western Front: The British Third Army and the Defeat of Germany in 1918* (Cambridge University Press, 2014)

Harris, J.P. with Niall Barr, *Amiens to the Armistice: The BEF in the Hundred Days Campaign 8 August-11 November 1918* (Brassey's 1999)

Lloyd, Nick, *Hundred Days: The End of the Great War* (Viking, 2013)

Montgomery, A.A., *The Story of the Fourth Army in the Battles of the Hundred Days August 8th to November 1918* (Hodder and Stoughton, 1919)

Prior, Robin and Trevor Wilson, *Command on the Western Front: The Military Career of Sir Henry Rawlinson 1914-18* (Blackwell, 1992)

Sheffield, Gary, *Forgotten Victory: The First World War, Myths and Realities* (Review, 2002)

Stevenson, David, *With Our Backs to the Wall: Victory and Defeat in the Great War* (Allen Lane, 2011)

Terraine, John, *To Win a War: 1918, the Year of Victory* (Sidgwick & Jackson, 1978)

Chapter 2

German Defeat and the Myth of the 'Stab in the Back'

By Jack Sheldon

Any analysis of the performance of the German army in the second half of 1918 has to begin with an examination of its manpower resources and, almost as important, the availability of horses and fodder. Of course, with the exception of the army of the United States, which was flooding into Europe at the time at a rate of 250,000 per month, all the other belligerents faced serious manpower shortages, but by far the greatest problems were those confronting Germany, by then in complete and irredeemable crisis. This subject has been discussed in some detail elsewhere,[1] but the main points to note are:

- The shortage of manpower, hitherto cushioned by the flood of wartime volunteers in 1914 and exploitation of the *Ersatz Reserve* in 1915, began to bite hard in 1916. The class of 1897, which was due to be called up in October 1917, had to be made available in July 1916[2] and, with certain restrictions, year group 1898 was called up from November 1916, a full two years ahead of what would normally have been the case.[3]
- The manpower bill for 1917, to meet the demands on the home front of the Hindenburg Plan and the needs of the field army, could only be met by use of the most stringent and far-reaching methods of management. These included repeatedly combing out rear-area and support troops for usable manpower under the age of thirty-five and hollowing out the formations on the Eastern Front.
- Such was the effect of overdrawing resources that the German Ministry of War and the entire High Command were fully aware by December 1917 that the manpower deficit during 1918 would increase at a rate of 42,000 per month, meaning that from July 1918 the army would only be able to call on returning wounded to boost its strength. All other sources would be exhausted, so, effectively, the war could not be continued beyond that summer.

None of this had anything to do with losses arising from the German offensives of spring and early summer, but of course the casualties suffered led to a rapid escalation of the crisis. In total, between March and July, 227,000 were killed, 765,000 wounded and 1,966,000 were sick, most victims in their weakened state to Spanish 'Flu. About 2,000,000 returned to duty, but net casualties had been 950,000 and the overall shortages at the front had reached 420,000 – a totally unbridgeable figure.[4]

Set against this background, the German offensives can be seen not simply as a gamble, but a desperate last throw of the dice. If the attempt were to fail, the game was up – small wonder that Ludendorff, exhausted and overwrought, collapsed as a result of the Amiens assault of 8 August. Following closely on the heels of the major setback of Second Marne from 18 July when Allied troops under the French General Mangin recaptured Soissons and inflicted a further 168,000 casualties, including 27,000 prisoners, on the German army, it was all too much for him.[5] Acutely aware that the tide had turned, that events were slipping rapidly out of his control, Ludendorff was henceforth gripped by paralysing depression. His behaviour and decision-making became increasingly erratic. The coming three months were to see numerous arbitrary sackings of commanders or chiefs of staff in a vain attempt to draw attention away from Ludendorff's own shortcomings. It was certainly a dubious way to manage a deteriorating military situation, as was the ceaseless shuffling of divisions up and down the line. The 11th Bavarian Infantry Division, for example, was redeployed no fewer than fourteen times from Verdun in one direction to Flanders in the other, interspersed with a return to Soissons from positions near the Dutch border in May. This experience was by no means untypical and, apart from wearing down their fighting ability more quickly than might otherwise have been the case, it was simply an exhausting experience for the troops involved.

As events unfolded on the Marne, this major French offensive was effectively a massive counter to a failed assault by the German Seventh, First and Third Armies. The intention of *Oberste Heeresleitung* (OHL – Supreme Army Command) on 15 July had been for Seventh Army to advance west of Reims towards Epernay, with First and Third operating east of the city, either side of Châlons. To have attempted to launch such an offensive on an eighty-kilometre frontage, with the field army already badly worn down, was certainly ambitious. Though the stakes were high, had it succeeded, Reims would automatically have fallen. However, the French had advance warning of what was going to happen. *Generalmajor* von Loßberg blamed the betrayal on 'German deserters and statements made by German prisoners captured during minor enemy operations'.[6]

There was no surprise, forward positions were evacuated, and attempted gas attacks resulted in the clouds blowing back at the attackers. In addition, large numbers of German soldiers were stricken with flu and the weather was extremely hot. Exhausted and suffering badly from thirst, the dejected survivors fell back to their start lines and what turned out to be the very last major attempt at offensive action by the German army was cancelled.[7] Further north, due to the fact that his army group was not involved in this final large-scale operation and so received no replacement manpower, Crown Prince Rupprecht noted in a diary entry of 13 July, how serious the lack of infantry manpower had become: 'The fighting strength of our companies that have not been reinforced is fifty men on average'.[8] With the prospect of further heavy fighting to come, this was far from encouraging.

The French attack came as a rude shock. It was supported by tanks (to which German commentators later attributed its success), that is tanks thrusting into the flank of the German Seventh Army from the wooded area around Villers-Cotterêts. It certainly put paid to any lingering hopes by OHL to move strong forces north for operations in Flanders at this time and, despite rushing reserves to the area to stabilise the situation, eventually there was no alternative but to pull the defending forces back behind the Vesle. There was considerable reluctance at the highest level to acquiesce in this, mainly for reasons of prestige, but clear thinkers could see that there was no alternative. Hermann von Kuhl noted in his diary on 20 July, 'It's a turning point in the war! . . . I had long doubted the wisdom of the [offensive] operations and could not understand the manner in which OHL wished to conduct the continuation of the war.'[9]

That same day, Ludendorff despatched his outstanding defensive expert, *Generalmajor* von Loßberg, to Army Group German Crown Prince to assess the situation and make recommendations. It did not take him long to make up his mind, then returning north, having gained, inter alia, a very poor view of loosened discipline behind the front,[10] he reported, first, to OHL in Avesnes, then Army Group Crown Prince Rupprecht, that:

> The only possible solution is a radical one. Around Soissons and to the east of it, [we must] pull back behind the Aisne and then the Vesle, otherwise we shall constantly be in an unfavourable position.[11]

Despite extreme reluctance on the part of OHL, Ludendorff in particular, who had to be forced by Hindenburg to issue the necessary orders,[12] battlefield pressure built up further and the defence was forced back regardless. For OHL there was nothing for it but to go over to the strategic defensive, but just as tactical success during the German offensives led to no operational gains, the way the remainder of the war was conducted was equally aimless.

In the wake of the major setback of 8 August, the mass deployment of tanks advancing, screened by extensive use of smoke, was blamed for the reverses of Second Army astride the Amiens–St Quentin road. Once more, despite the loss of a considerable amount of ground, it proved possible to shore up the defence and prevent an Allied breakthrough. However, concerns about declining morale amongst the German infantry began to be voiced; the accusation being that far too many front-line units had buckled and allowed themselves to be pushed back easily and that the extent of the surrenders, some of which were 'arranged' on a large scale by junior officers and NCOs, was already worrying. These surrenders would eventually reach a total of at least 340,000 men during the final weeks of the war[13] and, by other estimates, were as high as 385,000.[14]

General von Gallwitz, by this stage commanding an army group, simply could not understand what Ludendorff was trying to achieve. One of his diary entries, written on 30 August, reads:

> I am at a complete loss to try and understand Ludendorff's thinking in the wake of the complete turnaround in the situation. A step by step withdrawal from one position to another will not achieve anything. The enemy has the complete initiative.[15]

Nevertheless, that is what happened. The lengthy retreat had begun and Gallwitz was quite correct in that from that moment the operational initiative was in Foch's hands and it was never wrested from him.

Others had seen it all coming long previously. As early as 8 September 1916, following a conversation with Ludendorff, General von Kuhl, chief of staff to Army Group Bavarian Crown Prince, noted in his diary:

> We agreed that a great and positive success is no longer possible. All we can do is hold on and seize a favourable opportunity to make peace. This year we have made too many serious errors.[16]

In the wake of the early German 1918 assaults, Kuhl was once more recording negative thoughts in his diary. On 9 May, he wrote:

> Our supply of reinforcements and replacements is virtually exhausted . . . I doubt if further major offensives will be possible . . . The Americans are on their way. I am really doubtful if we shall be able to force a decision. We are not going to achieve a breakthrough – and then there is the issue of horses and the supply of oats . . .[17]

A month later, he struck an even more pessimistic note:

> We are at the end of our personnel resources. All that is left are the returning wounded and the class of 1900 which is about to be called up and which cannot be deployed before spring 1919 . . . I simply cannot explain how the OHL thinks that decisive results can be achieved and the war brought to an end.[18]

By mid-August, enormous pressure was building up on the defence. Foch concentrated his efforts on the flanks of the huge salient so the German Seventeenth Army was involved in heavy fighting on the Somme between Albert and Bapaume, then, on 21 August, Ninth Army, which had been deployed around Noyon and Soissons since July, was pushed out of its relatively well-prepared defences and forced back across the Oise-Aisne Canal at Chauny. In an attempt to improve the manpower situation, OHL transferred a number of Austrian and Hungarian divisions to the Western Front, deploying them in the Meuse, Moselle and Vosges sectors. From the start they were of questionable motivation and very limited fighting ability. Furthermore, the move weakened the Italian front, a situation made worse when, in summer 1918, the Austro-Hungarian high command had to deploy forces to Albania where the Italians were advancing and also to the western flank of the Bulgarians in Macedonia.[19]

Indicative of the way OHL was now thinking was the outcome of a visit by the newly appointed Foreign Minister, Paul von Hintze. After the war there was some dispute about what actually passed between Ludendorff and Hintze during a private discussion on 13 August, but a statement made by Hintze on 14 August before the Privy Council, and recorded in the minutes, is probably a fair reflection of growing concern amongst the army leadership:

> The Chief of the General Staff of the Field Army has defined the war situation thus: we can no longer hope through military operations to break the will of our enemies to continue the war; rather the objective of our conduct of the war must be gradually to wear down our enemies' will to fight by going over to the strategic defensive.[20]

The question of oats and other fodder for the horses was always of great importance and by now was becoming seriously problematic. Overworked, weakened through lack of food, teams towing guns in particular were having to be augmented and large numbers of horses were dying in harness from sheer exhaustion. All manner of steps were taken to mitigate the problem, including the use of feed substitutes. In a letter home on

8 August, *General der Kavallerie* von der Marwitz, commander Second Army, wrote: 'The *Intendant* [an administrative official] brought me a bag of *ersatz* horse food. It smelled of snuff and looked like a greyish peat. I fed it to my horses and I must say that they ate it readily.'[21] Quite how much nutritional value it contained is an open question. It did nothing to halt the wastage of horses and the strictly limited numbers of motor vehicles were insufficient to compensate for their loss.

Operationally, such was the pressure being exerted all along the line that, by the beginning of September, OHL was forced to direct Seventeenth, Second, Eighteenth and Ninth Armies to pull back to the Hindenburg Line. Worse, what relatively few reserve formations there were by this stage, had all had to be deployed to relieve fought-out and severely-weakened divisions; all this at a time when the Allies were able to deploy ever greater quantities of artillery and conduct complex all-arms battles with increasing skill. Morale was beginning to sag substantially. On 2 September, reports of poor morale reached as high as Crown Prince Rupprecht who noted in his diary: 'A military train has been seen in Nuremberg bearing the inscription, "Slaughter cattle for Wilhelm and sons"!', adding 'Morale is not only very poor in Bavaria; the same is true in north Germany.'[22]

Manifestly this was true. Then, a few days later, he received a report on an assessment of letters sent home by men of 183rd Infantry, 3rd Marine, 26th Reserve and 83rd Infantry Divisions which showed that the morale of the troops was bad and that they lacked confidence. That same day, 5 September, he wrote that: 'General von Below reported this morning that an exhausted battalion of the otherwise reliable 44th Reserve Division simply scattered at the shout of "Here come the British" – this despite the fact that the attack was not going in against it, but rather against neighbouring troops.'[23] The German army, which for some time had been sending worn out, so-called *Schrott-Divisionen*, to man the front opposite the Americans, began to notice the extra impetus the arrival of large numbers of reinforcements was giving the American operations. In mid-September, the St Mihiel salient was eliminated and then, on 26 September, and in association with the French army, a major assault was directed against the German Third and Fifth Armies.

Although the French army did not gain a great deal of ground in fourteen days of battle, on the very first day the Americans pushed the German front line back substantially between the Argonne and the Meuse. The defenders did inflict enormous casualties and were able to prevent a breakthrough, but the Americans pushed on until they were fighting on the east bank of the Meuse. They had suffered serious losses, but the same was true proportionately of the German army which was ill placed to take large-scale casualties. The terrible shortage of draught horses was a major problem and, within a short time, mobility was severely reduced, as was the ability to conduct an active defence. *Leutnant* Otto Lais, a machine-gun company commander with Infantry Regiment 169, deployed in the area, commented on events at the beginning of October:

Weak, decimated infantry companies, machine gun companies that were so small that the weight of the ammunition, without which a machine gun has no value, utterly exhausted the spiritually spent, starving, gunners, fought against freshly introduced American battalions and regiments right up to war establishment. Tens fought against hundreds or more; our few hundreds against thousands from over there. Most of the infantry close support batteries, now reduced to two guns, had no horses left. Sweating and straining, the gunners hauled on ropes to drag their guns through the swampy crater field of the wooded valley to positions where they could engage oncoming tanks.[24]

Despite everything, the more courageous and well-led front-line forces continued to offer stout resistance, but the same could not be said of the men back along the lines of communication or engaged in rearward administrative duties. A man in amongst a crowd gathered at Mons railway station as Hindenburg's train pulled out on 20 September was heard to shout, 'Kill him; we want peace'.[25] Against this unpromising backdrop, Ludendorff realised on 28 September that with the fall of Bulgaria, the last hope of salvaging something from the wreckage had gone. Following a lengthy discussion with Hindenburg, the two men came to the conclusion that it was essential to seek an armistice. They were now both sure that even if they were to succeed temporarily in holding along the Western Front, the situation could only continue to deteriorate. There followed difficult discussions with the Kaiser and others, but eventually, and bowing to the inevitable, the newly-formed popular government despatched the offer of an armistice the day it took office on 1 October; Vienna and Constantinople being informed confidentially at 9.40 pm about what had been done.

That same evening, at 10.00 pm, Ludendorff addressed the staff of OHL. After pointing out that the Bulgarian collapse ruled out the transfer of any more forces from the east, he continued:

> We have no reserves left to transfer to the West . . . I should be no better than a gambler if, in view of the gravity of the position, I did not insist upon ending the war by asking for an immediate armistice. This has been done. I have come to this conclusion in complete agreement with *Generalfeldmarschall* von Hindenburg. An administration, broadly based, is essential to conclude the war. The *Generalfeldmarschall* and I make this statement with the greatest reluctance, but it is essential that it should be made . . .[26]

Nevertheless, the war had to continue for the time being in order to buy time for armistice arrangements to be concluded so, on 29 September, OHL was forced to issue a directive stating that in contrast with accepted practice for the past eighteen months, 'Neither amongst the infantry, nor the artillery must the need for deployment in depth be over-emphasised. Given its weakened strength, the infantry must close in on the main defensive line . . . it will not be possible everywhere to man a zone of advanced posts.'[27] For many of the recipients this was fiddling while Rome burned and meanwhile the endless attrition of the defending forces continued to make itself felt. Despite continuing to score successes against the advancing American forces, losses even on that sector were becoming unsustainable and irreplaceable. Worse, morale continued to slump. Crown Prince Rupprecht met General von Carlewitz, commander Second Army, at Maubeuge on 12 October, only to be told of worsening morale among the men under his command. 'In expectation of imminent peace, many of the men are making it known that they would be stupid to allow themselves to be shot dead now' and he added that if only morale were better, the British attacks would be easier to beat off.[28]

DEPTH   POSITIONS

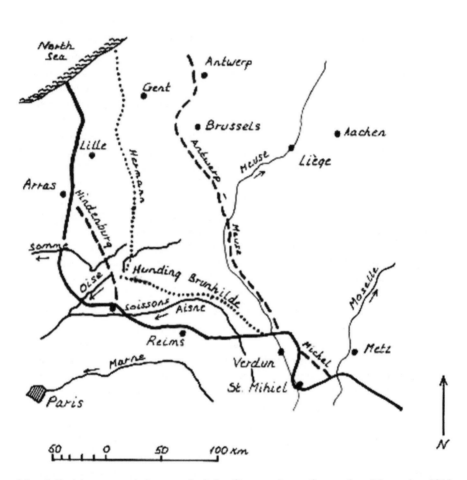

Map 2. Positions occupied successively by German Army, September–November 1918.

As a result of the catastrophically weak manpower situation, on 13 October, Army Group Gallwitz gave up trying to balance manpower within some of its divisions and ordered the complete disbandment of 197th Infantry Division.[29] The older, more experienced surviving soldiers were posted into other formations, but the latest recruits were returned to a field recruit depot, a move which possibly saved their lives and certainly gave them the opportunity to improve their standard of training. That same day, Hindenburg issued a directive designed to stiffen resolve within the remaining fighting formations.

Diplomatic negotiations aimed at ending the war have begun. The outcome will be most favourable the more the army succeeds in remaining cohesive, maintaining captured territory and inflicting damage on the enemy. In particular:

- Should there be breakthrough of the Hermann–Gudrun Position, it is essential that the thrust be halted as soon as possible . . .
- The construction of the Antwerp–Meuse Position and the backloading of all stores and equipment that can be spared is to be accelerated.
- Each withdrawal is simply a costly makeshift measure. It is damaging to the morale of the troops and means the loss to us of irreplaceable stocks . . .
- We should not underestimate the enemy. However, we must not overestimate them.[30]

At the other end of the Western Front, in Belgium, the German Fourth Army was subjected to immense pressure in October. On 14 October, during a powerful Allied thrust between Zarren and Werwik, 1st Bavarian Reserve Division was simply overwhelmed. Already extremely weak in infantry, when the blow fell, the defence was soon splintered into small groups fighting for their lives. Reserve Infantry Regiment 15, Bavarian Ersatz Division, which had been subordinated to it to bolster its numbers was rapidly surrounded around Dry Masten to the north-northwest of Kortrijk, whilst of the divisional organic Bavarian Reserve Infantry Regiments 1, 2 and 3, a mere handful of troops was lucky enough to break out. When they assembled later at Landlede, they numbered fewer than one hundred, all ranks. Yet another division had been fought to complete extinction[31] and there were numerous other disbandments at this time.

The previous couple of weeks had also witnessed a spate of attacks by the British army against the Hindenburg Line between Cambrai and St Quentin. A break-in, near Cambrai, was swiftly expanded southwards as October opened. It proved to be impossible for the defence in its parlous state even to hold around St Quentin and in heavy fighting the line was gradually pushed east. By the second half of October, there was a further fall back to the barely developed *Hermann-Hunding* Position. All in all, the German military situation was nothing short of desperate. Already by the end of September, nobody in a position of authority, certainly none in OHL, was in any doubt that the war could no longer be won. As October wore on, ever more extreme measures had to be taken to compensate for the lack of reserves. For many senior commanders, this was a waste of effort, mere tinkering at the edges of what was an escalating problem and the same criticism applied to endless shuffling around of divisions in the hope of stemming the tide of the general Allied advance.

The highly-experienced *Generaloberst* von Einem, commanding Third Army, complained in his diary:

> I simply do not understand the thinking of OHL. They are operating with a lot of 'divisions', but those I have here are pitiful remnants, some of which barely equate to the strength of battalion at war establishment [1000+]. Bulgaria has collapsed and will be followed by Turkey and Austria. That means that war against overwhelming odds will be more hopeless than ever. The thought that all the blood has been spilled for nothing is appalling.[32]

The size and number of artillery batteries continued to diminish and pressure on infantry manpower was unrelenting. On 20 October, 115th and 236th Infantry Division, whose battalion strengths had fallen to below 400 on average, in a procedure that was being mirrored the full length of the Western Front, applied to Army Group Gallwitz to reorganise their regimental structures from three battalions of twelve rifle companies each down to two with only three rifle companies. In effect this was halving their ability to hold the front or conduct offensive operations.[33] In a way it was remarkable that these divisions still contained reasonable numbers of infantry. Elsewhere it was becoming common for companies to muster no more than twenty to thirty men, a situation exacerbated by a sharp increase in shirkers, malingerers and outright deserters. For obvious reasons, exact figures are hard to come by, but one commentator subsequently drew attention to an increased tendency for men who found themselves in Germany for reasons such as wounds, ill-health or even leave, simply not to return and the same observer stated that 'a reliable source suggests that in the last days of October there were 50,000 deserters in Berlin'.[34]

Meanwhile, in the field, the situation continued to worsen with increasing rapidity. On 24 October, General von der Marwitz, having been removed from Second Army and now commanding Fifth Army, reported that of its twenty five divisions, twelve were capable of further action, a further nine required immediate relief or had not yet been reconstituted, two others were in the midst of recovery and reconstitution and two were totally fought out.[35] On the same day, tensions between government and OHL came to a head when Hindenburg, reacting to the third note sent by President Wilson, issued a statement to the army, without consultation:

To be brought to the Attention of all Troops: Wilson states in his answer that he wishes to propose to his Allies that they enter into ceasefire negotiations. However, the ceasefire must render Germany militarily so defenceless that it can never again take up arms. He would only discuss peace with Germany if it agreed totally to all demands of the Allies concerning its internal affairs; otherwise there could only be unconditional subjugation. Wilson's answer is a demand for military capitulation. For us soldiers it is, therefore, unacceptable. It is proof that the will for annihilation of our enemies, who unleashed the war in 1914, continues undiminished. Further it proves that our enemies have only used the expression 'a just peace' to deceive us and break our powers of resistance. To we soldiers, therefore, Wilson's answer can only act as a challenge to continue to resist with every last bit of strength we can bring to bear. Only if the enemy recognise that the German front cannot be broken regardless of the greatest sacrifice, will they be prepared for a peace which will secure a future for Germany appropriate to the broad mass of its people.
In the Field 24 October 10.00 pm Signed von Hindenburg[36]

For Crown Prince Rupprecht, this statement made no sense. Of Wilson's reply he wrote:

It is painful for us, but there is nothing else for it, but to accept it. We have just lost the war . . . Ludendorff does not see it that way. Shortly before his departure for Berlin at 11.00 pm, he spoke to my chief of staff [von Kuhl], who put across my position, complaining about governmental weakness and stating that Wilson's conditions were unacceptable. Quite apart from the military situation, Ludendorff ought to consider internal politics. If we reject Wilson's conditions, in a short time we shall be facing a revolution.[37]

Of course it soon transpired that Hindenburg's statement in no way chimed with the reply issued by the government. Ludendorff, who countersigned it, later claimed that he had been misinformed about the thrust of the governmental response. His conversation with von Kuhl does not suggest that that was a true reflection of the situation. In any case, it caused an enormous row and two days later at Spa, during an audience with the Kaiser that was so stormy that a truculent Ludendorff had to be reminded forcefully in whose presence he was, he tendered his resignation and it was accepted. The two never met again. Ludendorff proposed von Kuhl as his successor but, to the relief of the latter, the choice fell on General Groener.[38] All that Ludendorff stated subsequently was that the interview constituted 'some of the bitterest moments of my life. I said to His Majesty respectfully that I had the painful impression that I no longer possessed his trust and therefore begged him humbly to release me. His Majesty acquiesced.'[39] After the war, *Generalleutnant* von Moser commented of him, 'The more prominent his role became during 1917 and 1918, the higher he climbed, the more profound his fall'[40] and went on to praise his contribution and service.

He was now finished, however, and it fell to Prinz Max von Baden to move to acceptance of the terms offered by the Allies. Thus it could subsequently be claimed that responsibility for this lay with civilian politicians, rather than the military; a sophistry that was to continue to have influence well into the post-war period. From 27 October, though the war had two weeks left to run, Germany's fate was sealed, both politically and strategically. All that was left was a determination to prevent total collapse before the requested armistice could come into effect. Privately, key figures on the Western Front were fully aware that it was all over. In the morning of 3 November, General Groener, who had been appointed in succession to Ludendorff, met General von Kuhl and the chiefs of staff of Fourth and Sixth Armies. That same afternoon, in Charleroi, he and Kuhl had further discussions with the chiefs of Seventeenth, Second and Eighteenth Armies. Kuhl remembered:

> I put forward the view that we could hold for a further eight days in the *Hermannstellung* along the Schelde, but that then a swift decision would need to be made to determine if we could risk holding any longer, or if by then we should be too worn down to arrive in the Antwerp-Meuse Position able to fight at all . . . Groener stated that, according to the Chancellor [Prinz Max von Baden], a response from [President] Wilson was expected in about three days' time. It was especially important for us, therefore, to maintain our positions and not to give the enemy the impression that we were utterly shattered.[41]

All three chiefs of staff reported 'many instances of indiscipline', i.e. mutiny or near mutiny, and altogether more serious than issues such as widespread drunkenness which had afflicted mainly line of communications troops earlier in the year and, in isolated cases, fighting formations. After the war and related to this, in the search for explanations for the defeat and scapegoats to blame for it, one of the more bizarre accusations came in a 1924 pamphlet by Professor Hans Schmidt of the University of Gießen. Issued under the auspices of the temperance movement and under the title 'Why did we lose the War', he blamed its outcome on French wine and the inability of

German soldiers to resist the attraction of the demon drink during the 1918 offensives in particular. This polemic infuriated many senior German generals, who were anxious not only about their own reputations, but also that of the army which had lost the war. So, as a result, within months, no fewer than twenty eight of them had combined to produce their own pamphlet, 'That was not why we lost the War'. Though something of a curiosity, it is interesting in as much as in countering Schmidt, the contributors highlighted those times when he was correct and thus the pamphlet provides some concrete proof of disciplinary problems which affected the German army towards the end of the war.

Alcohol clearly had a role in the stalling of the German advance in and around Albert on 27 March; drunkenness amongst the troops of a complete division having been noted subsequently in British intelligence reports.[42] This was in fact a reference to the 3rd Marine Division, described by General von Kuhl in 'That was not why we lost the War' as 'a division recognised as extremely efficient'. However, he admitted that there were major disciplinary lapses that day, before adding that drunkenness was not the primary reason why the advance stalled; that had more to do with general exhaustion after several days of continuous fighting and the fact that enemy resistance had stiffened greatly.[43] Adding credence to this version of events was the testimony of *Generalmajor* von Gleich, commander at the time of 18 Reserve Infantry Brigade, 9th Reserve Division. Of this division, attacking Albert just to the south of the Marine Division, Gleich recalled that only slow progress was made through Albert because the enemy had concentrated a great deal of artillery and was occupying favourable positions in strength. Furthermore, the advance came at the end of five days and nights of continuous action, during which time the brigade had suffered casualties of 110 officers and about 2,000 other ranks.[44]

In general, while condemning Schmidt for inaccuracy, frequent wild exaggeration and continual deployment of hearsay evidence, Kuhl was prepared to admit where the charges were correct. So, for example, he rejected accusations such as, 'Two complete divisions were drunk' and 'Following excessive alcohol consumption near Soissons two divisions that were still battleworthy had to be disbanded.' Nevertheless, he accepted, for example, that, 'Infantry baggage trains blocked the roads in Ham during the March offensive because the personnel were drunk.' Similarly, the statement that a similar situation occurred in Estaires, 'was certainly correct'. Both service support personnel and men of follow-up columns were found to be drunk, but another report, also quoted by Schmidt, stated expressly that: 'The progress of the leading troops, the assaulting infantry had in no way been prevented because of alcohol.'[45] The best assessment is probably that abuse of alcohol caused problems and disciplinary lapses, especially amongst support troops, that were at times serious, but which did not impact fundamentally on the ability of the German army to go on fighting to the end.

Second Army reported at the beginning of November that it could probably withstand the next major thrust, but the Eighteenth stated that it could not. Another Allied attack would probably have meant breakthrough. There could hardly be clearer proof that the German army had reached the end of the road. Already on 30 October and to their self-evident relief, all remaining Austro-Hungarian troops (now being described by their German liaison officers as of 'rather doubtful quality') were withdrawn, to be replaced as far as possible with more reliable German formations. However, all was not well there either, with obvious signs of deteriorating morale and slackening discipline. General von Gallwitz noted in his diary that same day:

> In a regiment belonging to the 18th Landwehr Division, which was due to relieve 10th Infantry Division, a very large group of men from Alsace-Lorraine led by an *Offizierstellvertreter* [officer deputy] . . . declared that they did not want to fight here and had marched back without permission to Thionville. A criminal investigation is underway. That evening it was also reported that a battalion of another regiment of this division had refused to move forward into the positions. This was something that was unheard of in the German army. *Armee Abteilung* C had decided to place it well away from the firing line and to impose special measures on it . . . A trainload of reinforcements intended for the Saxon 241st Infantry Division had been the scene of ugly disturbances, such that one hundred men had to be arrested. 1st Landwehr Division which had always fought well reported that recently many men had deserted to the Americans. They were mainly from Alsace or belonged to the latest batch of young reinforcements.[46]

With only days of the war left, the bulk of the field army pulled back raggedly into the so-called Antwerp-Meuse Position where the situation was near crisis. Once again the line chosen, as was the case for most of the earlier ones, was, in the words of Crown Prince Rupprecht: 'More of a geographical description than a position.'[47] American pressure increased against the severely weakened Fifth Army, so, on 4 November, OHL decided to withdraw its right flank there as well, but insisted that it continued to fight hard.[48] In the rear areas, things went from bad to worse, as disruptive elements, whether imbued with left-wing tendencies or just accumulated war-weariness, continued to cause widespread problems. In the German homeland, by 7 November, Hanover, Braunschweig, Frankfurt am Main, together with Munich and the cities on the coast, were all under revolutionary control.

On 9 November, the day that Prinz Max of Baden announced the abdication of Wilhelm II as Kaiser and King of Prussia, word reached Army Group Crown Prince (Rupprecht) of a, 'mutiny affecting reinforcement troops of the Marine Corps at Beverloo Camp [at Leopoldsburg, seventy-five kilometres northeast of Antwerp]. 1st Bavarian Reserve Division, 11th Bavarian Infantry Division and another Prussian one, together with aircraft and tanks have been despatched to surround the mutineers and defeat them.'[49] Given that 1st Bavarian Reserve Division was the formation utterly destroyed in mid-October, this response was probably little more than a token effort and one, which at a time when OHL was reduced to directing its subordinate commanders to negotiate with soldiers' councils where these existed, such as in Brussels, it is most unlikely that any action actually occurred. By now the Imperial Navy had for days been gripped by mutiny, but the army was also simply disintegrating, even if its forward elements were attempting to hold as they had been directed.

In fact, it was remarkable in the face of rapidly-mounting difficulties that, to the very last day of the war, elements of the German army remained such a dangerous prospect for the Allied armies as the latter doggedly pushed the front eastwards throughout the summer and autumn from village to village and wood to wood. Part of the explanation is the fact that although the Hindenburg Plan swallowed huge quantities of manpower, it did manage to deliver the arms and ammunition required to carry on the fight. Furthermore, the battlefield was becoming increasingly automated, concentrating tremendous fire power in the hands of relatively few men.

Thus, provided that four or five stoutly-manned machine-guns, which would be easy to conceal and difficult to neutralise, could be placed in and around places of tactical importance, a huge toll would be taken of the attackers, forced to move across open ground to capture these places; something which is grimly confirmed by the presence of so many 1918 cemeteries dotted all over the routes of the advancing British armies. All of them are full of young conscripts and NCOs often previously decorated for bravery, but who fell encouraging their inexperienced men forward. A glance at a snapshot of German machine-gun production figures during the summers of 1915 – 1918 illustrates starkly how this was achieved:

Period	MG Production
4.7. – 31.7.15	611
2.7. – 5.8.16	1,608
7.7. – 3.8.17	8,676
2.8. – 30.8.18	11,354[50]

However, right at the end of hostilities, the logistic system faltered badly. On 10 November, the day when the Kaiser crossed the border into exile in the neutral Netherlands and Brussels descended into armed chaos, Crown Prince Rupprecht noted in his diary: 'Because the rail links with the homeland have been cut, neither ammunition nor rations are getting through. We have stocks of food for only three days. We are completely defenceless and, unfortunately, have lost our honour.'[51] He resigned his command the following day; his men and those of the other army groups held their positions grimly until the guns fell silent. Fought to a standstill, incapable of further action; the German army on the Western Front had been utterly defeated in the field.

As has been noted, virtually all commanders were well aware of what had happened and exactly how it had come about. Based on the undeniable and increasing problems faced by Allied logisticians if the general advance were to be continued, here and there in the literature are to be found claims or suggestions that the field army could have fought on.[52] In the short term this was in the undoubtedly forlorn hope that so to do would lead to an improvement in the armistice conditions and, had it been possible to consolidate, perhaps along the Antwerp-Meuse Line, an extended pause in operations might have enabled them, following such stabilisation, to carry the war on into 1919. However, even these optimists fail to answer the question 'To what end?' American troops arriving in huge numbers in late 1918 and a cascade of new and improved Allied arms and equipment scheduled for spring delivery, would have made short work of finishing off the weakened defence in 1919 had it been necessary.

The fact of the matter is that it was immensely difficult for the whole of German society, both military and civilian, to come to terms with what was a crushing defeat. For years, immense sacrifices had been made in pursuit of what was portrayed as a defensive war and a successful one at that. It was not long in the wake of the withdrawal across the Rhine, therefore, before different groups in Germany were attempting to rationalise what they had experienced and to pin down responsibility for this unprecedented humiliation. The political situation throughout the Germany to which returning troops came, was extremely precarious. Revolution was in the air, soldiers' councils were springing up everywhere and *Generalmajor* von Loßberg saw almost nothing but red flags flying over Stuttgart when he returned there in late 1918.[53]

With the army melting back into civilian life at breakneck speed, truly reliable units were a rarity, even amongst those who marched back in recognisable formed bodies to their garrison towns there to receive an enthusiastic reception from waiting crowds. Facing a dangerous situation, with a real risk of a descent into an all-out revolution, General Groener despatched to Berlin nine divisions he felt that he could trust. They were complete in the capital by 10 December when they put on a major parade, almost a show of strength, along *Unter den Linden*, with a saluting base near *Pariser Platz*. In the hope that these men would rally to his support, the then chancellor and later president of the republic, Friedrich Ebert, addressed them, stating: 'Welcome with all my heart, comrades and citizens. Your sacrifices and actions are unprecedented. No enemy has overcome you. We only gave up the fight when the superiority of the enemy in men and equipment was unstoppable.'[54]

Despite the fact that he did *not* state that they had been 'undefeated in the field', that was how his words were later twisted by supporters of the 'stab in the back' myth. In any case, his appeal did no good.[55] These troops too soon dispersed and Ebert, who was forced to tread an extremely precarious route, felt that he had no choice but to throw his lot in with dubious rightwing elements and *Freikorps* formations, a move which subsequently brought a torrent of criticism down on his head from socialists or communists who accused him of 'betraying the revolution'.

Those of a conservative disposition who remained loyal to the concept of empire and long-established institutions seized on the myth that the army had been 'stabbed in the back' by unreliable elements in society and out of this sprang the more extreme proponents of this approach, who swiftly began to shift the blame onto the Jews and to embrace Nazism.

By no means all who were attracted to the 'stab in the back' myth as an explanation for the 1918 defeat would have aligned themselves with such views, but a great many could not bring themselves to accept the defeat in the field and were therefore willing to accept some version of it, especially after Hindenburg used the phrase in November 1919, during his much-publicised and carefully stage-managed evidence to the Reichstag Commission investigating the causes of the collapse.[56] Among them, significantly, were those to be found manning the *Reichsarchiv*, the institution charged with guardianship of the archives and production of history. It was staffed almost exclusively by approximately one hundred former members of the Great General Staff, which had been forcibly disbanded under the terms of the Treaty of Versailles. General von Kuhl, who wrote and published opinions which were enormously influential, was one of its prominent members and a key witness to the *Reichstag* Sub-Committee charged with investigating the 1918 collapse. A modified form of 'stab in the back' was certainly an interpretation of history to which he subscribed.

The *Reichsarchiv* not only kept alive the ethos and techniques of the Staff, it also maintained a firm grip on the way the records were used and by whom. Concerned to defend its own performance and to brush over any deficiencies in the way the war had been conducted, it set out to ensure that a lost war was portrayed in such a way as to show the German armed forces, and by extension, the newly-formed *Reichswehr*, in the most favourable way possible. This applied not only to the writing of official history, but also to its semi-official publications, which continually and quite openly emphasised the performance of the strongly motivated individual soldier triumphing against overwhelming odds. Prominent amongst these was the 36-volume series *Schlachten des Weltkrieges* that appeared between 1921 and 1930. Writing in the Foreword to the final volume, which concerned events of 8 August 1918, the President of the *Reichsarchiv*, *Generalmajor Ritter* Mertz von Quernheim, stated bluntly:

> Despite all limitations, the objective has, without doubt, been achieved; namely to give not only those who fought in the World War a description of the individual battles in context, but also to provide the rising generation with an eternal image of German heroism . . . so I present to the readership the last volume of the series in the hope that from the limited selection of battles, they will be able to build up a picture of the unforgettable mighty deeds of the German army and of the German soldier in the World War.[57]

Any fair assessment of the fighting ability of the German army during the First World War has to give it credit; nobody would realistically doubt the courage of those who served but, as an organisation, by November 1918 it was overwhelmed and comprehensively defeated. Unfortunately, widespread institutionalised refusal to accept that plain fact, coupled with propagandistic distortion of history during the interwar years, led to a universal feeling that the outcome had been rigged, that there remained unfinished business and so, tragically, the seeds were sown for the drift to war in 1939.

Notes

1. Jack Sheldon, *The German Manpower Crisis of 1918* (The Douglas Haig Fellowship Records, 2011).
2. BA.-MA. Freiburg RH 61/51716 Kriegsministerium M.J. 14864/16 A.1. Geheim dated 17.7.16.
3. BA.-MA. Freiburg RH 61/51716 Kriegsministerium Nr 817/16g. Clb dated 6.10.16.
4. Martin Kitchen, *The German Offensives of 1918* (Stroud, 2001), pp. 208–9.
5. William Philpott, *Attrition: Fighting the First World War* (Little, Brown, 2014), pp. 323–4.
6. *General der Infanterie z.D.* Fritz von Loßberg, *Meine Tätigkeit im Weltkriege 1914-1918* (Berlin, 1939), p. 343.
7. *Generaloberst* von Einem, *Erinerungen eines Soldaten 1853-1933* (Leipzig, 1933), pp. 187–8.
8. Rupprecht, *Kronprinz* von Bayern, *Mein Kriegstagebuch: Zweiter Band* (Berlin, 1929), p. 420.
9. BA.-MA. Freiburg RH 61/505652 *Persönliches Kriegstagebuch des Generals der Infanterie a.D. von Kuhl* [KTB Kuhl], p. 170.
10. Loßberg, *op. cit.*, pp. 348–50.
11. KTB Kuhl, p. 171.
12. Loßberg, *op. cit.*, p. 350.
13. Dennis Showalter, *Instrument of War: The German Army 1914-1918* (Oxford, 2016), p. 267.
14. Gary Sheffield, *Forgotten Victory: The First World War, Myths and Realities* (London, 2001), p. 220.
15. Jakob Jung, quoted *Max von Gallwitz: General und Politiker* (Osnabrück, 1994), p. 96.
16. KTB Kuhl, p. 23.
17. Ibid., pp. 151–2.

18. Ibid., pp. 156–7.
19. *Oberst* Immanuel, *Siege und Niederlagen im Weltkriege* (Berlin, 1919), p. 147.
20. Quoted *Oberarchivrat Oberstleutnant a.D.* Wolfgang Foerster, *Der deutsche Zusammenbruch 1918* (Berlin, 1925), p. 71.
21. *General der Infanterie* von Tschischwitz (ed.), *General von der Marwitz: Weltkriegsbriefe* (Berlin, 1940), p. 303.
22. Rupprecht, *Kronprinz* von Bayern, *op. cit.* p. 439.
23. Tschischwitz (ed.), *op. cit.* p. 441.
24. Otto Lais, *Ein Regiment stirbt den Heldentod* (Karlsruhe, 1936), pp. 181–2.
25. Rupprecht, *Kronprinz* von Bayern *op. cit.*, p. 448.
26. Karl Tschuppik, *Ludendorff: The Tragedy of a Specialist* (London, 1932), p. 251.
27. *General der Artillerie* Max von Gallwitz, *Erleben im Westen 1916-1918* (Berlin, 1932), p. 398.
28. Rupprecht, *Kronprinz* von Bayern, *op. cit.*, p. 459.
29. Gallwitz, *op. cit.*, p. 415.
30. Ibid., pp. 415–16.
31. Bayerischen Kriegsarchiv, *Die Bayern im Großen Kriege 1914-1918* (Munich, 1923), p. 563.
32. *Generaloberst* von Einem and Julius Alter (ed.), *Ein Armeeführer erlebt den Weltkrieg* (Leipzig, 1938), p. 443.
33. Gallwitz, *op. cit.*, p. 427.
34. Immanuel, *op. cit.*, pp. 160–1.
35. Gallwitz, *op. cit.*, p. 434.
36. Erich Ludendorff, *Meine Kriegserinnerungen 1914-1918* (Berlin, 1919), pp. 614–15.
37. Rupprecht, *Kronprinz* von Bayern. *op. cit.*, p. 466.
38. Not that any trace of this appeared in his post-war writings. KTB Kuhl, p. 199.
39. Ludendorff, *op. cit.*, p. 617.
40. *Generalleutnant z.D.* Otto von Moser, *Kurzer Strategischer Überblick über den Weltkrieg 1914-1918* (Berlin, 1921), p. 119.
41. KTB Kuhl, p. 201.
42. Alexander Watson, *Enduring the Great War: Combat, Morale and Collapse in the German and British Armies 1914-1918* (Cambridge University Press, 2009), p. 196.
43. Deutchlands Heerführer, *Deshalb haben wir den Krieg nicht verloren!* (Hannover, 1926), pp. 9–10.
44. Ibid., p. 39.
45. Ibid., pp. 12–13.
46. Gallwitz, *op. cit.*, p. 442.
47. Rupprecht, *Kronprinz* von Bayern, *op. cit.*, p. 474.
48. Tschischwitz, *op. cit.*, p. 330.
49. Rupprecht, *Kronprinz* von Bayern, *op. cit.*, p. 475.
50. *Generalmajor a.D.* Ernst von Wrisberg, *Wehr und Waffen 1914-1918* (Leipzig, 1922), p. 8.
51. Rupprecht, *Kronprinz* von Bayern, *op. cit.*, p. 476.
52. See, for example, *Generalleutnant* Max Schwarte et. al., *Der Weltkampf um Ehre und Recht: Der Deutsche Landkrieg, Dritter Teil* (Leipzig, 1925), pp. 591–3 and *General d. Inf. a.D* Hermann von Kuhl, *Der Weltkrieg 1914-1918 Band II*(Berlin, 1929), pp. 508–11, though Kuhl was careful to caveat his remarks and to emphasise the short-term nature of any such attempt to fight on.
53. Loßberg, *op. cit.*, p. 363.
54. George S. Vascik, and Mark Sadler, *The Stab-in-the-Back Myth and the Fall of the Weimar Republic* (London, 2016), pp. 86–9.
55. 'Undefeated in the field' would have been *Im Felde unbesiegt*, but what Ebert actually said was *Kein feind hat Euch überwunden*, i.e. 'No enemy has overcome/prevailed over you.'
56. Vascik and Sadler, *op. cit.*, pp. 122–5. Hindenburg never saw any reason to modify his view, concluding his memoirs with a comparison of the fate of the worn-down front-line soldiers with Hagen son of Alberich's treacherous spear thrust into Siegfried's back at the climax of Wagner's *Götterdämmerung*. See *Generalfeldmarschall* von Hindenburg, *Aus meinem Leben* (Leipzig, 1934).
57. *Major a.D.* Thilo von Bose, *Schlachten des Weltkrieges Band 36: Die Katastrophe des 8. August 1918* (Oldenburg, 1930), p. 8.

Suggested Further Reading

Boff, Jonathan, *Winning and Losing on the Western Front: The British Third Army and the Defeat of Germany in 1918* (Cambridge University Press, 2012)

Stevenson, David, *With Our Backs to the Wall: Victory and Defeat in 1918* (London, 2011)

Vascik, George S. and Mark R Sadler, *The Stab-In-The-Back Myth and the Fall of the Weimar Republic* (London, 2016)

Watson, Alexander, *Enduring the Great War: Combat, Morale and Collapse in the German and British Armies 1914-1918* (Cambridge University Press, 2008)

Chapter 3

The Royal Navy: Securing Victory and Coping with its Consequences

By Duncan Redford

On the morning of 21 November 1918, HMS *Cardiff* met the German High Seas Fleet and led them towards the Grand Fleet; in Versailles, the following spring, the victorious Allies were to debate what to do with the German ships. Forty miles east of May Island in the Firth of Forth, the two fleets met. Not since 31 May 1916, off Jutland, had these two massive symbols of national power and pride met: then it was in anger, now it was as part of the Armistice.

As the German High Seas Fleet approached, it met the full might of the Grand Fleet, representative warships from Allied navies and all the British home naval commands, drawn up in two long columns six miles apart, which shaped courses to pass either side of the dirty, demoralised and defeated warships and their crews. All in all, there were thirteen squadrons of battleships, battlecruisers, armoured and light cruisers and the obligatory screen of destroyers – some 370 ships to take the Germans into custody. The British were not taking any chances; the Grand Fleet was at action stations ready to react if the Germans showed the slightest hostile intent. Then, on a command from the Grand Fleet's flagship, HMS *Queen Elizabeth* – the signal 'ML' – the British fleet turned through 180 degrees to take station on either side of the German ships, conveying them to their anchorage in the Firth of Forth. Admiral Beatty, the Grand Fleet's commander, ordered that 'The German flag will be hauled down at sunset today, Thursday, and will not be hoisted again without permission.' Such was the importance of the event that *The Graphic* even produced a souvenir issue of the surrender of the High Seas Fleet, calling it the 'most striking symbol of Germany's utter failure to attain that World Power for which she really undertook the Great War on August, 1914'.[1]

Yet this was not just a victory that left a feeling of incompleteness, it was one that had long-term ramifications which were still being felt in the 1930s, not just for the Royal Navy, but also in the public and political spheres. The First World War heralded a sea change in Britain's attitude to its navy, and towards war itself. This chapter will explore the impact victory had on the Royal Navy and British sea power. Central to this was the absence of a second Trafalgar – Jutland, while a British victory, was no Trafalgar – and, to almost all but the most astute, the invisible nature of the pressure of sea power that had forced Germany to seek peace, lacked national satisfaction. Victory also brought with it new challenges – demobilisation, retrenchment, disarmament – to complement the traditional peacetime challenges of little wars and naval diplomacy in the hope that sea power might deter aggression that was detrimental to British interests.

It is this author's contention that the war had been won by sea power, sea power which not only manifested itself in the long lines of dreadnoughts which had fought and won at Jutland, but was also found in the economic blockade which, made possible by British sea power, starved Germany out of the war. While the blockade in the early years of the war had not been enforced as rigorously as the Admiralty wanted, by the end of 1916 it had become much tighter. However, the Germans could and did receive goods and foodstuffs via neighbouring neutral states, but thanks to the efforts of the Ministry of Blockade, diplomatic pressure had ramped up against neutral trading with Germany.

The increasing effectiveness of the blockade through both diplomatic measures and the continuing patrols by the Navy to catch blockade runners, as well as the day to day interception of neutral vessels to ensure they were not carrying contraband, meant that in the winter of 1916–17 Germany experienced real food shortages. Before the war, the average calorie consumption per person, per day, in Germany was 3,215; by autumn 1916 it had fallen to 1,344 before rising very slightly in November to 1,431 calories when an average working man would need about 2,500 calories to remain healthy. Some, involved in heavy manual labour, might need up to 4,000. Around 763,000 people died prematurely in Germany as a result of the economic blockade.

The shortage of fertilisers and fodder which had been previously imported and were now covered by the blockade only made the German situation worse. Fortunately for the Allies, the Germans had experienced poor weather and a poor harvest during 1916 too, which was exacerbated by a lack of agricultural labour. Indeed, the restrictions on fertilisers would continue to compound German woes: the amount of wheat, oats and potatoes produced in 1918–19 was only half what it had been in 1912–13. Germany's

German imports of foodstuffs (in thousands of tonnes)[2]

		Average net imports 1912–13	Imported 1917	% decrease
Breads/cereals		5,538	17.6	99.7
Animal fats		161.6	5.2	96.7
Fish		361.3	161	55.4
Eggs		169	40	76.3
Leguminous vegetables		310.8	1.7	99.5
Fruits		850	220	74.1
Vegetable fats & oils		155.3	Not given	
Oilseeds		1,595.4	17.1	98.9
Cattle foods (not including pig fodders like maize)	– oilseeds	1,571.9	14.8	99.1
	– bran	1,744.9	10.2	99.4
	– oilcake	532.5	2	99.6
	– other	359.2	18.6	94.8

inability to feed itself forced it to surrender, even though its army was still in the field and still fighting.

The invisible nature of this victory was deeply unsatisfying for the Royal Navy and for the British people. Hidden and misunderstood, British sea power was perceived – wrongly – as not having pulled its weight in the conflict. Admiral Rosslyn Wemyss, the First Sea Lord, thought there was a 'feeling of incompleteness' and he clearly believed that Beatty and his Grand Fleet felt themselves cheated by the small matter of there not being a second Trafalgar to cover the Navy in glory, and a select few in personal triumph.[3] Yet Wemyss also understood that the victory gained by the Royal Navy was greater than any 'second Trafalgar' decisive battle, and, furthermore, had been achieved without the losses that would have been associated with such a momentous clash of dreadnoughts at sea.[4] Yet the feelings of the Navy on the subject were far less pertinent than the opinions of the British more generally. Here public opinion was firmly against the naval contribution to victory. The lack of the promised decisive sea battle weighed heavily against sea power. Public and politicians alike were united in their lack of understanding about how sea power really worked. The Navy's much-vaunted dreadnoughts had not only failed to deter a war in the first place, but had not won it either.[5] The small fact that the dreadnoughts and sea power had in fact won the war was not appreciated.

The German ships only remained anchored off Rosyth for a few days before they were transferred in small groups to the Grand Fleet's main wartime anchorage at Scapa Flow. There they sat and waited and rusted in isolation while the negotiations to turn the Armistice into a treaty to end the war dragged on at the peace conference in Paris. The deadline for the treaty to be signed was noon on 21 June 1919, although it was extended at the last minute by a couple of days. However, it seems that the German officers at Scapa Flow were determined to avoid handing over their ships to the Allies for either destruction or use by allied navies. At 1000hrs on 21 June, before the nominal expiration of the deadline, the Germans put in action a well-organised plan to scuttle their ships. All bar one of the battleships and battlecruisers, over half the cruisers and thirty-two out of fifty destroyers, were successfully scuttled. The German High Seas Fleet had ceased to exist, but the Royal Navy's Grand Fleet was no longer around to witness the event; early in 1919 it had been broken up into the Atlantic, Home and Reserve Fleets.

Victory at sea and the removal of the German threat brought a series of challenges for the Royal Navy and its supporters at they came to terms with the new post-war world. At the end of the war the Royal Navy's strength was 37,636 officers and 400,975 enlisted men, excluding of course the Royal Naval Air Service which had been transferred to the Air Ministry as part of the RAF on 1 April 1918. Pre-war it had just 150,000 officers and men. Clearly, the Navy was going to have to shrink in terms of its size and the amount of money spent on it. At the same time, the men who had volunteered for service during the war – both reservists and hostilities only personnel – needed to be returned to their peacetime employment, not only to reduce the cost of the Navy, but also to start the process of returning the wider economy to a peacetime basis.[6]

In what was perhaps an all-too-rare appreciation of possible feelings on the lower deck, the Admiralty was at pains to explain to the fleet the demobilisation scheme and to help men prepare for civilian life before the order to demobilise was given in mid-January 1919. The Admiralty even produced a pamphlet for prospective employers of ex-naval personnel, explaining the ranks and rates of different specialisations and what general skills a man of a particular rate and specialisation might have, such as experience of managing men, or particular machine-tool skills. In the highly-charged political atmosphere of late 1918 and early 1919, where industrial unrest was rife, where troops had been used against strikers in Glasgow, and civil and military militancy was widespread, demobilisation and lower-deck pay and other issues were extremely important. If it were mismanaged in any way, mutinies and disorder like those suffered by the British and Dominion Army units in Calais, Southampton, Folkestone, Rhyl and Cardiff, might follow, or worse – sailors had been at the centre of the Russian and German revolutions after all.

Fortunately, the Admiralty moved quickly to deal with lower-deck concerns. Pay and pensions were increased, despite opposition from the other services and the Treasury, demobilisation went smoothly on the whole and in order to forestall the development of a ratings union, the Admiralty developed a welfare committee system to provide an outlet for grievances. As a result, unrest in the Navy was slight, and even the most serious events – auxiliary service crews refused orders or the raising of the red flag on the patrol boat *Kilbride* in Milford Haven – were isolated acts.

The knife was wielded quickly on the uncompleted war emergency construction programmes too, as defence spending was slashed. One of three 'E'-class light cruisers was cancelled, as were thirty-eight modified 'V&W'-class destroyers, two 'S'-class destroyers, and thirty-three submarines during 1918–19. Also, three out of the four *Hood* class battlecruisers, whose construction had been suspended in 1917, were scrapped on the slipways. However, new ships would be needed in the light of war experience if the strength of the Navy were to be maintained. Naval airpower demanded new ships and rebuilds of existing ones – 'aircraft carriers' – from which to operate aircraft in support of fleet operations. Much of the existing fleet was worn out by war service or was obsolescent, hence the Admiralty's demands to keep most of the 'D' and 'E'-class cruisers under construction and the proposals in 1920 for four new battleships.

There was also the rather tricky problem of excess officers in the Navy; too many had been recruited as a result of the pre-war naval expansion and the practice of offering regular commissions to officers who joined during the war. In 1920 a voluntary redundancy scheme was implemented; the Admiralty hoped that 650 officers of lieutenant commander rank and below would take advantage of the scheme, but in the end only 407 did so. Nor did the Admiralty – rather hypocritically – do anything about the size of the Flag Officer's list. The shortfall in the 1920 scheme meant that in 1922 there was another attempt to reduce officer numbers – the 'Geddes Axe'. This scheme saw 200 lieutenants retire voluntarily and another 350 made redundant. However, even this was not enough as the Navy continued to contract through the 1920s. In 1926 and 1929 retirement inducements were offered to lieutenant commanders. On the whole, the redundancy packages were sympathetically dealt with by the Treasury; only when the Admiralty, in a self-serving moment, tried to get better terms for the most senior of officers did the Treasury dig its heels in. Ratings pay, too, was examined in the 1920s as the cost of living continued to fall. In 1925 it was decided that a new lower pay scale would be used for all men joining the Navy from October 1925, but that the 1919 pay rates would remain for those already serving.[7]

It was also clear that once demobilisation had been completed there would not be a return to 1914 levels of spending on the Navy. Instead, the Cabinet decided in August

1919 that, given the lack of potential enemies and the impact of the war, no major war was likely for the next ten years. This was the now notorious 'Ten Year Rule'. This rule was straightforward and, it has to be admitted, was not the cause of any British unreadiness for war in 1939. Put simply, the rule told all three branches of the armed forces that for the next ten years there was no likelihood of major war and that they should prepare their budgets accordingly. However, it also meant that at the end of the ten-year period, the armed forces should be ready to fight a major war. It was a financial, and even strategic, planning tool that should have allowed the armed forces to absorb the lessons from the previous war and tailor their procurement plans and doctrine accordingly to ensure that military readiness and reconstruction after the war was achieved in a reasonable time period.

However, the Royal Navy's success in the early to mid-1920s in persuading the Cabinet to back the replacement of its cruiser strength, and to maintain it at around seventy, as well as the campaign to develop Singapore as a major fleet base, led to political dismay in the Treasury. The problems with the 'Ten Year Rule' really started in 1925, when Winston Churchill, now Chancellor of the Exchequer, managed to persuade the Committee for Imperial Defence that the Admiralty was not to make preparations to base a fleet at Singapore that was equal to that of Japan. This effectively extended the Ten Year Rule to cover a war with Japan up to 1935. Then three years later – again as a direct result of the Admiralty's success in getting funding approved by the Cabinet – Churchill, with the approval of his Cabinet colleagues, decreed that the Ten Year Rule would now become self-repeating and would reset itself after each year to year zero. The impact of this was clear, straightforward and devastating. Instead of being at a point where all three armed services were just three years from when they had to be ready to fight a major war, overnight they were returned, in financial and procurement terms, to 1919. Procurement plans were dashed: work on the improved base at Singapore was

Defence spending 1919–1939[8]

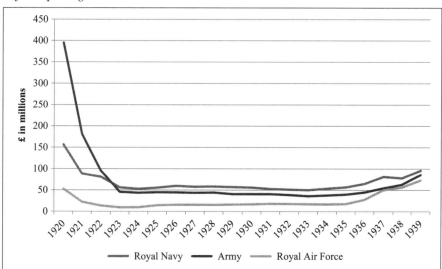

retarded, as was the modernisation programme for battleships.[9] The result was that the low point in spending on the Navy was not in the early 1920s as the service contracted after the Great War, but in 1932, due to the twin impacts of the self-perpetuating Ten Year Rule and further government retrenchment as a result of the collapsing economic situation.

Nor could it be said that the armistice of 11 November 1918 and then the formal treaties that brought the Great War to a close, actually ended war or the possibility of it. There was the widespread undeclared war going on in Russia between the Bolsheviks and the White Russians, the latter actively supported by almost everyone else, including Britain, making the civil war an international affair. There was also an ongoing crisis in the Near East caused by the collapse of the Ottoman regime.

With the end of the war against Germany and the Central Powers, Britain had to decide the line to take in the Russian Civil War between the Bolsheviks and the non-Bolshevik or White Russian forces. At the end of November, the Cabinet decided to intervene on the side of the White Russian forces and a cruiser squadron together with a destroyer flotilla were dispatched to the Baltic. Torpedo-armed Coastal Motor Boats (CMBs) were sent overland to the Caspian Sea, while HMS *Suffolk* at Vladivostok fitted out and manned an armoured train which supported the anti-Bolshevik forces in central Siberia along the Trans-Siberian Railway near Omsk – about as far from the sea as it is possible to get.

The main British effort was, however, in the Baltic, where not only were White Russia forces supported, but the establishment of independent Baltic states overseen, and the German forces in the area compelled to leave the Baltic states and Russian territory as demanded by the Armistice. The initial British force of five 'C'-class cruisers, nine 'V&W'-class destroyers and seven minesweepers suffered an early loss when the light cruiser HMS *Cassandra* struck a mine in the Baltic and sank, thankfully with only very light casualties. Soon submarines joined the naval forces and two CMBs commanded by Lieutennat A. Agar were also dispatched to the region by MI6 to run agents in and out of the Bolshevik-controlled areas. Agar soon got fed up with the relative impunity a minefield gave the Red warships while they shelled White forces in the forts near Kronstadt. He decided to exceed his orders and on the night of 16/17 June 1919 torpedoed and sank the Bolshevik armoured cruiser *Oleg*. He was awarded the Victoria Cross for his bravery and initiative.[10]

Agar's private war delighted the anti-Bolshevik forces in the region as well as Admiral Wemyss, the First Sea Lord, and Admiral Cowan, commander of the British naval forces, who thought it an excellent demonstration of what the Navy should be doing and argued as such to the Government. The Government was less impressed, but Wemyss got permission for a more offensive posture and Cowan received reinforcements: the aircraft carrier HMS *Vindictive*, more minesweepers and eight large CMBs. Cowan did not wait long before launching his forces at the Bolshevik naval forces in Kronstadt. In the early morning of 18 August 1919, under cover of an air raid launched by *Vindictive*'s aircraft, seven of the large CMBs, and Lieutenant Agar in a smaller CMB, penetrated the harbour at Kronstadt and caused mayhem.

The crisis in the Near East was a complex affair. Naval gunboat diplomacy was used in 1919 to persuade a reluctant Ottoman regime to sign the peace treaty with the

Allied powers – The Treaty of Sèvres. The Greek invasion of Asia Minor was given tacit support too. Yet the naval presence also helped shore up the Ottoman regime in the face of internal opposition from the nationalist uprising led by Kemal Ataturk. When in 1922 the Greeks threatened Constantinople, against the wishes of the other allies, the Royal Navy concentrated forces off the port in support of the French army units protecting the city. The Greeks, very aware of their vulnerable supply lines to their forces in Asia Minor, backed down.

The Kemalist forces were, however, beating the Greeks in Asia Minor. By September the nationalists were threatening the city of Smyrna, which despite its location in the Ottoman Empire had a large Greek population and character. The Mediterranean Fleet stood off the port and British citizens were evacuated by the Navy and in commandeered merchant ships, but the Navy's efforts to achieve an orderly surrender of the city to Kemal's troops failed when the city caught fire and was largely burnt to the ground. The nationalist forces then threatened the Dardanelles, which under the terms of the Treaty of Sèvres had been demilitarised and declared neutral. When Kemal's forces approached Chanak on the Asiatic shore of the Dardanelles, war threatened. The Mediterranean Fleet was sent to the region to support the few Allied troops in the area and stop Kemal's forces crossing the straits.

Careful diplomacy on the ground prevented any escalation and eventually a new treaty was signed at Lausanne in 1923 to replace the Treaty of Sèvres. However, at the threat of war in the Near East, Conservative backbench MPs, more dubious still about their role in upholding Lloyd George's wartime coalition government, took a long hard look at what continued association with Lloyd George was doing to their future prospects. They decided that they were not impressed and forced the Conservative Party to leave the coalition, consigning Lloyd George to the political wilderness.

With victory and peace came the almost continuous round of naval diplomacy, foreign visits, anti-piracy work, disaster relief and the protection of British citizens and interests around the globe. Yet these were effectively side issues when compared to the big question of where and against whom would the next war be fought?

The terms of the Versailles Treaty, notwithstanding the demise of the High Seas Fleet at Scapa Flow, meant that a new German navy was limited to 15,000 men, six 'battleships' no bigger than 10,000 tons, six cruisers no larger than 6,000 tons, twelve destroyers, twelve smaller torpedo boats and no submarines at all. In short, a force that could contest control of the Baltic with Russia, but was no threat to Britain. In naval judgement it was the United States Navy which should be used to set the size of the Royal Navy. However, when this idea was floated in Cabinet in August 1919 by the First Lord of the Admiralty, Walter Long, it only succeeded in provoking the Cabinet to declare, a few days later on the 15th that 'It should be assumed . . . that the British Empire will not be engaged in any great war during the next ten years, and that no Expeditionary Force is required for this purpose.' Nor could the Admiralty use conflict with the USA as basis for its war plans and the size of the Navy.[11]

Fortunately, the Admiralty, after much argument, managed to get the agreement of the Government that the Navy would not be inferior to any other navy – a one-power standard that included the USA. As a result, Cabinet approval for four new battleships was given in 1920. However, before work could commence on these new battleships, the

Naval Strength at the end of the First World War[12]

	Britain	USA	France	Germany	Japan	Italy
Battleships	61	39	20	40	13	14
Battle-cruisers	9	–	–	5	7	–
Cruisers	30	16	21	3	10	7
Light Cruisers	90	19	8	32	16	10
Flotilla Leaders	23	–	–	–	–	8
Destroyers	443	131	91	200	67	44
Submarines	147	86	63	162	16	78
Aircraft and seaplane carriers	4	–	–	–	–	–

Americans proposed a naval arms limitations conference. This did not of course solve the problem of who the Royal Navy should be preparing to fight even if the government were to have decided that any such war would be in ten years' time. Nevertheless the focus on disarmament spoke to a wider issue within British society – a change in attitude to sea power.

The Quest for Naval Arms Limitation
The Great War was seen by many as the war to end all wars. To make sure that this was indeed the case, many people asked why the war had started. The answer, felt by many in Britain and the USA, was not political determination to meet national aims even at the risk of a war, but the arms races before the war – and most clearly the *naval* arms race. Such a view may well have been erroneous, but it was a common view. There was also a more general aversion to war as a political tool. In July 1921, 'No More War' demonstrations took place across Europe on the anniversary of the outbreak of war; the rallies continued in Britain until 1924. 1921 also saw the foundation of the 'No More War Movement'. In the *Morning Post* it was reported that Lady Frances Balfour at the 'Women against War' meeting on 11 November 1921, had declared to loud cheers that:

> It is not a choice between good and evil: it is the choice between life and death to the world. Wars have miserably failed. It is for the women of the world to say, with one voice: 'Let's scrap the old battleships and launch a new order of things'.[13]

For the British, the American call for a naval arms limitation conference was a popular one with the public. It was also popular with the Government as it was a means of avoiding an expensive arms race. The Government may have decided that cuts in naval strength were needed to help the economy, but what was communicated in the press was a need for arms reduction not for economy but for peace.

The Washington naval conference in 1921–2 was a turning point in British naval history; Britain gave up the naval superiority that had been prevalent since 1815 and enshrined later in the two-power standard. Instead, parity or a 'one-power standard' was accepted with America, the latest challenger to British maritime pre-eminence. The Washington Treaty ushered in fifteen years of naval arms limitation, only ending with Britain's, at first secret, rearmament after 1933 and the failure of the 1936 London Naval Conference.

The 1922 Washington Naval Treaty did indeed see the USA, Britain, France, Japan and Italy all agree to limiting the size and composition of their navies for the next ten years, and suspending the construction of new battleships for the same period of time. Additionally, the total displacement of the battleship and aircraft carrier force, as well as the maximum size of each ship, was limited. This meant that while Britain was limited to a maximum displacement of its entire battleship force of 525,000 tons, no one ship could be larger than 35,000 tons or have guns greater in size than 14-inch calibre. Furthermore, no new battleships were to be built for ten years. As a special consideration, given the age of the Royal Navy's battleships and the more recent building programmes of the USA and Japan, Britain was allowed to build two new battleships which could have nine 16-inch guns. These two ships – HMS *Rodney* and HMS *Nelson* – finally entered service in 1927. The amounts set aside for aircraft carriers were smaller, only 135,000 tons with no one ship greater than 27,000 tons. The key to the treaty was the ratio between the powers: 5, 5, 3, 1.75, 1.75 in the order Britain, USA, Japan, France and Italy, ensuring that Japan, for example, only could have a battleship or aircraft carrier force three-fifths the size of that of Britain or the USA. Cruisers were given a maximum size of 10,000 tons displacement per ship and forbidden to have guns larger than 8-inch calibre, but the controlling ratio for battleships and aircraft carriers was not extended to cruisers and other warships.

At a stroke, Britain had accepted what was effectively naval parity with the United States, but the treaty still gave a two-power standard against the next two biggest naval powers – as long as everybody kept to the agreement. Perhaps surprisingly, given the strength of popular interest in the Royal Navy before the war, and a clear example of how the Great War had changed expectations inside and outside of Parliament, there was very little opposition to the treaty. Even the Navy League, the pre-war staunch defender of British naval supremacy, proclaimed itself in favour of naval arms limitation and then found itself under attack from its own members for placing its faith in collective security and international treaties rather than the strength of British sea power. Both the prospect of a treaty and the final agreement was seen as: 'The only hope of putting an end to a rivalry which is unhealthy and dangerous lies in the adoption of a policy of limitation.' The *Daily Telegraph* told its readers that: 'with the approval, as we believe, of the mass of the people, we have announced that we shall be satisfied if in future our Navy is not inferior to that of any other country.' The *Scotsman* concurred stating that: 'Agreement is, indeed, the only way out; and this country has shown by the moderation of its policy that it has no desire to resume naval rivalry.'[14]

However, the Royal Navy and Britain also benefited from this attempt to impose international limits for naval armaments. First, they had avoided an arms race with the USA and at the cost of parity with the United States Navy, with whom they were not prepared politically to fight, and had prevented the Americans and Japanese producing fleets based on more modern ships than the Royal Navy. Second, the Royal Navy alone had emerged with permission to build two new battleships. The Americans and Japanese at best could look forward to completing a couple of ships that had already been started, with the implication that the Royal Navy would be able to build in lessons from the recent war far better than its closest rivals. Furthermore, permission to build the two battleships helped preserve shipbuilding capacity from the full force of the treaty's battleship-building embargo. Third, it had prevented the Washington ratios being extended to cruisers and lesser warships; yes indeed cruisers were limited in size and gun-power, but there was no total tonnage limit, or limit on hull numbers, ensuring that for as long as Britain was prepared to spend money, it could protect its trade and maritime empire. Fourth, parity with the USA might have been accepted, but Britain still had the largest navy and the Washington ratios also gave Britain a two power standard against Japan and any European naval power that had signed the treaty or was bound by the Versailles Treaty. More importantly, the Royal Navy succeeded in replacing much of its cruiser force during the 1920s, a feat that was largely due to Beatty's adept political manoeuvring as First Sea Lord.

The flaw in the treaty concept was that the Washington naval treaty was supposed to herald a series of international agreements that could cover land and air warfare and these planned treaties were never pursued. After all, the single most powerful land army and air force belonged to France, who, thanks to the Versailles Treaty and an absence of a rival land or air power with whom to compete, saw no need for such treaties. Worse, the decision to do away with the Anglo-Japanese treaty in favour of the Washington process turned an ally into a potential rival in the Far East. The other flaw in the Washington process was that it relied on states obeying the rules and not cheating, something that became problematic in the 1930s. Britain's desire to avoid an expensive naval arms race in the early 1920s made the Washington treaty possible, not the promise of global arms reduction, and if fighting a real war were now frowned on, the Navy had the prospect of re-fighting the First World War, especially the Battle of Jutland, to entertain itself.

The Long, Stormy Legacy of Jutland and the Great War

The Battle of Jutland had been a deep disappointment to both the Royal Navy and the British public. Instead of the long hoped-for decisive battle that would destroy German sea power and give the British a victory to compare with Trafalgar, the Navy lost three of its prestigious battlecruisers – HMS *Indefatigable*, HMS *Queen Mary*, and HMS *Invincible* – all to horrendous magazine explosions, three older armoured cruisers and eight destroyers. The Germans lost just one battlecruiser, one obsolescent pre-dreadnought, four light cruisers and five torpedo boats. The Germans may have suffered a strategic defeat, but to casual observers it looked dreadfully as if the Royal Navy lost the battle. The legacy of the battle not only influenced debates during the War, but also long into the peace.

The failure of the Navy to meet public as well as its own expectations as to what would happen when the Grand Fleet actually managed to meet the German High Seas Fleet in battle, meant that the Royal Navy embarked on a round of enquiries and reports to try and find what went wrong, why, and what was to be done about it. Throughout the 1920s, the Royal Navy's staff college, its tactical school in Portsmouth, senior officers, the naval staff in the Admiralty and the staffs of the various commanders-in-chiefs afloat all pored over the battle in an effort to make sure all the ills were identified and corrected. To call the Battle of Jutland an obsession for the Royal Navy during much of the interwar period is not an overstatement.

Obsession with the Battle of Jutland did in fact cause some desirable changes and improvements that might be considered overdue. The idea that fighting at night between capital ships – the battleships and battlecruisers – was to be avoided at all costs and the destroyers fighting at night would pursue a defensive action, were rejected. A great deal of theoretical and practical effort was put into getting the Navy to feel happy about the idea of fighting aggressively and offensively at night – the payback for this investment was the crushing defeat inflicted on the Italian Navy at night during the Battle of Matapan in 1941. The command and control problems that Jutland had highlighted were also addressed by developing 'divided tactics' – a means of allowing decentralisation of command within the battle fleet thus reducing the communication problem Jellicoe and Beatty had faced while ensuring better co-ordination of efforts by subordinate commanders. Allowing officers to use their initiative was encouraged not disparaged.[15]

The fuzes in the Navy's large-calibre shells and the shells themselves, which had been highlighted as one of the main reasons the German's losses were not heavier, were improved as these had been found to fail when the British warships had actually managed to score a hit on the Germans. This, however, had an unfortunate side effect. By concentrating attention on the reliability of shells the inaccuracy of British gunnery during the war was in part disguised. What made the problem worse was that poor gunnery was highly localised to Beatty's Battle Cruiser Fleet, which being based at Rosyth during the war did not have easy access to the gunnery ranges that had been established in the Orkneys and were regularly used by the Grand Fleet. After the war, revised fire-control systems to control long-range gunnery duels were developed. This in itself was an avenue for dispute, given the Admiralty's poor pre-war relations with Arthur Pollen and his accusations that Frederick Dreyer had stolen his ideas for mechanical fire-control computers. Pollen took his case to the Royal Commission on Awards to Inventors in 1920 and 1923, which did not find in his favour, and had his case re-heard in 1925 where again it was rejected – only with regard to one part of his system, the Argo 'Clock', was an award made by the 1925 review. The Navy's new fire-control systems – the Admiralty Fire Control Table Marks 1–7 – which were fitted into all new cruisers and battleships from the mid-1920s onwards – were very much developments of the Dreyer system, although in part influenced by the Argo 'Clock'.

Unsurprisingly, after the war, Beatty, now First Sea Lord (he had intrigued against Jellicoe's successor in the post, Admiral Wemyss, and forced him out), was highly sensitive to any suggestion that failures at Jutland were down to him, or the efficiency of his ships. The result was that the efforts to find out what went wrong and what went right – especially at Jutland – ended up being construed in personal terms. The Navy and indeed politicians were divided over it. Was Admiral Jellicoe as the then Commander of the Grand Fleet, or his subordinate, Admiral Beatty, as the then commander of the Battle Cruiser Fleet, and their different approaches to gunnery, command and control as well as their tactical handling of the battle, more at fault? This dispute, which started soon after the battle, limped on well into the interwar period and polarised the Navy's officer corps, just as the Fisher-Beresford feud had divided the Edwardian Navy. The decision by Jellicoe's successor as First Sea Lord, Admiral Sir Rosslyn Wemyss, to commission an official account of the battle, based solely on the documentary evidence available, within a few weeks of the end of the war, provided a continual focus for antagonism between Jellicoe's and Beatty's supporters. This 'Harper record', so named after its chief author, Captain J. E. T. Harper, may have been started under Wemyss's tenure as the professional head of the Royal Navy, but was finished under his successor as First Sea Lord, Admiral Sir David Beatty – the former commander of the Battle Cruiser Fleet at Jutland.

Beatty took great exception to the Harper's draft of the official account and the positions shown on the accompanying charts of the battle which either did not tally with his recollections of the battle or that he felt portrayed the Battle Cruiser Fleet (and by inference him as its commander) in a less than attractive light. Some of Beatty's senior staff had also been with him in the Battle Cruiser Fleet at Jutland and they too opposed Harper's account. Admiral Chatfield disagreed strongly with the contention that it was the Battle Cruiser Fleet's poor gunnery rather than faulty shells that had resulted in so little damage to the German ships. Chatfield had been Beatty's Flag Captain at Jutland and was hardly impartial. Harper tried to resist the pressure to change areas for which he had documentary support, but in the end had to give in to Beatty's wishes. This upset Jellicoe who had not seen either the official account or the amendments Beatty had insisted on, and when he did see them he objected most strongly. In fact, Jellicoe refused to leave Britain to take up his post as Governor-General of New Zealand unless it were guaranteed that the published work would not contain the passages *he* objected to. Unable to reconcile the wishes of Beatty and Jellicoe and aware of the rumours about the official account circulating around the Navy and the gentlemen's clubs of St James, the Admiralty shelved the project indefinitely.

The Jutland controversy rumbled on through the early 1920s as Beatty's Admiralty tried various attempts to get its version of events published and was opposed by Jellicoe and his supporters. The controversy even enveloped the official Cabinet Office history of the war at sea, as the author, Sir Julian Corbett, had the temerity to criticise Beatty and by default side with Jellicoe. However, almost as soon as the volume of Corbett's official history that dealt with Jutland was finished, the author died, preventing Beatty from getting any changes through. The Admiralty had to be satisfied with a preface that stated they disagreed with the author's opinions. As the years went by the Jutland controversy occasionally sparked into life as memoirs were published by various politicians and retired Admirals. In the end the controversy died away with Beatty's retirement from the post of First Sea Lord in 1927 and the appointment of a perceived Jellicoe supporter, Admiral Sir Charles Madden, as Beatty's replacement. Jutland may have been the source of much change for the Navy, making sure the Royal Navy's performance in the Second World War was much better, but it was also an open sore and was too slow in the healing.

Victory, born out of sea power, heralded much change for the Royal Navy; some changes, like demobilisation and retrenchment were expected. Some, like disarmament and an altered attitude towards the Navy, were not. All had to be managed and some, by definition, took time. The consequences of victory were still being felt as the next war loomed and Britain rearmed itself for the new conflict. Some of the new developments were straightforward matters of material and professional concern – new shells and fuzes or new tactics as well as command and control procedures, but others were more fundamental in nature. Of these, the transformed public and political attitude to the Navy and sea power was the most important.

This transformation, as a result of the experience of the Great War, saw first an acceptance of a new naval standard, parity with the United States in place of the pre-war British supremacy, then second, widespread support for disarmament. The disenchantment with the war and the desire to ensure it was the 'war to end wars' by embracing disarmament even saw the self-proclaimed protectors of British naval supremacy, the Navy League, support the Washington Naval treaty, having already embraced collective security and the League of Nations, to the outrage of many members when they realised exactly what maritime future their organisation was embracing. If the Navy League were to see no reason to argue for continuation of British sea power in the aftermath of the war it is easy to see why few others thought it worth campaigning for.

Victory also brought painful divisions to the surface as the Navy first tried to learn from its war experiences and then senior officers tried to protect and justify their reputations. The refighting of Jutland did at least ensure that the fear of night-fighting and the command and control problems that manifested during the battle were addressed and overcome. Gunnery, tied up as it was between the Beatty and Jellicoe views of what went wrong, was a harder issue to resolve and was further poisoned by the dispute between Pollen and the Admiralty about patents, but resolved it was. However, for all the division and divisiveness centred on the Battle of Jutland, for the Navy, the legacy of the battle, and indeed of the war, was a strong desire to do better next time. Next time, the Navy did just that.

Notes

1. NMRN, RNM 2001/48/5, letter from Roger Talbot to his mother, dated 22 Nov 1918; S.W. Roskill, *Earl Beatty, the last naval hero: An intimate biography* (New York, 1981), p. 279; *"The Graphic" Souvenir of the Germany Navy's Surrender* (London, 1918), p. 4.
2. The National Archive [TNA], ADM 186/603, CB 1554 The Economic Blockade, p. 21.
3. A.J. Marder, *From Dreadnought to Scapa Flow* Vol. 5 (London, 1970), p. 176.
4. Rosslyn Wemyss, *Unpublished Memoirs*, quoted in Marder, *Dreadnought to Scapa Flow*, Vol. 5, p. 165.
5. B. Lavery, *Able Seamen. The Lower Deck of the Royal Navy 1850-1939* (London, 2011), p. 265.
6. S.W. Roskill, *Naval Policy Between the Wars*, Vol. 1 (London, 1968), p. 72.
7. Roskill, ibid., pp. 124–5; A. Carew, *The Lower Deck of the Royal Navy* (Manchester, 1981), pp. 143–9.
8. Figures from B. Mitchell, *British Historical Statistics* (Cambridge, 2011), pp. 591, 594. Figures for 1938 and 1939 do not show the value of Defence Loans.
9. C. Bell, *The Royal Navy, Seapower and Strategy Between the Wars* (Basingstoke, 2000), p. 22; O. Babji, 'The Royal Navy and the defence of the British Empire', in K. Neilson and G. Kennedy (eds), *Far Flung Lines* (London, 1997), pp. 173–6; Bell, *The Royal Navy, Seapower and Strategy*, pp. 22, 24.
10. A. Agar, *Baltic Episode* (London, 1963), pp. 80–97; G. Bennett, *Cowan's War* (London, 1964), pp. 33–6, 124–7; Roskill, *Naval Policy*, Vol. 1, pp. 144–50.
11. TNA, CAB 23/15, War Cabinet Minute 616A, dated 15 August 1919.
12. Roskill, *Naval Policy*, Vol. 1, p. 71.
13. *Morning Post*, 12 November 1921, p. 4.

14. D. Redford, 'Collective Security and Internal Dissent: The Navy League's Attempts to Develop a New Policy towards British Naval Power between 1919 and the 1922 Washington Naval Treaty', *History*, Vol. 96 (2011), pp. 48–67; *Scotsman*, 18 March 1921, p. 4; *Daily Telegraph*, 16 December 1921, p. 10; *Scotsman*, 18 March 1921, p. 4.

15. Roskill, *Naval Policy*, Vol. 1, p. 533.

Suggested Further Reading

Bell, C., *The Royal Navy, Seapower and Strategy between the Wars* (Basingstoke, 2000)
Farquharson-Roberts, M., *A History of the Royal Navy: World War 1* (London, 2014)
Marder, A., *From Dreadnought to Scapa Flow* Vol. 5 (London, 1970)
Roskill, S., *Naval Policy Between the Wars* 2 vols (London, 1968 & 1976)

Chapter 4

Kitchener or Lloyd George, The Architect of Victory?

By George Cassar

Reinterpreting the activities of well-known historical figures is common enough and an ongoing process that is dependent on one or more factors, among which are the discovery or accessibility of new source materials, changes in the world at large which affect the way historians look at the past, and fallacies in, or unsound reasoning behind, the 'historical facts'. In this chapter I have challenged the long-held view by most historians regarding the record of the two most dominant individuals in the British government during the First World War, Kitchener and Lloyd George.

Few reputations in recent history have changed as dramatically as that of **Kitchener**. Before the Great War he had spent most of his brilliant career as a soldier and administrator in the outer reaches of the Empire. His successful military campaigns against the Mahdists in the Sudan and the Boers in South Africa brought him such fame and influence that no other commander since Wellington had enjoyed. But post-war treatment of Kitchener as Secretary of State for War has been unkind and, while there have been attempts in recent years to reset the balance of how he is viewed, he continues to be portrayed unsympathetically in historical works as well as in feature films and television documentaries.

Open season for attacking Kitchener began with the publication of the memoirs and recollections of contemporary politicians. To expunge their culpability they blamed him for most of the mistakes that had been committed while he served as Secretary of State for War. He was a convenient scapegoat for he was not around to answer the charges brought against him. Nor did writers later try to correct the record even after the restrictions on classified information had been lifted in the 1960s and the personal papers of key politicians became available. His detractors have glossed over his list of accomplishments as though it were inconsequential, while dwelling on, and at times magnifying, what they considered were his misjudgments. They decry him as a bungler who mismanaged the war and hold him accountable, along with the commanders in the field like French and Haig, for callously sacrificing a generation of young men to no good purpose. It is sufficient to cite the names and conclusion of a few recent critics. John Gooch has no hesitation in saying that Kitchener's appointment was 'a grave mistake – perhaps Asquith's greatest during his wartime period of office'.[1] According to John Grigg, Kitchener's tenure as the nation's military chief 'turned out to be a disaster'.[2] William Philpott shares the prevailing consensus that 'Kitchener was not the right man for the job'.[3] Renowned journalist and TV personality Jeremy Paxman gave full vent to his negative feelings about Kitchener, both as an imperialist and as War Minister.[4]

Among Kitchener's present-day critics some are respected writers and they ought to know better. Is there an explanation for their myopia? Is it because of their dislike of Kitchener as a person or his ruthless campaigns in the Sudan and South Africa or that he embraced imperialism and the moral standards of his age? Whatever the cause, the only yardstick by which he should be measured was the quality of his work during the two years of his service at the War Office.

When the Great War broke out in August 1914, Kitchener, on leave in England from his posting in Egypt, was invited to 10 Downing Street where he was asked to join the government as Secretary of State for War.[5] Kitchener initially showed no interest as he was well aware of his limitations. He could lead and execute policy but he had misgivings about his ability to work as a member of a team, especially with men whose profession he held in low regard. What gave him further pause was his knowledge that he was deficient in the arts of oral expression and persuasion, assets vital to win over Cabinet colleagues who doubted or resisted his policy. However, Asquith overcame his reluctance by appealing to his patriotic duty. The appointment was greeted with relief and delight by the public and did much to unite the country which in the decade before the war had been wracked by a series of domestic crises. Standing like a rock, steadfast and stoical, he instantly became the living embodiment of Britain's will to win.[6]

The Cabinet entered the war without expecting fundamentally to depart from the strategic doctrine laid down before 1914. It proposed to conduct war with comparatively little cost to Britain. The idea was to confine the country's part to supplying money and munitions to its allies, send a token force to northern France and impose a blockade of Germany and its allies. The main burden of the fighting on land would be left to France and Russia. If France fared badly in the opening battles, the British Expeditionary Force (BEF) could retreat to the coast and be evacuated.[7] Implicit in Britain's policy of limited liability was its willingness to risk an Entente defeat.

Trained as an engineer, Kitchener instinctively looked at the broad picture when confronted by a problem and had the uncanny ability to judge accurately what needed to be done. He appreciated that Germany was thoroughly prepared for war, had a large population, great resources and, given its determination to avoid defeat, would not relinquish the struggle until it had exhausted the last vestige of its manpower and material. His own experience in the Sudan and South Africa and a careful study of the American Civil War reinforced his conviction that the war would be long and that victories would only be won by superior numbers.

Kitchener's colleagues were in awe of his legendary reputation and, bewildered by the first stirrings of war, were thankful to place the decision-making process in his capable hands. In the early months of the war no criticism of his methods or ideas was heard. 'When he gave a decision,' Churchill declared, 'it was invariably accepted as final. He was never, to my belief, overruled by the War Council or the Cabinet in any military matter, great or small. . . . Scarcely anyone ever ventured to argue with him in Council. All-powerful, imperturbable, reserved, he dominated absolutely our counsels at the time.'[8]

At the first Cabinet meeting Kitchener gave notice that the war would not be brief and was likely to continue for at least three years. He explained that Germany's defeat would come, not after a few land battles, but only when its manpower had been exhausted by a slow process of attrition. As Britain's miniature army would fall well short of tipping the balance in favour of the Entente, he stressed that, in order to discharge its obligation, the government must be prepared to place and maintain an army of a million men in the field.[9]

The Cabinet could hardly believe what Kitchener was saying. Sir Edward Grey, the Foreign Secretary, would later recall that Kitchener's prediction of a war lasting three years 'seemed to most of us unlikely, if not incredible'.[10] To the members of the Cabinet the war was expected to be over in a matter of a few months, well before the million-man army could be trained and equipped. That being the case, it seemed to them a frightful waste of effort and treasure. Yet the ministers accepted Kitchener's advice passively and, even more astonishingly, without discussion.[11] Lord Beaverbrook, a press baron and close friend of both Churchill and Lloyd George, wrote in his classic study, *Politicians and the Great War, 1914-1916*: 'No other Secretary of State would have imagined it [the scope and duration of the war], and so no other would have prepared for it; certainly no other man could have induced his colleagues to act on his conclusions or the public to accept them.'[12] By permitting Kitchener to transform Britain into a nation in arms, the Cabinet had taken the most far-reaching policy decision of the entire war.

As Britain, alone among the European great powers, had not embraced conscription before 1914, the New Armies (or Kitchener's Army as they were called) had to be built through voluntary enlistment. By lending his name to the drive for recruits, Kitchener gave an aura of respectability to a profession formerly regarded by the general public as the last refuge of riff-raff and the unemployed. Kitchener's first appeal for 100,000 volunteers on 7 August appeared in the British press and he obtained them in a few days. In the early months of the war recruiting posters were placarded all over the country. None was more effective than the call 'Your Country Needs You,' depicting above the legend Kitchener's imposing face, bristling moustache, outstretched finger and piercing eyes glaring directly at the onlooker. So great was the surge of patriotic enthusiasm that during the first eighteen months of the war before the adoption of conscription in 1916, nearly two-and-a-half million men enlisted, hitherto forming the largest volunteer army in the history of any country.[13]

At the very top of the priority list was the need to overhaul the peace-time recruiting apparatus which was not designed to handle the flood of men who came forward. To train the recruits Kitchener held back a number of officers and NCOs from the BEF to the dismay of its commander, Field Marshal Sir John French, and in addition used retired personnel and some 900 Indian Army officers who had been on leave in Britain at the time of the declaration of war. No less important, the War Office had to arrange suitable accommodation for the men, feed them, and supply them with equipment, uniforms and arms. Britain was unprepared for war and so much had to be improvised. Kitchener's great challenge was to acquire munitions to supply Britain's vastly expanding army. Already overburdened, he took on the added responsibility of negotiating and placing contracts, of inspecting firms and the quality of production and of finding new sources of supply. That the herculean task of creating the New Armies and their infrastructure was accomplished in the midst of a great war, must, to use Churchill's words, 'certainly rank among the wonders of the time'.[14]

As Britain had no war plan of its own, arrangements had been made to align the BEF on the left flank of the French army. Although Kitchener was no tactical wizard on the battlefield, he was, conversely, a first-rate strategist. The British High Command wanted the staging area of its troops to take place at Maubeuge, near the Belgian border, to act in unison with French strategic designs. Such a deployment, in Kitchener's view, would place the BEF in great peril. He predicted that the Germans would make a wide sweep through northern Belgium to roll up the Allied left flank and he warned that the BEF would be overwhelmed if it concentrated at Maubeuge. He recommended Amiens, seventy miles to the rear, where the BEF would be in a better positon to react to the German envelopment movement which he anticipated. He argued that Germany would not have invaded Belgium at the cost of driving Britain into the war unless it meant to exploit its tactical advantage to deliver a rapid knock-out blow at France. However, Kitchener had been absorbed in the East for decades and could not claim that his conclusions were based on his active involvement in, or careful study of, the complex problem of Continental strategic planning. The discussion lasted for three hours and with neither side giving ground the matter was ultimately referred to the Prime Minister who, as might be expected, came down on the side of his commanders in the field. Kitchener, although still unconvinced, gave way.[15]

As it frequently happened, Kitchener's military instinct and logic proved correct. On 23 August, the German First Army, attempting to sweep wide around the Allied left flank, ran headlong into the BEF near Mons. Although badly outnumbered, British riflemen, trained to deliver fifteen aimed shots a minute, exacted a terrible toll on the advancing German units and at day's end had held the field. Even so, with the French forces in full retreat, the BEF had no option but to follow suit. Kitchener's uneasiness at news of the BEF's retreat from Mons turned to alarm and dismay when its commander, Sir John French, informed him that he proposed to leave the battle-line and head south-west behind the Seine. For Kitchener, fleeing to Le Havre was not an option. In statements made on different occasions he made it clear that he did not intend to withdraw British forces from France until the German army had been crushed.

In the opening days of the war, Kitchener, as he would tell among others the sister-in-law of a former subordinate, General Archibald Hunter, claimed that it was 'the duty of civilization to crush the overbearing Prussians, and relieve the world of their constant menace. And we shall do it or die in the attempt.'[16] Given his uncompromising attitude, he was not about to yield to French's wish to retire to Le Havre. At Kitchener's request the Prime Minister summoned a Cabinet meeting where the Secretary of State read French's grim telegram. He explained the political and military ramifications that would result from French's intended move. It would have a disastrous effect on the solidarity of Anglo-French cooperation and almost certainly lead to the capitulation of France which, in effect, would mean that Britain would also lose the war.

There were several ministers who had assumed from the outset that, if France faced defeat, the BEF could retreat to the coast and be evacuated. They argued that it would be inconsistent with tradition to deny the commander-in-chief freedom of action in the execution of his duties. But Kitchener, backed by the Prime Minister, insisted that Britain could not desert France in its hour of greatest danger and his argument carried the day.[17] Authorized to go over to France to deal with the emergency on the spot, Kitchener hurried to Dover and took a fast cruiser to Le Havre where he boarded a special train for Paris arriving before luncheon. A meeting was arranged with French at the British Embassy on 1 September. There followed a stormy interview, the details of which are unknown, but in the end French agreed, presumably under the threat of dismissal, to conform to the plans of General Joseph Joffre, the French commander.[18] This opened the way for the BEF to participate in the Battle of the Marne which halted the German juggernaut and irreparably dislocated the Schlieffen plan.

In a series of fierce engagements after the Marne, the forces of each side tried to outflank the other to the north but only succeeded in extending the battle-line to the English Channel. Before the end of 1914, the war of movement had given way to siege warfare as the rival armies, facing one another, dug in along a twisting line that stretched over 450 miles from the Swiss Alps to the North Sea. The most puzzling and disturbing feature for the leading soldiers was that the study of nineteenth-century military doctrine offered no sure leads on how to deal with trench warfare. The French High Command, devoid of imagination and imbued by the spirit of the offensive, fastened on a policy of mass frontal attacks with the object of wearing down the Germans. Kitchener considered French strategy, to which the smaller BEF was inexorably tied, as the last resort of unimaginative generalship. He had enough experience in warfare to understand that one side launching frontal attacks against another holding strong defensive positions would suffer much heavier casualties. At the current rate of exchange in human lives, the result would be precisely the reverse of the one the French High Command had assumed.

Kitchener took a great deal of pride in his New Armies, which were beginning to take the field in the spring of 1915, and the last thing he wanted to see was their destruction in Joffre's senseless war of attrition. Although initially baffled by trench warfare, it was not long before he came up with an idea, the seeds of which may have been planted during his conversations with General Henry Rawlinson, a former subordinate. His concept of attrition differed from that of Joffre who aimed at a breakthrough in one battle. What he had in mind was an active-defensive strategy on the Western Front. Such a policy called for a series of surprise attacks, each of which was intended to seize a limited and lightly-defended area of the enemy's front. Once the Allies had attained their objective, they were to fortify their new position and inflict heavy losses on the Germans when they counter-attacked. By the time the British army had reached its maximum strength in 1917, the Germans would be so weakened that they would be unable to hold back a massive Allied offensive. But a war lasting as long as three, or possibly four, years did not resonate with Joffre and his British acolyte, French.[19] Nor indeed was the British Cabinet willing to exercise such patience. Emerging from Kitchener's shadow at the beginning of January 1915, members of the War Council[20] were anxious to play a major role in shaping the country's future strategy. In search of an alternative to the bloody stalemate on the Western Front, they looked for a short-cut to victory outside of France. Kitchener always believed that the war could only be won on the main front but he was not unsympathetic to the idea of a minor diversion that would boost morale at home, avoid frittering away the New Armies in Joffre's futile offensives and produce political and strategic benefits. Indeed he considered the possibility of a landing at Alexandretta in the Gulf of Iskenderun, with the object of severing the communications between Turkey and Syria as well as removing the threat to the Suez Canal. He did not anticipate that the British force would have much difficulty in gaining control of the area as the Turkish defenders were few and it was certain to be welcomed and assisted by the local Christian population.[21]

Kitchener's idea never entered the exploratory stage because it was preempted by Winston Churchill, the First Lord of the Admiralty, who advanced a plan to force the Dardanelles by ships alone. He argued that, once the fleet broke into the Sea of Marmara, Constantinople would surrender rather than face the prospect of a naval bombardment. A successful operation would render Turkey helpless, convince the neutral Balkan states to join the Entente and open a southern-sea route to Russia. Kitchener had serious doubts about the feasibility of such an enterprise as a week earlier he had indicated that it would also require about 150,000 troops, a number that was not remotely within his reach.[22] But now Churchill maintained that the Royal Navy could accomplish the task without the cooperation of troops. Kitchener was no naval expert and when Churchill unfolded his scheme he seemed to have the support of his senior admirals.[23] Besides, the Turks were not expected to put up much of a fight given their lamentable military performances prior to the war and their recent debacle against the Russians in the first week of January 1915. Churchill won over Kitchener and the other members in the War Council by assuring them that if the naval attack were to prove too difficult, or too costly, it would be called off, followed by a public announcement that it was a feint for a strike elsewhere. It is a virtual certainty that Kitchener would not have lent his support otherwise. There were strong nationalist movements in Egypt and India which had been openly active in opposing British rule before the war. After Turkey's entry in the conflict the Sultan had called for a *jihad*, and Kitchener feared that any loss of face in the Muslim world resulting from a British defeat world inspire a revolt, or at the very least, serious trouble in these countries.[24]

On 19 February 1915, three weeks after Churchill received the authority to go ahead, Allied ships opened their preliminary bombardment against the Turkish forts. Churchill, on his own initiative and without the consent or knowledge of the War Council, issued a press communiqué, revealing the attack and claiming its successful start even though the bombardment had caused little or no damage. Constantinople was emphasized as the ultimate objective.[25] It is impossible to exaggerate the extent of this blunder. One can only speculate on the reason which drove Churchill to make such a declaration. As Lloyd George later remarked to his mistress, Churchill's indiscretion meant that there could be no turning back if things went awry.[26] Unfortunately that is exactly what happened. Poor preparation and execution, as well as underestimating the risks involved, doomed the operation. Worried about the effect the admission of defeat would have In Egypt and India, Kitchener felt compelled to use what forces he could spare to try to pull the navy's chestnuts out of the fire.[27] It was one of the rare instances in which he acted contrary to his habit of carefully assessing the pitfalls before embarking on a project. It would prove to be the biggest mistake of his long career. At a terrible cost he learned too late that errors committed at the outset of an enterprise are practically impossible to repair. The failure of the military operation not only resulted in heavy casualties but did much to erode Kitchener's influence in the War Council.[28]

Before the Dardanelles campaign was liquidated the Cabinet leapt into another side-show, joining the French in an expedition to the Balkans to save Serbia from being overwhelmed. Kitchener understood that the obstacles, made more daunting by the rugged terrain in the Balkans, could not be overcome without a huge force but his argument against opening a new front was disregarded. The handful of Anglo–French troops sent – less than one-third of the number Kitchener had deemed necessary – was ridiculously insufficient to break through and assist the Serbs.[29] The sensible course would have been to withdraw but for the sake of domestic politics the French insisted on remaining and, against the advice of Kitchener, the British Cabinet, defying reason, followed suit, effectively putting an end to the Dardanelles campaign.[30] Establishing an entrenched camp around Salonika, the size of the Allied garrison kept growing, reaching an incredible 600,000 troops by 1917. Its mission was undefined and it remained relatively inactive until the last few months of the war.

The lesson to tread carefully after two costly enterprises which were either a failure or grossly ineffective somehow eluded the British politicians. They proposed to embark on yet another distant adventure in the Middle East. In the autumn of 1915 the British War Council, desperate for a victory, sanctioned a further advance in Mesopotamia to capture and hold Baghdad. Kitchener's warning that the Turks could hurriedly collect an army of 60,000 men to bar the way fell on deaf ears. The upshot was that the understrength British force was halted at Ctesiphon, driven back to Kut-al-Amara where it was besieged and forced to surrender on 26 April 1916.[31] It was the first time that a major British force had yielded to an enemy since the Battle of Yorktown in 1781.

The intervention by British ministers to direct the course of the war in 1915 had dreadful military consequences and tied down hundreds of thousands of troops which could have been used to greater profit elsewhere. Kitchener often felt that he was waging a war on two fronts, one with the Germans and the other with his colleagues against whom he was no match in debate. He could not make them understand that even if the operations undertaken in the secondary theatres were successful, the Allies would lose the war if defeated on the main front. Sir Edward Grey, with characteristic integrity, was one of the very few politicians who gave Kitchener his due. In hindsight he wrote that Kitchener had been correct in opposing the Cabinet's flawed policies in 1915 and he regretted that he had not lent him more support:

> The chief mistakes in strategy may, in my opinion, be summarized in two words: 'Side-shows.' In justice to Kitchener it must be recorded that he disliked them all, and my own particular regret is that I did not resolutely support every resistance he made to them It seemed to me to be a true criticism that we did not sufficiently concentrate attention on the one cardinal point: that it was the German Army which had to be beaten, and that this could be done only on the Western Front. For us to attempt it anywhere else was to give the Germans the advantage of interior and safe lines of communication compared with our own. Had this been grasped continuously as the central fact of the war, the side-shows – Gallipoli, Baghdad, Salonika – would either never had been taken or would have been kept within smaller dimensions.[32]

As differences deepened over the direction of the war, Kitchener's isolation from his colleagues grew more and more. Admittedly he was difficult to work with as he was aloof, secretive, and could not express himself clearly in debate but his leadership had paid enormous dividends during the early months of the conflict. The nation's fortunes, however, took a downward turn in 1915 after the politicians insisted on taking over the direction of the war. It did not help that Kitchener was unable to solve the riddle of the Dardanelles; that the Anglo–French attacks on the Western Front in the spring of 1915 had failed with heavy losses, and that *The Times* on 14 May broke a story that Sir John French's latest attack had been crippled by a want of high-explosive shells for which, it should be noted, Kitchener was unjustly blamed.[33] In the end, rather than look at the unfortunate consequences of their intervention in directing the war, some ministers held Kitchener responsible for practically everything that went wrong. Their confidence in him evaporated and he was now being judged with increasing criticism as a member of the team. He was relieved of responsibility for munitions and later for strategy but he continued to be idolised by the masses and remained a member of the Cabinet until 5 June 1916 when, at the commencement of a mission to Russia, he drowned when the warship on which he was travelling struck a mine and sank off the Orkneys.

It would be idle to pretend that Kitchener's judgement was flawless while he was at the War Office – no man who has ever waged war has been free from mistakes – but his errors of omission and commission pale in comparison to his accomplishments which paved the way for Allied victory. During the four months that he was in supreme charge of the war, he convinced the government and the nation to discard the concept of limited liability; forged a military organization that produced a huge army, one that would allow Britain to step into the breech in 1917 caused by the collapse of Russia and the exhaustion of France, and hold a formidable foe at bay until American power could be brought to bear; laid the basis for a great armament industry; and overruled French's intention to leave the battle line and, in so doing, not only avoided an Entente defeat but contributed indirectly to the victory at the Marne.

Now let us turn to **Lloyd George** who built his pre-1914 reputation as a social reformer and a man of action in the administrations of Henry Campbell-Bannerman and Asquith. Chancellor of the Exchequer since 1908, he took over the newly-established Ministry of Munitions in May 1915 and was later appointed to succeed Kitchener as Secretary of State for War. He connived with the Conservatives to oust Asquith whom he considered to be an ineffective war leader and became Prime Minister in December 1916.[34] Fifty-four years old, he lived and breathed politics and was unencumbered by fixed principles or loyalty to close associates. Trained as a lawyer, he not only lacked a formal education but made little effort to broaden his general knowledge – Asquith once found him looking for Gallipoli on a map of Spain. A brilliant orator with a razor-sharp mind, he had the rare ability in Cabinet discussions to make an absurd proposal appear plausible. No stranger to gutter politics, he was quick to claim credit for the achievements of others and to place the blame elsewhere for his mistakes. His character flaws aside, he should be judged on the three most significant areas under his control: mobilizing the home front, keeping up the nation's fighting spirit and devising a coherent military strategy.

As a skilful politician possessing indefatigable energy, Lloyd George achieved his greatest success in tackling problems, some unprecedented, on the home front. In the first place he met the needs of war production by changing the relationship between the state and labour. Resorting to a variety of tactful expedients, Lloyd George surmounted the difficult and perilous task of keeping labour unrest within manageable limits. He took a more active role in settling labour disputes, established cordial relations with powerful labour leaders, brought some into his government and appealed to their patriotism to head off strikes. In instances when strikes did occur he was prepared to make generous concessions as waiting-out the strikers was not an option. If the union were to prove unreasonable he brought pressure on it to lower its expectations by exploiting widespread public support for the war. While strikes were still seriously to bedevil industrial production, it is reasonable to conclude that no other politician in the country could have shown greater dexterity in managing labour than Lloyd George.[35]

An equally vital element in the war effort was to devise and implement a coherent and just food policy. Since Britain had to import about 60 per cent of its food before the war, it was in greater danger of starvation than any other European belligerent. During the first two years of the war, rural output in Britain declined on account of labour lost to the army and industry, insufficient fertilizers as a result mainly of the loss of potash imports from Germany, and the requisitioning of horses by the military. On top of this, the enemy in 1917 resorted to a renewed policy of unrestricted submarine warfare aimed at starving Britain into submission. The Admiralty could offer no remedy to avert crippling shipping losses which lasted until the convoy system was introduced in May, not least thanks to the persistence of Maurice Hankey, Secretary of the War Cabinet, and then, to a lesser extent, Lloyd George who, unsurprisingly, claimed the entire credit.[36]

Initially the government responded by adopting a programme to ease the shipping shortage. The nation's dependence on imported food was reduced and measures were taken in hand to bring grassland and derelict areas back into production. Agricultural workers were encouraged to remain in place by receiving higher pay and exemption from military service. Unconventional sources were found to supplement labour on the land. The services of large numbers of schoolboys and women, in addition to prisoners of war, were used at harvest time. More reliance was placed on machines such as tractors to lessen the dependency on labour. New chemicals, in place of the pre-war standard ones, were used to produce fertilizers. The cumulative measures paid off. The total production of food for 1917, though below the desired goal, was 6 per cent higher than in the previous year. If the increase were not dramatic, at least the decline, in danger of deepening, had been halted and reversed.

The other aspect of Lloyd George's food programme was to provide for equitable distribution. Here he can be faulted for showing excessive caution. He was reluctant to commit to a practical plan, allegedly because the public, especially the working class, was adamantly opposed to a rationing system. Instead, his government relied on symbolic gestures such as encouraging meatless days and prescribing the size of a bread roll. However, voluntary appeals had little effect as the public's anger over shortages and rising prices, triggering a series of strikes in May 1917. Lloyd George's government tried different expedients to avoid rationing but conditions only worsened. The diversion of merchant ships to transport American troops to France in the last quarter of 1917 caused acute food shortages with predictable consequences. Prices of commodities in short supply rose sharply and in many parts of the country long queues formed outside shops. The ministry worried not only about the effect of the food shortages on the war effort but also about the rising revolutionary feeling among a segment of the working class which was being galvanized by events in Russia after the Bolshevik takeover. Heavy pressure from different quarters of society finally induced the government to take unprecedented action. Compulsory rationing was introduced at the local level on a few commodities in November 1917 and was gradually extended nation-wide so that by July 1918 it covered all items except bread which was plentiful. Eventually prices stabilized and long queues disappeared. As it happened, the rationing and distribution system worked better in Britain than in most countries where it was introduced.

Lloyd George also showed a lack of political will in adopting a manpower policy until late in the war. Although conscription had become law before Lloyd George seized the reins of government, the growing requirements of industry, transportation, shipbuilding and agriculture, all of which competed openly with the armed forces for the services of the men, retarded the development of a balanced and comprehensive policy. The obvious solution would have been to approve of a system that would effectively distribute men between the civilian workplace and the armed services. However, the main barrier to introducing a draft bill lay with the union leaders who were strongly opposed to allowing the state to decide whether a skilled man should serve in the army. The government was unwilling openly to confront the syndicates and initially relied on voluntary enlistment and the transferral of labour to war work. The idea was to encourage men physically unfit for military service, or engaged in non-essential trades, to volunteer to work in vital industries as substitute for those who would be drafted into the army. The results were disappointing as the number of enrolments fell far short of the projected goal. Other ad hoc measures proved no more successful until finally the unions, realizing the gravity of the situation in the army, relented and permitted the enrolment of the youngest men in the not-too essential industries. Thereupon a new Military Service Bill was hurried through Parliament and gained royal assent in February 1918. By its terms the government was empowered to cancel exemptions allowed in certain industries and to call up men based on occupation, age and marital status. The government's tardiness in putting into effect a coherent scheme to control manpower however had prevented maximum efficient utilisation of human resources.

With the fortunes of the Allies sinking steadily in 1917, Lloyd George did what he could to sustain the nation's morale and resolve. Although few could match his oratory, he lacked the means of mass communication which Churchill would enjoy during the Second World War. It must be remembered that twenty-five years before Churchill's personal leadership achieved legendary distinction, films were silent and public broadcasting by radio lay in the future. Still, in trying to project an image of a dynamic man of action single-mindedly committed to winning the war, Lloyd George embraced techniques that, if not novel, were carried out with great effect. He was constantly on the move, addressing crowds, negotiating with trade union leaders, visiting the front and attending inter-Allied conferences. Wherever he went he made sure that a bevy of reporters and photographers was on hand to record and publicise his activities. During his first nine or ten months in office, the Press helped shape his image as an ideal war leader and contributed to imbuing the public with determination and confidence in ultimate victory. That perception would change as the misfortunes of the Entente deepened, causing the Press to turn against Lloyd George. This undoubtedly affected his standing with the public.

Still, Lloyd George deserves to be commended for his overall good work in the nation's civilian sector and he should also be credited for his political acumen and persistence in working out arrangements with Allied leaders, something which clearly contributed towards victory. He was the main driving force in the establishment of a Supreme War Council which was empowered to watch over the general conduct of the war and to ensure the co-ordination of military action. He was instrumental in the creation of a unified Allied command under Marshal Ferdinand Foch, a move which helped to contain the German offensives in the spring of 1918. Additionally, he collaborated with the French to assist the Italian army in stabilizing and holding a new defensive line after the crushing Italian defeat at Caporetto in October 1917.

Where Lloyd George failed, and rather miserably so, was in crafting a sensible British military policy. He had never shown any interest in the study of warfare prior to 1914, but, supremely confident in his own ability, he had convinced himself that he could conduct war effectively without the advice of his generals. He likened strategy to politics, that it was based on rules and common sense and essentially a simple exercise which was 'unnecessarily complicated by professionals'.[37] However, as a novice, he did not understand that war does not follow a preconceived scenario. Nothing in war, or very little, is predictable. To devise a coherent strategy is a difficult art and even capable and experienced soldiers make errors. It certainly was beyond the grasp of amateurs as Lloyd George proved repeatedly.

Lloyd George embraced a peripheral strategy as a means of escaping from the costly offensives on the Western Front and to win inexpensive victories by attacking Germany's allies. He calculated that the defeat of the weakest members of the Central Powers would undermine German strength and bring about its collapse. He was wrong. It was Germany propping up its partners, not the other way around. He flitted from one half-baked scheme to another without taking into consideration such relevant factors as logistics, terrain, interior versus exterior lines and probable enemy response. There were instances where operations were carried out successfully but they were not worth the distraction and investment in human and material resources. The Prime Minister never seemed to understand that there was no short cut to victory. The war could only be decided on the Western Front and the price of beating the Germans would have been tragically high even if there were to have been the possibility of attacking by different methods in France from those employed in 1916 and 1917.

Although still favouring an Eastern strategy, Lloyd George involved himself in a rare and brief venture in relation to the Western Front. He had no use for Haig whom he considered rigid, unimaginative and delusional with no idea of how to win the war other than to charge like a bull at the enemy's impregnable front. In attempting to steer British military methods in a new direction, Lloyd George frequently clashed with Haig. One answer to the problem would have been to replace Haig but the Conservatives made his retention a condition of their entry into the coalition. That being the case, the next step could have been to place Haig on trial and if his generalship were to continue to prove unsatisfactory the Prime Minister would have been justified in sending him home. Instead, he left Haig in command but undermined him at every opportunity, an ill-considered manoeuvre scarcely likely to further the interests of the Entente.

The Prime Minister initially sought to change the command structure by placing Haig under the orders of General Robert Nivelle, the newly-appointed French Commander-in-Chief. Such an arrangement would have reduced the British Empire forces to a component of the French army and forced Haig to comply to a plan about which he might disapprove. Charming and fluent in English – his mother's native tongue – Nivelle had captivated Lloyd George, exuding unbridled confidence that his novel tactics would shatter the enemy's front and end the war. Neither Haig nor Sir William Robertson, Chief of the Imperial General Staff, had any faith in Nivelle's proposal. Nevertheless the War Council, under the sway of the Prime Minister, overrode their dissent and endorsed Nivelle's scheme and his request for the assistance of the BEF. Haig acceded to the arrangement after assurances that his subordination to Nivelle would be limited simply to the forthcoming offensive and that the BEF would keep its identity.[38]

Incredible as it may seem, a group of men, none of whom was experienced in the study of warfare, had consented to embark on a major operation contrary to the advice of their military experts and without pausing even to investigate its feasibility. As it happened, most of the high-ranking French generals were also highly critical of Nivelle's plan.[39] A case in point was the reaction of the Minister of War, General Hubert Lyautey, one of France's most distinguished soldiers, who ridiculed the scheme, describing it as 'a plan for the Grand Duchess of Gerolstein' and considered sacking Nivelle until told that it would have an unsettling effect on the army.[40] Nivelle played the British card in defending his scheme. He noted that cancelling his offensive would dismantle all the completed arrangements for British cooperation and ruin the prospect of unity of command. Although the French government caved in when Nivelle threatened to resign, it is a safe bet that without the support of Britain, no longer a junior partner, Nivelle's offensive would not have taken place.

With the British beginning a diversionary attack on 9 April 1917 to draw off German reserves, Nivelle's main blow was delivered a week later against a prominent ridge, the Chemin des Dames. Security had been compromised by Nivelle's indiscretion and by the enemy's capture of his operational plans in a trench raid. Consequently the Germans, with knowledge of the forthcoming attack, had strengthened and deepened their defences in the key sector to absorb the initial shock. After initial gains, Nivelle's attack stalled and by the time it ended on 24 April French casualty figures were estimated to have reached 134,000.[41] For the French soldiers whose hopes were raised by Nivelle's wild promises of a breakthrough and victory, the bloody repulse was the last straw, triggering mutinies which affected nearly half the divisions in the French army. The mutinous soldiers were patriotic enough to agree to defend their trenches but refused to participate in any more futile attacks, leaving the BEF to carry the bulk of the burden on the Western Front for the remainder of the year.

Perhaps the most damning indictment of Lloyd George was his failure to take seriously British intelligence reports that the Germans were planning to strike in force in the spring of 1918 before the Americans concentrated in great numbers in France.[42] He maintained that the Western Front was 'overinsured', and that Haig would have no difficulty in holding the line against an enemy assault. On the other hand, he reasoned that troops piled in France would only encourage Haig to fritter them away in senseless frontal attacks. It is true that the manpower pool in Britain was shrinking rapidly and that the needs of war production required to be taken into consideration but, given that the fate of the war was possibly at stake, it would have behoved him to err on the side of caution. He could have directed Haig to remain on the defensive and supplemented home drafts with troops brought back from overseas. Haig's reinforced army would have offered more resistance and might have mitigated, if not prevented, the damage done by the German breakthrough. At least partly because Lloyd George did not react to the exigencies of war with a sense of urgency, the BEF came perilously close to defeat.

The Prime Minister's running battle with Haig had drawn criticism from some publications in the latter part of 1917, and the *Spectator* in particular went so far as to suggest that he had outlived his usefulness and cited several politicians who, it claimed, could do a better job of leading the nation.[43] The faultfinding continued and widened, at times with virulence, in the aftermath of the severe battering received by the BEF during the first German spring offensive in March 1918. The Press came down hard on Lloyd George, accusing him of endangering the security of the Western Front by diverting badly needed reinforcements overseas. The *Globe*, among the most strident in berating Lloyd George, claimed that the hundreds of thousands of troops squandered in eccentric operations of little strategic value should have been concentrated on the Western Front where they might have made a difference in producing a victory. It attributed the present military predicament to the national folly of 'allowing the war to be managed by men who know nothing of war'.[44] If there were to have been a viable candidate in waiting at the time, it is doubtful whether Lloyd George could have survived in office until the end of the war. However, Germany's capitulation came with surprising suddenness in the autumn of 1918 and all the Prime Minister's mistakes and underhanded deviousness were forgotten. He was hailed 'as the man who won the war', not least by himself. It was an absurd claim and overlooked the fact that the war was not won by Britain alone but by a coalitions of powers, in addition to other factors that weighed more heavily than Lloyd George's leadership: the naval blockade of the Central Powers; Kitchener's foresight and response to the war; American help; and Haig who learned from his defeats and produced a series of brilliant victories in 1918.

An inexplicable feature has been the myth of Lloyd George's supposedly decisive role in winning the war and it survives to this day. It was aided in large measure by Lloyd George himself. In retirement, he wrote his *War Memoirs* in which he represented himself as calm and calculating, as the only person who invariably discerned, with unerring judgment, the correct thing to do. Memoirs are of course self-serving but what was unusual was that they were accepted almost as gospel by the academic community and solidified his reputation as a brilliant politician and strategist. For example, the late A.J.P. Taylor considered Lloyd George a greater war leader than Churchill, an opinion that John Grigg would not have disputed.[45]

Academics are overwhelmingly liberal or well left of centre and one has to wonder whether they were swayed by their devotion to the political tradition with which the Welshman was identified. In short, did their admiration for Lloyd George's contribution in setting up the foundations of welfare state in Britain colour their assessment of his management of the war? Whatever their reasons, their elevation of Lloyd George almost to the status of cult figure is not warranted. His record between 1916 and 1918 was mixed. On the home front his performance on the whole was good but there were others in his Cabinet such as Milner who could, in all likelihood, have obtained similar results. He also made important contributions to the war effort but on the most important issue of strategy, he was undeniably a failure. It can be argued that in evaluating his entire body of work during the war he did more good than harm, but the margin is far too narrow for the veneration he is customarily accorded.

By contrast, Kitchener's control of the war effort during the last four months of 1914 was crucial to winning the war against Germany. I have been researching and writing about various aspects of the Great War for nearly half a century and know of no other figure in that conflict who even approaches, let alone eclipses or equals, Kitchener's impressive record of accomplishments. In my book *Kitchener's War: British Strategy from 1914 to 1916* (2004) I asserted that while 'it would be a fallacy to point to any single person as having won the war, it can be fairly claimed that Kitchener did more than any other individual to bring about the defeat of Germany.' I went further and concluded by saying: 'One thing is indisputable. Without Kitchener, the Entente would have lost the war.' Several reviewers, kind enough to judge the book favourably, hinted that in this instance I had perhaps overreached myself. To those scholars and others who may feel the same way, I can only point to the facts which firmly support my position. I do so in the form of a series of questions. Who took steps to make long-range preparations for a war which he alone maintained would last at least three years? Who induced the British Cabinet to abandon its short-sighted policy? Could the Entente have emerged triumphant without Britain's full participation? Who created the New Armies in the midst of a great war and whose reputation was mainly responsible for pulling in an unprecedented flood of recruits during the first eighteen months of the war? Could anyone else have accomplished this feat? Could the Entente have won the war without the New Armies? And finally who alone could have overruled Sir John French's decision to leave the battle-line during the retreat, and by his courageous action averted a disaster? I rest my case.

Notes

1. John Gooch, *The Plans of War: The General Staff and British Military Strategy, c. 1900-1916* (London: Routledge and Kegan Paul, 1974), p. 299.
2. John Grigg, *From Peace to War, 1912-1916* (London: Methuen, 1985), p. 157.
3. William J. Philpott, *Anglo-French Relations and Strategy on the Western Front, 1914-1918* (New York: St. Martin's Press, 1996), p. 52.
4. Jeremy Paxman, *Empire: What Ruling the World Did to the British* (London: Viking, 2011), *passim*; and *Great Britain's Great War* (London: Viking, 2013), pp. 173–9.
5. Michael and Eleanor Brock (eds), *H. H. Asquith: Letters to Venetia Stanley* (Oxford: Oxford University Press, 1882), p. 157.
6. George H. Cassar, *Kitchener: Architect of Victory* (London: Kimber, 1977), pp. 177–80.
7. David French, *British Strategy and War Aims 1914-1916* (London: Allen and Unwin, 1986), pp. xii–xiii, 20–1.
8. Churchill before the Dardanelles Commission. Cited in Martin Gilbert, *Winston S. Churchill, The Challenge of War 1914-1916*, Vol. 3 (Boston: Houghton Mifflin, 1971), p. 313.
9. George H. Cassar, *Kitchener's War: British Strategy from 1914 to 1916* (Washington, DC: Potomac, 2004), pp. 22, 32.
10. Viscount Grey of Fallodon, *Twenty-Five Years*, Vol. 2 (New York: Frederick Stokes, 1925), p. 71.
11. Asquith did not even mention the adoption of this critical measure in his summary of the day's Cabinet proceedings which was sent to the King.
12. Lord Beaverbrook, *Politicians and the War 1914-1916* (London: Oldbourne, 1960), p. 171.
13. On the subject of the New Armies the most recent works are Peter Simkins, *Kitchener's Army* (Manchester: Manchester University Press, 1988); Ray Westlake, *Kitchener's Army* (Tunbridge Wells: Nutshell Publishing Co., 1989); and A.J. Smithers, *The Fighting Nation* (London: Leo Cooper, 1994).
14. W.S. Churchill, *The World Crisis* (New York: Charles Scribner's Sons, repr, 1951), Vol. 1, p. 254.
15. Philip Magnus, *Kitchener: Portrait of an Imperialist* (New York: Dutton, 1959), pp. 280–1: C. Brad Faught, *Kitchener: Hero and Anti-Hero* (London: Tauris, 2016), pp. 193–4.
16. Cited in Archie Hunter, *Kitchener's Sword-Arm: The Life and Campaigns of General Archibald Hunter* (Staplehurst: Spellmount, 1996), p. 220. See also a note by General Archibald Murray (Sir John French's Chief of Staff), 14 August, 1914, Murray papers, WO 79/62.
17. Cassar, *Kitchener's War*, p. 89.
18. George H. Cassar, *The Tragedy of Sir John French* (Newark, DE: University of Delaware Press, 1985), pp. 134–7.
19. Cassar, *Kitchener's War*, pp. 163–4.

20. In November 1914 the Prime Minister set up a special Cabinet committee charged with the central direction of the war. All decisions taken by that body had to be ratified by the Cabinet as a whole.

21. Cassar, *Kitchener's War*, p. 120.

22. Minutes of the War Council, 8 January 1915, CAB 42/1/12.

23. Cassar, *Kitchener's War*, pp. 123–7.

24. As consul-general in Egypt from 1911 to 1914, Kitchener, unlike his predecessor, had been able to keep the nationalists in check, a task made easier because he was revered by the masses. But he was no longer in Egypt and his temporary replacement (Sir Henry McMahon) was a professional bureaucrat and practically unknown to the general population, not to mention that he did not speak Arabic, was indecisive and unfamiliar with the country's politics. Conditions in India were more uncertain. Prior to the war the nationalist movement, aided by the Germans who fanned anti-British feeling, was gaining in strength and some of its supporters had engaged in violence, acts of terrorism and even tried to assassinate the Viceroy, Sir Charles Hardinge. See my most recent work, *Kitchener as Proconsul of Egypt, 1911-1914* (London: Palgrave Macmillan, 2016), pp. 117, 134–8.

25. See for example the article in *The Times*, 22 February 1915.

26. A.J.P. Taylor (ed.), *Lloyd George: A Diary by Frances Stevenson* (New York: Harper and Row, 1971), p. 50.

27. Minutes of the War Council, 24 February 1915, CAB 42/1/42.

28. The number of books on the Dardanelles operation are enough to fill a bookcase. Patrick Gariepy, *Gardens of Hell: Battles of the Gallipoli Campaign* (Potomac Books: University of Nebraska Press, 2014); and Robin Prior, *Gallipoli: The End of the Myth* (New Haven: Yale University Press, 2009) are two recent readable books.

29. Cassar, *Kitchener*, pp. 398–9. Kitchener estimated that even if Greece decided to enter into the fray, in addition to its 180.000-man army the Allies would require to place no fewer than 300,000 men in the field. The British and French governments, however, committed only 150,000 to the operation.

30. Roy A. Prete, 'Imbroglio par excellence: Mounting the Salonika Campaign, September-October 1915', *War and Society*, 19 (2001), pp. 47–70.

31. A.J. Barker, *The Bastard War: The Mesopotamian Campaign of 1914-1918* (New York: Dial Press, 1967), Chapters 3–4. The debate over whether or not to advance to Baghdad can be followed in *Report of the Mesopotamian Commission*(London: HMSO, 1917), pp. 20–8, Paul K. Davis, *Ends and Means: The British Mesopotamian Campaign and Commission* (Cranbury: Associated University Presses, 1994), Chapter 6, and Cassar, *Kitchener's War*, pp. 232–4.

32. Grey of Fallodon, Viscount, *Twenty-Five Years*, Vol. 2 (London: Hodder and Stoughton, 1925), pp. 74–5.

33. After early spring fighting in 1915, French assured Kitchener on 14 April and again on 2 May that he had enough ammunition on hand to participate in his next forward movement. But following the repulse of the British attack at Aubers Ridge on 9 May, he sought to pre-empt the possibility of being recalled by laying the blame on Kitchener. He gave an interview to *The Times* correspondent whose telegram to his newspaper was published in a leading article on 14 May, attributing the cause of the defeat to a shortage of high-explosive shells. The disclosures were disturbing enough but what made matters worse was that the Prime Minister, on the basis of information supplied by Kitchener, had categorically refuted widespread rumours in a speech at Newcastle on 20 April that military operations in France were being conducted with insufficient ammunition. Throughout the crisis, Kitchener behaved with dignity and restraint and made no effort to defend himself as he could easily have done by revealing French's statements on 14 April and 2 May. Cassar, *Sir John French*, pp. 239–40.

34. Besides Grigg's multi-volume work, Travis L. Crosby, *The Unknown Prime Minister* (London: Tauris, 2014) and Roy Hattersley, *David Lloyd George* (London: Little, Brown, 2010) are two recent books on the Welshman.

35. George H. Cassar, *Lloyd George at War 1916-1918* (London: Anthem Press, 2009), Chapter 3.

36. Ibid. For the entire story see Chapter 6.

37. John Ehrman, 'Lloyd George and Churchill as War Leaders', in *Transactions of the Royal Historical Society*, ser. 5, Vol. 11 (London: Royal Historical Society, 1961), pp. 101–2.

38. Cassar, *Lloyd George*, pp. 88–95.

39. For the details see Robert A. Doughty, *Pyrrhic Victory* (Cambridge: Cambridge University Press, 2005), pp. 338–44.

40. André Maurois, *Lyautey* (New York: Appleton, 1931), trans. by Hamish Miles, pp. 303–4.

41. Doughty, *Pyrrhic Victory*, p. 354

42. Cassar, *Lloyd George*, p. 247.

43. *The Spectator*, 17 November 1917.

44. Cited in David Woodward, *Lloyd George and the Generals* (Newark, DE: University of Delaware Press, 1983), p. 292.

45. In a lecture on the rise and fall of Lloyd George delivered on the campus of the University of New Brunswick in 1961, A.J.P. Taylor maintained that the Welshman was a greater war leader than Winston Churchill. Taylor expressed similar opinions in his writings. See for example *English History, 1914-1945* (Oxford: Oxford University Press, 1965), pp. 87, 192; and his introduction to Kenneth O. Morgan's biography of his hero, *Lloyd George* (London: Weidenfeld and Nicolson, 1974). I know from my personal contact with John Grigg as well as his inferences in his last volume on Lloyd George, which he had nearly completed at the time of his death, that he considered him no less the equal of Churchill.

Suggested Further Reading

Barnett, Margaret, *British Food Policy During the First World War* (London: Allen and Unwin, 1985)

Bourne, John M., *Britain and the Great War, 1914-1918* (London: Edward Arnold, 1989)

Cassar, George H., *Kitchener's War: British Strategy from 1914 to 1918* (Washington, DC: Potomac Books, 2004)

Cassar, George H., *Lloyd George at War, 1916-1918* (London: Anthem Press, 2009)

Dewey, P.E., *British Agriculture in the First World War* (London: Routledge, 1989)

French, David, *The Strategy of the Lloyd George Coalition, 1916-1918* (Oxford: Oxford University Press, 1995)

Gilbert, Martin, *Winston S. Churchill: The Challenge of War 1914-1916* Vol. 3 (Boston: Houghton Mifflin, 1971)

Graves, Keith, *The Politics of Manpower, 1914-1918* (Manchester: Manchester University Press, 1988)

Grigg, John, *Lloyd George: War Leader, 1916-1918* (London: Allen Lane, 2002)

Wilson, Trevor, *The Myriad Faces of War* (Cambridge: Polity Press, 1988)

Woodward, David R., *Lloyd George and the Generals* (Newark, DE: University of Delaware Press, 1983)

Chapter 5

British Industry and the First World War

By Matthew Richardson

As in so many other areas of British life, the First World War was a watershed moment in the industrial landscape of the United Kingdom. Old certainties, assumptions and working practices were changed irrevocably by the impact of a total war. It was a war for national survival, and of such unprecedented scale that it demanded that every sinew, every fibre of the national being should be bent in the effort towards victory. Although the British experience on the battlefields is increasingly understood by both historians and the general public alike, that on the home front is still obscure to many. Victory in this theatre rested upon two great pillars, industry and agriculture. Only the former is the subject of this chapter, but both witnessed government intervention and control on a scale which could never have been imagined by the liberal-minded free-market politicians of the Victorian age. Engineering, railways, shipbuilding and coal mining all came under varying degrees of state control. At the same time, industry was unionised in a way which had not been seen before, and women entered the workplace in numbers in which they had never done previously. The short and longer-term effects of the Great War on the British industrial workplace are to be examined in this chapter, as well as the experience of waging war on the industrial front at a personal level.

Upon the outbreak of war in 1914, Great Britain was governed by a Liberal Party which was strongly wedded to ideas forged throughout the previous century of individual personal freedom and above all of economic liberty. Freedom of trade and freedom of the capitalist system to make profits unfettered by government interference were central tenets of their creed; this freedom had been intruded upon only marginally by the Victorian Factory Acts. In 1914, across great swathes of industrial Britain, iron masters, mill owners and coal magnates were the supreme overlords of what they surveyed, able to hire and dismiss at will, set wages and, if they so chose, to be largely indifferent also to the welfare of their workers. Again, this freedom had scarcely begun to be curtailed by the challenge of Britain's embryonic trade unions which in the Victorian era had mainly taken the form of trade societies anxious to protect skilled occupations from intrusion by unskilled labour rather than to confront the excesses of capitalism.

At first, those in power in Britain saw the war as providing little justification to abandon their long-cherished tenets. Just as participation on the battlefield was to be a matter of personal choice with armies raised by voluntary enlistment rather than conscription, so it was with industry. Prime Minister Herbert Asquith's Liberal administration felt it had no mandate to direct or control Britain's means of production. Only in the areas of shipbuilding and railways was there any immediate intervention. On Clydeside, three shipyards, Beardmores at Dalmuir, Browns of Clydebank and Fairfields at Govan, were placed under Admiralty control – others would follow in due course. Most of Britain's railways, however, came under immediate government control. In 1871, following the Franco-Prussian War, the British Government had taken by Act of Parliament the power to acquire by Royal Proclamation any or all of the railways of the United Kingdom in time of war. A committee of railway managers was already in existence to deal with such a situation. This body, known first as the War Railway Council and afterwards as the Railway Executive Committee, was to act as a central organisation, to give instructions, and to co-ordinate the activities of the different railways in wartime. Working in co-operation with it was the Engineer and Railway Staff Corps – a volunteer organisation of railway workers whose purpose was to develop schemes, methods, and personnel for the War Railway Service. It was composed of general managers of the leading railways, leading contractors, engineers, and other railway men.

Thus it was then that on the same day that war was declared, 4 August 1914, the railways of England, Wales and Scotland, but not Ireland, were taken over by the Government. The managers opened their sealed instructions and proceeded to carry them out. It had been provided in the Act of 1871 that full compensation should be paid to the owners for any loss incurred. The Government, however, did not at the beginning announce any terms with the companies. This was left for a later date. Government control, it is important to note, did not mean Government ownership. The lines remained the property of the companies. They retained the management of their own concerns, subject to the instructions of the Executive Committee, and the whole machinery of administration went on as before. At the beginning of the war, the sole purpose of government control was to facilitate the movements of troops. However, as the war developed, and as the national economy became more and more essential to the war effort, the scope of the Railway Executive Committee became greatly extended.

In other fields, the approach of the Government hindered industrial output by encouraging factory workers and miners to join the army in large numbers. However, in the textile trades, quite often the opposite situation pertained, at least initially. Thousands of pounds worth of contracts were quickly written for supply of army boots, uniforms and similar items, and in places such as Leicester with strong footwear and hosiery industries, the overtime being paid by factories struggling to keep up with government orders actually worked against recruiting. In the town's knitwear industry it was very much business as usual, one company historian writing:

> By 1913 black cardigans, pullovers and children's jerseys had built for J. Pick and sons a fine new factory at the corner of Dover and Wellington Streets . . . The Great War swept over it, transforming the business without seriously affecting the volume of trade. From black to khaki cardigans was not a difficult switch, and of necessity quality improved. Production was steady, contracts assured.[1]

In fact, urgent pleas were made by the great and the good of Leicester to try to shore up the town's reputation in the light of what was seen as a poor response to recruiting appeals. The same was reported of Leeds and Halifax. Recruiting rallies were held in theatres and other venues, patriotic speeches were made and martial music was played. Newspapers carried advertisements and appeals for recruits for various branches of the armed forces. Whilst joining in with these appeals, Leicester's Mayor, Jonathan North, and nine other members of the borough council, acknowledged in an open letter to the *Leicester Mail*:

> We are well aware that many men in Leicester are working on Government contracts, and that they are doing their duty by remaining at their work of making boots, hosiery etc which are necessary for our forces.[2]

Likewise a Leicester clergyman, Reverend J.T. Coward, told his congregation that:

> All young and eligible men ought not to be termed cowards for not forthwith joining the forces, seeing that the excessive stress of local employment called for prompt and strenuous aid to help in adequately equipping both Navy and Army, and that was especially so in this district, hence their labours were essentially serviceable to those engaged in fighting our country's battles abroad.[3]

It was a similar situation in the Colne Valley woollen industry in West Yorkshire, though here the work involved much more female labour. In the early months of the war, textile production increased against previous levels, and thus much overtime was necessary to meet the growing demand for cloth, much of which was for military uniforms, particularly khaki serge. Wartime production levels relied heavily on overtime and as with pre-war practice, weavers, and many other textile operatives, were not paid overtime rates. Workers made representations to officials of the General Union of Textile Workers (GUTW) about low rates of pay and the strain brought about by this overtime. At a meeting of the Heavy Woollen District Trades Council, Ben Turner, a representative of the GUTW, raised the issue of females working overtime in the mills. He stated that women textile operatives had to:

> . . . stand all day from 5.30 in the morning until 8.30 at night. In the interests of womanhood and motherhood . . . they should, during the crisis have at least two nights a week, as well as Saturday afternoons free from overtime.[4]

There was to be much unrest in the West Riding textile trade due to this practice of employers not paying overtime rates. In December 1914, male and female weavers at three Marsden mills met and agreed that they would stop working unpaid overtime after Christmas, if their employers were to refuse to pay enhanced rates; they were fully supported in this by the union. The weavers were to finish work at 5.30 pm rather than continuing to work overtime until 7.30 pm. Throughout the Colne Valley, members of the union held meetings and urged trade union officials to negotiate with employers. The weavers were demanding a limit on overtime of two hours a night with no work on Saturdays. Weavers in other Colne Valley mills also followed the example of the Marsden weavers, in refusing to work overtime. However, trade declined in January 1915, and this had the effect of preventing the unrest spreading further.

Interestingly, the Dundee jute industry, which had been in decline prior to the First World War due to competition from the establishment of a rival industry in Bengal, saw demand rocket as Government contracts for sandbags filled order books. During 1915, in a period of just two weeks, some 150 million sandbags were sent to the different theatres of war. At the same time the Dundee factories were protected by a temporary government ban on the import of Indian jute. With a shortage of labour caused by the war, a series of strikes succeeded in wringing concessions on wages from employers who, with full order books, had little choice but to concede. Wages rose by an average of 20 per cent in 1915, but it is estimated that the cost of food and fuel rose by 42 per cent during the same period. Dundee was one of the poorest places in Britain; whilst child mortality rates in England had fallen prior to the First World War, those in Scotland had increased, and in Dundee they were the worst. This was directly connected to the fact that the industry overwhelmingly employed women, who both worked and lived in appalling conditions. Malnutrition and rickets were commonplace. It was also standard practice for children to be employed in this industry, so exposure to the harmful fibres produced by jute spinning began at an early age. Lizzie Duncan must have been typical of many. She remembered starting work during the war:

> . . . my mother had six at home . . . I got my exemption from full time education and started work as a shifter, and had to go to the night school until I was fourteen, three nights a week.[5]

By contrast, in Lancashire, the cotton industry was hit hard by the war. Alice Foley grew up in Bolton and her early years were spent as a weaver before she became a trade union official. At that time, much of the output of the mills in her locality produced fine goods for export, particularly to India. Unlike the woollen trade, the raw material for which was home produced, the Lancashire mills relied upon a raw material – cotton – which had to be imported. These mills would naturally be hard hit by the disruption of supply caused by the war. Alice remembered later:

> As hostilities dragged on, more and more looms were commandeered for war purposes; khaki suitings, air-plane cloths and hospital denims replaced the sari trade. Later the toll of sinking cargoes on the high seas alarmingly reduced the supplies of raw cotton and textile exports dwindled almost to zero. Those workers drawn into munitions and the engineering industry escaped much of the paralysis and ruthlessness that overtook Lancashire. Unemployment, under-employment and short-time working grew apace; looms and spindles stood idle and there was no State aid or wage guarantees to cushion operatives against the worst effects of a disastrous depression.
>
> It is to the credit of the industry that, at rock bottom, a Cotton Board was established and a scheme of out-of-work-donation created by the imposition of a levy on all running machinery. This Fund was jointly administered by [the] Employer's Association and Trade Unions and I vividly recall those weekly visits to factories distributing money payments to workless operatives. Almost two million pounds was disbursed in this way; in a period of total war the scheme, never to be repeated, could be criticised as unsound economic policy, but in essence it was a humanitarian

effort to meet a crying need of a hard-hit community. It helped to keep in being a drastically reduced cotton industry.[6]

As early as March 1915, it had become abundantly clear that the Government's laissez-faire approach in many areas of industry was failing disastrously. The munitions crisis of that month, when it emerged that a major offensive on the battlefield had failed due to a lack of artillery ammunition, demonstrated clearly that the existing methods of procurement were totally inadequate. A more robust approach towards mobilising industry for the war effort was obviously needed. The result was the creation of the Ministry of Munitions, in May 1915, under the energetic David Lloyd George. This gave the Government control of supply, procurement and prices. Another milestone in government control would come almost exactly a year later, with the introduction of the Military Service Act, which allowed the state to decide who would serve in the army, and whose skills meant that they were better placed to help the war effort in a factory. Through its 'star' system the Government also differentiated between different trades and occupations, rating some as more essential than others.

The contribution of Leicester in particular to the mobilisation of industry towards the war effort – which was one of the key factors in Britain's victory in the conflict – was an interesting one. In early 1915, when the shortage of artillery ammunition for the army became a political scandal, it emerged that the government before the war had obtained its shells mainly from Woolwich Arsenal and a few private contractors, which were now unable to cope with the demand. In response, the Government now indicated that it was prepared compulsorily to remove trained engineers from private firms and install them in newly-built munitions factories. However, a group of Leicester engineering firms came together and insisted that there was a better way. The removal of their workers and the disruption that this would cause, they argued, would be counter-productive. Instead they offered to turn their own factories and employees over to munitions, working together to overcome any shortcomings which they might individually have had in terms of machinery. This co-operative arrangement was so successful that it set a pattern which was emulated in other parts of Britain. In the official account of Leicester's munitions work, under the heading *An Experiment in Engineering Co-Operation*, is recorded:

When the history of Leicester and District Engineering Trade is written, no brighter chapter will be found than the one dealing with the part Employers and Employees played in the Great War. Without experience, and without time in which to gain experience, they were called upon at a moment of crisis to help in the supply of ammunition to the Allied Forces. Indeed, they were pioneers in the great movement for the manufacture of High Explosive Shells, which spread throughout the country early in 1915 ... Major General Mahon, who represented the War Office, had grave doubts as to their ability to do the work. In his opinion, shells could only be made properly after many years' experience . . . but the Employers stood firm. [They] saw no difficulty in the way of local manufacture, provided the different firms were willing to pool their resources. By division of work into processes, the manufacture of shells might be carried out by the firms in the district.[7]

The expansion of the engineering industry to cope with soaring demand for munitions was not limited to existing factories. New, government-owned facilities were established from scratch, such as the enormous Chilwell works near Nottingham – officially National Filling Factory Number 6 – or the UK's largest munitions plant, HM Factory Gretna. Both facilities employed a high proportion of women workers. As the war progressed, the requirements of the ever-demanding conflict on the Western Front, together with the increasing need for workers on the Home Front, threatened a manpower crisis in Great Britain. How could she sustain a mass army on the battlefield and keep it adequately supplied with reinforcements, if she were not at the same time to denude her factories of the men needed to operate them? This particular circle was squared by the mass mobilisation of women. Women entered British factories in a way which had never been seen before. It is true that female labour had been predominant in some industries such as textiles in the north of England, and herring production in Scotland prior to the war, but what was different now was the types of industries which were seeing women enter for the first time, such as engineering and railways, and also the sheer number of females who were working.

While this could be an exciting challenge, some women found it hard. May Brew, aged just 17, left home to work at Coventry Ordinance Works, many miles away. She recalled:

Three sisters and myself left Douglas during the first months of the Great War, our destination being Coventry to work on munitions. There was no work of that kind being done in Douglas. We soon found out there was really a war on. We started work at 6am and continued to 6pm, worked one week night shifts and one week day shifts with 1½ hours off per shift for meals. The wages were 2½d per hour (weekly wage 13s 1d days, 16s 9d nights) Sundays included. The Coventry Ordnance Works were under Government control, and the girls had to keep their jobs or otherwise be out of work for six weeks. The control was taken off in 1916, and wages went up to £1 4s and £1 10s. The Zeppelins always paid their terrifying visits while we were on night shift. Lights would go out, and girls would faint by the dozen. The persons to be pitied on those occasions were the nurses, who were always in attendance. It was a nightmare those four years of war . . .[8]

For many, however, it was a liberating experience. For the first time they were able to escape from male domination, living away from their fathers or older siblings and enjoying a new freedom. Others left the drudgery and low wages of domestic service and entered an occupation which was both adequately paid and which carried the respect and admiration of the nation. The highly-regarded novelist Hall Caine wrote a glowing tribute to the so-called 'munitionettes' in his book *Our Girls*, published in 1916. It is also true to say that middle-class women – who had traditionally stayed at home to manage the house and servants – entered the workplace in significant numbers for the first time during the war. A typical example was that of Alice Gibb, of Ramsey, on the Isle of Man. A member of a wealthy ship-owning family,

Alice became a supervisor at Chilwell. She had been educated at home by a governess, and had never worked before in her life. She also never worked again afterwards. It is significant that a contributory reason for Germany's defeat was that, as a country, she never succeeded in mobilising her female population to anything like the same degree as Britain did.

Another consequence of the growth in the industrial workforce was increased union membership. In Leicester, as across much of Britain, a new trade union was gathering strength. Previously in the town, only craftsmen, and the boot and shoe and hosiery workers, were unionised. In the engineering trade, only the very skilled were organised; the semi-skilled and labourers had no voice at all. However, unlike most other unions, which were narrowly based upon a trade or craft, the Workers' Union, later to become the Transport and General Workers' Union, appealed to the mass of unskilled or semi-skilled workers, many of them women who had previously been unrepresented by the existing unions and who were now flooding into industry. Prominent in this organisation was Sydney Taylor. Taylor had previous experience in the Amalgamated Society of Carpenters and Joiners, and as an enthusiastic trade unionist and a socialist he began to try to organise a Leicester branch of the Workers' Union. Initially he had just thirteen members, but the conditions produced by the war encouraged rapid expansion. Taylor recalled later:

In April 1915 I was invited by Mr J. Beard the National President of the Workers' Union to take on a job as District Organiser at the large wage of 35/- per week. After giving it thought with my wife I accepted and in 6 months I got 1000 new members and a 5/- per week rise.[9]

Much of Taylor's work focused upon the engineering industry, and his first real fight was with the engineering employers. Eventually a 23/- minimum wage for unskilled labourers was agreed, with an additional 4/- for some semi-skilled men in engineering works and foundries. He also fought for and won overtime pay for foundry labourers. In the early part of the war there was a great deal of dilution in engineering, as fit men joined the army and semi-skilled men or women were put onto machines in their place. Taylor insisted on the dilutees receiving the full rate for the work that they were doing. This brought him into conflict with established engineering unions which also complained that the contributions required by the Workers' Union were lower than their own, and who insisted the newcomers should have joined them. Ironically, in these early days the majority of members joined the Workers' Union precisely because no other union was interested in them. On the whole, these men and women were not concerned with political struggles; their main objective was improving their wages. A good example of this is given by Tom Barclay, who was a labourer in a dye works in 1915:

At the aforesaid Works I was but a casual hand, a dyer's labourer, an old man. Well the dyers who were Trade Unionists, obtained an advance in wages, and that made some of the rest of us discontented. We began to agitate, and the heads of the firm came to hear of it and summoned one of the ring-leaders.

"You've been trying to get the men to join the Union' said a 'head.'

'Yes,' said the ring-leader, 'I believe in a living wage, and we're not getting it."

"Do you know what we do with hands that agitate like that?"

'You can do what you like, Sir; if you sack me I can get another place, and my Trade Union'll defend me till I do.'[10]

In the event, the troublesome hand was not sacked, suggesting that either labour was in such short supply that the firm could not afford to lose the man, or that they feared the backlash from his union. Far from fighting the rise in trade unionism during the war, the British Government actively encouraged it, as having one or two major unions for each industry to which most workers belonged was seen as more efficient for the purposes of collective bargaining. Lloyd George met the leaders of most of the main unions at the Treasury in 1915, and was able to extract agreements from them that for the duration of the war they would act in the national interest. In turn promises were made by the Government in regard to wages in an effort to dampen the embers of potential industrial disputes. For example, on the railways an agreement was reached with the unions which in its final form meant that all employees of 18 years or upwards were given a bonus of 5s. per week, those of under 18, 2s. 6d. The understanding at the time was that this arrangement was finally to settle the wages question until the end of the war. A definite undertaking was given on that point by the mens' organisations, which ran as follows:

The National Union of Railwaymen and the Associated Society of Locomotive Engineers and Firemen undertake that during the pendency of this agreement they will not present to the railway companies any fresh demands for increased bonus or wages, or general alterations in conditions of service, and that they will not give countenance or support either to a demand on the part of any of their members to reopen the settlement now made or any strike that might be entered upon in furtherance of such demand.[11]

In the notoriously hierarchical world of the railways, these rapid rises in the wages paid to the men came in for much criticism. It was pointed out that the increase of 1916 was nearly equal to wiping out the dividends on the ordinary stock. The *Railway Magazine* declared:

Under no other system but State control would a war bonus be paid on an all-round basis alike to lads of eighteen years of age and the oldest employee, and single and married men placed on the same plane, no matter what may be their financial responsibilities or comparative wages.[12]

However, certain considerations have to be borne in mind here. Rising wages were not peculiar to the railways, but were a general phenomenon across industry, caused by the shortage of labour. Furthermore, under the war labour regulations, railwaymen could not leave their employment for other work. It was felt therefore that they could not reasonably be expected to continue under far lower wages than other men in allied industries in the same districts. Above all, there was the outstanding fact that the old scale of wages was inadequate given the rise in prices due to the war. The average cost of food of the kind mainly purchased by working men had doubled; clothing was much dearer; all the incidental expenses of living, except rent and rates, had gone up, and men could not maintain their families decently on the old wage scale. The idea of making the rise the same for all ranks was to benefit most those who needed it most – the lowest-paid men.

Up to the beginning of the war British railways had been very reluctant to employ female labour, even for office work. Booking clerks, head office staff, ticket collectors, attendants in dining-cars, were in nearly every case male. Nevertheless, the shortage of men, and the desire to release as many as possible for service with the Colours, caused the introduction of women workers early in 1915. The experiment was a great success. Women were then employed on an ever-growing scale, not only for purely clerical duties, but for manual work of many kinds. Soon everywhere in the industry there were women, working as engine or carriage cleaners, porters, ticket collectors, booking clerks, and many other occupations besides. The railway trade unions were uneasy about this, and pressed for a definite understanding about the wages the women were to receive. Furthermore, they asked for assurances that the employment of women in capacities in which they were not formerly employed was an emergency action, arising out of circumstances created by the war and would not, on the conclusion of the war, prejudice in any way the undertaking given by the railway companies as to the re-employment of men who had joined the Colours. The pay of women in grades in which they were not engaged in August 1914 was fixed, at the minimum pay of the grade. At first, women were not granted a war bonus, but in November 1916, it was arranged that women of 18 years of age and over should be given a bonus of 3s. a week and those under 18 years of age, 1s. 6d. This amount was later increased to 5s. 6d. a week for the seniors and 2s. 9d. for the juniors.

In July, August, and September 1918, the number of workers employed in munitions was probably the maximum for the whole period of the war. During the third quarter of 1918 it was estimated that the number of men and women working on munitions was, in round figures, about 2,871,000, with women accounting for 825,000 of this number. These figures are lower than some other totals which were quoted, but stand for munitions in a narrower sense than the one which was commonly used. They relate solely to the metal and chemical industries. Munitions in the broader sense embraced workers in the coal mines, as well as those employed in, for instance, the manufacture of boots, uniforms and bedding. Indirectly even those concerned in special tramway work on behalf of munition factories might be described as munition workers and also those concerned in building and repairing factories for the manufacture of munitions. If those indirect munition hands were added in, then the total above would of course be much higher. This total was put at 3,400,000, including both sexes.

These are astonishing figures, not least when set against a peacetime British population of around 46,000,000. This massive expansion of the engineering and steel production industries could only be achieved through 'dilution' – introducing unskilled labour, usually, but not always, female. It caused recurring problems through 1915 and 1916, and even later, though on paper it seemed to have been solved at quite an early stage. It was probably the most contentious and divisive issue affecting British industry during the war. Other labour questions became formidable at various times during the conflict; disputes over wages, hours, food, drink, discipline, and anti-war movements all reared their head but perhaps none of them was so difficult or so delicate to handle as dilution. Though he could not try to ride roughshod over trade union sensitivities without inviting disaster, Lloyd George, through the Munitions of War Act, showed his hand plainly as to the powers he meant to take over both sides in industry, employers and unions alike.

Among written trade union regulations which he intended to overcome, Lloyd George mentioned the provisions that one man must not attend to more than one machine, and that women must not take the place of male workers. The unwritten rules were still more restrictive, making it impossible, for instance, for a man to do more than a specified amount of work without bringing about the displeasure of his fellows. Lloyd George was forced to back down in some areas, notably that of the 'leaving certificate' which the Act introduced into war industry. It forbade employers to give work to a man who within the previous six weeks had been engaged elsewhere on munitions work, unless the applicant could show a certificate proving he had left that work with the employer's consent. Devised to prevent one acquisitive firm from drawing away workers from another, a common grievance at the time, it caught a good many innocent firms by surprise. Also it was galling to the workers; and, after being amended by a later Act, it had to be abandoned altogether. Yet Lloyd George succeeded in introducing lasting changes to British working practices which had existed for years. George Dewar, who inspected many British munitions factories during the course of the war, wrote:

> What a change was worked by dilution in a year or two! Customs, which it had taken the men decades to secure, were by 1918 dead letters. I recall a visit to Messrs. Hans Renold's chain-making works near Manchester in that year, and watching a whole roomful of women, each in some cases taking charge of two or three automatic or semi-automatic machines; and that experience was a familiar one all over the North and Midlands in the latter part of the war.[13]

Another of Britain's great industries was coal mining, and here was one of the few situations where women were seldom used to replace male labour. The consequences of the lack of labour in the industry were far reaching. By 1916, hundreds of thousands of men had left the mines for the Forces, at the same time as demand for coal for munitions was soaring. The result was that labour was scarce, and what there was, was used as far as possible upon immediately productive work. As a result, the 'roads' within the mines were to some considerable extent neglected, and the effect of this was to be felt for many years after the war. It should not be imagined that the coal owners were acting in any selfish manner in neglecting this form of development. The capital of a colliery is largely represented by its 'ungotten' mineral. It was therefore to the coal owner's interest to bite into this capital as little as possible during a period when profits were very strictly limited. The coal owners fully realised this, but there is no evidence to show that they acted in this narrow, unpatriotic way. On the contrary during the war period, while profits were limited by the operation of the Excess Profits Duty and the Coal Mines Excess Payment, they still diverted labour to win coal rather than do 'dead work' which would not be immediately productive, but which would place them in a position to earn high profits when, as all then believed would be the case, profits were no longer limited, that is after the war.

But not only was output adversely affected by the restriction of this particular form of development, it was equally affected by the absence of many other kinds of infrastructure work. The need for immediate production during the war tended to bring about the winning of the coal which was most easily reached. 'Dead work', such as driving long drifts through faults, which in normal times would be undertaken and which would eventually result in fresh coalfaces being opened up, was usually not attempted, and in fact could not even be undertaken without the sanction of the Coal Mines Department. As a result, in the 1920s there was considerably less coalface being worked upon than would otherwise have been the case.

For speedy clearance of hewn coal to be possible, it was necessary not only for the roads inside the mine to be in good condition, but also for the rails and rolling stock to be well maintained. This was not possible during the war years. Steel was in short supply, and other materials were hardly obtainable; metal and wood were required for purposes more immediately connected with the war. What would, in normal times, have become colliery rails became light rails for use behind the lines in France; the steel which in pre-war years would have gone to make colliery tubs was turned into shells. Precisely the same difficulty was experienced by the railways, with the result that they had greatly decreased in efficiency and speed by the war's end. However, in a colliery, lack of speed naturally meant reduced output, for all other things being equal, if the speed of the tubs on the roads were reduced, then fewer tubs reached the lifting cage in any given hour.

Although keeping the unions 'on-side' was an integral part of Lloyd George's policy, and days lost to strikes had indeed dropped in 1915, an astonishing 5,600 working days were lost in 1917, with a similar figure for 1918. Most of these were in mining, with shipbuilding a close second. From 1914 to 1918, trade union membership in the United Kingdom doubled, from a little over four million to a little over eight million, and work stoppages and strikes became more frequent in the second half of the war as the unions became increasingly aware of the strength of their position. Often it was those lower down in the union hierarchy who led these walkouts, resulting from grievances over rising food prices, liquor control, pay disputes, 'dilution', fatigue from overtime and from Sunday work, or inadequate housing. One of the most serious of these disputes was the May 1917 Engineers' Strike, which lasted three weeks. Also called the Shop Stewards' Strike, one of its chief causes was the flood of unskilled workers into the industry; however, there was also a strong political dimension to this strike. Many of the shop stewards were emboldened by events in Russia, where the February 1917 revolution had briefly promised a workers' democracy, and the strike was in many ways a protest against their own union leadership, which had disavowed it. Eventually the Government lost patience with the ringleaders and had them arraigned under the Defence of the Realm Act. One of them, Dave Ramsay, was a committed Bolshevik and was one of those who, with the Clyde Workers' Committee, was attempting to build a network of socialist 'workers' committees' across Britain.

Yet even in spite of the reputation of 'Red' Clydeside for strikes and anti-war agitation, Lloyd George had also succeeded in harnessing the industrial muscle of the

Glasgow shipyards. Indeed, Clydeside companies benefitted greatly from the wartime boom, with the three leading yards winning orders worth over £16 million. Between 1914 and 1918, 481 warships were built on the Clyde. Great pride was felt among the shipyard workers for their skills and abilities, and in 1918 John Brown's on Clydebank broke its own record by producing the destroyer HMS *Scotsman* in under six months from contract to delivery. It was believed that the pride the workforce felt in the vessel's name played a considerable part in this feat. Another story of massively significant industrial achievement is that of the north-east shipyards, on the Tyne for warships, and on the Wear producing merchant vessels in astonishing numbers to replace those being lost to U-boats. British shipbuilding had declined alarmingly during the first two years of the war, and before the war British shipyards had become dangerously reliant upon imported steel, especially that produced in Germany. However, British shipbuilding had other advantages, in that its two main manufacturing centres, western Scotland and north-east England, along with Barrow, Belfast and Birkenhead, had built up a skilled workforce of world renown, such as no other country, allied or enemy, possessed. Just before the war, historian Frederick Talbot commented that:

> The native workman in the German shipbuilding yard is the product of one generation; his colleague in the British yard is the product of centuries. In marine engineering hereditary qualifications go a very long way. Son has followed father in the yards of the Clyde and Tyne for so many generations that shipbuilding has developed almost into a sixth sense, and this is the sole reason why Germany cannot secure a footing as a builder of ships outside her own borders.[14]

There were sixteen working yards on the River Wear at Sunderland during the First World War and most of the 360 ships built on the river during that time were merchant ships. Initially output suffered as many skilled workers went to war, and in the early months of hostilities Sunderland was accused in *The Times* of shirking its responsibility to increase shipbuilding production by tolerating inflated rates of pay and irregular time-keeping and attendance. The men who were left often worked twelve-hour shifts, during which meal breaks of one hour were taken. This meant a 55-hour week, based on a five-day week without weekend work. After a while, 'standard' ships began to be built to make up for the U-boat losses. These ships were of a basic design which could be constantly reproduced, improving the rate of completion from laying-down the keel to launching. Each of the Wear yards could produce a 'B' style standard ship in a 39-week period which helps to account for the Wear's phenomenal wartime tonnage of ships launched, approximately 900,000 tons. Towards the end of the war, construction materials were in even shorter supply, and the industry was forced to look for alternatives to steel. The war had the effect of spurring on many technological developments which in peacetime might have happened either more slowly or perhaps not even at all, and in one example of wartime innovation, the Wear Concrete Building Company Ltd in Southwick was contracted to produce concrete-hulled tugs for the Admiralty.

An interesting parallel of this phenomenon can be found in the Sheffield steel industry. Prior to the war, although electric furnaces for smelting were known, they were not widely used, first because it was believed that the high cost of electricity made them uneconomical, and second because of the inertia of an industry wedded to the traditional Bessemer or crucible system. However, the demand produced by the war for large quantities of steel overcame these obstacles, and it was under these circumstances that a Sheffield metallurgist, Harry Etchells, came up with a new and refined electrical smelting process. Etchells wrote of it:

> It is well known that previous to the War there were huge accumulations of steel turnings, and especially alloy steel turnings, in various parts of the country. Although one or two enlightened open hearth steel metallurgists had found a way of dealing with these at that time, the majority had not, and it required the strenuous War conditions to force them into using a proportion of turnings instead of all pig iron and heavy scrap. Shell production increased the proportion of turnings more and more, and though thousands of tons went into the blast furnaces as well. It was evident that true economy and increased production would only be realised when these could be converted into finished steel. The electric furnace was, and still is, the only ready and flexible instrument for accomplishing this.[15]

During the war, Etchells and his business partner developed a half-ton electric furnace, a type which was subsequently installed in many Sheffield steel works. It was of simple construction, easy to operate, and the workers could quickly be trained how to use it. As an illustration of how rapidly this technology spread, one Sheffield works which had a single electric furnace in the early part of the war had nine in a row by the end of it. In 1919, there were around 1,000 electric furnaces worldwide, of which around seventy were in Sheffield. In the 1920s Echells had personal success in supplying the technology to the Ford Motor Company in Detroit, Peugeot Frères in France, and the Lancia company of Turin, among other companies too.

Overall, however, despite these individual technological advances, and leaving aside short-term gains resulting from wartime bonuses or government contracts, in the long term British industry was badly affected by the First World War. By 1919, though there were 31,000 more men employed in the coal industry than there were in 1914, the post-war miners were not, for various reasons over which they had no control, as efficient as were the men who were employed in 1914. To understand the reason for this lack of efficiency it is necessary to consider the method of promotion in the mines, whereby a 'boy', as they were called in the industry, after a certain length of time underground, became a collier. This pattern of promotion was disturbed by the war, for a large proportion of the younger men – the 'boys', who were actually 18, 19 and 20 years of age – joined the Army. They came in many cases off the 'roads', or from the 'stalls' (a working place) where they were acting as 'drawers', pushing tubs of coal. They left the collieries in large numbers in the early years of the war, for the majority of mineworkers joined up before the Conscription Acts were passed. They served on the battlefield for nearly four years and then they, or those of them who were left, returned. Nearly 100,000 would never return.

In some cases they returned to their old work, but in many other cases they returned to the work they would have had had they never left the pit. In other words, their service in the forces counted for promotion. In permitting or assisting in these arrangements, it must be realised that the miners' leaders and the coal owners acted with the best motives and in the earnest desire to see that the demobilised soldier did not suffer for having served his country, but it must also be understood that such an arrangement meant two things; first the replacement of the man who, before the soldier's return, was actually doing the work, and second the continuation of the work by a man who though he might have served his country bravely on the battlefield, was somewhat inexperienced as a miner. The result was a degree of ill-feeling among the displaced men, as well some loss of efficiency and as a consequence, there was a decline in output.

Britain's coal industry also suffered in the 1920s from the fact that many of the world's navies (Britain's included) and shipping lines were in the process of converting from coal power to fuel oil as a means of propulsion, thus greatly reducing the demand for solid fuel. At the same time, many overseas territories which had before the war been importers of British coal had, when the war interrupted supplies, found alternative sources or developed their own domestic coal industry to fill the void. Britain's weakness in the international coal market as a result of the First World War would ultimately lead to the 1926 General Strike, when coal owners whose profits were under pressure succeeded in forcing the workforce to accept reduced terms. Likewise, international sea trade slumped after the war, with a consequential effect on the the shipbuilding industry. Orders for new ships dried up and unemployment rose. High unemployment in the Scottish shipbuilding industry also led in the 1920s to unemployment in Scotland's iron and steel industries which largely relied on shipbuilding.

Britain's railways had performed remarkably during the war. There had been no previous major conflict in which the service of railways owned and managed by private companies had been directly pitted against the service of railways owned and managed by governments; the foremost representative of militarism, Germany, had proceeded on the assumption that, primarily for military reasons, railways ought to be in the hands of the state. Austria, the other great Central Power, had done likewise. The railways of Belgium were also government-owned, as were 60 per cent of those of Russia. On the other hand, in Britain at the outbreak of the war, all the railways were in private hands, while in France, five of the seven great companies, having over 80 per cent of the total mileage, also were under private management. It was the railways of these six countries which had to perform the great feats of military transportation in the early stages of the conflict. The war showed that railway transportation was not just significant to military operations but demonstrated that twentieth-century warfare could not be conducted without railways. One contemporary observer noted:

> . . . before the war began the manager of one of the large English systems predicted that the railways of his country would be able to bear any burden that the government might ever put upon them in connection with military operations; and after the war had been in progress some time, the chairman of one of the largest British systems made a public statement, which stands uncontradicted, that the railways were better prepared at the start to perform their part and did perform it better than any department of the government.[16]

Yet the British railway system also paid a heavy price for its success in the war. With chronic underinvestment, little maintenance and overuse during the conflict, by 1919 the rail network and its infrastructure were on their knees. In order to assist the industry to recover from the effects of the war, the coalition government passed the Railways

Act of 1921. Also known as the Grouping Act, it was intended to stem the losses being made by many of the country's 120 disparate railway companies, and to retain some of the benefits which the country had derived from a government-controlled railway during and after the war. Devised by Sir Eric Geddes, the railway man who had held sway over the system during the war, the Act was also designed to remove some of what he saw as damaging internal competition within the industry, though it stopped short of full nationalisation. The English and Scottish companies were thus organised into four groups, which became the 'Big Four' companies: London, Midland and Scottish (LMS), London and North-Eastern (LNER), Southern (SR) and Great Western (GWR).

Overall, the experience of harnessing and directing industry during the First World War, and the lessons learned from it, would directly influence Britain's approach to industry during the Second World War. Indeed it might be argued that the legacy of government control and direction of industry between 1914 and 1918 was actually much further-reaching, and that it influenced the policy of nationalisation which followed the election of the 1945 Labour government. Nationalised railways, steel, vehicle and coal production were to be a feature of the British industrial landscape until the 1980s. Other legacies of the industrial war between 1914 and 1918 were social. Union membership peaked in Great Britain in the 1970s and has been in decline ever since, but ideas of female equality, and of the place of the female being in the workplace as much as in the home, have had far greater longevity, indeed permanence. Even in matters as apparently trivial as women's fashions – such as short hair and wearing trousers – or of it becoming socially acceptable for women to smoke, the legacy of their work in the factories from which these things derive, is still discernible. It was largely this work which delivered the greatest legacy of all – the reward of female emancipation in 1918, albeit at the time only for women over 30.

Notes

1. J.B. Pick, *The Pick Knitwear Story 1856-1956* (Leicester, 1956), p. 20.
2. *Leicester Mail*, 27 November 1914.
3. *Leicester Mail*, 23 November 1914.
4. *The Worker*, 14 November 1914.
5. Anthony Cox, *Empire, Industry and Class* (Abingdon, 2013), p. 70.
6. Alice Foley, *A Bolton Childhood* (Manchester, 1973), p. 84.
7. Leicester and District Armaments Group, *An Experiment in Engineering Cooperation 1915-1918* (Leicester, 1919).
8. Matthew Richardson, *This Terrible Ordeal* (Douglas, 2013), p. 162.
9. Matthew Richardson, *Leicester in the Great War* (Barnsley, 2014), p. 50.
10. Tom Barclay, *Memoirs and Medleys* (Coalville, 1995), p. 59.
11. F. A. McKenzie, *British Railways and the War* (London, 1917), p. 15.
12. Ibid., p. 16.
13. George A.B. Dewar, *The Great Munition Feat 1914-1918* (London, 1921), p. 38.
14. F.A. Talbot, *Steamship Conquest of the World* (London, 1912), p. 335.
15. *Birmingham Metallurgical Society Journal*, Vol. VII, Part 3 (March 1919), p. 126.
16. Samuel O. Dunn, *The Railways in Peace and War* (Yale, 1918), p. 365.

Suggested Further Reading

Barclay, Tom, *Memoirs and Medleys – the autobiography of a Bottlewasher* (Coalville, 1995)
Cox, Anthony, *Empire, Industry and Class* (Abingdon, 2013)
Dewar, George A.B., *The Great Munition Feat 1914-1918* (London, 1921)
Dunn, Samuel O., *The Railways in Peace and War* (Yale, 1918)

Foley, Alice, *A Bolton Childhood* (Manchester, 1973)

Leicester and District Armaments Group, *An Experiment in Engineering Cooperation 1915-1918* (Leicester, 1919)

McKenzie, F.A., *British Railways and the War* (London, 1917)

Pick, J.B., *The Pick Knitwear Story 1856-1956* (Leicester, 1956)

Richardson, Matthew, *This Terrible Ordeal* (Douglas, 2013)

Richardson, Matthew, *Leicester in the Great War* (Barnsley, 2014)

Stone, Gilbert, *The British Coal Industry* (London, 1919)

Chapter 6

'Do Good by Stealth': British Propaganda and the First World War

By David Welch

The Great War holds an unique position as the milestone by which the heroism, brutality and futility of modern industrialised warfare has come to be measured. Having begun with the promise of individual honour and nationalistic glory, it ended after four bloody years of trench, air and naval warfare with huge question marks hanging over whether the sacrifices were to have been justified and worthwhile. As Philip Taylor has observed, it is often viewed in the victorious powers as an 'end of innocence' or a 'rite of passage' into the modern world.[1]

Once the war had begun, the belligerents rapidly began publishing accounts of how the war had been caused. They did so, as Hew Strachan has pointed out, because the issue of responsibility was the key element in the propaganda battle.[2] Propaganda dates back 2,400 years to Sun Tzu's *The Art of War*, but the First World War witnessed its first use by governments in an organised, quasi-scientific manner. Writing in 1919, General Eric Ludendorff praised British propaganda. In Ludendorff's famous phrase, the German home front had been hypnotized by the enemy propaganda 'as a rabbit is by a snake'.[3] In contrast, his views on German propaganda were scathing. Ludendorff was attempting to justify the failure of his final offensive in 1918 and the post-war *Dolchstoss* (stab-in-the-back) legend. Nevertheless, he was reflecting the widespread perception held by all the protagonists that British propaganda had been the most effective at home, in enemy countries and among neutral nations. Britain unquestionably emerged from the First World War with the reputation for having conducted propaganda on a wider and more successful scale than other belligerent. Why should this be? The explanation can largely be found in the diplomatic events leading to the outbreak of war in August 1914. The unique circumstances surrounding Britain's entry into the war shaped its response to and recognition of the importance of propaganda. Britain was the only major belligerent power in which there had been serious argument as to whether to enter the war at all and then with but a small professional army Britain was not in a military position to face an army on the German scale. With America remaining neutral, propaganda assumed an increasingly important position in securing military victory.

* * *

One of the most enduring images of the Great War remains the distinctive recruitment poster of Lord Kitchener's heavily moustachioed face and intimidating finger imploring the British population that 'Your Country Needs YOU'. Kitchener had been appointed Secretary of State for War on 5 August 1914 and was already a war hero with the public for his military exploits in the Sudan. The poster became a symbol of the national resolve and will to win. Kitchener's message and the manner in which it was disseminated also reflected the change in the nature of warfare and the recognition that 'Total War' would require the deployment of the twin weapons of propaganda and censorship to justify war aims and to impose rigid controls over public perceptions of the nature and course of the war. It was also the first war in which the mass media played a significant part in disseminating news about the war from the fighting front to the home front with the result that the gap between the soldier at the front and civilian at home was considerably narrowed.

Britain, as with all the belligerents, was compelled, therefore, to recognize that it had to justify the righteousness of its cause; in short that propaganda was an essential part of the war effort. By the end of the war, the evolution of Britain's propaganda apparatus provided the model for other states subsequently to follow. Tracing this development is particularly interesting because it was conducted by an evolving democratic system still coming to terms with the idea that the people, and not simply elites (mass opinion as opposed to elite opinion) now demanded a voice in the political process as a quid pro quo for their participation in the war effort. Out of these tensions, Britain evolved an extraordinary approach to the conduct of propaganda that would help secure ultimate victory but would leave also a bitter taste in the aftermath of the peace settlements. Given this extraordinary legacy it is surprising therefore to discover that Britain's first steps in setting up its propaganda machinery were tentative and uncertain. There is little evidence, for example, that there was any pre-war planning of how propaganda should be organised. In Germany, on the other hand, the entry of the civil government into the field of propaganda began under Bismarck's chancellorship with the establishment of the Press Office (*Presseamt*), an early example of an official bureau set up to monitor news coverage and release information favourable to the German government. Owing to extensive pre-war preparation, Germany, unlike Britain, was not caught by surprise at the outbreak of hostilities and responded with extraordinary vigour. Posters, pamphlets, leaflets and other forms of pro-German propaganda poured out from Berlin to Europe and the rest of the world – notably the United States of America. Sir Rennell Rodd, the British Ambassador in Rome, observed: 'German preparedness for the eventuality of war was revealed by the amount of literature with which the office and agencies in Italy were immediately inundated.'[4]

The initial antipathy of the Government to propaganda can be explained partly by the fact that Britain, as indeed all the belligerents, was working towards a short war and specifically by the different circumstances surrounding Britain's entry into the war. Thus at the outset of hostilities the mobilisation of opinion behind the war effort was left initially to the voluntary/private sector, with the activities of individuals and groups such as the 'Fight for Right Movement', the 'Atlantic Union' and the Anglican clerics for example, co-ordinated by the Central Committee for National Patriotic Organisations (CCNPO) under the chairmanship of Sir Henry Cust, one-time editor of the *Pall Mail Gazette*. Its Honorary President was the Prime Minister, Asquith, with

Lord Rosebery and A.J. Balfour as Vice-Presidents. Established in November 1914, its chief objectives were to keep British public opinion informed and fortified and then to lay before neutral countries a clear statement of the British case.[5] The Committee invited prominent establishment figures to lecture or write on the causes of the war and to justify Britain's position in the conflict. It published the so-called 'Oxford Pamphlets' – almost a hundred in number – including a publication from members of Oxford University's History faculty entitled 'Why We Are at War: Great Britain's Case'. The most obvious value of such organisations lay in their usefulness as distribution agencies thereby providing a cover for 'official' propaganda disseminated by the Government. Nevertheless, the CCNPO proved a constant irritant to official propaganda departments until July 1917 when it was eventually absorbed by the Government.[6]

However, the traumatic experience that Asquith and Grey had encountered within the Cabinet over whether Britain should enter the war convinced senior figures within the Government that propaganda was too important to be left to the private sector and groups such as the CCNPO. While the need for Britain to conduct official propaganda in foreign countries was recognised, there was no blueprint in place for the control and influence of foreign opinion. The Government's initial plans were therefore cautious and uncertain as it attempted to construct (or 'muddle through') the necessary organisational machinery. To achieve its objectives two organisations were set up. At the Foreign Office, a News Department had been established shortly after the outbreak of war to respond to the increased demand for news concerning the war from Allied and neutral correspondents in London. It was originally made directly responsible to the Foreign Secretary, Sir Edward Grey, but by the end of 1914 it had been placed under the general supervision of the Parliamentary Under-Secretary of State for Foreign Affairs, Frederick Acland. Although initially viewed with suspicion within the Foreign Office, once the preoccupation with secrecy and censorship had subsided (largely after it was conceded that the war would *not* be over by Christmas), the small group of permanent officials within the News Department improvised an autonomous approach which stressed 'information' and news rather than propaganda and 'views'. The News Department saw its role therefore as a supplier of official information on demand. Journalists, for their part, were expected to publish sensitive material with discretion, otherwise an important source of information would suddenly dry up. Eventually the News Department would serve as a general co-ordinating centre for other government departments which were taking an interest in propaganda, furnishing daily news telegrams together with instructions to diplomatic and consular missions abroad. A general policy was adopted from an early stage to avoid a sense of exhortation. Overseas representatives were encouraged instead to make use of the information for propagandist purposes in the foreign press and elsewhere as they thought appropriate according to local conditions. The more obvious forms of propaganda involving attacks upon the enemy and the British justification for war, continued to be left to unofficial patriotic organisations such as the CCNPO.

The second organisation to be established was the Neutral Press Committee (NPC), formed under the aegis of the Home Office on 11 September 1914 in connection with the Press Bureau, the Government's principal wartime censorship organisation.[7] The Committee was placed under the direction of G.H. Mair, the recently-retired assistant editor of the *Daily Chronicle*, one of the earliest examples of a newspaperman being recruited to serve in the official machinery of propaganda. Under Mair's leadership the NPC organised its work under four main areas: promoting the exchange of news services between British and foreign newspapers, the sale of British newspapers abroad, the dissemination of propaganda articles among friendly foreign newspapers and journals, and the transmission of news abroad by cables and wireless. In October 1915, Mair was able to extend his activities beyond neutral countries to encompass Allied countries as well.

Having set up the machinery to deal with foreign opinion, there was an even greater need to convince the British public, the Empire and neutrals, above all the United States, of the justice of the British case. The Cabinet was particularly alarmed at the virulence of the German propaganda campaign in the States and it became apparent that immediate countermeasures were urgently required. At the end of August 1914, Lloyd George, the Chancellor of the Exchequer, raised the issue of war propaganda and the need to set up an organisation for this purpose. Asquith reported to the King that, at the most recent meeting of the Cabinet, Lloyd George had urged the 'the importance of setting on foot an organisation to inform and influence public opinion and to confute German mis-statement and sophistries'.[8] As a result, Asquith invited Charles Masterman ('Mr Masterman was requested to take the matter in hand'), the Chancellor of the Duchy of Lancaster and the Chairman of the National Insurance Commission, to establish an organisation along the lines suggested by Lloyd George.[9]

The War Propaganda Bureau was based in a block of flats at Buckingham Gate known as Wellington House which had previously been the headquarters of the National Insurance Commission. Henceforth, it would invariably be referred to as Wellington House. The Bureau, which operated under the supervision of the Foreign Office, was Britain's principal propaganda department for the initial two and half years of the First World War. Its function was to make the British case in Allied and neutral nations. It was not however engaged in propaganda directed at the enemy or to the home front. Nor was it to be concerned with supplying news to the press, which remained the responsibility of the News Department of the Foreign Office.

Charles Frederick Masterman has been described as 'one of the inventors of twentieth century propaganda'.[10] He was arguably the most important government propagandist in Britain during the First World War – although Lords Beaverbook and Rothermere would later take much of the credit. Masterman had been a strong supporter of British intervention in August 1914 and his brief at the War Propaganda Bureau was to put Britain's case for entering the war and to justify wartime policies to neutral countries and to the Dominions. There was, however, neither precedent nor blueprint for such an experiment. Masterman distinguished himself by the speed with which he addressed the task and the manner in which he formulated general principles for his work which largely endured until the end of the war. These principles can be summarised as follows; the need for secrecy in order to disguise the source of the propaganda, that propaganda should be based upon accurate information and measured argument, and that propaganda should be directed towards the opinion-makers rather than to the masses. The latter is perhaps the most surprising though it should be remembered that at the time, the concept of mass public opinion was still largely incomprehensible to the exclusive senior officials in the Foreign Office. This perception would slowly change during the course of the war.

The Bureau began its propaganda campaign on 2 September 1914 when Masterman invited twenty-five leading British authors to Wellington House to discuss ways of best promoting Britain's interest during the war. Those who attended were all part of the Edwardian establishment and included J.M. Barrie, Arnold Bennett, G.K. Chesterton, Arthur Conan Doyle, John Galsworthy, Thomas Hardy, John Masefield, Gilbert Murray, G.M. Trevelyan and H.G. Wells.[11] Rudyard Kipling and Quiller Couch sent their apologies but offered their services.[12] Masterman's aim was to organise a manifesto of support in response to that signed by a group of prominent German academics defending the attack on Belgium.[13] Gilbert Murray drafted a statement that was eventually signed by fifty-two authors and published in *The Times* on 18 September, calling upon Britain and 'all the English speaking race' to defend the 'ideals of Western Europe against the rule of "Blood and iron" . . .'[14] Four women were among the signatories; Jane Ellen Harrison, May Sinclair, Flora Annie Steel and Mrs Humphry Ward, a rare example of participation by women in official propaganda during the war.

The second meeting, convened on 7 September, was attended by leading editors such as Sir Edward Tyas Cook, Robert Donald of the *Daily Chronicle*, Geoffrey Dawson, A.G. Gardiner of the *Daily News*, J.L. Garvin, then of the *Pall Mall Gazette*, Sidney Low of *The Standard*, Thomas Marlowe of the *Daily Mail*, Geoffrey Robinson of *The Times*, J.A. Spender of the *Westminster Gazette* and St. Leo Strachey of the *Spectator*. Four resolutions were unanimously adopted. It was agreed that censorship should be minimal, that a government co-ordinator should be appointed for disseminating government news, that help should be provided to journalists reporting on the Dominions and neutral countries, and that British diplomats should enlist the help of journalists when correcting errors in foreign news reporting.

The work of Wellington House was highly secret, so much so that few were aware of its existence at the time.[15] Partly this was determined by a belief on the part of Masterman that propaganda stood a greater chance of success if the recipients were ignorant of its provenance and also because official propaganda was a sensitive political issue and there was some anxiety when Wellington House was established about the way both public and parliamentary opinion might respond to the truth of its operations. Its single most important section, however, was the American branch, headed by Sir Gilbert Parker, the Canadian-born writer and MP for Gravesend, who volunteered his services free of charge.[16] Wellington House's campaign in the United States had, in fact, been greatly assisted by an action which had been undertaken before a shot had been fired. This was the cutting, within hours of Britain's ultimatum to Germany expiring, of the direct transatlantic cables from Germany to the United States by the *Telconia*. Thus all news from Germany, with the exception of wireless reports, had to proceed via London, the cable centre of the world. One of the most important consequences of this action can be seen in 1917 when the British intercepted and deciphered the infamous Zimmermann Telegram and leaked it to the US press. It stands as a perfect example of intelligence and propaganda working hand-in-hand and did much to bring the United States into the war.[17] This recognition of the relationship between propaganda, censorship and intelligence-gathering provided Wellington House with an important advantage in the battle for hearts and minds in that it meant that the majority of news reaching America was disseminated through British filters, not German. This almost instinctive action also established the blueprint for how modern states should go about conducting a global propaganda campaign in a changing world that was already witnessing what is now referred to as the globalization of mass communications.

Having formulated a number of operational ground rules, Masterman set about applying them in pursuit of a number of key objectives such as the righteousness of Britain's cause, mobilizing hatred of the enemy, maintaining the friendship of allies and procuring the cooperation of neutrals – particularly America. Under Masterman's direction, Wellington House developed into the most active of all propaganda departments, arranging for the production and dissemination of books, pamphlets and periodicals as well as films, photographs, lantern slides, cartoons and picture postcards. Interestingly enough, British propaganda policy was not explicitly designed to get America into the war on the Allied side, but rather to allow them to make up their own minds. Recognising the counter-productive effects of the German approach, which was to bombard American public opinion with pro-German propaganda, Wellington House decided to eschew exhortation in favour of explanation and furthermore to target American opinion-makers, individuals who were in a position to influence others. Mass opinion was to be influenced only indirectly. The Wellington House objective was to persuade Americans to 'take a right view of the actions of the British government since the commencement of the war'.[18]

Such an angle required delicate direction. Having decided to target elite opinion – politicians, civil servants, writers, industrialists, academics, teachers and journalists – it was imperative that an educated American elite should remain unaware that the material they were receiving was in fact propaganda, hence, the importance of maintaining the secrecy of the publishing operation at Wellington House. Masterman believed that propaganda directed at opinion leaders would have less chance of succeeding if they were aware of the source of the information. For this reason the material was also distributed under the imprint of commercial publishing houses such as Hodder and Stoughton, Methuen, John Murray and Macmillan. He was so successful that for the next two years even most Members of Parliament were unaware of its activities. As Philip Taylor has pointed out, today we would label Wellington House-inspired propaganda at the least as 'grey' or perhaps even as 'black' propaganda, which purports to emanate from either an unidentifiable source or from someone or somewhere other than the true source.[19] Masterman appears not have had any moral misgivings over the policy of secrecy and to have viewed the clandestine approach as a necessity of wartime.[20] However, one of the implications of secrecy was that Masterman and his Wellington House staff were bound by a necessary code of silence and frustratingly unable to respond to complaints that nothing was being done to counter German propaganda.

The second related operational ground rule which governed the work undertaken at Wellington House was that it should always attempt to disseminate neutral facts or objective information so as not to appear to be propaganda which the target audience could then dismiss. Masterman's principle was to avoid known falsehoods or fabrication in the belief that the truth will invariably come out and could damage the credibility of the source. 'We have determined to present facts and general arguments based on facts' stated the first report on the work of Wellington House.[21] Masterman was not opposed, however, to the selective re-packaging of the 'facts' in the interest of the British cause. He also stressed the importance of subtlety and close attention to the culture and mentality of the target audience. To ensure these principles were implemented, Masterman appointed the historians Arnold Toynbee, Lewis Namier and J.W. Headlam-Morley as advisers and guardians of the Wellington House conscience. In the years that followed, written material produced by some of the finest writers of the time poured out of Wellington House to the homes of America's opinion-forming elite with no indication that it had been commissioned by Britain's foremost propaganda organisation. As far as the American target audience was concerned, it appeared that Britain's intelligentsia had spontaneously mobilised itself in a patriotic cause. Accompanying much of the literature was a personal letter from Gilbert Parker, then a well-known author. These letters were measured and discreet and intended to provide a personal approach. Typical is the following from March 1915:

Dear Sir,

   I am well aware that American enterprise has made available reprints of the official papers relating to the present European war, but the original British prints of these publications may not be accessible to those persons of influence who would study them for a true history of the conflict. I am venturing to send to you under another cover several of these official documents. I am sure you will not consider this an impertinence, but will realise that Britain's desire that their cause may be judged from authoritative evidence.

   In common with the great majority of Americans, you have, no doubt, made up your mind as to what country should be held responsible for this tragedy, but these papers may be found useful for reference, and because they contain the incontrovertible facts, I feel that you will probably welcome them in this form.

   My long and intimate association with the United States through my writings gives me confidence to approach you and I trust you will not think me intrusive or misunderstand my motive.[22]

British propaganda policy in the United States was summed up by Lord Cecil as one of 'stealth'.[23] Wellington House's 'invisible' achievement was greatly facilitated by a series of inept German mistakes that allowed Gilbert Parker to capture the moral high ground. The most obvious propaganda blunder was perpetrated in August 1915 when the nurse Edith Cavell, who had been working at a Red Cross hospital in German-occupied Brussels, was found guilty by a German court martial of helping British and French soldiers to escape into neutral Holland. She was sentenced to death and executed by firing squad. British propaganda spared no effort to ensure that Cavell's execution was given the widest possible publicity in the United States and of course in Britain. American newspapers and magazines printed full accounts of the 50-year-old devoted nurse's calm and courageous composure as she faced the German firing squad. Rapidly American opinion – much of it previously pro-German and suspicious of the atrocity stories about German behaviour in Belgium – now turned in favour of the Allies and against Germany whose action in executing Cavell was seen as the height of Hunnish barbarism. The emotional impact of the execution of Cavell was sustained and kept alive by Germany's decision to impose unrestricted submarine warfare in order to break Britain's naval blockade of Germany. The German naval campaign which led to the sinking of the passenger liner *Lusitania* was another serious body-blow in the struggle to win the hearts and minds of American public opinion. *Lusitania* was sunk by a U-boat without prior warning on 7 May 1915 with the loss of 1,198 lives, 128 of them American. Gilbert Parker went on the offensive the following day by declaring in the *New York Times* that the sinking of the liner was a 'most inhuman crime committed by an inhuman nation which has placed itself outside the bounds of civilisation'.[24] The *Times* described the event as worthy of being 'placed side by side with the sack of Louvain and Dinant, the cold-blooded slaughter of innocent Belgian and French citizens, the outraging of helpless women and girls, the unnumbered acts of bestiality and torture'.[25] The Germans attempted to justify the sinking of *Lusitania* on the grounds that it was carrying weapons and that they had placed in the American press explicit warnings of the danger of boarding British vessels in the war zone.[26] However, the incident had inflamed anti-German sentiment and was widely condemned in the American press as an act of barbarism.

Wellington House had also discovered that an inflammatory medal had been struck privately in Munich by a metal worker, Karl Goetz, to commemorate the sinking. On one side the medal depicted *Lusitania* laden with weapons beneath the words 'No Contraband!' (*Keine Bannware!*), and on the other it showed the figure of Death selling tickets to passengers with the motto 'Business before Everything' (*Geschäft über Alles*). Photographs of the medal were eventually published in *The New York Times* on 7 May 1916, the first anniversary of the sinking. They attracted so much attention that Wellington House, under the guise of the '*Lusitania* Souvenir Medal Committee', decided to produce a boxed reproduction for propaganda purposes. Over 300,000 were eventually produced and were sold with an explanatory leaflet which sought to demonstrate the bestiality of German actions. Referred to as 'German Naval Victory', the leaflet cites the *Kölnische Volkszeitung* on 10 May 1915: 'With joyful pride we contemplate this latest deed of our navy' and continued:

> The medal has been struck in Germany with the object of keeping alive in German hearts the recollection of the glorious achievement of the German Navy in deliberately destroying an unarmed passenger ship, together with 1198 non-combatants, men, women and children . . . The picture seeks apparently to propound the theory that if a murderer warns his victims of his intention, the guilt of the crime will rest with the victim, not with the murderer.

Thousands of these boxed replicas were purchased in the United States where, in order to mask its propagandistic purpose, the British government asked Selfridge's department store, which had been given responsibility for production and distribution, to announce that all profits from the sale of the medals would go to the Red Cross.[27]

The propaganda impact of the incident was immensely powerful in rousing American, and indeed global, indignation against Germans. By seizing the opportunity, Wellington House and Gilbert Parker had demonstrated the critical importance of exploiting German military naivety and building an incremental campaign underpinned by moral parameters. The British version of events invariably prevailed; Americans would have no choice but to view the Germans as the Allies wanted: demonic barbarians with no regard for basic human rights. The moral considerations should not be underestimated when taken together with the widely-believed atrocity stories emanating from Belgium and the use of poison gas on the battlefield. It would appear that even members of the British government had succumbed to such propaganda. Dr Christopher Addison, parliamentary secretary of the Board of Education, later Minister of Munitions, wrote in his diary on 7 May concerning *Lusitania*: 'One good thing, however, may come out of it. Not only belligerent nations but neutrals ought to be anxious that there should be no half measure in terms of peace and that the war should be carried through until savageries of this description, the use of poison gas and such like, are made impossible.'

Five days after the sinking of *Lusitania* the infamous Bryce Report on *Alleged German Atrocities in Belgium* was published. Wellington House had seen to it that large numbers of copies had been printed to ensure the widest-possible circulation in the United States. Viscount James Bryce, the former Ambassador to the United States, presided over the committee which included the eminent jurist and constitutional historian Sir Frederick Pollock and the distinguished lawyers Sir Edward Clarke MP and Sir Alfred Hopkinson.[28] Due largely to Bryce's reputation in America and to its prestigious membership, the report was accepted as fact and made headline news in the United States. As Masterman informed Bryce in June 1915: 'Your report has *swept* America. As you probably know even the most sceptical declare themselves converted, just because it is signed by you! It was a great idea of the P.M.'s to ask you to do this piece of work, which will stand as a historic document – hideous enough. God knows.'[29]

The stories of the alleged German atrocities in Belgium, the execution of Nurse Cavell and the sinking of *Lusitania* allowed Britain to project an image to many Americans of Germany as a nation prepared to flout recklessly moral and civilised codes of conduct. Wellington House did not sink *Lusitania* but it certainly exploited the incident together with the execution of Cavell and the stories of atrocities carried out by German troops in occupied Belgium to appropriate the moral high ground, which successfully undermined clumsy German attempts to make propaganda capital, that is counter-propaganda, out of the British naval blockade and the crushing of the 1916 Easter Uprising in Ireland.

The campaign for American public opinion was only one aspect of the work carried out by Wellington House – albeit the most pressing and important. At the decision-making level, the senior officials and advisers that Masterman had assembled into an elaborate division of labour, met several times a week and was known as 'the Moot'. Divided into various branches along linguistic lines, these sub-divisions scoured foreign newspapers and periodicals for information which could be used as propaganda either in support of the British cause or against Germany. Once it was ready for distribution, the material, together with advice on how to use it, was passed on to the Foreign Office News Department, which in turn gave it to diplomatic and consular officials abroad.

By June 1915, Wellington House had produced some 2.5 million books, official publications, pamphlets and speeches in seventeen languages. According to the first annual report which Masterman provided for the Cabinet, these materials 'were not circulated promiscuously but ... either ... sold or sent with a personal letter to some man or woman of importance, placed in public libraries or distributed amongst a selected list of those to whom the particular literature was suitable'. Just over twelve months later, Wellington House was also distributing six fortnightly illustrated newspapers which had a total printing of one million copies and 300 books and pamphlets in twenty-one languages, almost entirely without the readers' knowledge that this material was sponsored by the British government. In addition, 4,000 photographs a week were being circulated to the press in all parts of the world.[30] An increasingly important awareness of visual propaganda saw Wellington House campaign for war artists to visit the front, starting with Muirhead Bone in 1916, as well as film cameramen. Film, which was still in its infancy but would become, partly as a result of the war, *the* mass-medium of the first half of the twentieth century, was another visual medium that interested Masterman. Wellington House produced the very first official documentary film, *Britain Prepared*, which was exhibited in neutral countries and premiered in London in December 1915. The premiere, held on 29 December and attended by a cross-section of the ruling Establishment – with the First Lord of the Admiralty offering a ringing endorsement of the film in an address during the interval – was described by an observer as 'unquestionably the most influential gathering ever collected under one roof to witness the exhibition of a film'.[31] The following day in its review of the film, which attempted to demonstrate Britain's preparedness for war, the *Manchester Guardian* claimed that the cinema was much more than 'a mere amusement . . . and its importance is destined to increase with time. The moving picture is the new universal language.'[32]

Wellington House also commissioned the hugely successful documentary film, *The Battle of the Somme*, which appeared in August 1916. The film draws on the footage shot by two official cameramen, Geoffrey Malins and J.B. McDowell, and included footage of Rawlinson's Fourth Army on the opening day of the offensive. The completed film, which ran for an hour and a quarter, was enthusiastically endorsed by Lloyd George, recently appointed Secretary of State for War, and after a private screening for the King at Windsor Castle, George V urged people to see it. *The Battle of the Somme* was a huge propaganda and commercial success quite without precedent in the history of the British cinema and it has been estimated that 20 million saw the film in its first six weeks.[33] By the end of 1917, official British films had been sent to some forty foreign countries.[34] Although Masterman recognised that the new visual medium of film could be utilised to reach mass audiences, the bulk of Wellington House's output continued to be the printed word directed at an elite audience overseas based upon rational argument rather than emotional appeals.[35] The propaganda campaign in the United States, for example, continued to concentrate on lecture tours, a constant stream of pamphlets sent to a mailing list that by 1917 numbered 170,000 influential Americans and carefully selected material which regularly found its way into over 550 syndicated American newspapers. Gilbert Parker reported that Wellington House had established 'an extraordinary widespread organisation in the United States, but which does not know it is an organisation. It worked entirely by personal association and inspired by voluntary effort . . . The quiet and subterranean nature of our work has the appearance of a purely private patriotism and enterprise.'[36]

Not that Wellington House's effectiveness, especially in the United States, saved it from being buffeted by political interference, personal feuds and inter-departmental rivalries. As early as December 1915, the Army Council signalled its concern at the lack of a central controlling authority and proposed an interdepartmental conference to discuss ways of improving matters. Over a year later in January 1916, the long-awaited meeting took place at the Home Office presided over by the new Home Secretary, Sir Herbert Samuel. The meeting degenerated into a stand-off between the War Office and the Foreign Office and to some extent marked the beginning of the end for Masterman and Wellington House. At the time, however, Masterman clearly thought that he had won a reprieve and that Lord Robert Cecil had seen off the demand from the War Office for the creation of a separate organisation which would control all government propaganda. The intense bitterness of the power struggle unfolding is encapsulated in a letter Masterman wrote to Cecil a few days after the meeting: 'Heartiest congratulations to you and the Foreign Office and Grey [the Foreign Secretary] for having slaughtered your enemies last Wednesday in what I think is the most effective destruction that any Office has given to any of its critics during the eighteen months of the war.'[37]

At the heart of this interdepartmental rivalry was a 'news versus views' debate whose roots and antecedents can be traced back to the beginning of the war when the Government divided responsibilities of propaganda and censorship along ad hoc lines with no real terms of reference nor any specific definitions of duties. In August 1914, for example, Winston Churchill set up the Press Bureau which essentially performed a negative function of providing 'trustworthy information' supplied by the War Office and the Admiralty which was also responsible for postal, cable and wireless censorship. The dissemination of individual news stories was undertaken by the Foreign Office News Department and by the Neutral Press Committee under the direction of the Home Office. By the end of 1915 a major rift was growing between civilians at the Foreign Office and the Home Office and the military leaders at the War Office and the Admiralty because of each department's desire to control the public's perception of its work.[38] The 'invisible' successes of Wellington House on the other hand went largely unnoticed not least because so much of the propaganda undertaken was being conducted secretly.

While Asquith remained Prime Minister the bureaucrats continued to fight among themselves about who should assume overall responsibility for propaganda, with two broad strategies emerging from the different interpretations of propaganda techniques. The Foreign Office and the Home Office favoured placing most propaganda activities under the control of the Foreign Office on the grounds that the majority of official propaganda was directed at foreign audiences. The War Office and the Admiralty, on the other hand, pressed for the creation of a new, separate department of propaganda to be staffed by emerging experts. When Lloyd George succeeded Asquith on 7 December 1916, this resolution was given a new impetus as a result of the Prime Minister's interest in propaganda and the role it played in modern political life.[39] It was Lloyd George, after all, who in August 1914 had first suggested the idea of an official propaganda bureau; ironically, a proposal which led to the establishment of Wellington House. Two days after assuming office, Lloyd George raised the issue at his first War Cabinet and indicated that propaganda was in need of early consideration.[40] Not surprisingly, given the Prime Minister's well known distrust of diplomats, as well as of generals, he wanted to reduce the role of the Foreign Office and instead cultivate the press barons such as Lords Beaverbrook and Northcliffe. Masterman's fate was sealed.

In February 1917, following a report that Lloyd George had commissioned from his friend Robert Donald, editor of the Liberal *Daily Chronicle* and a man critical of Masterman, the Prime Minister appointed John Buchan head of the new Department of Information (DOI). Although independent, the DOI would consist of four sections, including an emasculated Wellington House which now dealt only with printed materials, photographs and the works of war artists. Moreover, the chief *raison d'être* of Wellington

House activity, the United States, had disappeared when President Wilson declared war on the Central Powers in April 1917. Although Masterman continued at Wellington House, his influence within the wider British propaganda apparatus waned rapidly.

The establishment of the DOI represented a blow to the Foreign Office and a vindication of the views of the War Office for a centralised, co-ordinating body. However, the blow to the Foreign Office was less severe than had initially been anticipated – partly because the reorganisation had not been as radical as Donald had envisaged. As well as being a famous author, John Buchan had been a former News Department official and chose to locate his headquarters in the Foreign Office building where it effectively functioned as the administrative division. The fact that Buchan and Masterman liked and respected each other served also to minimise the disruption caused by the change of leadership. Moreover, both men shared similar views on the nature of official propaganda, namely that it should be based upon so-called neutral facts or objective information. Such beliefs exposed Buchan to criticism from many quarters that, like Masterman, he lacked leadership and dynamism, failed to use whatever means necessary to attack the enemy and that he refused to adopt a more emotional style of propaganda that would appeal to the masses. In May 1917 for example, Buchan was severely criticised for not exploiting a story that had appeared in *The Times* alleging that the Germans were running a factory which converted human corpses into animal food. Buchan stood his ground when his officials, including Masterman, reported that there was insufficient evidence to substantiate the story. After the war, in a parliamentary debate, it was acknowledged that the *Times* story had been faked.[41]

Although Buchan was directly responsible to the Prime Minister, he did not in fact have direct access to him. Indeed it was one of Buchan's own suggestions, the setting up of an Advisory Committee, that led eventually to his downfall. This advisory committee consisted of leading newspapermen such as Robert Donald, C.P. Scott and Lord Northcliffe (later to be replaced by Lord Beaverbrook). Having sold the idea of an advisory committee to the War Cabinet, Buchan chose not to consult it, preferring instead to receive advice from the Foreign Office. In September 1917, Buchan suggested that in the face of continued interference from the committee and his own failure to gain access to the Prime Minister, the department be placed under a member of the War Cabinet with whom Buchan could have regular contact. Sir Edward Carson, who had recently entered the War Cabinet, was immediately assigned this function. However, Carson was too preoccupied with Irish matters to provide Buchan with the support that he needed. Donald's dissatisfaction with Buchan soon reached the Prime Minister who intervened on behalf of the committee. Consequently Lloyd George turned once again to his friend Robert Donald who was invited to examine the situation and make recommendations. In his second report to the War Cabinet, in December 1917, Donald repeated many of the criticisms that had been levelled at Masterman: the dominance of the Foreign Office, the lack of co-ordination and Buchan's failure to centralise his organisation.[42]

Donald's report coincided with the changing demands of the military and economic situation. The opening of the Brest-Litovsk negotiations between Germany and the Bolsheviks in December effectively took Russia out of the war. Moreover, the failure to make a decisive military break-through had led to widespread war-weariness. For many observers the situation now required a more adventurous propaganda campaign that focused on an all-out psychological offensive against the enemy and a more coherent exposition to the home front of Britain's war aims. Critics argued that for too long the Foreign Office had supervision of Britain's overseas propaganda and had concentrated on propaganda for Allied and neutral countries at the expense of propaganda direct into enemy countries. Following the resignation of Edward Carson in January 1918, the arguments long advocated by the War Office now held sway and the way was open for the establishment of a Ministry of Information that would force the Foreign Office to relinquish its remaining control over propaganda.

On 25 January 1918, Buchan had written to Lord Northcliffe, an ally of the Prime Minister, suggesting that that the DOI needed a head with real authority in the War Cabinet. In February, Lloyd George consolidated and centralised British propaganda for the final time by establishing a Ministry of Information (MOI) with Lord Beaverbrook as Minister and Buchan as his Director of Intelligence. A separate organisation responsible for enemy propaganda was set up under the direction of Northcliffe. Both Beaverbrook at the MOI and Northcliffe at the Enemy Propaganda Department at Crewe House were directly answerable to the Prime Minister and attempted immediately to improve the effectiveness of British propaganda by re-focusing on why Britain was fighting a protracted war. Determined to widen the debate beyond 'poor little Belgium', the press barons simply were not prepared to counter Foreign Office interference or even accept dictation from the Foreign Office on matters of foreign policy. In this respect they were aided by Lloyd George's increasing personal involvement in foreign policy and diplomacy at the expense of the Foreign Office and his belief in the power of propaganda.[43] For the remaining period of the war, Beaverbrook and Northcliffe switched the emphasis from elite, indirect propaganda, favoured by the Foreign Office, to direct mass persuasion. Both recognised the power of propaganda over mass opinion and the importance of what today would be termed 'official public relations'. More specifically, as journalists, both believed that the Government needed to present a more coherent statement of its war aims and that public opinion should be targeted directly.

Northcliffe had famously, or infamously, been quoted as saying: 'God made people read so that I could fill their heads with facts, facts, facts – and later tell them whom to love, whom to hate and what to think.'[44] He wasted no time in using propaganda to convince the enemy of the futility of their cause and the certainty of an Allied victory.[45] Crewe House targeted initially Austria-Hungary, as the fragmenting empire offered the prospect of immediate success. However, the question of 'oppressed minorities' within Austria-Hungary raised the controversial issue of national self-determination and drew Crewe House and the MOI into the realm of foreign affairs and the previously exclusive domain of the Foreign Office. Indeed many within the Foreign Office, including Balfour, the Foreign Secretary, feared that British diplomacy was being shaped more by propaganda than by policy. The ensuing struggle would weaken the work of propaganda during the remaining part of the war and prompted Northcliffe to conclude that: 'As a people we do not understand propaganda ways . . . Propaganda is advertising and diplomacy is no more likely to understand advertising than advertising is likely to understand diplomacy.'[46] The Foreign Office, on the other hand, felt slighted now that it had been forced to hand over its control of propaganda to the press barons. Since the establishment of Wellington House, the Foreign Office had worked on the principle that propaganda and foreign policy – the image and the reality – should operate hand-in-hand. Not surprisingly other government departments closed ranks and united behind the Foreign Office in opposition to any further dilution of Whitehall responsibilities to Fleet Street. Beaverbrook later recalled that, like Northcliffe, he too found himself engaged in 'a remorseless battle . . . without compensations'.[47]

The creation therefore of the MOI and Crewe House in 1918 actually led to an intolerable situation for all concerned. This is often overlooked when the accepted version of events unfolded in the post-war period: namely, that three years of failure was compensated by a final period of qualified success under the leadership of the press barons. As we have seen, nothing could be further from the truth. However, given the secrecy within which Wellington House operated, the nature of the propaganda disseminated and the restrained personalities of Masterman and Buchan, it is not surprising that Beaverbrook and Northcliffe were able to construct such a myth unchallenged.[48]

Having said that, it should also be conceded that the looming presence of Beaverbrook and in particular Northcliffe energised propaganda in the final period of the war. Their prestige and support unquestionably increased co-operation between government departments and those of other countries.[49] Moreover, the move away from targeting elite opinion as favoured by the Foreign Office to mass public opinion as favoured by the press barons reflected the manner in which the war was unfolding. With the entry of the United States into the conflict it was no longer necessary to target Allied and neutral opinion. Both the MOI and Crewe House recognised the need to cultivate foreign opinion as an adjunct to military success. Crewe House directed its propaganda to the mass populations of the Entente nations in order to drive a wedge between the ruling political and military elites and the war-weary ordinary citizens who had borne the brunt of the fighting.

In a perceptive memorandum drafted by Beaverbrook in September 1918, which set out the functions of the MOI, he famously referred to propaganda as 'the popular arm of diplomacy' and talked about total war as a struggle in which 'the munitions of the mind become not less vital for victory that fleets or armies'.[50] Recognising that a military victory could only be secured by undermining enemy morale, British propaganda in the final stages of the war focused on persuading the German people that to continue the war was futile and to force their ruling elites to sue for peace on Allied terms. Certainly from the German perspective, the press barons were credited with having played a major role in undermining German morale. Much of this was part of a post-war inquisition undertaken by the far right to justify the so-called *Dolchstoss* (stab-in-the-back) legend and to cover-up for Germany's military defeat. As the proprietor of two mass circulation newspapers which reflected unambiguously his strident anti-Germanism, Northcliffe had been viewed in Germany as the most powerful unofficial propagandist in Britain during the war. Having been placed in charge of enemy propaganda in 1918, *Simplicissimus*, the German satirical magazine, depicted Northcliffe in collusion with the devil. In a cartoon reminiscent of a medieval woodcut, Satan is shown wearing an inquisitor's robe while Northclifffe, who is holding a copy of *The Times* in one hand and a copy of the *Daily Mail* in the other, is dressed in a garish suit reminiscent of British commercial travellers of the period. With one arm round the paunchy press baron, the devil is quoted as saying: 'Welcome, Great Master! From you we shall at least learn the science of lying!' In a similar vein, the deposed Kaiser is quoted as saying immediately after the war had been lost: '*Ach, diese Propaganda von* Northcliffe! *Es war ko-loss-al!*'.[51] The post-war German perspective on the decisive roles played by Beaverbrook and Northcliffe in the propaganda war helped perpetuate the myth that the two press barons had assiduously been cultivating in Britain.

Interestingly, Buchan stayed on within the MOI working with Beaverbrook, largely writing articles and lecturing and he proved particularly effective in improving relations with American newspaper reporters. In October 1918, when Beaverbrook resigned as Minister of Information ostensibly on health grounds, Buchan once again took charge of propaganda – albeit briefly. Two days after the Armistice had been signed, he was instructed by the Cabinet to close down as much of the Ministry as possible. Charles Masterman continued in his post as director of the literary section within the MOI, on a reduced salary and largely ignored by the public and politicians who remained unaware of his contribution to the propaganda war effort.[52]

Nevertheless, the history of Wellington House is remarkable in many ways; not only did it establish a structure and strategy that systematically employed modern technology for the dissemination of official propaganda, it also laid down certain operational ground rules. The most important one was to be absolutely clear about one's objectives; namely what the propagandist wants his audience to think and do. On this there can be no vagueness – objectives must be as precise as possible. The second major operational ground rule was that British propaganda should be based upon selective, but objective, information. During the Second World War this principle would be refined by the British and encapsulated in the working phrase that it was always best to 'tell the truth, nothing but the truth and, *as near as* possible, the whole truth'. Wellington House's legacy can be detected in the reactions in the United States once the full extent of British propaganda had been revealed after the war. At the heart of the campaign in the United States was the personal touch. Inter-war isolationists in particular seized upon the work of Wellington House to claim that America had been 'duped' into entering the war. In 1927 the novelist and activist Upton Sinclair claimed that 'I am one of the hundred and ten million suckers who swallowed the hook of British official propaganda'.[53] In 1939, as Europe was once again about to plunge into war, *Life* magazine reminded its American readers how wartime British propaganda had enticed America to send two million men to Europe in the last war.[54]

When Charles Masterman was setting up Wellington House he warned his colleagues that when their work was finished 'it is highly probable it would go completely unrewarded and unacknowledged'.[55] Masterman clearly thought deeply about the nature of propaganda in wartime and its relationship with censorship and truth. In many ways he was in advance of his time. It is important also to remember that new techniques of persuasion were being tried for the first time and that the so-called psychology of the masses was in its infancy. Masterman never possessed the political gravitas or the necessary support from within the War Cabinet to have become director of the newly-formed Ministry of Information. He was accused by his critics of elitism and effeteness and of adopting a too literary approach to propaganda. It was said of him that he was unwilling to fabricate stories of the enemy for the raw edification of the masses. After the war, Masterman was never effusive about his wartime experiences as a propagandist, preferring instead to return to Parliament and to write a number of books on themes he had explored in *The Conditions of England* (1909). He died in 1927. Buchan paid tribute to Masterman as 'one of the most brilliant, misunderstood, and tragically fated men of his time'.[56]

* * *

Britain emerged from the First World War with the double-edged distinction of having employed propaganda better and more successfully than any other nation. It is difficult to say why this should be as there appears to be no clearly thought out or co-ordinated plan to such an end. Indeed, the Ministry of Information was not finally established until 1918. Whatever one might think about the content of British propaganda during the First World War, it was undeniably an impressive exercise in co-ordination. By means of strict censorship and tightly-controlled propaganda campaigns, the press, films, leaflets, and posters, were all utilised in a co-ordinated fashion – arguably for the first time – in order to disseminate officially approved themes. Having entered the conflict with nothing that could be described as an official propaganda department, Britain finished the war with a highly-respected MOI which proved to be a classic model on which other governments were subsequently to base their own propaganda machinery.

The emergence of propaganda as the chief instrument of control over public opinion was the inevitable consequence of 'total war'. At home, it became the fifth arm of defence. In short, propaganda became an indispensable part of the equipment of the modern state at war. However, in December 1918, six weeks after the end of the war, the MOI was dissolved. It was, as one official wrote in the 1920s, 'a good word gone wrong – debauched by the late Lord Northcliffe'. It was only to be revived as an official agency of propaganda in 1939 with the outbreak of the Second World War.

Notes

1. P.M. Taylor, *British Propaganda in the Twentieth Century. Selling Democracy* (Edinburgh, 1999), p. 1.
2. H. Strachan, *The First World War. A New Illustrated History* (London, 2003), p. 35.
3. E. Ludendorff, *Meine Kriegserinnerung 1914-1918* (Berlin, 1919), p. 369.
4. M. Sanders and P. Taylor, *British Propaganda during the First World War* (Macmillan, 1982), p. 38. For a detailed analysis of German propaganda during the First World War see D. Welch, *Germany and Propaganda in World War I. Pacifism, Mobilization and Total War* (I.B. Tauris, 2014).
5. Its key objectives were reported as widely as the United States of America. See *The New York Times*, 22 November 1914.
6. Links between public and private propaganda organisations had been firmly established in the 1880s with the rise of pressure groups such as Imperial Federation League, the British Empire League and the Navy League, founded to lobby Parliament for increased military expenditure and to disseminate the values of the Empire. For an account of the various unofficial propaganda agencies see J.D. Squires, *British Propaganda at Home and in the United States from 1914 to 1917* (Harvard University Press, 1935), pp. 16–25.
7. Established in August 1914 under the Defence of the Realm Act (DORA), the War Office Press Bureau was placed under the control of F.E. Smith and would censor news and telegraphic reports from the British army and then issue them to the press. For a contemporary analysis of the work of the Press Bureau see Sir Edward Cook, *The Press in Wartime* (London, 1920).
8. Asquith to the King, 31 August 1914, CAB 41/35//38. Also cited in Sanders and Taylor, *British Propaganda*, pp. 38–9.

9. According to Lucy Masterman, Lloyd George had approached him informally after a luncheon earlier in the month. L. Masterman, *C.F. G Masterman* (London, 1939), p. 72.

10. G.S. Messinger, *British Propaganda and the State in the First World War* (Manchester, 1992), p. 25.

11. The meeting has been described as 'probably the most important gathering of creative and academic writers ever assembled for an official purpose in the history of English letters'. P. Buitenhuis, *The Great War of Words* (London, 1989), p. 14. A description of the meeting can be found in L.Masterman's *Masterman*, p. 272.

12. Kipling was despised by the Foreign Secretary, Sir Edward Grey, who even threatened to resign if the government backed Kipling's visit to the United States in late 1914. See L. Masterman, *Masterman*, p. 277.

13. Ninety-three German scholars, writers, scientists and artists signed the manifesto *'Es ist nicht war!'* ('It is not true!'). See Welch, *German Propaganda*, p. 66.

14. Messinger, *British Propaganda*, p. 36.

15. Even Lord Northcliffe seemed unaware of its activities. In a letter to Asquith in November 1914 he compared British propaganda efforts unfavourably to the initiatives undertaken in Germany. In Germany, he claimed, xenophobia was being whipped up by co-ordinated propaganda campaigns that included posters and the new medium of the cinema, whereas the British people were offered 'nothing but casualty lists'. Quoted in H.Y. Fyfe, *Northcliffe, An Intimate Biography* (London, 1930), pp. 174, 205.

16. J.C. Adams, *Seated with the Mighty: A Biography of Sir Gilbert Parker* (Ottawa, 1979). Overall, according to Lucy Masterman, the experiment cost the British taxpayer £2 million. See L. Masterman, *Masterman*, p. 294.

17. The telegram, sent by Arthur Zimmerman (head of the German Foreign Office), to his Ambassador in Mexico City, instructing him to offer Mexico the states of Texas, Arizona, and New Mexico if it would join Germany in any future war against the United States. See N. Cull, D. Culbert and D. Welch, *Propaganda and Persuasion. A Historical Encyclopedia, 1500 to the Present* (Santa Barbara, 2003), p. 453. For a more detailed analysis see B. Tuchman, *The Zimmermann Telegram* (New York, 1956).

18. INF4/5, 1st report of the work of Wellington House, 7 June 1915 cited in Sanders and.Taylor, *British Propaganda*, p. 42.

19. Taylor, *British Propaganda in the Twentieth Century. Selling Democracy*, p. 36. See also Chapter 2 for a more detailed analysis of 'grey' and 'black' propaganda.

20. Lucy Masterman claimed that secrecy was not an issue with her husband or his staff because 'already in certain circles there was a kind of *chic* in a civilian refusal to benefit by the war'. L. Masterman, *Masterman*, p. 273.

21. INF4.5, 1st report of the work of Wellington House, 7 June 1915.

22. Cited in Sanders and Taylor, *British Propaganda*, p. 169. A similar letter from Parker can be found in H.C. Peterson, *Propaganda for War: The Campaign against American Neutrality, 1914-17* (Norman, 1939), p. 52.

23. Note by Cecil, 29 December 1916, CAB 24/3, G.102. Quoted in Taylor, *British Propaganda in the Twentieth Century*, p. 39.

24. Cited in Adams, *Seated with the Mighty*, p. 170.

25. *The Times*, 8 May 1915.

26. After the war, it emerged that *Lusitania* had been carrying munitions: 4,200 cases of cartridges containing ten or eleven tons of powder and 1,250 cases of shrapnel. See J.M. Read, *Atrocity Propaganda, 1914-1918* (New York, 1972), p. 200.

27. Interestingly, Lucy Masterman implies that her husband had not been a party to the distribution of the medal. L. Masterman, *Masterman*, p. 280. This claim seem unlikely, given his close links during the period with British intelligence. For further details of the *Lusitania* medal, see Peterson, *Propaganda for War*, pp. 108-33.

28. The report was 600 pages long and sold for 1d, about the price of a newspaper and significantly cheaper than the German White Book, which investigated alleged atrocities committed by Belgian civilians.

29. Masterman to Bryce, 7 June 1915, Bryce Papers, MS 248, cited in Messinger, *British Propaganda*, p. 74.

30. NA. INF4.5, 1st report of the work of Wellington House, 7 June 1915.

31. N. Reeves, *Official British Film Propaganda During the First World War* (London, 1986), p. 223.

32. *Manchester Guardian*, 30 December 1915, p. 4. When it was premiered in the USA in July 1916, the *Moving Picture-World* reported that it had been 'widely acclaimed' all over America.

33. N. Reeves, *The Power of Film Propaganda. Myth or Reality* (London, 1999), p. 26. See also S. Badsey, 'Battle of the Somme: British war-propaganda', *Historical Journal of Film Radio and Television*, Vol. 3, No. 2 (1983), pp. 99–115.

34. For a discussion of the overseas distribution of the films see N. Reeves, 'Film propaganda and its audience: the example of Britain's official films during the First World War', *Journal of Contemporary History*, Vol. 18 (1983), pp. 463–94.

35. Lucy Masterman claimed Wellington House was so successful in concealing the source of its propaganda that a number of its pamphlets were actually reviewed in the German press. L Masterman, *Masterman*, p. 288.

36. The comment can be found in Wellington House's first report to the Cabinet. See Adams, *Seated with the Mighty*, p. 164; and Taylor, *British Propaganda*, p. 39.

37. Masterman to Cecil, 31 January 1916, FO 371/2835, 20631, cited in Taylor, *British Propaganda*, p. 15.

38. The tensions continued throughout the summer of 1916. In August, Brigadier General Charteris referred in his diary to ' a little war within a war between the War Office and the Foreign Office all about films' and commented that 'the trouble is that the Foreign Office, Home Office, War Office, Admiralty and Masterman's absurd committee are all working separately and each is jealous of the other'. Brig-Gen. J. Charteris, *At G.H.Q.* (London, 1931), diary entries for 2 August 1916 and 19 September 1916.

39. In 1912, when in charge of the Insurance Commission, Lloyd George had been responsible for an innovative publicity campaign that hired a corps of lecturers to tour the country explaining the intricacies of the National Insurance Act.

40. Messinger, *British Propaganda*, p. 49.

41. In a debate in the House of Commons, an MP suggested that steps should be taken to 'make it known as widely as possible in Egypt, India, and the East generally, that the Germans use dead bodies of their own soldiers and of their enemies . . . as food for swine.' Hansard, 5th series, HC, XCIII (30 April 1917), p. 27.

42. Robert Donald, 'Inquiry into the extent and efficiency of propaganda: reports on various branches of propaganda work, and recommendations', 4 December 1917, INF 4/4B.

43. A.J.P. Taylor suggested that, in contrast to the majority of his contemporaries who were suspicious of propaganda, Lloyd George, 'if anything, rated the influence of propaganda and the press too highly'. A.J.P. Taylor, *Beaverbrook* (London, 1972), p. 137.

44. Cited in H. Cudlipp, *The Prerogative of the Harlot* (London, 1980), p. 82.

45. Tom Clarke alluded to the intensity with which Northcliffe assumed his assault on the enemy once he became director of Crewe House; 'The rigour with which he conducted this "paper offensive" against the Germans is a matter of history. It was too rigorous for the more internationally minded H.G. Wells, who helped Northcliffe for but a week or two before a quarrel as to the methods led to his resignation'; T. Clarke, *My Northcliffe Diary* (London, 1931), pp. 115–16.

46. Northcliffe to C.J. Phillips, 12 July 1918. Cited in G. Harmsworth and R. Pound, *Northcliffe* (London, 1959), p. 653.

47. Lord Beaverbrook, *Men and Power, 1917–18* (London, 1956), p. 290.

48. This myth was perpetuated in Germany by Ludendorff and Hitler, and also in Britain by, among others, Lloyd George. In his war memoirs published between 1933 and 1936, the former Prime Minister wrote: 'The disintegration of the home front in Germany is attributed largely to the "lying propaganda" which the Allies organised. But the deadliest quality in the propaganda was its truth . . . Our Ministry of Information arranged for a good deal of propaganda of this order . . . It was done with great skill and subtlety. The credit for its success is due to Lord Beaverbrook and Lord Northcliffe'. D. Lloyd George, *War Memoirs*, Vol. II (London, 1936), p. 1873.

49. On 14 August 1918, for example, Northcliffe chaired a four-day inter-Allied propaganda conference at Crewe House where he urged representative to share their insights and information.

50. Memorandum by Beaverbrook, 'The organisation and functions of the Ministry of Information', September 1918, INF/4/5, also cited in Taylor, *British Propaganda*, p. 28.

51. Both the cartoon and the Kaiser quotation are cited in Pound and Harmsworth, *Northcliffe*, pp. 671, 669.

52. By the end of the war, Masterman was barely on speaking terms with Lloyd George.

53. Cited in Messinger, *British Propaganda*, p. 68.

54. Taylor, *British Propaganda*, p. 44. The extent to which this suspicion lingered in the United Stated can be gleaned from Peterson's *Propaganda for War*. One of the long-term consequences of this was that British propaganda directed at the United States between 1939 and 1941 had to be even more

unobtrusive than it had ever been during the Great War. Cf. N. Cull, *Selling War: British Propaganda and American 'Neutrality' in the Second World War* (Oxford, 1997).
55. L. Masterman, *Masterman*, p. 273.
56. J. Buchan, *Memory Hold the Door* (London, 1940), p. 170. Also cited in Messinger, *British Propaganda*, p. 97.

Suggested Further Reading

Badsey, S., 'Battle of the Somme: British war-propaganda', *Historical Journal of Film Radio and Television*, Vol. 3, No. 2 (1983), pp. 99–115
Buitenhuis, P., *The Great War of Words* (London, 1989)
Messinger, G.S., *British Propaganda and the State in the First World War* (Manchester, 1992)
Read, J.M., *Atrocity Propaganda, 1914-1918* (New York, 1972)
Reeves, N., *Official British Film Propaganda During the First World War* (London, 1986)
Sanders, M., and Taylor, P.M., *British Propaganda during the First World War* (Macmillan, 1982)
Taylor, P.M., *British Propaganda in the Twentieth Century. Selling Democracy* (Edinburgh, 1999)
Welch, D., *Germany and Propaganda in World War I. Pacifism, Mobilization and Total War* (I.B.Tauris, 2014)
Welch, D., 'Images of the Hun: The Portrayal of the German Enemy in British Propaganda in World War I', in D. Welch (ed.), *Propaganda, Power and Persuasion. From World War I to Wikileaks* (I.B. Tauris, 2015)

Chapter 7

The Commonwealth Contribution to Victory on the Western Front

The Australians *by* Peter Burness

On the first day of the twentieth century the nation of Australia was created by the federation of the six states, the former colonies of Tasmania, Victoria, Western Australia, New South Wales, South Australia and Queensland. The new nation of less than five million people occupying a continent was confident, socially advanced and optimistic. However, the Great War lay just over the horizon.

In 1914 Australia had only a compulsory-service militia and a small permanent cadre for home defence, so a new and separate army, called the Australian Imperial Force (the AIF), had to be raised for the war. By 1918, more than 300,000 men and nurses had left Australia as members of the AIF, most of them to serve on the Western Front. The Royal Australian Navy, whose main units had only been delivered the previous year, was placed at the disposal of the British Admiralty.

The AIF was late in arriving on the Western Front as the Australian and New Zealand Army Corps (ANZAC) had spent most of 1915 in the Middle East and had concentrated its fighting on the Turkish Gallipoli peninsula. Finally, between March and November 1916, five Australian divisions landed in France from camps in Egypt or England. Some of the men were veterans of the ill-fated Gallipoli campaign and others were fresh arrivals and reinforcements. The troops were brimming with confidence and satisfied, at last, to be at the main front of the war.

The Australian divisions were split between I ANZAC Corps under Sir William Birdwood and II ANZAC Corps (which included the New Zealand Division) under Sir Andrew Godley. Both commanders were from the British army as indeed was the majority of their staff, although Birdwood's Chief of Staff was an outstanding Australian, Brigadier General Brudenell White, who was to remain with him for the rest of the war.

In their first year in France and Belgium, four of the divisions were thrown into very heavy fighting. The casualties suffered at the battles of Fromelles in French Flanders and at Pozières on the Somme during July and August were almost more than a volunteer army could endure.

Casualties for the Australians through 1917 were even worse. The Third Battle of Ypres in the later part of the year engaged all five divisions and the appalling losses were felt across the whole of the AIF in Europe. In the last six months of that year the

Australians in France and Belgium received 12,036 new reinforcements. Against this, in the same period, there were 6,972 deaths and 26,184 troops were lost from wounds, sickness and other causes.[1] Most of the keen and available volunteers from Australia had joined up early and now the pool of willing recruits was drying up.

In November 1917, there was a morale-boosting organisational change although its full effect would not be felt for several months. In this, the five Australian divisions were nominally shifted to Birdwood's I ANZAC Corps which was then renamed the Australian Corps. The consolidation into a single national corps further improved the cohesion of the AIF. It created a large corps of experienced divisions with an established reputation as fighting troops. The corps remained an all-volunteer force despite two unsuccessful attempts by the government in 1916 and in 1917 to introduce conscription.

In January 1918 there were about 110,000 Australian troops, including nurses, on the Western Front. Their identity and character had been forged in the earlier years of the war. They were better paid than most, they had their own uniform and the familiar slouch hat was being seen almost as a national dress. The men were now calling each other by the popular name of 'Digger'. Each one of them had little chance of seeing their far-off homes until the war was won, that is if they survived.

The 'Diggers' did draw criticism for their poor discipline when out of the line, and the rates of venereal disease and charges of absence without leave were high. However, Australians insisted that they had good battle discipline and that was what mattered most. Field Marshal Sir Douglas Haig and others, including some Australian generals, felt that the introduction of the death penalty would improve the AIF's discipline, but the Australian government refused to sanction it. During the war no member of the AIF was executed under military law.

Captain George Mitchell of the 48th Battalion, summed it up:

We Diggers were a race apart. Long separation from Australia had seemed to cut us completely away from the land of our birth. The longer a man served, the fewer letters he got, the more he was forgotten. Our only home was our unit, and that was constantly being decimated, and rebuilt by strangers. Pride in ourselves, in face of a world of friends and enemies, was our sustaining force.[2]

When on 21 March 1918 the great German offensive struck in France and was soon heading towards the old Somme battlefields, the Australians were well away from the action. The widely-spread divisions were soon needed. Suddenly all leave was stopped, officers were recalled to units and training cancelled. The AIF was about to face its most important actions of the war.

Sir John Monash later recalled:

The whole five Divisions [had become] widely scattered, and, for a time, the Third and Fourth divisions served under the VII British Corps, the Fifth Division under the III Corps, and the First Division under the XV Corps. It was not until April 1918 that four out of the five Divisions again came together under the control of the Australian Corps Commander, at that time General Sir William Birdwood.[3]

The troops were soon heading south. The first to go were the 3rd and 4th Divisions which were then resting out of the line. This would be the first time that Major General Sir John Monash's 3rd Division had been on the Somme. The old soldiers in the other divisions already knew the region well.

The men of the 4th Division under Major General Ewen Sinclair MacLagan were mostly drawn from the more rural Australian states. They had had a hard time through the previous year. With heavy losses and dwindling reinforcements it was felt that it might have to be the first division to have to be disbanded. These thoughts were swept aside as it was called on once again to face a stern test.

Sinclair MacLagan, a Scot, was a British army officer who had spent considerable time on loan to the Australian army before the war and was considered an 'adopted' Australian, at least by the AIF. He had come away with the first troop convoy in 1914 and had commanded the first brigade to go ashore on the Gallipoli Peninsula the following year. He was promoted to the command of his division in 1917 and remained with the AIF throughout the war.

Travelling south in a lorry convoy, the 4th Division could see smoke coming from the direction of the old 1917 battlefields ahead. Then its 4th Brigade was suddenly detached to go to Herbuterne to assist with the defence there. It arrived in time to help repulse an enemy attack on 27 March. The brigade would stay there facing any further threat throughout the following weeks.

The rest of MacLagan's division (the 12th and 13th Brigades) went into positions at Dernancourt close to the familiar Somme town of Albert. There they witnessed the sad stream of French refugees fleeing the German onslaught. In a heavy clash on 28 March the two brigades held off a German attack.

Meanwhile Monash's 3rd Division, after having travelled to Doullens by train, boarded old London buses to be delivered to a spot along the road from Amiens which overlooked the Ancre valley. While fighting went on nearby, the division went up the forward slopes of the valley to take possession of the plateau north of the Somme River.

The movement across hastily-abandoned fields was a welcome change to the old trench warfare of a few years ago. The considerable time spent in training over the recent quieter months was paying off. The modern infantry tactics well-practised since the previous year, were proving effective.

With the Germans approaching, worn-out British troops tried to form a defensive line. North of the Somme River the Australians took over the ground from Morlancourt Ridge to Dernancourt. Meanwhile, in the scramble to fill gaps and place brigades where they were needed most, Monash detached his 9th Brigade to be under British command south of the river at Villers-Bretonneux where it went into reserve.

The orphan brigade was soon in action when one of its battalions was called on to hold ground against the oncoming enemy. Then a few days later on 4 April, in miserable weather, a strong German attack penetrated as far as the town itself only to be driven back by a bold charge by the brigade's 36th Battalion. Weakened by its efforts, the brave battalion had to be disbanded soon afterwards.

On 5 April, the Germans made their heaviest attack in the war so far against the Australians with a further attempt to break through at Dernancourt. They were on one side of the railway embankment and the Australians on the other. This ground had been a hot spot for the past week until at 9.30 in the morning, in heavy fog, the enemy advanced with strong numbers and well supported by artillery.

The Australians suffered casualties and fell back but stayed engaged. The fighting went on all day until successful counter-attacks restored the position. The Germans were beaten and would make no further attacks here. Soon the 2nd Division, having shifted down from Messines in Belgium, relieved the tired 4th. Meanwhile the 5th Division, which had already provided a brigade to assist the 3rd, was spread from the north of Villers-Bretonneux, astride the Somme River.

The 1st Division's fate had taken a different course. The division had been led since Gallipoli by Major General H.G. 'Hooky' Walker of the British army. It had no sooner reached the Somme than it was turned around and sent back north on 10 April to meet a fresh German threat in Flanders. It reached Hazebrouck in time to reinforce the desperate defences there and in the following weeks played its part in halting the enemy. It was three months before the division re-joined the rest of the corps on the Somme.

More British troops were arriving on the Somme and the German offensive was running out of energy. General Ludendorff was shifting his attention to Flanders but he was too close to Amiens to give up just yet. By now Australian divisions were beginning to be relieved and the diggers were struck by the youth and inexperience of the British reinforcements. Then, on 24 April, on a dull misty morning, the Germans struck once again, and this time they had some tanks.

The ragged posts of British troops holding Villers-Bretonneux were hit hard and the enemy's slab-sided tanks penetrated deeply. The situation became desperate with the town on fire and the enemy getting through to the far side. Troops behind the town met young soldiers withdrawing who said that the enemy was coming in waves. At some points hard-pressed troops managed to hold on, but the Germans once again appeared to be in the ascendancy.

Everything depended on a successful counter-attack and two Australian brigades from separate divisions were rushed in for the task. At Querrieu, several kilometres away, Brigadier General William Glasgow and his 13th Brigade, veterans of the recent Dernancourt battle, were ordered forward and Brigadier General 'Pompey' Elliott's 15th Brigade, which was closer and anxiously awaiting the chance to get involved, was sent too. No Australian commanders were tougher than these two veterans.

No reconnaissance was possible and the ground was unfamiliar to the brigades which were to attack on each side of the town in a pincer movement in the dark. That night they attacked yelling as they went forward silhouetted by burning buildings. They were met with heavy fire, much of it from machine guns. The Germans fell back. By the morning of 25 April, Anzac Day – the anniversary of the AIF first going into action on Gallipoli in 1915 – Villers-Bretonneux was back in British hands.

The German offensive on the Somme had effectively ended and Villers-Bretonneux, and the city of Amiens just 12 kilometres away, were safe. General Birdwood would later write: 'From that day the Germans never advanced a foot. For them it was the beginning of the end. I have always maintained that this action was the great turning point of the war.'[4] The claim was, of course, not correct. However, it was a reflection of the general's pride in his Australians.

Over the next several weeks the British consolidated and the Villers-Bretonneux front was transferred to the Australians. They held the right of the line of the British army and stood side-by-side with the French. Meanwhile the Australians stole territory in aggressive patrolling and raids wherever they could. In May and June, the 1st Division, which was still in Flanders, was taking ground almost every day.[5] These tactics were called 'peaceful penetration'.

Meanwhile the British Fifth Army had been re-formed and in May Birdwood was promoted to command it. This created a vacancy at the head of the Australian Corps, which was now part of the Fourth Army under General Sir Henry Rawlinson. Birdwood's move provided the opportunity sought by the Australian government to replace many senior British officers within the corps with Australians. Sir John Monash was selected to command the corps effective from 31 May.

Monash had been born in Melbourne and was of German-Jewish descent. He was not a regular soldier but he did have long and extensive experience as a senior militia officer. In 1914 he had been given command of the AIF's 4th Brigade and over the past two years had shown his skills and knowledge as a divisional commander. He had impressed Sir Douglas Haig and he had the support of most of the other divisional commanders. Monash's exceptional gifts were his sharp intellect, a commanding personality, confidence and the fact that he was superbly articulate. His civilian career as an engineer also complemented his military training. He had experience in large-scale projects, embraced technological innovation and understood the need for effective management.

In the months following the halting of the German advance, the enemy-held village of Le Hamel near Villers-Bretonneux remained a problem. An attack had been under consideration for some time and, when sufficient numbers of the new Mark V tanks became available for Monash's use, fresh plans were made.

The first important task for Monash and his corps was a division-strength attack on a frontage of about seven kilometres using the tanks and aircraft and plenty of artillery. He also had four companies of United States infantry which he added to the battle. The attack was launched under MacLagan on 4 July to acknowledge the Americans' involvement.

Firepower, surprise and timing were essential to Monash's plan. He took advantage of every resource and technological innovation available to him. Sixty tanks would have a central role. Monash decided that the tanks would attack along with the infantry and behind the barrage rather than ahead of it. Aircraft were used for spotting, reconnaissance and aerial photography, and he also had them dropping ammunition supplies. He took full advantage of the increased sophistication in the use of artillery. By this time gunnery had become scientifically still more advanced and was the dominating factor in any fighting and the Australian general drew lessons from other recent battles.

Monash's first battle commenced at 3.10 am on 4 July in the early morning mist. Ninety three minutes later it was over and he had established his reputation as a corps commander. The attack had unleased the potential in using artillery, tanks, aircraft and well-trained infantry in concert. Importantly, it gave the British a good line from where to launch a much larger offensive and a chance for Monash's ideas to be a model for future success.

August 8th 1918 was chosen as the date for a big push that would become known as the battle of Amiens. Rawlinson's Fourth Army was to attack on a 20-kilometre front astride the Somme River. The Australians were in the centre, the Canadian Corps was on the right and the British III Corps was to the north on the other side of the river. Each of the three corps would fight to their own plan.

The battle began after a day of drizzling rain and in heavy fog. At 4.30 am the artillery opened up, engaging the enemy's guns and providing a creeping barrage behind which tanks and infantry advanced. Monash had two divisions push on to the first objective. They advanced from behind two divisions on the front line which in turn later would come through them in a double leap-frog. By 6.20 am the first objectives were reached. During a pause, more tanks came up and the field artillery shifted their guns forward so that the further advance would not get beyond their range.

> Through the fog came the jingle of trace-chains as the teams brought their guns forward to help the battalions and brigades in the second and third stages. Through the mist also were heard the panting engines and creak of the tanks earmarked for those stages.[6]

When the sun came up, it revealed the battlefield over which could be seen the tanks, guns, cavalry and the strings of infantry going forward in artillery formation. The Australians had the unusual experience of penetrating so far that they were overrunning German artillery positions, even capturing a monster 38cm railway gun.

By afternoon most of the objectives had been taken. For the Australians' part it had been a great success at the cost of 2,000 casualties. Again, good planning, fighting spirit, firepower and the combination of arms had been decisive factors. The Australians acknowledged the support of British troops working with them including the tank crews, gunners, and airmen of the Royal Air Force.

In the following days, the Australian Corps shifted its advance to both sides of the Somme and for the rest of the month fought its way towards the town of Peronne which was protected by the Somme River, its wide marshes, and the fortified hill of Mont St Quentin. Here the Germans could make a stand and possibly delay further British progress.

Monash was operating with greater command flexibility than would have been extended to a corps commander earlier in the war, and his troops had battle-hardened experience. He did not wait long. He ordered his men across the Somme River and, without tanks or a creeping barrage, in the early hours of 31 August, set the 5th Brigade (2nd Division) against Mont St Quentin. Like others the brigade was tired and low in numbers, but it was made up of confident and well-trained infantrymen. The Germans managed to hold them just below the summit.

General Rawlinson's chief of staff, Sir Archibald Montgomery, later described the brigade's fighting as 'a soldiers' battle'. He wrote:

> With only hastily arranged artillery support and without a creeping barrage, [it] ranks as one of the most notable examples of pluck and enterprise during the war. Confronted with the task of storming a very strong position defended by picked

troops, this brigade . . . overcame every difficulty and gained a footing on Mont St. Quentin, which it maintained in spite of the enemy's numerous counter-attacks.[7]

The division's 6th Brigade entered the fight and by next day it had captured the hill. Meanwhile, on the river flat, the 5th Division entered Peronne. It was a fine feat of arms from units thin in numbers.

The British were now moving across their whole front, and the Australians' advances through September brought them up to the outposts of the Hindenburg Line. Monash was driving his men hard. He later acknowledged: 'I was compelled to disregard the evident signs of overstrain which were brought to my notice by the Divisional Generals and their Brigadiers, and which were patent to my own observation of the condition of the troops.'[8] Monash was feeling the strain too.

On 18 September, the 1st and 4th Divisions, which had been recovering for the past few weeks, made a very successful attack, penetrating deeply and capturing 4,300 prisoners. Clearly German morale was now fragile. These two divisions were then withdrawn to rest. As events would have it, they would not fight again.

Monash now took on the task of attacking the Hindenburg Line with only his 3rd and 5th Divisions readily available to him. To this however he was able to add two keen but inexperienced American National Guard divisions, the 27th and 30th. They would lead an attack set for 29 September. The attack, which was across a land-covered canal, began at dawn. The American troops advanced meeting deadly resistance in some places and pushing well forward in others. But when the Australians came forward behind them they ran into heavy fire from uncleared posts. This was a tough action that did not go smoothly. The situation was improved when a British division on the right managed to cross the open end of the canal and threaten the Germans' flank. In the end Monash had another victory, but this one had taken longer than planned.

A few kilometres on, the last Australian action was fought by a few battalions, including pioneers of the depleted 2nd Division, when they captured Montbrehain on 5 October. The diggers were now all withdrawn to rest areas and they had not come back into action when the war ended on 11 November.

The war correspondent and later historian, Fred Cutlack, recorded General Rawlinson's appreciation in those final weeks of the war:

> The story of what they have accomplished as a fighting Army Corps, of the diligence, gallantry, and skill which they have exhibited, and of the scientific methods which they have so thoroughly learned and so successfully applied, has gained for all Australians a place of honour amongst nations and amongst the English-speaking races in particular. It has been my privilege to lead the Australian Corps in the Fourth Army during the decisive year to a successful conclusion at no distant date.[9]

The Australian Corps finished the war with a reputation as reliable and bold assault troops, but it was a tired and under-strength force. The sense of adventure and excitement displayed by the men in the war's early years had long ago evaporated. Many of them had become fatalists with little expectation of ever going home. By then, one's mates, the men of the battalion, and a determination to defeat the enemy, were what mattered most.

Major General John O'Ryan of the US 27th Division had closely observed the Australians. He noted that they had the characteristics of all good soldiers as well as their own unique features. He saw that long combat experience had given them an edge. He later wrote:

> The operations and supply technique of the Australian divisions were of the very best, and so it was that the rough-and-ready fighting spirit of the Australians had become refined by an experienced battle technique supported by staff work of the highest order.[10]

By the final year of the war the recruits' physical requirements had been lowered. The minimum height standard was now only five feet and many older men were filling the gaps in the ranks. Eleven proud battalions had to disband and those men now joining up were almost exclusively directed to the infantry to replenish the remaining battalions. Numbers were reduced even further when, for the first time, the survivors from among those men who had enlisted in 1914, were finally given home leave to Australia.

On the other side of the ledger, the Australians looked back on a year of success. At no other time had they made such an impact on the main fighting. They had been at the forefront in blunting and then reversing the German offensives on the Somme and in Flanders. In the following months they re-took ground in small raids and in major battles culminating in their part in the battle of Amiens, the capture of Mont St Quentin, and in the breaking of the Hindenburg Line.

There had been many proud achievements. However, the long years of the war had brought tragedy, waste, and disruption from which the young nation was a long time recovering. Charles Bean, the Australian official war historian, saw the war as a test and confirmation of the newly-conferred nationhood. He would write: 'Australians watched the name of their country rise high in the esteem of the world's oldest and greatest nations.'[11]

The legend of the Anzacs' fighting spirit on Gallipoli still stands high in Australians' perceptions of the First World War, usually overlooking the later fighting in France and Belgium. Now, a century on, the 'Diggers'' achievements of 1918 are receiving renewed recognition. In the final critical year of the war, a distinctive national corps under Australian command had fought a series of decisive battles which made a most worthy contribution to the Allied victory.

Notes

1. A.G. Butler, *The Australian Army Medical Services in the War of 1914-1918*, Vol. III (Canberra: Australian War Memorial, 1943), p. 909.

2. G.D. Mitchell, *Backs to the Wall* (Sydney: Angus & Robertson Limited, 1937), p. 168.

3. Sir John Monash, *The Australian Victories in France in 1918* (London: Hutchinson & Co., 1920), p. 9.

4. Field Marshal Lord Birdwood, *Khaki and Gown* (Melbourne: Ward, Lock and Co., 1941), p. 322.

5. C.E.W. Bean, *Anzac to Amiens* (Canberra: Australian War Memorial, 1968), p. 455.

6. Ibid., p. 471.

7. Sir Archibald Montgomery, *The Story of the Fourth Army* (London: Hodder and Stoughton, 1919), p. 101.

8. Monash, *The Australian Victories in France in 1918*, p. 202.

9. F.M. Cutlack, *The Australians: Their final campaign, 1918* (London: Sampson Low, Marston & Co. Ltd., 1918), p. 328.

10. Major General John F. O'Ryan, *The Story of the 27th Division* (New York: Wynkoop Hallenbeck Crawford Co., 1921), p. 340.

11. C.E.W. Bean, *Official History of Australia in the War of 1914-18* Vol. VI (Sydney: Angus and Robertson, 1942), p. 1095.

Suggested Further Reading

Bean, C.E.W., *Anzac to Amiens* (Penguin Books, 2014)

Beaumont, Joan, *Broken Years: Australians in the Great War* (Allen and Unwin, 2013)

Monash, John, *The Australian Victories in France in 1918* (Black Inc. (Schwartz Publishing), 2015)

Pederson, Peter, *The Anzacs: Gallipoli to the Western Front* (Penguin Books, 2010)

The Canadians *by* Tim Cook

'We absolutely fought him to a finish and beat him at every turn': The Canadian Corps and the Hundred Days Campaign.

Canada went to war on 4 August 1914 at Britain's side as a loyal Dominion and Prime Minister Sir Robert Borden promised a voluntary war effort. He would have to break his promise in mid-1917, which led to deep divisions across Canada, but some 620,000 Canadians enlisted or were conscripted during the war from a country of fewer than eight million. The Canadian Corps was the symbol of the country's war effort. By late 1917, the corps had fought through the battles of Second Ypres, Mount Sorrel, the Somme, Vimy, Hill 70, Passchendaele, and several minor engagements. Throughout this time, the Canadians had been ably supported by the British, who had provided experienced staff officers to guide the Canadians to maturity, as well as the first two corps commanders, E.A.H. Alderson and Julian Byng.[1] The appointment of Canadian-born militia officer Arthur Currie to command the corps in June 1917, when Byng, the current commander, was elevated to Third Army, was another symbol of the corps's evolution as an increasingly independent fighting unit.

Arthur Currie had proved himself in the war, showing a keen mind and an ability to learn from others. The 41-year-old did not look the part of a senior general, as he was overweight and without a moustache, but he was a methodical planner and not shy about demanding more resources from his superiors.[2] He could be stubborn and even spiteful, but he had tremendous personal courage, and he often spoke his mind to those in more senior positions.

In the aftermath of the grim Passchendaele campaign, with its roughly 16,000 Canadian causalities, the corps limped back to Vimy Ridge.[3] There was a manpower crisis throughout the BEF. The battlefield losses of 1917 were difficult to replace and British divisions were forced to reorganize, with the War Office taking the severe step of reducing the number of battalions in a division from twelve to nine to create new, albeit weaker formations.[4] This desperate measure cut the fighting units of the infantry divisions by a quarter, while also ripping battalions from their home divisions and placing them in other formations.

BEF High Command pressured Currie to follow suit: by reducing the four Canadian divisions' battalions from twelve to nine, they would create two new divisions. To placate Currie, it was hinted that he might be given command of the six-division, two-corps Canadian army.[5] This would make Currie the only Dominion army commander, but he surprised his superiors by refusing to accept the reorganization. Even with pressure from officers in his corps and in the United Kingdom who were aching for promotion, Currie knew that diluting his divisions would provide no additional fighting effectiveness. He had honed the combat strength of his formations and by early 1918 it was an effective machine of war. The semi-permanent structure of the corps, whereby its four divisions usually fought together, allowed for the easier transmission of lessons and the grouping of support units, especially artillery and machine guns.[6] 'While technically an Army Corps of the British Army,' wrote Currie of the Canadian Corps, it 'differed from other Army Corps in that it was an integral tactical unit, moving and fighting as a whole, retaining the same Canadian troops though British Divisions and troops were often attached to it'.[7]

Canada had also recently passed through the bruising conscription crisis over the summer of 1917 which had led to much vitriol and venom at home. Conscription had been passed and confirmed in the December 1917 election, but the 100,000 conscripts in the first call-up would take time to be trained and deployed.[8] Six weaker divisions would be put into the line more frequently and suffer more from the regular wastage of trench warfare. In the end, Currie's principled stand allowed his four infantry divisions to retain their twelve battalions and he even broke up the 5th Canadian Division in England, freeing up thousands of trained soldiers to bring the corps's infantry units up to full strength.[9] While Currie's stand was neither popular from within the High Command nor among many Canadians in England, he had ensured that the Canadian Corps' fighting units were up to strength for the final year of the war, and furthermore he added more trucks, increased engineering units, and more mortar teams to provide added combat power.[10]

Amiens Preparation

The Allied forces withstood the German onslaught from March to July 1918, and even counter-attacked at the Second Battle of the Marne in July 1918. That battle, with French and American troops delivering a severe blow, revealed that the Germans, who had lost some 800,000 soldiers in their multiple offensives since March, were worn down and unable to absorb heavy punishment.[11] The new Allied supreme commander, the French General Ferdinand Foch, ordered the Commander-in-Chief BEF, Sir Douglas Haig, to strike east of Amiens. The Canadian and Australian Corps would form the spearhead of the BEF's Fourth Army's assault.

In a logistical marvel, the 100,000-strong Canadian Corps arrived at the Amiens battlefield in time for the offensive on 8 August.[12] 'You had the feeling that everything was well planned, well organized,' recalled infantryman G.S. Rutherford.[13] A strategic deception plan also threw off the enemy, as a number of Canadian signals' units were sent north to the Ypres front, where they engaged in deliberately sloppy work so that the corps was identified there. The Germans had long regarded the Canadians as an attack formation and sign of them at the front was often an indication of the approach of an offensive. Posted into each Canadian soldier's paybook was an emphatic message: 'Keep Your Mouth Shut.'[14]

The German divisions opposite Fourth Army were weak and exhausted. Influenza and curtailed rations had damaged morale, as did the withering effects of the failed offensives earlier in the year and the ongoing naval blockade that was choking off food and supplies to German civilians at home. The trench system to the east of Amiens was poorly constructed and not prepared in depth, although there were hundreds of machine-guns along the front.

The successful Canadian way of battle, honed after years of hard lessons, was the combination of artillery and infantry. While the assembled 646 artillery pieces would hammer the enemy trenches and locationally-identified batteries behind the lines, this Battle of Amiens would also see the unleashing of a massed tank attack. To date, the Canadians had little experience with tanks, fighting with only a handful on the Somme on 15 September 1916, and then with eight more at Vimy, almost all of which broke down in the boggy, cratered terrain. While the Canadians had engaged in some tank-infantry combined-arms tactics over the previous two months, the 168 tanks attached to Currie's corps were not easy to incorporate into the Canadian attack doctrine.[15]

The Battle of Amiens

The silence was broken at 4.20 am as the Allied artillery opened fire. The German defenders were caught unprepared and their weak defences did little to hold up the surging British, French, Australian, and Canadian troops. Along the Canadian front, three assault divisions got away rapidly, encountering little immediate resistance as the infantry followed their rapid-moving creeping barrage. A heavy fog also obscured much of the front, which aided the attackers, who followed the explosions of their barrage, while the surviving defenders strained their eyes into the murk.

The tank charge shocked the enemy, but the Germans had effective anti-tank defences, doctrine and weapons. Mortars and field guns were used in a direct-fire role and brave teams of German defenders stopped many of the Mark V tanks and the faster and smaller Whippets. The tanks were nonetheless much appreciated by the infantry, with the official reports highlighting their work in turning the tide of battle in many places.[16] The enemy's porous front-line trench system was rapidly overrun, but after a few kilometres, increased enemy shell and mortar fire began to fall among the Canadians. The machine-gun nests of MG 08/15s which anchored the front were particularly lethal, and each had to be knocked out by Canadian platoons using in fire and movement tactics.[17] The fighting became more intense and Canadian losses mounted, especially as the infantry outdistanced the protective artillery barrage. Nonetheless, the assault on the 8th, which lasted for much of the day, saw the Canadians advance an astonishing 13 kilometres. The Germans had been rocked. But the challenge for the Allies was mounting another set-piece battle the next day, in order to transform the break-in to a break-through.

By the early hours of the 9th, the Canadian infantry were spread over the battlefield, artillery was in the process of moving forward, and communication from front to rear was sporadic. Everywhere behind the lines there was activity. Amid this chaos, the attack on the morning of the 9th was slow in forming and most Canadian units did not begin advancing until late in the morning. It was immediately clear that the Germans had recovered and were making a concentrated stand. Surprise was lost. Machine guns continued to plague the Canadians, and there were far fewer tanks running on the 9th. Units like the 29th Battalion reported destroying and capturing over forty Maxim heavy machine guns, almost all of them in fierce infantry-led battles.[18] Currie's soldiers snatched another six kilometres from the enemy on the 9th, but suffered 2,574 casualties, adding to the 3,800 casualties on the first day.[19] Private A.E. Smith of 116th Battalion offered a soldiers' view of the battle: 'The whole thing gave one the impression that a chunk of hell had broken loose.'[20]

Intense combat raged for several more days with less ground gained and fewer prisoners captured. By 13 August, Currie and the Australian Corps commander, John Monash, appealed to Army commander Sir Henry Rawlinson to call off the operation.[21] More fighting would only lead to greater losses. Rawlinson convinced Haig of this and Haig stood up to Foch's bullying to keep driving forward no matter the cost.

Amiens proved that a surprise operation launched with aggressive troops employing sophisticated all-arms tactics could rupture the enemy lines. However, the challenge of achieving and developing open warfare was not easily overcome, and organizing a second phase to a set-piece battle eluded the Allies. The victory was nonetheless significant. On the Canadian front alone, the corps's four divisions met and defeated elements of fourteen German divisions, capturing 9,311 prisoners, 201 guns, 152 trench mortars, and 755 machine-guns.[22] There were no easy victories and the Canadian Corps, a little over 102,000-strong, suffered 11,822 casualties, with most of these losses falling on the infantry.[23] The Germans were demoralized from the blow, with the Kaiser remarking with melancholy realism that 'The war could no longer be won.'[24]

Arras

The shattered Canadian battalions were soon restored to almost full strength. The conscripts from Canada were now trained and ready for battle, along with other soldiers culled from non-combat units.[25] The Canadian Corps moved to the Arras front, east of Vimy Ridge, to spearhead Sir Henry Horne's First Army. The Hindenburg Line to the east of Arras was an enemy fortress consisting of multiple trench lines, in all some 30 kilometres deep. The defence in depth was based on isolated strongpoints anchored on concrete pillboxes, reverse slope positions, and deep rows of barbed wire. The most formidable trench of many was the Drocourt-Quéant Line and further to the east was the unfinished Canal du Nord which incorporated marshland and numerous trench systems into its defences. Beyond that was a series of trenches, all of which protected Cambrai, a key logistical hub.

Currie was ably supported by Horne. The two were very different in nature and experience, but they had a strong relationship, with Horne giving Currie wide leeway to plan his operations. Their staffs also worked well together and they had fought and won operations at Hill 70 in 1917. Because of the depth of the German defences, Currie ordered a two-division attack for 26 August, with rotating infantry brigades from each the 2nd and 3rd Division bearing the brunt of the fighting for three days. If the Canadians were not to have broken through at that point, two fresh divisions would rotate into the line for a final push on the Drocourt-Quéant Line. The Arras front was not suitable for armour, and so this would be an infantry and artillery frontal assault, although there would be support from machine guns, mobile mortar teams, and from the air. Horne was able to marshal tremendous firepower for the Canadian Corps, which remained, in the words of one senior British staff officer, the 'backbone of the army'.[26]

The attack at 3.00 am on 26 August went in behind a barrage from 762 Allied guns. Canadian and British counter-battery fire was effective and heavy calibre guns smothered enemy batteries in high explosive, shrapnel and gas clouds. At zero hour, the Canadian infantry followed their creeping barrage through the enemy lines, breaking the outer crust defence, before engaging in tougher, small-unit actions. The Germans fought hard, often long after their positions were surrounded, especially if machine-gun teams survived to anchor the defence. Lieutenant Ivan Maharg of 1st Canadian Mounted Rifles, noted that: 'The Hun seemed to be depending upon the large number of his machine guns rather than his artillery to hold us back.'[27] There was no walkover as at Amiens. The fighting was nearly continuous for three days, with the Canadian units steadily worn down as they assaulted the Germans and withstood counter-attacks. The Canadians advanced a few kilometres through multiple trench systems, but at the cost of 6,000 casualties.[28]

Currie had pushed his soldiers hard – perhaps too hard, some of the 'poor bloody infantry' grumbled – and he paused on the 29th for several days to unleash a new set-piece operation against the Drocourt-Quéant Line. The tempo of battle and recovery was far faster now than in the previous years of fighting, and the artillery was in place and ready to shoot the Canadian infantry forward at 4.50 am on 2 September.[29] The Canadians slowly bashed through the enemy lines. The Germans launched a series of counter-attacks, but could not reverse the tide. Infantryman J.P. Van de Water wrote that: 'Fritz had his best troops against us and very strong positions . . . Our casualties were very heavy and some of the best have gone, but we absolutely fought him to a finish and beat him at every turn.'[30]

The day ended in mass German surrenders and a withdrawal along the line. During the Arras battle, elements of at least seven German divisions had been met and defeated, with 10,492 prisoners captured. Attesting to the German machine-gun defence, 927 were captured on the Canadian front[31] but 12,000 Canadians had been killed or wounded, almost all from sharp-end units.

Canal du Nord

The Canadian Corps had inflicted significant defeats on the enemy at Amiens and Arras, but had suffered more than 25,000 casualties.[32] Despite these losses, the Canadians continued to reinforce their formations from conscripts and men training in England, and most infantry battalions – those hardest hit in combat – were up to about 900 strong by the end of September.[33] However, the edge of the blade was dulling from over-use and there was open anger in the ranks as it appeared that the Canadian Crops would not be pulled from the line. War-weariness was becoming a problem and the 'poor bloody infantry' felt they had been pushed too hard for too long.[34]

The breaking of the Drocourt-Quéant Line forced the enemy to retreat to the Canal du Nord, which formed a powerful barrier behind which a series of deep trench systems protected Cambrai. This was the last significant line of defence for the Germans and it was to be held at all costs.[35] Currie studied the battlefield and did not like it. Much of the terrain on the Canadian front was boggy marshland. Intelligence patrols and air reconnaissance photographs indicated a dry gap of about 2,600 yards, but that was a very narrow space through which to send his 100,000-strong corps. Eight German divisions held the front, echeloned in strength.[36] But Currie had faith that his infantry, supported by the gunners and engineers, could breach the position, cross the 40-foot canal, and fan out on the eastern side before the Germans could respond with fire or reinforcements. It would be exceedingly dangerous and Horne intervened with Currie to warn him off. Currie listened but refused to change his plan.

After two weeks of intense planning and preparatory artillery bombardment, the 1st and 4th Divisions attacked at 5.20 am on 27 September, behind a creeping barrage supplied by 785 guns. German strongpoints and gun batteries were saturated with shrapnel, high explosive and gas, and the Canadians drove forward throughout the day, overcoming areas of resistance or bypassing strongpoints to allow follow-up forces to snuff them out. It was a fast-paced drive and Bourlon Wood, a key feature in the enemy defences, fell by the end of the day.

The Germans responded to the assault, rushing forward reinforcements from six divisions and thirteen machine-gun companies.[37] Battles on the 28th, 29th, and 30th, witnessed see-saw engagements. Currie wrote that the combat to the east of the canal was 'the bitterest fighting we have ever experienced . . . It was attack and counterattack'.[38] The carefully-planned set-piece battle on the first day of the assault broke down rapidly, with infantry battalions and brigades struggling through the defensive grid, often with haphazard communication to the rear and with only sporadic artillery support. George Bell of the 58th Battalion wrote that the intense fighting often degenerated into a series of 'frontal attacks. We were really butchered.'[39]

There was little time to plan and all operations were rushed. From the 29th, two fresh divisions, the 3rd Canadian and 11th British Division, were fed into the line to provide a new push for the tired units still at the sharp end. However, the battle broke down into dozens of daily skirmishes that were ultimately won at the platoon and section level where infantrymen displayed remarkable skill, grit and courage. Cambrai finally fell on 8 October and fighting eased off. The German Army's vaunted Hindenburg Line had been broken on the Canadian front, and along other parts of the line. The Kaiser's armies were battered into retreat.

Final Push

The Canadians had suffered over 42,000 casualties since Amiens. While there was pride in the Canadian battlefield triumphs, the soldiers groused that the victory cost too much. Much of the anger was directed towards Currie. The general was accused of raising his own reputation by sacrificing his soldiers. It was an unfair charge. Currie had always tried to ration lives in combat by preparing thoroughly for battles and using shells instead of flesh, but even successful battles on the Western Front came with a crippling cost in lives.[40]

The Canadians chased the retreating German forces throughout October, engaging in many small unit actions, usually against sacrificial rearguard formations. The liberation of dozens of French towns, where the cruelty of the German occupation was revealed, further hardened attitudes among the front-line soldiers. There were documented cases of German soldiers attempting to surrender being 'executed', especially during the final set-piece battle of the war at Valenciennes from 30 October to 2 November.[41] The capture of the symbolic city of Mons on 11 November 1918, the place from where the BEF began its retreat in 1914, was the capstone of the Canadians' victorious battles of the Hundred Days campaign.

During the campaign, the four Canadian divisions met and defeated elements of fifty German divisions, a truly remarkable number even if these divisions were severely understrength. Currie crowed, 'No force of equal size ever accomplished so much in a similar space of time during the war.'[42] However, they paid for their success with more than 45,835 casualties, an eighth of the total losses for the entire BEF, which stood at 379,000.[43] It is small wonder that Gunner Walter S. Woods wrote of the Armistice: 'Instead of feeling full of joy that we had won the "war to end all wars," I was consumed with a sickness of the soul.'[44]

Notes

1. On staff officers, see Douglas E. Delaney, 'Mentoring the Canadian Corps: Imperial Officers and the Canadian Expeditionary Force, 1914–1918', *The Journal of Military History* 77.3 (July 2013), pp. 931–53; on Alderson, see Andrew Iarocci, *Shoestring Soldiers: The 1st Canadian Division at War, 1914-1915* (Toronto: University of Toronto Press, 2008); on Byng, see Jeffrey Williams, *Byng of Vimy: General and Governor General* (London: Leo Cooper, 1983).

2. There are four biographies of Currie: D.G. Dancocks, *Sir Arthur Currie: A Biography* (Toronto: Methuen, 1985); A.M.J. Hyatt, *General Sir Arthur Currie: A Military Biography* (Toronto: University of Toronto Press, 1987); H.M. Urquhart, *Arthur Currie: The Biography of a Great Canadian* (Toronto: Dent, 1950); Tim Cook, *The Madman and the Butcher: The Sensational Wars of Sam Hughes and General Arthur Currie* (Toronto: Allen Lane, 2010).

3. Daniel Dancocks, *Legacy of Valour: The Canadians at Passchendaele* (Edmonton: Hurtig, 1986).

4. Chris McCarthy, 'Queen of the Battlefield: The Development of Command Organisation and Tactics in the British Infantry Battalion during the Great War', in Gary Sheffield and Dan Todman (eds), *Command and Control on the Western Front: The British Army's Experience 1914-1918* (Staplehurst: Spellmount, 2002), p. 185.

5. Desmond Morton, *A Peculiar Kind of Politics: Canada's Overseas Ministry in the First World War* (University of Toronto Press, 1992), pp. 152–7.

6. For the corps, see Tim Cook, *At the Sharp End: Canadians Fighting the Great War, 1914–1916, volume I* (Toronto: Penguin, 2007) and *Shock Troops: Canadians Fighting the Great War, 1917–1918, volume II* (Toronto: Penguin 2008).

7. Library and Archives Canada (LAC), Sir Arthur Currie papers (CP), MG 30 E100, v. 10, file 29, undated note in file.

8. On manpower, see J.L. Granatstein and J.M. Hitsman, *Broken Promises: A History of Conscription in Canada* (Toronto: Oxford University Press, 1977); Richard Holt, *Filling the Ranks: Manpower in the Canadian Expeditionary Force, 1914-1918* (Montreal: McGill-Queen's University Press, 2017); William F. Stewart, *The Embattled General: Sir Richard Turner and the First Word War* (Montreal: McGill-Queen's Press, 2015).

9. William Stewart, 'Frustrated Belligerence: The Unhappy History of the 5th Canadian Division in the First World War', *Canadian Military History* 22.2 (2013); Patrick Dennis, 'A Canadian Conscript Goes to War—August 1918: Old Myths Re-examined', *Canadian Military History* 18.1 (2009).

10. See Urquhart, *Arthur Currie*, pp. 195–203; Shane Schreiber, *Shock Army of the British Empire: The Canadian Corps in the Last 100 Days of the Great War* (Westport, Conn: Praeger, 1997), pp. 20–2; Kenneth Radley, *We Lead, Others Follow: First Canadian Division 1914-1918* (St. Catherines: Vanwell, 2006), p. 115.

11. Martin Kitchen, *The German Offensives of 1918* (Stroud: Tempus, 2005); James McRandle and James Quirk, 'The Blood Test Revisited: A New Look at German Casualty Counts in World War I', *Journal of Military History* 70 (July 2006), p. 686; LAC, RG 9, v. 4032, 1/11, Change in the Discipline and Moral of the German Army.

12. On logistics, see Neal Porter, 'From Logistics to Open Warfare: The State of Logistics in the Canadian Corps, August to November 1918' (MA Thesis: University of Ottawa, 2002).

13. CWM, Military History Research Centre, CBC Radio Flanders Fields transcripts, episode 14, 5.

14. G.W.L. Nicholson, *Canadian Expeditionary Force, 1914-1919: Official History of the Canadian Army in the First World War* (Ottawa: Queen's Printer and Controller of Stationery, 1962), p. 389.

15. Andrew McEwen, '"A useful accessory to the infantry, but nothing more": Tanks at the Battle of Flers–Courcelette, September 1916', *Canadian Military History* 20.4 (2011); Dean Chappelle, 'The Canadian Attack at Amiens, 8-11 August 1918', *Canadian Military History* 2.2 (1993).

16. See for example, LAC, Online digitized War Diary (WD), 19th Battalion, Report of Capture of Marcelcave, 8 August 1918; F.W. Noyes, *Stretcher Bearers at the Double* (Toronto: Hunter Rose Company, 1937), pp. 213–14; Canadian War Museum (CWM), Sir Arthur Currie papers, 58A 1.60.3, Extract from G.H.Q. Summary of Information, 26 August 1918.

17. LAC, Records of the Department of Militia and Defence (RG 9), III, v. 4810, file Medical Arrangements, Records of Canadian Medical Services During Last Hundred Days; RG 9, v. 3893, Medical Arrangements during the Second Battle of Amiens, August 8th to 20th, 4.

18. LAC, War Diary online, 29th Battalion, Narrative of Operations for 8-9 August 1918; H.R.N. Clyne, M.C., *Vancouver's 29th* (Vancouver: Tobin's Tigers Association, 1964), p. 63; LAC, War Diary online, 5th Brigade, Narrative of Operations, 8th, 9th, 10th August 1918.

19. Nicholson, *Canadian Expeditionary Force*, p. 414.

20. Percy Climo (ed), *Let Us Remember: Lively Letters from World War One* (Colborne: P.L. Climo, 1990), p. 285.

21. McGill University Archives, H.M Urquhart papers, 4027, box 1, file 12, T. Stewart Lyon to Urquhart, 15 August 1934; for the letter, see RG 9, v. 3854, 73/5, Currie to Rawlinson, 13 August 1918.

22. LAC, Records of the Department of National Defence (RG 24), v. 1844, 11-5, Amiens; on prisoners, see Canadian War Museum, Sir Arthur Currie papers, 58A 1 60.3, Special Order [by Currie], 12 August 1918.

23. LAC, RG 24, v. 1844, 11-5, Amiens.

24. Daniel Dancocks, *Spearhead to Victory: Canada and the Great War* (Edmonton: Hurtig, 1987), p. 59.

25. On manpower, see Richard Holt, *Filling the Ranks: Manpower in the Canadian Expeditionary Force, 1914–1918* (Montreal: McGill-Queen's University Press, 2017).

26. Hastings Anderson, 'Lord Horne as an Army Commander', *Journal of the Royal Artillery* LVI.4 (January 1930), pp. 416–17.

27. J.L. Granatstein, *The Greatest Victory: Canada's One Hundred Days, 1918* (Toronto: Oxford University Press, 2014), p. 95.

28. Nicholson, *Canadian Expeditionary Force*, p. 432.

29. G.W.L. Nicholson, *The Gunners of Canada: The History of the Royal Regiment of Canadian Artillery, Volume I* (Toronto: McClelland and Stewart, 1967), pp. 352, 355.

30. Canadian Bank of Commerce, *Letters from the Front: Being a record of the part played by officers of the Bank in the Great War, 1914-1919* (Toronto: Southam Press, 1920), p. 298.

31. LAC, Sir Arthur Currie papers, v.2, file M-R, Currie to Morrison, 11 September 1918; LAC, WD online, 4th Division, Report on the Scarpe Operations.

32. Dancocks, *Spearhead*, p. 119.

33. CWM, Sir Arthur Currie papers, 58A 60.4, 1st Division Report of Operations, [Canal du Nord operation], Strength Return.

34. See Jordan Chase, 'Unwilling to Continue, Ordered to Advance: An Examination of the Contributing Factors Toward, and Manifestation of, War Weariness in the Canadian Corps during the Hundred Days Campaign of the First World War' (MA Thesis: University of Calgary, 2013).

35. Sir James Edmonds, *Military Operations France and Belgium 1918*, Vol. IV, p. 312.

36. For enemy defences, see Major General Sir W. Hastings Anderson, 'The Crossing of the Canal du Nord', *Canadian Defence Quarterly* 2.1 (October 1924), p. 65.

37. Overseas Military Forces of Canada, *Report of the Ministry, Overseas Military Forces of Canada, 1918* (London, 1919) p, 162.

38. LAC, Sir Arthur Currie papers, v.1, file A to F, Currie to Borden, 26 November 1918.

39. LAC, Records of the Canadian Broadcasting Corporation (RG 41) B III 1, Volume 15, Interview with George Bell of the 58th Battalion, Interview 2 of 2, Page 4.

40. On the Currie rumours, see Tim Cook, 'Black-hearted Traitors, Crucified Martyrs, and the Leaning Virgin: The Role of Rumor and the Great War Canadian Soldier', in Michael Neiberg and Jennifer Keene (eds), *Finding Common Ground: New Directions in First World War Studies* (Leiden: Brill Academic Publishers, 2010), pp. 21–42; Tim Cook, *The Madman and the Butcher: The Sensational Wars of Sam Hughes and General Arthur Currie* (Toronto: Allan Lane, 2010).

41. Granatstein, *The Greatest Victory*, p. 152; Tim Cook, 'The Politics of Surrender: Canadian Soldiers and the Killing of Prisoners in the Great War', *Journal of Military History* 70.3 (July 2006), pp. 637–65.

42. Dancocks, *Sir Arthur Currie*, p. 174.

43. LAC, RG 24, v. 1844, file 11-5, Casualties, [Hundred Days]; Peter Simkins, 'Building Blocks: Aspects of Command and Control at Brigade Level in the BEF's Offensive Operations, 1916-1918', in Gary Sheffield and Dan Todman (eds), *Command and Control on the Western Front: The British Army's Experience, 1914-1918* (Staplehurst: Spellmount, 2004), p. 165.

44. Walter S. Woods, *The Men Who Came Back: A Book of Memories* (Toronto: Ryerson Press, 1956), p. 57.

Suggested Further Reading

Chase, Jordan, 'Unwilling to Continue, Ordered to Advance: An Examination of the Contributing Factors Toward, and Manifestation of, War Weariness in the Canadian Corps during the Hundred Days Campaign of the First World War' (MA Thesis: University of Calgary, 2013)

Cook, Tim, *At the Sharp End: Canadians Fighting the Great War, 1914–1916, volume I* (Toronto: Penguin, 2007)

Cook, Tim, *Shock Troops: Canadians Fighting the Great War, 1917–1918, volume II* (Toronto: Penguin, 2008)

Cook, Tim, *The Madman and the Butcher: The Sensational Wars of Sam Hughes and General Arthur Currie* (Toronto: Allen Lane, 2010)

Dancocks, Daniel, *Spearhead to Victory: Canada and the Great War* (Edmonton: Hurtig, 1987)

Granatstein, J.L., *The Greatest Victory: Canada's One Hundred Days, 1918* (Toronto: Oxford University Press, 2014)

Holt, Richard, *Filling the Ranks: Manpower in the Canadian Expeditionary Force, 1914-1918* (Montreal: McGill-Queen's University Press, 2017)

Humphries, M.O. (ed.), *The Selected Papers of Sir Arthur Currie: Diaries, Letters, and Report to the Ministry, 1917-1933* (Waterloo: LCMSDS Press of Wilfrid Laurier University, 2008)

Nicholson, G.W.L., *Canadian Expeditionary Force, 1914-1919: Official History of the Canadian Army in the First World War* (Ottawa: Queen's Printer and Controller of Stationery, 1962)

Porter, Neal, 'From Logistics to Open Warfare: The State of Logistics in the Canadian Corps, August to November 1918' (MA Thesis: University of Ottawa, 2002)

Schreiber, Shane, *Shock Army of the British Empire: The Canadian Corps in the Last 100 Days of the Great War* (Westport, Conn: Praeger, 1997)

Urquhart, H.M., *Arthur Currie: The Biography of a Great Canadian* (Toronto: Dent, 1950)

New Zealand in the Great War *by* Christopher Pugsley

At 3.00 pm on the afternoon of 5 August 1914, in the forecourt of the Parliamentary buildings in Wellington, the Governor, the Earl of Liverpool, announced Britain's declaration of war on Germany. New Zealand found itself at war. Britain had spoken for us and that was enough. There was a general belief that German aggression had to be met and that this was as much New Zealand's war as Great Britain's.[1]

Commitment to Imperial Defence was a role for which New Zealand had prepared. This was initiated by the 1909 Defence Act and further refined after Field Marshal Lord Kitchener's visit in 1910. The Territorial Force was established and sustained by peacetime conscription. Its role was to defend New Zealand but the commitment of an Expeditionary Force to assist the Empire was always part of the planning. Major General A.J. Godley, a British officer, was an adept organiser and administrator. He imported British officers on secondment, many with links to New Zealand, and set out to raise a Territorial Force which would be fully effective by 1916. It was anticipated that a quarter of this force would be committed as volunteers to an Expeditionary role. It was also envisaged that there would be a joint Australian and New Zealand commitment as New Zealand alone could not raise the numbers needed to sustain a divisional organisation.[2]

War saw New Zealand working to script and committing a 1,400-strong Advance Party of the New Zealand Expeditionary Force (NZEF) to seize German Samoa, which was occupied on 29 August 1914.[3] The 8,400-strong Main Body NZEF mobilised concurrently.

Forging a National Army for Overseas Service
New Zealand's first crisis of the war was over the sailing of the Main Body convoy in August 1914. Lord Liverpool pressured the Prime Minister, William Massey, to accept British Admiralty advice and sail despite the possible presence of the German East Asiatic Squadron. Massey threatened to resign over the issue. War is a political act and the New Zealand government was suddenly conscious that imperial advice had to be weighed against national interests and the sailings were delayed until naval escorts arrived.[4]

This was the first of a series of issues which forced a growing political awareness that imperial decisions had to be tempered by national realities, particularly as Massey's government had a knife-edge majority in Parliament. Questions of national command over the administration and chains of communication between the government and the NZEF featured in the deployment of the Main Body, its sailing to Egypt and the formation of a combined New Zealand and Australian (NZ & A) Division, under Godley's command, as part of the Australian and New Zealand Army Corps (ANZAC) under the command of Lieutenant General Sir William Birdwood.

Godley used his time in Egypt to whip his division into shape with hard training and strict discipline.[5] As Commander NZEF, he was in a unique situation with his responsibilities to Birdwood for the training, discipline and administration of his division and answerable to his government for its administration. It was a learning process for both Godley and for James Allen, the Minister of Defence. Allen wanted all communications and requests on issues relating to NZEF reinforcements and equipment to be channelled through the War Office. This did not allow for the inevitable questions and complaints raised by soldiers in letters home and for public concerns for 'their boys in Egypt'. By trial and error an umbilical cord was forged between Godley and his government on matters of national administration such as welfare, reinforcements, pay, hospitalisation and mail.

Gallipoli 1915

By late March 1915 Godley's New Zealanders were itching for action. Godley believed they were ready. This came with the landings on the Gallipoli Peninsula on 25 April 1915. Godley's NZ & A Division landed with its two infantry brigades with the New Zealand Mounted Rifles Brigade and the Australian Light Horse remaining in Egypt. The initial landings were carried out before dawn by the 1st Australian Division, followed by the New Zealand Infantry Brigade from 10.00 am onwards at what became known as Anzac Cove.

Australian tactical decisions saw the New Zealanders thrown in to support the northern flank in fierce fighting for Baby 700 at the junction of the first and second ridges which became the Anzac front line for the next eight months. The Anzacs hung on by their fingernails. It became trench warfare at close quarters with the nearest opposing trenches sometimes less than five metres apart. Short of artillery ammunition, defence stores and supplies, Gallipoli was a poor man's war waged by the richest empire on earth. Within a fortnight the New Zealand Infantry Brigade was reduced to less than half-strength with some of its battalions no longer combat effective. The New Zealand Mounted Rifles deployed, along with the Australian Light Horse, in an infantry role and held the northern perimeter at Anzac. In July, they were joined by the 500-strong Maori Contingent which was the first Maori unit to see operational service overseas.[6] A lack of water, fresh food, medical supplies, poor sanitation and the massed dead in No Man's Land, saw sickness rates soar in the summer heat.

The chaos of the landings meant long delays in casualty reporting. This caused enormous disquiet in New Zealand and a growing belief that the government was deliberating holding back casualty details. In fact the issue was beyond the government's control, but it became a factor in the formation of a National Government in August 1915 with Massey and Sir Joseph Ward of the Liberal Party, effectively co-leaders, despite their strong dislike for each other.[7]

The climax of the campaign was the August 1915 offensive. The New Zealand Mounted Rifles Brigade seized the foothills overlooking a new landing at Suvla Bay and the New Zealand Infantry Brigade formed the Right Assaulting Column in the attack on the high ground of Chunuk Bair which, though taken, was lost in the Turkish counter-attack of 10 August. Brigadier General A.H. Russell stood out in his command of the Mounted Rifles Brigade. Lieutenant-Colonel W.G. Malone, commanding the Wellington Infantry Battalion, had distinguished himself at Quinn's Post before being killed on Chunuk Bair. He and LieutenantColonel W Meldrum of the Wellington Mounted Rifles stood out in the fighting for Chunuk Bair on 8–9 August 1915. The struggle in August, including the attacks on Hill 60, destroyed the combat effectiveness of the NZEF. The scale of the casualties impacted on every New Zealand community.[8]

The Gallipoli Campaign was voracious in its demand for men. Some 17,000 New Zealanders landed on the Peninsula to support an 8,400-strong NZEF that was reduced to some 1,000 all ranks after the August offensive. Even with reinforcements it was only at half-strength at the evacuation in December 1915. It put the Territorial-based volunteer reinforcement system under strain with provinces such as Otago and Southland unable to meet the manpower demands to keep their regimental quotas up to strength. With something over 17,000 men overseas and 8,000 in training, New Zealand geared itself for a long war with the passage of the National Registration Bill imposing a census on all males between the ages of 20 and 40 years. It was a national stocktaking of manpower properly to assess New Zealand's capacity to send men to war while still maintaining essential national industries. By the year's end, the Trentham Regiment, later the New Zealand Rifle Brigade (Earl of Liverpool's Own), 5,000-strong, was raised as the third infantry brigade to bring Godley's NZ & A Division up to the organizational strength of a standard British infantry division.

In January 1916, Massey's Manifesto to the New Zealand people stated that New Zealand's Gallipoli graves would be protected and he argued for the annexation of the Gallipoli Peninsula under Imperial control as part of the peace settlement. There was open criticism by the New Zealand government of the management of the Gallipoli Campaign. Sir Thomas Mackenzie, the New Zealand High Commissioner in London, a member of the Dardanelles Commission charged with responsibility for examining the causes of the campaign's ignominious failure, was dissatisfied with the Enquiry. He wrote a highly critical dissenting view as an addition to the Commission's final report. The Anzac Day commemoration on 25 April 1916 became the public expression of unforgotten grief and that inexplicable mix of dismay and pride which continues to be felt today at the cost of New Zealand's imperial service.[9]

New Zealand found itself mourning its casualties from Gallipoli but enjoying an economic boom brought on by the war and the British government's purchase of the entire output of wool, frozen meat and dairy produce. Labour was scarce and wages soared along with the cost of living, but for those not limited to fixed pensions, these were prosperous times with money in most people's pockets.

Formation of the New Zealand Division, 1916
Withdrawn to Egypt, the rapid expansion of the Australian Imperial Force (AIF) to five divisions saw the New Zealand Government reluctantly endorse the formation of a New Zealand Division of three infantry brigades, commanded by Major General Sir Andrew Russell, totalling some 20,000 men. It consisted of the original New Zealand Infantry Brigade, now titled 1st New Zealand Infantry Brigade, a newly-raised 2nd Brigade formed out of reinforcements and recovered convalescents, and the 3rd New Zealand Rifle Brigade.[10] A separate Headquarters, NZEF (Egypt), was established answerable to Godley. It was commanded by Brigadier General E.W.C. Chaytor who commanded the New Zealand Mounted Rifles Brigade which saw distinguished

service in Sinai and Palestine for the rest of the war. Chaytor would command the ANZAC Mounted Division in 1917 as part of Lieutenant General Harry Chauvel's Desert Mounted Corps.[11]

This demanded a manpower commitment far beyond what Allen, the Minister of Defence, had ever thought possible. Providing enough trained reinforcements for the duration of the war became his principal concern. New Zealand established two major training camps in Trentham and Featherston and by 1916 sent 2,000 reinforcements a month. The New Zealand Division's experience in France in 1916 and the losses on the Somme in September/October of that year confirmed this need. In November 1916, New Zealand became the first Dominion in the Empire to follow Britain's lead and introduce conscription for overseas service.[12] Two flying schools were also established, one in Christchurch and one, using flying boats, in Auckland to train pilots for the Royal Flying Corps and the Royal Naval Air Service.[13]

The 'Nursery Sector' of the Western Front

The New Zealand Division was shipped to France in April–May 1916, initially as part of Birdwood's I ANZAC Corps and then part of Godley's II ANZAC Corps. It deployed to the Armentières or 'nursery sector' where new divisions were introduced to trench warfare. It was a learning experience.[14] The approaching Somme offensive saw heightened activity. Intensive patrolling and trench raids tested inexperienced officers and men to their limits and beyond. Courts-martial and sickness rates soared as the inexperienced division grappled with the demands of the Western Front. New Zealand followed the Canadian Expeditionary Force's lead in the rigorous discipline it imposed. Twenty-seven soldiers were sentenced to death and five were to be executed, four after sentence by New Zealand courts-martial.[15]

The Battle of the Somme

After a month's training out of the line, the New Zealand Division became part of XV Corps for the renewed offensive on the Somme which opened on 15 September 1916. The New Zealand Division, attacking with four tanks in support, gained more ground than any other division on that day. It played a major part in suppressing German resistance in High Wood on its left flank and in regaining the village of Flers on its right. It was a day of hard fighting and heavy losses. The New Zealanders would remain in the line from 15 September until 2 October, a period of twenty-three days, the longest unbroken spell of any division in this battle. The Division suffered 7,959 casualties, 2,111 dead and some 5,848 wounded.[16]

Godley wrote to Allen and reported the praise the Division had received, 'and a thing with which they were all particularly pleased, was that the Division, though it was kept in the line longer than any other Division has been yet, made no bones about it and did not ask for relief. They also told me that a thing they liked very much was, that after they got their orders, nothing more was heard of them, till a report was sent that they had gained their objective.'[17] The New Zealanders also adopted the term 'Diggers' to identify themselves after the Somme. In 1917 the term spread to the Australian divisions. The Australian official war historian, C.E.W. Bean, acknowledged its New Zealand origins in his official history of the AIF in France.[18]

The transfer of the New Zealand Division to Europe saw the establishment of a Headquarters NZEF (UK), under the command of Brigadier General G.S. Richardson who commanded the various training camps and hospital establishments in the United Kingdom. Sling Camp at Bulford became the main New Zealand reinforcement depot with subsidiary camps for the New Zealand Rifle Brigade and various corps. During the Somme battles, 300 New Zealand wounded a week arrived in England so that by December 1916 there were 1,764 New Zealand patients in four New Zealand hospitals, 1,473 in the convalescent camp at Hornchurch and 3,449 in Codford Camp.[19]

By 1918 there were 6,495 NZEF hospital beds in the United Kingdom, each of the general hospitals, Walton-on-Thames and Brockenhurst, having over 1,500 beds with 1,000 at the Convalescent Hospital in Hornchurch. To cater for those permanently unfit awaiting evacuation back to New Zealand, a New Zealand Discharge Depot was opened at Torquay in May 1917. It became a centre for agricultural activity where men were rehabilitated with farming work on leased land. This also provided fresh food for the New Zealand camps.[20]

Conscription in New Zealand was introduced in November 1916. The public generally accepted this 'first gamble in human life'. Allen, under pressure from the War Office, raised a fourth infantry brigade from reinforcements and returning convalescents in the United Kingdom. Russell saw it as an unhappy addition to his division as it made his organisation the odd-one-out as the extra brigade was detached on labouring tasks that hindered its training.

Passchendaele

Early 1917 saw Russell prepare his division for the attack on Messines under II ANZAC in Plumer's Second Army. Russell demonstrated his tactical excellence in the planning and execution of his attack to secure Messines within the limits imposed by II ANZAC and Second Army. It demonstrated the division's growing professionalism.[21]

The opening of Haig's Third Battle of Ypres in the Flanders offensive saw the division involved in a series of minor attacks on La Basseville in what was an exceptionally wet August. It attacked on 4 October 1917 in the Battle of Broodseinde, which was the first time that both Birdwood's I ANZAC and Godley's II ANZAC attacked side by side. It was an outstanding success. There was a follow-up attack with the two British divisions of II ANZAC on 9 October which failed. The New Zealanders attacked in the first battle for Passchendaele on 12 October 1917 – New Zealand's blackest day of battle. It was a rushed attack without preparation on waterlogged ground with insufficient artillery support. Eight hundred and forty two New Zealanders died on 12 October 1917 with another 2,000 wounded or taken prisoner. The October battles cost 6,000 casualties, including at least 1,900 dead. This and the conditions faced when they wintered in the desolation of the Ypres Salient came close to breaking the spirit of the New Zealanders.[22]

1918

By March 1918, after a period in reserve, Russell's New Zealanders were at full strength and trained in open warfare tactics. On 23 March the division was rushed to the Somme to fill a dangerous gap between the British IV and V Corps. The ad hoc New Zealand formations held the German attacks in the critical days of late March and early April 1918. Then, as part of the British IV Corps, the Division held the line from April to August 1918.[23]

Between 21 August and 6 November 1918, the New Zealand Division spearheaded the advance on the IV Corps front. This climaxed with the outflanking and capture of the fortress town of Le Quesnoy on 4 November 1918. This was New Zealand's last offensive and they were withdrawn on 6 November 1918.

Circumstance determined that the New Zealand Division was treated more like a British division than any other Dominion division. It fought on the Somme in 1916 as part of XV Corps, fought throughout 1917 at Messines and in the October battles before Passchendaele as part of II ANZAC, and throughout 1918 as part of IV Corps. The cumulative cost of this for the NZEF since its arrival in France was 12,483 dead and 35,419 wounded; 47,902 out of the total of 59,483 casualties suffered by New Zealand in the First World War.

New Zealand in four years mobilised 124,211 volunteers and conscripts from an eligible male population of some 243,376 drawn from a population of 1,158,436 (based on 1914 estimates); 100,444 sailed overseas suffering 18,166 deaths and 41,317 wounded. The nation furthest removed from the centre of the fighting sent to war 9 per cent of its total population. This was 40 per ecnt of its eligible male population, suffering casualties amounting to 25 per cent of its eligible male population. Six out of every ten who sailed overseas became a battle casualty, thousands more were debilitated by sickness and disease.[24]

For many of the New Zealanders who were in France at the Armistice on 11 November 1918, soldiering in war was the only occupation they knew. Like everyone else, the New Zealanders were stunned by the rapid end to a campaign that was anticipated to go on into 1919. Three months as part of the Cologne garrison showed them the human face of the enemy they were fighting. There was a universal feeling of thankfulness for having survived and a great longing to see home. Massey proved an adept wartime Prime Minister whose ability to gauge the popular mood disturbed Lord Liverpool, his Governor–General. He was well served by Sir James Allen who, with Ward and Massey often overseas attending the Imperial War Cabinet in London, proved an effective acting prime minister and a very efficient Minister of Defence. Despite delays and frustrations, the demobilisation of the NZEF was complete by early 1920.[25]

New Zealand accepted the transfer of the Anzac area to the control of the Imperial War Graves Commission as an acceptable compromise to its demands for the annexation of the Gallipoli Peninsula by Britain. It also insisted on battlefield memorials to the New Zealand Division on all of the principal battlefields including Chunuk Bair on Gallipoli, which is the only national memorial other than Turkey's on the Peninsula. In the same way it insisted on New Zealand Memorials to the Missing on each of its battlefields in Turkey, France and Belgium. There are no New Zealand names on the Imperial monuments to the missing at Cape Helles, the Menin Gate at Ypres, or Thiepval on the Somme.

Notes

1. 'War Declared,' *Evening Post*, Wellington, 5 August 1914, p. 8.
2. Peter Cooke and John Crawford, *The Territorials: The History of the Territorial and Volunteer Forces of New Zealand* (Auckland: Random House, 2011), pp. 154–201. Christopher Pugsley, *The ANZAC Experience: New Zealand, Australia and Empire in the First World War* (Auckland: Oratia Books, 2016), pp. 51–63.
3. 'New Zealand's military role in Samoa,' Ian McGibbon (ed.), *The Oxford Companion to New Zealand Military History* (Auckland: OUP, 2000), pp. 475–7.

4. Gavin McLean, *The Governors: New Zealand's Governors and Governors-General* (Dunedin: Otago University Press, 2006), pp. 176–7.
5. Major Fred Waite, *The New Zealanders at Gallipoli* (Wellington: Whitcombe and Tombs, 1919), p. 31. Christopher Pugsley, *On the Fringe of Hell: New Zealanders and Military Discipline in the First World War* (Auckland: Hodder & Stoughton, 1991), pp. 15–33.
6. Christopher Pugsley, *Te Hokowhitu A Tu: The Maori Pioneer Battalion in the First World War* (Auckland, Libro Press, 2015), p. 36.
7. Ian McGibbon, *The Path to Gallipoli: Defending New Zealand 1840-1915* (Wellington: G P Books, 1991), pp. 194–209. Charles Ferrall and Harry Ricketts, *How We Remember: New Zealanders and the First World War* (Wellington: Victoria University Press, 2014).
8. Christopher Pugsley, *Gallipoli: The New Zealand Story* (Auckland: Oratia Books, 2016).
9. Steven Loveridge, *Call to Arms: New Zealand Society and Commitment to the Great War* (Wellington: Victoria University Press, 2014).
10. Ian McGibbon, *New Zealand's Western Front Campaign* (Auckland: Bateman, 2016), pp. 30–2.
11. Terry Kinlock, *Echoes of Gallipoli: in the words of New Zealand's Mounted Riflemen* (Auckland: Exisle, 2005). Terry Kinlock, *Devils on Horses: in the words of the Anzacs in the Middle East 1916-1919* (Auckland: Exisle, 2007).
12. Paul Baker, *King and Country Call* (Auckland University Press, 1988).
13. David Mulgan, *The Kiwi's First Wings: The Story of the Walsh Brothers and the New Zealand Flying School 1910-1924* (Wellington: Wingfield Press, 1960), pp. 28–32. Peter Aimer. 'Aviation', *Te Ara – the Encyclopedia of New Zealand*, updated 21-Sep-2007 URL: http://www.TeAra.govt.nz/EarthSeaAndSky/SeaAndAirTransport/Aviation/en. E.F. Harvie, *George Bolt: Pioneer Aviator: Foundations of a Future* (Wellington: A H & A W Reed, 1974), p. 61.
14. Andrew Macdonald, *On My Way to the Somme: New Zealanders and the bloody offensive of 1916* (Auckland: HarperCollins, 2005), pp. 35–41. McGibbon, *New Zealand's Western Front Campaign*, pp. 58–67. Colonel H. Stewart, *The New Zealand Division, 1916-1919* (Wellington: Whitcombe & Tombs, 1921), p. 58.
15. Pugsley, *On the Fringe of Hell*, pp. 350–1.
16. Macdonald, *On My Way to the Somme*, p. 269.
17. Godley to Allen, letter dated 15 October 1916, Godley Papers, WA1 252/3, Archives New Zealand.
18. C.E.W. Bean, *The Australian Imperial Force in France 1917* (ninth edition) (Sydney: Angus & Robertson, 1939), pp. 732–3.
19. A.D. Carbery, *The New Zealand Medical Services in the Great War* (Christchurch: Whitcombe & Tombs, 1924), pp. 264–5.
20. Lieutenant Colonel Myers, 'New Zealand Hospitals in the United Kingdom' in Lieutenant H.T.B. Drew (ed.), *The War Effort of New Zealand* (Auckland: Whitcombe & Tombs, 1923), pp. 115–26. Carbery, *The New Zealand Medical Services in the Great War 1914-1918*, pp. 274–6. John R. Pike, 'The New Zealand Discharge Depot in Torquay, 1917-1919', *The Volunteers: The Journal of the New Zealand Military Historical Society* 42:3 (March 2017), pp. 8–20.
21. Jock Vennell, *The Forgotten General: New Zealand's World War 1 Commander Major General Sir Andrew Russell* (Auckland: Allen & Unwin, 2011). Pugsley, *The ANZAC Experience*, pp. 204–44.
22. Glyn Harper, *Dark Journey: Three key New Zealand battles of the Western Front* (Auckland: HarperCollins, 2007). Andrew Macdonald, *Passchendaele: The Anatomy of a Tragedy* (Auckland: HarperCollins, 2013). McGibbon, *New Zealand's Western Front Campaign*, pp. 120–57.
23. Harper, *Dark Journey*: McGibbon, *New Zealand's Western Front Campaign*, pp. 298–359. Pugsley, *The ANZAC Experience*, pp. 278–99. Nathalie Philippe *et al* (eds), *The Great Adventure Ends: New Zealand and France on the Western Front* (Christchurch: John Douglas, 2013).
24. Lieutenant Colonel John Studholme, *NZEF, Record of Personal Services during the War* (Wellington: Government Printer, 1928), p. 18.
25. Barry O'Sullivan and Matthew O'Sullivan, *New Zealand Army: Personal Equipment 1910-1945* (Christchurch: Willson Scott, 2005), pp. 318–20.

Suggested Further Reading

Cooke, Peter, and Crawford, John, *The Territorials: The History of the Territorial and Volunteer Forces of New Zealand* (Auckland: Random House, 2011)

Crawford, John (ed.), *The Devil's Own War: The First World War Diary of Brigadier General Herbert Hart* (Auckland: Exisle, 2008)

Crawford, John (ed.), *No Better Death: The Great War Diaries and Letters of William G. Malone* (Auckland: Exisle, 2014)

Crawford, John, and McGibbon, Ian (eds), *New Zealand's Great War: New Zealand, the Allies and the First World War* (Auckland: Exisle, 2007)

Ferrall, Charles, and Ricketts, Harry (eds), *How We Remember: New Zealanders and the First World War* (Wellington, Victoria University Press, 2014)

Harper, Glyn, *Dark Journey: Three key New Zealand battles of the Western Front* (Auckland: HarperCollins, 2007)

Kinlock, Terry, *Devils on Horses: in the words of the Anzacs in the Middle East 1916-1919* (Auckland: Exisle, 2007)

Kinlock, Terry, *Echoes of Gallipoli: in the words of New Zealand's Mounted Riflemen* (Auckland: Exisle, 2005)

Loveridge, Stephen, *Call to Arms: New Zealand Society and Commitment to the Great War* (Wellington: Victoria University Press, 2014)

Macdonald, Andrew, *On My Way to the Somme: New Zealanders and the bloody offensive of 1916* (Auckland: HarperCollins, 2005)

Macdonald, Andrew, *Passchendaele: The Anatomy of a Tragedy* (Auckland: HarperCollins, 2013)

McGibbon, Ian, *New Zealand's Western Front Campaign* (Auckland: Bateman, 2016)

McGibbon, Ian, *The Path to Gallipoli: Defending New Zealand 1840-1915* (Wellington: G P Books, 1991)

McGibbon, Ian (ed.), *The Oxford Companion to New Zealand Military History* (Auckland: OUP, 2000)

Chapter 8

Sideshows to Strategic Victory: Defeating Germany, Bulgaria and the Ottoman Empire in South East Europe, Asia and Africa in 1918

By Robert Johnson

Sir William Robertson, the forthright Chief of the Imperial General Staff (CIGS), had spent a great deal of his time trying to persuade the British government that the centre of gravity of the entire war was Germany, not the 'sideshows' of Africa, the Middle East or the Balkans. It was on the Western Front, he argued, that the war would be won or lost. Jealously protecting the resources of manpower and munitions for this theatre of operations, he would not permit his political masters to pursue an 'Eastern Strategy' which had ended in the disastrous Dardanelles and Gallipoli operations of 1915. His former ally and subsequent rival, Prime Minister David Lloyd George, believed that Robertson and his protégé in France, General Sir Douglas Haig, had wasted the lives of thousands of men in fruitless offensives on the Western Front. The future lay not in the wastes of Flanders, he reasoned, but in the potential of the British Empire. In his typical and impassioned way, he delivered his verdict with all the mastery and eloquence he could muster:

> The British Empire owes a great deal to 'side-shows'. During the Seven Years' War, which was also a great European War—for practically all the nations now engaged . . . were then interlocked in a great struggle—The events which are best remembered by every Englishman are not the great battles on the Continent of Europe, but Plassey and the Heights of Abraham; and I have no doubt that, when the history of 1917 comes to be written, and comes to be read ages hence, these events in Mesopotamia and Palestine will hold a much more conspicuous place in the minds and memories of the people than many an event which looms much larger for the moment in our sight.[1]

The dichotomy of views was not always so clear cut. There were times when Robertson would relent to permit limited operations in the Middle East, but this could only be done, he maintained, if it were not to interfere with the main effort in France. He gave General Stanley Maude the opportunity to advance in Mesopotamia in December 1916, and he had encouraged the diligent if rather slow-moving Sir Archibald Murray to be audacious in attacking and exploiting the Ottoman forces in Palestine in the spring of 1917. For his part, Lloyd George understood that only close co-operation with the French offered any hope of making progress in Western Europe, and he sanctioned support for the Italians, after their decisive defeat at Caporetto in 1917, in order to counterbalance the threat to the Western Front.

The Allies understood the depth of the problems they faced in early 1917. The first attempts at co-ordinated offensives in 1916, agreed at the Chantilly conferences in 1915, had produced some positive effects. The Russian Brusilov offensive in Galicia had achieved some astonishing early successes, but was ultimately halted. The Anglo-French pressure on the Somme had at least brought the German Verdun offensive to a conclusion. But in the spring of 1917, despite the entry of the Americans into the war, the situation for the Allies was bleak. British shipping was being sunk at an alarming rate; the Germans were achieving air superiority over the Western Front; Russia was in revolutionary tumult; the French soldiers on the Chemin des Dames were going on strike; and the British offensive into Palestine had been checked at Gaza. In Macedonia, the Greeks were divided about their participation in the war which created great uncertainty about the prospects of an Allied advance from its base at Salonika. Attempts to break the Central Powers, primarily Bulgaria, at the battles of Lake Prespa (March 1917) and Vardar (May 1917) were unsuccessful, and diseases increased the suffering and losses of the Allied armies.

There were, however, glimmers of success and some hopes for the future. The fabled city of Baghdad had been captured in March 1917 and British and Imperial forces lay not far from Jerusalem. Conscious of the war-weariness of the British people, Lloyd George implored General Allenby in Palestine to take the city as a 'Christmas present for the nation'.[2] Preparations therefore began to break out of Gaza and take the ancient city. In South East Europe, a Bulgarian offensive, the Battle of Florina, had been checked in the autumn of 1916, and General Maurice Sarrail, the French commander of the Allied forces, had driven back the attackers. Encouraged by this success, Romania joined the Allies in the war. Moreover the Italians broke through in Albania, linking the Allied fronts. After setbacks in early 1917, hopes were raised again when the Greeks finally came in on the Allied side in June. At the end of the year, the appointment of the energetic General Adolphe Marie-Louise Guillaumat brought the prospects of greater inter-Allied co-operation and a complete reorganisation of the front. There was optimism on other fronts. In Africa, most of the German forces in the colonies had been neutralised by 1917. Togoland, Kamerun and German South-West Africa had been seized. Only in East Africa did German resistance continue.

Strategy and Operations in East Africa, 1917–1918
Colonel Paul von Lettow-Vorbeck, the German military commander of East Africa, could command a force of 10,000 at the outbreak of war, and he vastly outnumbered the small British garrisons along the Uganda Railway to the north. Two Indian expeditionary

forces (Force C and D) were defeated with relative ease when they attempted to land at Tanga. The Germans hoped to tie down more Allied troops by maintaining a harassing resistance using guerrilla tactics against the British colonies. Obliged to conduct a strategic defence of their colonies, there was little choice but to reinforce the cordon around German East Africa. With reinforcements, Lieutenant General Jan Smuts, who had actually served with the Afrikaner guerrilla forces that had resisted the British army in 1900–2 in South Africa, knew that the Germans would seek to avoid fixed positions and engagements. Smuts therefore flooded the region with troops from Britain South Africa, India and the West Indies, and attempted to co-ordinate an envelopment that would leave nowhere for the Germans to escape. The terrain and climate tended to mitigate against the Allied forces. It was relatively easy to conceal the smaller German contingents and their African partners in the tangle of vegetation and topography.

Smuts therefore drove columns into the interior of East Africa on multiple axes. This was designed to prevent the Germans from being able to operate with the depth and protection of a large hinterland. While Smuts advanced from the north, paralleled by Major General van Deventer's force, the Nyasaland and Rhodesian Field Force came up from the south, and the Portuguese were enjoined to close the southern border. From the west came a Belgian force from Congo. The most remarkable element of the scheme was the arrival of amphibious forces on the coast and the transfer of two maritime vessels that formed a gunboat flotilla on Lake Victoria. Under the enterprising command of Commander G.B. Spicer-Simpson, the gunboats *Mimi* and *Tou-Tou* had been hauled by traction engine from Cape Town, traversing rivers and across the bush, they were then assembled on the shore of the lake, and in due course they were to sink two German vessels in close combat.

Smuts' operations drove Von Lettow-Vorbeck away from the northern highlands, prevented him from threatening the Uganda Railway. As the cordon began to tighten, a third of the German force was cornered in the south-east of the colony and compelled to surrender on 28 November 1917. Confusion and communications problems amongst the Portuguese allowed Von Lettow-Vorbeck and the remainder of his command to escape into Portuguese East Africa. Regardless of the losses amongst the African labourers, the Germans kept on the move, evading their pursuers.

Although many commentators regard Lettow-Vorbeck's activities as a successful guerrilla campaign, this is merely to make a virtue of his endless flight. The German forces could not threaten the Allied control of their colonies after 1916, and, when the war came to an end, he could muster just 175 Europeans and 3,000 Africans. With this Lilliputian contingent, his resistance was of little strategic significance. The best that can be said is that he tied up thousands of Allied troops, but the conflict he had prolonged led to the death, directly and indirectly, of an astonishing 250,000 African civilians.[3] Strategically, Germany lost in other ways. It was stripped of its colonies and its presence in Africa was permanently at an end. By contrast, the British were able to argue that, thanks to Smuts, the Central Powers were unable to capitalise on their African possessions and could not menace the strategic nodal points of Egypt and Suez, or the East African coast. Britain's position in Africa was strengthened as a result of the war, and Smuts emerged as a member of the imperial elite with a strong grasp of the art of strategy.

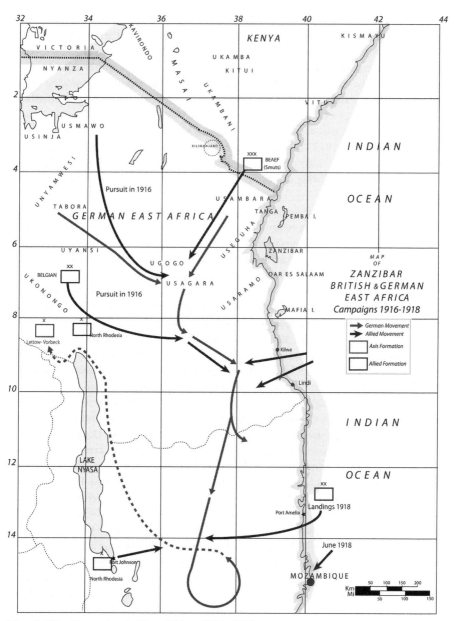

Map 3. The Campaign in East Africa, 1916–1918.

Strategy in South East Europe and the Mediterranean, 1917–1918

South East Europe had been the crucible of the Great War. It was the fate of Serbia that had driven the collision between Austria-Hungary and Russia, and it was the desire of the Ottomans to recover lost territories that had driven the regime in Istanbul into the conflict. Conscious of the need to develop the coalition against the Central Powers, Britain and France and courted the neutral powers of the region. Part of the calculation to force the Dardanelles and land troops on Gallipoli had been to persuade Greece, Bulgaria and Romania, old enemies of the Ottomans, to come in on the Allied side. If Bulgaria and Romania could be enlisted, in all likelihood the Ottomans would be cut off from the munitions and support of the Austrians and the Germans, and, fatally disabled, it was thought that the Ottomans would then have to sue for peace. The consequence of this would be that the isolated Austro-German bloc would have to submit to Allied terms. As late as mid-1915, the Entente powers still hoped that Bulgaria might join an anti-Ottoman coalition, and, when the Gallipoli campaign stalled, a new landing was proposed at Salonika to bring the Greeks and other Balkan states into the war on the Allied side.

This strategy of coalition-building was only partially achieved. The official Italian position until May 1915 was neutrality and there was negotiation with both sides to ascertain the greatest concessions to Italian national interests. Finally, Antonio Salandra, as Prime Minister, declared war against Austria-Hungary, but there were political divisions in Italy that only deepened when economic hardships increased.

In Greece the situation was even more complicated. The King, Constantine, had been educated in Germany. In Greece he was deeply unpopular. The Prime Minister, Eleutherios Venizelos, inclined towards the Allies and in early 1915 offered to assist in the support of Serbia. The King intervened and demanded the resignation of the Prime Minister, but a royalist government was defeated in elections. Delaying the reappointment of the Prime Minister, the King ignored Greece's treaty obligations towards Serbia in the face of a Bulgarian offensive. The Allies landed at Salonika in northern Greece in accordance with Venizelos' earlier invitation, but the fall of his administration and fresh elections returned a pro-German government. Paramilitaries stirred violence between factions and Greek divisions permitted the Bulgarians to seize border positions unopposed. Venizelos gathered an alternative government, to which many patriots flocked. A new Army of National Defence was formed, and with Allied assistance, a blockade was imposed in January 1916 on Athens. In June 1917, the Allies went further and demanded the King's abdication. Venizelos was returned to power in June 1917 and amongst his government's first decisions was to declare war on the Central Powers. Nevertheless, the divisions in Greek society were so severe as to delay full mobilisation until April 1918. Constantine continued to intrigue against the Greek government, and there were some mutinies against the new authorities in Athens.

The original objective of the Entente had been to support Serbia, but Serbia was all but overrun by the autumn of 1915, save for a small enclave in the far south-west. Even then, its defiant government refused to surrender and seek terms. Austria-Hungary and Bulgaria divided the occupation between them and their repression of Serbians, especially those who tried to resist, was uncompromising. Thousands of refugees fled southwards, and there are estimates that as many of 200,000 died in the flight. The Serbian army also evacuated and redeployed to the main Allied effort at Salonika. The greater strength this gave them encouraged Serbian leaders to consider the idea of a united southern Slav kingdom under Serbian direction. As the idea of liberation became a reality, so the concept of a Jugo-Slavia seemed more tangible, but there was immediately resentment and resistance from Croats and Bosnians. This anger would smoulder for decades.

The Allied offensives of 1916 had failed to make headway and there were prolonged periods of inactivity in 1917 because of the formidable defences established across the mountainous terrain around the Salonika salient. Instead, it was decided patiently to build up resources and to strengthen the inter-operability of the partner nations now involved. The French commander, General Adolphe Marie-Louise Guillaumat, had replaced the abrasive Sarrail, and was able to smooth the diplomatic path. He integrated the Greek formations within the Allied order of battle and with patience prevented friction between the various armies. The Greeks enjoyed an operational success at Srka de Legen (30 May 1917) which inoculated them to the conditions of the war. Guillaumat was recalled to France in the spring of 1918 to organise the forces in Paris against the German onslaught, and he was replaced by the energetic General Louis Franchet D'Espèrey ('Desperate Frankie' to the British soldiers). Franchet D'Espèrey had exhibited tremendous resolve throughout the war, but he knew the Balkans well from his pre-war travels, and he was conscious of the limitations on his army. His forces had also suffered severe casualties during the overwhelming German offensives along the Chemin des Dames in May 1918, but he brought tireless energy and encouragement to the Balkans Front.

On 14 September 1918, Franchet D'Espèrey unleashed a great three-day bombardment on the Bulgarian lines right along the front – from the Albanian hills to Lake Doiran, which lies due north of Salonika, some eighty miles in total. Against this barrage, the Bulgarians could have no idea where the main thrust would come. In fact, on the 17th, the Italians near Monastir, the French and Serbians around Nidje,

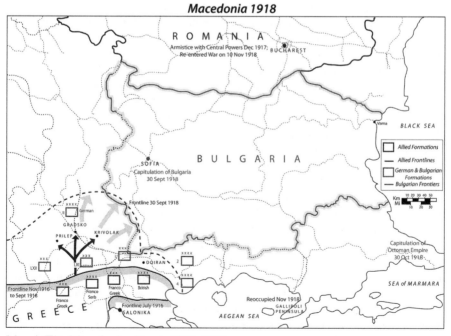

Macedonia 1918

Map 4. The Macedonian Front, 1916–1918.

and the British and Greeks at Lake Doiran, all attacked together. The Bulgarian troops could not hold in every sector and their centre and left flank gave way. As the Allied armies advanced, the Bulgarian resistance began to collapse. Prilep was seized before the Bulgarians could remove or destroy its vast stores. Strumitza fell to the British and by the end of the month the French were in Uskub in central Serbia, which cut the Bulgarian forces in half. The result was a chaotic Bulgarian rout. An estimated 100,000 prisoners fell into allied hands during the offensive. One brief attempt was made to hold the line in the hills at Kriva Lakavitza, north of the River Vardar, but the hastily-dug trenches were overrun and the retreat continued. On the 26th, the Bulgarians, now fearful that their country would be occupied, offered a ceasefire, but the Allies insisted on capitulation. Three days later, the Bulgarians concluded an armistice and accepted all the terms insisted upon by the Allies.

The strategic effect of the defeat of the Bulgarians was far-reaching. Serbia and Montenegro were immediately liberated; Germans in the Bulgarian army were made prisoners of war; and the Allies, driven by Franchet D'Espèrey's unstoppable determination, severed the strategic railway into the Ottoman Empire and considered a new offensive deep into Austria-Hungary and even southern Germany.

The collapse of the Bulgarians rattled the Germans and the Austrians, already concerned by the failures on their own fronts but it had the most profound effect on the Ottomans. Cut off from the vital line of supply from Central Europe, the Ottoman war machine, already exhausted, was now grinding to a halt. The end was coming.

Strategy and Operations in the Middle East, 1917–1918

At the outbreak of war, Britain had moved an Indian Army expeditionary force to the head of the Persian Gulf to secure the oil refineries in southern Persia, since oil was already emerging as critical to the functioning of the Royal Navy and Britain's war economy. But it was not just a concern to acquire reserves of oil that drove the British into Mesopotamia; it was the far older pre-war anxieties of regional and Great Power influence that they needed to forestall during the war and after.[4] The 'Great Game' had dominated British thinking about the region in the late nineteenth century and concerns about German and Ottoman schemes against British interests in Persia, the Gulf and India drove the strategy of 1914–18 in the region. The subsequent appearance of the Bolshevik threat ensured continuity of policy in this area.[5]

In 1915, there had seemed to be an opportunity to seize Baghdad when the performance of the Ottoman garrison was particularly weak. The Government of India had encouraged the local commanders to press forward on a tenuous line of communication and the result was that the British division on the Tigris was bundled back to Kut where it was besieged. All efforts to relieve the division were a costly failure and the British government stepped in to demand an end to offensive action.

From late 1916 onwards, the British army in Mesopotamia made significant improvements. There were steady increases in the manpower available. There was development in combined-arms operations (including integration of the new air arm), with the import of ideas from the Western Front.[6] There was more artillery, providing a superiority in firepower. There were improvements in logistics and river transport, more efficient staff work, and increased intelligence collection. In short, it was a very different army in 1917 from that which had made the ill-fated offensives in 1915. More proficient in combat, more efficient in supply, and arguably more realistic about its capabilities and limits, the British and Indian forces in Mesopotamia were far more combat-effective.[7]

When the Russians advanced south from Persian Azerbaijan to Khanaqin, within the Ottoman borders, there seemed a possibility that the Tsar's forces, rather than the British, might actually seize Baghdad. General Halil, commander of the Ottoman Sixth Army, therefore immediately diverted a portion of his army to reinforce Khanaqin and on 1 June 1916 he checked the Russian advance. Emboldened by the success, he ordered his men to counter-attack into Persia. They subsequently seized Kermanshah on 1 July and then Hamdan on 10 August, but this only took them deeper into Persia and away from the defences on the Tigris. With the Ottoman forces around Kut reduced to 20,000, there seemed to be a new opportunity for a British offensive. The CIGS, Robertson, always eager to preserve resources for the main theatre in France and Flanders, argued that, even if it could be taken, Baghdad had no value from a strategic point of view, and therefore no advance could be contemplated. The War Cabinet agreed. For now, the British and Imperial forces on the Tigris remained where they were.

General Stanley Maude was not prepared to accept the inactivity implied by his appointment to command in Mesopotamia in August 1916. He had fought at Gallipoli, and had seen action in France, where he had been wounded, so he was fully aware of the risks and implications of the conflict. He was no 'Chateau General' of the popular imagination, and his approach to operations mirrored the developing experience of the Western Front. He had the measure of the character of this war, and knew that it required overwhelming firepower, close co-ordination of all arms, and resolution throughout every level of the army. Training and preparation were crucial. He would not be hurried, but would proceed with methodical and relentless calculation towards his objectives in his own time.

Preparations were meticulous. Reinforcements were introduced, acclimatised and trained, and formations rehearsed. His divisions would enjoy a stronger ratio of artillery to provide crucial fire support. Basra was redeveloped as a port, greatly increasing its capacity to handle large volumes of stores and munitions. A light railway was constructed up to the front lines, while new river boats and hundreds of Ford motor lorries were brought in to speed up the supply system. Depots were opened up along the route to the front, and a precise approach was adopted to the question of logistics.

At the strategic level there was much better organisation. On 1 October 1916, General Charles Carmichael Monro, the Commander-in-Chief of the Army in India, assumed overall direction of the theatre, integrating it into the strategy of the Middle East and the rest of the war effort against the Central Powers, which offered the opportunity for truly co-ordinated action against the Ottoman Empire. Monro was served by an experienced staff.[8] While the CIGS continued to insist that the theatre commanders make do with what they had, the Russian General Staff agreed in principle that there should be co-ordination between the Army of the Caucasus and the British forces in the Middle East.[9]

On the night of 13/14 December, the Ottoman positions were subjected to the full weight of an intense artillery barrage. The fire was overwhelming, yet carefully controlled. In a methodical series of belts of fire, the barrage was mathematical in its obedience of timing. Ottoman trenches were subjected to a rain of shells, while rear areas were blasted to prevent reinforcements coming up. Then, close, came British and

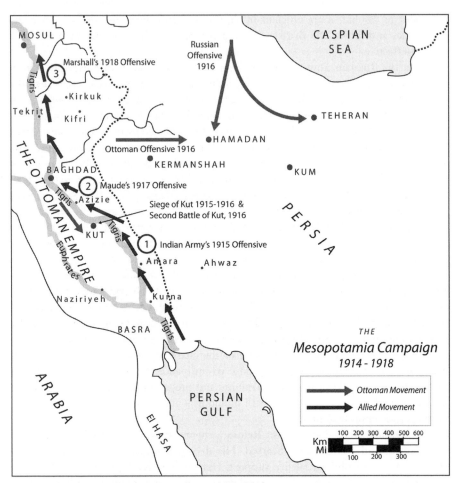

Map 5. The Mesopotamian Campaign, 1914–1918.

Indian troops, bayonets levelled, moving across the exploding hell of No Man's Land. Yet, the opening bombardment, intense though it was, could not guarantee success. Some infantry units were pinned down by Ottoman machine-gun fire, others took heavy losses as they tried to get forward. In some locations, more fortunate bands penetrated the lines and started to consolidate. But this was a battle that would not be decided in one day. As had been found on the Western Front, engagements lasted days, weeks and even months. The stoic Ottomans were not so easily dislodged.

Maude had opened his assault with two corps advancing in parallel up both banks of the Tigris. Heavy rain had impeded progress as the ground dissolved into mud but it was really Maude's concern to minimise casualties and proceed methodically from one objective to the next that actually slowed the force. Day after day, he pounded the Ottoman defences, then carefully pushed his advanced units into the gaps. After two months of relentless pressure, Maude had secured the entire western bank below Kut.

Hammering the Ottomans was not the limit of Maude's abilities, for his next manoeuvre displayed true imagination. While the defenders concentrated all their attention to their front, Maude transferred part of his force across the Shumran Bend on a pontoon bridge on 23 February 1917 and assaulted the right of the Ottoman line. Simultaneously, his corps attacked the Ottoman left, opposite the Sanniyat position. The crossing of the Shumran Bend, which enabled a force to establish a position some five miles upriver from Kut, threw the Ottomans completely off-balance. The bridgehead was expanded quickly and the Ottomans were in danger of complete encirclement. They pulled back, but the British pursuit was inspired. Captain W. Nunn of the Royal Navy led the chase with a flotilla of five British gunboats, seizing Kut and then steaming upriver. The Ottoman rearguard caught Nunn's little fleet in an intense crossfire at point blank range from the banks, but his crews pressed on regardless, ran the gauntlet, and then steamed parallel to the main body of retreating Ottoman troops. The result was carnage, and the entire Ottoman force was destroyed or dispersed. Barely 5,000 Ottoman troops escaped Maude's offensive.

He consolidated the advance at Aziziyeh, restocking every item, resting the troops and preparing to bring his great battering ram to bear once again. Meanwhile, Halil, confronted by the British success at Kut, was compelled to recall troops from western Persia. The grandiose Ottoman scheme to acquire Persia had to be abandoned entirely as Halil sought to shore up the defence of Baghdad.

The War Office and War Cabinet were divided about the next move. Robertson was adamant that there should be no further advance. While insisting the War Cabinet left the direction of the war to the military, he reasoned that if Baghdad were taken, how would it be held and to what purpose?[10] If the Ottomans were to reinforce the front, there was a risk that the British would merely repeat the siege of Kut but in the more exposed and extended location of Baghdad. He would permit raiding by cavalry, the extension of 'influence' into the province of Baghdad, but he cautioned against any situation that would compel a withdrawal of British forces because of the 'objectionable political effect' that might ensue.[11] He repeated his determination that the war would be won or lost on the Western Front against the main adversary Germany, and continued to regard Mesopotamia as an expensive and wasteful sideshow.

General Monro in India took a diametrically opposite view. He urged Maude to press on and seize Baghdad while the Ottomans were broken on the Tigris. He argued that taking Baghdad would prevent the Ottomans from reforming at this nodal point and it would provide an important prestige victory for the British amongst their Muslim subjects.[12] Maude concurred with Monro, but the deciding factor was the prospect that the Russians might extend their own area of control from the Caucasus to Mosul and northern Mesopotamia.[13] A renewed Russian offensive toward Baghdad also could not be ruled out, particularly with Ottoman troops so significantly reduced. In a post-war settlement this would give Russia enormous influence across the Middle East, and such empowerment left British officials in India concerned. Robertson relented. He permitted an advance if Maude were to judge it prudent, but with all Robertson's previous caveats.[14]

Maude therefore resumed his offensive on 5 March 1917 and it took just three days to reach the Diyala River where Halil had prepared defences on the confluence with the Tigris. On 9 March, the initial British probing attacks were repulsed and Maude opted to outflank the river positions and threaten Baghdad directly. The city was 226 miles (365km) away but Halil could not protect it if Maude's force were to move around his defences. The British manoeuvre forced Halil to readjust his line, and shift the bulk of his force to face the new threat, leaving the defences in the hands of a single regiment. Maude then switched axis again, assaulted the Diyala defences frontally and overwhelmed them. On 11 March, Maude was able to secure Baghdad without resistance. Some 9,000 Ottoman troops were captured in the confusion and resistance in the area had been broken. It was an enormous encouragement to the British government: with this achievement, might similar progress be made in the Near East?

After the capture of Baghdad, Maude's concern was to prevent the remainder of Halil's force north of the city joining with the 15,000-strong corps led by Ali Ihsan Bey, a formation that was withdrawing from Persia under Russian pressure. The solution was to seize the rail junction at Samarrah, some 80 miles (130km) to the north. Marching out with 45,000 men, Maude planned four short attacks and his first objective was to prevent any attempt to flood the Euphrates plain and thus render further British operations impossible. The secondary objective was to secure the western approaches to Baghdad. The first thrust to the north was resisted strongly but the British drove the Ottomans back 22 miles (35km) to the Adhaim River.

Halil thus withdrew to a much stronger series of prepared defences at Istabulat, which lay between the Tigris and the Ali Jali Canal. Maude made a series of attacks along the defensive lines on 21 April, and some positions changed hands several times in close-quarters fighting. The Ottomans were eventually pushed out, and occupied a low ridge some 10km from the Samarrah railway junction. Maude kept up the pressure and when the Ottomans realized their position could no longer be held, Maude's force secured the town. His offensive had been a complete success.

The German and Ottoman strategic dilemma in late 1917 was how to make best use of the new reserves that had been released from Europe and the Caucasus following the collapse of the Russian war effort. With the Bolsheviks in power, Russian resistance was melting away. The divisions now available from South East Europe gave Constantinople a strategic reserve, the *Yıldırım* (Lightning) Army Group, and this could be committed either to the recovery of Baghdad or to bolster the Palestine front against an expected British offensive. The German contribution was the seasoned and well-equipped brigade, *Pasha II*, which was armed with a generous scale of machine guns and field artillery. This force was designed to support an Ottoman offensive to retake Baghdad, although General Falkenhayn, effectively now in command of the Middle Eastern theatre, was conscious that any attack in that direction would first have to ensure the security of Jerusalem and Palestine lest the Allies break through and threaten the Turco-German lines of communications in Syria.

Just as the Central Powers agreed on where the strategic weight of the Ottoman Empire would be committed, namely in Mesopotamia against Maude, General Allenby commenced his operations in Palestine and the Ottoman *Yıldırım* Group had to be diverted. The strategic situation therefore altered again, and further operational successes for the British in both theatres began to alter the balance irrevocably in their favour.

To the west of Baghdad, Maude took Fallujah on 19 March 1917 and units fanned out to pacify the area. When operations were resumed in March 1918, the 15th Indian Division took Hit without resistance, as the Ottoman garrison gave way in its path.

In September, Ramadi was taken in a brilliant mobile operation that had cavalry, horse artillery, armoured cars and infantry in motor transport working in close co-operation. Swinging around the Ottoman positions, a series of cut-off groups decimated their attempts to make a tactical withdrawal.

To the north, the final phase of the Mesopotamia campaign fell to Maude's successor, Sir William Marshall. The strategic direction was the British government's desire that Mosul and its valuable oil resources should be in British hands at the end of the war. This was to be a vital diplomatic advantage for London in any peace negotiations, for it was anticipated that with Bulgaria soon to be out of the war and an Ottoman peace overture imminent, the conflict would soon be at an end. However, Marshall's Tigris force had been denuded of some of its transport by the need to convey 'Dunsterforce', a detached contingent, to Baku, where it could provide security against a final Ottoman attempt to control the oil resources of the Caucasus and Trans-Caspian region.[15] Resources also had to be diverted to Palestine for Allenby's offensive beyond the Judean Hills, so the final push in Mesopotamia was made by a much diminished force.

Marshall nevertheless pressed on, defeating the remnants of Halil's Sixth Army, restyled as the *Dicle Grubu* (Tigris Group) in a series of engagements that culminated in the Battle of Sharqat. The armistice was declared when Marshall's force was just a few miles short of Mosul, but the city was taken as ordered. The survivors of the Ottoman army were at the end of their endurance, with too few horses and mules to move, short of ammunition, in rags of uniforms and ravaged by disease.

In contrast, the confident British and Imperial troops, supported as they were by modern aircraft and motor transport, had achieved a significant victory. They had fought their way over 600 miles (1,000km) up the Tigris and Euphrates, against determined resistance and a hostile climate. They had endured floods, sandstorms, choking dust and deep mud. They had broiled under the sun, and frozen in the exposed plains. They had suffered debilitating sicknesses, such that more lives were lost through disease than combat. The Ottomans had fought for virtually every mile, hurling at them every available weapon of war. And yet, still the irrepressible 'Tommy' and his Imperial comrades had turned up, fighting with endurance and imagination, to secure the entirety of Mesopotamia by the war's end. It was a remarkable and sadly now forgotten achievement.

Victory in Palestine and Syria

Although they were in strong positions and had repulsed two British offensives in 1917, severe supply problems affected the Ottoman troops dug in at Gaza. The relative weaknesses of the Ottoman forces were not the immediate concern of the British War Cabinet or of the CIGS. Robertson informed the headquarters at Cairo that their request for two divisions would be denied and that, while 'every opportunity should be taken' to defeat the forces to their front, the Egyptian Expeditionary Force (EEF) in southern Palestine would not be required to conduct major offensive operations.[16] However, given the grave situation in Russia and on the Western Front, the Prime Minister could not permit inactivity, and more mounted troops were despatched. The whole mobile contingent of the EEF was then reorganised as three distinct divisions, with supporting artillery.[17] Moreover, the two infantry divisions requested were eventually despatched. Rail and water supply lines were extended to support the EEF's lines and the troops were subjected to intensive training, incorporating lessons derived from operations on the Western Front.

The British EEF therefore had the 'means' to achieve its 'ends', namely to break through at Gaza and drive the Ottomans out of the Near East. It had been expanded to ten infantry divisions and four mounted divisions, and possessed 116 heavy guns. This force was supported by new aircraft, particularly the Bristol Fighter plane, which gave the EEF a technological advantage on their front. The EEF was grouped into three corps: The XXI Corps of three infantry divisions, facing Gaza and its south-eastern approaches, was commanded by Lieutenant General Edward Bulfin. Opposite Beersheba, Lieutenant General Chetwode commanded the XX Corps, with three infantry divisions with an attached Yeomanry division, while Lieutenant General Harry Chauvel's Desert Mounted Corps faced Beersheba's south-eastern approaches.

The arrival of the new commander, General Edmund Allenby, seemed to herald the end of the stasis of the previous months, with all the hardships of trench warfare, and the soldiers believed there was every likelihood of an advance into the more temperate landscape of Palestine. His physical presence, his experience, his willingness to talk to soldiers and his intolerance of oversights amongst his officers had a positive and energizing effect across the army.[18]

The strategic situation was becoming more serious. There was growing concern that, with the situation in Russia deteriorating, more Ottoman troops might be released from the Caucasus front. According to Lloyd George, Allenby was expected to defeat and then pursue the enemy to the limit of his resources. Robertson was more cautious and wrote to Allenby that 'it will be a good thing to give the Turk in front of you a sound beating, but that the extent to which we shall be justified in following him by an advance into Northern and Central Palestine is a matter which for the moment must be left open'.[19] Referring to the Clausewitzian problem of a culminating point, he added: 'The further we go north the more Turks we shall meet; and the greater will be the strain upon our resources.' He added a 'PS', in which he pointed out it was not so much going forward that he opposed, but how to 'maintain ourselves after going forward and to a useful purpose'.

The Third Battle of Gaza (31 October–8 November 1917) opened with a sustained artillery bombardment on the defences of the town, and was then extended by Chetwode's XX Corps against Beersheba. The infantry of the 60th and 74th Divisions approached methodically from the south-west, the troops following just 30 yards behind a curtain of explosions, but they suffered some casualties from Ottoman retaliatory fire. Significant features such as Hill 1070 were captured, but progress was slow because of the resistance shown by Ottoman units.[20] It was not until the evening that all their objectives were secured.

The Desert Mounted Corps used the cover of darkness overnight on 30–31 October to ride around to the east of Beersheba. As planned, the XX Corps' attack from the south-west and west had compelled the Ottoman III Corps commander, Colonel Ismet Bey, to push his reserves against Chetwode's infantry. As a result, Chauvel's Mounted Corps outnumbered the Ottomans. The Australian 7th and 5th Light Horse regiments drove back the Ottoman 3rd Cavalry Division north of Beersheba, while the 6th Light Horse acted as a reserve in support of the New Zealanders' attack on

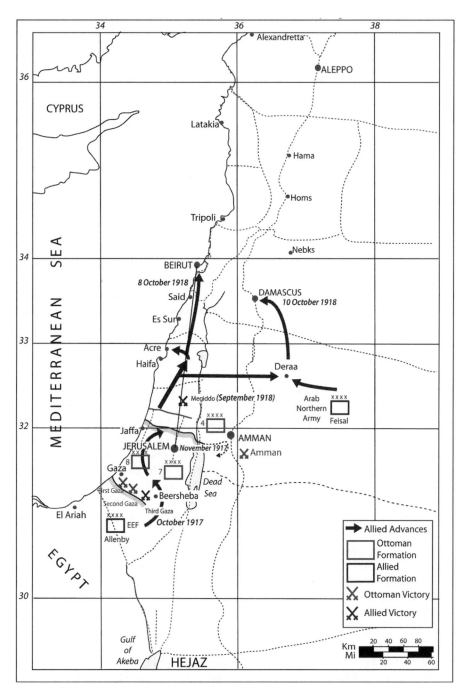

Map 6. The Allenby Campaign in Palestine, 1917–1918.

the hill at Tel es Sabe. An Ottoman battalion was dug-in on this high ground, whose commanding position gave it wide fields of fire across Beersheba's eastern approaches. It took the New Zealand Mounted Rifles brigade most of the day to assault and capture this tactically-vital position.[21]

Clearing this feature made it possible for the Australian 4th and 12th Light Horse Regiments that evening to charge through the twilight, 800 strong, towards the town. Under machine-gun and small-arms fire, the leading squadrons dismounted when they reached the Ottoman trenches and engaged in a close-quarters battle, mostly with bayonets.[22] The squadrons behind them continued to fight their way into the town on horseback. The result was the capture of Beersheba and a haul of Ottoman prisoners.

The attack on Gaza itself began on 1 November with Bulfin's XXI Corps artillery hammering the Ottoman defences, before mounting an infantry assault with the advancing troops keeping just behind the exploding shells. Attacks were made on the advanced strong points, and raids made against others, but the full weight of the offensive had not yet come.[23] Bulfin's artillery barrage was the largest outside Europe to date in the war, with 15,000 rounds smashing into the ground around the settlement before the infantry reached the position, but, despite the staggering volume of fire, the Ottoman garrison defended their collapsing trenches with courage and determination.[24] Believing that the British would press home the attack, more Ottoman units were rushed into the defences, while the line beyond Hebron was stripped of manpower. Allenby had succeeded in weakening the Ottoman positions in their centre, at the 'hinge' of Hareira and Tel el Sheria, two settlements at the heart of the Ottoman defences. On 6 November, the main attack went in against this section, and the Ottoman line was cut.[25] A gap seven miles wide was opened up, through which his reserves now marched.

After Third Gaza there was continuing debate between Robertson and Lloyd George over the ends and means of the Palestine campaign, and how the campaign fitted into the overall strategy of the war. Impatient with the CIGS, the Prime Minister forced Robertson out in February 1918. In December 1917, Robertson had stated: 'it is for serious consideration whether the advantages to be gained by an advance [in Palestine] are worth the cost and risk involved'. He added: 'The answer depends to some extent upon whether the conquest of Palestine would put Turkey out of the war.'[26]

Nevertheless, on 9 December 1917, it was Allenby's entry into Jerusalem that mattered to the Prime Minister. It was strategically important, not least for Britain's prestige and its bargaining position in the post-war world. Lloyd George told the House of Commons: 'The capture of Jerusalem has made a most profound impression throughout the whole civilised world . . . the name of every hamlet and hill occupied by the British Army . . . thrills with sacred memories.'[27] Allenby, conscious of the sensitivities in the city and globally, chose to walk in on foot in simple khaki service dress. After a brief ceremony lasting 15 minutes, he returned to the soldiers' business of finishing the Ottomans in the Near East.

Allenby had been instructed to resume his offensive in February 1918 but he could not progress north into Syria until he had neutralized the 20,000 Ottoman troops on his eastern flank in Amman. His first manoeuvre, to take Jericho, was successful, with the town falling to Allied troops on 21 February. Next, Allenby seized the hills above Wadi Auja, which put Jericho and its line of communications beyond the reach of Ottoman artillery. In March, an attempt to raid towards Amman met with defeat, largely because of the weather and topography, but a second attempt was delayed, in part because divisions were being withdrawn for service in France to face the massive German offensive of the spring. A second raid in May also met with failure. Nevertheless, these thrusts convinced the German and Ottoman commanders that more reinforcements must be sent to this city that commanded the British right flank. If the British could not secure Amman, it was reasoned, they would not be able to press on into Syria.

In fact, Allenby went to great lengths to conceal the direction of his intended offensive. Some 15,000 wooden and canvas horses were built and dummy camps erected to persuade intrusive reconnaissance pilots that the EEF intended to attack from the Jordan valley towards Amman. Units were moved at night, and camouflaged by day. Air patrols did their best to deny access over Allenby's formations. Bridges were built across the Jordan to give the impression of an impending thrust, and false wireless traffic was generated to support the idea of preparations. Jafar al-Askari and the Arab Northern Army played their part in creating the deception. With the bulk of the Arab force laying siege to Ma'an, one contingent advanced to within 50 miles (80.5km) of Amman. On 16 September, covered by aircraft of the Royal Air Force, Colonel T.E. Lawrence ('of Arabia')'s Arab irregulars conducted a series of guerrilla actions on the railway line either side of the railway junction of Daraa. This inspired more local Arab tribes to join the revolt and drew in Ottoman reinforcements to defend the area. On the 17th, the Arab Northern Army made another attack on the line, north of Deraa.

The Battle of Megiddo, which opened at 4.00 am on 19 September 1918 with a tremendous artillery barrage, was fought between the three corps of the EEF and the remnants of the Ottoman Fourth (near Amman) and the Seventh and Eighth Armies of *Yıldırım*. Allenby had concentrated 35,000 infantry, 9,000 cavalry and 400 heavy guns on a 15-mile (24km) front close to the Mediterranean coast, north of Jaffa. The shelling was the most intense delivered outside a European theatre, with 1,000 rounds a minute detonating on the Ottoman positions.

The engagement developed as Allenby had planned. The infantry assault of the XXI Corps carried the first two Ottoman lines and overcame the resistance of the third and fourth lines soon after. In just two and a half hours, they had penetrated 7,000 yards into the Ottoman positions, and broken open a wide gap in their defences. Chauvel's cavalry exploited the gap perfectly, chasing the routed Ottoman troops up to Tulkarm, which was captured. The cavalry pressed on with aircraft above them, seizing depots, rounding up prisoners and destroying the telephone communications' nodes on which the *Yıldırım* depended to allocate its reserves. The speed of the advance seemed to exceed all expectations: the British 4th Cavalry Division covered 70 miles (113km) on 20 September, while the Australian Mounted Division in one bound advanced 11 miles (18km) in just sixty minutes. The Ottoman forces began to disintegrate in the confusion: entire Turkish battalions found themselves encircled or under relentless air attack. A key manoeuvre was the decision of the cavalry to switch to a new axis to the south-east, from Nazareth and Beth Shean, which cut off the retreat of the Ottoman Seventh Army. On 23 September, British and Indian cavalry took Acre and Haifa. Resistance from Ottoman forces in Palestine was ebbing away.

British and Indian cavalry circled round to cut off Ottoman forces making for Beirut and Homs. By 30 September, the combined British and Arab force was on the edge of Damascus. A ceremonial entry was arranged for the Arab Northern Army, accompanied by T.E. Lawrence. The British entry was more prosaic, but Emir Feisal was accorded the honours of a conqueror for a short time before being informed, by Allenby, that the city was under British military occupation. It had been a whirlwind campaign which had driven the Ottomans pell-mell out of the Near East. The pursuit continued and Aleppo was taken on 26 October, but resistance had almost ceased altogether by that stage. Just four days after Aleppo was captured, on 30 October, the Ottomans concluded an armistice, agreeing to all the Allied terms.

Robertson's successor as CIGS, Sir Henry Wilson, wrote to Allenby soon after the victory and he concluded that the German strategic plan had been 'command of the sea [and] the Near and Middle East'. Wilson believed Britain had prevented German command of the sea and 'I was always casting about in my mind how this second objective [German domination of the Middle East] could be frustrated.'[28] He concluded: 'You [Allenby] and [General] Franchet [D'Espèrey, the commander in the Balkans] did that. The collapse of the main theatres followed almost automatically.' In 1918, in all three theatres, East Africa, South-East Europe and the Middle East, the Allies had achieved decisive operational and strategic victory.

Notes

1. John Grigg, *Lloyd George: War Leader* (London: Allen Lane, 2002), p. 150.
2. Archibald Wavell, *Allenby: A Study in Greatness* (London: 1940), p. 186.
3. Edward Paice, *Tip and Run: The Untold Tragedy of the Great War in Africa* (London: Phoenix, 2008).
4. S.A. Cohen, *British Policy in Mesopotamia, 1903-1914* (London: Ithaca, 1976; repub., 2008), p. 308.
5. Robert Johnson, *Spying for Empire: The Great Game in Central and South Asia, 1757-1947* (London: Greenhill, 2006), pp. 218–22; Keith Neilson, '"For Diplomatic, Economic, Strategic and Telegraphic Reasons": British Imperial Defence, the Middle East and India, 1914-1918', in G. Kennedy and K. Nielson (eds), *Far Flung Lines: Essays on Imperial Defence in Honour of Donald Mackenzie Schurman* (London: Routledge, 1996), pp. 103–23.
6. Kaushik Roy, 'The Army in India in Mesopotamia from 1916-1918: Tactics, Technology and Logistics Reconsidered' in I.W.F. Beckett (ed.), *1917: Beyond the Western Front* (Leiden and Boston: Brill, 2009), pp. 131–58.
7. This is also the verdict of E.A. Cohen and J. Gooch, *Military Misfortunes: The Anatomy of Failure in War* (London: Macmillan, 1990), pp. 156–63.
8. George Barrow, *The Life of General Sir Charles Carmichael Monro* (London: Hutchinson, 1931), p. 132.
9. F.J. Moberly, *The Campaign in Mesopotamia* III (London: HMSO, 1924–7), pp. 79, 86–90; William Robertson, *Soldiers and Statesmen, 1914-1918*, II (London, 1926), pp. 79, 227; Paul Guinn, *British Strategy and Politics, 1914-1918* (Oxford: Clarendon Press, 1965), p. 219.
10. Guinn, *British Strategy*, pp. 113–14.
11. Moberly, *Campaign in Mesopotamia* III, pp. 204–11.
12. Guinn, *British Strategy and Politics*, p. 157; Robertson, *Soldiers and Statesmen* II, p. 74.
13. Moberly, *Campaign in Mesopotamia* III, pp. 125–6, 159, 199; Robertson, *Soldiers and Statesmen* II, p. 77; Guinn, *British Strategy*, p. 200.
14. Eugene Rogan, *The Fall of the Ottomans: The Great War in the Middle East, 1914–1920* (London: Allen Lane, 2015), p. 323.
15. Major General Dunsterville, the inspiration for Kipling's 'Stalky and Co', was tasked to secure northern Persia and Baku on the Caspian with a brigade known as 'Dunsterforce'. L.C. Dunsterville, *The Adventures of Dunsterforce* (London: E. Arnold, 1920).
16. Lt-Gen. Sir George McMunn and Captain Cyril Falls, *Military Operations, Egypt and Palestine* (London: HMSO, 1927), I, pp. 355 and 356.
17. Ibid., p. 357.
18. Matthew Hughes (ed.), *Allenby in Palestine* (Stroud: Sutton, 2004), p. 8.

19. General Sir William Robertson to Allenby, 10 August 1917, Robertson Papers 8/1/69, Liddell Hart Centre for Military Archives, King's College London, cited in Hughes, *Allenby in Palestine*, p. 51.
20. Cyril Falls and A.F. Becke, *Military Operations, Egypt and Palestine* (London: HMSO, 1930) II, p. 50.
21. Ibid., p. 56.
22. Ibid., p. 59.
23. Ibid., pp. 66–9.
24. Ibid., p. 64.
25. Ibid., pp. 95–101.
26. Sir William Robertson, *Future Operations in Palestine*, 26 December 1917, CAB/24/37/12, The National Archives.
27. Cited in Grigg, *Lloyd George*, p. 344.
28. Wilson to Allenby, 7 December 1918, Wilson Papers, HHW2/33B/1.

Suggested Further Reading

Barr, James, *Setting the Desert on Fire: T. E. Lawrence and Britain's Secret War in Arabia, 1916–1918* (New York: W. W. Norton, 2008)

Erikson, Edward, *Gallipoli and the Middle East, 1914–1918: From the Dardanelles to Mesopotamia* (London: Amber, 2008)

Glenny, M., *The Balkans 1804-1999: Nationalism, War and the Great Powers* (London: Granta, 2000)

Hughes, Matthew, *Allenby and British Strategy in the Middle-East 1917–1919* (London: Frank Cass, 1999)

Johnson, Robert, *The Great War and the Middle East* (Oxford: Oxford University Press, 2016)

Karsh, Efraim and Karsh, Inari, *Empires of the Sand: The Struggle for Mastery in the Middle East, 1789–1923* (Cambridge MA.: Harvard University Press, 1999)

Kitchen, James, *The British Imperial Army in the Middle East: Morale and Military Identity in the Sinai and Palestine Campaigns, 1916-1918* (London: Bloomsbury, 2014)

MacMunn, Lt. Gen. Sir George, and Falls, Capt. Cyril, *Official History of the Great War. Military Operations: Egypt and Palestine* (London: HMSO, 1927–9)

Moberly, F.J., *The Campaign in Mesopotamia* 4 vols (London: HMSO, 1924–7)

Rogan, Eugene, *The Fall of the Ottomans: The Great War in the Middle East, 1914–1920* (London: Allen Lane, 2015)

Strachan, Hew, *The First World War* (London: Simon and Schuster, 2003)

PART TWO

Chapter 9

The United States and Britain's Victory

By Ross A. Kennedy

The United States entered the First World War late, almost three years after the conflict began, and its belligerency was relatively brief, lasting only about nineteen months. But the United States nevertheless had an enormous impact on the conflict. Prior to its declaration of war in April 1917, the United States provided massive material and financial aid to the Allies, largely accommodated Britain's blockade of the Germans, and American neutrality not only directly helped the Allied war effort, it also contributed to Britain's refusal to talk peace in late 1916 and to Germany's decision to initiate unrestricted submarine warfare in February 1917. Germany's choice marked a turning point in the war, as it triggered America's entry into the conflict on the Allied side.

Subsequent economic, naval and military assistance from the United States helped Allied forces defeat Germany's U-boats and to go on the offensive on the Western Front after July 1918. More significantly though, American belligerency influenced the decision-making of Britain and Germany, the two most important members of the opposing coalitions. For the British, the entry of the United States into the war reinforced Britain's will to fight, leading them to reject peace feelers from Germany in late 1917. For the Germans, America's presence in the war contributed both to their decision to risk all on an offensive in March 1918 and then to their appeal for an armistice in October 1918 – decisions that set the stage for their defeat.

America's contribution to the Allied cause began while the United States was ostensibly neutral, during the period from August 1914 to April 1917. First, the Wilson administration reinforced Britain's maritime supremacy by doing little to interfere with its blockade of Germany. To be sure, President Wilson did protest against aspects of the blockade that violated international law, such as Britain's interception of American commodities bound for neutral states near Germany. In part because of these protests, Britain's blockading efforts made only limited impact in 1915. Nevertheless, Wilson could have done a lot more to contest Britain's maritime strategy. He made no protest whatsoever over Britain's illegal North Sea minefield. The protests he sent to London on other components of the blockade were mild and unthreatening; one in December 1914 even implied that Britain could interfere with legitimate neutral trade if doing so were justified on grounds of national safety. Wilson also might have attempted to coerce Britain into respecting American neutral rights by partially or completely embargoing munitions sales, the vast bulk of which went to the Allies, as many in Congress wanted to do in early 1915. Alternatively, Wilson could have requested authority from

Congress to curtail Britain's access to American ports and discourage American banks from extending credit to the belligerents. In fact, Wilson did take both of these steps in later 1916 after Britain tightened the blockade. By that point, however, American acquiescence in the blockade had gone on for over two years.[1]

The President also buttressed the naval supremacy of the Allies by adopting a confrontational posture against Germany's submarine warfare, which the Germans initiated in retaliation for Britain's blockade. After a German submarine sunk the British liner *Lusitania*, leading to the loss of 1,200 lives – over a hundred American – Wilson demanded that Germany follow international law in its submarine campaign; any further violations of American neutral rights would be regarded as 'deliberately unfriendly'. Wilson claimed that these rights included the right of American citizens to travel in safety on armed belligerent merchant ships. No other neutral nation adopted this position yet Wilson stuck to it into spring 1916, to the point of threatening Germany with a break in diplomatic relations unless it were to change its submarine practices.[2]

The partiality in favour of the Allies shown by the United States from 1914 to 1917 materially aided their war effort. Gradually over the course of 1915 and then more substantially in 1916, Britain turned to the United States for the supplies it needed to conduct a war of attrition against Germany. By October 1916, 40 per cent of all the British government's war purchases were made in North America. From August 1914 through December 1915, Britain imported 3.5 million artillery shells from the United States; in 1916, that figure jumped to 20.9 million, almost 50 per cent the amount of Britain's own home production. In 1915, Britain imported 54,500 tons of finished munitions from the US; in 1916, those imports increased almost ten-fold, to 547,000 tons. Other crucial war-related goods flowed into Britain as well. Forty per cent of British flour came from America; Britain also heavily depended upon the US for nitrocellulose, lubricating oil, petrol, cotton, grain and other foodstuffs. This torrent of supplies made Britain's 1916 offensives possible. By the end of the year, indeed, Britain's leaders concluded in a formal review of their nation's ties to the United States that any interruption in the US supply line would be disastrous for Britain's prosecution of the war.[3]

American creditors provided much of the money necessary to buy this war material. To be certain, Britain also lent extensive funds to its allies, especially Russia; it ended the war, in fact, as a net creditor. But Britain's ability to act as banker for the Entente while also funding its own war effort depended upon loans it raised in the United States. As imports from the United States climbed in 1915, Britain found it increasingly difficult to maintain the value of sterling against the dollar and to find the dollars necessary for its war orders. In September 1915, the British and the French governments had to raise an unsecured loan of $500 million from American investors. This bond offering, largely bought up by American corporations and banks, stabilised the exchange rate and so allowed Britain to make its war purchases in 1916 at more affordable prices. However, it did not meet Britain's financial needs. The British government therefore had to take out short term loans from Wall Street in 1916 and early 1917, using American securities it held as collateral. It also ran up an overdraft of $358 million with J.P. Morgan & Co., the Financial Agent of the British government. By this point, in late 1916, British officials perceived that they had to raise almost half of their daily war expenditure through loans in the United States. In contrast, few US loans went to Britain's enemies: in the neutrality period, American creditors lent the Allies about $2.125 billion but only around $35 million to the Central Powers. The Allies, in other words, received about 98.4 per cent of all the money Americans lent to the warring antagonists from 1914 to early 1917.[4]

As the British increasingly exploited their access to American credit and resources, they simultaneously intensified their efforts to cut off Germany from the outside world. Emboldened by Wilson's evident unwillingness to confront them over the blockade and alarmed by Germany's ability to evade it, in 1916 they moved to tighten its enforcement. Among other measures, they started detaining all goods destined for neutral ports near Germany in excess of normal peacetime imports, a procedure called 'forcible rationing'. Consequently, American exports to the 'near neutrals' fell in 1916, in some cases by over 40 per cent, helping to produce shortages of various goods in the Reich. Hunger riots broke out in Hamburg in the summer of 1916. As autumn turned to winter, conditions deteriorated even more, with millions of German civilians subsisting on turnips to avoid starvation.[5]

To retaliate against the blockade and disrupt Britain's supply line to America, Germany tried to use its submarines against Allied shipping. But in 1915 and 1916 this effort was hobbled by Germany's fear of war with the United States. In September 1915, in the midst of Wilson's continuing demands that Germany disavow illegal submarine warfare, the Germans suspended all submarine operations against merchant ships. This halted what had been quite an effective campaign. From June to September 1915, U-boats had sunk an average of about 133,000 tons of ships per month, enough to affect insurance rates and raise the spectre of paralysing trade. The Germans resumed submarine operations against Britain in March 1916 and again had some success, sinking 141,193 tons in April. However, once more the Germans pulled back, this time because Wilson threatened to break diplomatic relations after a U-boat mistakenly attacked the liner *Sussex*. Only in October 1916 did the Germans resume the campaign in earnest. This effort, using in part newer, longer-range, submarines, inflicted damaging losses on the Allies, sinking an average of about 326,000 tons a month from October 1916 through January 1917. These figures give an indication of what the Germans might have been able to accomplish even with a campaign sparing neutrals and passenger liners had they not been deterred by Wilson's threats against them.[6]

The war-fighting advantage the United States gave to the Allies through its neutrality policies had political consequences and they also benefitted the Allies. In December 1916, first Germany and then Wilson attempted to get negotiations going to end the war. The British displayed no interest in either initiative. In part, this position reflected their conviction that Germany was a menace to Britain's status as an independent great power and that peace now would simply reward German aggression. But it also stemmed from their view that the Entente was gradually gaining the upper hand over the Central Powers. Britain's ability to draw on supplies from the United States and the increasing effectiveness of its blockade – a blockade tacitly tolerated by the United States – were central to this calculation. In addition, British leaders also perceived that the United States was now so financially intertwined with Britain that Wilson was unlikely to try to coerce them into peace talks by cutting off their war supplies. In different ways, then, Wilson's pro-Allied neutrality policy reinforced Britain's resolve to press on with the war in late 1916.[7]

Wilson's policy simultaneously contributed to Germany's commencement of unrestricted submarine warfare in early 1917 – the 'worst decision of the war,' in one historian's words, an 'extraordinarily stupid' choice that probably sealed the Reich's fate by triggering American entry into the conflict on the Allied side. Most fundamentally, Germany pursued unrestricted submarine warfare because of the commitment of Generals Paul von Hindenburg and Erich Ludendorff, Germany's de facto preeminent leaders after August 1916, to achieving territorially expansionist war aims for the Reich. These aims, in turn, derived from domestic political considerations and Hindenburg's and Ludendorff's vision of Germany's post-war security needs, neither of which had much to do with the United States or its neutrality policy.[8]

Nevertheless, there is no question that Wilson's approach to the war from 1914–16 significantly affected Germany's decision fully to unsheathe its submarine weapon. From late 1914 onwards, the Germans saw the war as a competition in attrition in which access to resources was crucial to victory. In this contest, the United States clearly helped the British. The longer this situation persisted, the more likely the war would end, in Admiral Henning von Holtzendorff's words, 'in the mutual exhaustion of all parties and thus in disaster for us'. Ludendorff especially feared 'a second Somme battle' sustained by American munitions. At the least, unrestricted submarine warfare offered some hope of staving off this development. It offered too a way to vent Germany's anger and resentment against both Britain and the United States for the pain they were inflicting on the German people. Finally, America's partiality toward Britain spurred on the submarine decision because it disqualified Wilson as a mediator, thus closing off a pathway to peace that German Chancellor Bethmann Hollweg sometimes saw as an alternative to unleashing the U-boats, and because it led the Germans to discount the significance of American entry into the war. As Vice Admiral Franz Ritter von Hipper reckoned in early 1917, the United States 'could not possible work any harder against us in the future than it has already done to date'.[9]

This estimation turned out to be wrong. During the time of its formal belligerency, from April 1917 to November 1918, the United States provided even more assistance to the Allies than it had during the neutrality years. The United States intervened in the war just as the Allies entered a period of prolonged crisis that lasted into late 1917. In the spring, Britain confronted a looming financial catastrophe. As of 1 April, Britain had about $577 million in securities and gold in New York plus less than $350 million in gold in the Bank of England and other British banks. Against these assets, Britain had the overdraft of $358 million with J.P. Morgan. With expenditure in the United States running at $75 million a week, Britain could thus keep funding the Entente and its own US purchases for only about three more weeks, if it were to hold back its gold in England; ten weeks if it were to cash that out too. Without American help, the Entente's Atlantic trade, the lifeblood of its war effort, would soon run dry.[10]

Britain's military situation also deteriorated in 1917. Allied losses to German submarines leapt to over 500,000 tons in February and March to 860,334 tons in April. Losses fell back below 700,000 tons in May and June but remained prohibitively high. On the Western Front, France launched an unsuccessful offensive on the Chemin des Dames in April, losing 130,000 men killed and wounded, precipitating mutinies in the French army which did not fully end until late in the year. Italy likewise pursued costly and demoralising offensives against Austria-Hungary in the spring and summer, then suffered a devastating defeat at Caporetto in late October. Most ominously, revolution

1. British troops advancing under cover of smoke, July 1916 on the Somme. (Museum of the Green Howards)

2. Green Howards advancing with tanks on the Somme in 1916. A photograph from the album of Lieutenant J.S. Purvis of the 5th (T) Battalion Yorkshire Regiment, the Green Howards. (Museum of the Green Howards)

3. Soldiers from the 5th Battalion Yorkshire Regiment, the Green Howards, fusing the detonators of Stokes bombs before marching up to the front line, during the Battle of the Somme, September 1916. A photograph from the album of Lieutenant J.S. Purvis of this battalion. (Museum of the Green Howards)

4. The Battle of Cambrai, November 1917: a painting by Ernst Zimmer of 'British troops advancing against the enemy'. (Anne S.K. Brown Military Collection, Brown University, Providence, Rhode Island, US)

5. British troops march into Lille at its liberation, 18 October 1918: soldiers of the 8th Battalion King's Liverpool Regiment accompanied by a French boy 'newly-equipped' with rifle and steel helmet. (US Library of Congress, Bain News Service)

6. Troops of No. 1 Platoon, A Company, 10th Battalion, Duke of Cornwall's Light Infantry, breakfasting on their way up to the line. Near Le Quesnoy, 27 October 1918. (Public Domain/IWM)

7. (*Left*). Field Marshal von Hindenburg and First Quartermaster-General Ludendorff, the German command team for the second half of the war. (Public Domain)

8. (*Right*). Crown Prince Rupprecht of Bavaria, Army Group Commander Western Front (North). (Public Domain)

9. German machine-gun crews from Ninth Army moving into position near Noyon, August 1918. (Public Domain)

10. German Company Aid Post near Soissons, September 1918. (Public Domain)

11. Effect of Allied shelling at Bruges, November 1918. (Public Domain)

12. The backbone of German defence during the final days of the war. An MG 08/15 crew in a hastily-improvised defensive position. (Public Domain)

13. 'The End of the German Destroyer Flotillas – some of the 50 surrendered boats steaming in line to Inchkeith in the Firth of Forth, 21 November 1918', a view portrayed from an escort ship by the Official War Artist, Oscar Parkes. (IWM/Public Domain)

14. The scuttling of the German High Seas Fleet at Scapa Flow, the Orkneys, 21 June 1919 and only the upperworks of the battlecruiser SMS *Hindenburg* above the water. (Public Domain)

15. Vice Admiral Sir David Beatty as Commander of the Battle Cruiser Squadron at Rosyth in 1916. (US Library of Congress)

16. Wearing the uniform of Admiral of the Fleet, the 1st Earl Jellicoe, circa 1920, Governor General of New Zealand 1920–4. (Bain Collection, US Library of Congress)

17. Lord Kitchener, Secretary of State for War, leaving the War Office to meet his House of Commons critics. (Illustrated London News)

18. Prime Minister David Lloyd George speaking at the Welsh National Eisteddfod in August 1917 at Birkenhead. (Illustrated London News)

19. HM Queen Mary visits the Sunderland shipyard, Doxford's, on the River Wear, June 15 1917. Note the female workers and boy riveters. (Sunderland Museum and Winter Gardens)

20. Sunderland's sixteen shipyards on the River Wear specialised in building merchant vessels with an average of about 4,000 gross tonnage each. With warships completed too, 360 vessels were launched into the small river during the war years, over 900,000 tons of shipping. Here, on 26 August 1918, the destroyer HMS *Shamrock*, is being launched from Doxford's yard. To her left, the keel of a cargo ship, SS *War Astor*, is in place. (Sunderland Museum and Winter Gardens)

21. A Leicester woman in the uniform of the Great Central Railway, c.1918. (M. Richardson)

22. Dave Ramsay, a shop steward of the Amalgamated Society of Engineers. He was one of the leaders of the 1917 Engineers' Strike. (Courtesy of Graham Stevenson)

23. Workers at the Pelabon munitions factory. Started by a private individual, this factory near Twickenham was rare, like the one in Birtley near Gateshead, in that it employed almost exclusively Belgian refugees. (M. Richardson)

24. Female labour in the coal industry: these women are working at the Malton Cokeworks near Lanchester, County Durham, where coal was transformed into coke, essential in the forging of high-quality steel. (Durham Mining Museum, Spennymoor)

THE MURDER OF MISS CAVELL
INSPIRES GERMAN "KULTUR..

TAKE UP THE
SWORD OF JUSTICE

25. (*left*). A 1915 British postcard portraying the execution of Nurse Edith Cavell as the ultimate barbaric act of a debased German culture, in which the land of Bach and Beethoven gives way to the music of death – note the Pickelhaube on the piano. (British Library Postcard Collection)

26. (*Right*). This British poster shows a figure rising from the sea to offer a sword, with the sinking *Lusitania* and drowning victims in the distance. (Imperial War Museum)

27. 'The Gentle German'. British anti-German cartoon depicting a Prussian soldier bayoneting the Angel of Mercy. The Kaiser's Garland, Edmund Sullivan, 1915. (Public Domain)

28. 'Britain Prepared (1915)'. Advertisement in *The Moving Picture World*, July 1916. (Public Domain)

29. 'Once a German – Always a German!' (1918). Poster showing post-war caricature of Germans, including wartime scenes of past violence, cruelty, and drunkenness, and then a charming German businessman of the day. Also a vignette of martyr Edith Cavell's grave and the caption, '1914 to 1918. Never again!' and an evocation of the *Lusitania* sinking. (Imperial War Museum)

30. Lieutenant Rupert Downes of the 29th Battalion (5th Australian Division) addresses his platoon before entering the fighting in the Battle of Amiens on 8 August 1918. Low in numbers, the platoon is still heavily armed with rifles, bombs and two Lewis guns. Four of these men were killed or died, and a similar number wounded, in the weeks before the end of the war. (Australian War Memorial, E02790/Public Domain)

31. Infantrymen of the 6th Brigade (2nd Australian Division) move through old trenches on a battlefield dotted with poppies to attack the heights on Mont St Quentin on 1 September 1918. Some men are carrying ammunition for the Lewis gunner, fourth in line. (Australian War Memorial, E03139/Public Domain)

32. On 14 September 1918, the commander of the Australian Corps, Lieutenant General Sir John Monash, accompanied the Australian Prime Minister, W.M. 'Billy' Hughes, over some sites of recent successful fighting. Although proud of their achievements Hughes went on to insist the divisions be rested before the on-coming winter. (Australian War Memorial, E03851/Public Domain)

33. Young Canadian soldiers watch younger German prisoners moving to the rear during the Battle of Amiens. (Library Archives Canada 0-2953)

34. Canadian infantrymen stop for a rest and a smoke in a ditch during the Battle of Arras in late August 1918. (Library Archives Canada 0-3166)

35. Canadian infantry advancing under fire as they sweep through Valenciennes, 1 November 1918. (Library Archives Canada 0-3504)

36. A picture for the folks at home: Two Otago soldiers fresh in the front-line trench at Anzac with a spotter and sniper busy behind them. (A.A. Perry Collection, Auckland War Memorial Museum, New Zealand)

37. Soldiers of the New Zealand Division now wearing 'Lemon Squeezer' headdress at the end of their trek to the Somme battlefield in early September 1916. Photographed by Lieutenant Ernest Brooks who last met the New Zealanders on the Gallipoli Peninsula. (Imperial War Museum, Q1243)

38. Troopers of the New Zealand Mounted Rifles Brigade on trek in the hills of Palestine. (Alexander Turnbull Library, Wellington, New Zealand, 066833)

39. New Zealanders march past the Royal dais, 3 May 1919, in the parade of Dominion troops. The photograph was taken by Sergeants H.H. Green/L.G. Hahn, NZEF. (Green and Hahn album, Te Papa Tongarewa – Museum of New Zealand)

40. Newly-captured Jerusalem and the reading of General Allenby's proclamation of the establishment of Martial Law, 11 December 1917. A Franciscan monk is reading it in French translation. (Matson Photograph Collection, US Library of Congress)

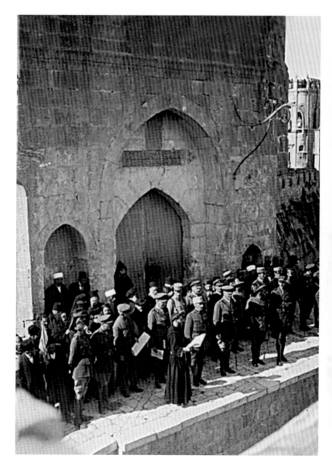

41. An arranged propaganda photograph but one which accurately illustrated the composite nature of the Entente forces in Macedonia. From left to right there is a soldier from Indochina, one from France, a Senegalese, a Briton, a Russian, an Italian, a Serb, a Greek and an Indian. (Wikipedia)

42. Sikh soldiers during the desert campaign in Mesopotamia in 1918. They have with them the sacred book, the Guru Granth Sahib, central to their faith and accompanying a Sikh regiment wherever it were to serve. (Gurdwara Sahib, Pulapol, Kuala Lumpur)

43. Congolese Belgian soldiers of the *Force Publique* campaigning in East Africa under conditions which tested the multi-national forces combatting the German-led native troops, similarly tested. (Public Domain)

44. President Woodrow Wilson in 1913. (US Library of Congress)

45. American troops arriving in France, November 1917. (US Library of Congress)

46. (*Left*). The office of J.P. Morgan and Co. in Manhattan, New York City: Britain's financial agent in the US. (US Library of Congress)

47. (*Right*). US Food Administration poster, 1917. (US Library of Congress)

48. Jazz music for American wounded in a hospital in Paris, 1918. 369 Infantry Regiment Band directed by Lieutenant James R. Europe. (US Library of Congress)

49. Paris on Armistice Day: an American sailor and an American Red Cross nurse celebrate among the crowd near the Paris Gate, Vincennes. A photograph taken by an American official photographer. (Public Domain)

50. Ferdinand Foch, Commander-in-Chief of the Allied Armies, photographed on 23 October 1918 at the ceremony of his being officially honoured as a Marshal of France. (Wikipedia)

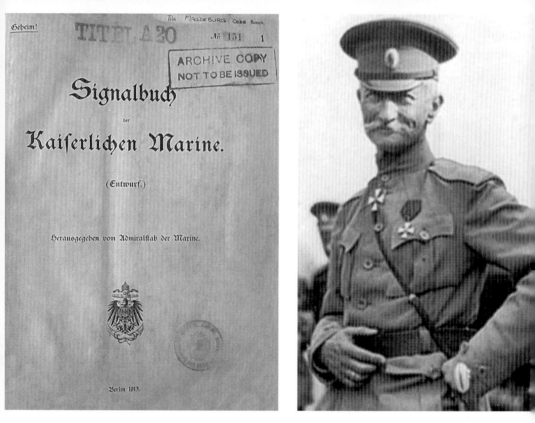

51. (*Left*). The German Naval Signal Code Book recovered by the Russian Navy from the cruiser *Magdeburg* which ran aground in the Baltic. The Russians kept the two Code Books thrown overboard but, after examination and annotation in blue pencil of this third copy taken from the captain's safe, handed it to the British. (Chris Bellamy, by kind permission of the National Archives, Adm137/4156)

52. (*Right*). General A.A. Brusilov in 1916 when in command of Russia's most successful offensive of the war, from June to August of that year. (Wikimedia Commons)

53. The enormous Russian bomber and reconnaissance aircraft, the Sikorski *Il'ya Muromets*, the first four-engined bomber ever built. It had a wingspan of 88ft, a length of 65ft, a range of up to 300 miles, a crew of three, and had at least three machine guns mounted for self-defence. Between 1913 and 1918 eighty-three were built and of those which saw action only one was shot down having run out of ammunition when attacked by several enemy aircraft. (Wikimedia Commons)

54. Australian solders searching German prisoners of war for 'souvenirs' following their capture during fighting around an outpost of the Hindenburg Line near Hargicourt, France, in October 1918. (Wikimedia Commons/AWM)

55. German delegates to the Paris Peace Conference pose for a photograph shortly before leaving for the Hotel Trianon in early May 1919. From left to right: Robert Leinert, Dr Carl Melchior, Johannes Giesberts, Ulrich von Brockdorff-Rantzau, Otto Landsberg, and Professor Walther Schücking. (Bundesarchiv/via Wikimedia Commons)

WILSON E LA PACE.

A Wilson.
Nobile Wilson che dal mar venisti
dal mare di Colombo con Tua Pace,
La Grande Roma, Madre del Diritto,
lieta le braccia t'apre come a Figlio.

56. An Italian postcard welcoming President Wilson bringing Peace and its reward to Italy.

Noble Wilson, you came from the sea
   You came from Columbus's sea with your Peace
   The mother of the Law, the Great Rome,
   Is happy to welcome you as a son, with open arms
   (*Museo Baracca*, Lugo, Italy)

57. A similarly laudatory Italian YMCA postcard. (*Museo Baracca*, Lugo, Italy)

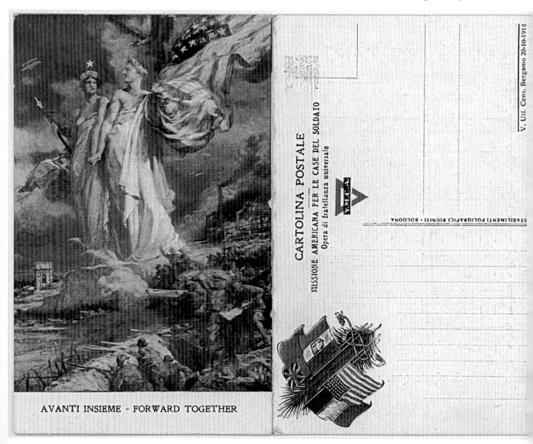

AVANTI INSIEME - FORWARD TOGETHER

58. Italian disillusionment sets in: a postcard cartoon portrays President Wilson offering as a gift to Italy from Britain and the United States a tiny parcel of coal, telling the Italians:

> This is your ration of coal – if it is not enough for the railways, then try, if you can, to go by foot. (*Museo Baracca*, Lugo, Italy)

Quest'è la tua razione,
ITALIA, di carbone;
Se per i treni non ti basta, vedi
se puoi andare a...piedi!—

...gnori miei scusate, vi domando:
Per me non c'è più posto all'alleanza?...

59. A postcard illustrating Italian resentment at being treated as of no account at the Paris Peace Settlement with 'Italy', somewhat pathetically, appealing to Clemenceau, Lloyd George and Wilson: 'Gentlemen, excuse me but I have to ask you, is there no place for me in the Alliance?' (*Museo Baracca*, Lugo, Italy)

60. Suffragette Christabel Pankhurst, of the Women's Social and Political Union, in Manchester to speak at a rally, 1909. (Wikimedia)

61. Ivor Gurney (1890–1937), English poet and composer. Served in the ranks in the army in the war. (The Ivor Gurney Society)

62. (*Left*). William Denis Browne (1888–1915), British composer, A photograph of Browne at his parents' home in Leamington, Warwickshire. Browne, an officer in the Hood Battalion, Royal Naval Division, was to be killed in action at Gallipoli on 4 June 1915, at the Third Battle of Krithia. (Public Domain)

63. (*Right*). Frederick Septimus Kelly (1881-1916), Australian-born and British-educated, musician, composer and GB Olympic rower. He won a Gold Medal at the 1908 Games. An officer in the Hood Battalion, Royal Naval Division, Kelly was twice wounded at Gallipoli, earned the DSC, but was to be killed in action in France on the Somme in November 1916. (Public Domain)

lfred Edward Housman (1859–1936), an English
ical scholar and poet. (Wikimedia Commons).

65. George S.K. Butterworth (1885–1916), English composer. Served in the Great War as a commissioned officer in the 13th Battalion, Durham Light Infantry. He was wounded on the Somme, awarded the MC, but was killed in action on the Somme in August 1916. Photograph first published in the George Butterworth Memorial Volume, 1918 (Wikipedia.org)

66. A postcard of citizens at work in devastated Bethune in the aftermath of the War. (Public Domain)

3288. Ruines de BÉTHUNE — Rue d'Arras

67. A truckload of French refugees outside the American Red Cross canteen at the Gare du Nord, Paris. They are about to start on the second leg of their journey to the south of France. June 1918. (US Library of Congress, American National Red Cross Photograph collection. The photograph was taken by Lewis Wickes Hine)

68. A member of the American Red Cross making friends with Belgian children at an American hostel for refugees in Paris at 46 Rue du Dr Blanche, June 1918. (US Library of Congress, American National Red Cross Photographic Collection, The photograph taken on 16 June 1918 by Lewis Wickes Hines)

69. British Prime Minister David Lloyd George, Vittorio Orlando, Prime Minister of Italy, Georges Clemenceau, Prime Minister of France, and the President of the United States, Woodrow Wilson, in Paris at the Peace Conference, 27 May 1919. (US Library of Congress, George Grantham Bain Collection)

70. Clemenceau, Wilson and Lloyd George leaving the Palace of Versailles after signing the peace treaty, 28 June 1919. (Keystone View Company)

71. Captain Poyntz, an early battlefield tour guide, advertises his services in the 1920s Pilgrim's Guide to the Ypres Salient. (Author's collection)

72. A group of veterans and their wives, the veterans from the 12th Eastern Division, revisiting the 'old front line' in 1931. (Clive Harris)

73. One of the many tanks still on the Ypres battlefields and remaining there up to the Second World War, this one photographed by a returning veteran in 1931, near Poelcappelle. (Clive Harris)

74. Visitors and volunteers inspect the Great War Centenary Exhibition mounted in Ellastone Parish Church, Staffordshire. (Ian Whitehead, courtesy of Margaret and Nick Taylor)

engulfed Russia in March, paralysing its army on the Eastern Front. On 1 July, Russia's Provisional Government attempted a major attack against the Germans with disastrous results. Many units refused to fight and Germany's counter-attack essentially destroyed the Russian army's offensive capability. In early November, the Bolsheviks overthrew the Provisional Government, denounced the war aims of the Allies as imperialistic, and called for peace talks with the Central Powers. Finally, Britain itself, in part to cover the wavering French, attacked the Germans repeatedly on the Western Front from the spring into the autumn. However much these offensives wore down the German army, they failed to achieve a breakthrough and the British themselves suffered well over 300,000 casualties.[11]

The persistent military stalemate combined with the Russian revolution to fray Britain's pro-war consensus at home. The Union of Democratic Control (UDC), a left-liberal organisation that had called for a negotiated peace since late 1914, was attracting more support. Between March and May 1917, strikes involving around 200,000 workers broke out, in part to protest against conscription which had in fact now been in force for a year. In May, the Petrograd Soviet, the voice of the Russian revolution outside the Provisional Government, appealed for a negotiated peace on the basis of no annexations, no indemnities, and self-determination, and called for an international socialist conference to meet in Stockholm to promote an end to the fighting. After some hesitation, Britain's Labour Party voted in August to support attending. Some Conservatives began to doubt the war as well; on 29 November, the *Daily Telegraph* published a letter from former Conservative Foreign Minister, Lord Lansdowne, essentially depicting the war as not worth the cost. The Labour Party and the UDC applauded the letter; Prime Minister David Lloyd George observed that it made 'a profound impression on the country'.[12]

The war effort by the United States provided a strong counterforce to the war pessimism enveloping Britain during the second half of 1917. Before the end of April, the US treasury extended a short-term loan of $200 million to the British to deal with their immediate financial needs. In late July, the Americans agreed to a more regular schedule of advances even as negotiations with British officials over how to spend the money remained tense; the British received $185 million in August and $400 million in September. This money – and the over $4 billion that followed – stabilised British war finances and the value of sterling against the dollar.[13]

As US government loans began to flow into Britain, the United States Navy provided crucial support for a new British initiative to defeat Germany's U-boats, the convoy system. When the British first began using convoys in late April, they calculated that at least thirty-two more destroyers were needed than what they had available fully to implement the system. The US began to fill this gap in May, sending eighteen destroyers to Britain. By the end of August, thirty-five US destroyers had arrived. Over the course of 1917–18, the United States provided 27 per cent of Atlantic convoy protection forces; by the end of the war, about 25,000 US Naval Air Service personnel served in European waters as well, helping to guard coastal convoys. The convoy system almost immediately blunted Germany's submarine campaign: losses in July 1917 declined by about 140,000 tons from June. In August, the Germans sank 472,372 tons compared to the peak of 860,334 tons back in April. In January 1918, Allied losses were below

300,000 tons. Late in the war, the United States also spearheaded the building of a huge North Sea minefield, the 'Northern Barrage', designed to destroy submarines trying to reach the Atlantic. It probably was not worth the $40 million that went into creating it, but it did destroy or damage around ten U–boats.[14]

In addition to the contribution of the US Navy to the convoy system, the entry of the US into the war brought with it a sudden increase in the merchant ships available for the Allied war effort. Soon after the break with Germany, the Wilson administration confiscated several hundred thousand tons of German shipping in American ports. Previously neutral states such as Brazil who either followed the US into the war or broke relations with Berlin, confiscated German shipping in their ports as well, and used them in trade with the Allies. The administration also initiated a massive merchant marine building effort. Although slow to get going, over the course of 1918 this programme produced 2.6 million deadweight tons of seagoing merchant shipping, almost 50 per cent of total Allied construction.[15]

Together, the financial and maritime assistance the United States provided to the British allowed them and their allies to step up their imports of US war supplies in the second half of 1917 and on into 1918. American wheat and flour exports to the British were crucial in later 1917 in covering a shortfall caused by lagging harvests and losses from the U–boats. Britain's dependence on the US for this commodity grew over time; in 1918, over half of British imports of wheat and flour came from the United States. For bacon and ham, the figure was 83.7 per cent; for dairy products, almost 40 per cent. Outside of foodstuffs, oil was the most important resource provided by the US for the Allies. By 1917, around half of Britain's navy burned oil for fuel, and petrol powered the aircraft, tanks and trucks that increasingly became part of the Allied war machine. British oil imports rose 41 per cent from 1916 to 1917, then jumped another 39 per cent in 1918. Almost all of that oil came from the United States. From April 1917 to November 1918, the US also produced as much propellant for artillery as France and Britain combined and delivered enough steel to the French alone for 160 million shells. America's own finished weapons production, to be sure, lagged until late in the war but without American resources, the Allies never would have produced and deployed the firepower they did in 1917 and 1918.[16]

The entry of the United States into the war also led to a sharp tightening of the blockade, which helped to contract Germany's economic output. American exports to neutrals near Germany had been a major hole in the blockade prior to 1917. In early October 1917, this hole closed when the Wilson administration implemented a complete embargo of all American goods to the European neutrals. This forced the neutrals to curtail their exports to Germany and also made them more willing to comply with Britain's blockade policies. Germany still managed, with difficulty, to attain most of its munitions production targets in 1917 and 1918, but overall its net national product in those years declined about 25 per cent compared to 1913. The blockade exerted its main impact, then, upon German food requirement and production. The Reich's imports of bread grains, for example, fell from 240,750 tons in 1916 to 42,598 tons in 1918; its imports of meats fell even more sharply. Far from making up the gap, Germany's own agricultural production fell, in large part because it could not import the fertilizer it needed. Malnourishment and endless searching for food became a way of life for

Germany's civilian population during the last two years of the war while on the Western Front, by spring 1918, even its combat troops were hungry.[17]

The material assistance the United States provided the Allies after April 1917 was matched by diplomacy which undercut rising domestic questioning of the war in Britain. First, President Wilson opposed negotiating with the existing German government and rejected peace terms designed to restore the *status quo ante bellum*. He wanted to defeat Germany's armies and see its government transformed before any negotiations could even be considered. Peace now, he declared in mid-June 1917, would solidify the existing Reich's power and leave it in position to threaten the world in the future. Those who supported peace talks were therefore simply 'tools' of Germany. Consistent with this view, Wilson denied passports to American socialists who wanted to attend the Stockholm conference. At the same time, though, Wilson endorsed, if vaguely, the anti-imperial, progressive peace programme of the left. He, too, opposed 'indemnities,' he insisted to the Russians, 'except those that constitute payment for manifest wrongs done'. He stressed in August that peace could not securely rest 'upon vindictive action of any sort'. The peace he wanted, he declared in his Fourteen Points Address in January 1918, would be based on 'the principle of justice to all peoples and nationalities'. He reiterated this vision a month later in his Four Principles speech, denouncing 'balance of power' politics and calling for the satisfaction of 'well defined national aspirations'.[18]

The political significance of both the concrete aid the United States provided the Allies and Wilson's diplomatic pronouncements became clear in late 1917 and early 1918. Wilson's strong opposition to the Petrograd Soviet's peace formula and to the Stockholm conference probably made the British and Allied governments feel more secure in facing down their anti-war left in the summer of 1917; all of them, by mid-August, refused to grant passports for attending Stockholm, effectively closing off that route to negotiations with Germany. More significantly, except for Russia, none of them substantively modified their peace terms or their wariness of peace talks in any form. The British came closest to doing so when they learned of peace feelers from Germany apparently based on German concessions in the west in exchange for a free hand in Eastern Europe and Russia. French and British leaders discussed this possible deal in late September 1917, with Lloyd George pushing the hardest to consider it. Nearly everyone else disagreed, however. In part, they feared such negotiations with Germany would divide and demoralise their coalition; in part they feared a settlement giving Germany dominance in the East would make it an overpowering threat in any future war. They also, though, saw no reason to pursue talks given that the ever increasing aid the United States gave them only strengthened their position in the war. As France's Alexandre Ribot put it on 30 September: 'until the United States has made the decisive effort it is preparing, we shall not be in a favourable position to negotiate'. British leaders felt the same way. 'With the vast potential supply of men in America', commented Chief of the Imperial General Staff, Sir William Robertson, in January, 'there should be no doubt of our winning.' Wilson's Fourteen Points and Four Principles speeches also rallied the left to the Allied war effort, diminishing any domestic political need to consider peace talks.[19]

American belligerency likewise shaped German decision-making in late 1917. By June 1917, German leaders perceived that their submarine campaign was not going to force Britain out of the war. At first, this realisation, along perhaps with concern over British attacks on the Western Front, led Germany's key policymakers, Hindenburg and Ludendorff, grudgingly to allow the civilian leadership to feel out Britain about peace negotiations based on minimal German concessions in the west. When those contacts went nowhere, the German Army Command (OHL) reverted to its commitment to expansionist aims to fend off democratic reforms at home and to give the Reich security in future wars. With the submarine campaign a failure, Ludendorff knew that the longer the war went on, more American troops would arrive in Europe, making it impossible to achieve the decisive military victory necessary to attain those political objectives. The collapse of Russia, however, meant that Germany might still win if it could transfer forces to the west, launching an offensive with decisive numerical advantage over the Allies. But Germany would have to act quickly. 'Our overall position requires the earliest possible blow,' Ludendorff warned an army conference in mid-November 1917, 'if possible at the end of February, or the beginning of March, before the Americans can throw strong forces into the scales.' Determined to exploit Germany's window of opportunity for victory before the United States shut it, Ludendorff made the high-risk choice to throw all of Germany's remaining resources into a massive offensive on the Western Front in early 1918.[20]

The German attack, which began on 21 March 1918, set off a sequence of events that ended in October with a new German government deciding to seek an armistice. Because the United States insisted upon building up an independent army under American command, its direct military contribution to defeating the German offensive was slow to materialize. By November 1917, only 77,000 American troops were in France while British combat forces there numbered nearly one million. On the day the German offensive started, US forces still numbered below 300,000, with only three divisions actually in the line. In response to the German attack, however, American deployments rapidly increased. In April, over 100,000 troops crossed the Atlantic; beginning in May, over 200,000 American soldiers landed in France every four weeks. About 46 per cent of these men made the trip in US ships, nearly all of them escorted by the United States Navy. By 10 May, American divisions occupied 55 kilometres of quiet sectors of the front. Under Allied pressure, General John J. Pershing, commander of the American Expeditionary Force (AEF), allowed some American troops to be brigaded with the British and French armies, which meant that they began to play a role in combat in late May. By mid-July, the AEF numbered more than one million. On 12 September, it launched its first major independent action, an attack at St-Mihiel involving 550,000 American troops. Two weeks later, the AEF led a co-ordinated Allied assault on Germany's battered forces, attacking at Meuse-Argonne with nearly 1.2 million US soldiers, more than the entire Confederate Army in the Civil War. By the time the war ended, the AEF, at about two million men, was bigger than British forces in France both in numbers and in the length of its front – a far cry from the situation that had prevailed at the beginning of the year.[21]

The AEF had a varied impact on the climactic battles of 1918. Early on, from about January through May, deployments of American troops to quiet sectors of the front freed up veteran Allied divisions to join in the ultimately successful defence against the series of German offensives. From late May to early June, two US divisions brigaded with the French Sixth Army helped to halt the German offensive driving toward Paris. The American forces, according to one observer, were like a 'blood transfusion' for French soldiers, who cheered their arrival. French Premier Clemenceau had a similar response: 'I told you on my first day,' he declared to other officials on 3 June, 'I am gambling the war on American intervention which will bring us such resources that we cannot fail to finish the Germans off.' Brigaded American divisions fought with French armies spearheading the first major counter-attack against the Germans on 18 July. Three weeks later, on 8 August, one US division joined in a spectacularly successful British attack at Amiens, which included aircraft, tanks and lorries powered by American oil.[22]

In its own offensives, however, at the St-Mihiel salient and at Meuse-Argonne, the AEF had a mixed performance. The St-Mihiel operation achieved its immediate objectives, but communications problems, lax discipline and inexperienced commanders all contributed to a failure to destroy the opposing German forces; 80 per cent of those in the salient escaped. At Meuse-Argonne, the American advance almost immediately ground to a halt in the face of German resistance. Again, poorly-trained and led troops and ill-conceived tactics hurt the AEF. Massive logistical tangles, compounded by influenza striking down troops just as the attack began, further hampered the Americans. Still, simply the presence of large-scale US forces at the front provided crucial help to the Allies, allowing them to attain numerical superiority over the Germans by July and giving Ferdinand Foch, the supreme Allied commander, the manpower he needed to launch the joint Allied offensive of late September.[23]

Two days after the co-ordinated attack began, on 28 September, Ludendorff abruptly decided that Germany needed to seek an armistice. 'The OHL and the German army are finished,' he declared. 'No more reliance could be placed on the troops . . . Continually, units have proved themselves so unreliable that they hurriedly had to be withdrawn from the front.' The demoralisation of German troops so alarming to Ludendorff was rooted in the failure of Germany's last-ditch offensives – a failure produced, we have seen, partly by the material and psychological boost the United States gave Allied forces and by the AEF's take-over of quiet sectors of the front, which made available the more experienced Allied soldiers for offensive operations. In addition, OHL's own morale was shaken by the rapid influx of US troops beginning in May. German intelligence officers had not anticipated this development; they could not even believe it was happening until late June when they realised American forces were approaching one million. In the context of huge German losses in the fighting from March through July, when Germany suffered 977,555 casualties, the spectre of fighting such a huge army was deeply disheartening. Sharp increases in the number of Germans surrendering after 8 August added to Germany's manpower disadvantage, which only magnified the disturbing implications of the never-ending arrival of more American troops. Perceiving that his own men had lost their will to fight and that the Americans provided an 'almost inexhaustible reserve' for the Allies, Ludendorff concluded that Germany needed to stop the war.[24]

A desire to get peace, though, would not have mattered much if German leaders had not also seen a way to implement it. In this respect, President Wilson's statecraft exercised a decisive influence on the Germans. Throughout the period of American belligerency, Wilson had publicly, though by implication, criticised Allied war aims and stated a willingness to negotiate with a democratic German government. German leaders certainly noticed Wilson's pronouncements. On 29 September, Foreign Minister Paul von Hintze, Ludendorff, and Hindenburg agreed that the best way to attain an immediate armistice was to broaden Germany's government to include representation from the Reichstag majority parties, including the socialists; accept the Fourteen Points as the basis for peace talks; and appeal directly to Wilson to take steps for a ceasefire.

Hintze in particular favoured this plan because he thought it might tempt Wilson into offering lenient terms to Germany. The head of the new German government, however, Prince Max of Baden, feared Wilson might press for German territorial concessions and questioned the need for an immediate armistice. In the debate over what to do, two key members of the new cabinet, the socialist (SPD) Philipp Scheidemann and the Centre Party's Matthias Erzberger, provided support for Hintze's approach. Both the SPD and especially Erzberger had favourably viewed Wilson's peace principles since February 1918 and believed that peace terms based on them need not compromise German territory. Reinforced by the Kaiser, who expected Prince Max to follow the lead of OHL, Scheidemann's and Erzberger's endorsement of an appeal to Wilson forced Max to go along with it, and he sent a note to Wilson on the night of 4/5 October.[25]

This decision led to the collapse of Germany's war effort. In his replies to its armistice appeal, Wilson demanded that Germany withdraw from all invaded territory, leave the precise ceasefire terms to US/Allied military representatives, and enact more sweeping changes to its political system. German leaders reluctantly accepted Wilson's position, partly because they doubted Germany's ability to keep fighting and partly because they continued to hope that Wilson's peace programme might in the end lead to a reasonable peace treaty for their country. Germany's armistice appeal and subsequent dialogue with Wilson accelerated the demoralisation of German troops and the disintegration of the Reich's chief ally, Austria-Hungary. The exchanges with Wilson also alienated the German naval leadership. They saw no need for an armistice and feared for the future of the German Navy if the war were to end without the High Seas Fleet engaging in battle with the British Grand Fleet. They therefore decided to send the fleet into the Thames estuary for such a maritime Armageddon. When preparations for the operation began to go forward in late October, German sailors rebelled. On 4 November they took over Kiel and revolution began to spread throughout the rest of Germany. With domestic order in peril, allies gone, and the enemy continuing to advance in the west, Prince Max's government resolved on 6 November to agree to whatever terms necessary to get a ceasefire. Five days later, German representatives led by Erzberger signed the armistice agreement.[26]

Given their command of the battlefield by this point, the Allies might have decided not to pursue an armistice and instead continue to press forward toward the German frontier until the Germans capitulated. Several considerations influenced their rejection of this course. The armistice terms essentially gave the Allies everything they wanted; France and especially Britain were suffering from continued casualties and declining manpower; and French and British politicians to some degree feared exposing their troops to revolutionary ideas inside Germany. The United States also factored into their eagerness for an armistice, however. Wilson opposed an invasion and extensive occupation of the Reich if it could be avoided, fearing it would humiliate the German people and alienate them from his peace programme. In addition, British leadership feared that the longer the war went on, the more the United States would dominate the peacemaking, as its power was on the rise while Britain's was in decline. With Wilson hostile to some of the British war aims, such as taking over Germany's colonies, the Lloyd George government wanted to avoid prolonging the war if at all possible.[27]

With the armistice, Britain secured the decisive victory it had been fighting for since 1914. It is highly unlikely this outcome would have occurred without the help Britain and her allies had received from the United States. The material assistance the United States provided – the financial credit that allowed the Allies to buy war supplies for their offensives, the destroyers that allowed them to operate the convoy system which defeated the U-boats, and the nearly two million soldiers who poured into France in 1918 – gave the Allies the edge in resources necessary to win a war of attrition. The assistance also stiffened Britain's resolve to fight in late 1916 and, more crucially, again in late 1917. It almost certainly boosted Allied morale, both in late 1917 and during the fighting that stopped the German offensive in spring 1918. In short, without the United States, the Allies would have lacked the means and the will to defeat Germany; most probably, without American entry into the war, they would have chosen to settle for an unfavourable compromise peace in late 1917.[28]

American policies also led to disastrous German decisions. The financial credits and supply sales to the Entente, Wilson's accommodation of Britain's blockade and his protests against the U-boat campaign all undermined Germany's ability to win the war. Perceiving that the United States stood in the way of their victory, the German leadership had to choose between modifying their war aims or taking a high-risk gamble on winning by unrestricted submarine warfare. The leaders chose the latter, driven in part by an intense animosity towards, and distrust of, Wilson. America's entry into the war as a consequence of this decision gravely worsened the German strategic situation, even with Russia's collapse in the east. Fearing the arrival of the AEF and still unwilling to reconsider their expansionist war aims, the German leadership decided to risk everything on what they hoped would be a war-winning offensive on the Western Front. This gamble failed to pay off. The attack hastened American troop deployments and its failure seriously damaged morale. Nevertheless, Germany still had options remaining even after it became clear on the battlefield that it could not win the war. For example, it could have withdrawn to more defensible positions while rallying its troops to fight by publicising France's desire to dismember the Reich. Wilson's peace programme and his apparent differences with the Allies, however, enticed Germany into making the armistice appeal of 4 October, an appeal which essentially led to the collapse of what remained of its war effort.[29]

The policies of the United States then fundamentally shaped the trajectory of the war, both before and after it became a belligerent. This largely reflected the immense economic power it possessed relative to the other combatants. Because of that power, whatever the United States did or did not do would inevitably affect the course of the fighting. Ironically, Wilson had hoped to use America's power to mediate an early end to the war on the basis of a 'peace without victory'. However, by assisting the Allies, he made the United States the decisive factor in prolonging the conflict and in making it possible for them to crush Germany completely – the exact opposite of Wilson's stated objectives.[30]

Notes

1. Eric W. Osborne, *Britain's Economic Blockade of Germany 1914-1919* (London: Frank Cass, 2004), p. 115 and see pp. 61–109; John W. Coogan, *The End of Neutrality: The United States, Britain, and Maritime Rights, 1899-1915* (Ithaca, NY: Cornell University Press, 1981), pp. 155–67, 194–200, 203–7, 210–13, 223–31; Thomas A. Bailey and Paul B. Ryan, *The Lusitania Disaster: An Episode in Modern Warfare and Diplomacy* (New York: The Free Press, 1975), pp. 28–31; Robert W. Tucker, *Woodrow Wilson and the Great War: Reconsidering America's Neutrality, 1914-1917* (Charlottesville, VA: University of Virginia Press, 2007), pp. 103, 140; Justus D. Doenecke, *Nothing Less Than War: A New History of America's Entry into World War I* (Lexington, KY: University Press of Kentucky, 2011), pp. 53–7; Arthur S. Link, *Wilson: Campaigns for Progressivism and Peace* (Princeton, NJ: Princeton University Press, 1965), pp. 65, 70–1, 202–3.

2. Woodrow Wilson to Robert Lansing, 21 July 1915, in Arthur S. Link, *et al.* (eds), *The Papers of Woodrow Wilson* 69 vols (Princeton, NJ: Princeton University Press, 1966–94), 33:548 and pp. 545–8, *passim*. Hereafter *The Papers of Woodrow Wilson* will be abbreviated *PWW*. See also Wilson to W.J. Stone, 24 February 1916, *PWW* 36:214; Bailey and Ryan, *Lusitania*, 39; Arthur S. Link, *Wilson: Confusions and Crises 1915-1916* (Princeton, NJ: Princeton University Press, 1964), pp. 222–79.

3. David Stevenson, *Cataclysm: The First World War* (New York: Basic Books, 2004), pp. 184, 190, 200; Hew Strachan, *The First World War Volume I: To Arms* (Oxford: Oxford University Press, 2001), pp. 1106–8; Kathleen Burk, 'J.M. Keynes and the Exchange Rate Crisis of July 1917', *The Economic History Review* 32:3 (August 1979), p. 406; Sterling Kernek, 'The British Government's Reactions to President Wilson's "Peace" Note of December 1916', *The Historical Journal* 13:4 (December 1970), pp. 749–50.

4. Strachan, *First World War Vol I*, pp. 956–7, 967–9, 972; Niall Ferguson, *The Pity of War* (New York: Basic Books, 1999), p. 328; Stevenson, *Cataclysm*, p. 184; Kathleen Burk, *Britain, America, and the Sinews of War, 1914-1918* (Boston: George Allen & Unwin, 1985), pp. 61–2, 81, 95.

5. Osborne, *Britain's Economic Blockade*, p. 122; Mark Jefferson, 'Our Trade in the Great War', *Geographical Review* 3:6 (June 1917), p. 479; Alexander Watson, *Ring of Steel: Germany and Austria-Hungary in World War I* (New York: Basic Books, 2014), pp. 331 and 330–74; Avner Offer, *The First World War: An Agrarian Interpretation* (New York: Oxford University Press, 1989), pp. 27–34.

6. Paul G. Halpern, *A Naval History of World War I* (Annapolis, MD: Naval Institute Press, 1994), pp. 299, 308, 335, and 291–335. See also Karl E. Birnbaum, *Peace Moves and U-Boat Warfare, A Study of Imperial Germany's Policy towards the United States, April 18, 1916–January 9, 1917* (New York: Archon Books, 1970); Arthur S. Link, *Wilson: The Struggle for Neutrality 1914-1915* (Princeton, NJ: Princeton University Press, 1960), pp. 355–454, 551–84, 655–81; Link, *Confusions and Crises*, pp. 85–100, 155–89; 222–74; Link, *Campaigns for Progressivism and Peace*, pp. 113–15, 165–86.

7. David French, *The Strategy of the Lloyd George Coalition 1916-1918* (Oxford: Clarendon Press, 1995), pp. 3, 6, 33–4; V.H. Rothwell, *British War Aims and Peace Diplomacy 1914-1918* (Oxford: Clarendon Press, 1971), pp. 3–4, 18–20, 24, 53–5, 59; Kernek, 'The British Government's Reaction', pp. 724–5, 751–2, and *passim*; Link, *Campaigns for Progressivism and Peace*, p. 77. See also Osborne, *Britain's Economic Blockade*, pp. 126–7, 140–2.

8. Watson, *Ring of Steel*, pp. 416–17. See also Martin Kitchen, *The Silent Dictatorship: The Politics of the German High Command under Hindenburg and Ludendorff, 1916-1918* (New York: Holme and Meier, 1976), pp. 18–19, 102–3, 106; H.E. Goemans, *War & Punishment: the Causes of War Termination and the First World War* (Princeton, NJ: Princeton University Press, 2000), pp. 74–118; Stevenson, *Cataclysm*, pp. 109–11.

9. Dirk Steffen, 'The Holtzendorff Memorandum of 22 December 1916 and Germany's Declaration of Unrestricted U-Boat Warfare', *The Journal of Military History* 68:1 (January 2004), p. 219; Ludendorff quoted in Watson, *Ring of Steel*, p. 423; Hipper quoted in Holger H. Herwig, *Politics of Frustration: The United States in German Naval Planning, 1889-1941* (Boston: Little, Brown, 1976), p. 124. See also Stevenson, *Cataclysm*, pp. 105, 110–11, 131, 208–14; Watson, *Ring of Steel*, pp. 226–39, 295–311, 324–6, 331, 339, 416–24; Birnbaum, *Peace Moves and U-Boat Warfare*, pp. viii–ix, 12–13, 19–20, 30–1, 39, 48–9, 53, 98, 105–7, 143, 253–61, 336–7; Osborne, *Britain's Economic Blockade*, p. 161; Offer, *Agrarian Interpretation*, pp. 363–4.

10. Burk, *Sinews of War*, p. 95.

11. Halpern, *Naval History*, p. 341; Stevenson, *Cataclysm*, pp. 142–3, 253–4, 267–77, 308–9, 312–13.

12. Lloyd George quoted in French, *Lloyd George Coalition*, p. 200 and see pp. 199–201; Rothwell, *British War Aims*, p. 96; Stevenson, *Cataclysm*, p. 286; Rex A. Wade, *The Russian Search for Peace:*

February–October 1917 (Stanford, CA: Stanford University Press, 1969), pp. 51–6, 106–10; W.B. Fest, 'British War Aims and German Peace Feelers during the First World War (December 1916-November 1918)', *The Historical Journal* 15:2 (June 1972), pp. 303–4.

13. Strachan, *First World War*, pp. 977–8; Burk, *Sinews of War*, pp. 133–4, 196–213; Burk, 'J.M. Keynes', *passim*; Patrick O. Cohrs, *The Unfinished Peace after World War I: America, Britain, and the Stabilisation of Europe 1919-1932*(Cambridge: Cambridge University Press, 2008), p. 68.

14. Halpern, *Naval History*, pp. 341, 351, 355–6, 359, 362, 365, 424–5, 438–41; Stevenson, *Cataclysm*, p. 365; David Stevenson, *With Our Backs to the Wall: Victory and Defeat in 1918* (Cambridge, MA: Belknap Press, 2011), pp. 311–15. See also Holger H. Herwig and David F. Trask, 'The Failure of Imperial Germany's Undersea Offensive Against World Shipping, February 1917-October 1918', *The Historian* 33:4 (August 1971), pp. 611–36, *passim*.

15. David M. Kennedy, *Over Here: The First World War and American Society* (New York: Oxford University Press, 1980), p. 311; Halpern, *Naval History*, p. 435; Stevenson, *Cataclysm*, p. 297; Stevenson, *With Our Backs to the Wall*, pp. 337–9.

16. Stevenson, *With Our Backs to the Wall*, pp. 343–4, 356–8, 360–3, 391.

17. Osborne, *Britain's Economic Blockade*, pp. 163, 167–8; Ferguson, *Pity of War*, p. 249; Stevenson, *With Our Backs to the Wall*, pp. 431–3. See also Offer, *Agrarian Interpretation*, pp. 28–61; Watson, *Ring of Steel*, pp. 330–41, 359–74.

18. Woodrow Wilson, 'Flag Day Address', 14 June 1917, *PWW* 42:502–3; Wilson to the Provisional Government of Russia, 22 May 1917, *PWW* 42:367; Wilson to Edward Mandell House (enclosure), 23 August 1917, *PWW* 44:35; Wilson, Address to a Joint Session of Congress, 8 January 1918, *PWW* 45:539 and 534–9, *passim*; Wilson, Address to a Joint Session of Congress, 11 February 1918, *PWW* 46:323 and 318–24, *passim*. See also Ross A. Kennedy, *The Will to Believe: Woodrow Wilson, World War I, and America's Strategy for Peace and Security* (Kent, OH: Kent State University Press, 2009), pp. 128–45.

19. Ribot quoted in David Stevenson, 'The Failure of Peace by Negotiation in 1917', *The Historical Journal* 34:1 (March 1991), p. 84 and see pp. 76–7, 84–5; Robertson quoted in French, *Lloyd George Coalition*, p. 202 and see pp. 142–7. See also Wade, *Russian Search for Peace*, pp. 62, 78, 107–10, 116; David Stevenson, *The First World War and International Politics* (New York: Oxford University Press, 1988), pp. 158–61, 168, 170; Rothwell, *British War Aims*, pp. 105–9; David R. Woodward, *Trial by Friendship: Anglo-American Relations, 1917-1918* (Lexington, KY: University Press of Kentucky, 1993), pp. 99–103; John L. Snell, 'Wilson's Peace Program and German Socialism, January-March 1918', *Mississippi Valley Historical Review* 38:2 (September 1951), p. 208; Stevenson, *Cataclysm*, p. 376. The United States also advised Britain not to pursue the peace feelers. See W.B. Fowler, *British-American Relations, 1917-1918: The Role of Sir William Wiseman* (Princeton, NJ: Princeton University Press, 1969), p. 93.

20. Ludendorff quoted in Gregory Martin, 'German Strategy and Military Assessments of the American Expeditionary Force (AEF)', *War in History* 1:2 (July 1994), p. 179. See also Halpern, *Naval History*, p. 368; Herwig and Trask, 'Failure of Imperial Germany's Undersea Offensive', pp. 618–19; Stevenson, 'Failure of Peace by Negotiation', pp. 78, 82; Gordon A. Craig, *Germany 1866-1945* (New York: Oxford University Press, 1978), pp. 358–64, 382–93; Stevenson, *With Our Backs to the Wall*, pp. 31–6; Wilhelm Deist, 'The Military Collapse of the German Empire: the Reality Behind the Stab-in-the-Back Myth', *War in History* 3:2 (April 1996), pp. 189–90; Watson, *Ring of Steel*, pp. 514–15.

21. Stevenson, *With Our Backs to the Wall*, pp. 49, 245, 247–8; Stevenson, *Cataclysm*, pp. 301, 342, 358–60; David F. Trask, *The AEF and Coalition Warmaking, 1917-1918* (Lawrence, KA: University Press of Kansas, 1993), pp. 42, 53, 60, 106–14, 119–30; Jennifer D. Keene, *Doughboys, the Great War, and the Remaking of America* (Baltimore: Johns Hopkins University Press, 2001), p. ix.

22. Quotes in Stevenson, *With Our Backs to the Wall*, p. 87 and see pp. 118–22. See also Trask, *AEF and Coalition Warmaking*, pp. 20, 42, 55, 60, 70–1, 88, 95–7, 175; Stevenson, *Cataclysm*, p. 347.

23. Trask, *AEF and Coalition Warmaking*, pp. 100–14, 123–30, 175; Martin, 'German Strategy and Military Assessments', pp. 178, 186; Carol R. Byerly, *Fever of War: The Influenza Epidemic in the US Army during World War I* (New York: New York University Press, 2005), pp. 108–19; Stevenson, *With Our Backs to the Wall*, pp. 130–3.

24. Ludendorff quoted in Watson, *Ring of Steel*, p. 534 and see pp. 524, 529, 532–4; OHL quote on reserves in Trask, *AEF and Coalition Warmaking*, p. 135. See also Martin, 'German Strategy and Military Assessments', pp. 179–80, 193; Stevenson, *Cataclysm*, pp. 359–60; Stevenson, *With Our Backs to the Wall*, pp. 290–1.

25. Watson, *Ring of Steel*, pp. 534–5, 547–8; Kitchen, *Silent Dictatorship*, pp. 254–9; Klaus Schwabe, *Woodrow Wilson, Revolutionary Germany, and Peacemaking, 1918-1919: Missionary Diplomacy and the Realities of Power* (Chapel Hill, NC: University of North Carolina Press, 1985), pp. 22–4, 28, 32–8; Klaus Epstein, *Matthias Erzberger and the Dilemma of German Democracy* (Princeton, NJ: Princeton University Press, 1959), pp. 250–5, 260–1, 264; Snell, 'Wilson's Peace Program and German Socialism', pp. 189–92, 208; Stevenson, *Cataclysm*, pp. 381–3; Stevenson, *With Our Backs to the Wall*, pp. 513–14.

26. R.A. Kennedy, *Will to Believe*, pp. 148–52; Epstein, *Matthias Erzberger*, p. 264; Schwabe, *Woodrow Wilson, Revolutionary Germany, and Peacemaking*, pp. 47–50, 55–8, 95–8, 101–11, 114; Kitchen, *Silent Dictatorship*, pp. 260–4; Watson, *Ring of Steel*, pp. 549–50; Stevenson, *Cataclysm*, pp. 386, 391–2, 394–404.

27. Bullitt Lowry, *Armistice 1918* (Kent, OH: Kent State University Press, 1996), pp. 166–8; Stevenson, *With Our Backs to the Wall*, pp. 521–8, 539–43; R.A. Kennedy, *Will to Believe*, pp. 148–56; David French, '"Had We Known How Bad things Were in Germany, We Might Have Got Stiffer Terms": Great Britain and the German Armistice' in Manfred F. Boemeke, Gerald D. Feldman and Elisabeth Glaser (eds), *The Treaty of Versailles: A Reassessment after 75 years* (Cambridge: Cambridge University Press, 1998), pp. 69–85; Stevenson, *Cataclysm*, p. 388.

28. Stevenson makes this point as well; my interpretation has largely followed his. See *With Our Backs to the Wall*, pp. 20, 535; *Cataclysm*, pp. 296–300.

29. On German options, see Ferguson, *Pity of War*, p. 317.

30. Wilson, Address to the Senate, 22 January 1917, *PWW* 40:536 and pp. 533–9. See also R.A. Kennedy, *Will to Believe*, passim.

Suggested Further Reading

Burk, Kathleen, *Britain, America, and the Sinews of War, 1914-1918* (Boston: George Allen & Unwin, 1985)

Kennedy, David M., *Over Here: The First World War and American Society* (New York: Oxford University Press, 1980)

Kennedy, Ross A., *The Will to Believe: Woodrow Wilson, World War I, and America's Strategy for Peace and Security* (Kent, OH: Kent State University Press, 2009)

Kennedy, Ross A. (ed.), *A Companion to Woodrow Wilson* (Malden, MA: Wiley-Blackwell, 2013)

Stevenson, David, *Cataclysm: The First World War* (New York: Basic Books, 2004)

Trask, David F., *The AEF and Coalition Warmaking, 1917-1918* (Lawrence, KA: University Press of Kansas, 1993)

Trask, David F., *Anglo-American Naval Relations, 1917-1918* (Columbia, MO: University of Missouri Press, 1972)

Chapter 10

France Leads the Way to Victory

By William Philpott

The role of France and the French army in the second half of the First World War has been underplayed. It served Britons at the time, and Anglophone historians afterwards, to compose a narrative of a tiring France, her army bled white at Verdun and her people increasingly war weary, sustained by her Anglo-Saxon allies. In this history, a partly-ready British army stepped up on the Somme, struggled on through 1917 with increasingly conditional French support, bore the brunt of the German offensive in 1918 and then played the major part in the subsequent advance to victory.[1] By 1918, masses of American troops were flooding into France to take up the fight from the war-weary Europeans and to deliver the *coup de grâce* to Germany. It is certainly true that France bore the weight of the war (with Russia) in its first two years and that British, Italian and American effort became increasingly significant from summer 1916. However, in 1918 the main theatre of the war remained France, the French army was still the largest Allied army in the field, and strategic and political leadership of the coalition remained in the hands of Frenchmen, Ferdinand Foch and Georges Clemenceau respectively, the managers of an increasingly effective coalition command and directive structure. A century on, chauvinistic history may still prevail, although it is appropriate to acknowledge that the First World War was fought and ended in France, by France and for France; and that a key element of French strategy and policy was to ensure that her partners were managed to that victorious outcome.

Influential early historical works such as Charles Cruttwell's 1936 Lees-Knowles lectures established the parameters of the supposed shift in relative power between Britain and France during 1917.[2] As a consequence of the heavy French casualties of 1914–16 the British army would become the leading military force in the west. After the Nivelle offensive failed in spring 1917, the French army was in crisis and went on the defensive under its new leader General Philippe Pétain, who was 'waiting for the Americans and the tanks'. Without an aggressive British policy this would have handed the initiative back to the Germans and risked their defeating the French army.[3] (In this contention there is an inherent, if untestable, assumption that in late 1917 the German army was actually capable of doing this.) Cyril Falls, an official historian of 1917's early operations, popularised this perception: 'To aid the process of regeneration by Pétain . . . France's British ally had to bear a heavy burden.'[4] French weakness in 1917 would become a post-facto rationale for the launch and continuation of the controversial Flanders offensive. (A similar rationale has also been used to explain the previous year's

Somme offensive.) By 1918, although the French army was fighting again, it required the British army to lead by example. The British commander-in-chief, Sir Douglas Haig, focused poorly-conceived French operational plans on the main goal, enabling victory in 1918 and avoiding another year's campaign.

In essence this historical judgement derives from Haig's own self-serving assessment of the 1917 and 1918 campaigns, chronicled in his contemporary diary record of coalition relations, on which British historians have been over-dependent for their view of French military performance.[5] It was formalised immediately after the war in the Haig-sponsored account of his period of command co-authored by the journalist George Dewar and Haig's former private secretary John Boraston.[6] In this narrative, the French are treated as a reason for Haig's own strategic decisions, rather than as strategic actors in their own right who largely determine Haig's contribution to coalition operation in his role of an Allied army group commander. For example, the Third Battle of Ypres was prolonged into the autumn 'largely in order to ward off a crushing attack on the French'.[7]

This chapter will endeavour to correct this skewed narrative by examining three themes: first, the real experience and growing military effectiveness of France in 1917, a year in which Douglas Haig seemed to be trying to fight 1916's battles better, while Pétain was starting to practise the 'winning formula' that would bring victory in the field in 1918; second, the proper organisation of the coalition to push to victory in 1918; and third, the military contribution of French leaders and forces to checking the German spring offensives and organising and sustaining the subsequent advance to victory.

1917 would be a difficult year for France, just as it would be for all belligerents as war weariness set in and political structures faltered as new populist agendas spilled into Old Europe from the New World and a renewed Russia.[8] Like Britain, during 1917 France would pass from a 'spring of hope' through a 'summer of discontent' and into an 'autumn of resolve' as a process of military reorganisation, political regrouping and popular remobilization took place.[9]

Arguably, by the end of 1916 France had a mature and effective army. Under General Robert Nivelle's leadership, Second Army had reversed French fortunes on the Verdun battlefield, and directed by Foch and led by General Marie-Émile Fayolle, Sixth Army had given the Germans their own bleeding on the Somme.[10] In 1916, France had had an effective military leader, General Joseph Joffre, and followed a coherent plan executed by a tactically effective army with strong allied support. Although it had not broken the German army, there was a real belief that Joffre's General Allied Offensive had brought France and her allies to the brink of victory. Joffre's intention had been to follow up quickly in 1917 and deliver the *coup de grâce*. However, political short-termism led to his being replaced by Nivelle in December 1916. Still, the parameters of French strategy remained essentially those set by Joffre in the first half of the war, and once Nivelle's former superior, Pétain, and Foch resumed responsibility in May 1917 they would organise and prepare for defeating the German army in a sustained battle of attrition on the Western Front. In the meantime, however, the army had to be readied and motivated for this final titanic engagement.

First, there was to be a test of resolve. Military morale was a matter of increasing concern for all armies by 1917. During the Somme offensive there had been signs of indiscipline in overtired troops, for example a mutiny at the end of July 1916 among

Colonial Army troops who had spent a month in a difficult sector of the line.[11] Research by Len Smith and François Cochet suggests that this was the way the republican system operated in France, through the periodic renegotiation of the parameters of discipline and duty, sacrifice and reward between the rank and file and their leadership.[12] Nevertheless, both Joffre and Nivelle were anxious about the influence of pacifist agitators on soldiers on leave by the turn of the year and asked the government to clamp down. This was a sign of the times: liberal revolution in Russia and growing economic protest on the French home front formed the background to these events. More generally, however, after the twin efforts and obvious successes on the Somme and at Verdun there was a hope for a rapid end to the war. This meant that the French rank and file began the year with relatively high morale: they knew that they could beat the enemy and that their leaders knew how to use them to beat him. Nonetheless, Nivelle's brash promises that he could turn localised tactical successes into decisive victory offered a hostage to fortune.

When it was belatedly launched in April 1917 the limited success of Nivelle's grand offensive, which delivered another strong tactical blow with no immediate operational or strategic outcome, catalysed a change in the mood of the nation and the army. This military false start was enmeshed with an ongoing political crisis. One French government had already fallen that year, and the new ministry had been too pusillanimous to cancel Nivelle's attack, despite the misgivings of his subordinates.[13] Falls suggested that: 'French politicians in their eagerness to discredit Nivelle circulated fantastically high figures for the losses. The soldier was given the impression that he had been defeated, whereas he had won a success greater than in many battles which had been proclaimed smashing victories.'[14] This lost opportunity provoked a reaction among the soldiery, the so-called 'mutinies'. These rippled along the front for the next two months, but were largely concentrated in divisions told off for the trenches behind the Chemin des Dames front, where Nivelle's partial penetration of the German defences in that sector had condemned the troops to another gruelling attritional fight for local tactical advantage. It was this reversion to '1916-style' fighting as much as the lost opportunity of the new campaign that convinced the troops that their leadership did not know how to win the war, and would go on throwing their lives away in vain. It was the job of their new commander, Pétain, to convince them otherwise.

Now that the promise of a quick decision had evaporated, the war, in which the *poilus* had made perhaps the greatest effort and sacrifice so far, seemed to be going to grind on interminably. It would entail a second test of stamina. Could the army sustain a return to a strategy of attrition that became the agreed policy on 4 May?[15] Falls suggests that: 'The French army cracked under the tensions to which it was exposed: disappointment, disillusion, losses, the weakness of the Government, the confusion of the Press, the campaign of agitators, the flood of rumour, the Russian revolution.'[16] In truth, the army did not crack, when compared with the Russian armies after the summer's Kerensky offensive or the Italian Second Army at Caporetto in October. The mutinies occurred behind the lines and, unlike the Italians after Caporetto, the troops did not stop defending their positions. There may have been the rhetoric and symbols of revolution in the ranks, a sign of the times, but the combat troops essentially went on strike for better conditions and better management, and their leadership acknowledged their grievances. In effect this was an internal 'army' issue, not a national crisis or an anti-war outbreak. Once their grievances had been acknowledged, the soldiers returned to duty, while the senior commanders took remedial action.

This short-term crisis in the French army was used at the time as a makeweight in Haig's argument for an offensive in Flanders; and afterwards as an excuse for its lack of success. More generally, it would furnish an explanation for the French army not pulling its weight in the latter phase of the war as their Anglo-Saxon allies assumed the burden of winning the victory. In fact, the French army of 1917 and 1918 was a changed and modernized force, having assimilated the lessons of the early and middle phases of the war into an effective tactical and operational doctrine that bore fruit in cost-effective triumphs on the battlefield and which would underpin 1918's systematic destruction of the German army.[17] This was made possible by the appointment in mid-1917 of a 'winning team' of senior commanders. Thereafter military success would be determined by the application of proven methods by competent individuals.

In May 1917, Foch was appointed Chief of Staff in the French war ministry and de facto strategic advisor to the government (a position analogous to that held by General Sir William Robertson in London). This central role served as a springboard from which he could move to supreme command in 1918, but in 1917 his role was to equip the army for the coming fast-paced and material-intensive *bataille générale* which he had conceived in theory at the end of 1916 after the Somme.[18]

Pétain would be responsible for implementing that strategy on the battlefield. A 'soldiers' general' who had made his reputation in the defence of Verdun, Pétain was to lead the French army to victory in 1918. His immediate task in summer 1917, however, was to restore it to fighting fitness after its mutinies. 'The apostle of caution' in Cyril Fall's judgement,[19] Pétain might be better dubbed the 'taker of care' – that operations were realistic, properly prepared and morale-boosting for the war-weary *poilus*. Pétain earned Falls' judgment for his statement on taking command that France should 'wait for the Americans and the tanks'. Yet this was not a doctrine of passivity, even if the army's delicate situation meant that large-scale active operations would not recommence immediately. Once the Allies committed themselves to renewing a strategy of attrition pending the opportunity for more decisive operations, Pétain determined on a policy of careful but effective offence. This was more than active defence as the Germans, heavily attacked in Flanders, were in no position to attack the French army for the remainder of the year.

The army would fight with so-called 'Pétain tactics'. These were nothing new – they had been practised since 1916 on the Somme and at Verdun, and had their roots in 1915's offensive in Artois, in which Pétain had been an effective army corps commander.[20] A series of directives set the pattern of future operations. Pétain's tactical mantra, the 'artillery conquers, the infantry occupies', would be codified into a doctrine for the army, while a training regime was implemented to make sure every division could implement these methods effectively. As far as possible, surprise attacks would be launched on pre-prepared yet previously quiet sectors of the front: to that end the whole French front was to be prepared with logistical infrastructure to allow offensives at will. These operations would be limited in time and objective – so-called 'bite and hold' seizures of key sections of the enemy's defences lying within effective artillery range, which would replace long, repetitious and costly battles. Collectively such measures should contribute to the restoration of morale and offensive spirit.[21]

While these reforms were being implemented, however, the army had to sustain just such an attritional operation along the Chemin des Dames, where Nivelle's attack had left a zone of friction between the two sides. To handle this delicate battle the third member of the winning team, Fayolle, was appointed as the responsible army group commander. Fayolle had been one of Pétain's divisional commanders in Artois in 1915, succeeded him in command of his XXXIII *Corps d'armée*, successfully commanded Sixth Army on the Somme under Foch's direction in 1916, and was unfairly passed over for army group command by Nivelle (who perhaps saw him as a rival). 'A difficult task: Reims, Champagne, Verdun', he noted in his diary on appointment, 'the situation is worsened by the recent operations, although the Boche are also badly placed.'[22] Fayolle's principal subordinate, General Paul Maistre, had commanded the army corps that fought alongside Pétain's in Artois and would now lead Sixth Army in the Chemin des Dames sector. (Maistre would be promoted to army group commander in 1918 and alongside Fayolle direct the principal defensive and offensive operations in that year.)

English historians stress the quiescence of the French army between mid-May and mid-August 1917. Falls claimed that: 'In . . . the rest of the year 1917, the French army was in a parlous state. This was the cause of Pétain's appeals to Haig to keep the enemy engaged by every means in his power.'[23] Haig was informed on 2 June that the army would have to delay its next planned offensive until mid-July, and in fact large-scale offensive operations did not resume until late August.[24] However, these three months were a crucial and beneficial breathing-space for the French army as it adapted to the task of beating the German army. Pétain was remaking a modern army, in both doctrine and equipment. As well as waiting for the Americans, he was waiting for the tanks. These the war industries were producing in ever-increasing numbers along with aircraft, modern heavy guns and munitions in huge quantities.[25] Morale and discipline were slowly restored as Pétain addressed welfare and leadership issues. Fully to restore soldiers' morale, however, Pétain had to re-establish the troops' confidence in their leadership. To do so he considered an active but successful offensive policy to be essential, thereby building confidence that the army could attack and secure results with acceptable casualties.

Downplayed by Cruttwell as 'carefully planned local operations',[26] the offensives mounted under Fayolle's direction in the later part of 1917 were targeted at key sectors of the enemy's front, Verdun and the Chemin des Dames, and mounted on the same 'army sector' scale as the British army's set-piece attacks in the same period at Messines, Ypres and Cambrai. Where they differed from British methods was that they were deliberately limited in duration and targeted at key strategic ground, the seizure of which would improve the French army's positions relative to the Germans' by removing zones of friction. These short, sharp, smashing blows, with the infantry assault carried out under overwhelming protective artillery fire, allowed the stunned enemy no effective riposte, and presaged a new offensive method that would become the mainstay of 1918's operations.

In the now largely-forgotten Second Battle of Verdun (20–25 August 1917), in a matter of days, General Guillaumat's Second Army took back the eastern heights above the river Meuse, Mort Homme, Côte 304 and territory on the western bank that the Germans had taken weeks to secure in 1916, and captured 10,000 prisoners. Paradoxically, this very impressive feat of arms is perhaps forgotten because of its striking success. The long, gruelling 1916 battle of Verdun is a paradigm of the horror and suffering of the war.[27] More akin to the sort of operations that would characterise mid-twentieth century warfare, the second battle simply does not fit such a model. Yet even Haig had to acknowledge that their 'defeat should have a great effect on the Enemy because *they* thought the French army had become a negligible quality'.[28]

Before that, General Anthoine's First Army participated in Haig's Flanders offensive,[29] covering the northern flank of the British advance. Today written out of the narrative of the axiomatic horror story of 1917, Passchendaele,[30] French forces contributed one-third of the offensive capacity in the first phase of the offensive, and delivered another stunning shock to the enemy when the battle opened. Thereafter, there was not a great deal to do but to press forward as Gough's army advanced. In the battle, Falls noted: 'Anthoine's French Army, with a minute role and the heaviest artillery support ever yet assembled – nearly double that of Nivelle's relative to infantry – returned the astonishingly low figure of 8,525 [casualties].'[31] This figure compares starkly to the 244,897 British casualties during the course of Third Ypres,[32] and demonstrates that the material-intensive method achieved result with acceptable casualties.

The best example of this was the final French offensive of the year, Maistre's Sixth Army's seizure of the Chemin des Dames in the Battle of Malmaison. 'All', Falls suggested with hyperbole, 'went like clock-work: the "Perfect Offensive".'[33] No Western Front battle ever went entirely according to plan, but Malmaison certainly showed what was possible using a well-equipped, trained and confident army. It was above all a victory for France's artillery. 'What a terrain! It's frightful, everything is devastated, we stumble into huge craters, German corpses everywhere blown to pieces, others overcome by gas, dying. It's dreadful, but superb', one French infantryman boasted.[34] Tanks were employed to assist the infantry forwards once the artillery barrage had fired them through the German front defences, sustaining the momentum of the advance which was to be limited to the range of artillery cover.[35] By the afternoon of the first day, all objectives were in French hands. There had been little fight left in the enemy on the shell-swept plateau, and most survivors were led into captivity, demoralised and exhausted, from the dugouts and quarries in which they had taken shelter from the French firestorm. Twelve thousand German prisoners, 200 guns and 720 machine guns were taken, and the enemy suffered another 38,000 killed, wounded and missing. The French suffered 14,000 casualties, less than one-third of the enemy's total. Having flanked the Germans' defences along the ridge, the field-grey-uniformed troops were obliged to abandon it over the following week under intensifying enfilade fire. A position the German army had been contesting tooth-and-nail with the French since General Nivelle's failed attempt to take it in April 1917, and which it had held since the retreat from the Marne in September 1914, fell in under a fortnight. 'It was an experiment which the Commander-in-Chief trusted would prove a tonic,' Falls continued.[36] Certainly the tanks were being properly tested for the first time after their relative lack of success in Nivelle's offensive, and proved their worth in an infantry support role. However, unlike the British Battle of Cambrai a few weeks later, Malmaison was more a vindication of tried and tested methods than a trial of new ones:

As a result of the preliminary bombardment the plateau had become a huge, flat, dreary expanse of monotonous brown mud, blown into craters. A few twisted shreds of broken wire, a snag here and there of concrete, and the broken ragged ramparts of the fort were all that could be shown for the vast expenditure before and since the war of money, time and labour on this once beautiful but now forbidding spot . . . Save for the quarries, the caverns and the thick-walled concrete 'pill-boxes''', which had survived the bombardment, the enemy would seem to have been, as it were, blown back to the [river] Ailette by the guns alone.[37]

These battles have dropped from the historical record. They were short and effective, but one hundred years later the tendency is to dwell on long, costly indecisive offensives as epitomising the war.[38] Their course and outcomes support the contention asserted above that Haig's army was trying to fight the battles of 1916 better in 1917, while Petain's was already anticipating those of 1918. Douglas Haig certainly never altered his assessment of the French army as it resumed offensive operations. 'Their Army has ceased to be the main factor in the military problem, in fact ceased to be able to take the offensive on a large scale but according to Pétain's opinion, its discipline is so bad that it could not resist a determined German offensive,' he noted in September.[39] Dewar and Boraston dismissed these battles: 'compared to a real offensive, they were trifling . . . Except as restoratives of morale, these small operations were really not of great consequence. They had no strategic purpose.' Instead, they suggested that the French army should have been mounting a sustained offensive – 'a full offensive . . . to pin down and use up the German reserves', so that the Germans could not concentrate their firepower and reserves in Flanders. Failure to do so, they suggested, prevented a strategic success in Flanders![40] Other critics suggested material-intensive French methods were wasteful. General Percin, one post-war critic of the high command, extrapolated from the barrage fired at Malmaison that at that rate of expenditure of munitions it would cost 800 billion francs and use ten years' world steel production to liberate all of occupied France! However, Percin was thinking in terms of liberated ground. By that measure, 1,000 such battles would be needed.[41] However, by the prevailing strategic paradigm of attrition, at the rate of 50,000 German casualties a battle, only forty such blows would be needed to destroy the fighting strength of the German army, perhaps fewer. During 1918, many battle of this or lesser scale would be fought, bringing the war to an end. By the end of 1917, French leaders had found the method and the means for victory. All that was now needed was time and effort, plus ever more shells, effective leadership and reliable allies.

The last acts of 1917 showed that the latter were now being taken in hand. The Italian disaster at Caporetto saw Foch, Fayolle and subsequently Maistre spending time in Italy. The French, who along with their British allies were obliged to send divisions to the Italian front to support their shaky ally after one section of the line collapsed, took it upon themselves to educate the Italian army in modern methods through advice and example.[42] The other outcome of the diversion to Italy was the formal creation of inter-Allied directing machinery, the Versailles Supreme War Council (SWC). While the British Prime Minister, David Lloyd George, and the Chief of the Imperial General Staff, General Sir William Robertson, argued about civil versus military influence at the SWC, Foch was busy establishing himself as its leading military figure. In this he had the support of Georges Clemenceau, recently appointed to the premiership in France.

Clemenceau's coming to power represented the final addition to the winning team. Alongside the military wobble of the summer, the wartime truce between political parties and factions in France, the so-called *union sacrée*, had crumbled in the face of the war-weariness that was affecting all belligerents by 1917. Clemenceau was the fourth premier of that year, but a different sort of leader from those who had preceded him. Glorifying in the nickname of 'the Tiger', Clemenceau was a committed patriot, a determined fighter, and an avowed populist. Although he could offer the French people 'war, nothing but war', by the end of the year they were ready to follow him into the final trial of strength. With his generals ready, his people willing and his army able, Clemenceau could direct the alliance to final victory, however long it might take.

That the war came to an end in late 1918 may have surprised a lot of people: plans were being drawn up by the Versailles SWC for 1919's campaign when the Germans sued for an armistice. That it was going to end eventually in the Allies' favour, now that they had leadership, co-ordination, material, manpower and method, probably surprised few (not even their adversary Erich Ludendorff, although he seemed increasingly out of touch as the year went on). That the timing and decisiveness of this final victory owed much to France and her army may still surprise today, given the prevailing narrative. Falls suggested:

> The recovery of the army [in 1917] was almost miraculous, but it was also slow. Whether or not it was complete is hard to say. The French forces appeared in 1918 to be inferior to the British in defence; even in attack, traditionally their strongest side, some divisions seemed to lack the drive of the British and Americans.[43]

This judgment notwithstanding, the facts suggest that French effort contributed substantially to the victory achieved with the support of allies whose activities were increasingly managed by Frenchmen and geared to French objectives.

The French army had laid the foundations for their success in 1917's operations even if the first phase of the 1918 campaign might suggest otherwise. The German army still contested that battlefield in the first half of 1917, but by year's end the Allied armies controlled it, having seized much of the strategic high ground the enemy had occupied since 1914. Ludendorff's decision to go on the offensive might have owed something to the fact that he knew that Pétain's methods made a long-term defensive strategy unsustainable (as Foch would soon demonstrate). The powerful series of German spring offensives facilitated by temporarily superior numbers and the Germans' own effective artillery–infantry tactics scored impressive short-term successes, but were not co-ordinated to any operational purpose.[44] A prepared opponent could meet and contain them.

Foch, who was appointed Allied generalissimo after the German spring offensive struck its first and heaviest blow, appreciated that he could hold the offensive until the time came to counter-attack and sweep the German army from France. Although such a blow had been expected at some point at some time, and Pétain and Haig had made preparations for mutual reinforcement after a scheme to establish an inter-Allied general reserve under Foch's direction had collapsed, when 'Operation Michael' commenced on 21 March, Ludendorff achieved sufficient tactical surprise to throw the Allied field commanders into momentary panic. A more phlegmatic adversary was paying careful attention. Foch knew that it would take time to muster the reserves to meet each powerful attack; but also, as he explained to a British observer at Versailles at the height of the crisis, that in the face of strengthening Allied resistance and as the advancing German troops tired, the 'waves' washing forwards would gradually diminish until the momentum of the individual German blows was absorbed.[45] To that extent, the Allied line would never break, even if it would bend alarmingly on occasion. While this essential dynamic was playing out as the battered British Fifth Army retreated across the old Somme battlefields, Foch, largely at Clemenceau's behest,[46] was being ushered into a position of responsibly for co-ordinating the Anglo-French defence, from which he would consolidate his role as director of the final campaigns.

It was not that the Allies lacked reserves to meet the German blows, more that they needed a guiding mind to overcome inter-Allied rivalries and direct efforts towards an overall plan. Foch was a highly experienced coalition commander, and if this alone were to have been his contribution to the final battle, it would have been significant.[47] Yet he was also a military thinker who, after reflecting on his earlier battles, had conceived the way to engage and defeat the German army. His counter-offensive method comprised a series of powerful and carefully-sequenced battles, each on an equivalent scale to Malmaison, which would cumulatively destroy the fighting capacity of the German army once the *bataille générale* was underway.[48]

Pétain's armies were to be Foch's principal instrument for checking and counter-attacking the enemy, although his growing control of Allied forces – the by now-experienced and reliable British, the keen, numerous but inexperienced American, the improving Italian and even in time the reluctant Belgian armies – facilitated the progress of his grand scheme. When the campaign began, Foch had ten French and five British armies under his direction. Four Italian armies came under his authority in May: to save face the Italian government defined his powers as co-ordination and scrutiny rather than command.[49] Two American armies were formed in the late summer. Finally in September the King of the Belgians agreed to command a combined Belgian–British–French army group (with a French chief of staff very much managing affairs) which would join the expanding Allied offensive and liberate occupied Belgium.

The principal operational responsibility in the field devolved upon Fayolle. Called back from Italy in February in anticipation of the German offensive, when Operation Michael struck, Fayolle was assigned command of a newly-formed reserve army group, initially comprising the French First and Third Armies, which would be deployed on the French left wing to fill the gap between it and the retiring British Fifth Army. Fayolle understood the dynamics of the battle he was conducting:

> The Boche is strong, but unintelligent. He's making a huge mistake. After making a breach between the Oise and the Somme [rivers], on a 60-kilometre front, he has fanned out. The [southern thrust] has been stopped between Noyon and Montdidier . . . In the centre, nothing serious, the advance is dying out near the latter town. We will have time to prepare a riposte. If . . . he had pushed along the south bank [of the Somme] towards Amiens, France and England would have been beaten.[50]

By the end of March, ten days into the German offensive, the defensive line had been re-established, the British and French forces linking up in front of the major rail junction at Amiens, which Foch as well as Fayolle had identified as the *Schwerpunkt* of the battle. In case the German attack were renewed, General Maistre's Tenth Army was hurried back from Italy and concentrated north of Amiens, in reserve behind the British front.[51] Other French divisions were sent northwards into Haig's zone of operations after the Germans struck their second blow south of the Ypres salient in April. The failure of the French 28th Division to hold the high ground at Kemmel Hill would be held against them by the British,[52] but once again Foch's method of judicious but timely reinforcement shored up the shaky British line.[53] Haig's post-war contention that 'between 21st March and 15th April, the French did practically nothing and took no part in the fighting', is overdue for exposure as calumny.[54]

Thereafter the weight of the German offensive fell against the French sector of the front. The French dubbed the later phase of the German offensive 'the Battle of France', as for the first time since 1914 the German armies were advancing and Paris appeared threatened. In high summer, the French did most of the defensive fighting themselves, pulling in Allied formations as they could. Although British divisions resting on the Aisne front were caught up in the battle, Haig was reluctant to provide further support, contending that his troops were tired after taking the earlier German blows. Foch stripped the British sector of French divisions. Maistre's army was moved again to contain the expanding salient forced by the smashing enemy blow struck on the Aisne in late May, and on 12 June, Maistre became central army group commander, responsible for the defence of the most threatened part of the French line. Foch used Italian and American divisions to strengthen this defence: the resting British divisions had been badly mauled and had to be relieved. Foch could not persuade Haig to send more British divisions into the French sector until July. Indeed, when he instructed Haig to move his own reserve divisions to the south of the British sector where they might better support the French army if required, Haig asked the British government to intercede. However, the government supported the generalissimo. Nevertheless, the divisions that Haig did eventually send southwards were released only on condition that they would come back under Haig's control if he felt his own lines were threatened.[55] From June onwards Foch had effective control of all the allied forces. Although the armies would mainly fight in their respective sectors of the front, the movement of Allied formations into other nations' sectors and the placing of Allied divisions and on occasion even armies temporarily under different national command became accepted practice.

Foch and Pétain were learning German methods and developing effective countermeasures. Foch would use his reserves to strike back when the enemy was off balance after his first blow had been absorbed. A surprise Tenth Army counter-attack on 11 June commanded by Nivelle's rehabilitated subordinate, General Charles Mangin, brought the fourth German offensive on the River Matz west of the Marne salient to a premature end after three days. The momentum of the final German blow of 15 July, 'Marneschütz-Reims', would be absorbed by Maistre's armies using 'defence in depth' tactics prescribed by Pétain after the Aisne front had collapsed in May. On 18 July, at Soissons Mangin would deliver an even heavier blow against the flank of the German salient, obliging its evacuation. The desperate German bid for victory, its last phase over-optimistically dubbed by Ludendorff, the 'Peace Offensive', had been defeated with French skill and Allied support. Foch would now use these factors to deliver the victory that he had himself long been planning.

There were a number of guiding principles to Foch's planned counter-attack. First, that it should involve all Allied forces and fronts to develop the greatest pressure on the enemy's resources: 'to embarrass the enemy in the utilising of his reserves and not allow him sufficient time to fill up his units' as he explained it in his memorandum to the commanders of his forces.[56] Second, once the *bataille générale* began, it would continue to a final decision. Third, that operations should be conducted at a pace which would allow the enemy little time to rest, undermining German soldiers' morale. Although the actual offensive would develop as circumstances and events dictated, the guiding principles would be adhered to as the armies under his direction concerted their efforts to destroy the enemy once and for all.[57]

Haig sought to claim credit for shaping the development of operations and hastening the collapse of the German armies during the final advance. According to Dewar and Boraston: 'It was the British Commander-in-Chief who turned Foch's unscientific plan for a general Allied advance into a scientific plan.'[58] It was their contention that by refusing to carry on the advance after the battle of Amiens–Montdidier on 12 August, instead switching the focus of the British army's offensive northwards towards Cambrai, Haig turned a 'crude' frontal attack into 'an entirely different scheme, which, when accepted, broadened out almost at once into the series of brilliant operations which broke the German army at its centre'.[59] Certainly, this was a tactically-important advance, but it was just one of the many blows being delivered against the German front during these months. In fact, all the other operations conducted by British arms in 1918 would be coalition battles fought with French forces, as were almost all engagements throughout the previous years of the war.[60] Perhaps this so-called 'Battle of Bapaume' was singled out because this was the one element of the *bataille générale* mounted by independent British forces and over which Haig had sole authority.[61] Foch himself would not have been troubled by Haig's interjection. It was his policy to listen to the opinions of subordinates who better understood the actual situation in the field and to modify his intentions appropriately, as long as operations developed along the broad parameters which he had set towards the ultimate strategic goal.[62] Indeed, the effectiveness of Haig's thrust up to and through the Hindenburg Line was largely facilitated by the other blows delivered elsewhere along the front that drew German reserves away from their centre. Dewar and Boraston's attempt to dress up a timely change of emphasis in the developing offensive as the root of victory, as the key component of the counter-offensive scheme, does their former chief a disservice.

In his defence, Haig was not the only Allied commander who clashed with Foch on details during the advance. In September, the American commander, General John Pershing, insisted on using the newly-created American First Army to capture the St Mihiel salient, even though this thrust was eccentric to the main line of the Allied advance. General Armando Diaz in Italy constantly postponed taking the offensive against the Austrians until it was clear that the Germany army was collapsing. Foch's French subordinates also refused to be rushed, which to some observers suggested a reluctance to fight on their part. The relationship between three men who pursued the same goal but exercised different levels of responsibility could be difficult at times, as Fayolle recorded:

Pétain . . . talks of his relations with Foch, fraught at one time, now better. Essentially, if Pétain was responsible, we would not have attacked. This is all due to Foch. It is not that he has organised this series of victories, but he has ordered us

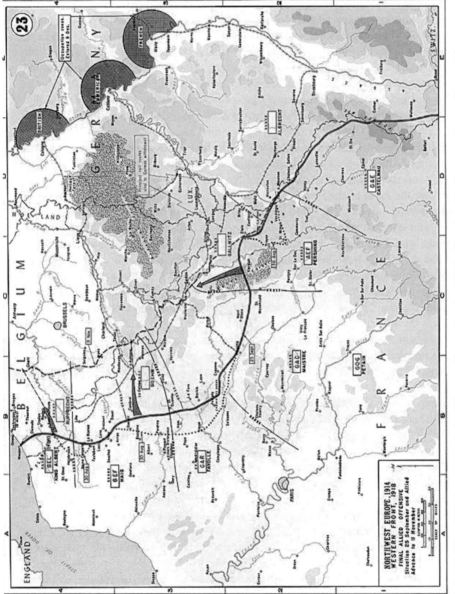

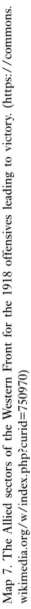

Map 7. The Allied sectors of the Western Front for the 1918 offensives leading to victory. (https://commons.wikimedia.org/w/index.php?curid=750970)

to fight. It is always the same: Foch says 'attack'; Pétain provides the wherewithal, sparingly as always, and I carry things out. It has been like that since the end of March. Foch leaves me in the shadows, because he does not object to it being said that he does everything, and Pétain does all he can to let it be believed that he directs the battle.[63]

Because the methods were sound and the executors, three future Marshals of France, were skilled, such inter-personal frictions were manageable: Foch, Pétain and Fayolle had worked with each other long enough to appreciate each other's foibles.[64] Under their management the French army's advance would be steady, effective and purposeful, while not too rushed: these were the offensive principles of 1917 in practice.

The French army's role in the Allied counter-offensive was prominent if now largely forgotten. In the first blow, the Battle of Amiens which began on 8 August, French XXXI Corps that came temporarily under command of General Henry Rawlinson's Fourth Army struck a blow as effective as those of the feted Canadian and Australian Corps on their left.[65] All Haig could note of the French contribution to 'his' victory in his diary on that famous day was that some French battalions had apparently run away in the face of enemy machine-gun fire.[66] The entry of the rest of Fayolle's First and Third Armies into the battle over subsequent days, expanding it southwards to capture Montdidier and pushing several kilometres beyond, is a feat of arms now forgotten. As the battle developed Haig only noted his problems with the French on his immediate right:

Debeney's[67] orders are framed for covering the British right: not for exploiting yesterday's success. I therefore sent for him to come to a conference in order to find out what his troops are really capable of doing . . .

The French met with no opposition owing to the determined advance of the British in front of their left . . .

. . . I asked Debeney to include in his front of advance Roye and 5 kilometres north of it. He said this would upset all his plans! I accordingly asked him to take Roye . . . This he agreed to.[68]

Haig's complaining comments might be dismissed as merely evidence of the inherent friction of inter-Allied co-ordination, were it not for the fact that they form the basis of the narrative of French operations which has come down to posterity. In fact, despite Debeney's formal subordination, Fayolle was responsible for the development of the French offensive thereafter, which he did without consulting with Haig,[69] whose diary suggests that he was oblivious to or uninterested in the developing operation to the south, more extensive than his initial attack at Amiens. His own focus was on trying to persuade Foch to expand the attack northwards along the British front.[70]

That Haig wished to represent that in the final campaign the French forces lacked dynamism and were gun-shy, owes a lot to his desire to justify his own policy and aggrandize his army's particular achievements. Certainly, the British forces fought better and division for division more than pulled their weight in the final campaign (something that could not be said of earlier years). Also, the strategic geography of the front, which meant that the British in the centre (and General Marie-Eugène Debeney's First Army) would have to make the deepest advance, placed the weight of effort most heavily on those

British armies which executed Haig's so-called 'grand design'.[71] Yet the French troops were far from dispirited or battle-weary, even if the method with which they now fought might suggest that to a poorly-informed observer.[72] The soldiers could see that victory was finally on the horizon, while their commanders were well aware that there was still much fight in the enemy and that slow, steady and cumulative pressure would have to be exerted as they were pushed out of France over the coming months.[73] Boraston describes the method now adopted in the British advance as if it were an improvement on the French:

> No more in the summer of 1918 than in the spring of 1917 did we believe that the war could be won by a sudden decisive stroke, such as Nivelle had planned, which would sweep all before it. Rather in 1918 as in 1916 and 1917 we pinned our faith to a continuous succession of attacks each with limited objectives, pressed one after another as rapidly as was consistent with due preparation and economy of troops, and persisted in week after week and month after month, so far as weather and our resources would let us, until either winter put an end to active hostilities or the power of the enemy was broken.[74]

Essentially this is an attempt to appropriate Pétain's tactics and Foch's strategy in place of Nivelle's. The implication that others still thought otherwise is fatuous.

Foch was directing and Pétain executing the July plan along these lines. Fayolle and Maistre's armies would play their part in the centre of the Allied advance, as well as in supporting other Allies' operations. Debeney's First Army would advance on the British right, up to and through the Hindenburg Line defences by early October, keeping pace with Rawlinson's army's movements. When the Hindenburg Line was assaulted it would engage in the large and costly battle for St Quentin. To Haig of course this smacked of French tardiness: 'The French on Rawlinson's right seem to be hanging back so . . . telephoned to Foch's HQ to ask him to urge Debeney to action!'[75] On Debeney's right, Third and Tenth Armies advanced towards the river Oise while Fourth and Fifth Armies in Maistre's army group retook the Aisne heights and followed up towards the Franco-Belgian frontier. All French armies were on the move during the final advance. When enemy resistance stiffened in front of one army, following Foch's conception, those on its flanks would attack to reinvigorate the advance and deny the enemy the chance to establish a new defensive line.[76]

When inexperienced allies took the field, it was with French support. In both battles fought by newly-formed American armies, at St Mihiel and in the Meuse-Argonne, the divisions of French Second Army and integrated tank, air and artillery formations closely supported and in places actively facilitated American progress. Striking as the American advance did towards the main German communications hub behind the eastern end of their front around Mézières, the American commander, General John Pershing, and American historians afterwards, liked to pretend that this vital blow broke the German army. 'By the morning of November 7 the US 1st and 42nd divisions were on the hills overlooking the city, to their rear Fourth Army continued their cautious advance,' wrote American historian Robert Doughty: 'the Americans raced and the French lumbered towards Sedan.'[77] In the wider scheme of things, however, the Meuse-Argonne offensive was just one of the carefully planned sequence of attacks that brought Foch's *bataillie générale* to a decisive conclusion in early November. In fact, troops of French Fourth Army liberated Mézières on 9 November, after the headlong

American advance had stalled. By then the war was effectively over; and as is well known, sometimes the tortoise beats the hare. French Sixth Army operated with the Belgian army as it advanced to liberate occupied Belgium in the final weeks of the war. Even the Italians required support in their final victorious offensive, Vittorio Veneto, for which Foch detached a French army corps. The British official historian of that campaign noted rather tartly that along with three British divisions already there, these Allied formations were the 'spearheads in the final phase'.[78]

While armistice preliminaries were taking place through October and into November, the armies under Foch's direction continued their advance. There was to be no let-up of the pressure that he was exerting to break the German army, and the final weeks of the war witnessed some of the most intense fighting of the whole conflict, all along the Western Front. Certainly, French troops were tired, but then so were all armies by that point; their morale remained high as they knew final victory was in sight.[79] On the night of 7/8 November, the Germans armistice delegation was allowed to cross the front, in Debeney's army's sector at the apex of the Allied advance. The German army had no illusions about who had beaten them and how they were beaten – Foch was delegated to lead the Allied armistice plenipotentiaries – even if their leaders were later to posit otherwise.

Fittingly, Fayolle was chosen to command the French army of occupation in the Rhineland. His troops would march, flags flying, across the German border in triumph. As he entered Germany, Fayolle would sound a rueful note: 'This country is beaten, but it is not broken. Its armies are retiring in good order . . . If they succeed in incorporating 12 million Austrian Germans, they will as before be a great Power that will continue to menace us.'[80] France had borne the burden of national defence on her own soil, while a country whose landscape had been unscarred by war would refuse to accept the verdict of the battlefield and would try to reverse it within a generation. France would then give a poorer account of herself. Her victorious generals knew the cost of victory and had no stomach for another such war. Two of the victorious Marshals of 1918, Foch and Fayolle, would not live to see that day. One can only speculate how they would have responded and whether they would have capitulated quite so easily as happened in 1940. With his old chief's spirit and method firmly in mind, Foch's protégé Maxime Weygand tried to salvage something from the debacle, but by then it was probably too late.[81] The third Marshal, Pétain, would be called on to lead France in her hour of anguish, along an uncertain and ultimately disastrous collaborationist path that would sully his nation's reputation and condemn him to end his days in prison, a discredited national hero. Viewed through the distorting lenses of rapid calamitous defeat and Vichy, it is no wonder that France's effort and achievement in bringing the First World War to a victorious conclusion has passed out of history.

Early on in his command of the British armies on the Western Front, Douglas Haig contrived the pretence that 'the British Army is on French soil saving France!!', something that the French resented.[82] Inevitably, he found it hard to admit that the French were using the British army (and others) to help them save France while undertaking the main military effort and co-ordinating coalition strategy themselves. His contemporary diary played up to this contention when he recorded the French army's activities and the attitudes of its leaders. Haig's self-centred narrative thereafter became the textual foundation of British histories of the Western Front, which emphasised the supposedly decreasing role played by the French in their own salvation. In Haig's defence, at the time and immediately after the war his conduct of operations came under intense critical scrutiny from British political leaders, Prime Minster David Lloyd George in particular, and he felt the need to justify his actions: this is the recurring subtext of Dewar and Boraston's narrative.[83] Equally, as the commander of the largest and most effective army Britain had ever mustered, Haig resented the fact that he was always acting in a subordinate capacity to Allied commanders whose motives he often questioned, not least because his political detractors often compared him unfavourably with Foch and others. Finally, and more personally, Haig found it necessary to make himself the hero of his narrative and his army the victors, in order to justify his methods and the sacrifice that it entailed over three years of intensive fighting.[84]

Haig's history has a kernel of plausibility. Certainly, the power and influence of the allies of France increased relative to that of France herself as the war was prolonged, grew wider and more complex. In its second half, allies had to be more carefully managed, and effort more fully co-ordinated, than in the first.[85] Fundamentally, however, the main effort to defend and to liberate France was made by the French themselves. France fielded the largest, most modern and best-equipped army throughout the war, and Frenchmen led the coalition in the field and perceived both the strategy and operational method that produced victory. The strategy of attrition Joffre had laid down in the first half of the war, Nivelle's folly being merely a brief diversion from this path; the operational method of using battles cumulatively to achieve this outcome was Foch's contribution to military success.

In recognising this fundamental truth, Douglas Haig's apologists sought to shift credit for defeating the Germans onto his shoulders. 'The importance of the elevation of Foch to the post of supreme commander of the Western Front was indeed immense', wrote John Boraston:

> It lay . . . in the fact that his appointment guaranteed that, so far as the influence of one man could effect it, the future policy of the French Armies would be the same as that which Joffre had been converted to in 1916 and had been the deliberate and unwavering policy of the British Armies ever since Douglas Haig assumed command of them.[86]

There is no magnanimity in victory, it seems. Haig resented the fact that he had been a subordinate in the greatest war British armies had ever fought and did his best to downplay and denigrate the role of the allies he fought alongside for over four years. He sought to take credit for others' insights and efforts, and to place himself and his army centre stage. 'Aided no doubt, by the prestige of his new position, the indomitable fighting spirit of France's greatest fighting general was able to inspire his own troops to co-operate effectively with the continued effort of their British Allies', Boraston continued.[87] One hundred years later, it may be impossible to correct the historical fabrications of the war generation. Perhaps, however, it is the true measure of Foch's genius, and a fitting epitaph of French leadership, that he got those allies to do exactly what he wanted them to in pursuit of a strategy he conceived, prescribed and managed, while letting them believe it was all of their own doing. That is how to win a coalition war.

Notes

1. For a forceful modern exposition of this narrative see G. Sheffield, *Forgotten Victory: The First World War, Myths and Realities* (London: Headline, 2001) which in challenging some myths about the British army's role on the Western Front endorses others.

2. C.R.M.F. Crutwell, *The Role of British Strategy in the Great War* (Cambridge: Cambridge University Press, 1936).

3. Ibid., pp. 61, 66–7.

4. C. Falls, *The First World War* (London: Longmans 1960), p. 263.

5. The construction and nature of this narrative is considered in W. Philpott, 'Unequal Sacrifice? Two Armies, Two Wars?', in R. Tombs and E. Chabal (eds), *Britain and France in Two World Wars* (London: Bloomsbury, 2013), pp. 47–61 and W. Philpott, 'Sir Douglas Haig's Command? The Image of Alliance in Douglas Haig's Record of the War', *The Douglas Haig Fellowship Records* 15 (2011), pp. 3–13.

6. G.A.B. Dewar and Lieutenant Colonel J.H. Boraston, *Sir Douglas Haig's Command, December 19, 1915, to November 11, 1918* 2 vols (London: Constable and Co., 1922).

7. Ibid., Vol. I, p. 344.

8. See W. Philpott, *Attrition: Fighting the First Word War* (London: Little, Brown, 2014), pp. 285–300, *passim*.

9. This model is presented in W. Philpott, 'Never over by Christmas: Meeting the Challenges of Interminable War', in D. Delaney and N. Gardner (eds), *Turning Point Year: The British Empire at War in 1917* (Vancouver: University of British Columbia Press, 2017), p. 19.

10. For the major and unrecognised contribution of the French army on the Somme see W. Philpott, *Bloody Victory: The Sacrifice on the Somme and the Making of the Twentieth Century* (London: Little, Brown, 2009).

11. Ibid., p. 256.

12. L. Smith, *Between Mutiny and Obedience: The Case of the French Fifth Infantry Division during World War* (Princeton NJ: Princeton University Press, 1994); François Cochet, *Survivre au front: Les Poilus entre contrainte et consentement* (SOTECA, Éditions 14–18, 2005).

13. Philpott, *Attrition*, p. 264.

14. Falls, *The First World War*, p. 261.

15. Philpott, *Attrition*, pp. 270–1.

16. Falls, *The First World War*, p. 261.

17. See M. Goya, *La Chair et l'acier: L'Invention de la guerre moderne 1914–1918* (Paris: Tallandier Éditions, 2004).

18. Philpott, *Bloody Victory*, pp. 441–2 and 515–16.

19. Falls, *The First World War*, p. 260.

20. See J. Krause, *Early Trench Tactics in the French Army: The Second Battle of Artois, May–June 1915* (Farnham: Ashgate, 2013).

21. Goya, *La Chair et l'acier*, pp. 371–2.

22. Fayolle diary, 2 May 1917, Maréchal Fayolle, *Cahiers secrets de la Grande Guerre*, ed. H. Contamine (Paris: Plon, 1964), p. 222.

23. Falls, *The First World War*, p. 262.

24. Haig diary, 2 June 1917, in G. Sheffield and J. Bourne (eds), *Douglas Haig: War Diaries and Letters, 1914–1918* (London:Weidenfeld & Nicolson, 2005), pp. 297–8.

25. On French industrial mobilisation see R. Porte, *La Mobilisation industrielle, 'premier front' de la grande guerre?* (SOTECA, Éditions 14–18, 2005).

26. Cruttwell, *The Role of British Strategy in the Great War*, p. 66.

27. See W. Philpott, 'The Trauma of Attrition: Verdun and the Somme', in P. Liddle (ed.), *Britain and the Widening War, 1915–1916: From Gallipoli to the Somme: The Central Years of the Great War* (Barnsley: Pen & Sword, 2016), pp. 48–64.

28. Haig diary, 20 August 1917, Sheffield and Bourne (eds), *War Diaries*, p. 320, author's italics.

29. Another coalition battle which, like the Somme, is remembered solely as a British feat of arms.

30. The opening French attack is covered in one sentence in the most recent study, N. Lloyd, *Passchendaele: A New History* (London: Viking, 2017), p. 106.

31. Falls, *The First World War*, p. 285.

32. This figure for the period 31 July–12 November 1917 includes trench wastage: Lloyd, *Passchendaele: A New History*, pp. 301–2.

33. Falls, *The First World War*, p. 285.
34. 24 October 1917, Henri Desagneaux, *A French Soldier*'s *War Diary*, trans. Godfrey Adams (Barnsley: Pen and Sword, 2014), p. 55.
35. T. Gale, *French Tanks of the Great War: Development, Tactics and Operations* (Barnsley: Pen and Sword, 2016), pp. 54–81.
36. Falls, *The First World War*, p. 285.
37. *The Times History of the War*, Vol. XVI (London: 1918).
38. For example they get a few sentences in David Stevenson's general history, *1914–1918: The History of the First World War* (London: Penguin, 2005), p. 329, while Third Ypres, which arguably achieved rather less for many more casualties, gets half-a-dozen pages.
39. Haig diary, 19 September 1917, Sheffield and Bourne (eds), *War Diaries*, p. 329.
40. Dewar and Boraston, *Sir Douglas Haig*'s *Command*, Vol. I, pp. 332–3
41. Général Percin, *Le Massacre de notre infanterie, 1914–1918* (Paris: Albin Michel, 1921), p. 121.
42. See 'Summary of a report on the situation of the Italian Army by General Fayolle, 26th December 1917', in Maj.-Gen. Sir J. E. Edmonds and H. R. Davies, *Military Operations. Italy, 1915–1919* (London: HMSO, 1949), pp. 143–5.
43. Falls, *The First World War*, p. 262.
44. See D.T. Zabecki, *The German 1918 Offensives: A Case Study in the Operational Level of War* (Abingdon: Routledge, 2006).
45. Maj.-Gen Sir G. Aston, *The Biography of the Late Marshal Foch* (London: Hutchinson and Co., 1929), p. 226.
46. Douglas Haig's claim that his personal intervention led to Foch's appointment has been refuted in E. Greenhalgh, 'Myth and Memory: Sir Douglas Haig and the Imposition of Allied Unified Command in March 1918', *Journal of Military History*, 68 (2004), pp. 771–820.
47. His career has been analysed from this perspective in E. Greenhalgh, *Foch in Command : The Forging of a First World War General* (Cambridge: Cambridge University Press, 2011).
48. W. Philpott, 'Marshal Ferdinand Foch and Allied Victory', in M. Seligmann and M. Hughes (eds.), *Leadership in Conflict, 1914–1918* (London: Leo Cooper, 2000), pp. 38–53.
49. F. Foch, *The Memoirs of Marshal Foch Memoirs*, trans. T. Bentley Mott (London: William Heinemann, 1931), p. 316.
50. Fayolle diary, 29 March 1918, *Cahiers secrets*, p. 265.
51. H. Bordeaux, *Le Général Maistre* (Paris: Les Éditions G. Crès, 1923), pp. 95–6.
52. As with British formations before them, the division was overwhelmed by a pulverising barrage and German 'storm troop' tactics, suffering over 5,000 casualties defending the hill. See E. Greenhalgh, '1918: The Push to Victory', in Tombs and E. Chabal (eds), *Britain and France in Two World Wars*, pp. 63–80: 68–70.
53. It was a method he had first employed while co-ordinating the Anglo-French defence of Ypres in 1914.
54. 'Notes on Operations on the Western Front after Sir D. Haig became Commander in Chief 1915', 30 January 1920, cited in Greenhalgh, '1918: The Push to Victory', p. 69.
55. R.A. Doughty, *Pyrrhic Victory: French Strategy and Operations in the Great War* (Cambridge MA: The Belknap Press, 2005), pp. 450–7 and 467.
56. Memorandum by Foch for the Allied Commanders-in-Chief, 24 July 1918, in Foch, *Memoirs*, pp. 425–9.
57. For an analysis of Foch's campaign see Philpott, *Attrition*, pp. 327–35. To categorise this as a 'strategy of opportunism' as first suggested by Basil Liddell Hart (Doughty, *Pyrrhic Victory*, p. 461), suggests a failure to appreciate the grand conception behind Foch's plan, although Foch was alert to opportunities when they presented themselves.
58. Dewar and Boraston, *Sir Douglas Haig*'s *Command*, Vol. I, p. 294, n. 1 and Vol. II, p. 270.
59. Ibid., Vol. II, p. 226.
60. The Battles of Arras (at a tactical level), Messines and Cambrai in 1917 are the only large-scale exceptions.
61. Dewar and Boraston, *Sir Douglas Haig*'s *Command*, Vol. II, pp. 257–62. Significantly, Bapaume had been the local objective that Haig had aimed for on the Somme in 1916.
62. Foch, *Memoirs*, pp. 444–8.
63. Fayolle diary, 26 August 1918, *Cahiers secrets*, pp. 298–9. After appealing to the French government in June Clemenceau had formally subordinated Pétain to Foch.

64. Their working relationship had begun before the war when they were all lecturers at the French army's staff college.
65. Philpott, *Bloody Victory*, pp. 552–3.
66. This was one instance of Douglas Haig altering his manuscript diary to make the French appear in a less favourable light. In the original the French army commander was 'pleased with himself' despite this event while in the transcribed diary he was 'much distressed' by it. Haig diary, 8 August 1918, in Sheffield and Bourne (eds), *War Diaries*, p. 440 and n. 2.
67. French First Army commander, temporarily under Haig's orders.
68. Haig diary, 9 August 1918, Sheffield and Bourne (eds), *War Diaries*, p. 441.
69. Fayolle dairy, 9 August 1918, *Cahiers Secrets*, p. 295. There is no evidence from their published diaries that these two army group commander fighting side-by-side had any direct relations; rather they took directions independently from Foch.
70. Haig diary, 10 and 11 August 1918, Sheffield and Bourne (eds), *War Diaries*, pp. 441–3.
71. Dewar and Boraston, *Sir Douglas Haig's Command*, Vol. II, p. 258.
72. Haig was not one for studying or learning from French methods, although on occasion insights that he claims to have had seem to follow ideas that the French had developed previously.
73. The process of defeating the enemy in the hundred days has only been evaluated from the British perspective. See J. Boff, *Winning and Losing on the Western Front: The British Third Army and the Defeat of Germany in 1918* (Cambridge: Cambridge University Press, 2012).
74. Dewar and Boraston, *Sir Douglas Haig's Command*, Vol. II, pp. 275–6.
75. Haig diary, 1 October 1918, Sheffield and Bourne (eds), *War Diaries*, p. 468. Debeney had been French army chief of staff in 1917 and drew up that year's tactical directives which he was following. His careful and methodical approach to operations also irritated his own army group commander: Fayolle diary, 1, 5 and 17 October, *Cahiers secrets*, pp. 304–5.
76. For the most recent account of French operations in the final advance see Doughty, *Pyrrhic Victory*, pp. 461–507. The manoeuvres are also well described in Foch, *Memoirs*, pp. 425–524 *passim*.
77. Doughty, *Pyrrhic Victory*, pp. 507–8.
78. Edmonds and Davies, *Military Operations: Italy*, p. 357.
79. Doughty, *Pyrrhic Victory*, p. 504.
80. Fayolle diary, 27 November 1918, *Cahiers Secrets*, pp. 316–17.
81. Philpott, *Bloody Victory*, pp. 578–88.
82. Haig diary, 20 February 1916, quoted in Greenhalgh, 'Push to Victory', p. 66.
83. For example, Dewar and Boraston, *Sir Douglas Haig's Command*, Vol. II, p. 258.
84. W. Philpott, 'Unequal Sacrifice?' pp. 54–7 and 'Sir Douglas Haig's Command?', *passim*.
85. See E. Greenhalgh, *Victory Through Coalition: Britain and France during the First World War* (Cambridge: Cambridge University Press, 2005).
86. Dewar and Boraston, *Sir Douglas Haig's Command*, Vol. II, p. 275.
87. Ibid., Vol. II, p. 277.

Suggested Further Reading

Doughty, R.A., *Pyrrhic Victory: French Strategy and Operations in the Great War* (Cambridge MA: The Belknap Press, 2005)

Foch, F., *The Memoirs of Marshal Foch*, trans. T. Bentley Mott (London: William Heinemann, 1931)

Gale, T., *French Tanks of the Great War: Development, Tactics and Operations* (Barnsley: Pen and Sword, 2016)

Greenhalgh, E., *Foch in Command: The Forging of a First World War General* (Cambridge: Cambridge University Press, 2011)

Philpott, W., *Attrition: Fighting the First Word War* (London: Little, Brown, 2014)

Philpott, W., 'Marshal Ferdinand Foch and Allied Victory', in M. Seligmann and M. Hughes (eds), *Leadership in Conflict, 1914–1918* (London: Leo Cooper, 2000)

Smith, L., *Between Mutiny and Obedience: The Case of the French Fifth Infantry Division during World War 1* (Princeton NJ: Princeton University Press, 1994)

Chapter 11

Redoubtable Adversary[1] – Bolshevik Catastrophe:[2] Imperial Russia's Forgotten Role in the Achievement of Allied Victory

By Chris Bellamy

If for a space we obliterate from our minds the fighting in France and Flanders, the struggle upon the Eastern Front is incomparably the greatest war in history. In its scale, in its slaughter, in the exertions of the combatants, in its military kaleidoscope, it far surpasses by magnitude and intensity all similar human episodes.

It is also the most mournful conflict of which there is a record. All three empires, both sides, victors and vanquished, were ruined. All the Emperors or their successors were slain or deposed. The Houses of Romanov, Hapsburg and Hohenzollern woven over centuries of renown into the texture of Europe were shattered and extirpated . . . [3]

Winston Churchill's first paragraph, prefaced 31 August 1931, could be a prophecy of the still greater 'struggle upon the Eastern Front', the 1941–5 Soviet-German war, which was underway ten years later. The fifth[4] and final volume of Churchill's *The World Crisis* (1923–31), is significantly subtitled *The Unknown War*. The original 1931 London edition omits that, but instead carries a telling and surprising dedication, also hinting, perhaps, at events as yet unforetold: 'To our faithful Allies and comrades in the Russian Imperial Armies'.[5]

As we mark the centenary of the Great War, the war on the Eastern and Caucasus Fronts and Russia's contribution may still be 'unknown' to some. However, the recommended further reading for this chapter shows that modern scholarship has stripped away that veil of unknowing. Churchill said his previous four volumes had 'centred upon the abiding quarrel between France and Germany and the attitude of Great Britain thereto'.[6] He was a key participant in that. However, his strategic vision drove him to investigate 'those sources of the World War *which arose in central, eastern and south eastern Europe*'.[7] As Dominic Lieven has observed, 'contrary to the near-universal assumption in the English-speaking world, the war was *first and foremost an eastern European conflict*'.[8] Writing in his acclaimed account of the war and the Russian

Revolutions to which it led, Professor Lieven 'places Russia where it belongs, at the very centre of the history of the First World War'.[9] The assassination of Franz Ferdinand, the heir to the Austro-Hungarian throne, by a Serbian nationalist in the Bosnian capital, Sarajevo, on 28 June 1914, led to a clash between the Austrian and Russian empires. Britain and France were drawn into this East European conflict primarily through fears for their own security, in case Austria, immediately reinforced by her ally Germany, won. The war was eventually won by the French, British and Dominion, and US Armies and their air components[10] in the West and the strangulation of the Central Powers by the Allied naval blockade, predominantly by the Royal Navy. But, as Dominic Lieven has rightly observed, with the defeat of *both* sides in the Eastern Front war, the Austrian and Russian (and also Ottoman) empires dissolved into a number of small states unfit to survive in an anarchic international system, leaving a gaping 'geopolitical hole in east-central Europe'.[11] That hole would be filled by the Russian Empire's heir, the Soviet Union. It is therefore essential to study Russia's role in the First World War because it played a cardinal part in international relations, a part so 'often misunderstood or sidelined',[12] and because it was, until mid-1917, at least, an equal component of the Coalition which triumphed a year after Russia left the Great War.

It is perhaps easy to see why the titanic struggle on the Eastern Front from 1914–17 and the 'thin, cold insubstantial conflict in the realms of Dis',[13] the Russian Civil War, into which it raggedly descended, have, until recently, been forgotten or ignored. Although the sources in German and Russian are abundant, many have not been translated into French and few into English. 'A whole library exists', wrote Churchill, 'into which the English-speaking world has scarcely ventured. Yet Britain's own fortunes were powerfully swayed by all that happened in the East, and it is there that we must look for the explanations of many strange and sorry turns in our fortunes.'[14] Material on the Caucasian front, (see Map 12) where the Russians fought a skilful campaign against the Turks and won, is even sparser.[15] In its briefing on 'other fronts and campaigns of the Allies', the British Western Front Association gives the Caucasus the distinction of being 'probably the least known European theatre of war in the First World War'.[16] However, it is 'one of the campaigns of the Allies'. And some ally!

The disintegration of government in the East after 1917 and the break-up of the former Russian, Austro-Hungarian and Ottoman Empires into fragmented fiefdoms have obviously erased traces of what happened there in the preceding Great War. But perhaps the most important factor in redacting the record of Russia's great fight against the Central Powers and Turkey lies with the Russians themselves in the Soviet period. It was clearly not in the Bolshevik Government's interest to advertise or promote the achievements of the Russian Empire and the Imperial Russian Army. Some of the senior Russian commanders who emigrated produced memoirs, notably former War Minister Sukhomlinov (1924), Quartermaster-General Yuri Danilov (1924) and Nikolai Golovin, who pursued a distinguished academic career in the United States and published his memoirs in English (1931). General Aleksey Brusilov, who reluctantly joined the Reds and remained in Russia until his death in 1926, had his memoirs published in 1929 and they were translated into English in 1930.[17]

In Soviet Russia there was plenty of analysis of Russian operations in the First World War, but it tends to be of a military-technical nature and it is all in Russian. The Soviet

Voyenno-istoricheskiy zhurnal (*Military-Historical Journal*) contains numerous articles on First World War operations, as does the splendid *Soviet Military Encyclopedia*,[18] but they are couched in a very Russian, military-theoretical way and, again, are in Russian. Finally, the Russian military thinkers who had experienced the Great War on the Eastern Front and helped build the new Red Army and Soviet strategy, including Aleksandr Svechin (1878–1938) and Mikhail Tukhachevskiy (1893–1937), were either terminated in Stalin's Great Purge or, in the case of Vladimir Triandafillov (1894–1931), died prematurely in an air accident.

Those who survived and were looking at that war experience to build a military industry and a Red Army which would not repeat the same mistakes, tended to look at the *mashinizm* (*sic*) of the war in the West as the paradigm for future operations. As one of them, writing in 1921, judged: 'In view of the development and superiority of technical weaponry in the west, it [the 1914-18 war] will, perhaps, influence preparations more than will our experience in the Civil War.'[19] There are also two superb accounts by English-speakers: Major General Alfred Knox, the British military attaché, and Stanley Washburn, a distinguished American 'cable-journalist' reporting, interestingly, for the London *Times*.[20]

Yet the Imperial Russian forces were a formidable combatant which remained robust until early 1917, and continued to tie down huge German forces until November. And, as we shall see, they displayed a number of military innovations. These included the biggest bomber of the war and the introduction of new tactics in the 1916 Brusilov offensive which the Germans copied. In three years of war the Imperial Russian Army lost to the enemy a tiny fraction of the territory lost to the Nazis in 1941. The Provisional Government's final offensive ground to a halt in July 1917, and the new Bolshevik Government effectively pulled Russia out of the war in November but until then, the Russian forces, now melting away because of the collapse of government and as a result of skilful agitation by Bolsheviks within their ranks, had conceded only Russian Poland, always the most rebellious of Russia's domains, Lithuania and part of Latvia (see Map 8). This might well be compared with the Red Army's and NKVD Border Guards' exit from a quarter of all European Russia including the Ukraine, White Russia (modern Belarus), the Crimea, the Don Valley, the north Caucasus, most territory around Leningrad (the Tsarist capital of St Petersburg, renamed Petrograd in 1914 and Leningrad in 1924), and all the territory west, north-west and south-west of Moscow.

A wartime estimate of the Russian soldier comes from an impeccable source, General Dr Baron Hugo von Freytag-Loringhoven (1855–1924), who was described in the Introduction to the 1918 British edition of his 1917 book *Deductions from the World War*, as 'the most distinguished soldier-writer of Prussia'.[21] For a major British publisher to bring out a translation of a work of German military history, theory and prediction when the war had reached unprecedented bitterness and intensity, and where the German people were universally vilified,[22] was quite remarkable at the time. The German general was writing just after the March 1917 Russian 'liberal' Revolution, but before the Russian Empire's military collapse.

> As a result of the reckless expenditure of the Russian troops, whose leaders were always spendthrift of the lives of their men, their army remained, notwithstanding their heavy losses and the defective training of the reserves, a redoubtable adversary.[23]

Size Matters, and the Operational Level of War

'The prime character', wrote Churchill of the theatre of military action, 'is its size'. He continued:

> In the West, the armies were too big for the country; in the east, the country was too big for the armies. The enormous masses of men who were repeatedly flung at each other were dwarfed and isolated by the size of the landscape. Sixteen or seventeen armies, each approaching two hundred thousand men, were in constant movement against the enemy, sometimes grouped in twos and threes, sometimes acting in convergent combination, yet always separated by undefended and almost unwatched country from one another. Everywhere and always the flanks and often the rear of these huge organizations were exposed to hostile strategy or manoeuvres. No large force on either side could advance far without intense and growing anxiety, lest some other powerful body were advancing swiftly from an unexpected angle and would suddenly manifest itself in unknown strength, marching upon the vital communications. Each of these armies comprised the population of a large city, consuming men, food and highly-refined, costly manufactures at an incredible rate. None could live for more than a week without a copious flow of supplies. The capture by surprise of some key fortress, the cutting of an important railway line, a blown-up bridge or a blown-in tunnel, the seizure of some mountain pass or gap in a chain of lakes, might spell not only the failure of gigantic operations but the ruin and disintegration of larger and far more highly organized forces than Napoleon had led from Europe into Russia.[24]

The extent and key features of the theatre are illustrated by Map 8. Its key feature at the start of the war was the Polish salient, 'Russia's sword arm sticking out into Europe', as Karl Marx described it, 'driven like a wedge between Russia and Austria'.[25] By August 1915, after the Gorlice-Tarnow operation, the Russians had been pushed back to a line roughly level with the base of that salient and the start of the Pripyat swamp, a primeval bog about the size of Scotland, where the villages were effectively islands linked by causeways, and dividing the Eastern Front in two.[26]

The scale of the war on both Eastern and Western Fronts led to the recognition of the 'operational level' of war, to which Freytag-Loringhoven drew attention. For millennia, armies had manoeuvered strategically to a fight which, in itself, was 'tactics'. By 1914, armies had become so big and the ranges of weapons so great that the land-air battlefield had expanded and split open to reveal a new alien life-form – the 'operational level'. In the West, Douglas Haig noted that the extensive and protracted battle from 1914 to 1918 conformed to all the classic phases of a 'tactical' engagement. Yet it would be ludicrous to call the conduct of that gigantic conflict 'tactics'.[27] Armed clashes broke up into a series of subordinate engagements or battles which were nevertheless linked by a common design. At the same time, 'strategy' was acquiring a new and higher meaning, especially as coalition warfare developed. Freytag-Loringhoven noted how:

> In the German army, starting in the general staff, the employment of the term *strategisch* has fallen more and more into disuse. We replace it as a rule, by the term *operativ*, 'pertaining to operations', and therefore define more simply and clearly

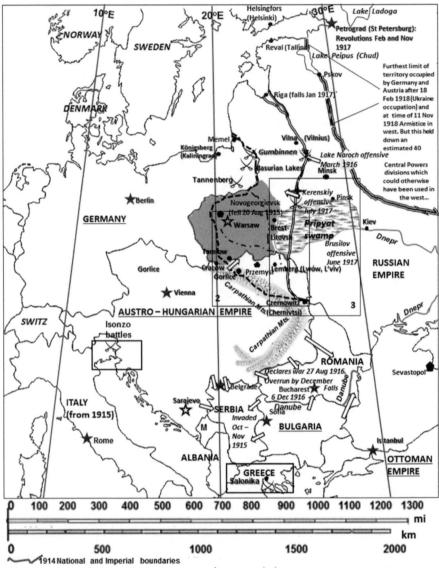

Map 8. The Eastern Front (Baltic to Black Sea), 1915–1918. 1914 battles referred to in the text are also shown.

the difference from everything tactical. All that pertains to operations as such takes place, on the whole, independently of actual combat . . . the term strategy ought to be confined to the most important measures of high command.[28]

The operational level is about campaign planning. In the First World War 'strategy', meanwhile, acquired elevated status as economic and social factors increasingly impinged on states' conduct of war, and as states orchestrated their national campaigns together as part of coalition war. The coalition warfare dimension was later dubbed 'grand strategy', aimed at attacking the opponent's government, society, economy and the fabric of alliances while securing one's own.[29] In the East, where higher-level ground manoeuvre remained possible, the operational level was perhaps more evident. Here, after all, 'was War in all its old unlimited hazard, but on an unexampled scale . . . It was the same fierce primordial game, multiplied fifty-fold and with whole ponderous armies instead of mobile brigades as counters.'[30] The recognition of the operational level was, in this author's view, a simple function of the expansion of the air-land battlefield in time and space, and by no means universally applicable.[31]

The story of Russia's later involvement in the First World War really begins with one of those uncharacteristic manoeuvre operations: the Gorlice-Tarnow operation of 2 May to 23 June 1915 (see Map 9). With continuous fronts from the Alps to the sea in the West and, though much less dense, from the Black Sea to the Baltic in the East, the traditional nostrum of outflanking and enveloping an opponent was ruled out.

Realising the impossibility of an operational encirclement of the extended Russian front, whether by the German Army in the north or the Austro-Hungarian KüK ('Royal and Imperial') Army to the south, the German Chief of the General Staff, Erich von Falkenhayn (1861–1922), developed the idea of the Gorlice-Tarnow operation, which became a pretty universal prototype for subsequent operational manoeuvres by big armies. As encirclement from without was impossible, you had to break through and then encircle from the inside out.[32]

By April 1915, the Russians were pushing through Galicia towards Hungary and the Austrians pleaded for help. Falkenhayn planned to surround the Russian Third Army and then turn on the rear of Brusilov's Eighth Army in the Carpathian passes to the south and threaten the rear of the Russian armies to the north. Falkenhayn even proposed to let Brusilov's Eighth Army break through if it attacked, so that the German armies breaking through to its west (see Map 9) could smash it from the back, a 'revolving door' movement.[33] However, the Austrians, perhaps understandably, did not like the idea of the Russians racing towards Vienna and Budapest and decided on a more conventional defence of the area. Falkenhayn emulated Napoleon in amassing a large concentration of artillery to create his breakthrough. This was not a large concentration by the standards of later in the war or of the Western Front, but was the largest concentration in the East up to that time, as the Russians later noted.[34] It was also the first time the Germans used a 'creeping barrage'.[35] Co-ordination of artillery fire with advancing infantry is extremely difficult and was one of the big challenges of the First World War, on both the Western and Eastern Fronts.

The Gorlice-Tarnow offensive began on a 25-mile (40-kilometre) front on 2 May. By the end of June, the Russians had been forced to withdraw 160 miles (250 kilometres). However, they avoided being trapped, which had been Falkenhayn's plan. The Russian and Soviet armies learned a great deal from this defeat, and it dominated the former's plans for the next year. With the Allies in the West relatively static or rather, unsuccessful, during the summer and autumn of 1915, the Russians faced an offensive by almost

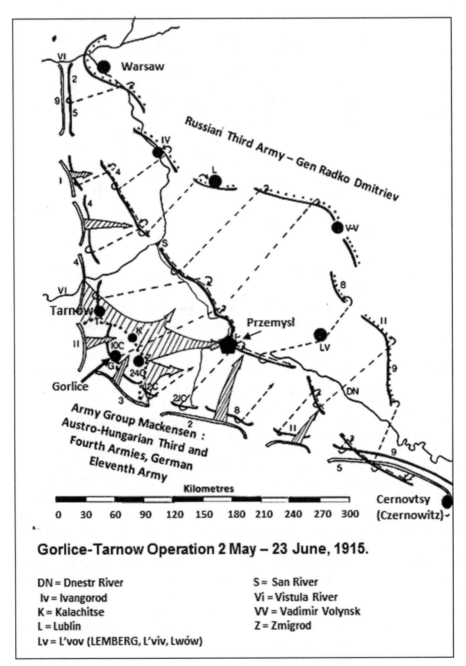

Map 9. The Gorlice-Tarnow Operation, May–June 1915.

all the Austro-Hungarian armies and some forty German divisions. On 5 August, the Russians evacuated Warsaw, at the centre of the Polish salient, but inexplicably defended the fortress of Novogeorgievsk, the only function of which was to defend Warsaw.

By 18 August, the Eastern Front ran virtually north-south through Riga, Kovno, Grodno and Brest-Litovsk (see Map 8). The Commander-in-Chief, Grand Duke Nicholas (1856–1929), was dismissed and moved to the Caucasus (see Map 12), where in fact he proved a successful commander, and the Tsar took over command directly.[36]

The Russian armies had been severely weakened and driven out of Poland, and were also at the nadir of their shell and rifle shortage. All the Western Allies suffered from munitions crises in 1915, but Russian industry was particularly poorly equipped to respond. No one had expected this to be a long war and although the Russian standing army had enough munitions and rifles to meet the foreseen demand, the requirements of this World War took them by surprise, unprepared. Enough rifles had been provided for the four-and-a-half million men to be called up in wartime, but that was all. Once they were issued, and men were then killed or taken prisoner, the Russian factories could only replace the lost rifles very slowly. By July 1915, four million more men had been called up. The story for artillery shells was similar. The Germans were producing four million rounds of artillery shell per month in summer 1915, of which three-quarters went to the Western Front, leaving a million for the East. Russian production rose from 450,000 shells in the first months of 1915 to 900,000 in July and more than a million in September, equalling German production.[37] The Russian Main Artillery Directorate (*Glavnoye Artilleriyskoye Upraveleniye* – GAU)[38] was responsible for supplying both artillery and small arms. GAU realised that it would be a longer and far costlier war than expected, but had little faith in the seventeen Russian industrialists who might be able to remedy the deficiency. Instead, they turned to foreign suppliers, with whom they had been doing business for some time. However, these foreign orders usually arrived late.[39]

Russia had been badly beaten, and lost her 'sword arm' of Poland (see Map 8). Now, more than ever, she needed the help of her Western allies, as she had acted generously but precipitately in her attack on East Prussia in August 1914. It was time for the efforts of the now Quadruple Entente – for Italy had joined on 23 May 1915[40] – to be fused in a grand-strategic plan for the defeat of the Central Powers.

Chantilly and the Coalescence of Coalition Warfare
The precedents for a concerted Coalition of France, Russia and the United Kingdom, which Italy later joined, had not been good. British russophobia can be dated back to a scare about a possible alliance between the mad Tsar Paul and Napoleon in 1801, and worsened throughout the nineteenth century. Lord Kitchener of Khartoum (1850–1916), the British Secretary of State for War, had been Commander-in-Chief of the Armies of India from 1903 to 1909. For the first four years, he had prepared the Indian Army to near-European standards primarily to counter the principal threat – Russia.[41] He was still more afraid of Russian than of French ambitions. Ironically, he met his death on 5 June 1916 on board HMS *Hampshire*, which struck a mine off the Orkneys, sailing to Russia to cement the developing coalition (see Map 11).

The British maintained a close watch on Russia despite the understanding between the powers reached in 1907.[42] France benefitted from her own treaty with Russia because it made up for France's demographic inferiority compared with Germany. And both Western Powers gained by their different agreements with Russia, which meant that Britain and Russia no longer had to prepare for war in Asia, as Elizabeth Greenhalgh explains in her recent definitive treatment of the coalition war.[43]

Although the French were grateful for this British *effort du sang*, the British did not really feature in their war plans.[44] The first inter-Allied military conference convened at Chantilly, the French Commander-in-Chief Joseph Joffre's headquarters, was not held until 7 July 1915. The catalyst was the entry of Italy into the war on the Entente side against its former allies, Germany and Austria Hungary.[45] British, French, Belgian, Italian, Serbian and Russian representatives attended. Joffre used the opportunity to stress the need for concerted and co-ordinated action by the Allied powers, but no specific commitments were made. It would be another five months before the Allies met again to plan co-ordinated action in 1916. The politicians met at Calais on 5 December and agreed temporarily to suspend operations to support the Serbians from Salonika. However, that decision was reversed just two days later, at the second Chantilly military conference, which took place from 6–8 December. Britain, France, Russia and Serbia were represented although the British Commander-in-Chief, Sir John French, was to be replaced that month by Sir Douglas Haig.

Joffre again stressed that 'the decision must be sought by combined offensives on the Russian, Franco-British and Italian fronts, carried out with the least possible delay'.[46] It was the first concerted attempt to forge a common strategy across the multiple fronts of the World War. The French began with a characteristically precise and meticulously argued memorandum, laced with the key points which dominated Allied strategy for the rest of the war:

> After the comparative failure of the operations against France and Russia, Germany, covered in the West by her main Armies and a powerful defensive system, and on the Russian front by similar dispositions of less strength, is employing in the East such forces as she still has at her disposal.
>
> The aims of the enemy in this new phase of the war are easy to understand:
>
> 1. To husband his resources in men, and by slowing down the process of attrition, to be in a condition to continue the struggle indefinitely: a policy made possible by the intervention of new allies, and by the intensive employment of those he already possesses in attracting its forces to secondary theatres by threats at particularly vulnerable points, to decentralize the efforts of the Coalition.
> 2. To pursue the realisation of the German imperial idea contained in the phrase 'Drang nach Osten" so as to increase his world prestige, raise the morale of his own people, and acquire so strong a position in the East that, whatever the issue of the struggle, he could not be forced to surrender it . . .
>
> To oppose Germany's aims we consider that the Coalition ought to:
>
> 1. Pursue its principal objective: the destruction of the German and Austrian Armies.
> 2. Foil Germany's attempt at imperial domination in the East . . .
>
> . . . The Allied armies ought to resume the general offensive on the Franco–British, Italian and Russian fronts as soon as they are in a state to do so . . .

All the efforts of the Coalition must be exerted in the preparation and execution of this decisive action, which will only produce its full effect as a co-ordination of offensives.

It must be borne in mind that an offensive by our troops in France would now be a very considerable undertaking, owing to the large forces of the enemy opposed to us. This operation would be facilitated if a Russian attack in force caused the Germans to move troops from the Western Front.

On the Western Front the enemy has developed and strengthened for more than a year past the strongest possible defensive system, held by very strong forces (110 divisions, all German). In Russia he occupies lines of vast extent, weakly held, which are probably not so strong owing to lack of time and means to make them so.

In these conditions, it seems that a breach in the German lines on the Russian front could now be easily converted into a strategic 'break-through', leading to the disorganization and retreat of the enemy Armies . . .

France, Great Britain and Italy should complete their organization and equipment and also supply Russia with the material she lacks, so that the Russian Armies may be raised to their full offensive value as soon as possible.[47]

The need to supply Russia with munitions is clearly highlighted. The final short paragraph of the document, is 'C., Economic War', 'The economic war will be organized and carried out to its fullest extent, the necessary steps being taken at once by common Allied agreement'. Russia would shortly play its part here, too.

The Russian representative, General Yakov Zhilinskiy (1853–1918), was extremely well-qualified. He had commanded the Warsaw Military District from 1910–11, and then served as Chief of the General Staff (1911–14). At the outbreak of war he had commanded the North-West Front (Army Group) and in August-September 1914 oversaw the sequential destruction of Samsonov's Second Army at the Battle of Tannenberg and the defeat and withdrawal of Rennnenkampf's First Army in the first Battle of the Masurian Lakes. Zhilinskiy tried to blame Rennenkampf for the disaster but was relieved of his command. After the defeat at Gorlice-Tarnow and Russia's fighting withdrawal from the Polish salient, Zhilinskiy argued for inter-Allied cooperation, which he felt, understandably, had been lacking in 1915. Russia had been left to face the Central Powers' 'Triple Offensive' in 1915 without her French and British allies mounting diversionary offensives on the Western Front. Perhaps blaming other people was a Zhilinskiy idiosyncrasy but he had a point. The assembled top brass agreed that Allied nations would launch their own offensives whenever any one of them came under serious threat. Immediately after Chantilly, the Russians held their own planning conference at Mogilev, still in December 1915, and it decided the plan for 1916.

The Russians proved over-enthusiastic in responding to their allies' calls for help. On 21 February 1916 the Germans launched their offensive against Verdun. The British, now with less French help than had been planned originally, launched the Somme offensive on 1 July. The Italians and the Russians moved quickly to try to help the French. The Italians launched another offensive on the Isonzo in March, and the Russians, responding directly to the French request, and hoping to expedite the flow of munitions from their allies, attacked at Lake Naroch in Belarus on 18 March (see Map 8).[48] Because the Germans had denuded the Eastern Front of troops to send them to Verdun, the Russians enjoyed a big numerical superiority: 550 battalions to about 200 German on a 400-kilometre front. Greatly increased Russian production and Allied imports had also started to remedy the 1915 shell-shortage. The attack went on for ten days, until 30 March, but nowhere achieved penetrations of more than two or three kilometres. This premature and poorly planned attack cost the Russians at least 78,000 casualties – estimates range up to 100,000 – to about 20,000 German.[49] Its prime aim of diverting German pressure on Verdun failed. If the Russians were to make a breach in the German lines on the Russian front they would have to do much better.

Brusilov's Offensive

The Lake Naroch offensive suggested that either even more ammunition was needed, or that there had to be another way, and that the Russians would have to plan more imaginatively. One of their most senior commanders, the best Russian general of the First World War and one whom Montgomery rated one of its seven best overall in the war, was General of Cavalry Aleksey Brusilov (1853–1926).[50]

On 14 April 1916, General Mikhail Alekseyev (1857–1918), the Chief of the General Staff who had replaced Grand Duke Nicholas the previous year and, after the Tsar, was effectively the head of *Stavka*, the supreme war-waging body,[51] called a meeting to discuss what the Russians could do to fulfil their promises to their allies at Chantilly.[52] To the south, the South-Western Front, of which he himself had been Chief of Staff, the Russian preponderance was less than in the north: 500,000 against 440,000. but the enemy here was not nearly in such good shape.[53] Brusilov, commanding the South-West Front, then intervened. He said he would attack in the summer, requiring relatively few reinforcements. His outstanding staff had studied previous Russian failures and devised solutions. 'The staff work and the orders in this army', Knox recorded, 'were said to be models.'[54] Brusilov received assent, although no-one expected much from him, let alone 'the most brilliant victory of the war', – on the Eastern Front, at any rate.[55]

In mid-May 1916, Austrians launched an offensive against the Italians. The Chantilly agreement was working, and on 20 May the Italians sent a telegram to *Stavka*. It was the first in a series of appeals culminating in a personal telegram from the King of Italy to the Tsar. The Russians had been planning an attack on all fronts on 4 June (22 May, Old Style[56]) but only Brusilov was ready. It was originally intended as a powerful auxiliary attack, with the main blow being delivered later by troops of the Western Front to the north. But this 'auxiliary attack' was brought forward to help the Italians. It succeeded beyond Alekseyev's wildest expectations.[57]

Brusilov's offensive took place between the Pripyat swamp and the Carpathians, in what is now Ukraine, to the west of L'viv (see Maps 8 and 10), pitting four Russian armies, Eighth, Eleventh, Seventh and Ninth, against four Austro-Hungarian and one German. It was so successful, by First World War standards, because it was prepared with great secrecy and thoroughness.

In order to confuse the enemy, Brusilov made preparations along almost the whole 220 miles (350 kilometres) of his front. Radio stations were set up near Baranovichi in western Belarus, formerly the Russian General Staff headquarters but now, after the 'great retreat', a front-line city, to make false radio broadcasts – electronic deception – to draw Austro-German attention away from the real concentration

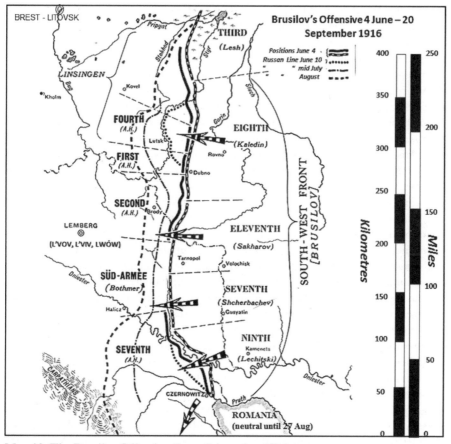

Map 10. The Brusilov Offensive, June–September 1916.

areas.[58] In defiance of conventional wisdom, and against his subordinates' advice, Brusilov prepared four separate breakthroughs of roughly equal weight. This meant the enemy could not determine the key breakthrough sector: 'there simply wasn't one'.[59] The breakthroughs were also unusually broad, to overcome the problem of enfilade fire.

Brusilov also used air reconnaissance on an unprecedented scale for the Eastern Front.[60] He had about 100 aircraft, roughly equal to the Austro-Hungarians and Germans. Compared with the Western Front this was a tiny number, but he prioritized reconnaissance, and there was little bombing or air-to-air combat. If we were to recall Churchill's comment about the size of the theatre, Brusilov needed aircraft with great range and endurance. This would not only enable them to spend more time over the target, but also to be based well to the rear of the Russian forward positions, out of sight and possibly out of reach of attacking Austro-Hungarian and German aircraft. The Russians had just such a plane.

It was the biggest heavy bomber of the war, the four-engined *Il'ya Muromets*, designed and first flown in 1913 by the aviation genius Igor Sikorskiy (1889–1972). Sikorskiy fled

Russia after the Bolshevik Revolution and, armed with a letter from a major general with the USAAF in France, emigrated to the United States in 1919 where he became renowned as a famous helicopter designer.[61] His giant 1913 aircraft was originally designed to use German engines which were unavailable after war commenced, and therefore used imported British and French engines.[62] During the next year, it was redesigned as a military aircraft.[63] For Brusilov's purposes the most important quality of this 'eye in the sky' was its range. It was slow and its service ceiling a mere 9,800 feet (3,000 metres), although both these limitations made it to some degree ideal for reconnaissance. It had a truly remarkable combat range for its era – about 500 kilometres.[64] In early 1916, a Combat Detachment was formed at Minsk to fly in support of the Russian summer offensive of 1916.[65] Although the *Il'ya Muromets* aircraft were tiny in number, they were very effective. They were uniquely and perfectly Russian, grandiose and a touch meretricious.

As Brusilov could not rely on superiority in numbers of guns or shells, he had to target his available artillery very carefully. The artillery preparation was calculated in terms of shells per metre of operation, a technique which the Red and Soviet armies developed further. Behind, a network of communication trenches, all signposted, enabled reserves to be brought up quickly. The Russians sapped forwards to just 75 metres from the Austrian positions. They then tunnelled under their own wire obstacles. As one Austrian officer said on 4 June, 'previously you could tell when they were going to attack because they took away the wire themselves'.[66] The Austrians had reserves in dugouts able to withstand artillery fire, but they were taken by surprise by the assault infantry which had been lurking so close and did not emerge, it seemed to the Austrians, until they were overrun. Therefore, the dugouts became traps, not strongpoints.

The most striking tactical innovation was the use of platoons of picked storm troops, whom the Russians called 'grenadiers', trained for close combat and infiltration. They were equipped with carbines, axes and hand grenades to work their way round defended positions. Following their success in Brusilov's offensive, Ludendorff took the idea for the German Army, and 'storm troopers' were a key component of the March 1918 Operation *Mars* in the West, initially making striking gains. Ironically, therefore, this innovative Russian contribution to tactics later rebounded against their former Allies.[67]

The Russian success took everyone by surprise. All observers attributed it in part to the poor morale of the Austro–Hungarian troops, many of whom were Slavs who surrendered at the first opportunity. The British Director of Military Intelligence wrote that if the Russians 'have obtained such results with so small a number of antique guns, what would they not have done if properly armed'.[68]

Brusilov's infinite capacity for taking pains and his innovative combined-arms tactics paid off, with his Front advancing up to 50 miles (80 kilometres) by the time the offensive was called off in the autumn. But the vastness of the landscape, again, and the problems maintaining momentum, caused it to run out of steam. Brusilov focussed on the principal problem hitherto – breaking through – but neglected what would and could happen if the opportunity for exploitation presented itself, which it did. As a cavalry general, Brusilov might have used far-reaching cavalry forces to exploit the breakthrough and convert tactical success into operational or even strategic success, but he did not, although Cossacks were used to exploit breakthoughs in the second phase of Brusilov's offensive. More critically, in spite of his brilliant initial tactical preparation, he sacrificed his own troops on an unbelievable scale.[69] Russian casualties were variously estimated at between half a million and a million. Austria-Hungary and Germany lost 600,000 and 350,000, respectively, making a total of a million casualties. Overall, combined with less effective Russian operations elsewhere, the Russians lost 1.4 million casualties in the period from June to September 1916, bringing their casualties in the war so far to eight million killed, wounded, captured and missing.[70] After a pause to regroup and redeploy his forces, including adding Third Army and a special Guards Army, drawn from other Russian armies, on 28 July 1916, Brusilov resumed his offensive – but this time with only limited success.

The Brusilov Offensive had a major impact on the course of the war. Along with the British and French attack on the Somme, it forced the Germans to withdraw troops – as many as eight divisions – from Verdun. This ended the great German offensive of 1916 and led to Falkenhayn's removal and replacement by Hindenburg. It also persuaded Romania to join the war on the side of the Allies. Additionally it broke the back of the Austro-Hungarian army, which had suffered the majority of the casualties in the Russian offensive. Thereafter, Austria-Hungary had to rely on the German army and German direction for any military success. Austria-Hungary ceased to be a major player in the war though it must be accepted that the German army had not suffered so severely from the operation and retained most of its offensive power.

It had been a Russian victory, but at a heavy cost. Imperial Russia was never able to repeat this level of success. Not even the Russians could take casualties on this scale, and most historians, including this one, contend that the casualties suffered in this campaign contributed significantly to the collapse of the following year.

Britain, Russia, and the 'Economic War': completing the Allied Naval Blockade, 1916

The Central Powers in the West did not collapse because of battlefield defeat. They were starved out by a ruthless blockade, again referred to in the Chantilly Conference proposal as 'Economic War', and primarily executed by the Royal Navy. By 1916, it was clear that the British economic blockade of the Central Powers was effective in cutting off supplies to the civilian populations of Germany and Austria-Hungary, as well as to their forces and war industries.[71] However, a critical gap in the blockade remained.

The Russians had already made a significant contribution to Britain's war at sea in 1914. On 26 August, the German light cruiser *Magdeburg* ran aground off Estonia. The Germans burned one of her four copies of the 1913 Signal and Code Book, *Signalbuch der kaiserlichen Marine*, and threw two overboard. The Russians recovered those two and found the fourth in the captain's safe. They offered one to the British, and the Admiralty eventually received it on 13 October. Churchill, then First Lord of the Admiralty, later recounted how Britain 'received from our loyal allies these sea-stained priceless documents'. In fact, the copy in the National Archives is not sea-stained at all. With characteristic generosity the Russians kept the two 'sea-stained' ones for themselves and gave the British the one from the captain's safe.[72] The Germans changed the codes but the British were able read the new codes through a simple substitution process. The ability to read German codes would become very significant later in the war, but it took time for the Admiralty to get its decryption operation, Room 40, working well.

That ability played a part in the Royal Navy's concentration against the German High Seas Fleet at the Battle of Jutland in 1916. The German surface fleet did not seriously threaten the British in the North Sea again and withdrew behind the narrow straits – the Kattegat and Skagerrak – leading into the Baltic. Iron ore from neutral Sweden was brought to Germany across the Baltic (see Map 11). To complete the blockade the British would have to interdict it. Thus began an extraordinary story of British-Russian cooperation, about which very little is known – until now.[73]

The British had sent six 'E'-class submarines into the Baltic through the straits, an extremely hazardous undertaking, between late 1914 and September 1915. Their initial objective was one of the Russian Baltic Fleet bases at Libau (Liepaja) in Latvia.[74] In the second half of 1915 these submarines enjoyed spectacular success in intercepting the iron ore trade between Sweden and Germany. The Swedes initiated a convoy system, which in fact pre-dated the British, but then winter set in.[75]

Then, in December 1915, the Russians wrote to the British Admiralty outlining an expected threat to the Russian right flank in the spring of 1915 and the importance of sea power protecting that flank (see Map 8). It asked for 'a serious demonstration' by the Allied fleets.[76] The timing clearly reflects the decision of the Chantilly conference of 6–8 December. The new First Lord of the Admiralty, Arthur Balfour, who had replaced Churchill, replied that he could not now reinforce the submarines in the Baltic through the normal entrances, but offered to send submarine crews.[77]

After Jutland the British decided to send more submarines. The 'C' class had been designed for coastal and harbour defence, and was probably thought suitable for the defence of Petrograd, which was the Baltic Fleet's principal role. But how would it be possible to get them there? The initial thought was to send them to Vladivostok and then west along the Siberian railway (see Map 11). However, they were too big to fit on the trains, even though the Russians were able to bring in eleven Canadian-built submarines by this route. The Russians then suggested sea conveyance of the submarines to Archangel (Arkhangel'sk), and then transporting them down the newly-broadened railway to Petrograd; but that would not work either.

Thus emerged one of the most extraordinary logistical achievements of the war, ably driven on the Russian side by one of its most charismatic characters, 'Captain Second Rank' (Commander) Roshchakovskiy (1876–1942). After an adventurous career, including punching a Japanese officer in the face when the latter tried to board his destroyer in a neutral Chinese port in 1904 and being taken prisoner at Tsushima, he was sent to Archangel in 1915 to establish a series of communications stations round the White Sea. In late summer 1916, he was commissioned to transport the British submarines from Archangel to Petrograd using the excellent Russian internal waterway system.[78] In his report to London, Roshchakovskiy wrote saying it was possible to transport the submarines by canal along the route.[79]

The 'C'-class submarines were towed to Archangel by four tugs, with crew who could not be accommodated on board another ship, the *Jumna*. The batteries were carried on four other ships, one set per ship. After picking up an escort, probably armed trawlers, at Lerwick, the ships continued another 1,649 nautical miles to Archangel.[80] The tugs and submarines arrived at a town of more than 40,000 people, where the British had accumulated 330,000 tons of coal, 60,000 tons of freight and 3,300 military vehicles. That summer, as Allied aid to hard-pressed Russia had picked up, Archangel had received more than 600 Allied vessels carrying a million tons of coal, munitions, food and other supplies.[81] Two new port complexes had been built and from the southern one, Bakaritsa, the newly-improved

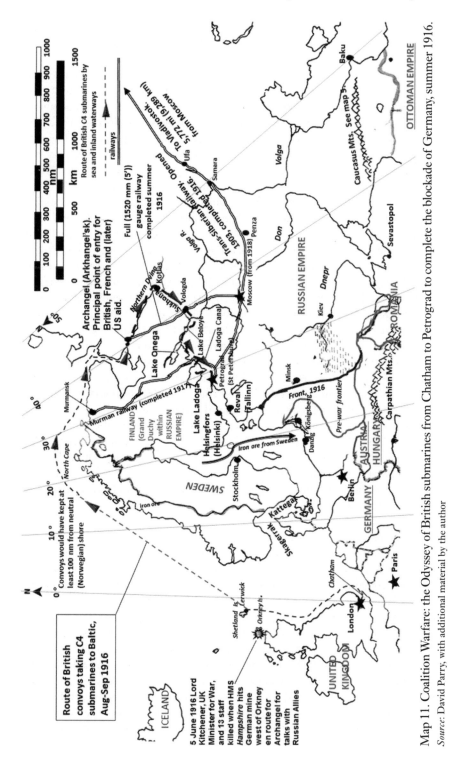

Map 11. Coalition Warfare: the Odyssey of British submarines from Chatham to Petrograd to complete the blockade of Germany, summer 1916.

Source: David Parry, with additional material by the author

broad-gauge railway[82] ran south to Vologda (see Map 11). The submarines and their tugs arrived in Archangel on 21 August. They reached the River Neva on 9 September and, the next day, the Baltic Works in Petrograd where they would be reassembled.[83]

However, by the time the submarines were ready for action, signs of the rot were already beginning to show in Petrograd, the cradle of the Revolutions. In spite of – or perhaps because of – Brusilov's offensive, and the less successful Russian operations on the other fronts, Petrograd was filling up with casualties and refugees. Food was becoming scarce, and sailors, soldiers and workers were becoming unhappy. The 'C'-class submarines arrived in the same month as Admiral Kanin's relative inactivity was cited at *Stavka* as leading to 'the extinction of the fighting spirit of the personnel'.[84] The Russian winter stalled military operations and during that severe winter of 1916–17 there were street protests against prices and against the war. At the front, the Russian armies were still holding on, but there were bread riots in Petrograd in early 1917.

Simultaneously with these riots, on 28 February, new recruits at the Torpedo and Mining Training Detachment mutinied.[85] Further west, at Reval, where the British boats were now based, things were calmer. But the Baltic Fleet ceased to exist as an effective fighting force. The 'C'-class boats, after all the ingenuity and effort needed to get them there, conducted only one short patrol before winter's icy paralysis descended.

In 1917 the Russians remained concerned about their right flank and the boats were used in support of defensive operations by the Baltic Fleet before it collapsed into its own paralysis. Then the Germans took the offensive in the Baltic. If they could push towards Petrograd that would put pressure on the new Kerenskiy government to sue for peace. In October they launched Operation Albion, known to the Russians as the *Moonsund* Operation, around the Gulf of Riga. The British submarines all took part. Then, in December 1917, after the Bolshevik Revolution, four 'E'-class and the remaining three 'C'-class were moved to Helsingfors (Helsinki) for the winter. They were never to leave. The Treaty of Brest-Litovsk, finally signed on 3 March 1918, provided for the British submarines to be handed over to the Germans, but the British, obviously, could not permit that. Negotiations with the Bolsheviks guaranteed the safe exit of the crews (and, now, some Russian wives), via Petrograd and Murmansk. The submarines were scuttled on 3 April.[86]

The Last Offensive, and the End on the Eastern Front

On General Alekseyev's advice, the Tsar had abdicated on 15 March 1917. The Duma formed the Provisional Government and elected Alexander Kerenskiy as Chairman. Kerenskiy was committed to continuing the war and managed to inspire the troops to some extent. At the start of 1917, Knox recorded that: 'The army was sound at heart', and that an Allied victory was possible by the end of the year.[87] On 1 July, however, on the eve of the Kerenskiy offensive on the South-West Front, where Brusilov had been so successful the year before, he wrote: 'There will be no success'.[88] The offensive began quite well, the troops buoyed up by the availability of unprecedented quantities of arms and ammunition, made possible by Russia's own greatly improved military industry and Allied imports. But the Russian attacks petered out if there was any serious opposition, and on 4 July Knox decided that 'no progress could be hoped for from the main offensive, and everything seen confirmed the previous impression that the Russian army had been irretrievably ruined as a fighting organisation'.[89] It was Russia's last great offensive of the Great War.[90] Knox was recalled to London to report to the War Cabinet. He opined that 'events in Russia since the Revolution had not only prolonged the war by a twelvemonth, but threatened . . . [to bring] a German victory within the bounds of possibility'.[91] No-one disagreed.

The fact that Russian withdrawal had put another year on the war underlines the importance of its contribution and how highly the British regarded its efforts. The Russian forces remained vitally important, however, because until after the Bolshevik Revolution on 7 November, the Germans had to keep huge forces in place in case the Russians did not sue for a separate peace, or in case another faction took power. Lenin then announced that the new regime would end the war, and hostilities formally ceased on 15 December. However, about a million German soldiers remained tied up in the East until the end of the war a year later (see Map 8). Germany's substantial gains had to be policed and defended against the new Red Army until peace was finally sealed at Brest-Litovsk in March 1918. The Turks regained much of the territory they had lost to Russia in its successful Caucasian campaign, while Georgia, now independent and fighting against the Reds, called in German help (see Map 12).

In the end, Germany and Austria lost all their captured lands, and more, under various treaties notably the 1919 Treaty of Versailles, signed after the armistice in November 1918. As late as April 1918, British Intelligence had marked six Prussian Army corps in position in the East, facing towards Russia.[92] At the height of Germany's effort in the East, in January 1916, there were fifty-five German infantry divisions and nine cavalry divisions on the Eastern Front. Brusilov's offensive drew eight German divisions from the West that could otherwise have been used at Verdun. Although the Germans transferred forty divisions to the West after hostilities ceased, they left another forty behind. The occupation of Ukraine tied down more than thirty divisions and during the war as a whole, 1.5 million German soldiers were killed, wounded or captured on the Eastern Front. The Russian effort, or even just the Russian presence, had tied down massive German forces until the United States was able to take over one of the four French sectors in France in 1918, making the timing so significant.[93] Had the Americans not come in at that stage, the position of the Allies would have been much worse, and possibly disastrous. Imperial Russia had remained, to the end, and even beyond, 'a redoubtable adversary'.

Full Circle, a Century On
Introducing his superb book on the end of Tsarist Russia,[94] Dominic Lieven warily explains that Ukraine was crucial to Russia's effort in the First World War, and that he was not emphasizing that to promote his work in the wake of the 2014 Ukrainian crisis. He was right. Ukraine provided much of the grain that fed Russia, and Brusilov's offensive took place there. The Baltic States, on Russia's right flank, were also key areas of fighting, and a century on, all members of the EU and NATO, they are anxious that a Russia might seek to swallow them up again. Indeed on, a resurgent Russia is again a cause for concern. Europe, unified for forty years by the European Union, which started as the Coal and Steel Community to prevent France and Germany going to war again, shows signs of breaking up. After decades of 'liberalist' emphasis on the role of international organisations like the UN to promote peace we have given

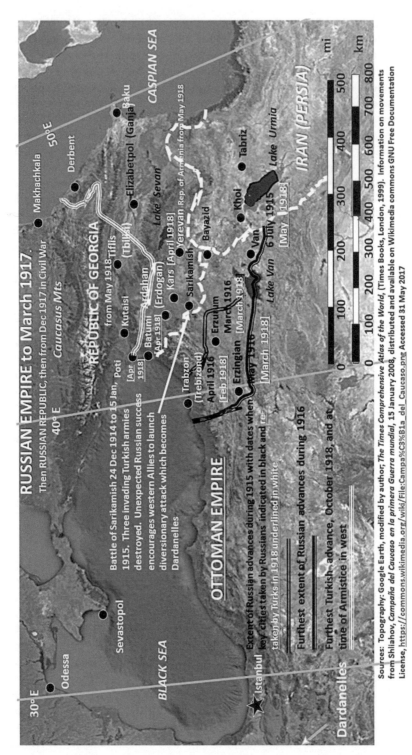

Sources: Topography: Google Earth, modified by author; *The Times Comprehensive Atlas of the World*, (Times Books, London, 1999). Information on movements from Shliahov, *Campaña del Caucaso en la primera Guerra mundial*, 15 January 2008, distributed and available on Wikimedia commons GNU Free Documentation License, https://commons.wikimedia.org/wiki/File:Campa%C3%B1a_del_Caucaso.png Accessed 31 May 2017

Map 12. War in the Caucasus, 1915–1918.

way to renewed 'realist' attitudes, in which states are independent actors fighting for themselves in an anarchic international system, more like the system that led to the Great War – 'America first' for example. The Caucasus, the scene of a ferocious campaign which this chapter has not had space to address, but shown in Map 12, has again become a contested frontier. Georgia fought the Reds in 1918, and was invaded by Russia again in 2008. And Turkey, Kemal Ataturk's secular masterpiece, has just voted to return to something that looks more like the Ottoman Sultanate. And, finally, there is Russia's long quest for access to the Mediterranean. The Gallipoli campaign arose out of the desire for easy access to Britain's Russian ally. A hundred years after the Great War, Russia is determined to try to keep the Assad regime in power in Syria. Why? Could it be that its only Mediterranean naval base is at Tartus, in Syria, and is being expanded?[95]

Notes

1. Infantry Lieutenant General Dr Freiherr Hugo von Freytag-Loringhoven ('Baron von Freytag Loringhoven'), *Deductions from the World War* (London: Constable, 1918), Introduction by 'J. E. M.', dated December 1917, p. 45. Translated from the German *Folgerungen aus dem Weltkriege* of mid-1917, which refers to the first, March 1917, Russian Revolution.
2. The term 'catastrophe' was often used at the time by those who opposed the Bolshevik Revolution, and especially those who thought that it had thrown Russia's political and economic development backwards. See Stanford University, *Centennial, Commemoration, Catastrophe: 1917-2017 as Past and Present in Russia and Beyond*, https://creees.stanford.edu/centennial-commemoration-catastrophe-1917-2017-past-and-present-russia-and-beyond, accessed 31 March 2017 and *Putin likes to pretend 1917 never happened*, https://www.theatlantic.com/international/archive/2017/04/russia-putin-revolution-lenin-nicholas-1917/521571/. Accessed 11 April 2017.
3. Winston S. Churchill, *The World Crisis. Volume V: The Unknown War* (London and New York: Bloomsbury Academic (Bloomsbury Revelations Series), 2015), p. 1. First published by Charles Scribner's Sons, 1931.
4. Sometimes referred to as Volume IV, or Volume VI, depending on the edition. Confusingly, *The World Crisis Vol. IV: 1918-1928: The Aftermath* (London and New York: Bloomsbury Academic, 2015) which covers the war's long shadow including the Bolshevik Revolution, the Russian Civil War and the Irish partition, precedes Vol. V, dealing with the Eastern Front. The latter finishes with the bourgeois Revolution of February 1917 and the abdication of the Tsar.
5. Churchill, *The World Crisis: the Eastern Front* (London: Thornton Butterworth, 1931), p. 5. This first edition does not carry the subtitle *The Unknown War*, and does not bear a number but five volumes preceded it, making it 'VI'. Emphasis added.
6. Churchill, *The World Crisis*, Vol. V, p. 1.
7. Ibid. Emphasis added.
8. Dominic Lieven, *Towards the Flame: Empire, War and the End of Tsarist Russia* (London: Penguin Random House UK, 2016). Also published as *The End of Tsarist Russia: the March to World War I & Revolution* (New York: Penguin Random House LLC, 2016; first published in the US by Viking Penguin, 2015), p. 2, emphasis added. The USAAF, having done strategic bombing (and nuclear bombing) in the Second World War, finally became the USAF in 1946.
9. Ibid., former version, p. 3. The second, US version has 'center' and 'World War I'.
10. Land-based aircraft were part of the armies, with the late exception of the independent Royal Air Force, created on 1 April 1918.
11. Lieven, *Towards the Flame*, p. 2.
12. Ibid., p. 4
13. Churchill, *The World Crisis*, Vol. IV, Chapter 12, 'The Russian Civil War', p. 232.
14. Churchill, *The World Crisis*, Vol. V, p. xii.
15. A good modern corrective is at http://www.turkeyswar.com/campaigns/caucasus.html. Accessed 11 April 2017.

16. Dr David Payne, The Other Fronts And Campaigns Of The Allies In The First World War at http://www.westernfrontassociation.com/the-great-war/great-war-on-land/battlefields/323-cam-other-front.html#sthash.yhcfeKs2.dpbs. Accessed 11 April 2017.

17. General Yuri Danilov, *Rossiya v Mirovoy voyne 1914-1915 gg* (*Russia in the World War 1914-1915*) (Berlin: Slovo, 1924), translated into German *Russland im Weltkriege* (Jena, 1925) and French *La Russie dans la guerre mondiale (1914-1917)* (Paris: Payot, 1927); General Nikolai Golovin, *The Russian Army in World War I* (New Haven, Ct.: Yale University Press, 1931); General Vladimir Sukhomlinov, *Vospominaniya* (*Memoirs*), also published in German as *Erinnerungen* (both Berlin 1924); A.A. Brusilov, *Moi vospominaniya* (*My Memoirs*) (Moscow-Leningrad, 1929), translated into English as *A Soldier's Note-Book, 1914–1918* (London: Macmillan, 1930, reprinted by Greenwood Press, Westport, CT, 1971). An outstanding up-to-date essay on the sources for the no-longer 'unknown' war is in David R. Stone, *The Russian Army in the Great War: The Eastern Front, 1914-1917* (Lawrence, KA: University Press of Kansas, 2015), pp. 345–7.

18. General Nikolay Ogarkov (ed.), *Sovetskaya Voyennay Entsiklopediya (SVE)*, 8 vols (Moscow: Voyenizdat, 1976–80).

19. The best translation of *mashinizm* is 'machine warfare'. 'Mechanization' usually refers to the large-scale introduction of armoured vehicles. See M. Batorskiy, '*Neskol'ko mysley o faktorakh, vliyayushchikh na formu budushchikh voyn*' ('Some thoughts on the factors influencing the form of future wars'), *Revolyutsiya i voyna* (*The Revolution and War*), 13/1921, pp. 59–68, this p. 67.

20. Major General Sir Alfred Knox, KCB, CMG, *With the Russian Army 1914-1917, Being chiefly extracts from the diary of a military attaché* Vol. I (London: Hutchinson, 1921. Digitised 2007 by The Internet Archive with funding from Microsoft Corporation, http://www.archive.org/details/withrussianarmy101knoxuoft); Vol. II (New York: E.P. Dutton and Company, 1921, Digitised 2015 by Internet Archives https://archive.org/details/withrussianarmy02alfr); Stanley Washburn, *Field notes from the Russian front* (London: A. Melrose, 1915) (Vol. 1); *The Russian campaign: April to August, 1915, being the second volume of 'Field notes from the Russian front'* (London: A. Melrose, 1915) (Vol. 2); *The Russian offensive, being the third volume of 'Field notes from the Russian front,' embracing the period from June 5th to Sept. 1st, 1916* (London: Constable, 1917) (Volume 3).

21. Freytag-Loringhoven, *Deductions from the World War*, p. iii.

22. Corroboration of this comes from Clare Mulley, *The Woman Who Saved the Children. A biography of Eglantyne Jebb, Founder of Save the Children* (Oxford: Oneworld Publications, 2009), p. 211.

23. Freytag-Loringhoven, *Deductions from the World War*, p. 45.

24. Churchill, *The World Crisis*, Vol. V, p. 47. 'The fronts and the combatants'. Freytag said much the same in *Deductions from the World War*, pp. 80–1.

25. Anonymous leader in the *New York Tribune*, 31 October 1854, in E.M. and E. Aveling (eds), *The Eastern Question. Letters written 1853-1856 dealing with the events of the Crimean War* (London: Swan Sonnenschein, 1897), pp. 489–90. The *Tribune* published many of Marx's articles anonymously as leaders. For others see also Paul Blackstock and Bert Hoselitz (eds), *From Karl Marx and Frederick Engels, The Russian Menace to Europe* (London: George Allen and Unwin, 1953), pp. 121–202. Scanned and prepared for the Marxist Internet Archive by Paul Flewers. Available on https://www.marxists.org/archive/marx/works/subject/russia/crimean-war.htm . Accessed 12 April 2017.

26. Churchill, *The World Crisis*, Vol. V, pp. 48–9, 58,

27. G.A.B. Dewar and Lt Col J.H. Boraston, *Sir Douglas Haig's Command, December 19, 1915 to November 11, 1918* (London: Constable, 1922), Vol. 2, pp. 354–6.

28. Hugo von Freytag-Loringhoven, *Generalship in the World War* (translated from the German *Generalfeldmarschall Graf von Schlieffen. Sein Leben u. d. Verwertg seines geistigen Erbes im Weltkriege* (Leipzig 1920)) (Washington DC: US Army War College, 1934), p. 34.

29. The Russians later recognised the concept of 'operational art' (*operativnoye iskusstvo*) as originally a German concept. In the 1920s it was assimilated into Soviet military thought. The former Imperial Major General Aleksandr Svechin proposed the division of military thinking into tactics, operational art and strategy in his definitive work *Strategiya* (*Strategy*) in 1926. It was the blueprint for the Soviet Union's conduct of the Second World War. His nemesis, the former Tsarist Lieutenant Mikhail Tukhachevskiy, who shared a cell at Ingolstadt, the First World War equivalent of Colditz, with Charles de Gaulle, proposed tactics, strategy (operational art) and *polemostrategiya* – 'war strategy'. Aleksandr Neznamov (1872–1928), who successfully transitioned from being an Imperial to a Soviet military thinker, also played an important part in transposing 'German views on operational art' to the Soviet Union.

30. Churchill, *The World Crisis*, Vol. V, p. 47.
31. Navies, for whom warships fight and defend themselves tactically, but can have strategic and political impact, even individually, found it difficult, and often quite inappropriate, to espouse the new jargon. In Peace Support Operations, similarly, an incident at a checkpoint (tactical) can immediately have politico-strategic impact, and the 'operational level' is squeezed out.
32. Falkenhayn (11 September 1861–8 April 1922) was Chief of the General Staff from September 1914 until 29 August 1916. He was removed in late summer 1916 after the German failure at the Battle of Verdun, the start of the Allied offensive on the Somme, the Brusilov Offensive and Romania's entry into the war. He later held important field commands in Romania and Syria. Hugo von Freytag-Loringhoven, '*Wandlungen im operativen und taktischen Verfahren Napoleons verglichen mit denjenigen des Weltkrieges*' ('Changes in Napoleon's operational and tactical methods compared with those of the Great War'), *Wissen und Wehr (Military Thought)* (1931), pp. 333–4. Freytag called this *operativen Umgehung* ('operational encirclement'). Ward Rutherford, *The Ally. The Russian Army in World War I* (London: Gordon and Cremonesi, 1975), pp. 125–8; *Soviet Military Encyclopedia* Vol. 2 (1976), pp. 607–8. The concept of breaking through the centre (attrition in its purest form), and then encircling outwards (manoeuvre) had of course been used often before, notably by Napoleon at the Battle of Austerlitz in 1805. Lure the Russians and Austrians round to the right, exposing their centre, and then smash through. Freytag, *Deductions from the World War*, pp. 81–2.
33. Freytag-Loringhoven, 'Changes. . . ', p. 338; Rutherford, *The Ally*, pp. 126–33.
34. V.D. Grendal', *Ogon' artillerii (Artillery Fire)* (Moscow: Voyenizdat, 1926), p. 48. This is a good example of how the Soviets drew on the Imperial Russian military experience, but in a very technical and exclusive way.
35. Captain Jonathan M. House, *Towards Combined Arms Warfare: a Survey of Tactics, Doctrine and Organization in the 20th Century* (Fort Leavenworth: Combat Studies Institute, US Army Command and General Staff College, 1984), p. 33.
36. Norman Stone, *The Eastern Front 1914-1917* (London: Penguin, 1998), Chapter 8, 'The Retreat, 1915', pp. 165–93, last point, p. 187; David R. Stone, *The Russian Army in the Great War: The Eastern Front, 1914-1917* (Lawrence, KA: University Press of Kansas, 2015), Chapter 7, The Great Retreat, 1915, pp. 146–77, last point, p. 173.
37. Ibid., Chapter 7: 'The shell-shortage 1915', pp. 144–64, this pp. 144–8.
38. As an aside, it was sometimes jokingly referred to in the Russian and Soviet armies and ministries as *Glavnoye Artilleriyskoye Smushcheniye* 'The Main Artillery Embarrassment'. The Russians and the British share the same punning sense of humour . . . But it did a good job, and survived right through the Soviet period.
39. Stone, *The Eastern Front*, pp. 150–3.
40. Italy had been part of the Triple Alliance with Germany and Austria Hungary before the war, but had not joined them in 1914. On 3 August 1914 Italy said it would not commit its troops because the Triple Alliance was a defensive one, and Austria-Hungary had been the aggressor. By May 1915 they had decided that the Entente was the better bet.
41. Chris Bellamy, *The Gurkhas: Special Force* (London: John Murray, 2011), pp. 157–8.
42. See for example the two outstanding War Office, General Staff *Handbook of the Russian Army*, 1908 and 1914. The British produced Handbooks on all major armies, but those on Russia are of particular interest as they deal with a Great Power that had, until 1907, been seen a principal threat, and because they straddle the period of Sukhomlinov's army reforms in Russia. UK National Archives (UKNA), WO 106/ 6222, Fifth Edition, 1908 and WO 106/6223, Sixth Edition, 1914. Both published for Her Majesty's Stationery Office by Harrison and Sons. For Official Use only. The 1914 edition incorporates corrections published in Russian Army Orders up to the end of 1913. Apparently, sometimes the compilers relied on German sources that were already a few years old.
43. Elizabeth Greenhalgh, *Victory through Coalition. Britain and France during the First World War*, Cambridge Military Histories (Cambridge: Cambridge University Press, 2005, rpr 2008), p. 13.
44. Samuel R. Williamson, Jr., *The Politics of Grand Strategy. Britain and France Prepare for War 1904-14* (Cambridge MA: Harvard University Press, 969), p. 316, cited in Greenhalgh, *Victory through Coalition* p. 16. The final plan which the French took to war, Plan XVII, anticipated that six British infantry and one cavalry divisions would deploy on the left flank, but France would attack into Alsace-Lorraine.
45. Greenhalgh, *Victory through Coalition*, pp. 17–41 covers the numerous problems and issues affecting British-French co-operation.

46. Ibid., p. 45. The minutes of the conference are in *Les Armées Francaises dans la Grande Guerre (AFGG)* 4/1 , Annexes 46, 47, 49. There is a copy of the conclusions in French in UKNA CAB 28/1.

47. *Plan of Action Proposed by France to the Coalition:Memorandum laid before the second Allied Military conference at Chantilly, 6th December 1915* (2009), at: http://www.firstworldwar.com/source/chantillymemo.htm Accessed 17 April 2017.

48. David Stone, *The Russian Army*, pp. 234–6; Norman Stone, *The Eastern Front*, pp. 227–31. The original Russian source in N.E. Podorozhniy, *Narochskaya operatsiya v marte 1916 g. na russkom fronte mirovoy voyni* [*The Naroch Offensive in March 1916 on the Russian Front of the World War*] (Moscow: Voyenizdat, 1938).

49. Ibid.

50. Field Marshal Viscount Montgomery of Alamein, *A History of Warfare* (World Publishing Company, 1968), p. 306. The others were Falkenhayn (later Hindenburg), Ludendorff, Mustafa Kemal (Ataturk), Plumer, Monash and Allenby. On Brusilov, L. Rostunov, *General Brusilov* (Moscow: Voyenizdat, 1964) and *Russkiy Front v Pervoy Mirovoy voyne* (*The Russian Front in the First World War*) (Moscow: Voyenizdat, 1976). David Stone, *The Russian Army*, pp. 232–71; Norman Stone, *The Eastern Front*, pp. 231–63. Also Brusilov's memoirs, *Moi Vospominaniya*, and English translations – see Note 17.

51. *Stavka* is often printed, quite wrongly, in block capitals, as if it were an acronym. It is an old Russian word for a warrior-chief's encampment or headquarters. Thus the Polovtsian chief's encampment in *Prince Igor* would be a *stavka*.

52. Norman Stone, *The Eastern Front*, p. 234.

53. Ibid.; David Stone, *The Russian Army*, pp. 236–7.

54. Knox, *With the Russian Army*, Vol. II, pp. 432–48, quotation p. 437.

55. Norman Stone, *The Eastern Front*, p. 235.

56. Until 1917 the Russians still used the Old Style Julian calendar, which by the twentieth century had slipped thirteen days behind the Gregorian calendar used in the west. That is why the 'Great October Socialist Revolution' occurred in . . . November.

57. Norman Stone, *The Eastern Front*, pp. 235–49; David Stone, *The Russian Army*, pp. 236–45.

58. V.A. Kirillov and V.P. Zhuravel, '*Radioelektronnoye protivoborstvo vlialo na khod operatsii Pervoy mirovoy voyny*' ('The influence of RadioElectronic Combat (REC) on the course of operations in the First World War'), *Voyenno-istoricheskiy Zhurnal (VIZh)* 8/2004, p. 48

59. David Stone, *The Russian Army* p. 239.

60. S.V. Averchenko, '*Brusilovskiy proryv, bor'ba v vozdukhe, chast' 1 – podgotovka*' ('The Brusilov breakthrough, war in the air, Part 1 – preparation"), *VIZh* 10/2011, pp. 11–15.

61. K.N. Finne, *Igor Sikorsky – The Russian Years*, Editors: Carl J. Bobrow, Von Hardesty; Translated and adapted by Von Hardesty (Washington, DC: Smithsonian Institution Press, 1987).

62. See *Sikorsky Ilya Mouromets V* at http://www.wwiaviation.com/bombers_Russia.html. Accessed 17 April 2017.

63. Scott W. Palmer, *The Russian Origins of Strategic Air Operations*, at http://russiasgreatwar.org/media/military/air_operations.shtml, Accessed 17 April 2017.

64. http://www.wwiaviation.com/bombers_Russia.html, Accessed 17 April 2017.

65. Imperial Russian Airpower WWI, at http://imperialairpowerrussia.blogspot.co.uk/ Accessed 17 April 2017.

66. Cited in Norman Stone, *The Eastern Front*, p. 249.

67. Nik Cornish, with illustrations by Andrei Karatchouk, *The Russian Army 1914–18* Osprey Men-at-Arms series 364 (Oxford and Long Island City, NY: Osprey, 2001), pp. 17, 37–9, Plate C4.

68. Minute by Macdonough, DMI, on WO 106/109, cited in Norman Stone, *The Eastern Front*, p. 251.

69. David Stone, *The Russian Army*, pp. 256–7.

70. John Keegan, *The First World War* (London and New York: Penguin/Random House, 2000), p. 306.

71. David Stone, *The Russian Army*, pp. 247, 255–6.

72. *Signalbuch der kaiserlichen Marine* Berlin 1913, Secret, known as '*The Magdeburg Codebook*', UKNA Adm 137/4156. The Russians had been through this one as well, as there are Russian annotations in blue pencil. Churchill, *The World Crisis*, Vol. V; Arthur. J. Marder, *From the Dreadnought to Scapa Flow; the Royal Navy in the Fisher Era, 1904-1919*, 5 vols (London: Oxford University Press, 1961–70), Vol. 2, p. 132, footnote 2,

73. I am profoundly grateful to my colleague, Commander (retd.) David Parry, with whom I worked on the MA in Maritime History at the Greenwich Maritime Institute, 2013–14. The detail of British submarine operations in the Baltic is examined in his unpublished paper *The Baltic C Class: Cooperation, Chaos & Courage* (September 2014), the source for what follows.

74. Ibid., pp. 4–5.

75. Ibid., p. 51.

76. Commodore G. von Schoultz [another Baltic German], *With the British Battle Fleet, War Recollections of a Russian Naval Officer* (London: Hutchinson, 1925), p. 69 and Appendix, quoted in Parry, *The Baltic C Class*, p. 6.

77. Parry, *The Baltic C Class*, p. 7.

78. Ibid., pp. 12–15.

79. Russian State Archive of the Navy (RGAVMF) Fond 418 Inventory 1 File 4966 p. 68, cited in Parry, *The Baltic C Class*, p. 16.

80. Parry, *The Baltic C Class*, pp. 17–25.

81. Ibid., p. 30.

82. The Russian broad gauge of 5ft, as distinct from the standard European and American gauge of 4ft 8½in.

83. Parry, *The Baltic C Class*, pp. 41–2.

84. Evan Mawdsley, *The Russian Revolution and the Baltic Fleet* (London: Macmillan, 1978), p. 3.

85. Ibid., p. 14.

86. Parry, *The Baltic C Class*, pp. 58–75

87. Knox, *With the Russian Army*, Vol. II, p. 552.

88. Ibid., p. 639. Kerenskiy offensive pp. 627–52.

89. Ibid., p. 648.

90. Ibid., pp. 679–80.

91. Ibid., p. 677.

92. War Office, General Staff, *The German Forces in the Field. Sixth Edition, April 1918* (MI8(9) April 1918). Maps at end after p. 239.

93. Timothy Dowling, 'Eastern Front', *International Encyclopedia of the First World War*, available at http://encyclopedia.1914-1918-online.net/article/eastern_front, accessed 20 April 2017. See also Dowling's *The Brusilov Offensive* (Indiana University Press, 2008).

94. Lieven, *Towards the Flame*, p. 1.

95. Rod Nordland, 'Russia Signs Deal for Syria Bases; Turkey Appears to Accept Assad' *New York Times*, 20 January 2017, at https://www.nytimes.com/2017/01/20/world/middleeast/russia-turkey-syria-deal.html?_r=0, accessed 20 April 2017.

Suggested Further Reading

Buttar, Pritt, *Russia's Last Gasp: The Eastern Front 1916-17* (London: Osprey, 2016)

Cornish, Nik, with illustrations by Andrei Karatchouk, *The Russian Army 1914-18*, Osprey Men-at-Arms series 364 (Oxford and Long Island City, NY:Osprey, 2001)

Churchill, Winston, *The World Crisis* First published 1923–31. Republished as five volumes, Bloomsbury Academic, 2015. Especially Vol. IV, *The Aftermath, 1918-1928*, and Vol. V, *The Unknown War*, originally just subtitled *The Eastern Front*.

Golovin, Nikolai, *The Russian Army in World War I* (New Haven Ct.: Yale University Press, 1931)

Greenhalgh, Elizabeth, *Victory through Coalition. Britain and France during the First World War*, Cambridge Military Histories (Cambridge: Cambridge University Press, 2005, reprinted 2008)

Knox, Major General Sir Alfred, *With the Russian Army 1914-1917: Being chiefly extracts from the diary of a military attaché*, 2 vols, originally published by Hutchinson, London and E P Dutton, New York, 1921. Available digitally at the Internet Archive, Vol. 1, http://www.archive.org/details/withrussianarmy101knoxuoft and Vol. 2, https://archive.org/details/withrussianarmy02alfr, respectively.

Lieven, Dominic, *Towards the Flame: Empire, War and the End of Tsarist Russia* (London: Penguin, Random House UK, 2016). Also published as *The End of Tsarist Russia: the March to World War I & Revolution*, also by Penguin, Penguin Random House LLC, New York, 2016. First published in the US by Viking Penguin, 2015.

Mawdsley, Evan, *The Russian Revolution and the Baltic Fleet* (London: Macmillan, 1978)

Stone, David R., *The Russian Army in the Great War: The Eastern Front, 1914-1917* (Lawrence KA: University Press of Kansas, 2015)

Stone, Norman, *The Eastern Front 1914-1917* (London: Penguin, 1998. First published London: Hodder and Stoughton, 1975)

Chapter 12

Italy and the Complex of the 'Mutilated Victory': Shared Myth and Party Mythology

By Irene Guerrini and Marco Pluviano

Thirty-five years may have passed since our student days, but we still remember the posters put up by the youth wing of the *Movimento Sociale Italiano*, the Italian neo-fascist party, showing the Winged Victory, or *Nike*, of Samothrace.[1] The young heirs of Mussolini adopted this iconic figure to personify the concept of the '*vittoria mutilate*', the 'mutilated victory', invoking it whenever they wished to protest against some or other offence to their nationalist ideals, as for example the Treaty of Osimo which settled the dispute with Yugoslavia, or the discussions over the return of the Obelisk of Axum to Ethiopia, or indeed to provoke a reaction against events or issues they perceived as threatening their idea of the nation – strikes, abortion, divorce.

The period in question constituted, chronologically speaking, the last public outing of the myth of 'mutilated victory', according to which Italy, despite being on the winning side in the First World War, had been robbed by its allies of its 'legitimate' aspirations to territorial expansion. The term, coined by Gabriele D'Annunzio during the final days of the Great War in protest against Woodrow Wilson's peace proposals,[2] gained currency in the months that followed the end of the war[3] and would survive until the final decade of the twentieth century. Widespread use was made of the myth by the nationalist/fascist Right both during the twenty years of fascist rule, as well as after the end of the Second World War.

Given the opening lines of this chapter, the reader might be forgiven for thinking that the myth of mutilated victory has always been the expression of nationalist, imperialist and revanchist far-right sentiment, but the reality is not as clear-cut. Analysis must begin by observing that the outcome of the Great War left almost everybody in Italy unsatisfied, albeit for different and in many cases opposing reasons. The forces that opposed intervention in the war and the way in which the war was conducted were dissatisfied at the failure to reform the country's social structures, while nationalist and conservative forces were disappointed at the failure of the Allies to honour the promises in the April 1915 London Pact of territorial gains for Italy after the war.[4]

Verifiable statistics attest the human scale alone of the Italian commitment to the war: of 7,000,000 men eligible for military service, 4,500,000 saw active service; at the lowest estimate, 652,000 were killed or died of wounds (the highest estimate stands at 709,000); 1,000,000 men were wounded; and with regard to the severity of Italian military justice, over 1,500 death sentences and summary executions were carried out. Small wonder that such figures provided ammunition for criticism from whatever perspective on the outcome of the war.

With the end of the conflict, both sides required a set of watchwords and rituals which, while preserving their respective demands, political on the one hand, and territorial on the other, would allow them to leave behind not only the war but also the 'culture of war', that is a demobilisation not only of soldiers, but also of minds, of attitudes, of the country's collective imagination. War needed to undergo a process of transformation from the daily experience of soldiers and civilians alike, into a collection of myths and rituals through which internal domestic issues as well as relations with other countries could be framed.

In this sense, the myth of 'mutilated victory' had for the Right the crucial function of identifying the internal and external 'enemy' guilty of compromising the integrity of the victory and betraying the sacrifices of the entire nation. Those who had opposed the war, largely on the Left, were aggrieved at how the conflict had been conducted – the harsh discipline, the enormous loss of life, the militarisation of Italian society, the curtailment of the rights of soldiers and civilians.[5] They wanted the post-war period to bring social change, either in a revolutionary sense or through a programme of radical reform. They also wanted those who had been responsible for the enforcement of merciless military discipline to be punished.[6] Dissatisfaction with the way the war had been conducted was not the exclusive preserve of socialists but was also expressed by many democrats and liberals who, although in favour of the conflict, opposed – albeit in hindsight – the way the army had been run until 9 November 1917 by its Chief of Staff, Luigi Cadorna. The dissatisfaction was widespread and sustained beyond the Armistice, influencing the findings of the commission set up to enquire into the Caporetto retreat, the *Regia Commissione di Inchiesta sul ripiegamento dall'Isonzo al Piave*.[7] The commission had been created with the tacit aim of demonstrating socialist responsibility for the crisis that had led to the collapse of the front but ended up assigning most of the blame to the way Cadorna conducted the war and led his troops.[8]

The camp of those dissatisfied with the way the war had been conducted thus constituted a diverse grouping, not just in terms of their political positions, but even with regard to their opinion of the war itself. As far as the socialists were concerned, the war had been a disastrous experience imposed by the ruling classes on a reluctant working class. For neutralist liberals and Catholics, it was a lengthy ordeal it would have been better to avoid but which, once embarked upon, it was necessary to follow through to the end. From the point of view of the 'democratic interventionists' meanwhile, the war had been a necessary choice made by an enlightened bourgeoisie which, by completing the work started by the *Risorgimento*, would lead to the complete integration and emancipation of the lower classes.

These divergences in interpretation constituted the biggest stumbling block to post-war collaboration between forces that – with the exception of the maximalist socialists – shared much common ground. The presence of a significant section of public opinion which had been hostile to the war and critical of how it had been conducted constituted an element of division in the country which prevented the consolidation of a shared reading of the war experience. The Right, in contrast, made no attempt to cultivate a culture of peace arising out of victory and instead viewed the war as an essential element of national identity.

Disappointment was also expressed by the nationalist-imperialist Right, which was centred around Gabriele D'Annunzio,[9] and the leaders of the liberal Right, Antonio Salandra, the Prime Minister, who had been the driving force behind Italian intervention in the war, and Sidney Sonnino, who held the post of Foreign Minister during the war up until June 1919. But there was support too from the Nationalist Party, and a group of movements amongst which, from 23 March 1919 onwards, the fascist movement led by Benito Mussolini began to emerge. This diverse grouping was marked by strong personal contrasts, as for example between D'Annunzio and Mussolini, and political differences too. The nationalist-imperialist Right drew the bulk of its support from among the lower and middle urban bourgeoisie and from landowners, but also enjoyed a degree of support among the working class as a result of the presence of a number of former socialists, first and foremost of course Mussolini,[10] and from anarchists and revolutionary syndicalists.[11] The various tendencies were held together by the shared experience of participating in the interventionist movement, then in the war itself, both at the front and as part of welfare organisations and/or propaganda initiatives, and by the shared belief in the concept of having been robbed of the victory manifestly earned. This conviction rapidly developed into a fully-fledged psychological 'complex', with recriminations directed at the other Entente states pervading both Italian foreign policy and internal propaganda.

Unsurprisingly the same attitudes swiftly found their way into private discourse as is testified in contemporary diary accounts, letters and memoirs. Emblematic of this tendency is a diary entry made by the Italian ambassador to Britain, Guglielmo Imperiali, who on 14 July 1919, noted: 'There are really no reasons to feel affection for the Allies and their associates (may God confound and punish them) who are poisoning our victory.'[12]

The disappointment expressed in such circles was, however, directed more at the results achieved at the peace negotiations than at the outcomes of conflicts within the arena of domestic politics. In this latter area there were, however, two important exceptions which, while having a significant impact in the country, were not – unlike those issues pertaining to overseas relations – subsequently included in the official reconstruction of the war experience. They were, first, the amnesty of 2 September 1919, decried by the Right as a gift from the government to draft evaders and deserters, when it was in fact an inevitable measure designed to remove the legal consequences of the extremely harsh military justice administered during the war,[13] and second, the protracted dispute regarding the failure to hold an official victory ceremony, as the other victorious powers had done.

Nationalists, regular and reserve officers, and many ordinary soldiers, found it incomprehensible that the government had not organized a major parade of the victorious troops between 24 May, the anniversary of Italian intervention in the war in 1915, and 4 November 1919, the anniversary of the Armistice. In his diary, Mario Piazzesi, quoting the opinion of an army officer, summed up the dissatisfaction that was felt:

Did you see what the French did? Their victorious troops marched under the Arc de Triomphe in Paris, to the cheers of a proud people [. . .] The English, Belgians,

Americans and everybody else did the same. Even the Germans showed their unity by acclaiming their troops as they paraded through the Brandenburg Gate [. . .] While we, after having single-handedly destroyed one of the biggest empires in history, a mammoth, exhausting undertaking – we were sent tiptoeing home under cover of darkness.[14]

The notion that the Italians had fought the Austro-Hungarian Empire on their own was of course false, ignoring as it did the contribution of the Serbs and more significantly the Russians – the latter until towards the end of 1917 – to say nothing of the post-Caporetto British and French commitment to the Italian struggle for survival. It was, however, one of the key tenets of the myth and was also employed by D'Annunzio: 'How did we win the war? On our own, ever more so from one year to the next.'[15]

But now to the issue of foreign policy, the central question for all of the forces of the nationalist Right, which supported an imperialist agenda aimed at securing territorial acquisitions in a range of geographical areas, namely the former German colonies in Africa, the Horn of Africa, the territories of the Eastern Mediterranean which had belonged to the Ottoman Empire, the Anatolian peninsula itself, the coastal regions of the Adriatic, the Dalmatian cities of Fiume and Zara, modern-day western Slovenia, and Albania.

As far as the new, post-war colonial division of Africa was concerned, at the Paris Peace Conference of 1919, the liberal Right and the Minister for the Colonies under the Orlando government, Gaspare Colosimo, sought to obtain fulfilment of Article 13 of the London Pact of 26 April 1915. It made provision for Italian 'territorial compensation' in Africa in the event of France and the British Empire acquiring colonies belonging to the German Empire. Accordingly – and with the goal of achieving predominance in East Africa – Italy advanced claims for a number of trading routes from France and oases from the British on the border with Libya; for Trans-Giuba, the port of Kisimayo and Somaliland from the British; and for Djibouti from the French.[16]

During the course of the conference, the strategy of the Italian delegation was confused and uncertain – at times unrealistic – and was frustrated by the attitude of France and Britain who, having annexed the German colonies in Africa and the territories in the Eastern Mediterranean which had belonged to the Ottoman Empire, refused to apply Articles 9[17] and 13 of the London Pact, claiming that one of the parties to the agreement, Russia, had withdrawn from the war, and that Italy had declared war against Germany a year too late. The behaviour of the Italian delegation, which abandoned the talks from 24 April to 7 May leaving behind only lower-level functionaries, proved ineffective if not downright counter-productive. When Orlando returned to Paris having obtained Parliament's approval of the line of action to adopt, he was presented with a fait accompli, the Allies already having determined on their own the fate of the German colonial empire. This Franco-British *coup de main* was facilitated by the failure of the Italians to comprehend the new system of 'mandates' being employed by Woodrow Wilson's League of Nations. The government in Rome was trapped in an old-fashioned notion of colonial expansion, which the changed international panorama had rendered unsustainable. Italy came to the Peace Conference exclusively with plans for annexation, with the additional objective of imposing a de facto protectorate on Ethiopia, an independent state that had remained neutral for the duration of the war.

Such a strategy met with puzzlement by the British, total opposition on the part of the French, and categorical refusal from President Wilson, who was opposed on principle to 'secret diplomacy'.

The Italian delegation did not insist on their demands with any great energy because the non-negotiable element of its strategy was not expansion in Africa but rather control of the Adriatic and acquiring a stable and lasting influence in the Danube/Balkans area, the ambition of the nationalists, the Right and the key financial and industrial sectors of the nation.

Regardless of the actual contents of the London Pact, the focus of attention of that area of public opinion which had desired and given its backing to Italian intervention was much closer to home: Trento, Trieste, Istria and Dalmatia, Fiume and, if possible, Albania. Essentially, the aim was predominance in the Adriatic. There were various reasons for this including the presence in the area of sizeable Italian-speaking communities, albeit all minorities, the historic overlordship exercised in the area by Venice until the eighteenth century, and a desire to control the access to the sea of the new states in the Danube/Balkan basin, over which Italy wished to establish its influence. This ideology, while remaining a minority one, drew support from all sectors of society, including those which previously had been within the socialists' sphere of influence.[18] Such thinking was a factor, both during the war and at the post-war peace talks, in the government's policies and relationships with the Allied powers. Once it had become evident that the American president did not support – and perhaps did not even comprehend – the full set of claims being put forward by Italy, and that making good on the promises made to Rome in 1915 was not a priority for its European allies, the Orlando government chose to sacrifice its secondary objectives in Africa and the Eastern Mediterranean in order to obtain its core demands, namely control over the Adriatic and a decisive role in the Danube/Balkans.

However, France also wished to become the dominant power with respect to the new states of Central and Eastern Europe, while President Wilson was wary of Italy's dangerous attitude of political and military hostility towards the newly-founded Kingdom of Yugoslavia, something which was exacerbated by a widespread anti-Slavic prejudice.

At this juncture, a key role was played by the city of Fiume (modern-day Rijeka in Croatia), the main seaport on the eastern side of the Adriatic and an important industrial and commercial centre inhabited by a diverse ethnic mix of peoples. In addition to Italians, the city was home to Croats, Hungarians, Germans and a large Jewish community. The Italian-speaking community of Fiume – the largest of the ethnic groups – was in the main in favour of becoming part of Italy, but this had not been promised under the London Pact. Moreover, Fiume was the only major Adriatic port not controlled by Italy and thus the only one that could be freely used by Yugoslavia and Hungary.

The Italian delegation to Paris made a request to annex Fiume which Wilson refused, point-blank. While it is true that the Italian demands only had partial legitimacy and represented an objective threat, the fact remains that the London Pact agreements of 1915 were being used by the Allies purely as it suited them. Where conflicts of interest arose, they were contested if they were to favour Italy, but justified if they were to thwart Italian demands.

Fiume thus became the focal point of the campaign led by the nationalist and fascist Right, which received support from large areas of the Italian military establishment, in particular the navy. A bitterly-fought campaign contesting the Italian handling and the outcome of the peace conference was further exacerbated with the arrival of the new government led by Francesco Saverio Nitti, who had little appetite for pursuing an expansionist foreign policy. The violence unleashed within the country by the fascist squads was, however, not directed against the government but rather against the forces of the Left and those who opposed the imperialist demands.[19] The nationalists and fascists enjoyed support from large sections of the worlds of business and agriculture. In addition, with elections approaching for which the socialists were well-placed, and the entire country gripped by the findings of the commission of enquiry into Caporetto – which had led to a great deal of criticism of the way the war had been conducted and of the leadership of the Italian military – the nationalists and fascists also operated with the tacit consent of the military[20] and of the state institutions.

The fascist campaign, based on an impenetrable mixture of territorial demands, violent opposition to socialists and trade unionists, and anti-Slavic racism, was marked by a series of events leading up to the occupation of Fiume, among which the attack on the *Camera del Lavoro* in Trieste on 4 August 1919[21] in particular, stood out. Then, on 12 September, Fiume was occupied by approximately 2,600 soldiers who had abandoned their units and placed themselves under the orders of D'Annunzio. Pending the definition of its status, the city had been presided over by troops from the Entente powers – a majority of whom were Italian – and from the end of June there had been clashes between French soldiers and Italian military and civilians. On 6 July, a group of Italian troops had attacked a small French unit, killing nine soldiers and wounding eleven. As a consequence, Italy had been obliged to reduce its contingent and to relinquish control of the mission, thus provoking further nationalist propaganda.

The occupation of Fiume, which was carried out by soldiers led in part by officers in active service, was the symptom of profound discontent at all levels of command. This feeling was fuelled by the unsatisfactory outcome of the peace talks and by waves of social unrest sweeping across the country, but was connected in particular to the uncertain peacetime prospects facing the officer class. While the ordinary troops were impatient for demobilisation, the officers feared it – particularly the large number of junior officers who, in the absence of good job prospects, were concerned that civilian society would not afford them the same social and economic status they had enjoyed in the army. The War Minister, General Alberico Albricci, in fact recognised that: 'The vast majority of officers view the Fiume endeavour favourably', while the President of the Council of Ministers, Nitti, noted bitterly: 'For the first time sedition has entered the Italian army – albeit for idealistic aims'. That this was indeed sedition and that among its objectives were the Entente powers was confirmed by Mussolini, writing on 13 September 1919: 'As the merchants of the West were unable to reach a conclusion and were dragging the question out ad infinitum, the use of violence was necessary.'[22]

On the face of things, the conquest of Fiume had been a *coup de main* organised by junior officers and their superiors in response to requests from the city's Italian populace, without any contact with Italian military leadership. In reality, not only did the local high command allow the action to take place, it directly facilitated it with those involved allowed to desert their posts with weapons, vehicles and supplies. In addition, the action had enjoyed the support of sections of the war materials and shipping industries, including that of the steel industrialist, Oscar Sinigaglia.[23]

The *impresa fiumana*, that is the Fiume endeavour, was initially monopolised by an assortment of nationalists and militarists convinced that only a show of force would lead to the defeat of the new 'Slavic enemy'. At home in Italy, these same forces celebrated the *coup de main* in the belief that it might deal a fatal blow to the government. As the situation unfolded however, a number of important developments occurred. The opposition of the Allies and Nitti's refusal to recognize the *fait accompli* and sanction the city's annexation to Italy, prompted D'Annunzio to transform Fiume into a fully-fledged state, albeit a temporary one, with the objective remaining that of annexation, known as the *Reggenza del Carnaro*, the Italian Regency of Carnaro. With the endeavour assuming a new political relevance, Mussolini halted economic and material support for the initiative, fearing the rise of a rival in the shape of D'Annunzio. In addition, the initiative had excited the curiosity of Europe's libertarian movements, as well as many of the Continent's artistic avant-garde and intellectuals. The Berlin-based Club Dada for example sent the following telegram to D'Annunzio at the Milan offices of the *Corriere della Sera* newspaper:

> Please phone the Club Dada, Berlin, if the allies protest. Conquest a great Dadaist action, and will employ all means to ensure its recognition. The Dadaist world atlas Dadaco already recognizes Fiume as an Italian city.
> Club Dada
> Huelsenbeck. Baader. Grosz.[24]

The spirit that animated the occupation of Fiume was multifarious, bringing together nationalists, fascists, anarchists, members of the cultural avant-garde, syndicalists and trade unionists, and was symptomatic of the political, moral and ideological confusion that the war had engendered in a section of Europe's intellectual avant-garde as well as of the hatred felt across a vast political area – but above all in intellectual circles – for liberal democracy and for the political system that had governed Italy as well as much of Europe before, during, and after the conflict.

These milieus, having previously promoted the interventionist movement, subsequently gave rise to the myth of 'mutilated victory'. Openly reactionary figures such as Guido Keller, Giovanni Giuriati and D'Annunzio himself, were joined by right-wing intellectuals such as the leader and the principal exponent of the Italian futurist movement, Filippo Tommaso Marinetti, and the writer Giovanni Comisso, but also by trade unionists such as Giuseppe Giulietti, who was the head of the Maritime Workers' Union, the *Federazione della gente di mare*, and the leader of the revolutionary syndicalists, Alceste De Ambris. Taken as a whole, they formed a movement which, rather than being truly subversive, championed a kind of fanciful, impractical subversion, and whose trademark was ideological confusion.

For many, this was simply a demagogic and populist tactic that could be exploited to win support even in traditionally less receptive areas of society. However, there was also no shortage of those who viewed it as a way of breaking free from old ideological classifications and forging a new nation and a new world. A not-insignificant number of syndicalists found their way to Fiume where they played an important role in securing for the initiative and its myths a degree of popularity which, though to a limited extent only, did extend beyond the confines of the imperialist Right. A factor in this was the progressive nature of a number of the articles of the *Carta del Carnaro*, the constitution of Fiume, as well as several audacious operations, such as the seizing of the cargo ship *Persia*. This freighter was transporting arms and supplies to Vladivostok for the anti-Bolshevik forces. She was hijacked on 4 October 1919 and brought to Fiume. Indicative of the variety of opinion present in the city were the words of Giulietti in the leaflets acclaiming the hijacking: 'Our action is in perfect harmony and continuation with the action we have carried out from the beginning of the European conflict for the freedom and defence of all peoples [. . .]. The supplies, which were to be used to fight the freedom and redemption of the Russian people, will be used to fight for the freedom and redemption of the people of Fiume.'[25]

From spring 1920, and then with increasing determination in the last six months of the Fiume affair, D'Annunzio sought to transform the city he governed into the spark that would bring down the Yugoslav state. With this aim in mind, he established relations with political and ethnic forces in Croatia, Montenegro and Albania which were opposed to the new state and the dominance exercised therein by the Serbian political class. Agreements were entered into with separatists, promising them arms in exchange for aid and territorial concessions to Italy.[26] In short, 'Fiume' was proving to be what it had been from the beginning – at least as far as its principal political and military sponsors were concerned – less an attempt to safeguard the specific characteristics of a city and its hinterland, and less a laboratory or workshop in which a new Europe, revolutionary in its own way, was taking shape, but instead more a way of destabilising the territorial settlements reached in the region and of preventing the 'mutilation' of the imperialist ambitions held by a significant section of the Italian elites.

As far as the Italian nationalists were concerned, in point of fact, the victory achieved in the war had been 'mutilated' by the existence of a unified south Slavic state which represented an obstacle to Italy's ambition of predominance in the Adriatic and the Balkans. The subversive character of the nationalist movement, which openly sought to overturn the international order established by the Versailles Treaty, was demonstrated by D'Annunzio's opposition to the treaty signed at Rapallo between Italy and Yugoslavia on 13 November 1920. By the end of 1920, however, the Fiume special circumstance had come to a conclusion. It no longer served the purposes of the Italian political and military classes, and even the fascists had abandoned it, declaring themselves satisfied with the diplomatic outcome and considering the agreement reached in Rapallo: 'superior to all those previously conceived'.[27] Accordingly, on 24 December 1920, following D'Annunzio's refusal to comply with the order from General Enrico Caviglia to surrender in accordance with the treaty, the Italian army attacked and in four days succeeded in forcing the *legionaries* to surrender.

In conclusion, we believe we have shown how war veterans and their families, regardless of political standpoint, were dissatisfied with the internal and external outcome of the war as far as Italy was concerned. This sense of dissatisfaction is particularly significant if we were to consider that in Italy the veterans' movements did not adopt nationalist positions. They were of course patriotic and loyal to the monarchy, but they still asked for social and economic reforms to compensate the war veterans, wounded, disabled ex-servicemen, widows and orphans. In the immediate post-war period, the veterans' associations demanded a politics of reform rather than of imperialist expansion. Once the 'Risorgimental' goals of Trento, Trieste and Gorizia had been obtained, they openly opposed suggestions of a show of force on the eastern border and called for rapid demobilisation. The war was considered over by the great majority of ex-servicemen and expectations were that it should now lead to the formation of a new ruling class that would draw its legitimacy from the enormous sacrifices made in the war and would be opposed to further hostilities.[28]

Few, in fact, were actually prepared to follow the nationalist vanguard, the fascists and ex-*Arditi* (assault troops), into new military adventures. On the contrary, strong calls were made for the discharge of all mobilised troops and for the end of those conflicts and disputes left unsettled. Indeed, the mass protests and strikes that broke out in the country at the announcement of new military expeditions against Soviet Russia[29] as well as against the continued occupation of Albania,[30] were, in contrast to opinions widely held on both the Right and Left, only in part the symptom of a wider revolutionary project and had more to do with opposition to new military adventures.

The above considerations bring us, however, to the question how was it possible that in the space of little more than a year, dissatisfaction and disappointment had become a legitimising basis for right-wing subversion? First of all, the behaviour of Italy's former allies, during and after the peace conference, had a decisive effect. The refusal to grant virtually any of Italy's territorial demands in both Africa and the Eastern Mediterranean, and above all in the Adriatic, was perceived as unjust and hypocritical. While the Allies made significant territorial gains not least through use of the mandate system – which in Africa envisaged no term for the granting of self-determination to local peoples, deemed too immature – Italy was not permitted to unite with the motherland Italian-speaking communities situated just some tens of kilometres from the country's eastern border. At the same time, however, France was permitted to establish, via a series of alliances, a ring of friendly pro-French nations around Italy in a way which severely compromised the latter's ability to conduct an independent foreign policy.

The USA, for its part, seemed bent on asserting its own 'moral hegemony',[31] a tactic masking political designs and real economic interests which were causes for concern among both the patriotic and traditionalist Italian ruling classes, and the church hierarchies and Catholic bourgeoisie. This American policy greatly disappointed public opinion in Italy, a feeling reflected in a large number of propaganda postcards published in the spring of 1919.[32]

The overall conduct of the Allies in taking advantage of Italy's indubitable weakness and the lack of authority of its post-war governments, eroded the country's sense of solidarity with the countries of the Entente, something which during the conflict had been strong and which had grown further in the last twelve months of the war and the first quarter of 1919 due in part to the immense popularity of the American president. This, notwithstanding, and in spite of the spread of the myth of 'mutilated victory', Italy's former allies in many ways continued to represent a role model and moral standard bearer, at least until the autumn of 1919.

As far as the fascists were concerned in these somewhat confusing alignments and standpoints, even in their circles a number of different positions co-existed. For example, an editorial of 16 July 1919 published in *Popolo d'Italia* read: 'We are not unmoved by the displays of affection towards our troops participating in the victory celebrations in Paris.' Mario Piazzesi however, writing at the same time, noted in his diary these words pronounced by an *Arditi* captain: 'No march on Vienna, no victory celebration; no colonies, no Fiume, no compensation, absolutely nothing.'[33]

The responsibility for the growing hostility towards Italy's former allies cannot simply be assigned to the victorious powers alone: the ruling class and governments which led Italy between 1918 and 1922 must be apportioned a greater share of the blame. On the one hand, there was a lack of a clear-cut strategy as far as Italy's territorial demands were concerned; one that recognized the country's actual weight on the world stage as well as the changed international panorama with the Soviet revolution, American intervention in the war, the end of the Austro-Hungarian Empire and the collapse of the Ottoman Empire. Italy had come to the peace talks without a programme drawn up by the government and with the endorsement of Parliament and public opinion, nor indeed one known fully to its allies.

On the other hand, the international tensions were being exploited by the Italian leadership to divert attention away from the country's internal political problems. At a time of severe social conflict, a significant section of the establishment chose to respond by stoking nationalist sentiment rather than by proposing social reform. Such reform, for example by obliging those who had profited from the war – big business and great landowners – to pay part of the costs of the conflict, might well have given genuine hope for improvement in living conditions compared with what the majority of servicemen and their families had experienced pre-war.

The Socialist Party (PSI) was not without its political responsibilities too, inasmuch as it failed to present a clear programme to the rural and urban popular classes. It proved unable to launch, and as far as a part of its leadership was concerned, was not interested in launching, a genuine revolutionary initiative. Furthermore, it was not able to make use of the war experience of the workers to legitimise its own status as part of the country's constitutional political process, as its European counterparts did. The PSI remained a prisoner of the slogan, *né aderire, né sabotare*, neither support nor sabotage, and was largely left out of the debate within the veterans' organizations, despite the decisive contribution made to the war effort by its supporters at the front and in the factories. Thus the PSI too played a part in allowing the set of watchwords and rituals that would lead to the formation of the myth of 'mutilated victory' to take hold.

While the spread of feelings of dissatisfaction at the outcome of the conflict was not unique to Italy, it was the only one of the victors in which this sentiment reached such dimensions, cutting across all social classes and political parties. However, it must be recognized that, even had the Allies been more generous with regard to Italy's confused and multifarious demands, the country would have experienced serious difficulty exploiting them due to its military weakness. We scarcely need reminding about the difficulties encountered in Libya and Albania and more particularly the long-term economic consequences of the forty-two months of hugely demanding warfare so recently endured.

The authors of this chapter are of the opinion that Italian feelings of dissatisfaction with the outcome of the Great War cannot be correlated in their entirety with the myth – or rather the complex – of 'mutilated victory', which initially and for a certain period was a minority view. However, the errors and short-sightedness of the leaders of Italy in both domestic and foreign areas of responsibility, as well as the self-interested calculations of a majority of the economic elites, did eventually allow the myth to take hold.

Italy, notwithstanding the undisputed territorial advantages obtained, in particular the strategic benefit from ending the Austro-Hungarian threat, experienced peacetime as a defeated country rather than as a victor. The real beneficiary of this paradoxical situation was Mussolini's fascist movement, which seized on its political potential, waging a bloody, low-level civil war[34] which came to an end only after the *coup d'état* of 28 October 1922, and the March on Rome. Europe thus saw the rise to power of a regime which made the revision and overturning of the status quo arising from the peace treaties its number one foreign policy objective, in a crescendo of militarism, anti-Slavic racism, anti-French and anti-Greek nationalism whose only possible outcome was the alliance with Nazi Germany and intervention in the Second World War.

Notes

1. On the identification of the 'mutilated victory' with the *Nike* of Samothrace, see G. Sabbatucci, 'La vittoria mutilata', p. 102, in G. Belardelli, L. Cafagna, E. Galli della Loggia and G. Sabbatucci, *Miti e storia dell'Italia unita* (Bologna, 1999), pp. 101–6.

2. The poet used these words for the first time in the ode *Vittoria nostra non sarai mutilate*, published by the daily *Il Corriere della Sera* on 24 October 1918.

3. On the idea of 'mutilated victory', see J.H. Burgwyn, *The Legend of Mutilated Victory. Italy, the Great War and the Paris Conference 1915-1919* (Westport, 1993); G. Sabbatucci, 'La vittoria mutilata'. G. Albanese, 'Versailles/Versaglia: la «vittoria mutilata»', in M. Isnenghi and D. Ceschin (eds), *La Grande Guerra. Uomini e luoghi del '15-18*, Vol. 2 (Torino, 2009), pp. 889–96; V. Demiaux, 'Dov'è la vittoria? Le role de la reference interalliés dans la construction rituelle de la sortie de la guerre italienne (1918-1921)', in *Mélanges de l'École française de Rome* (2013), pp. 355–70.

4. The London Pact was signed in London by Italy on one side and by the British Empire, France, and Russia on the other, on 26 April 1915. It was not a treaty, but rather an Italian memorandum accepted by the Entente governments. The Italian government did not submit it to Parliament, and it remained a secret until the Russian Soviet government published it at the end of 1917.

5. See G. Procacci, *Dalla rassegnazione alla rivolta. Mentalità e comportamenti popolari nella grande Guerra* (Roma, 1999), and *Warfare – welfare. Intervento dello Stato e diritti dei cittadini (1914-18)* (Roma, 2013); P. Dogliani, *Il fascismo degli italiani. Una storia sociale* (Torino, 2008), pp. 3–50; F. Fabbri, *Le origini della guerra civile. L'Italia dalla Grande Guerra al fascismo, 1918-1921* (Torino, 2009), pp. 3–70.

6. The Socialist official national daily *Avanti!* and some local Socialist newspapers printed a number of articles on this subject during the first eight months of 1919, until press censorship was established again after the D'Annunzio *putsch* in Fiume. Some liberal and progressive newspapers also published very critical reports regarding discipline in the Army. See M. Pluviano and I. Guerrini, *Le fucilazioni sommarie nella Prima Guerra Mondiale* (Udine, 2004).

7. The Royal Commission was established by the new Premier (in Italian *Presidente del Consiglio dei Ministri*) Vittorio Emanuele Orlando on 12 January 1918. With regard to its origin see: N. Labanca, *Caporetto – storia di una disfatta* (Firenze, 1997); G. Rochat, *L'esercito italiano da Vittorio Veneto a Mussolini* (Roma-Bari, 2006), pp. 38–77; A. Gionfrida, *Inventario del Fondo H-4 Commissione d'Inchiesta Caporetto*, http://www.esercito.difesa.it/storia/Ufficio-Storico-SME/Documents/150312/H-4-Commissione-d-inchiesta-Caporetto.pdf.

8. The Royal Commission paid this issue a great deal of attention, and was very critical, condemning a large number of the battles and actions that took place as '*infecondi sacrifici di sangue*' ('unproductive sacrifices of blood').

9. About D'Annunzio see P. Alatri, *Gabriele D'Annunzio* (Torino, 1983).

10. On Mussolini's role in the interventionist movement and his war experience, see R. De Felice, *Mussolini il rivoluzionario. 1883-1920* (Torino, 1965), and P. O'Brien, *Mussolini in the First World War. The journalist, the soldier, the fascist* (Oxford-New York, 2005).

11. Before the war, Mussolini was one of the main national leaders of the maximalist wing of the Italian Socialist Party (PSI) and was also the director of the Party's newspaper, *Avanti!*. Well before Italian intervention, during the first weeks of the conflict, his position on the war changed. Whereas up

until June 1914, Mussolini had been utterly anti-militarist and pacifist, he subsequently became an interventionist and was expelled from the PSI on 24 November 1914. He and other Socialists (among them Cesare Battisti, a Socialist member of the Austrian Parliament, where he represented his hometown of Trento), anarchists, republicans and syndicalists (the most famous of whom were Alceste De Ambris and Filippo Corridoni) joined the so-called 'interventionist left' After the war, some of them followed Mussolini into the Fascist movement, while others (Pietro Nenni, Gaetano Salvemini, Alceste De Ambris) became resolute opponents of Fascism.

12. E. Campochiaro (ed.), *Guglielmo Imperiali. Diario 1915-1919* (Roma, 2006), p. 656.

13. See Pluviano and Guerrini, *Le fucilazioni sommarie nella Prima Guerra Mondiale*.

14. M. Piazzesi, *Diario di uno squadrista toscano, 1919-1922* (Roma, 1981), p. 50.

15. G. Sabbatucci, 'La vittoria mutilata', p. 103.

16. Between the Armistice (4 November 1918) and the Fascist *coup d'état* (the so-called March on Rome, on 28 October 1922) Italy had five Premiers: Orlando until 19 June 1919, Francesco Saverio Nitti until 7 June 1920, Giovanni Giolitti until 27 June 1921, Ivanoe Bonomi until 22 January 1922, and Luigi Facta until 28 October 1922. Their governments had a confused and conflicting policy with regard to colonial issues, particularly in terms of post-war colonial claims. See. U. Frasca, *I rapporti italo-britannici e l'esecuzione del Patto di Londra nel Mediterraneo orientale* (Napoli, 1989); F. Onelli, 'Tittoni e lo scambio di note italo-francese del 12 settembre 1919 in materia coloniale', in *Africa: rivista trimestrale di studi e di documentazione dell'Istituto italiano per l'Africa e l'Oriente* (2003), n. 1, pp. 115–31; M. Isnenghi and G. Rochat, *La Grande Guerra 1914-1918* (Bologna, 2008), pp. 473–512; L. Monzali, 'La politica estera italiana nel primo dopoguerra 1918-1922. Sfide e problem', in *Italia contemporanea* (2009), n. 256–257, pp. 379–406 and 'Il governo Orlando-Sonnino e le questioni coloniali africane alla conferenza della pace di Parigi nel 1919' in *Nuova Rivista Storica* (2013), pp. 67–132; D. Ibra, 'From the London Conference to the London secret pact: the policy followed by Italy towards Albania', in *Mediterranean Journal of Social Sciences* (2012), pp. 95–102.

17. Article 9 of the London Pact stated Italy's right to occupy the area of Adana in southern Anatolia, in the event of the dismemberment of the Ottoman Empire or occupation of a part of its territory by one or more of the Allies.

18. There are several interesting studies regarding interventionism and its spread among workers and craftsmen, as well as on the 'political conversion' to the war of a number of former pacifists and subversives. See M. Mondini, *La guerra italiana. Partire, raccontare, tornare. 1914-18* (Bologna, 2014); M. Isnenghi, *Convertirsi alla guerra. Liquidazioni, mobilitazioni e abiure nell'Italia tra il 1914 e il 1918* (Roma, 2015).

19. See P. Dogliani, '*Sortir de la Grande Guerre, entrer dans le fascisme: le cas italienne*' in S. Audoin-Rouzeau and C. Prochasson (eds), *Sortir de la Grande Guerre. Le monde et l'apres-1918* (Paris, 2008), pp. 113–38; E. Gentile, '*La violenza paramilitare fascista e le origini del totalitarismo in Italia*' in R. Gerwarth and J. Horne (eds), *Guerra in pace. Violenza paramilitare in Europa dopo la Grande Guerra* (Milano-Torino, 2013), pp. 127–55.

20. See G. Rochat, *L'esercito italiano*, cit.

21. See F. Fabbri, *Le origini della guerra civile* , pp. 97–104.

22. These three quotations can be found in ibid., pp. 105 and 106.

23. Oscar Sinigaglia was an engineer and an industrialist. He also was an interventionist and a war volunteer. During the 1930s he restructured the Italian iron and steel industry for the Fascist government. Between 1932 and 1935 he was the chairman of the state-owned steel firm ILVA, but he was later excluded from the public sphere following the introduction of the 'racial laws' (1938). After the Second World War he continued to support the idea of the Italian character of Fiume and Dalmatia.

24. C. Salaris, *Alla festa della rivoluzione. Artisti e libertari con D'Annunzio a Fiume* (Bologna, 2002), p. 9. This book is an interesting and innovative, albeit not entirely convincing, evaluation of the Fiume experience in terms of its innovative ideas and as a break with the post-war bourgeois international order. For a much more critical evaluation of the Fiume adventure see P. Alatri, *Nitti, D'Annunzio e la questione adriatica* (Milano, 1959), an evergreen.

25. Ibid., pp. 140–1.

26. See G.N. Amoretti, *Il trattato italo-jugoslavo di Rapallo, la reazione di D'Annunzio e la mancata crisi adriatica*, in *Scritti in onore di Bianca Montale* (Genova, 2000), pp. 81–102.

27. See Mussolini's article, '*L'accordo di Rapallo*', in *Il Popolo d'Italia*, 12 November 1920.

28. During and after the war, the idea of *trincerocrazia* was widespread. Based on the notion that trench warfare had resulted in a selection of the best people who were most fit to lead the country, *trincerocrazia* produced both progressive and reactionary tendencies. While the first aimed to legitimize the access of the lower classes to government on the grounds that the war had freed them from any Socialist influence, the second supported the idea that trench warfare had bred a new élite of disciplined heroes, capable of imposing military order in peace time.

29. The government headed by V.E. Orlando had planned a military expedition to Georgia. This project was strongly supported by Great Britain, but Nitti's new government immediately decided (at the end of June 1919) to cancel it to avoid further conflicts with the PSI. See M. Petricioli, *L'occupazione italiana del Caucaso: "un ingrato servizio" da rendere a Londra* (Milano, 1972).

30. A detachment of *Arditi* (Italian assault troops) refused to leave Trieste for Albania on 11 June 1919. The most significant event, however, was the mutiny of the 11th Bersaglieri Regiment, who refused to leave Ancona for Albania, and were supported by local Socialists and Anarchists. Civilian and military rebels held control of Ancona from 26 to 28 June, and the authorities were forced to order the bombardment of the city from both land and sea in order to retake it.

31. For instance, Wilson proposed that the Allies establish 'Thanksgiving Day' as an international prayer day to celebrate the victory.

32. See. I.B.A.C.N. Emilia-Romagna, *La collezione di cartoline della Grande Guerra nel Museo Francesco Baracca di Lugo* (Bologna, 2015), especially I. Guerrini – M. Pluviano, *Cartoline della Grande Guerra: un'importante fonte storica*, pp. 47–56.

33. For both quotations, see V. Demiaux, *Dov'è la vittoria?*, pp. 362–3.

34. Some historians view the Fascists' violence as constituting a real civil war. See F. Fabbri, *Le origini della guerra civile*.

Suggested Further Reading

Gooch, John, *The Italian Army and the First World War* (Cambridge: Cambridge University Press, 2014)

O'Brien, Paul, *Mussolini in the First World War: the journalist, the soldier, the fascist* (Oxford and New York: Berg, 2005)

Rochat, Giorgio, 'The Italian Front, 1915-1918', in Horne, John (ed.), *A Companion to World War I* (Oxford: Wiley, 2010), pp. 82–96

Thompson, Mark, *The White War: Life and Death on the Italian Front, 1915-1919* (London: Faber and Faber, 2008)

Wilcox, Wanda, *Morale and the Italian Army during the First World War* (Cambridge: Cambridge University Press, 2016)

Articles about Italy in the *1914-1918-online. International Encyclopedia of the First World War*: http://www.1914-1918-online.net/

Chapter 13

'Brutal as Victors, Despicable as Vanquished'? Some Observations on the German Defeat in 1918

By Holger Afflerbach

By late September 1918 the Central Powers had clearly lost the war and would soon be unable to continue fighting. The German wartime alliance broke apart as all four states tried separately to make peace. The Bulgarians started the process, even seeking unsuccessfully to change sides at the very last minute, and an armistice was signed by their representatives on 29 September.[1] The Ottomans followed with such a signing at Moudros on 30 October[2] and the Austro-Hungarian government signed the armistice of Villa Giusti on 3 November. In this last case it has to be noted that it was impossible to separate the consequences of military defeat from those of internal dissolution.[3]

Germany too faced defeat, not simply because its allies were giving up despite all its attempts to keep them fighting, but also on its own account. Germany's request for an armistice and peace negotiations has remained a topic of intensive research ever since, involving questions beyond those raised by the 'stab in the back' legend[4] – for example, to what extent was the request militarily necessary? And to what extent was it the result of unrest at home?

Facing the consequences of a world war lost was a monstrous task. Indeed, trying to end a world war and to handle the enormous political consequences of defeat were without political precedent in the lifetime of any of those involved. The nearest comparable event was the end of the Napoleonic wars in 1814–15 which had seen France's defeat on the battlefields combined with the collapse of the regime.[5] Perhaps it could be said that Russia's defeat in 1917 and the negotiations at Brest-Litovsk were another and more relevant example of what might follow from defeat in a world war. Indeed, the Russian case was very present in everyone's mind in late 1918 as an awful warning. Both the internal and external consequences of Russia's defeat were considered to be so disastrous that in late 1918 all concerned, victors and vanquished alike, were desperate lest Germany follow Russia in adding social revolution and the overthrow of the existing order to military defeat.

In the event, the attempts of the German leadership to find a way out of the war were quite exceptional. They started on 5 October with the first note addressed by the newly-formed government of Prince Max von Baden to Woodrow Wilson.[6] It combined a request for an immediate armistice with one for peace negotiations on the basis of

Wilson's Fourteen Points. The Fourteen Points had first been proclaimed in Wilson's speech to the United States Congress on 8 January 1918 and amended with additional statements proposing a number of significant improvements of the international system, like a covenant – ideas that were highly popular in Germany on the brink of defeat.

If we were to look at the eventual results – the armistice of Compiègne which ended the fighting on 11 November 1918, and the peace conference to follow in Paris – we might conclude that the outcome of these negotiations in October and early November 1918 amounted to a straightforward German surrender on terms, even if the word 'surrender' was never used officially.[7]

The negotiations had been closely linked to dramatic reforms of government in Germany – 'a revolution from above',[8] according to Hintze, Secretary of State in the German Foreign Office and the chief initiator of the 'German way out of the war' and these reforms had soon been followed by a massive mutiny, originating with sailors in the High Seas Fleet, a revolution from below. In the meantime, many military and political leaders, both on the German and on the Allied side, thought that the negotiations were a mistake and that it would be better to fight on to get better conditions, or perhaps to adopt a totally different strategy for negotiations.

All this could be compared with events in France in 1814–15 – but there was one highly distinctive feature in the negotiations of 1918: the German leadership tried to thwart their conquerors by putting the American President Woodrow Wilson in charge of the negotiations, practically asking him for a guarantee that the peace would embody the principles of his Fourteen Points. The German 'Wilsonians', whose intentions were aptly analyzed by Klaus Schwabe,[9] put their hopes for a better world and a peace which would be acceptable to the vanquished nations too, on the President, and tried to circumvent those Allied leaders, like Georges Clemenceau, with a decidedly nationalist agenda. Even so, there was a serious risk that the attempt to end the war might fail, that hostilities would continue, and even worse, that an internal revolution might sweep away the government and destroy the structures of society.

If we were to consider the objectives of the German peacemakers and then compare them with the final outcome, it would appear that the German way of ending the Great War had at least been 'half successful'. To speak first about the success: the German initiative had ended the war. Fighting ceased on 11 November 1918; the Great War was finally over. As this was indubitably a benefit to mankind, the German way out of the war was far from a complete disaster, though of course self-interest rather than altruism was the motivation. To have prolonged the fighting would simply have resulted in even greater losses, more misery and ruination.

Even so, it is clear that in late September 1918 the German leadership had different hopes and expectations which were to be bitterly disappointed. Their goals were very different from what they were obliged to accept in November 1918 and in the Versailles Treaty of 28 June 1919. They had sought to avoid surrender but were able to do so in name only and their hopes of a 'Wilsonian peace' had been dashed. Nevertheless it may be of interest to examine some of the ideas, plans and hopes which the German leadership had cherished even in the days of defeat.

One might start with a question which was discussed in endless detail at the time and has been argued over ever since: how urgent was the request for armistice from a military point of view, and what exactly was the German General Staff seeking to achieve? This is, of course, an important part of the 'stab in the back' legend with its charge that the German military situation was not so bad as to require an immediate ceasefire, and that only the revolution at home forced the German army to give up.

The question was never discussed more urgently than in October 1918, when Prince Max von Baden, Chancellor since 3 October, sent Ludendorff several long questionnaires seeking to pin him down on the possibilities open to Germany and the prospects for continuing resistance.[10] He got only vague answers from Ludendorff, who said that war was not a mathematical science and everything was possible.

Despite all the wearisome arguments as to how dire the German military situation was in late 1918, there can be no doubt about the fact it was extremely serious.[11] There were three military factors determining the German decision to ask for terms. First, was the collapse of Germany's allies. As early as in 1915, the Germans had been afraid that their main ally, Austria-Hungary, might suffer a military or internal collapse and ask for terms, leaving Germany alone, forcing them to ask for terms too. By 1918, their concern about the state of their allies was only too clear. By then, indeed, all the European belligerents had over-extended their resources but there was a striking difference, quite apart from the American factor, in the manpower and material exhaustion of Germany and her principal ally. David Stevenson has recently established in his magisterial book on 1918, that the general perception that the Central Powers were decisively more drained than the Entente powers is by all the available evidence proven.[12] The problem became acute when the German leadership was unable to stop the Austro-Hungarian government from making its peace move of 14 September 1918. Although this offer of peace – *An alle* ('To all') – was a complete failure it was internationally understood as a sign that Austria-Hungary was on the brink of collapse.

By then, the German leadership was in fact preparing its own peace move, trying to use the Queen of the Netherlands as a mediator to broker a peace conference, preferably in the Hague. However, military events forced them to move more quickly. The British-French-Serbian-Greek *Armée de l'Orient*, which had been trapped from late 1915 until September 1918 in the enlarged bridgehead of Salonika, managed to break through the Bulgarian lines. Bulgaria was unable to halt the breakthrough in Macedonia and asked for an armistice at the end of September. For Bulgaria and its partners the consequences were dire: with Bulgaria, an allied army of around 500,000 men was lost, and the *Armée de l'Orient* threatened now the entire Balkan theatre, Constantinople, the German and Austrian supply lines with Turkey, and the uneasy peace with Romania.

At the same time, the German army in the West was under enormous pressure from constant Allied attacks. In June 1918, the Germans had lost the numerical superiority on the Western Front which they had enjoyed since Russia had dropped out of the war. On 15 July, the last German attack, Marneschutz-Reims, had failed. On 18 July, an allied counter-attack at Villers-Cotterêts, was successful, and on 8 August 1918, a British attack overran several German divisions which showed serious signs of combat fatigue and whose men surrendered in great numbers. To Ludendorff it was now clear that there was a growing problem and that his troops were losing fighting effectiveness and cohesion. It was a turning point and he spoke of the 'black day of the German army'. True, he talked of the need for political moves, but did not do so in terms of great urgency. Both Ludendorff and Hindenburg now admitted the serious setback, but still thought they could hold the German positions on French soil by defensive warfare and forcing the enemy to conclude peace. They judged that the German army was still strong enough to hold its positions and successfully resist attack, as it had done for the last four years.

Meanwhile, although German politicians were thinking of launching a peace initiative using the good offices of European neutrals like Spain or the Netherlands, it is probable that such approaches would have failed, as was the case with all Germany's previous peace feelers.

The German situation in the West was continuing to deteriorate as a constant stream of fresh American divisions flowed into France and German submarines proved unable to stop the transports. By the autumn of 1918, the Allies attained a superiority of nearly 2:1 as 3,527,000 German were engaged against 6,432,000 French, British, Dominion, American and Belgian soldiers.[13] The overall Allied commander, Foch, exploited this to keep the whole German Western Front under constant pressure and to deny the German troops even a moment of ever-more urgently needed rest.

This strategy was successful even though no Allied breakthrough occurred. The German army retreated in good order, but the German divisional reports show that not a single division on the Western Front was, according to their commanders, up to full fighting strength and all units on the Western Front were in urgent need of reinforcements and, especially, of rest. The dominant feature of the hard-pressed German soldier experience in the autumn of 1918 was sheer exhaustion,[14] and this resulted in the German army's loss of cohesion. Soldiers were surrendering to the enemy in ever-growing numbers or deserting into the hinterland, a process which Wilhelm Deist had called the 'hidden military strike' of the German army.[15]

September 1918 witnessed critical developments in the West. Ludendorff feared an Allied breakthrough and shouted practically every evening at the head of the Operations Department, Colonel Heye: '*Heye, jetzt sind sie durch!*' – ('Heye, now they are through!').[16] This did not happen, but the steady Allied advance continued until at the end of the month their divisions were able to pierce the Hindenburg Line. This fortification had been the most formidable obstacle on the Western Front and, according to Allied commanders, it would not have been possible to pierce it if the German defenders were to have retained their earlier tenacity and coherence. This was the moment at which it became clear that the game was lost. Ludendorff shocked those around him with his expressions of despair – his last desperate hope was an outbreak of the plague in the French army – and his underlings decided to inform the politicians that urgent action was needed.

True, the German army on the Western Front was still a formidable fighting force of 191 divisions, including four Austro-Hungarian ones,[17] but many of these divisions were under-strength, twenty-eight having battalions of 200–300 men, and the rest 400–500 men – the norm having been around 650. There was no longer the defensive capacity to hold up the Allied advance. There was no equivalent of the Hindenburg Line in the rear to give the German armies a new focal point of defence. The Antwerpen-Maas Line, for example, was not fortified and had inadequate railway connections.

Coinciding with the Bulgarian armistice, these developments in the West were, in Ludendorff's view, conclusive. On 28 September 1918, he admitted that an armistice was necessary to prevent a breakthrough in the West. In explaining his motives he focused on events in Bulgaria, but Crown Prince Rupprecht, commander of the army group named after him on the Western Front, considered this to be only 'a favourable excuse' to cover up the disaster in the West which was, in Rupprecht's eyes, the result of Ludendorff's failed strategy in 1918.[18]

Here it is worth noting that Ludendorff did not have a nervous breakdown, as has often been claimed. His decision to ask for terms was not the result of panic, but of a clear appreciation of the hopelessness of the situation. In fact, his psychological condition in September 1918 was better than in the previous months; he had been given medical treatment for overwork and the therapy had been successful.[19] Moreover, his decision was quite in line with what he had said before. He had repeated countless times that there was no third way between victory and defeat. He had tried to achieve victory and had failed; now he admitted defeat – albeit not without blaming the politicians for the poor state of morale in the army and in society and the poisoning of the fighting spirit of the army which was now forcing him to ask for an immediate armistice.

Although for both Hindenburg and Ludendorff an immediate armistice was now an absolute priority, the question remained: why should the enemy concede one to Germany? One of Ludendorff's officers, Albrecht von Thaer, asked him exactly this question. If he, Ludendorff, were in Foch's position, would he give Germany an armistice? Ludendorff answered. 'No, I wouldn't, I would press even harder; but in war everything is uncertain and it may be that our enemies are also in need of rest. We do not know and we have to try.'[20]

What exactly was Ludendorff hoping to achieve by an armistice? An attractive precedent might have been the armistice in the East in 1917 which actually provided a ceasefire and a demarcation line. One thing at least was clear: an armistice was not a surrender and not a disarmament. Of course, Ludendorff understood very well that he might have to pay a hefty price for an armistice and he was ready to do so, for example by offering to give up all occupied territories in the West and to withdraw all Germany's armies to the German frontier. He considered this a very significant concession, sparing those territories from the destruction of war and giving up very significant military advantages. He envisaged a retreat over a period of two to three months – a very tight schedule but one which would allow the German armies to bring back with them a large part of their heavy weapons, equipment and munitions. Such a retreat Ludendorff calculated, would not leave Germany defenceless. The armistice would be followed by peace negotiations, but if these were to break down, Germany could resume the fight at its borders, with regrouped armies.

In short, armistice was not surrender. The key difference was that a surrender leaves the vanquished party defenceless and at the mercy of the victor. Ludendorff's later opposition to the terms of the armistice therefore did not reflect, as is often said, an incomprehensible change of mind but the realization that the conditions for the armistice as they emerged during the negotiations with Wilson were very similar to surrender and left Germany unable to resume hostilities. Ludendorff regarded such an armistice as pointless. Rather than accept such terms, Germany would do better to fight on, for even if it were defeated and forced to surrender, it would in fact be no worse off.

As for the question of whether an immediate armistice were necessary, there is no doubt that Ludendorff erred massively in failing to take into account the devastating psychological consequence of requesting an armistice. His troops had already lost much of their cohesion and it should have been clear that if the army command were actually to admit defeat, disintegration would accelerate. Nobody wanted to be the last fallen soldier of a lost world war. It is also clear that others, among them the newly-appointed Chancellor, understood much better the political consequences of the request for armistice. But Ludendorff pressed relentlessly for an armistice as soon as possible and did not even want to wait for the formation of a new government.

Is it possible to say how urgently the German armies needed an armistice in October 1918? In his book, *The Last Four Months* (1919),[21] General Sir Frederick Maurice drew two conclusions: the German armies were defeated and unable to stop the Allies, but the Allies were unable, for logistical reasons and also owing to exhaustion, to pursue the Germans effectively for much longer. Hence, although the danger of an Allied breakthrough was there, it was less urgent than Ludendorff thought in late September 1918. Indeed, by October 1918, Ludendorff had changed his mind and considered the military situation to be somewhat better and that the German army could have continued co-ordinated resistance for several months, in the form of a retreat towards the German frontier.[22] This was also the opinion of Field Marshal Sir Douglas Haig and even Foch thought that the German armies might be able to continue resistance for some months. But the point was: to what purpose? As the head of the operations department of the German General Staff, Colonel Heye, replied to the question of the head of military intelligence, Lieutenant Colonel Walter Nicolai: 'Is our military situation indeed so catastrophic?' 'No, it is not catastrophic, but hopeless.'[23]

In short, as far as the German army was concerned, even if there were no longer any need for an immediate armistice there was also no future in attempting to continue the struggle. The position was different in the German navy, where, as to some extent it was not hindered in its operations and did not need an armistice or surrender at all, the naval high command was inclined to fight on. The sailors, however, were not, and the attempt to make a sortie with the entire fleet sparked off a revolution on board the battle fleet which then spread to the whole of Germany.

The German attempt to 'Out-Wilson' Wilson

Ludendorff's urgent request for an immediate armistice at last moved German politicians, who had been largely apathetic for years, to spring into action. During the war, Imperial Germany had been less a military dictatorship than a society more or less confident that military victory would eventually save the situation, and therefore a society accepting the dominant role of the army. In the end, it was not the elderly Chancellor, Count Hertling, but the Secretary of State of the Foreign Office, Admiral von Hintze, who took the decisive steps in presenting the appeal for an armistice to President Wilson.

Ludendorff had focused on an immediate armistice and no more. He had not even read the Fourteen Points. Hindenburg's stance was even worse; he wanted to link the armistice with the German annexation of Longwy and Briey, which even Ludendorff considered to be inappropriate in the extreme.[24] Hintze handled the peace initiative now with ruthless decisiveness. For a start, he had lost faith in Ludendorff who, after telling him in June that he was confident of enforcing peace on the enemy, and in August that he still thought the German armies could stay on French soil, was now asking for an immediate armistice. Hintze, being a military man himself, had had enough of these unreliable assessments. He had originally hoped to broker peace through the

Netherlands, but now he decided to entrust Germany's fate to Woodrow Wilson. True, the President had made speeches in September 1918 in which he had been extremely critical of the leaders of the Central Powers, describing them as 'without honour',[25] but he remained the hope of the more progressive German politicians.[26]

Wilson's idealistic ideas of a better system of international arbitration and fair settlement of unresolved political questions, which seemed to fit in with some of Immanuel Kant's ideas, was very attractive for German politicians and diplomats, especially at this time of defeat. His talk of 'Open covenants of peace' (Point 1 of the Fourteen), of 'Absolute freedom of navigation upon the seas' (Point 2) and 'removal, so far as was possible, of all economic barriers and the establishment of an equality of trade conditions among all the nations' (Point 3) and then of 'a general association of nations' (Point 14) were welcome to Germans who were apprehensive about the possibility of economic warfare after the peace,[27] while Wilson's points on Belgium, the Ottoman Empire, Italy or Russia seemed secondary in those desperate days. The German 'Wilsonians' wanted to use the President to broker a peace which, if he were to stick to his words, they had reason to hope would not be too bad for Germany.

To overcome the President's criticisms of Germany's military autocracy, Hintze thought that a new government was needed, and this as soon as possible. He decided that the 'inefficient' Imperial Chancellor, Count Hertling, must go and he even decided that he himself, as a man of the old system, would have to go, too – a rare case of a revolutionary who was prepared to sacrifice his own person. His idea was to create a new government which would have more democratic legitimacy and credibility than the old one and the attempt to reconstruct Germany's political system continued with amazing speed after his departure from office and throughout October. First, a new government was created, led by Max von Baden, a prince, but a man with the reputation of being a moderate and a protagonist of a peace of 'understanding'.[28] Reforms such as abolishing the three-tier electoral system in Prussia, or moving towards a parliamentary system that had been attempted for years without success, were now implemented in a matter of weeks. Germany became a parliamentary state, the power of the Emperor was limited and the Cabinet system abolished.

These political reforms were almost universally believed to be overdue and their implementation was greeted with relief by the vast majority of Germans. However, the reason that the reforms were adopted at this juncture was, of course, not democratic zeal, but the urgent need to establish a government with democratic credibility which could gain the sympathy of Wilson and his followers. The driving force was the hope for better peace conditions.

Needless to say, both Wilson and his European allies were suspicious about these precipitate changes.[29] Clemenceau had only bitter sarcasm for German moves towards democracy which he saw, with some justification, as a German attempt to escape responsibility for a lost world war. The *Times* of 6 October 1918 referred to Germany's 'camouflage democracy'.[30] In Germany meanwhile, the leader of the Centre Party, Matthias Erzberger, warned against exaggerated attempts to accommodate the victors. Germany, he said, had to appreciate that the victors considered these changes to be mere tactical manoeuvres and Germany would lose credibility instead of winning it by such moves. Indeed, her opponents might say: 'Germany is brutal as a victor, and despicable as vanquished.'[31]

Even so, attempts to accommodate the victors continued into November, the most striking example being the deposition of the Kaiser. Here two elements came together: Wilhelm II's own blunders and catastrophic failures had already rendered his position impossible, but although a timely abdication might have saved the monarchy, his stubborn insistence on continuing to rule forced a reluctant Max von Baden to depose him. Of course, most Germans saw in the Kaiser an obstacle to getting better peace terms; but here too it was a case of opportunism rather than real conviction. Once German officials drew the conclusion from the various Wilson notes that the President wanted to get rid of military autocracy in Germany, the Kaiser became simply a political liability. In fact, by now Wilson did not care about Wilhelm II and he even thought that a constitutional monarchy in Germany would be better than risking a communist revolution.[32] However, German desperation to accommodate Wilson's supposed democratic requirements knew no bounds, and any political baggage that seemed to stand in the way of getting better peace terms was dropped.

Only at Paris did the new rulers of Germany realize that all their efforts had been in vain and that democratic Germany was not to be treated any differently from Imperial Germany. This final recognition that all Germany's self-humiliation in the hope of gaining Wilson's support had been pointless may explain the cold rage and despair of Brockdorff-Rantzau, the Foreign Minister of the infant Weimar Republic and leader of the German delegation in Paris. There, Wilson had pretended to stick to his Fourteen Points, while he had in fact clearly failed so to do. Nobody put this point more forcefully than the British economist, Maynard Keynes, in his sardonic comments on the Paris conference.[33]

The German belief in a 'Wilsonian peace' faded quickly.[34] Indeed, anger at the failure of the attempt to 'out-Wilson Wilson' was boundless. But the question remains: had there been any viable alternative at the time than to turn to Wilson? The answer must be that, as events had turned out, and given the great haste to secure an armistice and start peace negotiations in September, no practical alternative existed. True, several ways forward were discussed, but all too late. The most serious attempt to pursue a different exit strategy was made by Max von Baden when, even before he became Chancellor, he tried to postpone the request for armistice. Had he succeeded the entire situation might just possibly have been different, but, threatened by the Kaiser with dismissal from the very start, he simply fell into line.[35]

Indeed, the linkage established in October between the request for an armistice and that for peace negotiations greatly weakened the German situation. Wilson's notes in reply became increasingly sharp and demanding. To make matters worse, Wilson handed over the task of formulating the armistice terms to his European allies who did their utmost to make Germany defenceless by extreme stipulations. Foch, for example, demanded not only a German retreat to the border within two weeks, knowing that this was impossible without the German army leaving practically all its heavy weaponry and equipment behind, but the handing over of a decisive number of guns, machine guns, aircraft, locomotives, and concession of bridgeheads on the right bank of the Rhine. While the British members of the armistice commission thought that the French demands went too far and might result in the Germans rejecting the conditions, the French were similarly critical of the British naval requirements which included the internment of the High Seas Fleet.

To reaffirm: Max von Baden did not want to ask for an immediate armistice but was overruled. Friends counselled him to take over the chancellorship and advised him that if the military situation were to become still more critical, it was the military who should 'approach the enemy with the white flag'.[36] It is also clear that among the German military and political leaders there was no calm discussion of different approaches towards the enemy. Everything was dictated by haste; the haste created mainly by Ludendorff wanting an armistice within 48 hours. But there were other possibilities which would have been more compatible with the Prince's original idea. Starting the negotiations with a request for armistice irredeemably weakened the German position. An offer of peace talks, the acceptance of the Fourteen Points, but no request for an immediate armistice, would have been along the lines of the industrialist and politician, Walter Rathenau's idea of threatening the enemies with a German *levée en masse*,[37] a fanatical fight by the German people for their very existence. Rathenau's idea was unrealistic; the German people were tired and even Ludendorff did not see much potential in it.[38] However, once the peace negotiations started, there was no escape from them – neither for Germany nor, albeit to a lesser extent, for the victorious powers who, faced with war-weary populations, could have resumed hostilities only if justified by exceptional circumstances.

Another possibility was considered by the experienced politician, Karl Helfferich, who had no trust in Wilson. He, like Max von Baden, had read the Fourteen Points carefully. It was evident for them that Alsace-Lorraine would be lost (Point 8). It was equally clear that the Polish-speaking provinces in the east of Prussia would be lost too. (Point 13). Helfferich suggested that if Germany were ready to make these sacrifices, it should offer them not to Wilson but directly to the interested European powers. This would have meant, instead of trying to 'Out-Wilson Wilson', and indeed the Allies, trying to negotiate, so to speak, from nationalist to nationalist. This could have meant offering, for example, Alsace-Lorraine directly to the French to see what happened. This idea could have been combined with Walter Rathenau's plan of a *levée en masse*, offering the enemy a choice between accepting the offer or having to fight *a l'outrance*. Schwabe, too, speaks of a 'European alternative' to appealing to Wilson, namely, to speak to Germany's European enemies instead.[39] However, any discussion of such plans must remain conjectural because the decision-makers at the time never gave Rathenau's and Helfferich's suggestions serious consideration.

Certainly, it would have been risky for two reasons. First, if the hardliners among the European enemies were to have got the upper hand, the fanatical *guerre à l'outrance* might have taken place. The collapse of Germany's allies in October 1918 would have made such a last stand at the frontier even more hopeless. Indeed, when the German government, seeking a second opinion to Hindenburg's and Ludendorff's on the possibilities of further resistance, consulted Generals Gallwitz and Mudra, it was told that the pivotal question was the attitude of Austria-Hungary: if the main ally gave up, any further German resistance would be hopeless.[40]

In short, the decision to end the war came too late to offer any realistic difference of approach from what was taken. Things might have been different if Wilson's Fourteen Points were to have been accepted in January 1918 when the German army was still formidable and well equipped. Indeed, tentative moves in this direction were in fact undertaken by Hertling but it is most unlikely that a formal German request to conclude peace on the basis of Wilson's Fourteen Points would have been accepted even in January 1918, because, as Wilson himself was to put it in a 'somewhat cryptic' statement ten months later: 'If Germany was beaten, she would accept any terms. If she was not beaten, he did not wish to make terms with her.'[41]

Conclusion: . . . despicable as vanquished?

By October 1918 Germany was in fact beaten and Wilson was ready to make terms with her. But the optimistic expectations that Germany might even keep most of Alsace-Lorraine and other territories, and that Wilson's Fourteen Points might save her from the consequences of a lost world war, sparing her a punitive peace, proved to be a vain hope.

The attempt to 'Out-Wilson Wilson' failed. But at least the war was over – or was it? We have to keep in mind that not even this was a certainty, and that if things were to have gone differently the fighting might have continued well into 1919 at the cost of goodness knows how many more lives. This justified the German attempt to appeal to Wilson. As for the precipitate democratic reforms in Germany which accompanied the appeal to Wilson, were they evidence of a serious desire for political change or simply an opportunistic manoeuvre? The answer is: both. The first did not exclude the second. The German desire for political change was enormous, and the wish to get the best peace conditions possible absolutely dominant. Most of the steps and reforms undertaken in October 1918 were considered by a vast majority to have been long overdue. They had been stopped by the opponents of change, in the main by Conservatives and National Liberals, whom the wartime governments were unable to overcome. Now, on the verge of defeat, resistance to change could be overthrown.

Given what was to happen in Paris, it may still be asked if it were a bad idea to try to broker a peace by using Wilson? Hintze had understood that Wilson was the only enemy leader who had bound himself to a programme of a universal nature. Appealing to him, in the hope that he could enforce it, certainly seemed a sensible decision. Anything else seemed to offer dire consequences. Hindenburg advised against appealing to Wilson's Fourteen Points when he learned that this would mean the loss of Alsace-Lorraine and the Polish provinces, and suggested simply requesting peace talks.[42] However, he was told, correctly, that the Allies had several times rejected unspecific requests for peace talks, and would continue so to do. Being specific, and agreeing to certain concessions, might limit the danger of eventually more radical demands from the victorious powers. Besides, Wilson's Fourteen Points had several clauses which even looked advantageous from a German perspective.

All other German approaches towards ending the war, from Rathenau's in October 1918 to that of the first leader of the government of the new Weimar Republic, Philipp Scheidemann, with his refusal to sign the Versailles treaty in June 1919, tended to imply rejection of the claims of the victors considered by the Germans exaggerated, and a readiness to resume hostilities. However this strategy had become increasingly unrealistic as both the military and the interior situation deteriorated from October 1918. Events transformed the erosion of political control into an avalanche, especially during the days when every German ally broke away. The German negotiating position diminished until in the end every demand had to be accepted, even an armistice which was so harsh that the victorious powers seriously feared that it would be rejected.

German options, if they were ever to have existed, had melted away. When Hindenburg started to talk about a fight to the last man, he was told that this might be possible for a battalion, but not for a people of 65 million.[43] Germany had lost the war and had failed to soften the consequences of defeat. From the victors' point of view, the downside was that their victory had only been made possible by destroying almost the entire European system. The Germans, even democratic Germans, felt betrayed by a peace that failed to follow Wilson's Fourteen Points and they never accepted the peace of 1919 as the final word. Only after another world war was Europe able to rebuild itself.[44]

Notes

1. Bullitt Lowry, *Armistice 1918* (Kent, OH, 1996), pp. 7ff.
2. Paul C. Helmreich, *From Paris to Sèvres: The Partition of the Ottoman Empire at the Peace Conference of 1919-1920* (Columbus OH, 1974). Armistice agreement is on pp. 341ff.
3. Manfried Rauchensteiner, *Der Erste Weltkrieg und das Ende der Habsburgermonarchie* (Wien, 2013), pp. 1043–52. (Anm. 2520) Armistice conditions (in English): http://www.forost.ungarisches-institut.de/pdf/19181103-1.pdf
4. Harry R. Rudin, *Armistice, 1918* (New Haven, 1944); Pierre Renouvin, *L'armistice de Rethondes: 11 Novembre 1918, Trente journées qui ont fait la France* (Paris, 1968); and the respective volumes Herbert Michaelis and Ernst Schraepel (eds), *Ursachen und Folgen. Vom deutschen Zusammenbruch 1918 und 1945 bis zur staatlichen Neuordnung Deutschlands in der Gegenwart. Eine Urkunden- und Dokumentensammlung zur Zeitgeschichte* (Berlin, 1958–80).
5. Michael Broers, '"Civilized, Rational Behavior?" The Concept and Practice of Surrender in the Revolutionary and Napoleonic Wars, 1792–1815', in Holger Afflerbach and Hew Strachan, *How Fighting Ends: A History of Surrender* (Oxford, 2012), pp. 229–38.
6. Lowry, *Armistice 1918*, p. 11.
7. Ibid., p. 26; Sally Marks: 'Mistakes and Myths: The Allies, Germany, and the Versailles Treaty, 1918–1921', *The Journal of Modern History* 85 (September 2013), p. 634.
8. Rudin, *Armistice*, p. 51.
9. Klaus Schwabe, *Deutsche Revolution und Wilson-Frieden. Die amerikanische und deutsche Friedensstrategie zwischen Ideologie und Machtpolitik 1918/19* (Düsseldorf, 1971).
10. Rudin, *Armistice*, pp. 77ff, 99ff, 141ff. *Ursachen*, p. 301.
11. The official German history of the First World War does not leave much doubt about it (and this may explain that the volume in question, Vol. XIV, was intended only for limited and restricted circulation) *Der Weltkrieg 1914-1918. 14. Band: Die Kriegführung an der Westfront im Jahre 1918. Erstausgabe durch die Kriegsgeschichtliche Forschungsanstalt des Heeres* (Berlin, 1944) (Nur zum Dienstgebrauch). Re-edited by Bundesarchiv Koblenz, 1956.
12. David Stevenson, *With Our Backs to the Wall: Victory and Defeat in 1918* (London, 2011).
13. Holger Afflerbach, *Die Kunst der Niederlage. Eine Geschichte der Kapitulöation* (Munich, 2013), p. 201.
14. Alexander Watson, *Enduring the Great War. Combat, Morale and Collapse in the German and British Armies, 1914–1918* (Cambridge, 2008); Afflerbach, *Die Kunst der Niederlage*, pp. 201–6.
15. Wilhelm Deist, 'Verdeckter Militärstreik im Kriegsjahr 1918?' in Wolfram Wette (ed.), *Der Krieg des kleinen Mannes. Eine Militärgeschichte von unten* (München, Zürich, 1992), pp. 146–67.
16. Albrecht Philipp (ed.), *Die Ursachen des Deutschen Zusammenbruchs im Jahre 1918. 4. Reihe im Werk des Untersuchungsausschusses*, 2 vols (Berlin, 1925), p. 262.
17. Heye, 17.10.1918, in *Amtliche Urkunden zur Vorgeschichte des Waffenstillstandes 1918* (2nd ed. Berlin, 1924), p. 140.
18. See Holger Afflerbach: 'A comfortable excuse? The Bulgarian Surrender and the German decision to ask for terms in October 1918', in Iannis Mourelis, *The Salonika Front in World War One* (Saloniki, forthcoming).
19. Manfred Nebelin, *Ludendorff. Diktator im Ersten Weltkrieg* (München, 2010), pp. 454–6.
20. Ibid., p. 467.
21. Sir Frederick Maurice, *The Last Four Months* (1919) http://www.firstworldwar.com/source/armistice_maurice.htm

22. *Der Weltkrieg 1914-1918*, Vol. 14.

23. Afflerbach, *Kunst der Niederlage*, p. 205.

24. *Ursachen*, p. 405.

25. Lowry, *Armistice 1918*, p. 33.

26. Schwabe, *Deutsche Revolution und Wilson Frieden*, pp. 88–104.

27. I. Open covenants of peace, openly arrived at, after which there shall be no private international understanding of any kind but diplomacy shall proceed always frankly and in the public view.

   II. Absolute freedom of navigation upon the seas, outside territorial waters, alike in peace and in war, except as the seas may be closed in whole or in part by international action for the enforcement of international covenants.

   III. The removal, so far as possible, of all economic barriers and the establishment of an equality of trade conditions among all the nations consenting to the peace and associating themselves for its maintenance.

   XIV. A general association of nations must be formed under specific covenants for the purpose of affording mutual guarantees of political independence and territorial integrity to great and small states alike . . .

   From Woodrow Wilson, 'Speech on the Fourteen Points,' *Congressional Record*, 65th Congress 2nd Session, 1918, pp. 680681.

28. Lothar Machtan, *Prinz Max von Baden. Der letzte Kanzler des Kaisers. Eine Biographie* (Berlin, 2013).

29. Adam Tooze, *The Deluge. The Great War, America and the Remaking of the Global Order, 1916-1931* (London, 2014), p. 223.

30. Rudin, *Armistice*, p. 90.

31. Gerhard Ritter, *Staatskunst und Kriegshandwerk. Das Problem des »Militarismus« in Deutschland* 4 vols (München, 1954–68), Vol. 4, p. 454.

32. Stevenson, *With Our Backs to the Wall*, pp. 516ff.

33. John Maynard Keynes, *The Economic Consequences of the Peace* (New York, 1920).

34. Lowry, *Armistice 1918* p. 34.

35. Rudin, *Armistice*, p. 76.

36. Ibid., p. 61.

37. Stevenson, *With Our Backs to the Wall*, p. 518; Michael Geyer, 'Insurrectionary Warfare: The German Debate about a *Levée en Masse* in October 1918' in *The Journal of Modern History* Vol. 73, No. 3 (September 2001), pp. 459–527, pp. 470, 482fff; Rudin, *Armistice*, pp. 86ff; *Vossische Zeitung*, 7.10.1918.

38. Stevenson, *With Our Backs to the Wall*, p. 518, and footnote.

39. Schwabe, *Deutsche Revolution und Wilson Frieden*, p. 99.

40. Stevenson, *With Our Backs to the Wall*, p. 522.

41. John N. Snell, 'Wilson on Germany and the Fourteen Points', in *The Journal of Modern History*, Vol. 26, No. 4 (December 1954), pp. 364–9; Colonel House claimed that the formula was his; see also Lowry, *Armistice 1918*, p. 36 (15 October 1918).

42. *Ursachen*, p. 424.

43. Ibid., pp. 424ff.

44. Ian Kershaw, *To Hell and Back. Europe 1914-1949* (London, 2015).

Suggested Further Reading

Deist, Wilhelm, 'Verdeckter Militärstreik im Kriegsjahr 1918?' in Wette, Wolfram (ed.), *Der Krieg des kleinen Mannes. Eine Militärgeschichte von unten* (München, Zürich, 1992), pp. 146–67

Lowry, Bullitt, *Armistice 1918* (Kent OH, 1996)

Renouvin, Pierre, *L'armistice de Rethondes: 11 Novembre 1918, Trente journées qui ont fait la France* (Paris, 1968)

Rudin, Harry R., *Armistice, 1918* (New Haven, 1944)

Schwabe, Klaus, *Woodrow Wilson, Revolutionary Germany and Peacemaking, 1918-19: Missionary diplomacy and the realities of power* (London, 1985)

Watson, Alexander, *Enduring the Great War: Combat, Morale and Collapse in the German and British Armies, 1914-18* (Cambridge, 2008)

PART THREE

PART THREE

Chapter 14

The Great War and British Identity

By Ian Whitehead

The centenary commemorations for the First World War have coincided with a period of marked uncertainty within the United Kingdom about the future shape of the nation and its place in the world. Internally, ambitions for Scottish independence continue to disturb the constitutional status quo, despite hopes that the issue would be settled for a generation following the referendum in 2014. Externally, as the result of another referendum, Britain has commenced the timetable of departure from the European Union, starting a process that in turn looks set to raise further challenges to the integrity of the United Kingdom. Together, these developments have both reflected uncertainty about the definition of British identity and doubts about its ability to retain any meaningful attachment for people who might more strongly identify as English, Irish, Scottish or Welsh. In his study of English and British identity, Krishnan Kumar argues that it has only been in such uncertain times 'when Britain is faced by threats from within and without, only when there is talk of "the break-up of Britain" that serious attention has turned to the character of the United Kingdom'.[1]

Attempts to define, defend and disseminate British identity have inevitably drawn upon the achievements of Britain's past. In this context, the commemorations of the First World War centenary have provided an opportunity to emphasise the bonds of British unity that were forged in the immense struggle for victory and to press the case for how Britain's involvement in the War reflected the values embodied by British identity. However, seen through the prism of victory, and reflecting nostalgia for a period when Britain's place in the world seemed more certain, it is all too easy to forget the divisions in British society prior to the War and the extent to which British identity was a contested idea.

On the eve of war, it was tensions between British and Irish identity, rather than the events in Sarajevo, which exercised the attentions of Britain's political leaders. Edwardian politics had been engaged in fractious debates over free trade, social reform, military conscription and constitutional change. In these debates, the Liberal and Conservative Parties projected fundamentally different visions of Britain. Alongside these tensions, the growth of trade unions and the emergence of the Labour Party were feared by the ruling elite as evidence of an industrial workforce which was increasingly thinking in terms of its class rather than its national identity.

Externally, Britain was in a state of semi-detachment from European affairs. Imperialists feared the growing threats to the British Empire, particularly from the rise of German power, and were concerned about the extent to which the British population either understood the Empire or were willing to defend it from attack. Division over foreign and imperial affairs was evident right up until the declaration of war, when the cause of Belgium provided a purpose around which most people were able to unite. However, it was a fragile unity and the popular view of the War was less enthusiastic than is often depicted to be the case. The nation was not gripped by 'war fever' or carried away in a mass outpouring of patriotism.

Once engaged in the conflict, Britain did remain largely united and in many respects British institutions were in due course able to bask in the glow of victory. Even in the 1930s, by which point wartime assurances that this would be a 'War to End All Wars', resulting in 'A Land Fit for Heroes', had begun to ring hollow, there was a remarkable degree of stability in British society and pride in Britain's achievements during the War. In the decades since then, a narrative of disillusionment and futility has come to dominate popular understanding of the War. Through remembrance ceremonies, there is a continued commitment to honouring the bravery of those who fought in the War, remembering the plight of those who were left disfigured by battle and the price paid by those who gave their lives. An increasing interest in family history also drives a curiosity in finding out how our ancestors coped with the challenges of the War. However, remembrance narratives tend to reinforce generalisations about incompetent British leaders inflicting needless suffering and death in pointless battles on the Western Front. The willingness of the British Tommy to suffer these hardships and to risk life and limb is a source of both admiration of their deeds and mystification as to why they were prepared to remain loyal to a national cause that required them to fight in a seemingly unnecessary badly-conducted war. All of these factors when combined present significant challenges for any attempt substantially to reinvigorate British identity through our collective reflections on the legacy of the First World War.

In October 2012, the Prime Minister, David Cameron, gave a speech at the Imperial War Museum to launch the proposals for the official commemoration of the First World War centenary. In his speech, Cameron set out his ambition for 'a commemoration that captures our national spirit, in every corner of the country, from our schools to our workplaces, to our town halls and local communities. A commemoration that, like the Diamond Jubilee celebrated this year, says something about who we are as a people.'[2] His ambition reflected a determination to ensure that the commemorations gave due regard to the immense national effort and sacrifice occasioned by the Great War. His speech captured the continuing public interest in the experiences of those who contributed to the war effort, both on the battlefield and on the Home Front. The bravery of those who fought, the sacrifice of those who died and the continuing legacy of the War for those who suffered the physical and mental scars of battle, have continued to shape not only our collective view of the 1914–18 conflict but also our understanding of wars in general. Despite intervening conflicts, not least the Second World War, the date and rituals of Britain's annual Remembrance Service remain those which were set in place after 1918. Images of those who fought and the literary legacy of the War, most often the particular voice of the soldier poets, continue to frame our reflections on conflict and thus ensure that the First World War remains a significant event in our collective memory.

Cameron's commitment of over £50 million to support the commemorations was evidence of how seriously he viewed the need properly to mark the centenary. Additional public funding, notably that from the Heritage Lottery Fund, has further helped to ensure his hopes for a programme of events which has reflected local and regional experiences of the conflict, as well as marking the key points in the national story. Particularly in 2014, communities across the United Kingdom held a range of events, many of which sought to ensure that the commemorations had broad appeal and reflected the variety of the war experience.

In July 2014, the author of this chapter gave a paper at a seminar in Ashbourne, Derbyshire, which formed part of a week-long programme of commemorative events in the town. Ashbourne's schedule of activities was typical of many held across the country and included the re-creation of a Red Cross Hospital and an exhibition looking at the role of women on the Home Front. There was a concert in the Memorial Gardens, a programme of Edwardian entertainments, fancy dress competitions and a display of children's art inspired by the War. The town also organised a 'boys' game' of its traditional Shrovetide football match to acknowledge the importance of football to the troops in the Great War.

Across the country, the centenary has inspired interest in understanding the War's impact on even the smallest communities. Ellastone, a Staffordshire village, on the border with Derbyshire, held an exhibition in its parish church, St Peter's, which used a range of photographs and memorabilia to reveal the extent of the War's impact on this small rural community. For example, despite its size and location, Ellastone became the site of one of only seventeen auxiliary hospitals in Staffordshire. The on-going commemorations in the village have highlighted the heroism of those who left to fight on distant shores, such as Edward Unwin and Arthur Charlesworth, who lost their lives in the Gallipoli campaign.[3] Thus, in such local commemorations, there is evidence of a community engagement that chimed with Cameron's ambitions, although this has arguably been most evident in localities where there were already existing networks of community activism.

To mark the centenary, the Arts and Humanities Research Council (AHRC) has funded five centres across the UK with the purpose of enabling academic researchers to engage with and support community commemorations of the War. One of these is the Centre for Hidden Histories, which has a focus on 'themes of migration and displacement, the experience of "others" from countries and regions within Europe, Asia and the Commonwealth, the impact and subsequent legacies of the war on diverse communities within Britain, remembrance and commemoration, and identity and faith'. Projects supported by the Centre include one involving Ramgarhia Social Sisters, a Sikh group in Leicester, which is creating a tapestry to tell the story of the Sikh contribution to the War. Another project, Britalians, highlights the role played by the Italian community in the East Midlands.[4] Such partnerships between academics and community groups have been important not only in widening engagement with the commemorations but also in ensuring that the centenary has provided an impetus for increasing our understanding of the diverse aspects of the War, giving voice to previously forgotten or neglected popular experience.

However, whilst research on the War has been drawing attention to diversity there has been a simultaneous desire in some quarters to see in the commemorations an opportunity to promote a more coherent sense of British identity and values. In 2014, the Secretary of State for Education, Michael Gove, provoked a debate when he attacked what he regarded as a left-wing bias in representations of Britain's part in the War. He particularly objected to the narrative of incompetence and futility that has informed popular representations of the War, such as the satirical series *Blackadder Goes Forth*. Gove acknowledged that there is 'no unchallenged consensus'. However, he set out the case for teaching a positive history of British participation in the War, which reflected Britain's pursuit of a just cause and her 'special tradition of liberty'.[5] In doing so, Gove was echoing the justifications for war which enabled the Liberal government of Herbert Asquith to remain largely united in 1914, with the resignation of but two of its members. What he was perhaps missing was the extent to which the apparent unity of Britain, as it entered the War, masked significant differences about Britain's place in the world and the values for which the British nation stood.

The divisions within Asquith's Liberal Party concerning foreign policy had threatened to destroy his government. At the Foreign Office, Sir Edward Grey had presided over a policy of greater diplomatic and military partnership with France, capitalising on the shift in relations which had occurred as a result of the 1904 *Entente Cordiale*. An increasingly noisy war of words with Germany, fuelled by a succession of diplomatic confrontations, had drawn Britain deeper into the tense and complex web of continental rivalries. In particular, the Moroccan Crises of 1905 and 1911 had provoked defiant responses from British ministers. Perhaps most noteworthy was the voice of David Lloyd George, the Welsh radical MP and former pro-Boer, who as Chancellor of the Exchequer made a significant intervention in foreign policy in his 1911 Mansion House speech. However, the radical wing of the Liberal Party, of which Lloyd George was generally seen as the most significant parliamentary figure, was generally uneasy about the direction of British foreign policy. The Liberal Foreign Affairs Committee had formed as an internal party opposition to the direction of Grey's policies whilst in numerical terms Asquith's Cabinet was dominated by pacifists and 'Little Englanders'. From their perspective, Grey's policy risked taking Britain down a profoundly anti-Liberal path, paved with nationalistic and militaristic influences. For them this threatened a reversal of everything that the Liberal Government had managed to achieve and represented a departure from Liberal philosophy.

Edwardian politics had been characterised by an intense struggle between Liberalism and its opponents over a series of issues, such as free trade, conscription, social reform and Home Rule for Ireland. Threatened by the apparent rise of socialism on the one hand and facing a steady stream of right-wing opposition to its policies on the other, the Liberal Party had been seeking to shape a vision of Britain as a peace-loving, free-trading nation in which the rights of the individual were protected. Instead, from the perspective of his Liberal opponents, Grey's conduct of affairs promoted belligerent nationalism and a heightened risk of war. In such a war, economic dislocation and the inevitable pressure for military conscription would represent a fundamental threat to Liberal principles. 'Untainted' Liberals were determined to prevent this from happening. However, their numerical strength did not translate into influence over policy-making. Suspicion of Germany's accumulating naval power, with its capacity to threaten British trading interests and the security of its far-flung Empire, had strengthened anti-German voices in the Foreign Office. Germany's diplomatic blundering and the mounting sense of potential continental conflict had also intensified the atmosphere of urgency. If France were to be left alone to fight Germany in such a war, there was a general assumption that she would face defeat for a second time at the hands of Prussian military might. The resultant German continental hegemony would destroy the balance of power in Europe, threatening Britain's position on its own doorstep. The British Government was not prepared to risk such an outcome.

The events of July 1914 thus presented Asquith and his Liberal colleagues with a huge dilemma. Understandably, like the bulk of his party, the Prime Minister was concerned to preserve the principles that underpinned the Liberal vision of Britain. Such a vision was hardly compatible with entering a conflict driven by nationalism and imperial rivalry, in which Britain would be aligning with Russia's illiberal Tsarist regime. On the other hand, France could not be abandoned to defend the continental status quo on her own against the perceived threat of German expansionism. What saved the Liberal Government, at least in the short term, was the necessity in German military planning for an invasion of Belgium as part of the Schlieffen Plan for a rapid knock-out blow against France. A war that Grey believed would have to be fought to preserve Britain's national interests, however uncomfortable it might be for his Liberal colleagues, could now be presented as a necessary step to preserve Belgian sovereignty. The cry of 'Poor Little Belgium' blunted the opposition to war from all but the most determined pacifists. There was now a morally-justifiable cause around which Britons could unite. The declaration of war on 4 August 1914 was confidently depicted as an affirmation of Britain's willingness to defend freedom and democracy. Propaganda capitalised on the righteousness of Britain's stand against the evils of aggressive German militarism. The British had been forced to take up arms in a just cause. It was an apparently unselfish act, which emphasised the spirit of fair play that defined the British national character. Indeed, from the perspective of the centenary commemorations, the Liberal Government's seizing of the moral high ground continues to provide a neat and palatable version of British motives, which sits comfortably with contemporary projections of British values and justifies Gove's stance.

However, Grey's view of the situation in 1914 reflected Britain's identity and purpose as an imperial nation; this imperial, nationalistic vision of British identity was at least as potent a force in shaping the decision to enter the War as the claim to be defending the rights of small nations. Many who had doubted the resolve of the Liberal Government were relieved that the Belgian issue had stirred Asquith and his colleagues into action. Those who had pressed for increased military expenditure, the introduction of compulsory military service and the need to prepare the economy for war against Germany now felt vindicated. Britain was engaged in a necessary war for the preservation of the British Empire against the threat of German aggression. It was a war for which they believed Britain ought to have been much better prepared, but which must now be fought in the national interest. Without any requirement for a reference to the violation of Belgian neutrality, the preservation of the existing order, upon which the British Empire's foundations were secured, was in itself regarded as a righteous cause.

The Empire was lauded as the means by which Britain's benign influence had been spread across the globe. It was a force for good that had to stand firm in the face of Germany's imperialism, which by contrast represented her oppressive *Kultur*. The idea of a morally superior Britain overcoming German evil became a central theme of British propaganda. Typical of the sort was the three act play, *Kulture*, which was performed in December 1914 at the Manchester Hippodrome. The play, described as a 'Spectacular Aqua-Drama', culminated in a cascade of water drowning the German troops, whilst an illuminated halo symbolised the triumph of the British as God's chosen people.[6] Such propaganda messages reinforced the legitimising myth of the British Empire as God's instrument for spreading Christian morality and civilisation across the world. The pre-eminence and rectitude of Britain and her institutions were unquestionable and this conviction shaped a sense of superiority within British identity that could be found across all sections of society. In particular, the violence and hatred towards the German population in Britain which the War precipitated helped to fuel a mounting xenophobia, a paranoia about immigrants and a more strident expression of national identity.[7]

As Linda Colley argues, British identity had been forged in the eighteenth century through 'a common investment in Protestant warfare and lucrative imperial adventure'.[8] It was through a combined effort by the peoples of the four nations of the United Kingdom that the Empire had been conquered and settled, reinforcing a common bond of British identity, which was able to contain and co-exist with Scottish, Welsh, Irish and English identity.[9] For the ruling classes in particular, this imperial British identity was a significant means of sustaining a strong sense of shared national interests and patriotism.

One of those who sought to stiffen the sinews of this patriotic feeling was Reginald Brabazon, the seventh Earl of Meath. He was an enthusiast for promoting military values amongst British youth and sought to ensure that the education system instilled a loyalty to the British imperial ideal across all classes. In particular, Meath championed the foundation of Empire Day, which was first celebrated in 1904 and quickly established itself across Britain as a fixture of the school calendar for more than fifty years. Jim English has demonstrated how 'Empire Day could be presented as the righteous celebration of what was generally held to be a set of social facts – the primacy and destiny of the Anglo-Saxon race, the virtuous progression of the British Empire, and the common bond of an "imagined community" inhabiting a vast and far flung empire.'[10] Programmes of civic events also ensured that Empire Day reached into the collective consciousness of the adult population, promoting the imperial spirit across the social classes and in all regions of the United Kingdom.[11]

The idea of popular identification with the Empire contrasts with the views of Bernard Porter, who questioned the extent to which the concept of empire had impinged on the minds of the working classes.[12] Indeed, as Catriona Pennell has shown in her study of popular responses to the War, across the social divide there were limits to the patriotic fervour that the propagandists had hoped to create. The population did not go to war unquestioningly in a spirit of enthusiastic nationalism. In fact, contrary to the impression that might be gained from photographs of crowds apparently embracing the news of war in London and other cities, the response was more muted. Pennell shows that across Britain 'people supported the war, but only because they felt it was the right thing to do in the circumstances'.[13] Rather than a 'war fever', a mix of emotions was evident in British towns and cities. As Adrian Gregory notes, the enthusiastic crowds, once the War had begun, reflected a desire to cheer on the departing troops rather than necessarily being evidence of a patriotic war enthusiasm.[14] It was the events of the War itself – reports of atrocity stories, the sinking of the *Lusitania* and the fate of Edith Cavell – that created a real sense of an inflamed popular patriotic feeling across British society.[15]

The limits of British popular patriotism were commented upon by the French writer, Robert Briffault, based upon his own experiences of serving alongside British troops:

I have no doubt that you know just how much patriotism entered into the motives which marshalled our wage-earners into the war. I happen to know that pretty well myself; I have spent some years with them in the trenches of France, Gallipoli and Flanders. And I know that the average wage-earner in khaki would have been, on the word of command, just as ready to fight the French, the Belgians, the Portuguese, or the Canadians, or the Australians as to fight Fritz or the Russians. Patriotism, enthusiasm for the British Empire or the Cause was not at all a prominent motive in the dim mind of the average khaki-clad wage-earner. He was actuated by very vague impulses. The chief was a certain eagerness to avail himself of any opportunity to escape from the drudgery of earning wages, even if it were a change from the frying-pan into the fire. He was foolishly glad to exchange the joys of his home for a sand-bag dugout in France. The prospect of change, together with the added glamour of khaki, which enhanced him immensely in the eyes of his female friends, the phrases of the hour, hypnotised and fascinated him – and compulsion further persuaded him.[16]

Certainly, a multiplicity of other factors – poverty, unemployment, boredom, peer pressure, the excitement of travelling to foreign lands – led men to war. However, Briffault's failure to detect overt expressions of patriotism might in part have reflected his antipathy to British culture. Even during the War he felt repelled by the inhabitants of France's ally, as is evident from his comments on a 1916 visit to Wimbledon, which he found to be:

> the dwelling-place of a well-to-do smug people suffering from complete atrophy of the brain – there is not a discordant note anywhere, everything speaks of artless English suburbanity undefiled – it appears to be peopled by chambermaids and Sunday-school-teaching shopboys. The girls are rosy-cheeked imbeciles. It is an unpatriotic place, because it makes one pro-German to look at it. Every flame of thought and living feeling is as surely extinguished there as in an atmosphere of carbonic acid.[17]

Seen from a more sympathetic perspective, however, such a scene might have been described as representing the image of Britain which some men felt they were fighting to protect.

The settled state of British imperial interests by the close of the nineteenth century ensured that Britain was contented with the global status quo. Britishness embodied stability, honour, respect for order and a spirit of playing by the rules. The British saw themselves as the defenders of all that was good in the world and the agents of the highest form of civilisation. Other nations were meant to be grateful for this gift of civilisation and to exist within the system of values and law that Britain had established. Nationalists and imperialists in Germany begged to differ and attacked what they regarded as the hypocrisy of Britain's claim to be the defender of liberty whilst the British selfishly secured their own economic and political interests. The growth of Germany's power fuelled British paranoia about her intentions whilst Britain's sated imperial appetites inevitably cast her as the righteous defender against Germany's aggression. As Germany emerged as the principal challenger to the British world view, her 'disruptive energy threatened the essence of Britain's accomplishment, which was the establishment of a measure of law and order in the world'.[18] During the War, the certainty that the British were the unique custodians of justice gained in currency. In his novel, *Mr Britling Sees It Through*, H.G. Wells wrote: 'It was not simply English life that was threatened; it was all the latitudes of democracy, it was every liberal idea and every liberty. It was civilisation in danger. The unchartered liberal system had been taken by the throat; it had to "make good" or perish.'[19]

The popular press was important in stoking opinions on the German menace, whilst adventure stories and spy novels depicted positive portrayals of British heroism alongside dire warnings of German aggression. These stories of future war 'served to fashion a new national legend',[20] perhaps most famously captured in *The Riddle of the Sands* by Erskine Childers. For the propagandists, if the British character were guilty of any flaw it was that of complacency. John Buchan was a Scot who had been 'raised in a culture that viewed the world in strongly dramatic terms and that saw life in Calvinistic categories of Good barely able to hold its own against Evil'.[21] Both before and during the War, the tension and excitement of his novels, such as *The Thirty-Nine Steps*, captured the precariousness of Britain's fight to preserve civilised values and the need for the British to be alive to their responsibilities. The journalist and writer Hall Caine reminded British readers of the selfish and untrustworthy traits in the German character that had been on open display prior to the War:

> I had, in common with the majority of my countrymen who travelled much abroad, been compelled to recognize the ever-increasing hostility of the German and British peoples whenever they encountered each other on the highways of the world – their constant cross-purposes on steamships, in railway trains, hotels, casinos, post and telegraph offices – making social intercourse difficult and friendship impossible. The overbearing manners of many German travellers, their aggressive and domineering selfishness, which always demanded the best seats, the best rooms, and the first attention, was year by year becoming more and more intolerable to the British spirit.[22]

From the 1890s there was a mounting clamour for Britain to prepare for a future war. A lack of military readiness was seen as a sign of complacency that would precipitate Britain's political and economic decline. Such concerns gained added vigour after the mixed fortunes of the Boer War drew attention to British weaknesses. There were increasing demands on the Government to expand Britain's armed forces with organisations such as the Navy League, which had 100,000 members by 1914, acting as increasingly vocal representatives of public opinion. Most notably, Edwardian Britain was riven by debates about the need for peacetime conscription. These debates reached into the heart of what it meant to be British, with the Liberal Government successfully making the case that the freedom of the individual from compulsory military service was a defining feature of the nation. To its opponents, the failure to introduce conscription was a sign that the Government could not be trusted to defend the British patriotic interest. These arguments persisted until the introduction of conscription in 1916. Austin Harrison, the editor of *The English Review*, had been a critic of the pre-war failure properly to recognise the German threat. In 1915, he attacked the opponents of conscription for betraying the essence of the British spirit:

> We call ourselves sportsmen. We are the sailors of the modern world. Our national pride is the youthful splendour of our athletes. The very name of Nelson still brings a lump into our throats. And yet we hesitate. Still, like schoolboys, we prattle about one volunteer being the equal of four conscripts. Still we talk about man and his rights, about liberty, about civilisation, about Empire, yet after a year of unsuccessful war we cannot even make up our mind to take the one step which can ensure our victory . . . Can any man hold that England is justifying her civilisation if she refuses to give her all to fight for it?[23]

Fears about a lack of military preparedness, combined with growing awareness of the extent and impact of poor health amongst the working classes, led to a particular focus on ensuring that British youth were not only imbued with an understanding of British virtues but were also physically prepared for the task of defending Britain's interests. Amongst the children of all classes there was a promotion of a muscular Christian ethos, which emphasised values such as duty, discipline and respect for order. The sports cult of the public schools trickled down across society, whilst organisations such as the Boys' Brigade, the Church Lads' Brigade and the Boy Scouts accustomed British youth to military structures and values. Jack Davis recalled: 'I was in the Boys' Brigade and was a member of an athletics club too, so I both accepted discipline and had an organised life. It meant the call of the army quite naturally attracted me.'[24] Popular juvenile papers, such as the *Boy's Friend* and *Chums*, inspired the young with tales of heroism in the distant reaches of the Empire.[25] Collectively this propaganda and the values of Edwardian Britain established a dominant form of British identity that was essentially masculine, encapsulating the virtues that would inspire young men to volunteer in 1914.

Whilst acknowledging the extent to which popular enthusiasm for the Empire was muted in ordinary circumstances, it is evident that the language and symbolism of empire had helped to establish a quiet sense of British patriotism across the social classes, which gained a louder expression on the outbreak of war. The industrial working class in Britain, as elsewhere in Europe, displayed the same patriotic feeling as other sections of society. The working-class rejection of the anti-war message of Ramsay MacDonald and the pacifist movement demonstrated that they saw the War from the perspective of a shared national interest. There was little criticism of empire and no sense that this was a conflict which merely served the interests of the elite.[26] In this sense, Empire Day had helped to achieve the purpose of its founders. National identity triumphed over class identity in 1914. Young, single working-class men did flock to the recruiting offices, which were also places of mingling between the classes. Working-class patriotism also showed itself in the badging system for industrial workers, which highlighted and protected the contribution to the war effort of men engaged in essential war work.[27]

It should be remembered, however, that there was a sizable but largely unrecorded minority of the poor and economically marginalised who remained untouched by any sense of patriotism or British identity. One woman who represented this strand of opinion was reported as saying: 'She did not see what difference it would make if the Germans did come and rule England. She had always been poor, and didn't suppose she would be worse off with them than without them.'[28] In fact, in the short term, the War did bring benefits for the working-class population. There were improvements in working conditions, pay rates and diet. There were improvements in life expectancy, a decreased incidence of deficiency diseases and an improvement in maternal and infant mortality rates. However, lest we fall too easily into the idea of the War as an engine of social progress, it is important to note the price that was paid in working-class lives. As John Bourne points out: '94 per cent of the British dead belonged to the "Other Ranks". These were overwhelmingly working class.'[29] Moreover, the apparent triumph of a shared British identity over social divisions was a limited victory. Class tensions were not eradicated by the War. By 1917, working-class discontent, as evidenced through industrial disputes and expressions of war-weariness, was becoming a concern for the Government. After three years of war, with its immense sacrifices, the patriotism of 1914 was no longer on its own sufficient to sustain the spirit of the masses. The formation of the Ministry of Reconstruction and the attendant promises of a 'Land Fit For Heroes' helped to redefine the War as the means towards the creation of a better society. Lloyd George's declaration of War Aims in 1918, in response to the popular mood, promoted the impression that Britain was fighting for international freedom and democracy, rather than narrow imperial self-interest.

As the War progressed, stridently patriotic depictions of British imperialism gave way to the idea of the Empire as a commonwealth of nations held together by shared values of liberty and justice. Joseph Thorp talked of the death of 'Jingoism as a national spirit'. He argued that Britain's Empire was now bound together in 'the unity of a shared spiritual passion for freedom'.[30] At the Imperial War Conference, in April 1917, Jan Smuts asserted that whatever post-war adjustments might be implemented in the relationship between Britain and her Dominions, the Empire must continue as an unquestionable force for good in world affairs:

> the only successful experiment in international government that has ever been made is the British Empire, founded on principles which appeal to the highest political ideals of mankind. Founded on liberal principles and principles of freedom and equality.[31]

In fact, although the War had seen the Empire reach its largest extent, it had also hastened the process of its decline. The contribution to the war effort by Britain's Dominions and colonies helped to fuel nationalism, whilst the conduct of the War had encouraged resentment of Britain.[32] In particular, the treatment of British colonial troops emphasised the extent to which they remained the victims of prejudice and inequality within the Empire which they were fighting to defend. The men of the British West Indies Regiment were dismissed as innately inferior to their white counterparts and they were not seen as suitable for front-line service on the Western Front. Caribbean troops were seen as fit only for labouring tasks and throughout the War suffered discrimination in terms of pay and living conditions.[33] Similarly, although manpower requirements did lead the British to deploy Indian soldiers in combat roles on the Western Front in 1915, they too were subject to discrimination and were feared as the racial 'other'. For example, walls were constructed in military hospitals to ensure Indian patients were prevented from mingling with their white counterparts.[34] After the War, despite their contribution to victory, the Black and Asian population in Britain was subject to institutional racism and widespread xenophobia. Black troops were encouraged to repatriate rather than settle in the UK, whilst their war service was firmly marginalised within the narrative of the British war effort. The British identity which emerged out of the War remained an exclusively White identity.

The Second World War further loosened the bonds of imperial unity and the subsequent dismantling of the Empire, from the 1940s onwards, 'removed a major prop to Britishness'.[35] However, the fact that Britishness did not crumble overnight, combined with the absence of popular concern about the loss of Empire, highlights how shallow had been the imperial identity for much of the population. In any case, other institutions, particularly the Monarchy, continued to provide a focus for British identity.

The Monarchy successfully re-invented itself for the post-imperial age and it was able to do so upon foundations of constitutional monarchy that had been securely laid by George V during the First World War. His assumption of the dynastic name Windsor, and the cutting of foreign ties, enabled him to achieve a 'fundamental repositioning of the British monarchy, away from the traditional and transnational royal cousinhood and the personal friendships that had gone with it, towards the British nation and empire'.[36] As a result, the War actually strengthened the Monarchy, in marked contrast to the situation in other countries. Tours of the Front, visits to hospitals and increased patronage of charitable activities, all helped to secure close bonds between the Royal Family and the British people, which were strong enough to survive the Abdication Crisis and were reinforced by the images of George VI standing with his people during the Second World War. The Monarchy was able to sit above politics whilst representing British liberties and democracy. In 1937, the editorial of the left-wing *Daily Herald* declared: 'The King is neither a dictator nor a Party man. He is a constitutional King in a Parliamentary democracy. And yesterday [the Coronation] was the celebration of that democracy by all people, irrespective of Party.'[37]

The War also proved to be a milestone for British democracy. The Representation of the People Act established universal male suffrage whilst finally making some concession on the issue of votes for women. The sacrifices and hardships of the War had helped to ensure that the evolution of British democracy could no longer be held up. In 1918, the general election was conducted in an atmosphere of patriotic fervour and triumphalism, with calls to 'Hang the Kaiser' and 'Make Germany Pay' being voiced from all sections of society, particularly the working class.[38] The result of the election gave the Coalition, under Lloyd George, a huge majority. During the election the abuse piled upon candidates who ran on pacifist platforms or who advocated a lenient peace settlement with Germany testified to the strong identification with the patriotic cause which the War had engendered. At the same time, Lloyd George's election campaign encouraged expectations that the progressive social changes which the War had stimulated would be built upon in peacetime through a significant programme of social reform. The War had apparently bequeathed a strengthened British democracy which was going to deliver a better and more prosperous society for all. However, by the end of the 1920s, Lloyd George was a spent force in British politics and the hopes he had raised had collapsed amidst economic decline, unemployment, industrial tensions and striking evidence of wealth inequality.

Yet, despite this picture of social division and economic stagnation, it is remarkable just how far British society remained stable, with limited attraction to the political extremes and little evidence of widespread disenchantment. The War had been a powerful force for social conservatism in British society and nothing reflected this better than the inter-war political domination of the Conservative Party. In particular, the steady leadership of Stanley Baldwin, with his 'Safety First' mentality and his suspicion of foreign ideas, appeared to personify the period.[39] As Jeremy Black has pointed out, the War had promoted a patriotism rooted in a strong sense of national pride, 'based on the eventual victory, which seemed to show that, despite her inter-war economic problems, Britain was exceptional in punching above her weight'.[40] The Monarchy, Parliament and the institutions and customs of British society were reinforced by the successful outcome of the War. The Conservatives were the party that most successfully represented these institutions and customs. Above all the Conservatives were the party of the Union.

However, the Conservative view of the Union was founded upon a belief in a homogenous British identity, which translated into a highly centralised polity for governing the United Kingdom. It was based upon a concept of parliamentary sovereignty that saw Westminster as supreme and was hostile to any idea of sharing sovereignty in federal or devolved power structures. The rigid Conservative view of British identity and of political power centralised in Westminster had been increasingly at odds with the pre-war reality of Britain as 'a multinational state'.[41] Whilst in retrospect there is a focus on the supposed crisis of Edwardian Liberalism there had been a crisis of Edwardian Conservatism as it faced this reality. No issue had demonstrated this more clearly than the difficulties posed for the Conservative vision of the nation by the prospect of Irish Home Rule.

The outbreak of war in 1914 took place in an atmosphere of crisis over the issue of Home Rule in Ireland. However, the invasion of Belgium, a Catholic country, enabled the Liberal government to enter the War with support from both sides of the Unionist and Nationalist divide.[42] The declaration of war ensured that Irish Home Rule was put on hold and in 1916 Nationalist discontent with continued British rule spilled over in the Easter Rising. The British response to the Rising and the controversy over conscription being extended to Ireland in 1918 both helped to drive moderate Nationalists into the arms of Sinn Féin.

By the end of the War, the divisions were apparent in the Irish newspapers, which greeted the Armistice with 'discordant tunes.' For example, whilst the Unionist *Belfast Newsletter* trumpeted its loyal support for Britain, the Nationalist *Connaught Telegraph* emphasised the vital role of America and the need for unity behind the cause of Home Rule.[43] The cumulative effect of the War was to stiffen Ulster Protestant resistance to rule from Dublin and to undermine any remnants of British identity amongst the Nationalist community. The events of the Anglo–Irish War, particularly the deployment of the Black and Tans, added further to the toxicity of Britishness in Ireland. In 1921, the partition of Ireland, following the establishment of the Irish Free State and a separate parliament for Ulster, effectively brought to an end the idea of a twin Irish–British identity that Home Rule had been intended to preserve in 1914. The legacy of this in Northern Ireland was a particularly narrow and sectarian form of Britishness that not only defined it against the Catholic south but also stood in contrast to the expressions of British identity that predominated in the rest of the United Kingdom.[44]

The controversial nature of the War and its relationship to the history of British rule ensured that a national war memorial was not built in Ireland until 1937. A reluctance to risk any displays of British military or imperial identity, combined with the onset of the Second World War, resulted in an indefinite postponement of the opening ceremony until 1988. However, it was not until 1995 that an official government-led ceremony took place at the memorial. More recently, the Irish National War Memorial has been one of the sites of public reconciliation between the British and Irish identities, following the successful visit of Elizabeth II to Dublin in 2011.[45] In Northern Ireland the memory of the War is now a factor in helping to bridge the sectarian divide. Whilst the precarious nature of the Province's unity during the War cannot be ignored, an understanding of how Irish Protestant and Catholic soldiers shared the same experiences is 'having positive impacts on community relations in [Belfast]'.[46]

Aside from Ireland, 'the "national unity" of the Great War seemed to confirm the cohesion of Britain'.[47] In Wales, where the plight of another small country resonated, the issue of Belgium had been significant in mobilising support for the War. In Scotland, 'the clergy of the Presbyterian churches in particular excelled themselves in depicting the war as a Homeric duel between Good and Evil'.[48] During the period of voluntary enlistment, Scotland responded positively, producing '320,589 recruits, the highest proportion of enlistments in the UK'.[49] The demand for armaments, steel, coal, ships and supplies meant that the heavy industries of Wales and Scotland were called upon to make a highly significant contribution to the British war economy. However, this contribution intensified the reliance in both countries on the older heavy industries. In the saturated international markets of the post-war years, their economies felt the chill of economic decline and unemployment. As this process of industrial decline gained momentum over the subsequent century, the attachment to British institutions has declined in both countries. A similar picture can be observed in the industrial regions of England, which have failed to keep pace with the growing prosperity in other parts of the country.

The political changes wrought by the War also had long term implications for perceptions of British identity. The Edwardian Liberal Party had championed Irish Home Rule. Its radical Nonconformist wing, under the leadership of Lloyd George, had been the pre-war political voice of Welsh Wales. In Scotland, which had retained its own institutions within the Union, such as separate legal and education systems, the Liberals had favoured further devolution. There had been the possibility of a looser, more federal structure for the United Kingdom, in which Scottish and Welsh identities might comfortably exist within and alongside a common sense of Britishness. The collapse of the Liberal Party, as a result of its wartime divisions, transformed the political landscape and ended any prospect of further constitutional reform. The War had radicalised working-class communities in areas such as Clydeside and the Welsh mining communities. Labour was increasingly their natural home as the old Lib-Lab loyalties died, but Labour's agenda was focused on national politics rather than voicing specifically Welsh or Scottish concerns. In that sense it did not pick up the mantle of the Liberals. More significantly, in an age where politics seemed increasingly divided between capital and labour, fears of socialism amongst the middle class made the Conservatives the principal beneficiaries of the Liberal decline across Britain as a whole. The Conservative vision for Britain was of a centralised Union, with Westminster as the heart of the political system. They represented a British identity that was in essence a very English vision of Britain. Indeed, it was a picture of Britain that reflected a London and Home Counties bias that was as alien to parts of the North and Midlands of England as it was to Wales and Scotland. Nevertheless, in the inter-war years, the Conservative vision offered reassuring stability in troubled times. After the Second World War, however, the end of empire alongside rapid social and economic change diminished the appeal of the Conservative constitutional model and the united British identity it represented.

As Wales has been more institutionally entwined with England, it was here rather than in Scotland where the cultural shifts were most immediately felt after 1918. Uncertainties about Welsh identity, which were reflected in regional and class divisions across the Principality, can be seen in the ambivalent attitudes towards the design of the Welsh National War memorial and the varied enthusiasm across the nation to raise the funds needed to pay for the memorial. As a result, 'the Welsh National War memorial seems to be only quite Welsh and not very national'.[50] The formation of Plaid Cymru, in 1925, was born from a determination to protect and assert a distinctive Welsh culture through its language and traditions.[51]

In Scotland, the emphasis of the post-war peace settlements on the principle of self-determination did lead to more serious political interest being given to the idea of Scottish Home Rule. However, the war had also been a force for reaffirming Scotland's place within the Union.[52] Thus, an assertive Scottish identity continued comfortably to co-exist with Britishness. Scotland and Scots remained at the heart of the British Empire, which gave outlets for expressions of Scottish identity. Scotland took pride in the design of its national war memorial and the fundraising effort inspired contributions from Scots across the Empire, 'who imagined themselves a national community'.[53]

There was, however, no specifically English national war memorial. As Kumar asserts, English nationalism is an imperial nationalism which asserted itself through its dominant role in the creation of the United Kingdom and the British Empire. It was in these 'larger entities and larger causes in which they found their role and purpose'.[54] It is precisely this English domination of Britishness which has helped to undermine its currency in other parts of the United Kingdom, particularly in the context of the centralised British state. However, as the post-imperial British state has tried unsuccessfully to be part of the European Union and as the integrity of the United Kingdom has come under strain from within, Englishness itself has experienced a crisis.

Thus, it is understandable that the centenary commemorations have been regarded as an opportunity to reinforce the common bonds of British identity and to celebrate the best of what that identity is seen to represent. The expression of national unity was always a significant factor in the rituals of commemoration and remembrance which emerged during and after the War. The wearing of poppies and observation of the two-minute silence became significant collective acts of remembrance which served to exert a unifying influence on British society. However, the format and tone of commemoration was not uncontested. In the 1920s, the Festival of Remembrance was the focus of an ideological conflict between internationalist and nationalist visions of how the War should be commemorated. The composer, John Foulds, motivated by pacifist views, premiered his *A World Requiem* in 1923 and it became the centrepiece of the British Legion's Festival of Remembrance for four years. However, Foulds' *Requiem* came under a steady onslaught from the *Daily Express*, which campaigned for a more nationalistic celebration of Britain's imperial achievements in the War. From 1927, the *Daily Express* gained control of the Festival and transformed it from an expression of 'international grief and mourning [into] a nationalist and pro-empire celebration of the war effort', whilst *A World Requiem* was no longer a part of the ceremony and has only recently seen a revival in its reputation.[55] The emphasis of official commemorations was on British unity and the shared sacrifice in pursuit of victory.[56]

The outbreak of the Second World War lastingly altered the way in which the First World War was remembered. Memories of victory had been replaced by perceptions of a flawed peace settlement which had resulted in another global conflict just twenty years after 'the war to end all wars'. By the 1960s and 1970s, post-imperial Britain was in an age of increasing individualism, industrial decline, mass immigration and changing social values. Old deferential attitudes were being discarded and this meant a rejection of the masculine ideals of leadership and duty that had shaped British identity.[57]

In the context of rapid post-war change, the First World War seemed an increasingly distant and inexplicable event, in which valiant men were depicted as having been led to their deaths by the incompetent British ruling class. Books like Alan Clark's *The Donkeys*, A.J.P. Taylor's *The First World War* and John Laffin's *British Butchers and Bunglers* helped to establish a dominant narrative of the War which emphasised futility and tragedy. Contrary to Michael Gove's assertion, such negative representations of the War have not been the preserve solely of a left-wing consensus. For example, Niall Fergusson, in *The Pity of War*, has argued from a quite different perspective that the War 'was at once piteous in the poet's sense, and "a pity". It was something worse than a tragedy, which is something we are taught by the theatre to regard as ultimately unavoidable. It was nothing less than the greatest *error* of modern history.'[58]

The negative histories of the War drew heavily on the war myth that emerged from the works of the disenchanted poets, such as Owen and Sassoon, or from the pages of *All Quiet on the Western Front*. These literary voices have come to be regarded as *the* authentic representatives of those who fought between 1914 and 1918. As Brian Bond points out, despite their, at best, partial versions of its history, these works came to be regarded as the definitive version of the War.[59] In the 1960s, the stage and screen productions of *Oh! What a Lovely War* further popularised this negative view, which also received comic reinforcement in the 1980s with *Blackadder Goes Forth*. Yet, in the ready acceptance of this version of Britain's experience in the War, what has all too frequently been missed is the extent to which the disenchanted writers offered highly individual accounts of the War, which were often far from typical of the whole. Stepping away from the excessive focus on disillusioned literature, it is clear that in the 1920s and 1930s there was a continued market for war literature which presented a more positive image. Hugh Cecil has shown 'how wrong it is to generalise, how different were people's reactions, and how infinitely varied were the routes by which they reached their conclusions, whether optimistic or pessimistic, about the nature and effects of the First World War'.[60] It is this more complex and diverse picture which historians are increasingly working to uncover as mainstream historiography has moved away from the *Blackadder* version of the War.

Brian Bond correctly identified the need for historians to liberate the First World War from the clutches of literary representations and to ensure that it is treated as a historical event like any other.[61] Caricatures of callous British generals and blanket assumptions of soldier disillusionment have increasingly been displaced by attempts to explore the variety of war experience and to understand how Britain achieved her victory in 1918. Historians such as John Bourne, Paddy Griffiths, Robin Prior, Gary Sheffield, Dan Todman and Trevor Wilson have helped to shape a less emotive history of the War, in which a balanced assessment of British military successes and failures emerges.[62] The factors which motivated British troops and sustained their morale are outlined, in contradistinction to the image of the pitiable or disillusioned Tommy. The relationship between officers and men is rescued from stereotypical representations. Above all, the characterisation of the British Army as being led by unthinking generals, incapable of innovation, is replaced by a narrative that demonstrates a capacity to learn operational and strategic lessons, develop and employ new technologies and ultimately to hone the battle tactics that were to bring victory in 1918. As a result, Douglas Haig, so often the cold-hearted villain of the war myth, has re-emerged as an historical character possessing diverse strengths and flaws who led the British forces to victory in 1918 and who was feted for his achievements up until his death.

Typical of this more balanced approach is the military historian Frank Vandiver, who wrote: 'In the tragedies of wars and battles there is room for criticism of Haig, as of Ulysses S. Grant and other great captains, but when they lead men to victory it gives one pause for thoughts beyond denigration.'[63] One of Haig's recent biographers, Gary Mead, also reminds us of the need to understand and appreciate changing principles and modes of behaviour and to bear these in mind before rushing to judgments based on the prevailing values of the present: '[Haig's] stoicism, self-discipline, courage and unshakeable determination to defend the inviolability of British interests are anachronisms in today's society, one in which public figures, at the drop of a hat, lay bare their souls, beat their breasts, thump tubs, even if they have little to say. Haig would have regarded such emoting as deeply vulgar and destructive of human dignity.'[64]

The course of historiographical conflicts on the War shows that the challenge for those who would like to see the teaching of British history promoting a greater sense of shared identity and collective achievements, lies not only in the difficulties of defining British identity but also in conflicting views about Britain's past actions and their consequences. The study of British history reveals the extent to which, beneath the ruling elite, the British nation which was forged in the eighteenth and nineteenth centuries never 'formed a monolithic identity'.[65] The diverse and shifting nature of responses to the First World War, combined with the continual re-evaluation of its purpose and legacy, are testament to this diversity. There were multiple justifications for Britain's involvement in the War, which shaped the individual perceptions and experiences of those who fought and lived through the 1914–18 conflict. In the century since its outbreak, the continued reinterpretation of the First World War has reflected these different, often antagonistic, yet co-existing views of Britain and what it means to identify as British. At a time of political uncertainty, as Britain reshapes its relationship with its continental partners, and as regional and national identities seek a stronger voice within the United Kingdom, it is understandable that some may have hoped the commemorations of the First World War would help to reinforce the bonds of a common British identity. However, it was always unlikely that such a contested event in our history would succeed in promoting a greater feeling of national unity or a more distinct sense of British values and shared characteristics.

Perhaps a more realistic ambition for the centenary commemorations might be that our collective understanding of Britain's part in the War may have become more nuanced and balanced. Most academic historians have moved on from the passionate and diametrically-opposed debates which once dominated writing on the First World War. It will be a significant achievement if the centenary commemorations were to have allowed this more even-handed and restrained academic debate to alter popular consciousness of the War, liberating it from the clichés of the *Blackadder* variety at one extreme or the national myth of British exceptionalism at the other.

Contradictory though it may seem, Britain's war for imperial self-preservation was also a war to promote freedom and justice. A war that produced a nation in arms on a scale previously unseen also established the right of the individual to make a conscientious objection to military service. A war that produced huge losses on the battlefields retained popular support until its conclusion. Understanding these apparent contradictions and tensions will give us a much better appreciation of Britain's complex war experience and its relationship to the nation we are today. If we could comprehend more fully the variety of British popular experience during the War and recognise the assorted emotions and motives which framed how the British people responded to this great conflict, then we would see beyond attempts to frame a monolithic definition of our collective identity. Instead, we would begin to grasp the remarkable capacity for British identity, at its best, to accommodate diverse identities and viewpoints.

Notes

1. Krishnan Kumar, 'Nation and Empire: English and British National Identity in Comparative Perspective', *Theory and Society*, Vol. 29, No. 5 (October 2000), p. 575.
2. David Cameron, Speech at the Imperial War Museum on First World War centenary plans, 11 October 2012.
3. *Ellastone Remembers*, http://www.ellastone.org/tourism/ellastone-special-events/ellastone-special-events-2013/
4. The Centre for Hidden Histories, http://hiddenhistorieswwi.ac.uk/

5. Michael Gove, 'Why does the Left insist on belittling true British heroes?, *Daily Mail*, 2 January 2014.
6. L.J. Collins, *Theatre at War, 1914-18* (London: Macmillan, 1998), p. 188.
7. Panikos Panayi, 'Anti-immigrant violence in nineteenth- and twentieth-century Britain' in Panikos Panayi, *Racial Violence in Britain in the Nineteenth and Twentieth Centuries* (London: Leicester University Press, 1996), p. 11.
8. Linda Colley, *Britons: Forging the Nation, 1707-1837* (London: Vintage, 1996), p. 393.
9. Paul Ward, *Britishness Since 1870* (London: Routledge, 2004), p. 24.
10. Jim English, 'Empire Day in Britain, 1904-1958', *The Historical Journal*, Vol. 49, No. 1 (March 2006), p. 249.
11. Ibid. pp. 253–60.
12. Bernard Porter, *The Lion's Share: A short history of British Imperialism, 1850-1970* (New York: Longman, 1977), p. 200.
13. Catriona Pennell, *A Kingdom United: Popular Responses to the Outbreak of the First World War in Britain and Ireland* (Oxford: OUP, 2014), p. 4.
14. Adrian Gregory, *The Last Great War: British Society and the First World War* (Cambridge: Cambridge University Press, 2008), pp. 25–7.
15. Bernard Waites, *A Class Society at War: England, 1914-1918* (Leamington Spa: Berg, 1987), p. 187.
16. Robert Briffault, 'The Downfall of Old Europe', *The English Review* (February 1920), p. 139.
17. Robert Briffault, cited in Arthur Searle, 'The Letters of Robert Briffault', *The British Library Journal* (Autumn 1977), p. 174.
18. Modris Eksteins, *Rites of Spring: The Great War and the Birth of the Modern Age* (London: Black Swan, 1990), p. 169.
19. H.G. Wells, *Mr Britling Sees It Through* and *In the Days of the Comet* (London: The Literary Press, n.d.), p. 175.
20. I.F. Clarke, *The Great War with Germany, 1890-1914* (Liverpool: Liverpool University Press, 1997), p. 22.
21. Gary S. Messinger, *British Propaganda and the State in the First World War* (Manchester: Manchester University Press, 1992), p. 94.
22. Hall Caine, *The Drama of 365 Days: Scenes in the Great War* (London: William Heinemann, 1915), p. 32.
23. Austin Harrison, 'Britain's Duty', *The English Review* (September 1915), p. 226.
24. Jack Davis, cited in Richard van Emden and Steve Humphries, *All Quiet on the Home Front: An Oral History of Life in Britain during the First World War* (London: Headline Book Publishing, 2003), p. 11.
25. Michael Paris, *Warrior Nation: Images of War in British Popular Culture, 1850-2000* (London: Reaktion Books, 2000), p. 91.
26. Michael Howard, *War and the Liberal Conscience* (London: Temple Smith, 1978), pp. 68–9.
27. Waites, *A Class Society at War*, p. 188.
28. Ibid., p. 187.
29. J.M. Bourne, *Britain and the Great War, 1914-1918* (London: Edward Arnold, 1989), p. 205.
30. Joseph Thorp, 'Democracy and the Commonwealth', *The Review of Reviews* (April 1917), pp. 367–8.
31. Jan Smuts, *War-Time Speeches* (New York: George H Doran, 1917), p. 11.
32. Philippa Levine, *The British Empire: Sunrise to Sunset* (Harlow: Pearson, 2013), pp. 183–4.
33. Richard Smith, '"Heaven grant you strength to fight the battle for your race": nationalism, Pan-Africanism and the First World War in Jamaican memory' in Santanu Das (ed.), *Race, Empire and First World War Writing* (New York: Cambridge University Press, 2013), pp. 269–70.
34. Ron Ramdin, *Reimaging Britain: 500 Years of Black and Asian History* (London: Pluto Press, 1999), p. 130.
35. Ward, *Britishness Since 1870*, p. 9.
36. David Cannadine, *George V: The Unexpected King* (London: Allen Lane, 2014), p. 60.
37. *Daily Herald*, 13 May 1937, cited in Ward, *Britishness Since 1870*, p. 30.
38. Waites, *A Class Society at War*, pp. 233–4.
39. Ward, *Britishness Since 1870*, p. 100.
40. Jeremy Black, *The Great War and the Making of the Modern World* (London: Continuum, 2011), p. 237.
41. Keith Robbins, 'An imperial and multinational polity: The scene from the centre, 1832-1922' in Alexander Grant and Keith J Stringer (eds), *Uniting the Kingdom? The Making of British History* (London: Routledge, 1995), p. 246.
42. Adam Hochschild, *To End All Wars: How the First World War Divided Britain* (London: Macmillan, 2011), p. 94.
43. Peter H. Liddle, 'Britons on the Home Front' in Hugh Cecil and Peter H. Liddle (eds), *At The Eleventh Hour* (Barnsley: Leo Cooper, 1998), pp. 80–1.

44. Ward, *Britishness Since 1870*, pp. 162–5. Frank Welsh, *The Four Nations: A History of the United Kingdom* (London: Harper Collins, 2002), pp. 345–51.

45. Jenny Macleod, 'Britishness and Commemoration: National Memorials to the First World War in Britain and Ireland', *Journal of Contemporary History* Vol. 48, No. 4 (October 2013), p. 648 and pp. 662–3.

46. Richard S Grayson, *Belfast Boys: How Unionists and Nationalists Fought and Died Together in the First World War* (London: Continuum, 2009), p. 184.

47. Robbins, 'An imperial and multinational polity' in Grant and Stringer (eds), *Uniting the Kingdom?*, p. 253.

48. J.D. Mackie, *A History of Scotland* (London: Penguin, 1991), pp. 357–8.

49. Edward Spiers, 'The Scottish Soldier at War' in Hugh Cecil and Peter H. Liddle (eds), *Facing Armageddon: The First World War Experienced* (Barnsley: Leo Cooper, 1996), p. 315.

50. Macleod, 'Britishness and Commemoration', p. 656.

51. Kenneth O Morgan, *Rebirth of a Nation: Wales 1880-1980* (New York: Oxford University Press/ University of Wales Press, 1981), pp. 206–9.

52. I.G.C. Hutchison, 'The Impact of the First World War on Scottish Politics' in Catriona M.M. Macdonald and E W McFarland (eds), *Scotland and the Great War* (East Linton: Tuckwell Press, 1999), p. 55.

53. Macleod, 'Britishness and Commemoration', p. 652.

54. Kumar, 'Nation and Empire', p. 589.

55. Anthony Butterworth, Thomas Debaere, Laura Jackson and Rickesh Patel, 'Requiem: Foulds, Beaverbrook and a "British" Festival of Remembrance' in Ruth Larsen and Ian Whitehead (eds), *Popular Experience and Cultural Representation of the Great War, 1914-1918* (Newcastle: Cambridge Scholars, 2017), p. 91.

56. Adrian Gregory, *The Last Great War* (Cambridge: Cambridge University Press, 2008), p. 255. Bob Bushaway, 'Name Upon Name: The Great War and Remembrance' in Roy Porter (ed.), *Myths of the English* (Cambridge: Polity Press, 1993), p. 158.

57. Ward, *Britishness Since 1870*, p. 52.

58. Niall Ferguson, *The Pity of War* (London: Penguin, 1998), p. 462.

59. Brian Bond, *The Unquiet Western Front* (Cambridge: Cambridge University Press, 2002), pp. 59–66.

60. Hugh Cecil, *The Flower of Battle: British Fiction Writers of the First World War* (London: Secker & Warburg, 1995), p. 338.

61. Brian Bond, 'British "Anti-War" Writers and Their Critics' in Cecil and Liddle (eds), *Facing Armageddon*, p. 829.

62. John Bourne and Gary Sheffield (eds), *Douglas Haig: War Diaries and Letters, 1914-1918* (London: Weidenfeld and Nicolson, 2005). Paddy Griffith, *British Fighting Methods in the Great War* (London: Frank Cass, 1996). Robin Prior and Trevor Wilson, *Command on the Western Front* (Oxford: Blackwell, 1992). Gary Sheffield, *Forgotten Victory* (London: Headline, 2001). Dan Todman, *The Great War: Myth and Memory* (London: Hambledon, 2007).

63. Frank E. Vandiver, 'Field Marshal Sir Douglas Haig and Passchendaele' in Peter H. Liddle (ed), *Passchendaele in Perspective* (Barnsley: Leo Cooper, 1997), p. 41.

64. Gary Mead, *The Good Soldier* (London: Atlantic Books, 2007), p. 406.

65. Ward, *Britishness Since 1870*, p. 37.

Suggested Further Reading

Beckett, Ian F.W., *The Great War* (Harlow: Pearson Education, 2nd edition, 2007)

Black, Jeremy, *The Great War and the Making of the Modern World* (London: Continuum, 2011)

Bond, Brian, *The Unquiet Western Front* (Cambridge: Cambridge University Press, 2002)

Bourne, J.M., *Britain and the Great War, 1914-1918* (London: Edward Arnold, 1989)

Eksteins, Modris, *Rites of Spring: The Great War and the Birth of the Modern Age* (London: Black Swan, 1990)

Gaffney, Angela, *Aftermath: remembering the Great War in Wales* (Cardiff: University of Wales Press, 1998)

Gregory, Adrian, *The Last Great War: British Society and the First World War* (Cambridge: Cambridge University Press, 2008)

Hochschild, Adam, *To End All Wars: How the First World War Divided Britain* (London: Macmillan, 2011)

Pennell, Catriona, *A Kingdom United: Popular Responses to the Outbreak of the First World War in Britain and Ireland* (Oxford: OUP, 2014)

Sheffield, Gary, *Forgotten Victory* (London: Headline, 2001)

Todman, Dan, *The Great War: Myth and Memory* (London: Hambledon, 2007)

Ward, Paul, *Britishness Since 1870* (London: Routledge, 2004)

Chapter 15

Women and the Great War: a Transient Transformation of their Place in Society?

By Phylomena Badsey

Before the War, women of the lower classes were the industrial drudges of the community, earning an average wage of 11s 7d per week, about a one third of the male average. For women of the upper classes it is true that professional opportunities were beginning to open, but by and large it could with equal literalness be said that these women were good for nothing – educated only sufficiently to grace a leisurely life.[1]

The social changes which women experienced in the Great War were of such a profound nature that in 1918 there could be no return to the status quo. This transformation for all women from all social classes was not transient but permanent, and British society benefited from the change. The historian Arthur Marwick, who wrote at length on the link between the pre-war Suffragist campaigns: the National Union of Women's Suffrage Societies (NUWSS) led by Millicent Garrett Fawcett (1847–1929) and the Women's Social and Political Union (WSPU), known as the Suffragettes and led by Emmeline Pankhurst (1859–1928), concluded that:

To say that the war brought votes for women is to make a very crude generalisation, yet one which contains essential truth. To understand it fully, one must see the question of women's rights not in isolation, but as part of a wider context of social relationships and political change.[2]

In August 1914, a woman's political, legal and social role in British society was prescribed and almost static from birth, that wealth, privilege and social status could do little to alter. Up until the 1870 Married Women's Act, a woman upon marriage lost her legal identity and was regarded as 'belonging' to her husband under the legal principle of 'coverture' – the husband had total control over her person, their children and property, and this only changed if she became a widow. The 1870 Act gave married women the right to be the legal owners of their own money earned as wages, any property they brought into the marriage, and any subsequent inheritance they received in their own right while married. But while single women did have a legal status, in reality, financial and other decisions in their lives would be made by fathers, brothers or other male family members or guardians. Education for women of any class was very limited. The 1870 Education Act created elementary education for all boys and girls aged 5 to 13 years old at Board Schools. For most working-class girls this was usually the limit of their formal education before going into employment in local factories, shops or domestic service. Some lower middle-class parents might pay for their daughters to attend a better type of 'Dame School' for primary education, followed by a local 'private' girls' school, often to become teachers themselves.

For the upper middle class, girls would be educated at home by a governess, and perhaps be sent to a girls' private 'boarding school'. But the object of this extra education was not employment but better marriage prospects. Middle-class respectability was based on the notion that daughters and wives did not engage in paid employment outside the home, while servants were paid to undertake the drudgery of housework. For the new wealthy industrialist class and the established aristocracy, daughters would be educated at home by a nanny, followed by a series of governesses to teach various subjects, French, music, drawing, and mathematics, before being sent to Finishing School, usually abroad, for eighteen months to two years. Here language skills would be practised, household management including accounts would be taught, and child management, together with other domestic skills required in order to become a successful society hostess and wife. The industrialists' daughters would return home, and around their 18th birthday be 'launched' on local society at 'Coming Out' parties in Manchester,[3] Liverpool or any other large manufacturing city in Great Britain and around the Empire.

At the aristocratic level, 'debutantes' were presented at Court to the King and Queen, and this marked the start of the social season in London, Edinburgh or Dublin. The object of this specialist form of education and training was marriage to a suitable eligible bachelor, by which means the daughter's own social status, connections and wealth could be improved.

However, some women and men had long been campaigning to change women's political status and so improve their legal and social position by the means of gaining the Parliamentary vote. One of the most important was Millicent Garrett Fawcett, a Constitutional Suffragist who believed in campaigning within the law to achieve women's rights, and who became President in 1897 of the National Union of Women's Suffrage Societies. The NUWSS was democratic in its structure, and the first umbrella organisation for different suffragist groups, whose individual members might or might not believe in the property qualification being removed entirely from local voting eligibility rights. By 1905 the NUWSS was comprised of 305 constituent societies and had nearly 50,000 members. Both men and women could be members, and by 1914 it had 500 branches and over 100,000 members, the majority of whom were middle class. Millicent Garrett Fawcett remained in post as the NUWSS President until 1919. Its colours and badge of green, white and red, which became a common sight, could be read as 'Give – Women – Rights'. It had active branches all over the British Isles, whose members might also support other social reform campaigns. They sought a gradual change of public opinion towards women's suffrage, in particular by cultivating the local 'great and good' by holding meetings, often in the homes of members, letter writing and the influencing of sympathetic sitting MPs. NUWSS members actively assisted Liberal and Conservative candidates or sitting MPs in their election campaigns if they were to support votes for women.

Many Conservative MPs were opposed to women's suffrage on principle but not all. Liberals were more open to the idea, in particular those on the Radical wing of the party. The Labour Party also supported women's suffrage but wanted the 'property requirement' removed as part of the voting criteria for both men and women in local and municipal elections.

It has to be recognised that many women from all social spheres took little or no interest in the long-running suffrage campaign, but when the war came, women, whether or not they had held and expressed political or social opinions, stepped forward to undertake the many and diverse roles opened up by the needs of this war. Motivation was from patriotic duty, a sense of community, yes, also a sense of adventure and change and perhaps linked to this, peer pressure too. The jobs which women took on both surprised, even shocked, British society, in particular, those who had opposed women's suffrage. But 'the national emergency', they had to accept, required extreme measures. Once the war was over, 'things would return to normal, surely?' was their belief.

Some suitably-educated women moved into clerical jobs in banks, post offices – the postman became the postwoman – and other commercial businesses, some of which had never employed women as clerks before the outbreak of the war. Women worked in transport as 'clippies' on buses and trams; some worked in road maintenance tarring roads, in heavy industry operating cranes in dockyards and on construction sites. Further fit and able women joined the Women's Fire Brigade, others worked as chimney sweeps and in the coal industry, an especially dirty and physically-demanding job, loading coal onto ships and railway wagons for example. The actual jobs which women undertook from what was on offer were influenced by economic status, education, social class, family commitments and of course inclination and aptitude. The war provided the opportunity for women, individually and collectively, to show what they were capable of doing outside the home. Those more aware of the long suffrage campaign wanted to prove that they should have the right to vote, and have equal rights with men.

Fully to appreciate the enormous contribution made by women, from all backgrounds and classes, to the Great War and wider British society, we have to grasp the pre-war history of women's suffrage campaigners in the United Kingdom, not least because of the part they were to play in the forefront of women's voluntary war work. The campaign for votes for women began when John Stuart Mill (1806–73) MP, philosopher and political economist, presented the first petition to Parliament for women's voting rights on 7 June 1866; it was ignored. Mill also wrote about the need for a 'principle of perfect equality' between the sexes in *The Subjection of Women* (1869), which stressed the urgent need for women's political rights, legal protection, and access to education and employment. By the 3rd Reform Act of 1884, a uniform franchise was brought in that tripled the electorate, but only men aged 25 or over could vote in Parliamentary elections; the principle of 'one man (or woman), one vote', would not be established until 1948. The 'Women's Suffrage' campaign found its focus from this Reform Act date.

The 'Cause' was supported by both men and women from all classes of society. The Women's Franchise League was founded in 1889 by Emmeline Pankhurst and Richard, her husband. The Men's League for Women's Suffrage was founded in 1907. The Women's Franchise League campaigned to secure the right for women to vote in local and municipal elections, which required eligible voters – men or women – to meet the property qualification, and they produced metal badges in green and white, with the motto 'Votes for Women'.

This was the start of Emmeline Pankhurst's[4] active role in the Suffrage movement. She would found the Women's Social and Political Union (WSPU) in 1903, breaking away from the NUWSS, the new group becoming widely known as the Suffragettes, who used civil disobedience and violence to promote the 'Cause'. The WSPU was a single-issue party, which men could not join. It supported property requirements for voting for both men and women, and this put it at odds with the Labour Party. From 1908, the WSPU started to use green, white and violet or purple as its official colours.

In July 1908, as a direct response to WSPU activities, the Women's National Anti-Suffrage League was formed, the Central Committee comprised of titled men and women. Its badge was pink with a gold clover, primrose and thistle in the centre, surrounded by a black border, and its newspaper was the *Anti-Suffrage Review*. Mrs Humphrey Ward (1851–1920), the very successful writer, was a member of the Central Committee, and spoke at many public meetings in favour of the League's aims. It supported women having the local and municipal vote but *not* the Parliamentary vote, on the argument that a wife might vote for a different political party from that supported by her husband, and this could promote marital discord. Forming branches all over the country, it had 104 by July 1910 when it merged with the National League for Opposing Women's Suffrage, and continued to campaign against women's suffrage until the end of 1918. It gave seven principle reasons why women should not receive the Parliamentary vote, linked primarily to the difference between men and women's spheres of influence, and the view that the women's sphere was properly domestic. One of its principles stated that women could not undertake military service, or work in key industries such as construction, transport or shipping, and were therefore unfit to receive the Parliamentary vote.

Advocating the converse, by 1913 the WSPU had a membership of 2,000, and although it was always relatively small, its leadership was skilled in public relations and the use of publicity such as mass rallies, the burning of public and private property, and hunger strikes when serving prison sentences. Their paper, *Votes for Women*, renamed *The Suffragette* in 1912, was widely read and subscribed to by members from all social classes. In 1913, the government introduced the Prisoners (Temporary Discharge for Ill Health) Act, colloquially known as the 'Cat & Mouse' Act, to break the pattern of suffragette imprisonment, hunger strike, force feeding, decline of health and release. The government did not want suffragettes to die in prison, but they wanted them to serve their full prison terms, so they were released to recover and then re-arrested to continue their sentences, a vicious circle which could have lasted for years.

In March 1914, Mary Richardson, a WSPU member, slashed a famous painting in the National Gallery, the 'Rokeby Venus', by Velazquez, in protest at the imprisonment of Emmeline Pankhurst. That Spring, the British domestic political atmosphere was tense with threats of escalating violence on the streets from the militant Suffragettes. Notices went up in shops: 'Votes For Women – Ladies, if we had the power to grant, you should have the Vote right away. Please don't smash these Windows, they are not Insured.'[5] The police guarded churches and railway stations, and patrolled museums, galleries and major public social events, for example the Chelsea Flower

Show. Women, whether declared Suffragists or Suffragettes wearing their respective colours or not, were excluded from political meetings. However, women wearing the Women's National Anti-Suffrage League badge would be admitted if accompanied by a man. In major cities, policemen followed women in the streets if they appeared to be about to post a letter, because it might be a cover for them to set fire to the contents of the pillarboxes!

The campaign for votes for women, waged as it was with determination, political influence and eye-catchingly staged incidents, was still considerably diminished in significance by the boiling cauldron of Irish politics. The Liberal government had introduced the Irish Home Rule Bill in 1912, which sought to devolve powers to an executive in Dublin. This was opposed by the Unionists (Conservatives) in Parliament, the Ulster Protestant population, and the 'Irish Protestant Ascendancy', the privileged social class of Protestant landowners, whose descendants had a long tradition of service in the British Army. But the Home Rule Bill was welcomed by the Irish Parliamentary Party and the wider Catholic population of Ireland. The Irish Parliamentary Party saw women's suffrage as a distraction from the Irish Home Rule question, and most were also opposed to the very notion of women being able to exercise political power and gain equal rights with men. It appeared that Ireland was on the edge of a civil war, with a breakdown in British Army discipline threatening, when, near Dublin in March 1914, the 'Curragh Incident' took place, with a group of British Army officers led by Brigadier General Hubert Gough, a member of the Protestant Ascendancy, threatening that they would not 'coerce' Ulster Protestants into accepting Home Rule, but would resign their commissions. Only the assassination of Archduke Franz Ferdinand of Austria and his wife Sophie, Duchess of Hohenberg, on 28 June, and the July crisis which followed, took precedence over all domestic issues.

Great Britain declared war on Germany on 4 August 1914, and the WSPU leadership met government representatives shortly afterwards. On 10 August, the Government publicly declared that all WSPU prisoners would be released from prison, with immediate effect. Emmeline Pankhurst announced that all militant action would now cease, and that the full resources of the WSPU national structure would be turned to support the war effort. Emmeline was a great Francophile, and was to develop over time an intense loathing of Germany. Both she and her daughter Christabel were involved in fundraising, recruitment drives and public lectures about war aims. Later they would both campaign for conscription to be introduced, which it was in January 1916, except in Ireland. They were very patriotic in their speeches and writings; their newspaper *The Suffragette* was re-launched again in April 1915 with a stress on women's contribution to the war effort, and changed its name again in October 1915 to *The Britannia*, which was extremely jingoistic in tone and content.

This strand of extreme patriotism found expression right at the start of the war in August 1914 when a few – a very few – WSPU members, including Emmeline and Christabel Pankhurst, were active supporters of the 'Order of White Feather' created by Admiral Charles Fitzgerald together with Mrs Humphrey Ward of the Women's National Anti-Suffrage League. The 'Order of the White Feather' sought by public shaming to encourage any man not in military uniform to enlist, by a woman handing him a white feather, a sign of cowardice. This contemptible and misguided campaign only lasted a few weeks, with incidents mostly taking place in London and in and around Folkestone in Kent but reports of such acts continued to circulate throughout the war, often of a vague and unverifiable nature. Folkestone harbour was to become the main embarkation port for the Western Front during the whole of the Great War, and it is estimated that 10 million troops passed along the harbour arm. In September 1914, thousands of Belgian refugees were landed at Folkestone harbour, fleeing from German invasion, occupation, real and reported atrocities, atrocities which greatly increased patriotic fervour in the area. The actions of a few WSPU members created a 'myth' that entered the public consciousness of the time, and no doubt which grew in the re-telling, that *all* women who campaigned for women's suffrage were part of, or supported. the 'Order of White Feather' activities. As a direct consequence of the public's anger and indignation, the Government introduced the 'King and Country' lapel badge, to be worn by men working in essential war industries, and in September 1916, the Silver War Badge, issued to servicemen who had been honourably discharged due to sickness or wounds sustained during their war service.

Millicent Garrett Fawcett, as President of the NUWSS, waited until the end of August 1914 before issuing a statement that she wanted the extensive NUWSS branch network, with its vast membership, to support the war effort. She also made it clear that the NUWSS had a duty to continue to campaign for women's suffrage, which it did throughout the war. The majority followed the guidance of their president, not just out of a sense of loyalty but also because the war provided an unanticipated opportunity for women to show ability, courage and skills at a time of national crisis. A sense of patriotism and the 'rightness' of the cause must also have been factors. The vast organised talent of the NUWSS became the backbone of many village and town war support committees and events designed to contribute to the war effort. For example such committees undertook the need to welcome and look after Belgian refugees, produce 'comforts' for the troops or British prisoners of war in the form of knitted socks, scarves and gloves, or sending parcels of soap, cigarettes or tobacco, and for fund raising for local hospitals.

The NUWSS set up an employment register, and as men were called up or enlisted, a woman would volunteer to replace them in their work. This system was soon replaced by a more formal government scheme, but the principle had been established of the absolute necessity of women's active contribution to the war effort: 'What can be said is that the "Domestic Front War", whether it were to economise against food shortages or produce more ships or guns, could not be lost or the war would have been lost – and, in the end, the war was won.'[6]

The NUWSS did not encourage working-class women to become members, and the wartime politics of women's suffrage was not of immediate importance to the majority of working-class women, although they would benefit from them in the course of the war. In 1914, working-class women employed in factories found themselves almost overnight producing goods for the war effort under government contracts. This process took place all over the country as the Government placed mass orders with private contractors for essential items, such as uniforms from the Yorkshire mills, jute for sandbags from Dundee in Scotland, and armaments from the industrial Midlands. Very few first-hand accounts or letters exist in which these women recorded their experiences. The women were often married and lived locally, their civilian working life continuing unchanged, at least for a time. But, following the Shell Crisis of March 1915 and the creation of the Ministry of Munitions, many more women were to become Munitionettes, producing armaments and weapons in designated factories and local workshops. The work was hard, the conditions dangerous and unpleasant, and the hours long, although well paid by the standards of the day – half a man's wage for the same work. One middle-class volunteer, Naomi Loughnan, wrote that:

> Though we munition workers sacrifice our ease we gain a life worth living. Our long days are filled with interest, and with a zest for doing work for our country in the grand cause of freedom.[7]

The Trades Unions, which in the main women could not join, sought to prevent 'dilution,' the de-skilling of their member's jobs and consequent pay reduction, threatened by the employment of women who could and would be paid less. 'Many male factory workers found women entering the munitions workforce in such large numbers threatening and intolerable and acted accordingly.'[8] However, many women, in particular former shop assistants, were members of the National Federation of Women Workers (NFWW) which became active in many munitions factories, particularly the largest, Woolwich Arsenal in London.[9]

The Government was keen to recruit women into the factories, but concerns had been raised in the popular press about the behaviour of women earning high wages, and their standards of morality without either a husband or parents to exert control over them. This problem was grossly exaggerated by the same popular press, which focussed on young unmarried Munitionettes, when in fact many were married with children. Working-class married women in towns and cities, with husbands serving in the Army, frequently found that the 'Separation Allowance' was insufficient to feed and clothe themselves, their children and sometimes their wider family. Food and rent costs increased during the war but becoming a Munitionette provided an income and also company, a source of comfort and solace in anxious times.

The sense of belonging, within the factory, was very strong, and encouraged by the management because it assisted good time-keeping (latecomers were heavily fined), reduced absenteeism and increased production. While the factories did not provide child care facilities, grandmothers offered support, as did the wider local community in the form of unofficial crèches and nurseries. However, many former domestic servants also changed jobs to become Munitionettes, attracted by the higher wages. In 1917, by which time 80 per cent of British armaments and weapons were being produced by Munitionettes, an official government film, twelve minutes long, was produced to be shown in local cinemas entitled 'A Day in the Life of a Munitions Worker', and depicting a young Munitionette. This showed the workers' hostel the women were living in, stressed the care and respectability of the factory, and the vital importance of the war work being done. Upper-class and middle-class women were also employed as Munitionettes. It became fashionable to undertake such war work as advertisements appeared in the *The Lady* and other upper middle-class magazines and newspapers.

In 1915, the poet and novelist Sylvia Townsend Warner (1893–1978) saw a notice seeking to 'train women of the leisured class in munition-making to relieve the regular hands, as factories were now working non-stop'; she applied and received a leaflet giving details, including the following information: 'low-heeled shoes are advisable, and evening dress is not necessary'.[10] She lived in a local hostel, and worked as a shell machinist at the Vickers' factory in Erith, South East London. She earned six shillings, including a bonus for each eight-hour shift with half-an-hour meal break, and remembered that:

> Through the open doors of the workshop came noise and light and warmth: it looked as gay as a ballroom. Once inside it, the place wrapped me round like a familiar garment. Up in the roof the big driving-belt slid over the rollers: I thought of them going on shift after shift, day after day like a waterfall sliding over the top of a crag. Shell-cases, 4.5s and 18-pounders were piled high against the walls and stacked on every spare foot of floor, with numbers and hieroglyphics chalked on their grey sides and sleek faces.[11]

In February 1916 she published an article based on her experiences as a 'Lady Worker' entitled 'Behind the Firing Line'. These upper and middle-class women would eventually make up 9 per cent of the total workforce, and became known as 'Lady Volunteers' or colloquially, the 'Miaows'. All the women from whatever background received the same training, were obliged to follow the strict conditions of employment and shift patterns, and were exposed to the same risks. All the Munitionettes shared the nickname of 'Canaries' because the toxic chemicals they worked with filling shells turned their skin yellow, and some were to die from this form of poisoning. Furthermore there were deaths for women in factory accidents and explosions too. For reason of morale and security these events were not widely reported. The most notable explosion was at Silvertown, West Ham, in London in January 1917, in which 73 women were killed and over 400 injured[12] but there were such tragedies in all the shell-manufacturing areas as, for example, the Barnbow explosion at Crossgates in Leeds when 35 women were killed.

In the same way that Munitionettes attracted public attention during the war, so did nurses, particularly those working in France, Belgium and in the Balkans. More significant for the status of women, the traditional caring role of nursing became a focus for change at the start of the war. 'Participation in the war effort replaced Votes For Women as the forces of suppressed female energy and ambition. Nursing in particular became *chic*.'[13] The NUWSS financed the Scottish Women's Hospital and associated units led by Elsie Inglis who had been a Suffragist in Edinburgh since the 1890s, and who had worked with the NUWSS. Many professional nurses were also supporters of women's suffrage, usually siding with the Constitutionalist and non-violent NUWSS. Before the war the middle classes actively discouraged their daughters from paid employment, and professional nursing was not regarded as a suitable or indeed respectable occupation for them. Nursing was the sort of thing the unmarried daughters of the clergy undertook, since it could be seen as a 'vocation', and an extension of their parish work. For example, Edith Cavell (1865–1915), the head matron of a nurse's training school in Brussels in 1914, was a vicar's daughter and a professional nurse.[14] The training for professional nurses was intensive, the hours long and poorly paid. Even in peacetime, nursing tasks were often unpleasant and dangerous, with nurses being constantly exposed to contagious diseases and infections.

Some nurses were in the Territorial Force Nursing Service (TFNS) founded in 1908. The TFNS consisted of civilian nurses who could be mobilised in time of war. During the war they worked alongside the Queen Alexandra's Imperial Military Nursing Service and Reserve (QAIMNS) in military hospitals at home and overseas, including on the Western Front on hospital trains and as far forward as at Casualty Clearing Stations (CCSs). Other women working on the Western Front included members of the First Aid Nursing Yeomanry (FANY), founded in 1907, who were all unpaid volunteers. They drove ambulances in France and Belgium collecting wounded from the CCSs and transported them to rail-heads for onward passage and further treatment. They also conveyed food, uniforms and other urgently needed equipment to the CCSs, and provided a mobile canteen and soup kitchens to feed soldiers at Calais. As Surgeon-General Tom Percy Woodhouse once described the FANYs, 'neither fish, flesh nor fowl but you're a dammed good red herring'.[15]

In Great Britain, many upper- and middle-class women undertook training as members of the St. John Ambulance Brigade or the British Red Cross as Voluntary Aid Detachment (VAD) nurses. Aristocratic women also trained as VAD nurses, the most well-known was Millicent, Duchess of Sutherland, who not only organised, staffed, funded but also nursed with her Ambulance Unit, which served in Belgium and later established a hospital on the French coast.[16] As the war continued, VAD nurses would find themselves working alongside the professional nurses in the network of Military Hospitals to which the Auxiliary and Convalescent Hospitals were linked. It might appropriately be mentioned that VAD nurses not only found themselves doing the more menial but of course necessary 'non-nursing' tasks in a hospital and that their training might well have been for cookery or driving rather than actually for nursing, but ironically, if predictably, those women actually engaged in nursing frequently found themselves looked down upon by the more thoroughly-trained professionals in the QAIMNS.

VAD nurses, some of whom worked part-time, were not paid, just given a uniform allowance. Men also undertook Red Cross training, some of them in reserved occupations while others were waiting to be called up, and when they enlisted they often served as ward orderlies or stretcher-bearers. Very soon, trained VAD nurses, both men and women, would be nursing in the Auxiliary and Convalescent Hospitals which were established in larger private homes or suitable public buildings all over Great Britain and Ireland. Also working alongside the medical staff were local people from all social backgrounds, all voluntarily and often part-time. They carried out the duties of cooks, ward maids, orderlies and cleaners, contributing their time and skills, in effect acting as the domestic staff in the running of 'their' Auxiliary and Convalescent Hospitals. The phenomenon of the 'Great & Good' and in particular titled ladies, 'mucking in', was wonderfully recorded in a cartoon by J.H. Dowd published in *The Bystander* in November 1918. It depicts a woman on her hands and knees scrubbing a hospital floor, with a nurse attending a patient behind her, addressing a patient in a dressing-gown and pyjamas as he walks past:

Hospital Worker: *"Would you be so good as to get me a pail of water, my man?"*
Patient: *"Dash me, woman, I'm a major!"*
Hospital Worker: *"Dash me, man, I'm a duchess!"*[17]

Only a minority of VAD nurses served on the Western Front, 1,587[18] out of a total figure of 82,857 women VADs serving at the end of the war.[19] One of these was Vera Brittain, who nursed on the Western Front in the large hospital complex at Etaples.[20] Professional nurses had expressed deep concerns about VAD nurses, in particular the aristocratic or society hostesses who were attracted by the 'glamour and romance of nursing', and though trained, were known as 'Limelighters' or 'VAVs' – 'Vicarious and Voyeuristic thrill-seekers'.[21] At the start of the war it was often feared that their lack of dedication, experience and level of skills could damage the reputation of nursing, but these fears proved groundless:

> The stoicism of the nurses is referenced in various wartime texts, and their power to endure broke all long-held prejudices and shibboleths about the physical and emotional frailty of women. Unfortunately, it had taken the War to demonstrate to the bigots and disbelievers that women, not just nurses, were equal to the task and the realisation added a new dimension to the tea rooms, public houses, parlours and parliamentary debates on women's suffrage.[22]

For all women in 1914, 'womanhood' – the qualities considered as being natural or desirable in a woman – were focused very firmly on the domestic sphere of home, family, children, and being a support to their husband. This soon changed as women were actively recruited into the newly-formed women's civil and military services, which like the Munitionettes and the various nursing organisations, played a highly visible part in the war effort.

At the very start of the war the civilian National Union of Working Women was formed, which had 5,000 women members who patrolled places of entrainment, cinemas and public houses. They operated in particular in large cities and had a watching brief to protect and prevent Munitionettes from lewd and drunken behaviour. Margaret Damer Dawson (1873–1920) founded the Women's Police Volunteers in Autumn 1914 (called the 'Copperettes' but not to their faces); to protect female Belgian refugees from attempts to recruit them into prostitution as they arrived penniless and unable to speak the language at London railway stations from Folkestone. They also focused on the conduct of Munitionettes, and the prevention of prostitution by patrolling parks and other open spaces after dark. The Women's Police Volunteers had no powers of arrest but they did patrol the streets and could call on policemen for assistance. Mary Allen (1878–1964) was the first women to sign up, and she was a Suffragette who had been imprisoned three times and force-fed. Edith Smith was the first woman police constable attested with the powers to arrest, at the discretion of her Chief Constable, in Grantham where she served. Many other Suffragette and Suffragist women were to join the Women's Police Volunteers, and in August 1915 the organisation was renamed the Women's Police Service. Its main concerns continued to be protecting public decency. It was always small, having only 1,080 trained and equipped members who came from a diverse range of backgrounds, with the largest group, 411, recorded as; 'Women of private means or of no [past] profession', suggesting a middle- or upper-class background.[23] They served by 1918 in all major industrial cities, many ports, and towns with large Army camps.

In September 1915, the official founding meeting of the first British Women's Institute (WI) took place in Llanfairpwill, Anglesey, with Madge Robertson Watts of the Women's Institutes of Canada in attendance.[24] During the Great War, the WI was to become a vital element in rural communities, its work sponsored by the Board of

Agriculture, which created a Women's Institute section.[25] The WI provided education and training for women to produce more food in the countryside, many of whom were running farms and smallholdings by themselves for the first time. As the war progressed, domestic management and the role of the 'Housewife' became a key element of the Home Front, and women were encouraged to grow their own vegetables and reduce waste. Short government official films were made giving advice on the best ways to cook; one entitled *The Secret* (1918) was about using potato to replace suet to make dumplings. WI branches were created in towns and cities all over the United Kingdom, the stated aims being to stimulate interest in the agricultural industry, develop co-operative industries, encourage home and local industries, study home–economics and provide a centre for educational and social intercourse and for all local activities.[26]

Many NUWSS members joined their local WI branch, which soon became the focus of all wartime-related activities, and by 1919 there were over 1,200 WIs in Great Britain.[27] All this frenetic activity was highly localised. 'Although it is still not fully recognised, place framed the experience of all on the Home Front to the point where it might be more appropriate to speak of local Home Fronts.'[28]

By late 1916, it was realised that women needed to play a more formal uniformed military role in the war effort. The opportunity actually to 'serve' was welcomed by women, and the different services offered good wages and wider experience. The women took great pride in wearing their respective uniforms, although by regulation uniform skirts could not be more than 12 inches from the ground. The Women's Army Auxiliary Corps (WAAC) was established in 1917. Millicent Garrett Fawcett was a great supporter, stating that: 'The dilution of the army by women can only successfully be carried out if the whole Mother wit of women can be brought to bear.'[29] The WAAC's members released men to fight in the front line, as they took over traditional female domestic tasks for the Army, such as cooking and serving food. They also undertook administrative and other general office work, including being switchboard operators. Many women were taught to drive and learned mechanical repair skills as they took over responsibility for transport and driving cars and lorries. By 1918, 50,000 women had enlisted in the WAAC, and women served in France, Belgium, Italy and Greece. The Women's Royal Naval Service (WRNS) was also formed in 1917, and by the end of the war they had nearly 6,000 members serving both on ships and in ports, carrying out administrative and clerical duties. When the Women's Royal Air Force (WRAF) was created in 1918, its members were all 'ground-crew' based at the aerodromes, providing support as cooks and waitresses, but also working as clerks and running the stores. Some women also undertook technical work on aircraft, but no one was trained to fly.

Again in 1917, the urgent need to increase food production, reduce food shipping and release military age men for service led directly to the creation of the Women's Land Army by the Board of Agriculture: 23,000 women were formally recruited into areas of agriculture, for example forage-haymaking for horses, and timber cutting – these women were called 'Lumber Jills'. An additional 260,000 women were working as farm labourers. The majority of women working in agriculture, ploughed fields, milked cows, picked fruit, planted and harvested crops. They were required as part of their uniform to wear 'breeches' made of hard-wearing corduroy. Some land girls started to wear trousers when not on duty, and this caused much local comment and occasioned caustic remarks in small rural areas, but a fashion had been started and it would continue.

Far from being transient, women's status during the war years was progressively being transformed. The historian, Maggie Andrews, has summarised the experience of British women:

> In many areas of voluntary work wartime gave women the opportunity to develop a range of new experiences, skills and confidence. Nevertheless in the main, women remained predominantly concerned with caring for or supporting men; domesticity expanded and was reworked to include care for men away from home and a range of domestic and caring tasks for others outside the parameters of the home.[30]

However, things had changed irrevocably. This was no 'transient' phenomenon in society: women's actions before and during the Great War broke the sword of misogynistic attitudes and patriarchy which had held them down for generations. This process of social change, which affected both men and women, should be acknowledged and remembered as an important element of the War and women's contribution to it.

It was in 1918 when a major exhibition, which was to become the core of the Imperial War Museum's 'Women's Collection', was held at the Whitechapel Art Gallery, in London. This exhibition was visited by thousands of people, and a photograph exists of three men sitting at a table introducing the collection: the first is a senior Army Officer in uniform, the second is the Town Clerk, wearing his chain of office and with the Borough mace on the table in front of him, and the third is a clergyman in formal collar and Anglican clerical dress. Before the Great War, all three institutions which these men represented had opposed women's suffrage; the Army because women could not fight, local government because the registration of women would be problematic, and the Church because women's interests in politics should mirror their fathers or husbands opinions. In 1918 such views seemed foolish and dated. A transformation had indeed taken place within society.

Notes

1. Arthur Marwick, *The Deluge – British Society and the First World War* (London: Macmillan, 1965), p. 87.
2. Arthur Marwick, *Woman At War 1914-1918* (Glasgow:Fontana, 1977), p. 157.
3. Vera Brittain, *Testament of Youth – An Autobiographical Study of the Years 1900-1925* (1933), Chapter 2 'Provincial Young-Ladyhood'.
4. Professor June Purvis has written an excellent biography of Emmeline Pankhurst which details not only her family life and campaigning career but also provides the background to the complex women's history of the time.
5. Maroula Joannou, *'Ladies, Please Don't Smash These Windows': Women's Writing, Feminist Consciousness and Social Change 1918-38* (Oxford: BERG, 1995), poster opposite Preface p. xi.
6. Peter Liddle, *Voices of War – Front Line and Home Front* (London: Leo Cooper, 1988), p. 66.
7. Gail Braybon and Penny Summerfield, *Out of the Cage - Women's Experiences in Two World Wars* (London: Pandora, 1987), p. 62.
8. Vivien Newman, *We Also Served – the Forgotten Women of the First World War* (Barnsley: Pen & Sword, 2014), p. 58.
9. Mary Macarthur (1880–1921) in 1901 became the Secretary of a Scottish Shop Assistants Union Branch; in 1903 she became Secretary of the Women's Trade Union League based in London. In 1906 she founded both the Anti-Sweating League and the National Federation of Women Workers. She was a Scottish Suffragist and trade union activist. In 1909 she led the women chain makers strike at Cradley Heath, in the Black Country. She wanted both men and women to have exactly the same voting rights with no property qualification.

10. Claire Harman, *Sylvia Townsend Warner – A Biography* (London: Chatto & Windus, 1989), p. 30.

11. Ibid., p. 31.

12. The novelist Pat Barker writes of the Munitionettes' experiences in her *Regeneration Trilogy* (1997). Another well-researched and readable fictionalised account written as a crime novel is by Edward Marston, *Five Dead Canaries* (2013). It provides a strong background and contemporary social setting for the story line.

13. J.M. Bourne, *Britain and the Great War 1914-1918* (London: Edward Arnold, 1989), p. 106.

14. Diana Souhami has written a well-researched biography of Edith Cavell which concentrates on her upbringing and professional nursing career, 1895 to 1915. See 'Suggested Further Reading' below.

15. http://www.historylearningsite.co.uk/the-role-of-british-women-in-the-twentieth-century/first-aid-nursing-yeomanry/ accessed 23rd May 2017

16. Newman, *We Also Served*, pp. 85–8 .

17. Ref10948676,MaryEvansPictureLibrary,http://www.maryevans.com/about.php?pageName=about7&prv

18. Yvonne McEwen, *In the Company of Nurses – The History of the British Army Nursing Service in the Great War* (Edinburgh: Edinburgh University Press, 2014), p. 180.

19. Marwick, *Women At War 1914-1918*, Table 7 Growth of the VADs, p. 168.

20. Brittain, *Testament of Youth*.

21. McEwen, *In the Company of Nurses*, p. 180.

22. Ibid., p. 156.

23. Marwick, *Women At War 1914-1918*, Table 5 Social Background of Women's Police Service, p. 167.

24. Linda Ambrose, *A Great Rural Sister-hood. Madge Robertson Watts and the ACWW* (Toronto: University of Toronto Press, 2015), p. 106.

25. Maggie Andrews, *The Acceptable Face of Feminism – The Women's Institute as a Social Movement* (London: Lawrence & Wishart, 1997), p. 21.

26. Ibid., p. 20.

27. Ian Beckett, *Home Front 1914-1918 How Britain Survived the Great War* (Richmond: The National Archives, 2006), p. 77.

28. Maggie Andrews and Janis Lomas, *The Home Front in Britain – Images, Myths and Forgotten Experiences since 1914* (London: Macmillan, 2014), p. 86.

29. http://www.historylearningsite.co.uk/the-role-of-british-women-in-the-twentieth-century/the-womens-army-auxiliary-corps/ accessed 23rd May 2017.

30. Andrews, *The Acceptable Face of Feminism*, p. 17.

Suggested Further Reading

Andrews, Maggie and Lomas, Janis, *The Home Front in Britain – Images, Myths and Forgotten Experiences since 1914* (London: Macmillan, 2014)

Beckett, Ian, *Home Front 1914-1918 – How Britain Survived the Great War* (Richmond: The National Archives, 2006)

Crawford, Elizabeth, *Enterprising Women – The Garretts and their Circle* (London: Francis Boutle, 2002)

Liddle, Peter, *Voices of War – Front Line and Home Front* (London: Leo Cooper, 1988)

McEwen, Yvonne, *In the Company of Nurses – The History of the British Army Nursing Service in the Great War* (Edinburgh: Edinburgh University Press, 2014)

Marwick, Arthur, *The Deluge* (London: Macmillan, 1965)

Newman, Vivien, *We Also Served – The Forgotten Women of the First World War* (Barnsley: Pen and Sword, 2014)

Purvis, June, *Emmeline Pankhurst: A Biography* (London: Routledge, 2002)

Souhami, Diana, *Edith Cavell* (London: Quercus, 2010)

Winslow, Barbara, *Sylvia Pankhurst – Sexual Politics and Political Activism* (London: UCL Press, 1995)

Chapter 16

The Middle East: From Coalition-Oriented to Imperial-Oriented Strategy

By Yigal Sheffy

The offensive launched by the Egyptian Expeditionary Force (EEF) on 31 October 1917 on the Ottoman Gaza–Beersheba defence line culminated in the entrance of General Edmund Allenby, the Commander-in-Chief, into Jerusalem on 11 December. The worldwide publicised entrance symbolised the watershed of a fundamental – albeit gradual – change in British Middle Eastern policy in the Great War. During the first three years of the war British political and military activity against the Ottoman Empire was dictated by several sets of imperatives, not necessarily coherent.

From a purely military perspective, the Middle Eastern theatre of war was a sideshow of the Western Front. The German army was the principal enemy to be defeated in order to win the war. As a matter of fact, if the war could have unfolded according to Britain's wishes before Constantinople joined in, the Middle East would have remained outside the circle of war. In principle, London continued to favour a post-war situation which would guarantee the continuous existence of a viable Ottoman Empire, even within shrunken borders. Such a state would continue the role of being a buffer between British territories on the one hand and her traditional enemies, Russia and France and the new imperial rival, Germany, on the other.

With the exception of the Gallipoli Campaign, the military strategy in the region was generally based on a defensive-preventive approach, originating in the traditional requisite of defending imperial interests, territories and communication routes in the East. The initial advance of the Indian/British IEF D Force, north of Basra, Mesopotamia after its landing at Fao to defend oil fields and installations and to 'wave the flag' in that region, as well as the EEF's advance eastwards in Sinai towards Palestine, were initiated as a forward-defence oriented policy. The shift to the offensive in both regions was a process of evolution, originating in local achievements and decisions as well as the change in London's decision-making priorities following from the establishment of David Lloyd George's government in December 1916. With regard to these offensives we might also remember the maxim, appetite grows with feeding, accurate here as in all strategic, operational and tactical considerations.

There was another highly influential factor affecting British policy: a maintained reluctance to transform the war into a Muslim–Christian religious conflict. Such a dangerous perception might lead other Muslim nations to join the war against the Allies and, even worse, Muslim subjects in Entente-controlled territories, including India,

Egypt, Sudan, and North Africa, to rebel. Allied propaganda efforts, therefore, were aimed at presenting the conflict to the Muslim world as a political-secular conflict, not a clash of faiths. British encouragement of Sharif Hussein in the Hijaz to take up arms against Constantinople, by commitments for Arab independence and by British military support after the rebellion broke out in June 1916, was considered, apart from its direct military tactical advantage, a counterweight to the Ottoman call for *Jihad* against the Allies.

British policy during the first period had been dictated by an adherence to coalition interests over traditional imperial ones, this from the necessity of keeping Russia, France, and Italy in united cooperation against the major enemies – Germany and Austria-Hungary – in the European theatres of war. London's prime concern was that the dire circumstances of the times might compel its allies to seek a separate peace with Berlin.

To thwart any such temptation, the British Government was prepared temporarily to put aside its traditional policy of zealously safeguarding its favourable position in the Middle East by frustrating attempts of other Powers to intensify their grip or find a foothold there. Thus, on the eve of the Dardanelles-Gallipoli campaign early in 1915, the British were unable to hold further secret talks with Ottoman envoys about a possible peace agreement, because they were already committed to St Petersburg's demand to occupy and control the Dardanelles-Constantinople zone in the event of an Allied victory – the Constantinople Agreement of March 1915.

Furthermore, the general notion of 'forcing the Dardanelles' came into being following an urgent Russian request to divert Ottoman forces from the Caucasus. Similarly, this coalition interest was at the root of the London Agreement of April 1915, by which Britain agreed to an Italian demand to occupy parts of southern Anatolia after the war. Indeed, it also played a significant part in blocking British plans to carry out amphibious operations against the Syrian coast, as the French objected to independent British operations in a region considered by Paris to be in its zone of influence. French pressure also played a part in the British decision to take part, even if reluctantly, in the Salonika expedition in October 1915.

The famous and controversial Sykes-Picot Agreement of 1916 was also born first and foremost out of the pressure applied by the strong colonial voice in the French government and British inclination to satisfy Paris in view of the stalemate, hardships and increasing number of casualties in the main theatre of the war. London, reluctantly again, was persuaded towards an agreement with the French on a conditional post-war colonial division of Ottoman territories between the two powers – Russia's share in the future booty had been agreed beforehand.

Change of Interests and Indecision
By early 1917, the EEF had completed its eastward advance from the Suez Canal across the Sinai Peninsula, crossing the administrative division line that separated the British-controlled Sinai district and the Ottoman Mutasarrifate (independent district) of Jerusalem. This line later became the international border between Egypt and the new territorial entity of British Mandate Palestine. The advance into southern Palestine and the subsequence military operations, including the first two failed battles of Gaza in March–April 1917 and the static campaign in the spring–summer in the Negev, were still considered sideshow efforts within the framework of the overall British strategic

priorities, and were carried out without clear operational objectives. Thus, Lloyd George's famous farewell parting wish to Allenby, upon his appointment as the new EEF C-in-C in June 1917, 'the Cabinet expects Jerusalem by Christmas',[1] should be considered more a wishful hope than a political-strategic directive.

Yet, the resumption of the mobile campaign and the third British offensive on the Ottoman Gaza–Beersheba Line in October 1917 occurred against the background of growing disagreement between Britain's political and military leadership about the war's strategic priorities. The roots of this heated 'clash of giants' was a fundamental civil–military power struggle between the political leadership, personified by Lloyd George on the one hand, and the General Staff, personified by General Sir William Robertson, the CIGS, on the other, in relation to overall control of the conduct of the war.[2] A particular focus of this dispute was the question whether, in view of the stalemate and difficulties in France, it would not be preferable to change priorities. One school of thought preferred a temporary pause in Western Front offensive operations, while sufficient strength was being built up there, including American troops from across the Atlantic, in order to prepare for a decisive victory against the Germans in due course. In the meantime, enough resources should be transferred to the Middle East to force the Ottoman Empire out of the war thus bringing within reach tangible imperial profit.

The opposing school of thought was that, notwithstanding the Middle Eastern temptations, the Allies should still stick to the existing strategy of investing all available resources against Germany, while making do with a defensive strategy and limited operations in the Middle East.

When the EEF launched its October 1917 offensive, this controversy was still raging, resulting in policy indecision regarding the Middle East. The offensive was launched without clear objectives – neither strategically by London nor operationally by the EEF. Consequently, the tactical-territorial objectives defined in Allenby's operational order for the offensive were vague and limited in scope to only a few kilometres beyond the front line: 'to take the offensive against the enemy at Gaza and at Beersheba, and, when Beersheba is in our hands, to take an enveloping attack on the enemy's left flank in the direction of Sheria and Hureira'.[3] To judge by the order's language, the aim of the offensive was to gain territory and inflict casualties on the enemy by steady and cautious advance more than by defeating him in a decisive battle.

Militarily, the occupation of Jerusalem in December 1917 was, to adopt Edward Erickson's definition for later operations in the region, a 'campaign of opportunities',[4] and unplanned exploitation of the tactical success on the battlefield. The retrospective tendency to draw a straight line connecting Lloyd George's request in June and the occupation of Jerusalem six months later is not supported by the historical evidence. A similar gap between the limited ground objectives set for the operations and the much more significant gains actually achieved on Palestine's battlefields would be demonstrated again during the decisive EEF offensive a year later.

Indecision and being in two minds characterized Ottoman conduct as well. Instead of agreeing on the location and direction of the main strategic effort and concentrating the dwindling strength of the army in one theatre of operations, disagreement among the Ottoman leadership caused a division of forces between two different theatres – Trans-Caucasus in the north-east and the Arab provinces, Mesopotamia, Syria, Palestine and the Hijaz, in the south of the Empire. There was no agreement and decision over priorities.

Furthermore, a dispute over priorities occurred within the southern front as well. Sometime between March and May 1917, Minister of War Enver Pasha decided to establish the *Yildirim* Army Group, consisting of the Sixth Army, then operating in Mesopotamia, and a new, Seventh Army whose strength would come from crack Turkish divisions returned from the Balkans. They would concentrate in northern Syria. *Yildirim*'s original goal was to launch a major counter-offensive in Mesopotamia to regain Baghdad and lower Mesopotamia. However, disagreement soon emerged as to *Yildirim*'s actual objectives: should it operate in Mesopotamia, as Enver insisted, or, alternatively, reinforce the Palestine front, where the British were gaining strength? The latter was recommended by General Erich von Falkenhayn, the German C-in-C of *Yildirim*, and Ahmed Jemal Pasha, Governor of Syria and Arabia and Commander of the Fourth Army there. By adoption of deliberate defence or even counter-attack, the latter two wished to frustrate Allenby's coming offensive, which, to their mind, endangered the Ottoman southern flank much more than the British actions in Mesopotamia.

The heated dispute paralysed much of the deployment and operational employment of even those few *Yildirim* formations which, despite almost insurmountable difficulties of transportation and movement in the sparse system of roads and railway communications, managed to concentrate in northern Syria during the summer.[5] By August 1917, the Ottoman high command agreed at last to accept the dominance of the Palestine front over Mesopotamia and to reinforce the former with *Yildirim*'s northern troops, but the time left before the EEF launched its much awaited offensive late in October against the Gaza–Beersheba Line was too short for them to have any impact on the battlefield.

By late January 1918, the EEF had conquered southern Palestine, consolidating a new front line north of Jaffa–Jerusalem. On the other side, the Ottomans managed to withdraw most of their field formations which, despite heavy casualties and loss of equipment, did not break up, retaining their ability to fight another day, albeit weaker and depleted.

Severe weather and heavy rain in Palestine in the winter of 1917/18 ruined much of the poor, undeveloped communication infrastructure, disrupting the EEF's logistics already stretched to the limit because of the unplanned rapid advance. If we were to add the troops' exhaustion, the large number of casualties (about 21,000[6]), the rapid recovery of the Ottomans in defence, and the British intelligence overestimation of the expected resistance the further the EEF would advance, Allenby's decision to call a halt to the offensive for recovery, reorganization, and 'battery-recharging', seems to have been right on time.

This author does not share the view expressed in the literature that 'had Allenby attacked through Gaza [instead of through Beersheba] and linked this to a correct assessment of Turkish capabilities and intentions, Palestine might have been occupied in late 1917'.[7] Ottoman defences in the Gaza sector were the most developed along the entire front line and were strongly defended, as it had been predicted that Gaza would again be the main avenue of attack. The difficulties met by the EEF in executing its plan in the weaker sector of Beersheba cast doubt on its ability to overcome the enemy's stronger Gaza defences. Furthermore, the intelligence overestimation – the deliberation over whether it was a genuine error or presented for political purposes in the power struggle in London, continues to this day[8] – had very little, if any, effect on the actual conduct of operations on the battlefield. Allenby's original plan might have been cautious and narrow, but its implementation was dictated – as in most operations once the first shot is fired – mainly by the tactical situation, the terrain, the weather, enemy reaction, troop performance, etc. developing on the battlefield. Such a favourably evolving situation enabled the EEF to reach a much more northern line than planned and much earlier than expected. It was the tactical situation again which prevented it from further advance in January–February 1918. Thus ended the first phase of the Palestine campaign.

Towards Decision – the Strategic Dimension

In the meantime, London's two-voiced intercourse regarding the preferred main effort was ended by the sacking of General Robertson on 18 February 1918 and a joint Allied decision reached a month earlier to consider the Turkish theatre the main theatre of operations during the coming year. Succumbing to Lloyd George's pressure, the Supreme War Council, an inter-Allied body established by Lloyd George in November 1917 to bypass Robertson, agreed that, while the Western Front would assume a defensive stance, 'The Allies should undertake a decisive offensive against Turkey with a view to the annihilation of the Turkish Armies and the collapse of Turkish resistance'.[9]

In a process not unlike the Ottoman/German deliberations over the preferable front, which ended in favour of Palestine following visits by Enver and Falkenhayn to that country, Lloyd George sent his associate, the South African general-turned-politician Jan Smuts, to the region on a fact-finding mission. He was to recommend how to implement the 'Middle East first' policy. Unsurprisingly, and perhaps due also to his acquaintance with the Prime Minister's inclinations, Smuts recommended Palestine over Mesopotamia for the British main effort in the region. The latter should yield three infantry divisions and support units to the EEF, resuming a defensive disposition.

Unlike Smut's operational-tactical recommendations to the EEF about the territorial objectives and avenues of advance, which were totally ignored by Allenby in his Bir Salem HQ and by General Henry Wilson, the new CIGS, in London, his endorsement of Palestine becoming the main front in the eastern Mediterranean was a push at an open door.[10] Preference of Palestine over Mesopotamia was accepted as almost self-evident by the political and military leadership in London, in Cairo and later in Jerusalem, and even, though not without some reservations, in Simla, already late in 1917 and then early in 1918.

The military motives were obvious: the main Ottoman forces in the Arab provinces were deployed in Syria and Palestine, and their defeat there would probably be more damaging to Constantinople than a setback in Mesopotamia; an advance in Palestine and Syria towards Turkey proper was easier as far as terrain and communications were concerned; the Allied capability to reinforce and supply the EEF from the UK was easier and shorter, based on maritime transportation through the Mediterranean; and the arrival of the EEF at the gates of southern Asia Minor would, in theory at least, be considered by Constantinople a greater threat to the heart of the empire than the appearance of an enemy force in the far eastern provinces of Asia Minor. Unlike the situation in Mesopotamia, the occupation of Palestine and Syria by the British would cut off the Ottoman army in Mesopotamia from its logistic hinterland, making defence of the entire region much more problematic, if not entirely hopeless, which was not the case if Mesopotamia were to have been chosen as the main battleground.

No less importance was to be attributed to the strategic effects of a 'Palestine first' policy. Among them were the further removal of the threat to Egypt and the vital waterway of the Suez Canal, a better and quicker possibility of getting Constantinople out of the war for which clandestine contacts with different Ottoman groups and personalities were being held at that time[11] and the potential impact on the position of Bulgaria and Austria-Hungary vis-à-vis their continued participation in the war. Finally, it would be a great morale-booster for the British people following the occupation of the Holy Land and an enhancement of British prestige in the Muslim world, contributing perhaps to the spreading of the Arab revolt in the Levant.

The first offensive phase of British military operations in Palestine was ended, as mentioned, by February 1918 and the campaign turned almost into positional fighting, with both sides preparing for the resumption of full-scale operations in the spring and summer. As far as the Ottoman army was concerned, it was increasingly drawn to the Transcaucasian front, while the leadership of the Committee of Union and Progress (CUP), the ruling party in Turkey, internalised an understanding that the prospects of keeping the Arab provinces within the empire were diminishing. As those provinces, unlike the Transcaucasian territories, were in any case less in the CUP's national focus, the fighting there was only aimed at holding the British off the Turkish hinterland. From this perspective, Palestine was viewed by the Ottomans, too, as more important than Mesopotamia. Consequently, the only meagre reinforcement dispatched southward to the Arab provinces during 1918 – a German infantry regiment and two under-strength Turkish infantry brigades from different divisions – was sent to Paestine.[12]

Towards Decision – the Operational-Tactical Dimension

Maintaining his step-by-step tactics, Allenby drew up his next phase plan for advance, assuming once more that it would not be a decisive act, but one in a long series of deliberate offensives which would end in occupation of all of Palestine, and, if the Ottomans were to continue fighting, Syria as well. The plan called for a gradual advance in the coastal plain of the Sharon and the mountainous area of Samaria which, by May 1918, would see the EEF advancing about twenty-five kilometres to the Hadera (Liktara in British maps)–Tul Karem line, or perhaps even to Nablus, west of the Jordan River, and to the Amman area, east of the river.[13] Thus, a solid operational base would be established along the entire line for the future large-scale offensive.

The 'big push' from that line northwards was to begin, according to the original plan, during June or July, once again as a limited-objective offensive in two phases. The first should bring the EEF to the line of Jezreel Valley/Afule–Haifa, whose port and railway to the east facilitated the force's logistics. In the second, the force would advance to the Akko (Acre)–Tiberias line on the sea of Galilee–Dara'a, where it would stop and consolidate a new defence line. All this might be achieved, according to the EEF C-in-C, by his existing force of seven infantry and three mounted divisions, reinforced by an additional Indian infantry division due to arrive from Mesopotamia. Allenby's mode of operation was to advance in two spearheads: the main effort in the western coastal plain on his left flank and a supporting effort east of the Jordan River on his right, based on the solid base he would occupy beforehand in the Amman–Salt area. By such a move he hoped to destroy the Ottoman army there in a 'Cannae-like' envelopment, a tactic he had endeavoured to employ at Third Gaza but without success in that respect.[14]

This was not enough for Lloyd George and the 'Easterners' in the Cabinet. They demanded a broader plan that would not make do with occupation of Palestine alone, an area defined by the Cabinet as 'the territory between Dan and Beersheba',[15] but interpreted by Allenby as the Banias area in Upper Galilee, at the foot of Mount Hermon. The 'Easterners' sought further advance and the occupation of Syria up to Aleppo in the north, near the then administrative border with Turkey proper. Allenby responded by warning the Cabinet that to reach the Damascus–Beirut line alone, which was half the distance suggested by London, he would require a force double the size of the one under his command, and even then the task could not be guaranteed owing to the difficulties in supporting it logistically. In other words, early in 1918, the EEF C-in-C did not consider the occupation of Syria a sound idea.

Between December 1917 and February 1918, the EEF carried out a series of small offensive operations which expanded the territory under its control. First, the front was moved a few kilometres north of the Jaffa–Jerusalem line in order to get the urban areas and logistic centres of Jaffa and Jerusalem out of enemy artillery range. Then, the British advanced to the Jordan Valley on their eastern flank and occupied the area of Jericho, north of the Dead Sea. By these operations the EEF stabilised a front line based on natural obstacles on its two flanks, from the Mediterranean to the Jordan River – 'the two Aujas line', so-called after the Arabic names of rivers on both flanks – and it also established a solid base for future operations. The occupation of the Jericho area and the Jordan crossing was a precondition for any action east of the river.

Study of the two failed EEF operations across the Jordan carried out in March and April/May 1918 and labelled, *post factum*, as 'raids', largely to minimize their significance and obscure their failure, still occupy the time of historians and tacticians. One of the harshest critics of what had been in fact the only two major combat actions carried out in 1918 by the EEF prior to September was no less than the officer who was in command of the first operation as corps commander, Lieutenant General Sir Philip Chetwode. Years after the events, he asserted that 'these two expeditions of Allenby's across the Jordan were the stupidest thing he did, I always thought, and very risky'.[16] Chetwode, a prominent EEF general and a talented soldier, aimed his criticism at the lack of military logic in initiating these operations in the first place. Others focused on the poor planning and faulty execution. Since we lack sufficient evidence of the perceptions and intentions of the EEF commander-in-chief, it is most likely that the discussion will continue. For the purpose of this chapter, these raids should be examined less within the tactical and more within the operational context of the campaign.

The term 'raid' was used by Allenby as early as January 1918, when he described to Robertson his intention to attack the Hijaz Railway, the main Ottoman communication artery between Syria and the Hijaz passing north–south along the ridges plateau about fifty kilometres, as the crow flies, east of the Jordan. He wished to destroy part of the railway and to link up, even temporarily, with the Arab forces which operated at that time in the Dead Sea–Tafila area.

The British had supported the Arab revolt since June 1916, when Sharif Hussein raised the banner against Constantinople. The Arab force, led by Hussein's son, Feisal, with T.E. Lawrence as advisor, gradually advanced northwards, conquered Aqaba at the northern tip of the Red Sea in July 1917, and in January 1918 reached the Dead Sea area, further north. Operationally, the meagre Arab force was unable to pose a real threat to the Ottoman flank, and the Turkish-German command did not consider it militarily more than a nuisance. However, its mere existence and activity so far north might, in the Ottomans' view, ignite the fire of rebellion in the Syrian hinterland too, and therefore must be eliminated. The EEF command was of the opinion that a Turkish attack was only a matter of time and would defeat the Arabs, most of them irregular Bedouins with no real military training.

The immediate purpose of the first operation, therefore, was to support and encourage the Arabs by hitting the Hijaz Railway through which the Ottomans were reinforcing and supplying their troops east of the Jordan by drawing the latter away from Feisal's force. However, the instructions given to Major General J.S.M. Shea, in command of the 60th Division and of the first raid, clearly demonstrated that, in addition to this tactical objective, the operation had a more long-range operational aim as well. After destroying the railway in the vicinity of Amman, the raiders were to leave a garrison in a-Salt, a large village between the Amman/Hijaz Railway and the Jordan River, establishing thereby a forward base for future operations of the eastern EEF arm towards northern Palestine and Syria.[17] Furthermore, a regular British presence east of the Jordan would probably enhance co-operation with Feisal's Northern Arab Army in securing the EEF's right flank. Finally, as affirmed by Eran Dolev, who has examined the medical aspects of the Palestine campaign, holding the higher and cooler area of a-Salt might have a worthwhile side benefit by enabling British troops to avoid the malarial Jordan Valley.[18]

The second attack across the Jordan was carried out less than a month after the failure of the first operation and in the midst of a massive transfer of EEF troops to the BEF in France, following the Ludendorff Offensive in March on the Western Front. It was launched despite London's directive that the depleted EEF should temporarily adopt only a defensive mode. Retrospectively, the vague rationale behind the raid has been given several explanations, of which only two have been verified by reliable evidence. It should be accepted that the others may have substance too: for example lessening the pressure on the Arab forces, which early in April were under threat of an Ottoman attack in the Ma'an district, and making a renewed attempt at creating a military option for an offensive in the east by occupying a-Salt and handing it over to Feisal. Other accounts mentioned a deterrence-oriented demonstration to compensate for the significant decrease in the EEF strength, and a face-saving compensation for the previous failure. The *Official History* even stated that one of the operation's purposes had been deception, to draw Turkish attention away from the coast 'to induce the enemy to concentrate his attention on the opposite flank' in the east, where the main British thrust would ostensibly be launched.[19] However, the archival documentation points to the fact that such an objective was first raised by Allenby only *post factum* in May, perhaps to justify the costly failure.[20]

Although the attacking force was increased from two divisions in the first raid to almost four, the second raid also failed to achieve any of its objectives. British historiography has attributed the failure mainly to British command decisions, intelligence failures in terrain and assessment of the strength of the enemy, severe weather conditions which, incidentally, could have been forecast by the existing British meteorological stations in the country, and the Arabs' incompetence or even treachery. Recently, Erickson has brought to the knowledge of English-speaking readers the Ottoman share in the

British failure, demonstrating that the defenders' upper hand in the field was gained by quick recovery of tactical balance, creation of locally-superior ad hoc battle groups, the employment of specially-trained assault troops, and better exploitation of the terrain and ground conditions.[21]

The tactical objectives and failure notwithstanding, the logic of the raids should probably be better examined in the light of Allenby's fixed operational perception. It had been demonstrated against the Gaza–Beersheba Line in October 1917 and was to be demonstrated again a year later, namely a deliberate offensive against both of the enemy's flanks, by a main effort on one flank and a supporting/secondary effort on the other. For this, a solid base had to be secured beforehand.

Towards Decision – the Political Dimension

In 1915–17 Britain found herself entangled in a web of promises to Middle Eastern protagonists. The commitments given to the Arabs, or interpreted by Arab nationalists as given, by the correspondence between Henry McMahon, the British High Commissioner in Egypt, and Sharif Hussein in 1915 regarding the creation of an independent Arab kingdom, its territory, and the accompanying preconditions, did not correspond with the Sykes-Picot Agreement. The latter divided the Levant between the Allies in the event of an Ottoman defeat. France recognized British dominance over most of Mesopotamia, southern Palestine and trans-Jordan where an independent Arab state was to be established under British 'influence'. Britain, in the agreement with France, acknowledged Syrian territory east of the Damascus–Aleppo line as part of a French 'zone of influence' over a future Arab state which would include the northern part of Palestine up to a line north of Acre–Safed–Sea of Galilee. The territory west of the Damascus–Aleppo line, including the entire area of Lebanon, was to come under direct French control. As the two parties were unable to agree over the future of central Palestine (less the strategic Haifa basin, which was to be given to Britain), it was agreed to bypass the issue by agreeing on mutual Allied control which would be examined after the war. This solution, attributed to Mark Sykes, the British member of the duo,[22] was accepted by London when it was first presented in mid-1916, as the coalition consideration was still dominant. Now, early in 1918, the strategic-political situation was significantly different and France's goodwill was considered by London to be less important. The 'day after the war is over' sense had already emerged, and with it the British awareness that their dependence on satisfying French imperial interests was diminishing with the increased strength of the BEF, the perception of the French forces on the Western Front not having fully recovered from their calamities of 1917, and the anticipated arrival of a massive US army in France.

Concurrently, British interest in post-war control of the whole of Palestine increased. Termination of the war in a clear-cut decision in favour of the Allies was as yet an uncertain result, while another option, that of a negotiated peace with Constantinople, was on the table. Such a political outcome, around which numerous overtures by official, semi-official and private Ottoman, British, and French envoys were made from mid-1917 onwards, would ensure the continued existence of the Ottoman Empire, even if within shrunken boundaries. This might, the British believed, leave a strong German presence in the Middle East, increasing its imperial appetite.

Another scenario, this time in the case of an Ottoman defeat and dismemberment of the empire, was the return of Russia, now a socialist-communist entity, as an imperial and ideological foe. Both potential scenarios made it necessary to establish a buffer zone in order to diminish the hazards of a renewed 'Great Game', to preserve British domination in the region and to secure the maritime and land routes between Britain and the East. The more British imperial troops were engaged in battle on Ottoman lands and the more they were present in former Ottoman territory, the easier it would be to gain direct or indirect control over this territory in the post-war settlement.

In this sense, a friendly Arab authority established in Syria would serve British interests better than a French-oriented regime. As Haggai Erlich concluded, 'by encouraging Arab nationalism and by the leadership of their Hashemite ally, the British hoped to gain influence there [Syria]'.[23] Practical implementation of such a policy in the field was demonstrated during the final EEF advance, when the Mounted Australian Division, arriving at the outskirts of Damascus on 30 September 1918, was ordered to stop and let the Sharifian troops be the first to enter the city.

However, even before the war ended, the contradictions began to make themselves felt. Such, for example, was the case when, simultaneous with strengthening the case of the Hashemites for an independent state by presenting Feisal as the 'first to Damascus' (actually, the Australians rode in first, defying their orders), the British, in compliance with the Sykes-Picot Agreement, hurried to stop Arab attempts to proclaim their authority in Beirut following its occupation and on 8 October installed in Beirut a French governor instead.

The web became still further entangled by the War Cabinet's decision on 31 October 1917 to publish a letter by Arthur James Balfour, Secretary of State for Foreign Affairs, to the Zionist leader of the British Jewish community, Lord Walter Rothschild, announcing the support of His Majesty's Government for 'the establishment in Palestine of a national home for the Jewish people', known thereafter as the Balfour Declaration.[24] The reasons for this move still serve as fertile ground for research, speculation and debate. They cover, for example, belief in the influence of 'world Jewry' on the leadership of America, revolutionary Russia and even Germany, or 'cultivation' of the Jewish community as a pro-British element in Palestine, which might assist their future claim to the land, in contrast to the Sykes-Picot Agreement. A recent account even asserted that the roots of the proclamation lay in an internal dispute within the British leadership about the post-war Middle East. On one side stood a 'reformist' group that sought a peace agreement with Constantinople which would maintain the integrity and independence of the Ottoman Empire. On the other side were the 'radicals', who wished to crush the Turks militarily and dismember the empire. The pro-Zionist approach – according to this account – was adopted by the 'radicals' who, by means of the Balfour Declaration, intended to frustrate the efforts of the 'reformists' to end the war with a peace agreement that would maintain the Ottoman territory intact.[25] Whatever the reasons for the Declaration, the Arabs have viewed it from the start as a harmful move against the natural rights of the Palestinian Arabs, and nationalistic Arab circles interpreted it as contradicting the British promise to include Palestine within the boundaries of the new Arab state.

Decision

The period between May and September 1918 was used by the EEF for reorganization, following the loss by transfer of two infantry divisions, several mounted regiments, most British infantry battalions, and a large portion of its artillery to the Western Front, for which it was compensated by Indian troops – two infantry divisions coming from Mesopotamia, thirteen cavalry regiments and about forty infantry battalions, many of them composed of unseasoned troops, to complete the war establishment of the British divisions which remained in Palestine. The general public image portrays the Australian cavalrymen as the troops which conquered Palestine, but most of the EEF's fighting force was composed of Indians – half of the cavalry and three-quarters of the infantry. The 'Indianisation' of the EEF, including the acclimatisation and training of the troops until, in less than five months, they were transformed by summer 1918 into an efficient and co-ordinated fighting machine, became the largest and most successful administrative achievement of Allenby and his staff.[26]

On the eve of the September offensive, the EEF C-in-C had at his disposal four cavalry/mounted and seven infantry divisions, totalling about 72,000 combat troops, assisted by about 720 guns, 100 of them medium and heavy, about 110 fighters, bombers and reconnaissance aircraft, many of them modern types, an extensive radio communication network, and an enhanced and mechanically-mobile logistic system. An Arab force, most of its men irregulars, operated east of the Jordan.

Opposing this impressive and relatively technologically up-to-date British imperial army stood an enemy whose combat inferiority in every aspect – manpower, equipment, and morale – increased every day. As a result of the low priority assigned by Constantinople to the Syria-Palestine front in comparison to Transcaucasia, the great numbers of Ottoman casualties inflicted from October 1917 onwards were not replaced, Turkish reinforcements sent to the region were weak in experience and small in number, their ranks depleted even before reaching the front due to desertion, while a third of the German reinforcements – the strongest and most able troops to augment Ottoman defence of Palestine in 1918 – were reassigned to the Caucasus immediately upon arrival.

By September, General Liman von Sanders, the German commander of *Yildirim* as of March 1918, had under him twelve poor, depleted divisions, each with a combat strength of no more than a brigade. Infantry battalions with 500–600 troops each before Third Gaza, as compared to 800 at full war establishment, consisted in the summer of 1918 of no more than 150–200 malnourished and inadequately-equipped men of low morale. Cannibalisation of units within divisions, carried out to overcome the manpower shortage, lowered the number of manouevrable units, limiting Turkish ability to maintain units in reserve, as most divisions and army corps could muster no more than a lone battalion for this purpose. Exacerbating the basic weakness of *Yildirim* was the failure of its only significant offensive operation initiated during the summer.

In July, a strong Turkish-German battle group attacked British positions in Musallaba, in the Jordan Valley. The attack was intended to create a chain reaction in which the British line in the valley would be pushed back southwards, the Ottoman defence line shortened, and Ottoman troops transferred from east to the west of the front. Although the plan bore operational logic, *Yildirim's* basic weakness made it impossible to assign enough reserves for its implementation, leaving the decision to carry it out debatable. The only tangible outcome from the Ottoman perspective was negative, the loss of about 1,000 much-needed combat-seasoned troops as casualties or taken prisoner, a substantial percentage of the dwindling fighting force under Liman von Sanders.

A similar weakness was evident in Ottoman fortifications as well. After eight months of work, the first defence line was comprised of detached sectors, each consisting of a mere forward main trench connected to a lone support trench, with almost no sandbags, revetments or barbed wire. After overcoming this line, the EEF would then not encounter any more prepared defensive emplacements as no second line was ever built.[27] The defenders could in theory be supported by five German and two Turkish air squadrons operating west and east of the Jordan, but towards the summer of 1918, the crisis that beset the German air arm in Europe affected Palestine too. The number of serviceable aircraft and available pilots dwindled, while replacements, reinforcements, spare parts and fuel failed to arrive. On the eve of the British offensive, the newly-established RAF Palestine Brigade gained complete air superiority, as proven during the campaign when almost no German aircraft succeeded in taking off for combat.

However, Allenby was not convinced that his next offensive would turn into a decisive battle. In mid-August, he still considered the coming operation in terms of a 'deliberate' offensive which at most would push the enemy to the line of Tul Karem–Nablus–Damia in the Jordan Valley.[28] Only on 21 August, that is a month prior to Z-Day, did he for the first time raise the idea of a deep mounted penetration by almost the entire EEF mobile arm – three cavalry divisions – further north, to the Afule–Bisan area, thereby bypassing the Ottoman forward defence line, enveloping the enemy, and clearing Palestine of Ottoman troops south of the Haifa–Jezreel Valley–Bisan line, where it would stop. The Arab northern advance east of the Jordan was to be employed to carry out a preliminary raid on the central railway junction in Dara'a. This would prevent the Ottomans from sending reinforcements from Syria to Palestine just prior to the offensive, and also assist in convincing them that the main effort would be launched in the eastern sector. Nonetheless, even at this relatively late date, the big breakthrough was, in the C-in-C's mind – according to his letter to the CIGS – only a raw idea.[29]

The September offensive ('Megiddo', 'Armageddon', or 'Opening the Gate' Campaign, as it was to be called later on) was supposed to be no more than another link in a chain of large-scale operations which would probably continue up to 1919, and certainly not be the decisive battle, as in fact it became. Only the instant collapse of the Ottomans due to the speedy and deep penetration of the cavalry as well as the prompt and constant advance of the infantry – at a rate not predicated in the first place – led to Allenby's decision in the midst of the fighting on 25 September (unsubstantiated evidence precedes the date to 21 September[30]), to expand the operation and decide on a much more ambitious objective, the Beirut–Damascus line. And at this point he still stuck to the strategy of a steady advance and declined the CIGS's suggestion of continuing the advance to Aleppo, 360 kilometres north of Damascus, even if only as a cavalry raid, since he viewed such an operation – which in reality was carried out in about a month – as impractical.[31]

The EEF 'blitzkrieg' of September–October 1918 has already been extensively examined in academic and popular literature, but two points may be emphasized:

1. Allenby and the EEF General Staff were well aware of the expeditionary force's overall dominance. Their intelligence picture regarding the enemy's strength and deployment in all sectors was detailed and accurate though with a slight

numerical overestimate.[32] Seemingly, it was enough to guarantee victory. Yet, this prima facie superiority had little effect on the meticulous planning, of which a crucial component was special activity prior to the attack and during its first hours, aimed to throw the defenders off their operational balance as soon as the offensive began by disrupting their command and control system and preventing them from recovering operationally.

Among the actions taken was a vast deception operation aimed to mislead the enemy regarding the time of the offensive and the sector of its main effort; a field propaganda campaign to lower morale of enemy troops and encourage them to defect; destruction of the main telephone switchboard in Afule by a night air attack, the first of its kind in Palestine; aerial bombing of field armies, corps headquarters and communication centres simultaneously with the first rounds of the ground attack; air interdiction over enemy airfields; and utilisation of the irregular Arab forces to attack the vital railway and road junction of Dara'a for the purposes of diversion and a holding action.

Finally, a surprise cavalry brigade raid far behind enemy lines on *Yildirim* HQ in Nazareth on the first night of the offensive aimed to capture Liman von Sanders and destroy his headquarters. Although it failed to capture the German general, the raid nevertheless paralysed the HQ's activity, and along with the disruption of the command and control systems of the subordinate formations, impaired *Yildirim's* ability to read the battlefield picture.[33] The question whether all this were indeed a prerequisite for success when there was such British force superiority remains a matter for debate but even if the answer were in the negative, it does not detract from the high standards of EEF thinking and planning at the operational level.

2. It was Brigadier Dudley Clark, the Second World War master of deception, who declared, according to the accepted narrative, that a successful deception should 'induce the enemy to *do* something, not just to *think* something'.[34] From this point of view, Allenby's deception, although considered to this day as an exemplary model of planning and implementing deception operations, achieved only limited success. The traditional claim that the Ottomans were deceived and assumed that the main effort would be launched in the eastern flank, away from the real western sector, and were also surprised by its timing and reacted accordingly, is only partially supported by the evidence. True, captured Ottoman documents showed that the Ottoman estimate of the opposing force facing them erred in underestimation of the British order of battle in the main western sector and overestimation of the force in other sectors. However, Erikson, based on Turkish documentation, has shown that Liman von Sanders deployed his strongest divisions in the western sector, narrowing their front in order to concentrate more power there, concentrated there his main artillery units, did not divert combat units to the eastern flank, and, on the eve of the offensive, advanced his small front-level reserve nearer the western sector, where the EEF indeed planned the breakthrough. Conversely, he did not divert troops from other sectors to the west, perhaps because he was unable to eliminate them as possible sectors for the British attacks, even as secondary efforts.[35]

It seems, therefore, that the deception's partial success was in enhancing ambiguity and in leaving the German commander on the horns of a dilemma, rather than in directing his attention to the wrong place, as was the planners' intention and as had been the case a year earlier at Third Gaza. Although Liman von Sanders indeed identified the western sector as the more dangerous one, and therefore reinforced it accordingly in advance contrary to the deception's aim, nevertheless, since he was uncertain where the main blow would fall and unable to leave other sectors undefended, he was forced to disperse his meagre forces along the entire front.

Considering the poor state of *Yildirim*, it stood to reason that even if he were to have known for sure where the enemy's main thrust would come, he would still have found it difficult to reinforce it more than he did. On the other hand, had the deception met with overall success, a small shift of forces away from the western coastal sector to the east would probably not have made any significant difference in favour of the attackers there, as was indeed demonstrated by the infantry's rapid breaching of the western sector defences and the speedy cavalry breakthrough. It seems, therefore, that at the end of the day Allenby's deception did not have any major significance.

Conclusion

British Middle Eastern war policy was dictated throughout most of the war period by a coalition-oriented strategy which gave higher priority to the interests related to European fronts than to those bearing upon the secondary theatre in the eastern Mediterranean. This might explain, at least partially, London's 'readiness' to accept the inconsistent Arab aspirations on the one hand and French territorial demands on the other, both related to the same 'sideshow'. Only during the last year of the war was this strategy gradually transformed into an empire-oriented one, focusing on post-victory considerations and adding the Zionists to the tangled web of promises. British promises and commitments to the French, Arabs and Jews, taken as a whole, as well as their interpretation by the involved parties, created much of the labyrinth in which the British administration was entrapped in the post-war Middle East. Its echoes and reverberations are still to be heard and felt today.

This shifting of strategies also explains why the conquest of Palestine and Syria was less the outcome of prior strategic decisions and clear definition of operational objectives, and more an evolving process – sometimes contrary to the 'advice' of the military leadership – based on theatre-level appreciations of the situation and on actual developments on the battlefield. During Third Gaza in 1917 and the Megiddo campaign a year later, the EEF gained territorial objectives it had not expected to reach at that stage. The completely superior strength of the EEF, integrated with professional planning and execution of the operational art at the theatre level, brought the British imperial army to the gates of Cilicia by the end of October 1918, months before the time originally predicated when the offensive began on 19 September.

However, the military decision in the Palestine-Syria campaign was not the only – probably not even the major – reason for the ceasefire request by the Ottomans on 30 October. From Constantinople's perspective, developments along the empire's western borders bore much graver risks. The entire Balkan front collapsed when Bulgaria withdrew from the war late in September and the Allies broke out of the Salonika enclave. The news reached the Turks that Germany and Austria-Hungary were conducting ceasefire negotiations. Turkey found itself without any allies, isolated militarily as well as politically and economically, and threatened from the west by armies approaching its capital. To preserve its existence and sovereignty it had no choice but to ask for an immediate ceasefire.

Notes

1. David Lloyd George, *War Memoirs* (London: Odhams Press, 1938), Vol. II, p. 1090.
2. See David French, *The Strategy of the Lloyd George Coalition, 1916-18* (Oxford: Clarendon Press, 1995); David R. Woodward, *Field Marshal Sir William Robertson: Chief of the Imperial General Staff in the Great War* (Westport, CN: Praeger, 1998).
3. General Sir Edmund Allenby, Commander-in-Chief, Egyptian Expeditionary Force, 'Force order No 54', 22 .10.1917, in Cyril Falls, *Military Operations Egypt and Palestine, from June 1917 to the End of the War* Official History of the Great War, Part II (London: HMSO, 1930), Appendix 7, p. 676.
4. Edward J. Erickson, *Palestine: The Ottoman Campaigns of 1914-1918* (Barnsley: Pen & Sword, 2016), p. 152.
5. Ibid., pp. 88–9; M. Talha Çiçek, *War and State Formation in Syria: Cemal Pasha's governorate during World War I, 1917-1917* (London and New York: Routledge, 2014), pp. 258–63.
6. Eran Dolev, *Allenby's Military Medicine: Life and Death in World War I Palestine* (London: I.B. Tauris, 2007), p. 105.
7. Matthew Hughes, *Allenby and British Strategy in the Middle East, 1917-1919* (London: Frank Cass, 1999), p. 62. See also Clive Garsia, *A Key to Victory: A Study in War Planning* (London: Eyre and Spottiswoode, 1940), pp. 203–20.
8. Yigal Sheffy, *British Military Intelligence in the Palestine Campaign, 1914-1918* (London: Frank Cass, 1998), pp. 286–92; Hughes, *Allenby and British Strategy in the Middle East*, pp. 53–5; Woodward, *Field Marshal Sir William Robertson*, pp. 163, 167–8.
9. 'Joint Note No. 12 Submitted to the Supreme War Council By its Military Representatives', 21.1.1918, in *History of the Great War, Military Operations Belgium and France, 1918*, Appendices volume, Appendix 9 (London: MacMillan & Co., 1935), p. 42.
10. James E. Kitchen, *The British Imperial Army in the Middle East: Morale and Military Identity in the Sinai and Palestine Campaigns, 1916-18* (London: Bloomsbury, 2014), p. 193.
11. Jonathan Schneer, *The Balfour Declaration: The Origins of the Arab-Israeli Conflict* (New York: Random House, 2010), pp. 239–302; Joseph Maiolo and Tony Insall, 'Sir Basil Zaharoff and Sir Vincent Caillard as Instruments of British Policy Towards Greece and the Ottoman Empire during the Asquith and Lloyd George Administrations, 1915-1918', *International History Review*, 34 (4) (2012), pp. 819–39.
12. Erickson, *Palestine*, pp. 142–3, 146.
13. Allenby to Robertson, 14.12.1917, in Matthew Hughes (ed.), *Allenby in Palestine: The Middle East Correspondence of Field Marshal Viscount Allenby* (London: Sutton Publishing for the Army Records Society, 2004), p. 113.
14. Allenby to Robertson, 2.12.1917, 3.1.1918, ibid., pp. 115, 124–5 respectively.
15. Robertson to Allenby, 18.12.1917, ibid., p. 114.
16. Chetwode to Wavell, 28.3.39, cited in Dolev, *Allenby's Military Medicine*, p. 107.
17. Falls, *Military Operations Egypt and Palestine*, Appendix 20, p. 705.
18. Dolev, *Allenby's Military Medicine*, p. 110. See also: Archibald P. Wavell, *The Palestine Campaign* (London: Constable and Co., 1941), p. 184.
19. Falls, *Military Operations Egypt and Palestine*, Part I, p. 365.
20. Yigal Sheffy, 'Institutionalized Deception and Perception Reinforcement: Allenby's Campaigns in Palestine, 1917-18', *Intelligence & National Security* 5 (2) (1990), pp. 204–5; General Sir Harry Chauvel to Allenby, 'The Palestine Campaign', 13.10.36, Allenby's Papers, 9/6, Liddell Hart Centre for Military Archives.
21. Erickson, *Palestine*, pp. 136–42.
22. 'British War Aims in Ottoman Asia: report of the De Bunsen Committee, 30.6.15', in J.C. Hurewitz, *The Middle East and North Africa in World Politics* Vol. II (New Haven, CT: Yale University Press, 1975), document 12, pp. 26–46.
23. Haggai Erlich, *Introduction to the Modern History of the Middle East* (Tel Aviv: Open University Press, 1987), Vol. V, p. 88 (in Hebrew).
24. For the text of the Declaration see Schneer, *The Balfour Declaration*, p. 341.

25. Daniel Gutwein, 'The Politics of the Balfour Declaration: Chaim Weizmann, the Zionist Movement and British Imperialism', *Israel: Studies in Zionism and the State of Israel History, Society, Culture* 24 (2016), pp. 63–142 (in Hebrew).
26. Dennis Showalter, 'The Indianization of the Egyptian Expeditionary Force 1917-1918: An Imperial Turning Point', in Ray Kaushik (ed.), *The Indian Army in the Two World Wars* (Leiden: Brill, 2011), pp. 145–63; James Kitchen, 'The Indianization of the Egyptian Expeditionary Force: Palestine 1918', ibid., pp. 146–90.
27. Erickson, *Palestine*, p. 151; Liman von Sanders, *Five Years in Turkey* (Annapolis, MD: United States Naval Institute, 1927), pp. 268–75.
28. Allenby to Wilson, 14.8.1918, in Hughes (ed.), *Allenby in Palestine*, p. 174.
29. Allenby to Wilson, 21.8.1918, ibid., p. 175.
30. H.S. Gullett, *The Australian Imperial Force in Sinai and Palestine, 1914-1918*, The Official History of Australia in the War of 1914-1918, Vol. VII (St. Lucia: Queensland University Press, 1984/originally 1923), p. 728.
31. Allenby to Wilson, 25.9.1918, in Hughes (ed.), *Allenby in Palestine*, p. 188.
32. TNA WO 157/731, Estimate Distribution of Enemy Forces, in GHQ Intelligence Summary 14.9.18.
33. On the raid: Yigal Sheffy, 'Destabilizing the Enemy: The Raid on Nazareth, 19-20 September 1918', in Eran Dolev, Yigal Sheffy and Haim Goren (eds), *Palestine and World War I: Grand Strategy, Military Tactics and Culture in War* (London: I.B. Tauris, 2014), pp. 172–204.
34. Thaddeus Holt, *The Deceivers* (New York: Scribner, 2004), pp. 51–2.
35. Erickson, *Palestine*, pp. 158–60; Von Sanders, *Five Years in Turkey*, pp. 273–4.

Suggested Further Reading

Dolev, Eran and Sheffy, Yigal and Goren, Haim, (eds), *Palestine and World War I: Grand Strategy, Military Tactics and Culture in War* (London: I.B. Tauris, 2014)
Erickson, Edward J., *Palestine: The Ottoman Campaigns of 1914-1918* (Barnsley, Pen & Sword, 2016)
Friedman, Isaiah, *British Pan-Arab Policy, 1915-1922: A Critical Appraisal* (New Brunswick, NJ: Rutgers University Press, 2010)
Grainger, John D., *The Battle for Syria, 1918-1920* (Woodbridge: Boydell Press, 2013)
Grey, Jeffrey, *The War with the Ottoman Empire* (Melbourne: Oxford University Press, 2015)
Hughes, Matthew, *Allenby and British Strategy in the Middle East, 1917-1919* (London: Frank Cass, 1999)
McMeekin, Sean, *The Berlin-Baghdad Express: The Ottoman Empire and Germany Bid for World Power* (Cambridge MA: Harvard University Press, 2010)
Rogan, Eugene, *The Fall of the Ottomans: The Great War in the Middle East* (New York: Basic Books, 2015)
Woodward, David, *Hell in the Holy Land: World War I in the Middle East* (Lexington, K: The University Press of Kentucky, 2006)

Chapter 17

'Do not forget me quite' – Music's War Poets

By Kate Kennedy

The purpose of this chapter is twofold: first, to argue for a body of war composers to parallel the war poets, and second, to explore how we might think about the rarely-made connections and parallels between these poets and composers. By doing so, a future analytical approach to the work of these often-neglected composers will be recommended. In literary studies, we have begun to look at early twentieth century literature's use of music as a way of analysing the work of writers such as Woolf, Pound and Forster. By using the same tools with which literary critics are already comfortable, it should be possible to find new ways of reading the war generation's music.

Moments of intense political crisis tend to generate moments of cultural crisis. These moments, and by moment, I mean the four and a half year 'moment' of the war, are played out across the arts. Literature and music intersect, of course, at all and every point in cultural history. But the intersections are, perhaps, that much more intense at a time of collective crisis in which society and the nation are being re-defined; that much richer than at other less strained moments. The First World War was a prolonged experience to which every affected artist, writer and composer had to respond in some way. To ignore it entirely in one's work was a 'lie in the soul', as Katherine Mansfield accused Virginia Woolf of committing when she barely referred to the war in her novel *Night and Day*.[1]

The First World War is now remembered through its literature perhaps more than any other art form; we are all familiar with the traditional canon of war poets, with Siegfried Sassoon and Wilfred Owen. However, we are considerably less familiar with the parallel response of classical musicians to the war, both during and after the conflict. If we were to take Mansfield's rather dogmatic view, we might assume that to ignore the war in music would also have been a 'lie in the soul', and therefore there must be an equally rich seam of war music to investigate as there is war literature.

Ivor Gurney, for example, combined identities as a war poet and a composer. The very fact of his work in both genres suggests that there might be a genre of composition that has not yet been defined – if we can accept the 'war poet', then were there in fact 'war composers'? The answer is yes, but, as in literature, there were many different voices writing music from many different perspectives, both civilian and combatant.

But first, can we establish the difference between a war poet or composer, and someone who happens to write at a time when there's a war on? The concept of a war composer has not really been defined. War poetry, and, it can be presumed, war music, concerns itself with the relationship between art and violence.[2] It tells the truth. It bears witness. And what that truth turns out to be is not necessarily what we might expect to hear. In order to define a body of war composers based on the model of the war poets, we need to widen our understanding of what war poetry actually can be. We are too used to sifting our war poetry to retain only those poets who, or poems which, register horror, regret and sorrow. We are not so used to tuning our ears to the voices extolling patriotism, exhilaration, beauty, the nobility of death, or heroism – they are not terribly 'trendy'. But they are there, in the war poets, and they are certainly there in the body of war composers.

Wilfred Owen wrote in his draft preface to his poems that a poet's duty was to warn. The poetry was in the pity. It is perhaps an over-quoted maxim. It has led to a tendency to narrow our readings of Owen to poems primarily concerned with pity and not to register the poetry that is fuelled by anger, homo-eroticism or joy. The same artificial narrowing of focus might be said to be true of our conception of what counts as a piece of war music. Some might be concerned with pity, some might be to do with warning future generations, but others are concerned with working out personal trauma, with militarism and destruction, with nostalgia, celebrating beauty or upholding concepts of heroism. Frank Bridge's piano sonata, Arthur Bliss' *Morning Heroes*, Ivor Gurney's song cycle *Ludlow and Teme* and Frederick Septimus Kelly's *Gallipoli* violin sonata, spring from wide-ranging sources of inspiration.

There is of course the practical problem for composition, in that if there were to be no text and no helpful title, how can it be unequivocally claimed that a work written during or just after the war was indeed concerned with war? Some composers embrace the ambiguity that wordless music can offer – some have read Ernest Moeran's G minor symphony as a war work, with its post-apocalyptic landscapes of the second movement, and the subtle references to the Norfolk folk song *The Shooting of his Dear* woven into the melodies. Moeran is at least toying with the idea of text, if not quoting it directly. However, what happens to the categorising of a war work when there is no text associated, or a composer chooses an instrument to speak instead of a voice? Elgar's cello concerto is an obvious example. What actual basis is there for reading it as an elegy for a lost generation? Similarly, with Frank Bridge's cello elegy, *Oration*, which the composer explicitly identifies as a war work, but one in which he ascribes the oratory to the cello itself. Apart from the obvious fact that there are no words to orate, the work and its title are in some ways in conflict with themselves – an oration is, strictly speaking, a formal, ceremonial speech, not the job one would give a cello perhaps, which is an intimate, understated and softly-spoken instrument. But elegiac works which may not elegise, or orations which do not orate, are only the foothills of the mountainous terrain that is the creation of a canon of war music. The act of canonising works written in response to an event, when the works are disparate, ambiguous, written over a long period of time, and by composers with varied and changing relationships to the war, is bound to be fraught with problems of definition.

Music is both a public and a private act. The writing of it is private; its performance can of course be intimate, and its intentions deeply personal. But a choral and orchestral work written for the purposes of mass commemoration, to touch a public mood, is undoubtedly a public act, however personal the sentiment behind it. For the composers unlucky enough to find themselves writing during the war, the question as to what is an artist's duty in wartime, had to be addressed.

There is perhaps a duty both to themselves and to those around them, and perhaps even to those who were absent. On the one hand the war composer might, as the war artists were explicitly commissioned to do, record the events, sounds and sights around him for posterity and to help civilians understand. He might be writing for the benefit of his fellow men, as Gurney claimed to do – to give back to them their own experiences in words, paint or music. Equally, a war composer might be writing to exorcise his own trauma, to articulate the unspeakable, and to make artistic sense, or not, of the inexplicable.

So, with all these questions and possibilities in mind, who might be chosen as potential candidates for the musical equivalents of Owen, Sassoon and Blunden?

The war had come at a time of transition for British composers. The older generation of Parry, Stanford and Elgar was at the end of its reign, and a younger generation (of enlistment age) was being 'trained up', largely by the Royal College of Music. Ivor Gurney, Arthur Bliss and Herbert Howells were all students there in 1914. Vaughan Williams, approximately a decade older than the undergraduate composers, interrupted his work to enlist. Of those composers who went to fight, at least five were killed: among them the glamorous Olympic rower, Frederick Septimus Kelly, and the precocious young Cambridge pianist, William Denis Browne, both of whom were at the forefront of new music in England. In May 1914, Denis Browne performed the London premiere of Alban Berg's first piano sonata. Browne had already written some ambitious orchestral works and some of the most beautiful songs in English: *To Gratiana, Dancing and Singing*, is a masterpiece. He was devoted to the poet, Rupert Brooke, who couldn't wait to get out to the front. Brooke's enthusiasm was infectious, sweeping Browne along in his wake.

He would be joined by Frederick Septimus Kelly, who, like Denis Browne, was pushing the boundaries of English song with a style that combined elements of Stravinsky and Strauss. His songs are dense, orchestral and expansive, and almost entirely unknown. (As it happens the author of this chapter is in the early stages of writing Kelly's and Browne's biographies, and has been editing Kelly's songs from manuscripts scattered in archives from Australia to Oxford.) There are some real gems among Kelly's songs that had they been mainstream repertoire, would have gone some way towards re-dressing the rather snooty assumption that English song was something of a late Victorian backwater.

Kelly continued to write during the war, with a *Gallipoli* violin sonata, written in a tent on the peninsula shortly after both Brooke and Browne had died. Kelly also wrote a piano sonata that trails off mid-phrase, left unfinished at his own death. The *Gallipoli* sonata is full of homesick beauty, a lyrical, exquisite piece, in stark contrast with the unfinished piano sonata, which is dense, dark and turbulent. Both are war works, but express the need for beauty, hope and escapism just as much as a desire to bear witness to the darkness of the times.

Kelly, Browne and Brooke all sailed together to the Dardanelles, forming a little enclave, a floating Cambridge college, as they travelled in the spring of 1915 on the troopship *Grantully Castle*, playing piano duets, quoting the Classics and writing poetry for each other. The fun didn't last long. Rupert Brooke died of septicaemia on the voyage, and Kelly and Browne buried him shortly before their own deaths. It was their heart-rending accounts of the burial that came to form part of the mythological status Brooke would so quickly achieve. The three inspired each other in their poetry and music: the connections between their musical and literary utterances are so close that it is amazing that the two genres have been so indelibly separated in our thinking about artistic and cultural responses to the war. Kelly wrote a string *Elegy for Brooke* as he lay dying on board ship. Browne even stepped into Brooke's shoes and wrote a poem, *To Rupert Brooke in his memory* – two elegies for the same poet, in two genres.

To Rupert Brooke, by William Denis Browne
 I give you glory, for you are dead.
 The day lightens above your head;
 The night darkens about your feet;
 Morning and noon and evening meet
 Around and over and under you
 In the world you knew, the world you knew.

 Lips are kissing and limbs are clinging,
 Breast to breast in a silence singing
 Of forgotten and fadeless things:
 Laughter and tears and the beat of wings
 Faintly heard in a far-off heaven;
 Bird calls bird; the unquiet even
 Ineluctable ebb and flow
 Flows and ebbs; and all things go
 Moving from dream to dream; and deep
 Calls deep again in a world of sleep.

 There is no glory gone from the air;
 Nothing is less. No, as it were
 A keener and wilder radiance glows
 Along the blood, and a shouting grows
 Fiercer and louder, a far-flung roar
 Of throats and guns: your island shore
 Is swift with smoke and savage with flame;
 And a myriad lovers shout your name,
 Rupert! Rupert!, across the earth;
 And death is dancing, and dancing birth;
 And a madness of dancing blood and laughter
 Rises and sings, and follows after
 All the dancers who danced before,
 And dance no more, and dance no more.

 You will dance no more; you will love no more;
 You are dead and dust on your island shore.
 A little dust are the lips where
 Laughter and song and kisses were.
 And I give you glory, and I am glad
 For the life you had and the death you had,
 For the heaven you knew and the hell you knew,
 And the dust and the dayspring which were you.

In general, war poets had the advantage on war composers – it was infinitely more practical to write a poem than a piece of music while on active service. This meant that although there were exceptions, the job of war composition was largely postponed until after the war, and so was left to the composers who returned. Browne didn't write any more music after 1914 and it will never be known what the musical equivalents of Owen, Sorley or Rosenberg would have written. The war composers who died did so largely before they had the chance to put 'their wars' into music. Kelly's final works hint at how he was already beginning to assimilate his war experiences into innovative, strikingly original work. Would he have changed the shape of post-war music, had he survived?

George Butterworth is perhaps the best known of the names of those who never returned. His pre-war settings of A.E. Housman's texts represent most of his legacy, and he is, in a sense, a perfect example of a composer whose readings of text are so compelling that one can scarcely read Housman without hearing the subtle rhythms of Butterworth's melodic lines. What would Butterworth's Housman settings have sounded like if he were to have continued to write them after the experience of the Somme? It is quite simply impossible to know how, in the light of his war service, he might have reinterpreted Housman's insistence on the glory of premature death.

Housman had written his poetry collection, *A Shropshire Lad*, back in 1896, with other, colonial, wars in mind, but the poems were adopted as one of the iconic texts that accompanied soldiers into the trenches. They became appropriated as First World War poetry even though that had never been the original intention. Housman in fact noted in his diaries with a rather ghoulish pleasure an instance in which two wounded soldiers, waiting to be taken out of the line, had been left together. One had taken his copy of *A Shropshire Lad* out of his pocket to offer to the other to take his mind off their circumstance, and the other pulled out his own bloodstained copy. It was the nearest thing to the Bible, and there were even instances of a copy in a breast pocket stopping a bullet. No wonder Butterworth's beautiful, delicate, pre-war Housman settings found such a strong resonance during and after the war.

Housman's texts are not, then, strictly speaking, war poetry. They don't bear witness to conflict. But they are works that serve as containers for 'others' emotion', to use psychoanalyst, Wilfred Bion's, terminology. They are deliberately timeless and non-specific. They address nostalgia, beauty, and early and violent death, in a way which allows any generation to read into it their own experiences.

As with those writers who claimed to write of war on behalf of their contemporaries, such as Vera Brittain and Wilfred Owen, Housman's poems speak for a generation, but years before that generation knew what it was it wanted to say. No wonder that it was to these 'containers', these moulds for war poetry, that composers turned during and after the war, to pour out and shape their war experiences. Butterworth's Housman settings pre-empted the conflict that would kill him, but they can still be re-defined in light of the war as musical war poems, exploring ideas of loss, anticipating a cultural crisis, and grieving for an era that had not yet quite ended.

And what of those who did return, and were faced with the awesome responsibility, or desperate emotional need, to speak through their music of what they had witnessed? In the post-war work of the surviving combatant composers – Gurney, Arthur Bliss, Vaughan Williams – we find a highly significant parallel to the poets and writers of the war. Gurney returned to England after fifteen months at the front, having been wounded and gassed. He had written nearly two collections of war poems, and composed five new songs, some written within reach of the front line.

Gurney's five songs written whilst in the army are war songs both in terms of where they were written, and with regard to their subject matter. Their texts, apart from one, are not his own words, but their relevance is obvious. What does it mean to die? Is it in fact a grand and noble thing? What is his relationship to his beloved countryside that he is fighting for, and has had to leave behind? They are all preoccupations which he explores in his own poetry, and, in practically the same breath, in his music, using texts by John Masefield, Walter Raleigh, F.W. Harvey and the much favoured Housman to mull over these questions. He also set his own poem, *Severn Meadows*, to which further reference will be made.

By 1919, Gurney was able to continue his musical explorations of the glory of death, in the cold light of the disappointments of peacetime survival. It was to Housman that he turned again for the stimulus. However popular Housman appears to have been at this time, his romanticised celebrations of premature death must surely have had a peculiar resonance for Gurney. He loved Housman's work, but it was perhaps a combination of reverence and anger at its sentiment that drew him to set Housman's words; to take them to task, to embrace and to attack them, as he does so powerfully in his post-war song cycle for tenor and piano quartet, *Ludlow and Teme*.

Literary critic Alex Aronson sees writers such as Forster, Virginia Woolf and Thomas Mann all turning to music as something 'embodying a primordial vision of human life expressed through rhythm or melody, pitch or volume, concord or discord. In their search for a faithful representation of the inwardness of experience, be it through individual consciousness or through the awareness of social identity', they discover 'in music a metaphor of harmonious coexistence'.[3] The idea of music as a representative model of coherence and harmony has become something of a cultural cliché, and there are many interesting examples of writers subverting it. Literary responses to the war are concerned in many ways with new methods of showing meaning, and of representing coherence and exploring incoherence.

The writer Ford Madox Ford created an ambiguous but powerful image when he described the First World War as a 'crack in the table of history'. If we were to take this to be true, then how would a search for harmonious coexistence work for poets drawn to music for a very particular range of expression, or indeed for composers drawn to poetry? How might music, apparently a model of coherence, be harnessed to literature to explore the dysfunctional and incoherent? Gurney, as a poet himself, is ideally placed to subvert such an expectation of coherence in subtle and nuanced ways. Where better to look for the dysfunctional than Gurney's 1919 song cycle, *Ludlow and Teme*; a post-war interpretation of Housman's 'lads who will die in their glory', composed by a suicidal ex-combatant?

Gurney's music and poetry probe Ford's 'crack in the table of history', this sense that both the harmoniously coexisting and the dysfunctional can be explored in the dialogue between music and poetry. *Ludlow and Teme* plays out the psychological drama between text and music. It dramatises Ford's claim, through the struggle enacted between Housman's words, metaphorically on one side of the table's crack, and Gurney's music on the other. Gurney strives to find the musical reconciliation that he himself so fervently desired in life – between beauty and the abject, and between decay and new life.

Gurney was aware of Butterworth's pre-war Housman settings, and the gulf, the crack, between their two interpretations of the same text is one that reflects the four-year tragedy that took place between their compositions. Butterworth's 1911 *Lads in their 100's*, is a lilting, whimsical version in a major key, entirely in keeping with Housman's pastoral nostalgia. Butterworth sets the text to a folksong-inspired melody, with delicate, unobtrusive accompaniment. He does not dwell on the possible implications of lines such as *the lads that will die in their glory and never be old*, but incorporates them seamlessly into his fluid melodic line. The gulf between Housman's lads who 'never return' and Gurney and his comrades' ignominious return – often, as was to be Gurney's own experience, to unemployment or to become a burden on those around them – colours Gurney's post-war interpretation of Housman's texts. How could a romantic notion of glorious sacrifice and uncomplicated devotion to England really be sustained in the light of the war and its inglorious aftermath?

Gurney wrote the cycle when he was angry, bitter and disillusioned, but still living in hope of taking his place in the musical and literary worlds after delaying his career whilst stuck in the army. He revised the cycle in 1925, making some crucial changes. By then, he had been certified insane, labelled suicidal and locked in an asylum for three years.

Forgotten and isolated, he despaired of his place in the history of music. As he put it in his letters appealing to his friends to release him: 'after the war, what hopes there were for music – but, now, well – it is no use thinking.' But he did continue to think, and to continue to write music, as well as make revisions such as those to the manuscript of *Ludlow and Teme*, which enhanced his work.

The 1919 version of *The Lads in their Hundreds* underpins the top G of 'glory' with an accented, hammering figure in the accompaniment, and high-pitched, ff scream in the quartet. When he came back to this crucial moment from the asylum in 1925, he wrote even more anger and even more emphasis into the setting of *the lads that will die in their glory*. He replaced the scream with a figure of continuing momentum in the strings, impelling the voice on to a second attempt to make the hollow claim of glory convincing, rising to a more emphatic A flat.

At the very point of claiming glory for *the lads that will die*, the accompaniment quite literally screeches to a halt and stops its own incessant march. It gives the listener the time to consider the message of the last line, *and never be old*, but not just invited to consider it, but to be grabbed by the lapels and shouted at by the tenor. Here, the implications of not growing old are so hideous that Gurney insists that it is given full consideration, and having considered, might the 'glory' being claimed for these deaths be reinterpreted; glory, as a sentiment, already ringing hollow in the hysterical accompaniment.

The brief instrumental postlude is back in tempo. The implication is that the march to the front can only be halted in fantasy, and there is in reality no time for contemplation of what it might mean in personal cost. The final figure of two semi-quavers and a quaver with which the strings so abruptly end the song recalls the stutter of machine-gun fire, with which Gurney, as a machine-gunner, was intimately familiar. Death and the unstoppable destruction of war have the final word. *Ludlow and Teme* is war poetry in sound – delayed, written in the aftermath of the war, but musical war poetry nonetheless.

In the same year in which *Ludlow and Teme* was written, 1919, Siegfried Sassoon was exploring his relationship to his traumatic memories of the war through thinking about music. Just as Gurney was torn between embracing and attacking Housman, so Sassoon cannot stop torturing himself with the ragtime music that had come to be the soundtrack to his wartime army friendships. He finds a form of solace in returning to the music hall tunes, but in the silence that must follow as the record ends, the absence of the dead is unbearable. For Sassoon, the consonance that music, high-brow or otherwise, could offer, simply served to highlight the 'gap in the table of history'.

Sassoon's poem, *Dead Musicians*, made the point clearly:

> From you, Beethoven, Bach, Mozart,
> The substance of my dreams took fire.
> You built cathedrals in my heart,
> And lit my pinnacled desire.
> You were the ardour and the bright
> Procession of my thoughts toward prayer.
> You were the wrath of storm, the light
> On distant citadels aflare.
>
> Great names, I cannot find you now
> In these loud years of youth that strives
> Through doom toward peace: upon my brow
> I wear a wreath of banished lives.
> You have no part with lads who fought
> And laughed and suffered at my side.
> Your fugues and symphonies have brought
> No memory of my friends who died.
>
> For when my brain is on their track,
> In slangy speech I call them back.
> With fox-trot tunes their ghosts I charm.
> 'Another little drink won't do us any harm.'
> I think of rag-time; a bit of rag-time;
> And see their faces crowding round
> To the sound of the syncopated beat.
> They've got such jolly things to tell,
> Home from hell with a Blighty wound so neat . . .
> And so the song breaks off; and I'm alone.
> They're dead . . . For God's sake stop that gramophone.

In the light of the war, Sassoon re-evaluates music through poetry, just as Gurney re-evaluates poetry through music. In *Ludlow and Teme*, Gurney plays both with music and with silence to develop and to disrupt the narrative of the poems. In *Dead Musicians*, Sassoon used the evocation of music and of its absence – the silence after 'gramophone', both to attempt to breach the gulf between the dead and the living, and to show how unbreachable it really is.

As author and professor of literature Samuel Hynes has observed, there was a ten-year gap between the return of the war poets and the publication of their larger-scale testimonies based on their war experience. A certain amount of time needed to pass before their experiences could be sublimated, and they could replace the immediacy of their trench poetry with some degree of perspective and objectivity. In literature, there was a testimony-boom from 1928 to 1933: this period including Vera Brittain's *Testament of Youth*, Robert Graves' *Goodbye To All That*, Erich Maria Remarque's *All Quiet on the Western Front*, Sassoon's *Memoirs of an Infantry Officer* and Blunden's *Undertones of War*, to name but a few. This phenomenon has often been noted, but few if any connections have been made between this pattern and the similar pattern that emerges in music.

Frank Bridge's work fits the same model as we see emerging in the 1920s for literature. War composers were not limited to those who had first-hand experience of combat, and although Bridge was a non-combatant, he wrote explicitly in response to the war. As with the war poets, he too had used his compositions to respond to the events of the war as they developed, with a *Lament* in 1915 and his piano sonata in the years immediately after the war, but it was *Oration*, monumental in the proper sense of the word, that represented his greatest achievement, written, like so many of the literary testimonies, in 1930.

Arthur Bliss's 1930 piece, *Morning Heroes*, a choral symphony on war, is particularly interesting as a work of literary war music. His brother, Kennard, was killed on the Somme, and Arthur was wounded in the same battle. After the Armistice, Bliss repeatedly dreamt that he was fighting on forever in a forgotten sector of the front, unaware that the war was over. During the 1920s he tried again and again to write a piece that would honour his brother's memory whilst exorcising his own trauma but works such as his *Battle Variations* were abandoned.

Vera Brittain, in parallel, tried unsuccessfully to write her war diaries into fiction and then non-fiction for much of the 1920s, to lay her own war ghosts to rest. Both Brittain and Bliss had to wait until a decade after the end of the conflict to find the epic formats that would at last achieve their sublimation of war experience. Bliss finally hit upon the idea for *Morning Heroes* in a moment of inspiration at Kennard's graveside in France, and wrote the work for choir, narrator and orchestra in 1930. It draws on war poetry for its voice – pulling together poets of wars from the Ancient Greek to the contemporary to shape a musical argument about heroism and about death on the battlefield. Brittain wrote of her deeply personal experience of loss in order to use her story to speak for, and to represent, the losses sustained by so many women. Bliss draws on the same combination of individual loss and universality in *Morning Heroes*, making it at once his own story of loss on the Somme battlefield (the final poem he sets is Robert Nichols's *Dawn on the Somme*), and by drawing on war poetry since the Greeks, providing a work that has the capacity to contain the grief and personal stories of any listener. *Testament of Youth*, *Morning Heroes* and Frank Bridge's wordless *Oration* are all 'containers' in a sense, to return to Wilfred Bion's term. They are cenotaphs, empty tombs, which can contain in imagination the bodies of any lost son, brother or lover.

Both Bridge and Bliss's works had a lasting effect on the course of future musical treatments of the war. It was Bridge's teaching, both politically and musically, along with the example of Bliss' *Morning Heroes*, which would sow the seeds for Bridge's only pupil, Benjamin Britten, to write his justifiably celebrated *War Requiem* in 1962. It was written in the light of another war, but Britten acknowledged his debt both to Bliss and Bridge. In *Morning Heroes*, Bliss had been the first composer to set Wilfred Owen, and by choosing Owen's poetry again for his own requiem, Britten placed his work firmly within the tradition of First World War musical memorials.

As critic Stephen Benson pointed out, 'the hermeneutic traffic in musico-literary studies tends to flow in one direction: from literature to music'.[4] In other words, when there is writing about literature that engages with music, the famous Beethoven in Forster's *Howard's End* for instance, one wants to have Forster giving a reading, a critique, an account of the music. However, if one were to look at a piece of music as an act of critical interpretation of a text, there is a tendency to limit oneself to a programmatic reading, seeing the music as an embellishment, a response perhaps, to the text, but not a critical reading of it. By extension, historical events are read through their literature, even through their representation in art, but there are few examples – Shostakovich or perhaps Sibelius excepted – where history is seriously read through its music. Obviously there are well-rehearsed reasons for this. Abstract music is harder to pin down; music is simultaneously 'the most direct and esoteric of the arts'.[5] But how might we re-assess composers who engage with text: Butterworth's 'readings' of Housman for example, or Gurney's songs, in which both notes and words are approached with the same critical framework, and the same intentions? It does seem convincing that the First World War, the crisis that it was and that it caused in the decades after it in every way – political, social and most important here, cultural – is an ideal point of departure from an outmoded perspective. A new way of thinking about the interdisciplinary nature of war music would be timely, one which stretches across the artificial academic boundaries between musicology and literary studies.

To conclude, it would be appropriate to offer some thoughts about Gurney's song *Severn Meadows*; an incontestable example of musical war poetry, or poetical war music. Written at the front, it is a rare instance of Gurney interpreting his own words – setting a poem he had written only a couple of weeks earlier. However, being Gurney, it is not what one might expect. It challenges our often narrow perceptions of what a war poem might look like as it is not concerned with mud and slaughter. It is far more interested in what matters, where wisdom, joy and beauty lie, and what might happen to those who dwell in shadows, but speak the truth.

Gurney is perhaps uniquely placed to explore the connections between his own words and his music, but he is only one of many poets like Sassoon, and Ezra Pound, who were interested in exploring the points of contact between music and poetry in the light of the conflict. Pound used music to suggest that 'poetry is not merely technique, but rather that it can and should be part of an almost mystical reconciliation of spatial and temporal dimensions'.[6] If we were to take his assertion as a starting point – that poetry should be a 'mystical reconciliation of spatial and temporal dimensions', then a song such as Gurney's *Severn Meadows* might be an example of such an achievement. It is a synthesis of words and music, with music that is so expansive that it slows the heartbeat and the breath and transforms any rhythmic drive within the poem itself into something almost trance-like. In its journey from poem to song, *Severn Meadows* becomes a work that exists in space as much as it does in time, transcending any sense that the differing metres of poem and song are in any way in conflict.

Only the wanderer knows England's graces, or can anew see clear familiar faces.
And who loves joy as he who dwells in shadows? Do not forget me quite – O Severn Meadows.

The poem makes the most humble of claims, 'do not forget me quite', but might perhaps represent something quite the opposite of humility – an indication of the riches we might reap when we engage with a broader reading of war poetry and war music together; two genres that intersect and enhance each other.

Notes

1. Mansfield to John Middleton Murray, 10 November 1919, Vincent O' Sullivan and Margaret Scott (eds), *The Collected Letters of Katherine Mansfield 1919-1920* Vol. 8 (Clarendon Press, 1993), p. 82.
2. See Tim Kendall, *Modern English War Poetry* (OUP, 2006), Introduction.
3. Alex Aaronson, *Music and the Novel: A Study in Twentieth Century Fiction* (Rowman and Littlefield, 1980), p. 32.
4. Stephen Benson, *Literary Music: Writing music in contemporary fiction* (Ashgate, 2006), p. 13.
5. Ibid., p. 1.
6. Brad Bucknell, *Literary Modernism and Musical Aesthetics* (CUP, 2001), p. 7.

Suggested Further Reading

Banfield, Stephen, *Sensibility and English Song* (CUP, 1989)

Cooksey, Jon, and McKechnie, Peter (eds), *Kelly's War: The Great War Diary of Septimus Kelly* (Blink Publishing, 2015)

Hart, Peter, *Gallipoli* (Profile Books, 2011)

Hurd, Michael, *The Ordeal of Ivor Gurney* (OUP, 1979)

Robertson, Alec, *Requiem: Music of Mourning and Consolation* (Praeger, 1968)

Sellers, Leonard, *The Hood Battalion* (Leo Cooper, 1995)

Sheffield, Gary, *The Somme* (Cassell, 2004)

Spicer, Paul, *Herbert Howells* (Border Lines, 1998)

Thornton, R.K.R. (ed.), *Ivor Gurney: Collected Letters* (MidNag Press, 1991)

Chapter 18

Loss and Devastation: The Costs of the Great War

By Nick Bosanquet

Universal, conscript military service with its twin brother universal suffrage has mastered all continental Europe with what promises of massacres and bankruptcy for the twentieth century. (Taine 1891)[1]

In 400 BC, Sun Tzu wrote that: 'There has never been a state that has benefited from an extended war.'[2] Kitchener had described the Western Front as an extended siege and as Sun-Tzu predicted: 'If you lay siege to a walled city you exhaust your strength.' What then was the nature and what was the extent of the loss suffered by Britain as a result of the Great War?

The casualty loss can be specified in all its grim detail but we should also recognize the achievements of those who worked, and worked successfully, to limit them. The author of one of the best municipal histories, that of Leeds, wrote of the: 'unparalleled endurance of pain and suffering shown by both sides and all classes' but also of the 'wonderful power of organization and initiative shown by our own country' in this regard.[3] The war might otherwise have made a still more grievous impact upon Britain with far more deaths.

The French historian, Jacques Becker, summarised data often quoted since: 'Thus out of 1,000 inhabitants France mobilised 168 and lost 34: the UK mobilised 135 and lost 16; Germany mobilised 154 and lost 30. In other words France was the most severely affected, followed closely by Germany.'[4]

What were the key factors which reduced the UK losses below those of other combatants?

1. The British war machine was in due course able to develop weapons for a more mobile army with greater air support and firepower. This together with some similar weapons development for the French army, shortened the war by making the Hundred Days offensive possible in 1918. As late as September 1918, it was widely believed that the war would last well into 1919 and plans were being developed for this. The American potential was indeed an important factor in the background but the actual week-by-week pressure upon the German Army in France was primarily exerted by the British and Commonwealth troops from

August 1918. If the BEF were not to have maintained almost constant aggression from 8 August, the Germans would have had time to prepare new defence lines and to exploit resources in the territory captured in the March offensive.

2. British Army health services were remarkably efficient both in the prevention of the onset of disease or ill-health and in the treatment of war wounds. On the Western Front 3.5 million non-battle casualties, as well as 2.69 million battle casualties, received treatment. The services prevented epidemics through rigorous sanitation and even in 1918 there were relatively few deaths from the Spanish 'flu epidemic.

3. At home there were food shortages but rationing introduced in 1918 was timely and generally regarded as fair. Living standards of many adults and children have been assessed as actually improving from 1915, a very different situation from that found in Germany.[5]

However, these achievements in minimizing losses and securing an earlier end to the war have had little impact on public opinion. The inescapable nature of the war determined the heavy price which inexorably would be paid but somehow even today this is still not generally accepted. There was awareness of the achievements during 1918, but the perception faded. Instead it was the horror of the casualties which governed public response to the war. A more balanced perception might have increased national self-confidence in facing post-war challenges and not least a more realistic response to the threat from totalitarian regimes.

There were something over 700,000 deaths from the British Isles in the four and a half years of the war. Apart from the French Revolutionary and Napoleonic conflicts, previous wars had been fought far from home and by 'professionals' who had little contact with the home population. There had been no home leave for British soldiers in the Peninsular War against Napoleon. Some 300,000 were killed over a longer period in the French wars of this period, with a much higher proportion of nearly one-third, 90,000, of these losses from the navy.[6] There was little public mourning. The soldiers who died were buried in mass unmarked graves. Many of the deaths were due to disease rather than to military action. There were no war memorials, only triumphal arches and statues of Wellington. In fact, the loss in the Napoleonic Wars was at least as high a proportion of the smaller adult male population as the loss in the First World War, but in an age which had only just embarked upon the concept of Census in 1801, this did not seem to have made major public impact.

Attitudes after the Napoleonic Wars in part reflected the social standing of the army, as such. The men in the ranks were recruited from distant parts of the realm in Scotland and Ireland and from those unemployed or 'on the run' in England. From ports, the merchant navy and from fishermen, the press gangs delivered the Royal Navy its essential 'recruits'. But the public's attitude towards the army and the navy was also influenced by victory in the French wars. The Napoleonic Wars opened a hundred-year period of national security and the cost seemed worth the price.

There was some re-assessment during the Crimean War with Florence Nightingale in particular drawing attention to conditions which the troops had to endure but there were still no marked graves for men in the ranks, nor indeed for officers. However, there was some sense of public gratitude. For the first time a medal was introduced for gallantry, the Victoria Cross. It was open to all ranks. The first local memorials appeared to all from that designated district who had served in the Crimea. Later, the wars in South Africa were commemorated with many memorials in the UK and there were graves for some in South Africa.

The First World War brought what might well be called a transformation in the whole subject of war awareness, recognition of debt to the armed forces and commemoration of those lost in the endeavour. This was one of the many surprises in this new, near, great and terrible war. Many of the deaths were close to home, in France and Belgium; the reporting was immediate and personal. Furthermore, the war made its distinctive impact by its sheer scale on so many indices. The distance of the far-flung fronts; the nearness of the front across the Channel, the latter made the more so not just by the newspapers but by soldiers on leave. Then the German naval shelling of British coastal towns, and the Zeppelin and Gotha aircraft raid, brought to the home population a compelling sense of unity with the soldiers and sailors: everyone in the nation was at war with the nation's enemy.

The affronting presence of the Germans deep in Belgium and France demanded an aggressive response which was made possible by excellent logistical support facilitating more offensive operations than in any of Britain's previous wars in Europe where there had been long lulls and much manoeuvring between battles. The colossal expansion of the army, realistically called for and presided over by Kitchener, had of course the effect of making families all too conscious of the disappearance of the long-held truism that our wars were fought by 'others for us'. Through so many letterboxes this changed circumstance was tragically brought home.

Eight million men were by voluntary or compulsory enlistment inducted into the armed forces with several million more working on munitions and other war employment. War front casualties were concentrated in terms of age groups. Research in the 1970s showed that 16.2 per cent of men in the Services aged 20–24 and 9.9 per cent of those aged 25–29 were killed.[7] In terms of date and location, these casualties were concentrated at times of major offensives and in certain areas which had recruited heavily into 'Pals' battalions. All this concentration meant that the shock effect on the home front was the greater. The dread telegrams might be arriving at many houses in the same district in the same weeks. There has been much written about 'Pals' battalions in England but there were also very large numbers of casualties in Scotland where the initial enlistment rates had been much higher and because of the high proportion of Scots in front-line infantry units.

There was one more concentration factor which further raised the sense of loss. This was the very heavy casualty rate among young officers and young people from wealthy backgrounds.[8] The theme of the lost generation, the mowing-down of Edwardian youth and promise, was one that was current quite early in the war.

For perhaps the first time since the Wars of the Roses, certainly since the Civil War, the sons of the rulers were falling on the battlefield – just for example, Asquith losing one son and Bonar Law two. The poetry of Rupert Brooke was a poignant elegy for this lost generation. Forty years on, the theme of the missing leaders was still there in the ruminations of survivors such as Harold Macmillan and Hugh Dalton.

However, for the English, there were also some factors worth noting. Within the British Isles, the English and Irish had the lowest casualty rates. Of the 700,000-plus

Service personnel deaths from the United Kingdom, at least 100,000 were from Scotland and Wales, and Ireland lost 4 per cent of its male population compared to 12 per cent for Scotland. The number from England, approximately 600,000 killed, was less than half the number of French deaths at 1.4 million from a smaller population. We must remember the far greater 'soldier' burden borne by France until mid-1916 but also note that British deaths were reduced by excellent medical services.[9] At least 100,000 of the French deaths were from the higher death rate among the wounded and from non-battle casualties. Another factor to be borne in mind was that Great Britain benefited enormously both in military effectiveness and in the sharing of loss from the support given by the Imperial Forces from the Dominions, India and the Empire.

Concerning the hugely important matter of the health of British expeditionary forces, a war was also being waged against an 'invisible enemy', the microbe, which can cause a range of fearsome diseases, and a very small one, the mosquito. Sanitation and prevention were key areas of defence.[10] The Macedonian front was where the battle against the anopheles mosquito had to be fought. Malaria became a serious issue here but ultimately was in the main overcome. With regard to dysentery, there were sanitation sections which had permanent postings in divisional areas and this helped reduce cases to low levels apart from the exceptional circumstances of the Gallipoli Peninsula. Inoculation largely eliminated typhoid, and methods of prevention, after a bad first year, were effective in reducing the new problem of trench foot.

Rapid access to medical treatment, first in the daily sick parades by the battalion medical officers, and then in hospitals, returned most of the 3.5 million non-battle casualties on the Western Front to active duty. It should be borne in mind that a considerable number of men could be rendered ineffective by the simple ailments of everyday life, such as diseases of the respiratory and digestive systems, rheumatic fever and its allied conditions, local and general injuries, skin diseases, minor septic infections and influenza. Royal Army Medical Corps (RAMC) doctors had these matters with which to deal as well as the new problems of prolonged siege warfare – soldier's heart, trench nephritis, trench fever and shell shock.

In dealing with battle casualties, the RAMC became the most effective of all the equivalent units serving the nations engaged in the war. Particularly distinctive was the early surgery carried out in Casualty Clearing Stations, sometimes quite close to the front lines, and then the later rehabilitation in special centres. Eighty per cent of British battle casualties returned to duty. The remarkable RAMC achievement is reaffirmed by the low numbers of deaths in the 1918 'flu epidemic – 1,000 out of 2.5 million men on the Western Front. Rapid access to hospital and complete rest were the keys to preventing progression of the 'flu to pneumonia.

The large investment in medical services with at least 200,000 personnel in the RAMC and field hospital provision, from stretcher bearers at the front to those working in rehabilitation units, made a great contribution to the war effort and reduced the 'human cost' of the war.

Another sign of the medical success was that the number of deaths from non-battle factors was 43,000 for the whole war, fewer than the 50,000 Americans in the AEF who died from disease. The American losses were considerably increased by Pershing's decisions on the location of his men – as far away from the British as possible – so the American troops were unable to use the British support services. The pride of the

RAMC in their work was quite properly reflected in the Official History of the Medical Services in the war.

Not to be neglected in any tabulation of British success in the war was the actual financing of it in ways which did not reduce living standards, albeit that this was considerably as a result of benevolent US neutrality. Costs for all war activities – on land, sea, including merchant shipping, and in the air, rose from £5.7 million a day in 1916 to £7.4 million a day from April through to November 1918. Specifically for defence activities, the increase over the war is shown by these annual figures:

1913 £91.3 million
1915. £716.6 million
1917. £1123.0 million
1918. £1,955.8 million[11]

Total expenditure during the war was £10.8 billion or five times GDP in 1914. About a third of this was financed by taxation, mainly increased income tax which rose steeply for those with high incomes. The remainder of what was needed was raised by borrowing, much of it through War Loans. The public response to War Loans and then to Tank Banks remained strong throughout the war. The National Debt rose from £707 million to £7.4 billion. Prices were to double but rationing and price controls on key foodstuffs helped to equalize the burden.

The Ministry of Munitions ran a highly-efficient procurement system based on comparison between costs in government-owned factories and private factories and it also showed how to use purchasing power flexibly to order the manufacture of new weapons and new aircraft. The increases in spending produced good value, despite the many complaints. The munitions price index actually rose more slowly than the consumer price index, and the nation got 22,000 aircraft and 1,000 tanks. Britain's was the most effective procurement system of any of the combatants because it was the most flexible.

In the short term the funding system worked well. The problems came after the war through the threat of default on higher interest payments for the new debt deflation increased the real debt burden.[12] There was also a renewal of the conflict between social spending and spending on defence as well as new challenges on taxation policy. After the war the level of government spending at around 20 per cent of GNP was double what it had been before 1914. The war had destroyed Gladstone's financial legacy and produced an entirely different view of taxable capacity.

The deep acceptance of the war by the vast majority of the population was still there in 1918, transformed of course from the early war enthusiasm to steely resolve. This was clear in ceremonies towards the end of the war notably the special event of national re-dedication called for by the King for the first Sunday in January 1918:

To My People.

The Worldwide Struggle for the triumph of right and liberty is entering upon its last and most difficult phase, the enemy is striving by desperate assault and subtle intrigue to perpetuate the wrongs already committed and stem the tide of a free civilisation. We have yet to complete the great task to which more than three years ago, we dedicated ourselves.

> At such a time I would call upon you to devote a special day to prayer that we may have the clear sightedness and strength necessary to the victory of our cause.[13]

Services were held across the Empire from the summer day in Auckland to the fog of Leeds and the winter of Vancouver. According to the history of Leeds in the Great War:

> In Leeds on the first Sunday afternoon in January, there was a most moving and memorable service held in the Town Hall where a representative gathering occupied every seat and yard of standing room, and even overflowed on to the steps of Victoria Square. The Lord Mayor (Mr Frank Gott) read the King's Proclamation and the vast concourse of people joined in the singing of the National Anthem. The organ boomed forth the solemn tones of the Dead March; the Last Post was sounded; and with thrilling effect the congregation hymned their intercessions for Divine protection for the sailors, soldiers, sick and wounded and anxious ones at Home.[14]

The erection or placement of Street Shrines was a local movement which started early in the war. These were a low-cost commemoration with wooden panels bearing the names of local men killed, the panels fixed to walls. Few survive today but they were an important focus for grief at the time and their widespread presence demonstrated the strength of regional commitment to the national war effort.

After the war the sense of loss impelled a wave of events of commemoration and the design, erection and dedication of memorials which represented collective memory.[15] The Cenotaph was finished in nine weeks by mid-1919 and on its completion, more than a million people came to see it in the first week. By that same mid-year, more than 4,000 memorials were planned or under construction. The burial of the Unknown Warrior in Westminster Abbey on 11 November 1920 brought crowds of over a million to central London. For this war, it was an unknown front-line combatant who came first rather than the statues of the commanders.

The sense of loss remained and influenced many decisions personal and national. Perhaps the most distinctive feature of the post-war period was that the sense of loss did not fade with time – what did fade quickly was the recognition of the achievement both by the armed forces and by civilians working in war industries. A factor which made for this continuing sense of loss was the large number of wounded survivors with disabilities. The war was certainly the first in which 90 per cent of the wounded survived, but 1.5 million of the survivors were claiming disability pensions. Sadly, large numbers of the disabled, and many more not so classified, were in poor health as a result of their war service.[16]

Though gas poisoning had not caused huge numbers of fatalities during the war, contamination led to respiratory damage among those affected with a consequence of many premature deaths. There were also lingering effects on the ability to function 'normally' in neurologically-damaged men, men who were 'never the same again'. For some, the war brought a disorientation which led to an inability to settle down. The high and often visible level of disability contributed to the sense of loss hanging in the atmosphere for the 1920s and 1930s.

As well as a sense of loss, there was also a new element – one of anger. Immediately after the war the Armistice was seen as a victory, but, notably stimulated by Churchill's account in *The World Crisis*, there was growing criticism of generalship on the Western Front. Churchill's account of 1917, however much it may now be discredited, includes a paragraph which must be one of the most powerful passages he ever wrote. At the time, and until recently, it was quite remarkably influential:

> Mr Lloyd George viewed with horror the task imposed on him of driving to the shambles by stern laws the remaining manhood of the nation. Lads of eighteen or nineteen, elderly men up to forty-five, the last surviving brother, the only son of his mother (and she a widow), the father, the sole support of the family, the weak, the consumptive, the thrice wounded—all must now prepare themselves for the scythe.[17]

The theme of unending casualties ground down in the mud by military bungling began in the 1920s but became much more powerful with Liddell Hart's book, *The Real War*, published in 1930, and Lloyd George's *War Memoirs*, published in 1935 but well promoted earlier.[18] The theme of loss became that of *unnecessary* loss brought about by incompetent leadership. Such emotional judgement had a significant influence upon political debate and upon public opinion concerning the way Britain should respond to the threat of another war. It is certainly ironic that the period of Appeasement is one generally viewed, until recently, with shame and yet it was giving a majority section of public opinion exactly what it wanted. From a safe distance we may perhaps judge, with the blessing of hindsight, that that majority had drawn a temptingly attractive but wrong lesson from the Great War.

In Britain there was also little recognition of just how much Europe had been affected by civilian losses. Britain's home front deaths from naval shelling and airship and aeroplane bombing totalled 1,207 compared with the thousands who had died in France both as a result of war action and of hardship in occupied areas. The most detailed study across Europe of the human costs of war was carried out by a senior official of the American Red Cross and was published in 1920.[19] It covered most of Europe but not Great Britain. Homer Folks, the wartime administrator of aid to refugees in France – some 1.5 million people displaced by the six German offensives of 1918 – was assigned to review the need for aid across Europe. Folks saw his job as 'essentially that of estimating, in such parts of Europe as could be reached, the net results of the war upon human welfare'. His role was to give some actual information on the losses from four years in which normal economic activity and social improvement had been suspended and replaced in many areas with the destruction of buildings and any vestige of pre-war local support.

> Everyone knew vaguely that the able bodied men of these countries had been at war for several years: that their usual work of getting food, clothing and shelter for their families must have been done in a makeshift way or left undone; that widowhood and fatherlessness had been spread broadcast; that millions of men had been made cripples; that millions of people had been driven from their homes and that these homes had been destroyed; that other millions had lived under the rule of the armies of their enemies; that many thousands had been forcibly deported to labour as slaves; that fatigue, underfeeding, indecent overcrowding and exposure to cold, rain and snow had been general; that prices had been fantastically high, many supplies unobtainable and transportation had broken down.[20]

The job of the enquiry led by Folks was to collect evidence on these effects. The nation studies covered Serbia, France and Italy. Serbia was a 'paralyzed' country. A description of the activities of the enquiry is essentially one of a succession of negatives. There was no source of food apart from American aid and almost no men between 18 and 50 and no children under the age of 3. To travel from Skopje to Belgrade was to follow 'a trail of destruction for three hundred miles with refugees in rags travelling southwards'. There was a doubling of the death rate from TB in Belgrade. The pre-war infant mortality of 146 per 1,000 became raised as did the death rate of children under 5. There was a serious typhus epidemic in 1915, with a high chance of a recurrence. Mortality from influenza in 1918 was estimated to be 50 per cent greater than found in the United States.

As has been stressed, France was the country which had the greatest losses. 'No previous losses which she has ever suffered can compare for a moment with the loss of her men in the Great War and the tremendous decline in her birth rate.'[21] The population had been reduced by 1.5 million. In addition there was the issue of the huge numbers of wounded – four million – many with serious disabilities. In effect, the adult male working population was reduced by 20 per cent.

> The evidence of France's supreme sacrifice are the millions of fatherless families and childless homes. In addition there were the losses by refugees driven from their homes. There were no homes for them to go to, no schools to accommodate all these additional children, no doctors to look after the sick, no extra supplies of food to meet these unusual demands.

The German offensives from the spring of 1918 brought another half a million refugees. They received support from the American Red Cross. The refugees in France now numbered some two million and they faced the hard winter of 1918/19 with soaring prices and food shortages. When they reached their homes, they were to find that most had been destroyed. The German withdrawal of early 1917 had entailed the destruction not just of buildings and industrial structures with any military or economic value but also that of churches and even the cutting-down of fruit trees. The social capital of centuries had been razed. In occupied cities there had been less destruction of property but there was a rising mortality rate as a result of shortages of food and fuel. There was also the distress in occupied France of the four years of separation from relatives on the other side of the line with no mail or even the possibility of sending urgent messages through the Red Cross.

The documentation of circumstances in Italy was similarly harrowing as Italy had suffered grievously too. Her military deaths have been estimated at well over 600,000, a figure which would include the 50,000 deaths among the 500,000 prisoners of war and the 100,000 deaths from disease. The birth rate in Italy had been high and it is likely that the war led to at least half a million fatherless children. Folk's estimates of the total losses were as follows:

Civilian deaths 1915–18, in excess of pre-war, 310,000
Deaths from influenza 1918, 540,000
Death of soldiers in action, 462,000
Deaths in excess of normal rate among prisoners of war, 50,000

Deaths in excess of the normal rate among civilians in occupied areas, 80,000
Total Deficit in births, 1,435,000
Total deaths, 2,877,000.[22]

How did the costs within Great Britain compare with 'material' losses in the rest of Europe? In the immediate term there was nothing like such loss as was suffered by the countries listed. In social capital and living standards there was simply no comparison.[23] There was a loss in the 'progress dividend' which had been there before the war. There was no further advance in the standard but there was some equalisation. Many families had in fact benefitted in the sense that there had been full employment and from the separation allowances which were paid to families of men who enlisted. Infant mortality had fallen during the war, even in the last two years. However, the elderly, that was the 4 per cent of the population over 65, were losers unless they were fit enough to work. The pension remained at 5 shillings a week even though prices were to double. Also losers in the war were the well-off, affected by the fall in bond and share prices and in the value of land.[24]

In effect the war led to betterment in the standard of living for poorer people. Overall, between 1911 and 1921, life expectancy at birth for men rose from 49 to 56 years and for women from 53 to 60 years. These increases were substantially greater than the gains registered in either the first or the third decade of the twentieth century. Infant mortality fell by 15 per cent, with declines of 25 per cent in poorer areas.[25] Standards of living were not only maintained but rose during the war and most notably for families in poverty. Wages rose fastest for less-skilled workers. In Germany after 1915, there was a very serious decline in living standards and a rise in the mortality rate. Again however, in Britain, there was to be little recognition after 1918 of the success of protecting living standards especially for the groups which had been in poverty before the war.

There were not just these changes but much locational movement. The munitions industry pulled many people from smaller centres into the cities: London, Birmingham, Leeds and Glasgow all expanded,[26] and hence there was considerable pressure there on the provision of sufficient housing. However, two points must be made on this matter; first that many of the movers were earning higher wages in munitions than in their previous occupations, and second, that housing often took the form of dormitories rather than of individual homes.

An interesting point is that there were significant gains in well-being from the reduced consumption of alcohol during the war. National consumption in a year went down from 31 million gallons to 15 million gallons, and it might be added that the beer was weaker too. Concerning food, much has been made of shortages of imported foodstuffs, like sugar for example, supplies cut by U-Boat sinkings, but even with rationing at the end of the war, the food available was enough to maintain activity and health.

The post-war period began with an additional new perspective on loss; not the loss from the war but the loss from the effects of industrial society on health. The Ministry of National Insurance issued a report on the health of 2.2 million men who had been examined medically for conscription. The data in the report, published in 1920, was known and discussed by senior ministers earlier than its date of publication.[27] It made grim reading, with only 30 per cent of the males between 18 and 45 being rated A in terms of their health. The findings in industrial areas were, to quote as an example the results for Manchester and Stockport, that 'the average man here is, for military purposes, an old man before he reaches the age of 40'. This was a 'physical census of a scale unprecedented in history'. The results had the curious effect of presenting the British Army in a more favourable light as 18-year-old conscripts, after six months of training with a good diet, were greatly improved in health and fitness.

There is little evidence about the longer-term effects of the war on children but there may be some pointers from the later evidence about the effects of the Great Depression on children in the United States.[28] This showed that the most negative effects were on very young children, especially on young boys from infancy to 6 years old. However, the fall in infant mortality does not point to similar effects on this age group from the wartime experience.

This West Coast of the United States study of older children and teenagers in the Great Depression is perhaps still relevant. It suggested that economic and social crisis drew families closer together and enhanced the role of teenagers at a time when the fathers were having such problems. Later follow-up showed that many of the teenagers had shown resilience and persistence in career-building. The effects of military service on these young Americans in the Second World War were generally positive in creating new opportunities for them and enabling them to develop self-confidence. Thus the longer-term result was strikingly different for teenagers in comparison with the impact on very young children.

The clearest impact of the war upon women was the reduction of their prospect of marriage. In 1917, the senior Mistress of Bournemouth High School for Girls stood in front of the assembled sixth form, nearly all of whom were dressed in mourning for some member of the family, and announced to them that: 'I have come to tell you a terrible fact. Only one in ten of you girls can ever hope to marry. You will have to make your own way in the world.' By the 1921 Census there were 19.8 females compared to 18.08 males in the country. Virginia Nicholson, in *Singled Out*, has traced the later careers of women of this generation shorn of the ready prospect of marriage and found however that they exhibited remarkable resilience.[29] They had indeed made their own way in the world.

The fifteen years following the war witnessed the return of problems of poverty and poor health. Other nations in Europe had suffered terrible immediate consequences of the war in terms of devastating damage and loss of productive potential but for Britain, suffering no such calamity, problems of adjustment emerged by slow gestation. For the seventy years before the war, unemployment had fluctuated in business cycles but had not shown any trend towards alarming increase, and that was despite the considerable rise in population. Nor in the latter third of those years with the development of new industries were there marked indications of a fall in the rate of unemployment.[30] After the post-war boom ended in 1921, the position changed dramatically. Unemployment rose and remained above 10 per cent in many areas of the country and after 1929 it climbed above 20 per cent.

The war had destroyed the chance which had been there for a more affluent society by the 1920s and it had led to dislocation, dangerously-raised unemployment and poverty, with consequent effects on mortality. In addition, and less predictable after victory, there was a loss of national self-confidence. Of course the national mood towards a pacifist international stand was entirely predictable. The image of world power sustained by the war had obscured the underlying reality of national decline, insecurity and wishful thinking.

The Great War had precipitated the collapse of the nineteenth-century economic framework based on the Gold Standard and free trade.[31] Efforts were made in the 1920s to turn the clock back but in 1931 Britain went off the Gold Standard and, soon after, introduced a full range of tariffs. Before 1914, Britain had been well set in markets across Europe. The economy had also benefited from German and Austrian investment through firms such as Siemens and Scheurer Kestner, the firm which introduced the electrolysis process to the UK, greatly expanding the supply of cheap bleach for disinfectant and cleaning. The war's destruction considerably reduced these markets and ended German investment. The war had also led to heavy investment in steel, coal, engineering and agriculture leading to post-war over-capacity, followed by bankruptcies and rising unemployment.

By the mid-1930s there was a rapid improvement in growth. New markets opened for housebuilding and for consumer goods. Tariff protection led to more trade within the Empire and monetary links which later became known as the sterling area. Protection worked for a time and certainly it worked well for Britain in the 1930s. Adverse effects in reducing competition and innovation were to come later. The 1930s recovery, together with the poor state of the American economy, meant that by 1938, for the only time in over a century, real income per head was higher in Great Britain than in the United States. However, these adjustments took time. For fifteen years there had been a difficult period leading to economic decline in Scotland, Wales and the North East.

The loss of economic strength also led to credit crisis and to pressure on public finances. The post-war period saw the then new phenomenon of 'cuts' in public spending. The first round was the 'Geddes Axe' in 1921, which passed off without political impact perhaps because it was seen as a sign of strong government in action. The next major round in 1931 led to the Invergordon mutiny in the Royal Navy and departure from the Gold Standard.

During the nineteenth century Britain had been in the fortunate position of being able to achieve and maintain her position as the dominant world power, protected by the Pax Britannica, and this for a relatively small outlay. Naval supremacy and the services of a reformed volunteer British Army and the far larger Indian Army were able to control Imperial coastal areas and communications. The twentieth-century challenge turned out to be very different with a struggle between inland populations for the control of Eurasia driven by authoritarian regimes. The key to such a challenge was to form alliances, and the worst effect of the post-war policy drift was the loss of alliances and firm commitments first to Japan and then to France and the United States.

In 1917, Labour's Arthur Henderson wrote of the political changes to come:

A new social order is taking shape even in the mist of the stress and peril of the time. The revolution is fundamental for it touches the springs of action in the great mass of the common people. War is possible only because the skill and bravery of the common people, their immense industry, their patient endurance, their direct and simple sense of right and wrong, give the rulers a feeling of power which they use, not to ensure the happiness and prosperity of the multitudes of humble folk, but to glorify their own names and to feed their insensate ambitions. The people have discovered this, and in learning they have discovered their own power. Never again, we may be sure, will the people allow themselves to be driven helplessly into war by these sinister forces.[32]

For some nations the war brought revolution; in Britain it brought widened democracy with the franchise for all adults and a new power of public opinion: 12.5 million people voted in the Peace Ballot of 1934/1935 and Prime Minister Baldwin saw this as a vote against re-armament, confirming the indications of the Conservative defeat in the 1933 Fulham by-election.[33] The legacy of the war was a revulsion against war and the moral and practical wrong-headedness of deterrence. Ironically, the effect of the casualties at the time they fell had been different: a stronger national resolve to see the war through and not to let down the fallen.

The Great War had seriously weakened both Britain's actual defence security through loss of alliances and delayed re-armament against what the nation would have face – Nazi German aggression – and also weakened the nation's moral fibre, mercifully not as suicidally as that of France. Sun Tzu was right – a long war had weakened the state. When Churchill later wrote of Dunkirk, though he might have had in mind surrenders too in Greece, Crete, Singapore or Tobruk, 'They did not fight like their fathers',[34] it certainly provides food for thought with regard to a legacy of the Great War to which we draw less attention.

Notes

1. H. Taine, *Origines de La France Contemporaine. 1891*, quoted in H. Nickerson, *The Armed Horde. 1793-1939* (GP Putnam, 1942).
2. Sun Tzu, *The Art of War* (Ballantine Books, 1993), p. 107.
3. W.H. Scott, *Leeds in the Great War* (Leeds City Council, 1923), p. 3.
4. J.-J. Becker, *The Great War and the French People* (Berg, 1985), p. 6. Also quoted in R. Doughty, *Pyrrhic Victory* (Harvard University Press, 2005).
5. J. Winter and J.-L. Robert (eds), *Capital Cities at War. 1914-19* (CUP, 1997), Ch. 11.
6. Q. Wright, *A Study of War* (University of Chicago Press, 1965), p. 674.
7. J.M. Winter, *The Great War and the British People* (Macmillan, 1985), p. 82.
8. R. Pound, *The Lost Generation* (Constable, 1965), p. 77.
9. T.J. Mitchell and G.M. Smith, *Casualties and Medical Statistics of the Great War* (HMSO, 1931), Ch. 11.
10. W.G. Macpherson, *Hygiene of the Great War* Vol. 1 (HMSO, 1923), pp. 1–29.
11. A.T. Peacock and J. Wiseman, *The Growth of Public Expenditure in the United Kingdom* (Unwin, 1961), p. 184. See also J.S. Stamp, *Taxation during the War* (OUP, 1932); see also S. Broadberry and M. Harrison, *The Economics of World War I* (CUP, 2005).
12. D. Stevenson, *1914- 1918. The History of the First World War* (Penguin, 2005), Ch. 20.
13. Scott, *Leeds in the Great War*, p. 58.
14. Ibid., p. 59.
15. A. Gregory, *The Last Great War* (CUP, 2008), p. 257.
16. Mitchell and Smith, *Medical Services Casualties and Medical Statistics of the Great War*.
17. W.S.C. Churchill, *The World Crisis* (Thornton Butterworth, 1927), Vol IV.
18. B. Liddell Hart, *The Real War* (Faber and Faber, 1930).
19. H. Folks, *The Human Costs of the War* (Harper, 1920), p. 1.
20. Ibid., p. 2.
21. Ibid., p. 120.
22. Ibid., p. 197.
23. Winter, *The Great War and the British People*, p. 213.
24. W.F. Gephart, *Effects of the War upon Insurance* (Carnegie, 1918), p. 91.
25. Winter, *The Great War and the British People*, p. 150.
26. N. Bosanquet, *Our Land at War* (History Press, 2014), p. 10.
27. *Ministry of National Service Report upon the Physical Examination of Men of Military Age by National Service Medical Boards 1917-19* (HMSO, 1920).
28. Glen H. Elder, *Children of the Great Depression* (Westview Press, 1999).

29. Virginia Nicholson, *Singled Out* (Viking, 2007).
30. H. Clay, *The Post-War Unemployment Problem* (Macmillan, 1930), Ch.1.
31. K. Polanyi, *Origins of our Time. The Great Transformation* (Gollancz, 1945).
32. A. Henderson, *The Aims of Labour* (Headley Bros, 1918), pp. 10–11.
33. R. Overy, *The Twilight Years: The Paradox of Britain between the Wars* (Viking, 2009).
34. W.S. Churchill, *The Second World War*, Vol II. *Their Finest Hour* (Cassell, 1949), pp. 78–9.

Suggested Further Reading

Bosanquet, N., *Our Land at War* (History Press, 2014)
Broadberry, S., and Harrison, M., *The Economics of World War 1* (CUP, 2005)
Folks, H., *The Human Costs of War* (Harper, 1920)
Overy, R., *The Twilight Years: The Paradox of Britain between the Wars* (Viking, 2009)
Pound, R., *The Lost Generation* (Constable, 1955)
Stevenson, D., *1914-1918. The History of the First World War* (Penguin, 2005)
Winter, J.M., *The Great War and the British People* (Macmillan, 1985)
Winter, J.M., and Robert, J.-L. (eds), *Capital Cities at War. 1914-19* (CUP, 1997)

Chapter 19

'That Quiet Place' – A Historiography of Visiting the Old Front Line

By Clive Harris

> It does not appear that this terrain, then entirely in military occupation, makes any appeal 50 years later to tourists of Italy, who by-pass it on their trips to Venice and northwards to Austria. Yet to us, with recent memories of the devastated plains of Flanders, it all seems altogether too attractive a part of the world to be experienced under wartime conditions only, in fact ideal for a walking holiday.[1]

When Charles Horton wrote his memoirs in 1970, 'the old front line'[2] lay forgotten by many. Visitors to the battlefields were at an all-time low and he could never have foreseen the change that lay just around the corner. Today's generation, spurred on by reading Rose Coombs *Before Endeavours Fade* (1976), began as a trickle of visitors which soon led to a steady stream with the forming of the Western Front Association in 1980, the creation of Tony and Valmai Holt's Tours in 1977 and Graham Parker's Flanders Tours in 1988.

This modern flow of pilgrims was in turn eclipsed by the explosion of interest in the Great War which occurred around the turn of the millennium. Driven by the internet, the last veterans and the national curriculum, anyone wanting to visit the battlefields of the Western Front, Gallipoli, Italy or Salonika has never had more choice. Whether travelling independently with the plethora of modern guidebooks or with one of the major specialist tour operators such as Leger, the War Research Society or Battle Honours, battlefield touring has never been easier or as popular. Today's modern battlefield guides are armed with Cloud-based war diary archives, linesman GPS trench maps and audio-visual aids accessible on mobile phones. Tours are conducted with an historical knowledge, accuracy and with technology unthinkable to the generations which fought the war a century ago. But long before the existence of today's battlefield tour companies, visits to the battlefields had been undertaken, in fact visitors were beginning to arrive before the guns had even fallen silent.

> The majority of visitors to the British War Zone on the Western Front discover that their visit may easily become simply a panorama of jagged ruins and collapsed cottages surrounded by acres of pockmarked ground. This desert of destruction is certainly enlivened by the cheerfulness of those who dwell there, but the prodigious exertions

and vast sacrifices of the past are apt to be overlooked owing to the impressiveness of the pictures of the present unrolled before the eyes of visitors as they make their rapid tour.[3]

The anonymous writer of those words had not exaggerated the conditions greeting the tour participants for the guide from which it was taken was issued to groups of 'representatives of British Labour in large numbers on a visit to the Western Front'.[4] Several of these tours took place in the spring of 1918 with the intention that:

> When the war is won, all classes will be proud to have shared in the victory – the whole rank and file of the nation, the men in the trenches abroad and the men in the mines, factories, and workshops at home. It is right that some of the those who are preparing the war material should be enabled to see the result of their work in the field. I feel assured that our visitors will return home with a fuller conviction that their hard and monotonous labours are vital to their countries success, and that the men in the fighting line are worthy of their best efforts. In this war of nations every piece of honest work, wherever done, has its value for operations in the field.[5]

The country was gripped in its fifth year of war, the British Army was recovering from its exhausting efforts of 1917, morale was perhaps as low as at any stage since the British Expeditionary Force had stepped ashore in August 1914 and, as far as the soldier could see, there was 'no end in sight'.[6] And on the Home Front too in 1917 there were signs of civil unrest when 'roughly 200,000 workers in 48 British towns went on strike. Their grievances however were largely non-political, relating to such issues as wages, food prices, war profiteering and exemption from military service.'[7]

For one participant in these early tours, J. Carrigan, a union activist, the brief glimpse of the front line he witnessed had a significant impact on his thinking. He left an unpublished typed account of his visit during which he recalled at Vimy Ridge:

> We came across a boot with a foot in it and a Shell hole with a boot showing itself. Pulling it out, the leg above the knee was there. It was a German boot, I tumbled across a pill box; it was egg shaped with a hole to get through and a slit half way round and was about ten inches deep to work the guns on the boys as they were going up. After the difficulties that have been overcome here, if they are supported as they ought to be, from home, the men that could drive the Germans out of this place will still be able to drive on again when the time comes to do so.[8]

It would suggest that on this one occasion at least the purpose of the tours had had the desired effect. However, the events of 21 March 1918 which saw the launching of the Kaiser's Spring Offensive were to cut short this patriotic tour programme. In point of fact there had been still earlier civilian visits. The Poet Laureate, John Masefield, had visited the Somme front in late 1916 whilst the battle still raged. He wrote his account of the ground, which in effect became the first battlefield guide when published in 1917, and it remains in print at the time of writing. On witnessing the devastation of the area, he predicted it would be some time before visitors would return:

> It may be some years before those whose fathers, husbands and brothers were killed in this great battle, may be able to visit the battlefield where their dead are buried. Perhaps many of them, from brooding on the map, and from the dreams and visions in the night, have in their minds an image or picture of that place. The following pages may help some few others, who have not already formed that image, to see the scene as it appears today. What it was like on the day of battle cannot be imagined by those who were not there.[9]

Some soldiers serving in the war made prophesy of future generations of visitors returning to the battlefields. Two examples are left for us in verse, the more famous believed to have been written by Lieutenant John Stanley Purvis (under the pseudonym Philip Johnstone). Purvis was wounded on the Somme with the 5/Yorks in 1916 and returned to the front with pupils of Cranleigh School as early as 1921. It was three years earlier, whilst still recuperating at home, that he wrote the following poem published by the *Nation*:

> Ladies and gentlemen, this is High Wood,
> Called by the French, Bois des Furneaux,
> The famous spot which in Nineteen-Sixteen,
> July, August and September was the scene
> Of long and bitterly contested strife,
> By reason of its high commanding site. Observe the effect of shell-fire in the trees
> Standing and fallen; here is wire; this trench
> For months inhabited, twelve times changed hands;
> (They soon fall in), used later as a grave.
> It has been said on good authority
> That in the fighting for this patch of wood
> Were killed somewhere above eight thousand men,
> Of whom the greater part were buried here,
> This mound on which you stand being . . . Madame, please,
>
> You are requested kindly not to touch
> Or take away the Company's property
> As souvenirs; you'll find we have on sale
> A large variety, all guaranteed.
> As I was saying, all is as it was,
> This is an unknown British officer,
> The tunic having lately rotted off.
> Please follow me – this way . . . the path, sir, please,
>
> The ground which was secured at great expense
> The Company keeps absolutely untouched,

And in that dugout (genuine) we provide
Refreshments at a reasonable rate.
You are requested not to leave about
Paper, or ginger-beer bottles, or orange peel,
There are waste-paper baskets at the gate.[10]

The words resonate with battlefield guides and tour operators a century on and this insightful if somewhat cynical view was not restricted to the Western Front, being shared by Sub Lieutenant A.P. Herbert of Hawke Battalion, Royal Naval Division, in his poem 'The Helles Hotel' published in 1919. In one of the verses, Herbert predicts: 'And tread old battle-fields where vineyards are; With scarred young veterans they'll amble round, The Turks' entanglements at Sedd-el-Bahr, And practise at a reasonable charge, Heroic landings in the hotel barge.'[11]

As early as March 1915, Thomas Cook placed an advertisement in *The Times* 'to put a stop to stray enquiries, that they would not be organising sightseeing expeditions to the battlefields, at least until the war was over, owing to French opposition'.[12] Trench newspapers, popular among the troops, carried mock adverts for battlefield tours, displaying ironic humour undimmed today by the intervening years and rather different circumstances. In a letter home dated 23 December 1915, John Walcote Gamble, then a Lieutenant in the Durham Light Infantry, predicted: 'Ypres will be flooded with sight-seers and tourists after the War, and they will be amazed by what they see. The ancient ruins of Pompeii and such places will be simply out of it.'[13] Gamble was to be killed the following May.

When peace did come to the world in November 1918 and the massive clean-up operation began, it was not very long before battlefield tourists arrived in France and Flanders. There were several swiftly-produced illustrated battlefield guides which hit the market and proved remarkably popular. Ward Lock and Co's 'Red Books' was an established series of travel guides before the war so to produce an updated volume titled 'Belgium and the Battlefields' was an obvious 'newcomer' which by 1921 had already run to its 7th edition. It lists numerous tourist hotels already plying trade in Ypres, mainly outside the Railway Station where the Trois Suisse's, Skindles and Hotel France could be found or outside the Menin Gate (still under construction) where the Ypriana, Splendide and Metropole all offered lodgings. The journey time from London is suggested as nine hours by train and the first class fare each way is quoted as £2, 13s, 4d.

The guide offers a limited historical narrative; typical of the detail included is the entry for Hill 60 which reads:

A ridge about 50 feet high and 250 yards long, facing the Allied trenches in the Zillebeke region, S.E. of Ypres. It was the scene of many fights. By their possession of it the Germans were able to establish an observation post, commanding a large part of what, in 1914, constituted the British position. The British drove under it six mines each ending in a chamber containing a ton of gunpowder. The mines were exploded in April 1915, and the hill was immediately captured. The next day the Germans regained a portion of it, but this was taken from them. For the greater part of the war the British held the trenches on one side and the Germans were on the summit, where now stands the monument to the Queen Victoria Rifles.[14]

In direct competition were Muirhead's 'Blue Guides' which included Belgium and the Western Front. This useful pocket guide certainly pipped the 'Red Guide' with regard to historical content, as it included a narrative of the war written by Major General Frederick Maurice, a formidable character who had served from Mons through to May 1918 when he was forced to resign for proving 'over-critical' of David Lloyd George. Maurice could also lay partial claim to playing an important role in the origins of today's Royal British Legion. His descriptions were of far more historical value to the early visitor; the entry for Passchendaele being typical:

> Passchendaele, once a village of 3300 inhabitants, lost in the first battle of Ypres, it was stormed by the 1st and 2nd Canadian Brigades on Nov. 6th, 1917. From the mound that was once the church we look down upon the Belgian plain, where in clear weather Bruges and Ostend may be distinguished. Passchendaele has given its name to the whole offensive movement which culminated in its capture. It is the symbol of a heroic and almost superhuman effort; of strategic failure but of splendid endurance under the most wretched conditions hitherto known in war.
>
> From the 78 German divisions engaged in the battle that ended here, the British captured 24,000 prisoners and 74 guns. On the Passchendaele ridge the sharpest fighting was at Crest Farm. Along the heights stood pill-boxes whose garrisons had been ordered to hold out to the last man. About 2 miles north is Westroosebeke (p. 47) which had witnessed some skirmishes early in the War, was captured by Belgian troops on Oct. 1st, 1918. The railway station (p. 44) lies between the two villages. Cemeteries near Passchendaele: Tyne Cot and Waterloo Farm.[15]

The most famous of the early guides, books which have been updated and reprinted for the centenary, are the *Illustrated Michelin Guides to the Battlefields*, published from 1919 onwards. In all they number fifteen volumes covering the entire front. They were available in German, French and English and trumped their rivals by offering an historical narrative at the front, itineraries and routes offering practical advice, illustrated with numerous 'then and now' photographs and ending with comprehensive orders of battle for the troops engaged. They were without doubt well ahead of their time. They also contained advertising, including in the 1920 edition, one for *Ypres an illustrated history and guide*, for the Imperial War Museum Photographic Section, Crystal Palace SE19. All editions recommended a pre-tour visit to the Michelin Touring Office, 81 Fulham Road, London SW3 where if offered free information and advice regarding tours, boasting: 'its purpose is to save the intending Tourist time and trouble and generally assist him in mapping out his tour, free of charge and irrespective of the make of tyres he uses'.[16]

As visitors and pilgrims began to arrive in the devastated areas they had a wide range of guidebooks and accommodation from which to choose. One early visitor, the Honourable Lady Maule Crichton Stuart, travelled in 1923 to find the final resting place of her husband, Lord Ninian Crichton Stuart, the MP for Cardiff, who had fallen commanding the 6/Welch at Loos in October 1915. Her typed diary of the tour recorded that:

> We reached Lille at 1650, found a strange little half English interpreter at the station with the name of our hotel on his hat and asked for the hotel bus. He told us it would

be coming back in a moment. We talked to him about a motor for tomorrow and he told us the best one was driven by an 'English Boy' and that he would not cheat us. So, we obtained particulars of his car and agreed to come and book him later . . . We found the English Boy Chauffer and arranged that he should fetch us at 0930 tomorrow. Charge was to be 2 francs a kilometre. He says roads are very bad and we can well believe it![17]

Lady Crichton Stuart recalls the moving visit to her late husband's grave:

We went to the Bethune Town Cemetery, I recognised the view from a photograph up from the gate between the Cypress trees. On our left as we went in was the caveau d'attente in which Ninian's body lay for a while. It was however badly damaged and it became necessary to bury the coffin. The Englishman in charge took us straight to the spot and he planted my white chrysanthemum while we stood by and put the red carnations in a vase. Ninian so loved bright flowers. I hope he felt pleased.[18]

Her journey continued up into Ypres: she was escorted by her second husband, Jock Ramsey, who had been wounded in 1916 with the 2/Coldstream Guards. The conditions worsened as they crossed the Belgian frontier:

But what an extraordinarily devested [sic] country. At Messines we stopped and went into the British Cemetery. It is a very pleasant little place with well-kept grass and nice flowers. We looked out over a fine expanse of country but oh how sad – every tree a skeleton some of them severely blackened stumps – and piles and piles of barbed wire, corrugated iron and iron posts, all over Messines Ridge concrete German pill boxes were groping out and still many deep shell holes full of water. New houses were springing up but not one of the original ones remain and there are rows and rows of queer little tin and wood shacks build of anything procurable in which the peasants live while they reclaim the scarred land.[19]

By 1923, however, Ypres had become a thriving hub for battlefield tourism. It is estimated that a British population of 10,000 sprang up during the 1920s. Many were employed in the clearance of the battlefields, the reclaiming of the land and rebuilding of the region but, for a growing number, tourism through the running of hotels, the supplying of vehicles or battlefield guiding, became a viable option for employment. A leading light in Ypres emerging from its own rubble to become a hub for tourism was the formation of the Ypres League as early as September 1920. Its patrons read like a *Debrett's* and *Who's Who* combined. They include the HM King George V, HRH Prince Edward (who had himself served there with the Guards) and Princess Beatrice (whose son, Prince Maurice of Battenberg, had fallen in the Salient). Its president was Field Marshal Lord French, Earl of Ypres, and within five years, Haig, Plumer, Allenby and Pulteney were also named as officers of the League.

Its membership, primarily veterans, began to visit in numbers and in October 1921 the League arranged for a group of 800 to return to commemorate the anniversary of the First Battle of Ypres. Though travelling independently of the main group, John Hall made his own pilgrimage the same month and privately published an account of the experience. It provides a real insight into the conditions which prevailed during those pioneering days of battlefield touring:

> Night approaching, we had to leave the place of destruction and make our way to Ypres, the route taking us through many ruined villages. I would explain that the amount of destruction seen gives the traveller some idea of the size of the village or town that formally existed. Eventually we arrived at 'Wipers', the name coined by our British boys whilst in occupation. Similar destruction appeared here, only on a much larger scale; a volcanic eruption or earthquake could not have caused more damage. Sacred buildings were raised to the ground, roads and streets obliterated and huge blocks of stone, weighing several tons, retarded the progress of vehicular traffic.[20]

The author does, however, comment on the green shoots of recovery, albeit still with an anger towards the enemy when he recalls 'temporary wooden buildings were erected here, also, for the folk who had returned to their native town. Workman were doing their utmost to erect new dwellings and repair the damage done by the so called cultured race, to homes that were once a pride.'[21] Such levels of destruction led Hall to speculate on the inability of the town ever fully to recover. He would have been astounded at seeing the Ypres we know today where bookshops vie with Great War-themed pubs, and hotels and restaurants flourish, quite capable of catering for the thousands of visitors – an unimaginable vision when Hall was writing:

> One building will never be restored – that is the well-known Cloth Hall. Part of the tower is still standing and at the base can be seen tons upon tons of fallen masonry. Stone figures of great men of the past, of beasts and birds, the work of sculptors of many generations, which previously formed the architectural beauty of that famous building, now lie broken into fragments beyond restoration. It is the reported intention of the Belgian Government to preserve the remaining portion of this once beautiful edifice as a token of love and respect for the two hundred and fifty thousand British soldiers who fell in defending the Ypres Salient.[22]

Thankfully the building which looked 'beyond restoration' now houses a significant Great War Museum and the town is a vibrant bustling centre for tourism. In reality and symbolically, however, the scars of the war remain on the rebuilt Cloth Hall.

Monuments were beginning to appear and Hall recalls that 'I have been informed that 42,000 soldiers are still to be accounted for – A Triumphal Arch is to be erected at Menin Gate and the name of every missing soldier is to be inscribed thereon.'[23] When Reginald Blomfield's Menin Gate was completed in July 1927, it listed almost 55,000 names with a further 35,000 more recorded on the panels at Tynecot Cemetery. The unveiling of the Menin Gate Memorial was attended by a crowd of thousands who gathered to hear Herbert Plumer proclaim, 'They are not missing, they are here'. The ceremony also marked the BBC's first-ever live outside broadcast.

Throughout John Hall's visit, his guide was a local man who dropped his price from 300 francs to 160 when questioned about his credibility. Opportunist guides of questionable quality led in 1925 to the Ypres League publishing its own guidebook. *The Immortal Salient, an Historical Record and Complete Guide for Pilgrims to Ypres* promised to be sold at the 'lowest possible price'[24] and 'Although intended to serve as a guide book for pilgrims visiting the graves of their relatives, the book has been greatly expanded to meet many requirements.'[25] The guide was accompanied by a very useful illustrated map, a map that remains in print to this day and, overall, this guidebook stands up to scrutiny almost a century on. Around the same time, Talbot House published its own guide, *The Pilgrim's Guide to the Ypres Salient*, and boasted that it:

> had been compiled and written entirely by ex-service men. It aims at giving those who desire to visit the Graves and Battlefields a dependable and comprehensive Guide to their actions from the moment when they decide to undertake the journey until the moment when they once more set foot in England. With this end in view every possible care has been taken to ensure that all facts stated are accurate, complete and up-to-date; and while it is inevitable, with conditions still in a state of flux, that certain omissions and inaccuracies should occur, it is confidently believed that such deficiencies have been reduced to a minimum and that the Guide will supply a real want.[26]

What stands out in this guide is the introductory essays to each chapter which cover the experiences of the Infantry, Artillery, Tunnellers, RAMC, Machine-gunners and RFC. The Foreword is written by Noel Mellish, an Army Padre who had been awarded the Victoria Cross at St Eloi in 1916 and had lost a brother at Loos. His writing seems to give rise to an almost spiritual cloud blanketing the battlefields:

> Later we can see helmeted platoons going steadily down the grim ruined streets of Ypres towards the Menin Gate, and the awful, deadly struggle up to Passchendaele Ridge. We can see them coming back again, soaked with mud, strained and exhausted, painfully stumbling with swollen feet over the torturing cobbles. These confessed that they were strangers and pilgrims on the earth, for they who say such things make it manifest that they are seeking a country of their own. Yours is a pilgrimage in memory of those who passed this way. You will tread reverently, for it is holy ground. It is the shrine of those who won the right for us all to have a country of our own.[27]

In contrast, and a necessary commercial reality, is the advertisement section of the guide book which features Rolls-Royce and their new Torpedo-Phaeton, ideal for visiting the battlefields. There is an advertisement for the Hotel Skindles which offers rooms and food in Poperinghe and Ypres and boasts 'homelike, electric light, bathrooms and central heating' and also for private battlefield tours 'from 10 guineas inclusive', offering First Class Travel and Hotels. These tours were being led by Captain Richard Poyntz with a BA from Oxford and experience with the BEF throughout the war. On researching this early guide further, we learn that Poyntz served with the Honourable

Artillery Company, survived the war unscathed, and was no run-of-the-mill character. His obituary in the *Daily Mail* in 1958 informs us that 'he was fanatical about the boat race and sulked for weeks if Cambridge won, he became a first-time father at 54 and in later life developed a love for Rock and Roll music'.[28] He seems likely to have been a lively battlefield guide.

As the 1920s came to an end one final guidebook is worthy of mention and it is one I still travel with today when visiting the Salient, Beatrix Brice's *The Battle Book of Ypres* (1927). It was in effect an updated Ypres League Guide, consisting of a useful travel guide and map, an historical narrative provided by the Historical Section (Military Branch) of the British Army, and a gazetteer assisted by the Curator and Staff of the Imperial War Museum. With the Foreword written by Herbert Plumer and William Pulteney, it led the field with regard to historical accuracy but what distinguishes it in particular are the regimental contributions to the gazetteer sections. Interestingly, despite almost a decade having passed since the guns fell silent, the book shows no tone of reconciliation;

> The substance of all these narratives is drawn from military records. Accounts of German treachery and brutality have been omitted from this book. The Briton is a clean-handed and debonair fighter, his handclasp ready after the bout. The Teuton is different. But strong man met strong man foot to foot; brave man fought brave man with unsurpassed valour. That the greater number, long prepared and armed cap-a-pie, did not prevail against the unprepared and lightly armoured, is the heart of the story of the Salient.[29]

Visitor numbers continued to grow. In August 1928, the British Legion pilgrimage attracted 10,000 people, receiving widespread media coverage. The *Morning Post* suggested that:

> Since the War there has been a revival of that reverent and adventurous spirit that inspired the Pilgrimages of the Middle Ages. The Ypres pilgrims have set an example that may well be followed for many generations, and the sons and grandsons of the men who fought in the Great War will likely enough visit on certain dates marked with a white stone, the battlefields where England and the Empire were saved.[30]

The vast majority of visitors remained ex-servicemen; the British Legion membership now reached 500,000, regions and branches led tours which for many servicemen provided the comradeship they had missed since the end of the war. However, as the infrastructure and, though temporarily, the economy, improved, pilgrims began to be joined by tourists. The potential in visitors to the area was being realised at home and overseas.

> All day long charabancs stop in the road opposite Hill 60, and tourists file past the melancholy little group of men and children standing, collecting box in hand, by the footpath entrance Along the footpath the pitches of the souvenir sellers begin.

Prices range from 50 centimes for a brass button to 20 francs for a Smith and Wesson revolver. About fifty Americans wearing names of their home towns on bands round their hats, arrived when we were there. I 'witnessed' a minor tragedy in one family, consisting of a big stout father, a large mother, and a very thin son in leather jerkin, plus-fours, horn spectacles, and white and brown shoes. 'Now what do you want with a gun? The darned thing may be loaded. See here, take a button'. The small boy made a decisive cut-away gesture of non-acceptance with his right hand. 'Aw, pop, you said I could have a gun.'[31]

Henry Williamson returned to his old stomping ground several times between 1925 and 1964, witnessing and recording the change from pilgrims to tourists, but he was among many in recording this development. *The Ypres Times* featured an article by E. Williams who described the arrival of a tourist group as:

In they come with a rattle and a clatter through the Menin Gate, all packed together in huge charabancs, and after a raucous voiced guide has pointed out the very obvious Cloth Hall ruins, they are whirled away again to one of the show places, perhaps Hill 60, and when they get back home they will have seen Ypres and the Salient, and perhaps begin to wonder what all the fuss was about.[32]

Servicemen began to lose patience with the new 'day trippers' and blamed the larger tour operators for the change. The St Barnabas Society accused them of block-booking accommodation in Ypres and 'preventing real pilgrims from staying in the city'.[33]

Books and guides were still being published during the 1930s. Graham Seton Hutchinson DSO, MC, had had a distinguished military career and by 1935 was a prolific writer in both fact and fiction. His *Pilgrimage* was clearly aimed at his comrades and their children:

As the war years recede, visits to the battlefields are becoming not less rare, but are increasing. There are literally thousands of histories of the Great War. This book provides a synthesis. It is not intended to be a history, nor does it enter into strategic or tactical controversy, for it is concerned with events as and where they happened. The book is written primarily for the pilgrim. It is intended also for the Public Library of every town and village.[34]

Thomas Cook continued to lead parties of interested tourists across the battlefields: many had a set route of sites to see, among the most popular being the 'Tank Cemetery' just off the Menin Road and today the site of a theme park. The twisted, rusting hulks of tanks provided a tangible reminder of the war to both veterans and tourists alike. It seems to have disappeared at some stage in the 1930s. Two explanations have been put forward, first that there was a scrap-metal sale by the land owner, and a less likely second that the Germans removed them for scrap value when they returned in 1940. One site that lay hidden for decades was the La Maison Blanche dugouts, re-discovered by the Durand Group in 2006. They are reached today by parking opposite the German cemetery at Neuville St Vaast, hidden in a field behind an old red brick farm, three rusting wriggly tin sheets cover the entrance down some steps to a cavernous dugout which housed hundreds of Canadians during the Battle of Arras. To study the carvings and graffiti on the walls makes one feel today as if having stumbled on a time capsule, unexplored for a century. Further examination of the graffiti and you realise that you are mistaken. The arrows guiding you through the caves are not for the benefit of troops to find the exits up to their assembly areas but courtesy of Thomas Cook for their tourist in the 1930s. As Henry Williamson recorded:

> Wandering around, I discovered the Canadian HQ dugout, where the generals waited while the barrage fire rolled up to the crest of Vimy and turned the sleet into steam on the morning of that April day years ago. Now all is silent. A little French girl produces stumps of tallow candles and leads the visitor rapidly through one of the big new barns of la Maison Blanche, and across the farm yard to three rust sheets of corrugated iron laid on the ground. Underneath is the entrance. Steps, walls, roof are of brick-recently made, for tourists are many, and the dugout is one of the sights of the battlefields. Down many steps, and we reach the caves of chalk. The candle flames throw a bewildering glimmer in the cold, quiet place. Only the water drops make a sound. Rum Jars lie on the floor. Many tunnels here, and regimental crests engraved in the chalk – Maple leaves predominate. The signatures and initials in indelible pencil might have been made yesterday. All drowned far under time! Candle flames have smudged the chalk where many curious hands have held them. the grease thickens on ones fingers. How warm it is outside again![35]

The largest organised battlefield tour of the 1930s to come from outside the UK to the Western Front was the Canadian Vimy Pilgrimage of July 1936, to coincide with the unveiling of the impressive Vimy Ridge Memorial. The 'official' participants numbered 8,000, though an estimated 100,000 more attended independently. Planning for this tour which would have required similar logistics to moving a 1918 BEF division, began as early as 1927. Originally intended for 1932, the Great Depression and a delay in the completion of the memorial accounted for the four-year slip to 1936, by which time the political and military situation in Europe had changed significantly. The tour, which was mainly attended by veterans, widows and mothers, not only remembered the dead and the past achievements of the living but concluded when 'in the name of these groups the pilgrims made a desperate call for peace'.[36]

Six liners were chartered to convey the pilgrims from Montreal and the gathering was further enlarged by 2,000 pilgrims from the UK. Large corporations and employers were encouraged to support the tour by subsidising or sponsoring spaces and guaranteeing full pay throughout the time employees were away. The event used media to reach further into the hearts and homelands of Canada. By moving the official ceremony, presided over by King Edward VIII, from the traditional 11.00 start to 14.15, many Canadians were able to listen to the live broadcast. Services across Canada were held at the same time, effectively turning the unveiling of the memorial into a mass participation event, similar to that seen in the UK on 1 July 2016. Few who were in attendance could have envisaged the scene when less than four years later the memorial was the start line for 7 Royal Tank Regiment when they launched a counter-attack against Rommel's advancing army.

The opening of the Villers Bretonneux Memorial in July 1938 was attended by 400 veterans of the Australian Imperial Force. Though two 'official' Australian pilgrimages had taken place during the decade, this time the veterans were almost entirely UK based. It was the largest pilgrimage made by Australian veterans yet to be made but was almost forgotten, in part due to the wider events of the world at the time but also due to the participants not being considered 'diggers' by the Australian public, L.C. Robson, the headmaster of Sydney Church of England Grammar School, who did attend, commented:

> We passed first through a guard of honour of Australian ex-soldiers. Where they had come from, goodness knows. They were a motley crowd: probably many of them were odds and ends who had jobs in England. It would perhaps have been better if a smart guard of British troops had been brought over, but no doubt room had to be made for Australians. They were all in civilian clothes.[37]

Just two years later the Memorial would be the scene of a defensive action by French troops that would see a German armoured vehicle shooting at its bell tower, the cross of sacrifice and Commonwealth War Graves Commission buildings still showing the honourable scars of battle to this day.

As war spread across the world once more, the Commonwealth War Graves Commission, where possible, maintained the cemeteries and played an integral role in the escaper/resistance network, but Battlefield Tourism, with the exception of the much-publicised tour of Adolf Hitler and Herman Göring, was put on pause.

When the 'clear up' in Europe began, some of the Great War battlefields had been re-fought over and had sustained damage. Visitors to France from the UK slumped from their pre-war numbers as the country was in the grip of an all-too-understandable 'war-weariness'. One exception was the 1947 FA Cup winning side, Charlton Athletic. During an exhibition tour of Belgium in November of that year, the team visited the Menin Gate, Tynecot and several sites in the Ypres Salient. The trip was very personal for many of the participants. Manager Jimmy Seed and his trainer Jimmy Trotter had both served in the Great War, Seed being gassed, whilst legendary goalkeeper Sam Bartram's father had been awarded a Military Medal in the war. The battlefield experience had a clear impact on the players as a club historian noted: 'they had had spent the morning walking around great war cemeteries in the pouring rain, but this depressing experience cannot account for such a clear-cut victory by a much faster side.'[38]

It was not until the epic BBC series *The Great War* was screened in 1964 that interest was rekindled in the 1914–18 years. The veterans were by now reaching retirement and many became keen to re-visit their old battlefields with comrades or family. The Royal British Legion ran regular tours throughout the decade with designated guides on board to present historical narrative at each stand. Early Western Front Association member John Dray, himself a Monte Cassino veteran, acted as a guide on many of these trips and often commented on how he 'listened as much as he talked' when is such illustrious company. The Café Central and Hotel Sultan were regular haunts for the veterans. Many veterans preferred to travel independently which enabled them to visit less obvious spots that were of personal interest to them. Basil Peacock of the Northumberland Fusiliers recalled:

> Our taxi, the only car on the road, ascended a little rising ground which quickly fell away and I shouted 'stop' as I saw that we were skirting a cutting with a light railway running along it. The driver pulled up at a small signal box which had been a pile of bricks when I last saw it on 21 March 1918. This was the place where the Germans had taken me prisoner.[39]

When John Nisbet of the Royal Engineers returned to the Somme in April 1965, he recalled his personal feelings when 'we reached the British Military Cemetery at Bouzincourt. With a feeling of great emotion, I stood once more by the graves of my old comrades who were buried there, I was back at "that quiet place" with them again once more.'[40]

To conclude: why did they, and we today, continue to visit? Perhaps we will never fully understand what draws us back but a clue can be found in the words of Don Price, a Royal Fusilier, who wrote in 1983:

> Having just returned again from one of my visits to the battlefields I begin to wonder what is it that calls me back? Surely it cannot be that I want to recall those ghastly days and experience the misery and agonies of mind which I suffered. I ask myself did it really happen or was it a dream, was I really there? And yet I have the scars to show of two wounds that it certainly was no dream. I can remember the life so well, but I can feel none of it![41]

Despite the fact that the generation which fought the Great War is itself a fading memory, 'we that are left to grow old' continue to tread in the footsteps of our ancestors, albeit in rather more comfort than the pioneers of the 1920s. Certainly current visitor numbers show no sign of battlefield tourism being under threat of diminishing interest.

Notes

1. C. Horton, *Stretcher Bearer* (Oxford: Lion Hudson, 2013), p. 84.
2. J. Masefield, *The Old Front Line* (London: William Heinemann, 1917), p. 1.
3. *A Souvenir for Visitors to the Western Front* (London: Clay & Sons, 1918), p. 1.
4. D. Lloyd George, *A Souvenir for Visitors to the Western Front*, Foreword.
5. Ibid.
6. I.F.W. Beckett, *1917: Beyond the Western Front, planning for the end game* (Boston: Brill, 2008), p. 24.
7. MUN 5/80/341/6, *Reports on imminent and existing strikes, December 1917-December 1918*, National Archives.
8. J. Carrigan, *My Experiences in France*, unpublished memoir, March 1918, p. 6.
9. Masefield, *The Old Front Line*, p. 31.
10. P. Johnstone, 'High Wood', *The Nation*, 1918.
11. A.P. Herbert, 'The Helles Hotel', *The Bomber Gypsy*, 1919.
12. *The Times*, 31 March 1915.
13. J.W. Gamble, personal letter, 23 December 1915, IWM, P.P. MCR 82.

14. Ward Lock & Co Limited, *Handbook to Belgium and the Battlefields* (London: Ward Lock & Co, 1921), p. 57.
15. F. Maurice, *Muirhead's Guide to Belgium and the Western Front* (London: Hachette & Co, 1920), p. 48.
16. Michelin Tyre Company, *Illustrated Michelin Guides to the Battlefields* (London: Michelin & Co, 1919), end piece.
17. M. Crichton Stuart, *Diary of my visit to France*, unpublished memoir, 1923, p. 4.
18. Ibid., p. 6.
19. Ibid., p. 7.
20. J. Hall, *My Tour of the Battlefields 1921* (London: Roberts & Newton, 1921), p. 8.
21. Ibid., p. 9.
22. Ibid., p. 10.
23. Ibid., p16
24. W. Pulteney, *The Immortal Salient – An Historical and Complete Guide for Pilgrims to Ypres* (London: Hassel, Watson & Viney, 1925), p. 5.
25. Ibid., p. 5.
26. Talbot House, *The Pilgrims Guide to the Ypres Salient* (London: Herbert Reiach, 1920), p. 1.
27. Ibid., p. 4.
28. *Daily Mail*, Obituaries, 9 March 1958.
29. B. Brice, *The Battle Book of Ypres* (London: John Murray, 1927), p. 53.
30. *Morning Post*, 6 August 1928.
31. H. Williamson, *The Wet Flanders Plain* (London: Faber and Faber, 1929), p. 94.
32. E. Williams, *The Ypres Times*, April 1927, p. 153.
33. D. Lloyd, *Tourism and Pilgrimage 1860-1939* (Oxford: Berg, 1998), p. 41.
34. G.S. Hutchinson, *Pilgrimage* (London: Rich & Cowen, 1935), p. 4.
35. Williamson, *The Wet Flanders Plain*, pp. 116–17.
36. D. Lloyd, *Battlefield Tourism, Pilgrimage and the Commemoration of the Great War* (Oxford: Berg, 1988), p. 199.
37. Ibid., p. 211.
38. A. Bristow, *A Charlton Athletic Handbook* (London: Famous Ltd, 1951), p. 73.
39. B. Peacock, *A Tinkers Mufti* (London: Leo Cooper, 1974), p. 206.
40. J. Nisbet, unpublished diary, 1965, author's collection.
41. D. Price, Private letter written to the author 25 June 1983,

Suggested Further Reading

(Though most of the books listed here are out of print, they are widely available in second-hand bookshops or through inter-library loan.)

Brice, B., *The Battle Book of Ypres* (London: John Murray, 1927)
Coombs, R., *Before Endeavours Fade* (London: After the Battle, 1976)
Hutchinson, G., *Pilgrimage* (London: Rich & Cowen, 1935)
Lloyd, D., *Tourism and Pilgrimage 1860-1939* (Oxford: Berg, 1998)
Masefield, J., *The Old Front Line* (London: William Heinemann, 1917)
Maurice, F., *Muirhead's Guide to Belgium and the Western Front* (London: Hachette & Co, 1920)
Michelin Tyre Company, *Illustrated Michelin Guides to the Battlefields* (London: Michelin & Co, 1919)
Peacock, B., *A Tinkers Mufti* (London: Leo Cooper, 1974)
Ward Lock & Co Limited, *Handbook to Belgium and the Battlefields* (London: Ward Lock & Co, 1921)

Chapter 20

Britain and the Post-War Settlement

By Alan Sharp

The peacemakers after the Great War faced an awesome task. A shattered world had to be rebuilt over much of which, for all their military and economic power, their control was limited. Four empires collapsed which for centuries had dominated Eastern and Central Europe and the Middle East, leaving a vacuum that new states, old empires and revolutionaries competed to fill. The British Treasury estimated that victory cost £24,000,000,000 (1914 gold values). Over ten million servicemen and six million civilians had died and industrialised warfare had devastated great swathes of territory, leaving a legacy of loss, bitterness and dangerous debris. Meanwhile their governments faced pressing domestic responsibilities for demobilising the forces and closing down agencies created to conduct total war and then to deliver reforms acknowledging the contributions of servicemen and the women and children who had replaced them in agriculture and industry.

All the 'Big Four' – Georges Clemenceau, David Lloyd George, Vittorio Orlando, the premiers of France, Britain and Italy, and American President Woodrow Wilson – carried a burden of expectation. France anticipated the return of Alsace-Lorraine, lost in 1871, and security against a powerful neighbour; Britain expected substantial payments to offset its war costs and the trial and execution of the ex-Kaiser, Wilhelm II; Italy demanded fulfilment of the 26 April 1915 Treaty of London which secured its support and, additionally, the port of Fiume (Rijeka) which was not part of that bargain; Wilson, whose 1918 speeches had inspired enormous hope across the battle lines, feared he had created impossible aspirations and that the outcome would be a 'tragedy of disappointment'.[1]

Commitments and Promises

Britain had made wartime promises – some contradictory – to gain or retain allies: to Belgium the restoration of its political and economic independence; to Serbia access to the sea and, together with Romania and Greece, an expansion of territory; to Poland and Czechoslovakia support for their independence; to Japan gains in the Pacific and China. Italy, technically an ally of the Central Powers (Germany and Austria-Hungary), declared neutrality in August 1914. It joined the Entente (Britain, France and Russia) in return for the Treaty of London's promises of *Italia Irredenta*, the unredeemed lands in Austrian possession required to complete national reunification, territory in the Balkans and a share of any spoils from the German and Ottoman Empires.[2]

The future of the Ottoman Empire, especially in the Middle East, was complicated. An agreement negotiated by Sir Mark Sykes, a Conservative MP, and François Georges-Picot, a French colonial administrator, signed on 31 January 1916, essentially divided the Middle East between Britain and France, leaving a possibility of an Arab state or states over which they expected to exercise control akin to their respective power in Egypt and Morocco. This perception was not shared by leaders of the Arab Hashemite clan whom Britain was encouraging to rebel against the Ottomans. Hussein Ibn Ali, the Grand Sherif of Mecca, sought to replace the Ottoman Sultan as Caliph, the spiritual leader of the world's Muslims, and to rule a large independent Arab kingdom. On 24 October 1915, the final letter of a correspondence between Hussein and the Egyptian High Commissioner, Sir Henry McMahon, envisaged such a kingdom but left uncertain the extent of French control over Syria or the fate of Palestine. Anglo-French leaders thought the Arab state a fantasy, attaching much greater weight to agreements between themselves. Hussein believed otherwise. On 5 June 1916, the Arab revolt in the desert began, led by his son, Feisal, and his British adviser, T.E. Lawrence. In Paris they now expected recognition of their claims.[3]

Matters were further complicated by the statement of the British Foreign Secretary, Arthur Balfour, on 2 November 1917, that 'His Majesty's Government view with favour the establishment in Palestine of a national home for the Jewish people'. The Balfour Declaration sought to encourage Jewish support for the Allies particularly in the United States and revolutionary Russia but also, with Britain becoming the supervising power in Palestine – now the twice or thrice-promised land – to amend the Sykes-Picot Agreement in its favour. According to Balfour, the rights of the existing inhabitants would not be affected by Jewish immigration. Later, on 7 November 1918, Britain and France claimed that they were fighting for 'the complete and definite emancipation of the peoples so long oppressed by the Turks'. It was a tangled web.[4]

Anglo-French rivalry dominated the eventual outcome. In London, in December 1918, Clemenceau asked Lloyd George if he had any particular request. Lloyd George replied: 'I wanted Mosul attached to Irak, and Palestine from Dan to Beersheba under British control. Without hesitation he agreed.'[5] His prioritising of a revision of the Sykes-Picot Agreement was significant, though his knowledge of Dan's location was sketchy. British negotiators later sought a revised frontier further north but his intention was clear, an extension of British power in a region rich in the new strategic resource of oil and containing the Suez Canal, a crucial imperial artery. Lloyd George also sought to overturn the agreement giving France control of Syria, exasperating Clemenceau, who, although not a great advocate of imperialism, was determined not to yield. When these matters were belatedly considered at San Remo in April 1920, Britain was awarded the mandate for Palestine, though many believed this a poisoned chalice of coping with deepening Arab-Jewish hostility. Under similar terms Britain also gained Iraq, whilst France took Syria and Lebanon. Serious uprisings in Syria, Iraq, Palestine and Egypt revealed the extent of Arab resentment against the settlement, the repercussions of which still echo today.[6]

Armistice and Wilson's 'Program for the Peace of the World'
The war had ended as suddenly as it had begun. Bulgaria on 29 September 1918, the Ottomans on 30 October and Austria-Hungary on 3 November concluded armistices. On 4 October, seeking a respite to regroup, Germany requested Wilson to arrange an

armistice with his co-belligerents[7] on condition that the settlement would reflect the values of his Fourteen Points speech of 8 January 1918. 'Have you ever been asked by President Wilson whether you accept the Fourteen Points? I have not been asked,' Clemenceau fulminated. 'I have not been asked either,' responded Lloyd George – but, dependent as they were on American money, food, munitions and, increasingly, men, they had little option.[8] Subject to reservations about the freedom of the seas and the definition of the restoration of Allied territories, they accepted. Wilson's terms proved tougher than expected, with crippling military and naval armistice conditions precluding any resumption of hostilities.

At 11 am on 11 November 1918, the Western Front fell silent, though violence continued across Europe as a constant backdrop to peacemaking.[9] The Treaty of Versailles was signed with Germany on 28 June 1919, Saint Germain with Austria on 10 September, Neuilly with Bulgaria on 27 November and Trianon with Hungary on 4 June 1920. The abortive Treaty of Sèvres of 10 August 1920 with the Ottoman Empire was renegotiated with the new secular state of Turkey in the Treaty of Lausanne signed on 24 July 1923. As the peacemakers discovered, signature was the start not the end of a process and the enforcement, revision and abrogation of the settlements dominated the next twenty years and beyond.[10]

Wilson followed the Fourteen Points with the 'Four Principles' on 11 February 1918, the 'Four Ends' on 4 July, and the 'Five Particulars' on 27 September – Clemenceau quipped 'the good Lord Himself only required ten points'. Wilson's prescriptions embodied the 'New Diplomacy' which many believed should replace the aristocratic and secret practices alleged to have plunged the world into war. He advocated open diplomacy, free trade, free passage for neutral shipping in international waters in wartime, armaments limitation, freedom for peoples to choose their allegiance and governments and an alternative security architecture based on a universal alliance for peace.[11] In their enforced endorsement of Wilson's inspirational but imprecise proposals which, particularly in terms of self-determination, had raised unintended and impractical aspirations, his allies further complicated the already daunting prospect facing them by setting themselves higher moral standards than any previous peace conference.[12] The possibilities were legion for disappointed and aggrieved parties to find hypocrisy in the inevitable disparities between Wilson's rhetoric and the complex realities of post-conflict Europe and the wider world.

Complications

Wilson was determined the United States would never again experience naval blockade, whether by Britain stopping and searching vessels on the high seas or German unrestricted submarine warfare. His pledge to create a navy 'incomparably the greatest in the world' threatened a contest that, given America's superior resources, Britain knew it could not win. Lloyd George conceded that the conference might consider the question (it never did) – though since maritime blockade was a key sanction for the proposed League of Nations, Wilson admitted the joke was on him.[13]

A more serious dispute arose over Germany's liability to compensate the victors for their damage suffered and expenditure incurred. On 5 January 1918, Lloyd George stated devastation must be repaired but 'This is no demand for a war indemnity such as that imposed on France by Germany in 1871.' Wilson, on 11 February, emphasised there would be 'no contributions, no punitive damages'.[14] The Allied note of 5 November 1918 sent by the American Secretary of State, Robert Lansing, agreeing to make peace based upon Wilson's principles, declared: 'compensation will be made by Germany for all the damage done to the civilian population of the Allies and their property by the aggression of Germany by land, by sea, and from the air.' Lloyd George drafted this with great care, substituting 'aggression' for the original 'invasion of Allied territory' to safeguard British compensation for shipping losses and damage from German sea and air raids, because, as he acknowledged, the note precluded any war costs claim. Was this a sincere acceptance of a limited British claim or a *ruse de guerre* concealing his intention to pursue substantial German contributions?[15]

During the 1918 election, facing an expanded electorate and seeking to revitalise a lacklustre campaign, Lloyd George demanded on 29 November that the Kaiser stand trial for his crimes. He added, on 11 December, 'We propose to demand the whole cost of the war', hinting that Germany's capacity was substantial. Other candidates proposed 'hanging the Kaiser' and squeezing Germany 'as a lemon is squeezed – until the pips squeak'.[16] Of the 707 House of Commons seats, Coalition supporters won 478, Liberals 133, and Labour 10, but significantly there were 335 Conservatives, nearly half new members. They constituted a majority because 73 Sinn Feiners, pledged to an independent Irish republic, refused to take their seats. Walter Long, the Tory First Lord of the Admiralty, predicted: 'George thinks he won the election. Well, he didn't. It was the Tories that won the election, *and he will begin to find that out.*' Both the campaign and the result constituted hostages to fortune.[17]

British Aims

Lloyd George sought a stable Europe enabling Britain to prioritise trade and its imperial role, including a new sphere in the Middle East. Disarmament, beginning with the defeated powers, but becoming universal, would promote peace. Britain should receive as much as possible of any German payments. He intended to prosecute Wilhelm and to extend international law to encompass those responsible for the political and military decisions that had occasioned the war and the manner in which it had been fought. He was sympathetic to reintegrating Russia into international society, but given the confusion of forces vying for control there, this was a distant prospect. German power must be diminished but not destroyed, in order that both Bolshevism and French ambition could be countered. Later, Clemenceau would accuse him of becoming anti-French from the time of the armistice. 'Well' he replied, 'was it not always our traditional policy?'[18]

In London, on 5 January 1918, he had anticipated much of Wilson's Fourteen Points speech, though restricting himself to three: 'First, the sanctity of treaties must be re-established; secondly, a territorial settlement must be secured based on the right of self-determination or the consent of the governed; and, lastly, we must seek by the creation of some international organisation to limit the burden of armaments and diminish the probability of war.'[19]

Peacemaking in Paris

In January 1919, Lloyd George, promoted and self-promoted, as 'the man who won the war', departed for Paris intent on winning the peace. He held a strong hand; Britain's air force was the largest in the world, Germany's capital ships were interned at Scapa Flow, nullifying the main pre-war threat to Britain's naval supremacy, and its submarines rusted in Harwich. Britain's imperial armies had spearheaded the Western Front offensives launched in the summer and autumn of 1918 and were the dominant force in the Middle East where General Allenby's campaign had destroyed Ottoman power. The empire's main external rivals, Russia and Germany, had been eliminated and its other potential competitors – France, Italy and Japan – were allies. In contrast to Wilson's setbacks in the recent American mid-term elections, it appeared that the polls had consolidated Lloyd George's authority.

His personality and skills were great assets. Quick-witted, able to absorb complex briefs rapidly, eloquent and sometimes unscrupulous, he revelled in the quest for solutions to recalcitrant problems. Installed in an apartment on the Rue Nitôt with his secretary, mistress and future second wife Frances Stevenson, he was supported by his political colleagues, notably Balfour, and a team of diplomats and experts from the Foreign Office and other government departments, armed with briefing papers on the many issues the conference might face. At its height the British Delegation numbered over 1,000, including 13-year-old Jessie Spencer, one of the Girl Guides hired as messengers. Housed in the Hotel Majestic, disappointingly fed on Anglo-Swiss cuisine and British coffee, because, for security reasons, the catering staff was recruited from home, this small world became famous for its amateur dramatics and Saturday dances. 'Why' asked Foch, after attending one, 'do the British have such sad faces and cheerful bottoms?' Later negotiations over unreliable Daimler cars, smashed crockery and a staggering £14,000 bill for replacement laundry rivalled the peace talks for obduracy.[20]

Paris, menaced by German forces as late as June 1918, bombed and shelled, and the capital of a country which had suffered substantial devastation and terrible manpower losses, was not a conference location conducive to reconciliation. Once Wilson decided that Switzerland, his and Lloyd George's original preference, was too open to revolutionary influences, there were few alternatives with the capacity to facilitate such a large gathering. It opened in the Quai d'Orsay, the French foreign office, on Saturday 18 January 1919, the anniversary of Bismarck's 1871 declaration of the German Empire in the Hall of Mirrors at Versailles after French defeat in the Franco-Prussian War. Clemenceau emphasised that the positions were now reversed, refusing to forsake his soft felt hat for the formal top hats of the other leaders. Embarrassingly, Lloyd George was late, arriving during Raymond Poincaré's welcoming address, necessitating an apologetic note to the French President, already furious at his exclusion from the real business of peacemaking.[21]

Although there was a nod towards the equality of states in the Plenary Conference in which all the Allies were represented, this met only nine times and the great powers dominated proceedings. The main decision-making body for the first two months was the Council of Ten – Lloyd George, Clemenceau, Orlando and Wilson, their respective foreign ministers, Balfour, Stephen Pichon, Sidney Sonnino and Lansing, and two Japanese diplomats, Prince Saionji and Baron Makino. Its work was hampered by the lack of an agenda – Wilson rejected the only formal French proposal since it relegated the League to the final item and declared his statements too imprecise to form the basis of treaties – and hampered too by the large numbers of advisers milling about – at one meeting there were fifty-five people in the room.

The Ten began hearing the submissions of the smaller powers but soon delegated this and other tasks to fifty-two expert commissions established to bring recommendations to the conference. Uncertainty about the format of peacemaking proved disastrous. The French suggested that the Allies should dictate their terms on frontiers, disarmament and reparations to the defeated powers, only afterwards permitting their participation in consideration of broader international issues, echoing the pattern of 1814–15 when the Congress of Vienna followed the Treaty of Paris with France. This was not agreed and the commissions functioned expecting their recommendations would be negotiated with German representatives. They tended to suggest maximum positions to allow for concessions but, as they struggled to reach agreement, thought of direct negotiations with the Germans was abandoned. Unaltered, the commissions' recommendations became the basis of a draft treaty more severe than many intended. Harold Nicolson, a young British diplomat, was to declare: 'We were never for one instant given to suppose that our recommendations were absolutely final. And thus we tended to accept compromises, and even to support decisions, which we ardently hoped would not, in the last resort, be approved.'[22] The Germans were permitted to make written submissions, which they did in abundance, to little direct effect, though they did encourage British disquiet.

The League of Nations

Wilson insisted the conference's first priority was the League of Nations Covenant. Lloyd George, though not an enthusiast, appointed two strong League supporters – the Conservative politician, Lord Robert Cecil, and the South African Defence Minister and British War Cabinet member, General Jan Smuts – as the British members of Wilson's commission. Preliminary Anglo-American consultation produced the draft proposal which formed the basis of the commission's deliberations and Cecil, as its vice-chairman, worked closely with Wilson. Meeting first on 2 February 1919, they produced the draft Covenant which Wilson presented to the Plenary Peace Conference on 14 February.[23]

The anticipated cornerstone of the new organisation was an automatic obligation to support any member attacked by another before exhausting the League's procedures. Wilson's first draft stated any transgressor would '*ipso facto* [automatically] . . . become at war with all the other members of the League'. His advisers and allies rejected this abrogation of members' sovereignty over such a fundamental decision and his new proposal, which became Article 16, declared any covenant breaker would 'be deemed to have committed an act of war' against the other members. Each state could now determine its own response but this devalued the League as a guarantor of members' security.

Article 10 required members 'to respect and preserve as against external aggression the territorial integrity and existing political independence of all members of the League. . . '. Cecil asked pertinently: 'Yes, but do any of us mean it?' Although Article 16 provided for automatic economic and cultural sanctions against an aggressor, the League could only recommend, not require, members to take military action. Leon Bourgeois, one of the French delegates, argued that 'Without military backing . . . always ready to act, our League . . . will be filed away . . . simply as a rather ornate piece of literature'. Wilson and Cecil preferred moral force – Cecil stated: 'What we rely upon is public opinion . . . and if we are wrong about that, then the whole thing is wrong.' In that context, their resort to the dubious procedural practice of demanding unanimity to thwart the Japanese proposal for a racial equality clause was embarrassing.[24]

Cecil feared that a system which precluded change would endanger the peace it sought to preserve and Wilson and Lloyd George saw the League as a correcting mechanism for the conference's inevitable mistakes. Article 19, which permitted reconsideration of treaties or of 'international conditions whose continuance might endanger the peace of the world', provided room for manoeuvre but also raised awkward questions about its compatibility with Article 10, since many of the disputed new European frontiers were potential threats to peace. Whether some borders were sacrosanct and others open to revision cast further doubt on the League as a provider of security.

The League divided British elite opinion. Lloyd George traded his support as a bargaining counter in his negotiations with Wilson over naval construction. He recognised its electoral appeal, but the League played little part in his post-war efforts to manage the enforcement or revision of the treaties. He was typical of many inter-war British leaders, who disguised their private disbelief for the benefit of an electorate which was offered an impression of whole-hearted support. Others were dismissive. Sir Henry Wilson, the Chief of the Imperial General Staff, thought it 'futile nonsense'. Lord Milner, the Colonial Secretary, declared it 'flapdoodle' and his deputy, Leo Amery, called it 'moonshine'. The diplomat, Lord Eustace Percy, stated that: 'As a matter of cold historical fact [the League] happened because Cecil and Wilson wanted it – and for no other reason!' For James Headlam-Morley, a British expert, the League was integral to the settlement, and he gave it a central role in the solutions he helped to devise to provide minority protection and to reconcile the principle of national self-determination with the conference's decisions over the fate of Danzig and the Saar. Cecil remained committed to his 'great experiment', working tirelessly throughout the inter-war years to make the League effective and to maintain public support.[25]

The Conference in Crisis
By mid-March disputes over reparations, Poland, Fiume, the Saar, the Rhineland, the Middle East and other issues, threatened to stall the conference. The Council of Ten seemed incapable of deciding – only the Covenant and the forfeiture of Germany's colonies had been resolved. The peacemakers feared that their indecision could allow Bolshevism to spread in eastern Europe and were mindful of domestic responsibilities. A new decision-making body and the offer of guarantees proved crucial. Clemenceau, Lloyd George, Orlando and Wilson began meeting, at first with only Paul Mantoux as interpreter, later with the invaluable organisational skills of Maurice Hankey, the British Cabinet Secretary. The Council of Four was bombarded with difficult questions, often in haphazard order; it made mistakes but it decided. Their foreign ministers, and Makino from Japan, became the Council of Five, drafting much of the Austrian and Bulgarian treaties and making territorial recommendations, most of which the Four accepted.

For Clemenceau, who had twice witnessed German invasions, the future security of France was paramount. Aware that its ageing population of 40 million faced 65 million Germans, he sought an Anglo-American peacetime alliance and the diminution, either directly or indirectly, of Germany's capacity for aggression. The two policies did not marry easily. He faced strong pressure from Poincaré and Foch to strip Germany of its territory on the left bank of the Rhine and either annex it to France or establish one or more Rhenish republics. Here, as with his desire to annex the Saar in compensation for the destruction of French coalmines, or to transfer as many German resources as possible to Poland, Denmark and other neighbours, he clashed over the principle of self-determination with Wilson or Lloyd George and frequently both. Suspicious of French annexationist ambitions and anxious to avoid creating 'Alsace-Lorraines in reverse', Lloyd George persuaded Wilson on 14 March to offer Anglo-American guarantees to France against German aggression. Clemenceau, after receiving commitments for a fifteen-year Allied occupation of the Rhineland, its permanent demilitarisation and the right to extend the occupation if Germany did not pay reparations, abandoned demands that Germany surrender the area. The sincerity of either guarantee, or Lloyd George's promise of a Channel tunnel, may be doubted, but, as Wilson's close friend and adviser, Edward House, pointed out, this 'satisfied Clemenceau and we can get on with the real business of the Conference'. The logjam began to ease.[26]

Concerned at the direction matters were taking, Lloyd George gathered his key advisers at Fontainebleau where they produced 'Some Considerations for the Peace Conference before they finally draft their Terms', delivered to Clemenceau, Orlando and Wilson on 25 March.[27] He warned that no matter what restrictions were placed on German power, 'if she feels she has been unjustly treated . . . she will find means of extracting retribution from her conquerors'. He believed 'that as far as is humanly possible the different races should be allocated to their motherlands', that 'the payments of reparations ought to disappear if possible with the generation which made the war' and that Germany must have access to raw materials and markets: 'We cannot both cripple her and expect her to pay.' He feared driving the Germans to despair and revolution, arguing they must 'offer to Germany a peace, which, whilst just, will be preferable for all sensible men to the alternative of Bolshevism'. He advised offering terms 'which a responsible Government in Germany can expect to be able to carry out' hoping this would release Britain from enforcement responsibilities.[28] As Clemenceau swiftly countered, Lloyd George's magnanimity was self-serving: he had secured his key objectives of a share of reparations and destroying German naval, colonial and mercantile power – any concessions would be at others' expense.[29]

Reparations

After six intense weeks of argument, crisis and compromise, the Four handed a draft treaty to the Germans on 7 May, assembled from decisions taken piecemeal on complex problems, without any attempt to review their overall effect. One proved particularly difficult. The American expert, Thomas Lamont, declared: 'The subject of reparations caused more trouble, contention, hard feeling and delay at the Paris Peace Conference than any other point of the Treaty.' No-one doubted that the Central Powers owed compensation, nor that the Allies had need of it. Industrialised warfare had wrought immense damage to the battlefields and invaded territories and the Entente had borrowed heavily from the United States, which expected repayment. Meanwhile, Germany, with its industrial infrastructure undamaged and with no foreign war debts, promised to be a formidable future trade competitor.[30]

Someone – either the defeated enemy or the victorious taxpayers – would have to finance reconstruction. Unsurprisingly, given that consideration, in January 1919 Clemenceau and Lloyd George claimed war costs, despite the pre-Armistice agreement. When, predictably, Wilson resisted vigorously and they remained adamant, a crisis loomed, particularly for Lloyd George. Following unrest amongst government supporters in March, he received, on 8 April 1919, an open telegram from 233 Coalition

MPs demanding he pursue full war costs from Germany. Although on this occasion a bravura performance in the Commons confounded his critics, it was a salutary reminder that his election victory carried a price.[31]

John Foster Dulles, a young American lawyer, resolved the crisis by a suggestion rich in unintended consequences. Article 231, 'the war guilt clause', asserted the moral responsibility of Germany and its allies to reimburse all Allied war expenditure but did not, as Germans chose to believe, assign sole responsibility for the war to Germany. Moreover, Article 232 limited liability to Allied civilian damage. Lloyd George then persuaded Smuts to convince Wilson that pensions paid to widows, injured soldiers or their dependents constituted a legitimate claim because soldiers were merely civilians in uniform. Appreciating that this was not logical, Wilson still conceded because he believed the Allies would agree a fixed sum – a compromise amount covering all Germany's liabilities. Hence his decision would not affect what Germany paid but could give Britain a greater share. No fixed sum was agreed, apparently because Lloyd George's negotiators, Lords Cunliffe and Sumner, irreverently dubbed the 'Heavenly Twins' because they were always together and demanded astronomical sums, refused to abandon exaggerated estimates of what Germany could afford. On 5 April 1919, the decision was postponed for a Reparation Commission to determine in 1921. Lloyd George claimed the Twins had thwarted his policy of a moderate settlement but the reality is that he insisted on the maximum demands, using them as a smokescreen.[32] Indeed, when the British Delegation met on 30 May and 1 June to express its disquiet at the draft treaty, the British Prime Minister suggested a realistic figure might lie between £5,000,000,000 (already close to the maximum acceptable to the Americans) and a massive £11,000,000,000. The Delegation authorised him to specify a fixed sum but he resisted Wilson's attempt to do so and Cecil thought him 'curiously reluctant to make any changes'. Lloyd George's rhetoric spoke of moderation but during and after the conference, whenever his ideas were quantified, the figures belied his words.

In May 1921 the Reparation Commission set Germany's liability at £6,600,000,000 to be paid in A, B and C bonds. The C bonds, which constituted over £4,000,000,000, could, said the Belgian premier, Georges Theunis, be stuck 'in a drawer without bothering to lock up, for no thief would be tempted to steal them'. This was 'phoney money' to satisfy Allied electorates: the real bill was £2,500,000,000, within Anglo-American estimates of Germany's ability to pay – economically, if not politically. Over the coming years reparations would bedevil Anglo-French relations and offer German politicians an excuse for all their shortcomings but the Allies did have a case for compensation, even if their presentation of it were to have been flawed.[33]

National Self-Determination
Lloyd George was perhaps too easily persuaded that Germany should forfeit the Saar, but the expectations raised by the prospect of national self-determination were hard to satisfy. Faced with areas where populations were hopelessly mixed, he sought borders that would alienate as few people as possible and, by providing minority rights for those left on the wrong side of revised frontiers, he hoped to minimise their resentment. With reluctance he backed Italian claims at the conference – as Balfour expressed, 'a treaty is a treaty'. When Orlando demanded Fiume in addition to Wilson's concessions on the Brenner frontier and Adriatic territories, the President was adamant that Yugoslavia

must have the port. Clemenceau and Lloyd George tried to conciliate but failed. Frustrated, Orlando quit the Conference in late April, only to return empty-handed in May – 'fiuming', in one of Wilson's rare jokes. Unresolved in Paris, the issue dragged on until Mussolini annexed Fiume in 1924.[34]

Lloyd George supported an independent Poland but was distinctly unsympathetic to what he deemed its excessive territorial demands, telling the Conservative leader, Andrew Bonar Law, 'I have never cared for the handing over of two or three million Germans to Polish rule'. Wilson's promise to resurrect Poland from territory previously under Austrian, German and Russian rule, with an indisputably Polish population and secure access to the sea, was not easily accomplished. Danzig was the obvious port but its population was German. To link it to the Polish heartland required a 'corridor', inhabited by a mixed population, dividing East Prussia from the rest of Germany. Lloyd George opposed the Polish commission's recommendations assigning Danzig to Poland and delineating the corridor. He persuaded Wilson that making Danzig a free city under League control was the president's idea and he achieved plebiscites resulting in Germany's retention of Marienwerder, Allenstein and, later, a substantial part of Upper Silesia. Germans still regarded the territory lost to Poland as unacceptable and 'the bleeding frontier' constituted a continuing grievance.[35]

Disarmament and War Crimes

The Allied military leaders recommended a German army of 200,000, with volunteer officers and conscripted other ranks. Lloyd George opposed peacetime conscription, proposing that all should be long-term volunteers. Clemenceau accepted, but insisted on a reduction to 100,000 men. Germany had to reach this target by April 1920 and disband its General Staff. Its air force was banned and its once formidable navy, stripped of dreadnoughts and submarines, was limited to 15,000 men. Lloyd George envisaged this as a prelude to universal disarmament but was concerned not to leave Germany vulnerable to Bolshevism nor, *sotto voce*, France unchallenged in Europe.[36]

Lloyd George and Clemenceau favoured arraigning Germany's military and political leaders as a deterrent to future aggression. Wilhelm was a prime target but Lloyd George required all his powers to persuade his Cabinet and international colleagues to try a head of state. Article 227 indicted Wilhelm 'for a supreme offence against international morality and the sanctity of treaties', to be tried by an international criminal court of five Allied judges. In the event the Netherlands, to which he fled, refused to surrender him – though Lloyd George was still pursuing this as late as March 1920. Articles 227 to 231 of the Treaty, the so-called 'shame clauses', caused deep offence to Germany. In June 1919, the German government unsuccessfully tried to make their omission a condition of signing the treaty whilst later attempts to implement them threatened the survival of the Weimar regime.[37]

Conclusion

The coruscating indictment of John Maynard Keynes' brilliant but flawed polemic, *The Economic Consequences of the Peace*, that this was a 'Carthaginian peace' designed to crush Germany as effectively as Rome had destroyed Carthage in 146 BC, has, despite its inaccuracy, continued to colour historical verdicts of the settlement. Reinforced by the recollections of Anglo-American participants, disappointed that Wilson had not fulfilled their expectations, the First World War peace settlement has not enjoyed a sparkling reputation, often being portrayed as setting the course for further global conflict.[38] After the archives of the major powers were opened in the 1960s and 1970s, the increasing, but not universal, scholarly consensus is that the peacemakers made the best of a bad job.[39] Inevitably they made mistakes and left much unresolved, often because, as in the case of Russia, resolution was impossible. For much of 1919 the most likely post-revolutionary outcome seemed the victory of one or more of the White leaders and, even after their defeats that autumn, a Bolshevik triumph was not inevitable. If it were not to have transpired, was coexistence possible?

In tackling their central problem of incorporating Germany into a new order, granting it proper standing without allowing it to overwhelm its neighbours, the peacemakers relied too much on suppositions that the new democratic state would accept defeat, execute the treaty and not seek revenge. It was not a Carthaginian peace, though that could have been a solution – as the American General Mark Clark wryly remarked in 1945 after the bitter Italian campaign, 'We don't seem to get too much trouble from those Carthaginians today' – rather, Versailles was the least severe of the treaties, though this was not the German perception. The peacemakers did not create a traditional settlement based on allocating territory and resources to balance power, though whether the League could nurture stability remained uncertain.

America's abnegation of responsibility for a settlement that its representatives had profoundly influenced, left Britain and France as reluctant guardians of Wilson's orphan, responsible for enforcing a treaty that, left to themselves, they would not have negotiated. As Lloyd George remarked in 1923, 'If I had to go to Paris again I would conclude quite a different treaty.' The British attempt to revise the draft treaty in June had only one significant result, the Upper Silesian plebiscite, but left a legacy of sympathy for German attempts to mitigate the effects of the settlement. The French thought otherwise.[40]

Lloyd George was relatively successful in achieving his short-term aims but failure to cement a firm Anglo-French partnership was a major weakness. His colleagues believed this would guarantee peace but could not agree on whether to offer France an alliance to replace the guarantee that had lapsed with America's refusal to honour its pledge. Some argued this would enable France to be more generous to Germany as Britain wished, others that it would strengthen French recalcitrance. Britain and France each took the view that an alliance was more important to the other and sought too high a price, allowing Germany to exploit their differences. Whether Germany would have accepted any settlement based on the premise of defeat remains doubtful, yet a new major conflict was not inevitable. The legacies of the pre-war period, the war and the settlements, presented challenges but also opportunities for international decision-makers in what need not have been the inter-war years.

Notes

1. George Creel, *The War, the World and Wilson* (Harper, 1920), pp. 161–2.
2. Spencer Di Scala, *The Makers of the Modern World: Vittorio Orlando: Italy* (Haus, 2010), pp. 52–7.
3. T.G. Fraser, Andrew Mango and Robert McNamara, *The Making of the Modern Middle East* (Haus, 2011), pp. 48–70.
4. Ibid., pp. 75–86; Michael Dockrill and Douglas Goold, *Peace Without Promise: Britain and the Peace Conferences 1919-1923* (Batsford, 1981), pp. 137–43.
5. David Lloyd George, *The Truth About the Peace Treaties* 2 vols (Victor Gollancz, 1938), Vol. II, p. 1038.
6. Fraser et al., *Modern Middle East*, pp. 103–94.

7. The United States' declarations of war stated it was an 'Associated Power'. For convenience 'Allied' replaces 'Allied and Associated Powers'.

8. Charles Seymour (ed.), *The Intimate Papers of Colonel House* 4 vols (Ernest Benn Limited, 1928), Vol. IV, p. 167.

9. Robert Gerwarth, *The Vanquished: Why the First World War Failed to End, 1917-1923* (Allen Lane, 2016), pp. 69–117.

10. Zara Steiner, *The Lights That Failed: European International History 1919-1933* (Oxford University Press, 2005); Robert Boyce, *The Great Interwar Crisis and the Collapse of Globalisation* (Palgrave Macmillan, 2009); Patrick Cohrs, *The Unfinished Peace after World War I; America, Britain and the Stabilisation of Europe 1919-1932* (Cambridge University Press, 2006).

11. See Wilson's 1918 speeches in H.W.V. Temperley (ed.), *A History of the Peace Conference of Paris* 6 vols (Oxford University Press, 1920–4), Vol. I, pp. 431–8.

12. Erez Manela, *The Wilsonian Moment: Self-Determination and the International Origins of Anticolonial Nationalism* (Oxford University Press, 2007).

13. Adam Tooze, *The Deluge: The Great War and the Remaking of Global Order, 1916-1931* (Penguin, 2014), pp. 268–9.

14. David Lloyd George, *War Memoirs* 2 vols. (Odhams, 1938), Vol. II, p. 1513; Temperley, *History*, Vol. I, p. 437.

15. Antony Lentin, *Lloyd George and the Lost Peace: From Versailles to Hitler, 1919-1940* (Palgrave Macmillan, 2001), pp. 14–15 and 20.

16. Robert Bunselmeyer, *The Cost of The War 1914-1919: British Economic War Aims and the Origins of Reparation* (Archon, 1975), pp. 124–48 and 154–6; Lentin, *Lloyd George*, pp. 28–9.

17. Bunselmeyer, *Cost of the War*, pp. 146–8; David Butler and Jennie Freeman, *British Political Facts 1900-1967* (Macmillan, 1968), p. 141; Frances Stevenson diary 5.3.19., A.J.P. Taylor (ed.) Frances Stevenson, *Lloyd George: A Diary* (Hutchinson, 1971), p. 169.

18. Lentin, *Lloyd George*, pp. 1–22; Alan Sharp, *The Makers of the Modern World: David Lloyd George: Great Britain* (Haus, 2008), pp. 90–164; Margaret MacMillan, *Peacemakers: The Paris Conference of 1919 and Its Attempt To End War* (John Murray, 2001), pp. 43–57. Georges Clemenceau, *Grandeur and Misery of Victory* (Harrap, 1930), p. 113.

19. Lloyd George, *War Memoirs*, Vol. II, p. 1517.

20. Erik Goldstein, *Winning the Peace: British Diplomatic Strategy, Peace Planning, and the Paris Peace Conference 1916-1920* (Clarendon Press, 1991), pp. 9–119; Sally Marks, 'Behind the Scenes at the Paris Peace Conference of 1919', *Journal of British Studies* Vol. 9, No. 2 (1970), pp. 154–180. MacMillan, *Peacemakers*, p. 158.

21. Esmé Howard, diary 18.1.19, Howard Papers, Cumbria Archive Service, Carlisle; Letter 21.1.19, Lloyd George Papers, Parliamentary Archive, London, F/51/1/6.

22. Harold Nicolson, *Peacemaking, 1919* (Constable, 1933), pp. 128–9.

23. Gaynor Johnson, *Lord Robert Cecil: Politician and Internationalist* (Routledge, 2016), pp. 99–120. Alan Sharp, *The Versailles Settlement: Peacemaking after the First World War, 1919-1923* (2nd edition, Palgrave Macmillan, 2008), pp. 42–67.

24. Ibid., p. 57; Ruth Henig, *The Makers of the Modern World: The League of Nations* (Haus, 2010), pp. 25–53.

25. Peter Yearwood, *Guarantee of Peace: The League of Nations in British Policy, 1914-1925* (Oxford University Press, 2009), pp. 88–137 and *passim*; George Egerton, *Great Britain and the Creation of the League of Nations: Strategy, Politics and International Organization, 1914-1919* (Scolar, 1979), p. 98; Percy to Harold Temperley, 10.11.20, in 'History of the Paris Peace Conference Correspondence 1919' File 16/2a, Royal Institute of International Affairs archives, London; Alan Sharp, 'James Headlam-Morley: Creating International History', *Diplomacy and Statecraft* Vol. 9, No. 8, (1998), pp. 266–83. Johnson, *Cecil*, pp. 121–250.

26. Antony Lentin, 'The Treaty that Never Was: Lloyd George and the Abortive Anglo-French Alliance of 1919' in Judith Loades (ed.), *The Life and Times of David Lloyd George* (Headstart History, 1991), pp. 115–28; Diary 20.3.19, Seymour, *House*, Vol. IV, p. 409.

27. Hankey stated he, Henry Wilson and Philip Kerr believed that 'while every exaction on Germany can be justified on its merits, the accumulation of these will put Germany in an utterly impossible position'. Hankey to Lloyd George, 19.3.19, Lloyd George Papers, F/23/4/39. 'Some Considerations for the Peace Conference before they finally draft their Terms' *Cmd. 2169 Papers Respecting Negotiations for an Anglo-French Pact* (HMSO, 1924), pp. 78–87.

28. Ibid., pp. 79–81.
29. Ibid., pp. 90–3.
30. MacMillan, *Peacemakers* p. 191; Sally Marks commented 'German economic dominance would be tantamount to victory. Reparations would both deny Germany that victory and spread the pain of undoing the damage done', in 'Smoke and Mirrors: In Smoke-Filled Rooms in the Galerie des Glaces' in Manfred Boemeke, Gerald Feldman and Elisabeth Glaser (eds.), *The Treaty of Versailles: A Reassessment after 75 Years* (Cambridge University Press, 1998), p. 338.
31. Lloyd George, *The Truth* Vol. I, pp. 563–77.
32. Sharp, *Versailles Settlement* pp. 90–8; Lentin, *Lost Peace*, pp. 23–46.
33. British Empire Delegation Meetings 32 (30.5.19), 33, and 34 (1.6.19) in Michael Dockrill (ed.), *British Documents on Foreign Affairs: The Paris Peace Conference of 1919* 6 vols (University Press of America, 1989), Vol. 4, pp. 91–116; Antony Lentin, *Guilt at Versailles: Lloyd George and the Pre-History of Appeasement* (Methuen, 1985), p. 96; Sharp, *Versailles Settlement*, pp. 98–108.
34. Sharp, *Versailles Settlement*, pp. 147–52.
35. Ibid., pp. 127–31. Sharp, *Lloyd George*, pp. 112–42.
36. Seth P. Tillman, *Anglo-American Relations at the Paris Peace Conference of 1919* (Princeton University Press, 1961), pp. 166–75; David Stevenson, 'Britain, France and the Origins of German Disarmament, 1916-1919', *Journal of Strategic Studies* Vol. 29, No. 2 (2006), pp. 195–224
37. James Willis, *Prologue to Nuremberg: The Politics and Diplomacy of Punishing War Criminals of the First World War* (Greenwood Press, 1982); Gary Bass, *Stay the Hand of Vengeance: The Politics of War Crimes Tribunals* (Princeton University Press, 2002); Alan Sharp, *Consequences of Peace. The Versailles Settlement: Aftermath and Legacy 1919-2010* (Haus, 2010), pp. 161–9.
38. John Maynard Keynes, *The Economic Consequences of the Peace* (Macmillan, 1919); Nicolson, *Peacemaking*; Robert Lansing, *The Peace Negotiations: A Personal Narrative* (Houghton Mifflin, 1921); Stephen Bonsal, *Unfinished Business* (Michael Joseph, 1944); Agnes Headlam-Morley, R. Bryant and A. Cienciala (eds.), *Sir James Headlam-Morley: A Memoir of the Paris Peace Conference 1919* (Methuen, 1972).
39. Marc Trachtenberg, 'Versailles after Sixty Years', *Journal of Contemporary History* Vol. 17, No. 3 (July 1982), pp. 487–506; 'Introduction' in Boemeke et al., *The Treaty of Versailles*, pp. 11–20; Steiner, *Lights That Failed*, pp. 15–79 and pp. 604–15; Mark Mazower, 'Two Cheers for Versailles', *History Today* 49 (1999); MacMillan, *Peacemakers*; Matthew Hughes and Matthew Seligmann, *Does Peace Lead to War?: Peace Settlements and Conflict in the Modern Age* (Sutton, 2002), pp. 23–45; Alan Sharp, 'The Versailles Settlement: The Start of World War II?' in Frank McDonough (ed.), *The Origins of the Second World War; An International Perspective* (Continuum, 2011), pp. 15–33; Sally Marks, 'Mistakes and Myths: The Allies, Germany and the Versailles Treaty, 1918-1921', *Journal of Modern History* Vol. 85 (September 2013), pp. 632–59. In contrast see Cohrs, *Unfinished Peace*. Neither David Andelman, *A Shattered Peace: Versailles 1919 and the Price We Pay Today* (John Wiley and Sons, 2008), nor Norman Graebner and Edward Bennett, *The Versailles Treaty and Its Legacy: The Failure of the Wilsonian Vision* (Cambridge University Press, 2011), show much awareness of recent scholarship.
40. Lord Hardinge of Penshurst, *Old Diplomacy* (John Murray, 1947), p. 240. Lentin, *Lloyd George*, pp. 67–88.

Suggested Further Reading

Gerwarth, Robert, *The Vanquished: Why the First World War Failed to End, 1917-1923* (Allen Lane, 2016)

Goldstein, Erik, *Winning the Peace: British Diplomatic Strategy, Peace Planning, and the Paris Peace Conference 1916-1920* (Clarendon Press, 1991)

Keynes, John Maynard, *The Economic Consequences of the Peace* (Macmillan, 1919)

Lentin, Antony, *Lloyd George and the Lost Peace: From Versailles to Hitler, 1919-1940* (Palgrave Macmillan, 2001)

MacMillan, Margaret, *Peacemakers: The Paris Conference of 1919 and Its Attempt To End War* (John Murray, 2001)

Marks, Sally, *The Ebbing of European Ascendancy: An International History of the World, 1914-1945* (Arnold, 2002)

Nicolson, Harold, *Peacemaking, 1919* (Constable, 1933)

Sharp, Alan, *The Versailles Settlement: Peacemaking after the First World War, 1919-1923* (2nd edition, Palgrave Macmillan, 2008)

Steiner, Zara, *The Lights That Failed: European International History 1919-1933* (Oxford University Press, 2005)

Tooze, Adam, *The Deluge: The Great War and the Remaking of Global Order, 1916-1931* (Penguin, 2014)

Notes on Contributors

Holger Afflerbach is Professor of Central European History at the University of Leeds. He specialises in late nineteenth and twentieth century German history; Austrian and Italian history, international relations, military history and in particular the two world wars.

Among his publications are a biography of Erich von Falkenhayn, a study of the Triple Alliance, a book on the history of the Atlantic Ocean, and an edition of sources from the German Headquarters in the First World War. He edited in 2012 with Hew Strachan, a volume on *The History of Surrender* and single-authored a book on surrender in 2013, *Die Kunst der Niederlage*.

In 2012/13 Holger was a Fellow of the *Historische Kolleg*, Munich, and in 2014/15 a member of the Institute for Advanced Study at Princeton. He is currently working on a history of German political and military strategies during the First World War.

Phylomena Badsey is a Visiting Lecturer at the University of Wolverhampton specializing in women and warfare. Dr Badsey is a frequent speaker for the Western Front Association, and has recently been appointed the Association's University officer.

Phylomena has written a chapter on the topic of 'Queen Alexandra's Royal Naval Nursing Service and Reserve Nurses and Care-giving at Gallipoli' for *Gallipoli: New Perspectives on the Mediterranean Expeditionary Force 1915-16* edited by Michael LeCicero and Rhys Crawley (Helion & Company Limited, 2017) and was a contributor to Gary Sheffield's book, *The First World War in 100 Objects* (Andre Deutsch, 2013). In 2012, she wrote a chapter on 'Vera Brittain as a War Reporter, 1939-45', for *War, Journalism and History – War Correspondents in the Two World Wars*, edited by Yvonne McEwen and Fiona A. Fisken (Peter Lang, 2012).

Niall Barr is Professor of Military History at the Defence Studies Department, King's College, London, based at the Joint Services Command and Staff College, Defence Academy UK. Educated at the University of St Andrews, he has previously taught at St Andrews and the Royal Military Academy, Sandhurst. He joined the Staff College in 2000, where he teaches on a wide range of military courses and conducts numerous staff rides. He has supported the Higher Command and Staff Course as the Land Warfare Historian for many years.

His main research interest concerns the fighting methods of the British Army in the twentieth century but he also has an enduring interest in the Scottish military tradition, having, for example, published a book on Flodden. With J.P. Harris, Niall wrote, *Amiens to the Armistice: the BEF in the Hundred Days Campaign, 8 August-11 November 1918*. His most recent major work, *Yanks and Limeys: Alliance Warfare in the Second World War*, was published by Jonathan Cape Ltd in 2015.

Chris Bellamy is Professor Emeritus of Maritime Security at the University of Greenwich, was Director of the Greenwich Maritime Institute from 2010 to 2014 and before that Director of the Security Studies Institute, Cranfield University, an Academic Provider to the Defence Academy of the United Kingdom. Previous to this, he had been Defence Correspondent of *The Independent* and *The Independent on Sunday* newspapers reporting on the 1991 Gulf War, the ensuing Kurdish refugee crisis, from Bosnia, 1991 to 1996, and from Chechnya and the Russian campaign there, in 1995.

Having read Modern History at Oxford and serving as a junior officer in the Royal Artillery, he obtained a Distinction in the MA in War Studies at King's College, London. Chris also gained an honours degree in Russian, studying part-time at the Polytechnic of Central London, now the University of Westminster. After seven years as a civil servant in the Ministry of Defence, where he worked for the Royal Navy and RAF, he moved to Edinburgh where he gained his PhD on The Russian and Soviet View of Future War under Professor John Erickson in 1991.

His major publications include being Associate Editor of the *Oxford Companion to Military History* (OUP, 2001) and *Absolute War: Soviet Russia in the Second World War* (Pan Macmillan, 2007). The latter has been translated into several languages and won the 2008 Westminster Medal for Military Literature. His book, *The Evolution of Modern Land Warfare: Theory and Practice* (Routledge, 1990) has recently been republished.

Nick Bosanquet is Emeritus Professor of Health Policy, Imperial College, London. Nick developed an interest in the Great War through research into health services in the 1914–18 years which led to a chapter on: 'Health Systems in Khaki: The British and American Medical Experience' in Hugh Cecil's and Peter Liddle's *Facing Armageddon* (1996 and 2016). He wrote *Our Land at War: Britain's Key First World War Sites*, published in 2014 and contributed a chapter entitled 'A Teenage War: British Youngsters and the Great War' to *Britain and the Widening War. 1915-1916*, edited by Peter Liddle *(*2016).

Peter Burness retired from the Australian War Memorial at the end of 2016 after forty-three years' service as a curator and senior historian. In these capacities he contributed to numerous permanent, travelling and temporary exhibitions. With a special interest in the First World War, he has written books and contributed to military history conferences and journals; he was a regular writer for the Memorial's journal *Wartime*.

For twenty years Peter led annual tours and accompanied specialist study groups to the Western Front. Throughout much of his career he was also a member of the Armed Forces Working Party for the Australian Dictionary of Biography and wrote over twenty entries for the dictionary. In 2010 he was appointed Inaugural Lambert Gallipoli Fellow and in 2015 was made a Fellow of the Australian War Memorial. He remains involved in a number of activities marking the Centenary of the First World War.

George H. Cassar obtained his PhD from McGill University and has been teaching for over half a century at Eastern Michigan University where he is a professor of military and modern European history.

Professor Cassar's many books include studies of Asquith, Kitchener and Lloyd George during the Great War, *Trial By Gas: The British Army at the Second Battle of Ypres* (2014) and *Kitchener as Proconsul in Egypt, 1911-1914* (2016). Having published work on the French at the Dardanelles in 1915, he is currently working on a fuller and more up-to-date consideration of this subject.

Tim Cook is an historian at the Canadian War Museum. He was the curator for the museum's First World War permanent gallery, and he has curated numerous temporary, travelling and digital exhibitions. Tim has written eleven books, winning literary awards including, twice, the C.P. Stacey Prize for Military History and the Ottawa Book Award. His most recent publication is *Vimy: The Battle and the Legend* (2017), which was a national best-seller.

In 2012, Dr Cook was awarded the Queen's Diamond Jubilee Medal for his contributions to Canadian history and in 2013 he received the Governor General's History Award. Dr Cook is a Member of the Order of Canada.

Irene Guerrini of the Library, the University of Genoa, has published essays on Italian popular writing during the twentieth century and on the 'organisation of consent' from 1915 to 1945. Dr Guerrini has devoted many years to the study of Italian military justice during the First World War. This research, with Marco Pluviano, led to the publication of books in 2004 and 2007. Previously she had also written with Marco, a biography of the famous Italian fighter pilot, Francesco Baracca.

Irene is a member of the Italian Society for the Study of Contemporary History (SISSCo) and of the *Collectif de Recherche International et Débat sur la Guerre de 1914-1918* (CRID 14-18).

Clive Harris served in the Royal Corps of Signals between 1985 and 1991, ending his military career at the Signals Wing RMA Sandhurst. He is a co-owner of the battlefield tour companies 'Battle Honours' and 'Staffride' and has a lifelong interest in the Great War. He has written three books, *The Greater Game – Sporting Icons Who Fell in the Great War* (2005), *Walking the London Blitz* (2001) and *A Wander Through Wartime London* (2009) and has contributed to other publications, notably *1914: Britain Goes to War*, edited by Peter Liddle (2015).

As a battlefield guide he has led hundreds of groups the length of the Western Front, Gallipoli, Salonika, Palestine and the Italian Front. He has lectured widely in the UK and at The National World War One Museum, in Kansas City in the United States. Clive has considerable experience of TV contributions and consultancy and in 2016 was on the advisory panel to the Department of Culture Media and Sport for the Somme 100 Commemorations. He achieved the Guild of Battlefield Guides Badge in 2007 and has recently been awarded a Master's Degree at the University of Wolverhampton, studying Britain and the Great War. He is a member of the British Commission for Military History.

Rob Johnson is the Director of the Oxford Changing Character of War Programme at Oxford University. This programme (www.ccw.ox.ac.uk) brings together academics, policy makers and armed forces professionals in the study of war, pursuing a variety of research themes including the future character of war, war and the state in a connected world, non-state warfare, strategy and war, and the moral-legal dimensions of war. Dr Johnson's primary research interests are in the history of strategy and war, and their contemporary applications.

A former British army officer, he is the author of *The Great War and the Middle East* (Oxford University Press, 2016) as well as several other works on conflicts in the Middle East, Asia and Europe. He has examined strategic decision-making in a variety of contexts and publications, and draws attention to the local perspectives as well as the difficulties of making strategy based on a selective reading of history.

Kate Kennedy has held a Research Fellowship at Girton College, Cambridge, a Leverhulme Early Career Fellowship at the English Faculty, Cambridge, and is the Weinrebe Research Fellow in Life-writing at Wolfson College, Oxford, and Deputy Director of the Oxford Centre for Life-writing. Dr Kennedy lectures in both Music and English, and specialises in interdisciplinary biography. Her biography *Dweller in Shadows: Ivor Gurney, poet, composer* will be published by Princeton University Press in 2018, and she is currently working on a triple biography of Rupert Brooke and composers F.S. Kelly and William Denis Browne, to be entitled *The Fateful Voyage*. She has published widely on British composers and writers in the early twentieth century, co-editing *The Silent Morning: Culture and Memory after the Armistice* (Manchester University Press, 2013) and *The First World War: Literature, Music, Memory* (Routledge, 2011) and contributing numerous chapters for books and journal articles. She is the editor of *Literary Britten*, a compendium of scholarship on Benjamin Britten's use of text, to be published by Boydell and Brewer in 2017.

Both her biographies have been featured on BBC Radio 3, and she is a regular broadcaster and academic consultant to the BBC, directing the commemorations for the First World War and for International Women's Day for Radio 3, among other projects. She is particularly interested in developing biographical research as performance: her opera libretto, 'Out of the Ruins', was a Royal Opera House commission in 2014, and her dramatized recitals for singer, pianist and actor have been performed in Literary and Music Festivals across the UK, and commissioned by the Wigmore Hall and Southbank Centre.

Ross A. Kennedy is a professor of American history at Illinois State University. He is the author of *The Will to Believe: Woodrow Wilson, World War I, and America's Strategy for Peace and Security* (Kent State, 2009), which won the Scott Bills Prize in Peace History. He also edited *A Companion to Woodrow Wilson* (Wiley-Blackwell, 2013) and has written extensively on American domestic politics and foreign policy during the First World War.

Professor Kennedy's current project, entitled *The United States and the Origins of World War II*, analyses how the policies of the United States contributed to the structure of Great Power politics from 1918 to 1939.

William Philpott is Professor of the History of Warfare at King's College London. A historian of Anglo-French relations and the British and French armies in the First World War, his publications include *Anglo-French Relations and Strategy on the Western Front* (1996), *Bloody Victory: The Sacrifice on the Somme and the Making of the Twentieth*

Century (2009) and *Attrition: Fighting the First World War* (2014). He is currently co-editing a study of France's First World War commanders which will be published by Pen and Sword in 2018.

Bill Philpott is a councillor of the National Army Museum and a former Secretary General of the British Commission for Military History.

Marco Pluviano is a member of the Italian Society for the Study of Contemporary History (SISSCo) and works in conjunction with the historical museum of Trento. He has published widely in the area of soldier welfare and worker compliance in the First World War and on the Italian people under Fascism. Dr Pluviano's book, jointly written with Irene Guerrini, on the celebrated Italian fighter pilot, Francesco Baracca, was published in 2000. In 2004 and in 2007 he worked with Irene to produce two books on Italian military justice during the Great War.

Marco is also a member of the *Collectif de Recherche International et Débat sur la Guerre de 1914-1918* (CRID 14-18).

Chris Pugsley is a freelance historian and an authority on New Zealand at war. He has authored/edited nineteen books. His first book, *Gallipoli: The New Zealand Story* is in its fifth edition (Oratia Books, 2016). Also in print are *The ANZAC Experience* (Oratia Books, 2016), *A Bloody Road Home* (Penguin, 2014) and *Remembering Gallipoli* (Victoria University Press, 2015).

A former Senior Lecturer in War Studies at the Royal Military Academy Sandhurst, Dr Pugsley is an Adjunct Professor in the School of Humanities, University of Canterbury, New Zealand; a Distinguished Alumni of the University of Waikato and a Fellow of the Royal Historical Society. He is a Vice President of the Western Front Association and was appointed an officer in the New Zealand Order of Merit in the 2015 New Year's Honours List.

Duncan Redford is a former Royal Naval officer, has held a senior post at the National Museum of the Royal Navy and was an Honorary Senior Research Fellow at the University of Portsmouth. As a naval historian, Duncan specialises in the history of the Royal Navy since the late Victorian period. His books include *Submarine: a cultural history from the Great War to Nuclear Combat* and *A History of the Royal Navy: World War 2*. He is currently researching the relationship between the Royal Navy and British National Identity.

Matthew Richardson is Curator of Social History at Manx National Heritage, Douglas, Isle of Man, a post which involves the care and interpretation of a diverse range of collections relating to the history of the Island. He has produced a number of highly regarded exhibitions in recent years, notably several reflecting the Island's strong association with motorcycle racing through the famous TT races, and he is currently engaged in developing a new permanent gallery, exploring the involvement of the Manx people in conflict, from the 1750s to the twenty-first century.

His abiding interest – and the stimulus for much of his research – is the First and Second World Wars as experienced by ordinary people, particularly in the British Isles. An early formative post was as assistant to Dr Peter Liddle in the Liddle Collection at the University of Leeds. He has published a number of books on the history of the Royal Leicestershire Regiment and in recent years has turned his attention to the home front in the First World War, with *Leicester in the Great War*, published in 2014, and *The Hunger War* (2015).

Alan Sharp is Emeritus Professor of International History at Ulster University from which he retired as Provost of its Coleraine campus in 2009. His books include *David Lloyd George: Great Britain* (2008); and *Consequences of Peace, The Versailles Settlement: Aftermath and Legacy 1919-2010* (2010) in the 32-volume Haus, Makers of the Modern World series on the major peacemakers in Paris, of which he was the general editor. In 2014 he edited and contributed to *28 June: Sarajevo 1914 – Versailles 1919, The War and Peace that made the Modern World* (Haus).

Yigal Sheffy is Associate Professor of History at Tel Aviv University and Tel-Hai College, Israel. Having retired from the Israeli Defense Forces (IDF) with the rank of Colonel, Yigal teaches and studies the military history of the modern Middle East, especially during the years of the Great War. He also runs a programme of intelligence studies.

Among his recent books are *Early Warning Countdown: The Rotem Affair and the Israeli Security Perception 1957-1960* (2008, in Hebrew), *Palestine and World War I* (2014, with Eran Dolev and Haim Goren), and *To Conquer Haifa: British Intelligence Tours in Palestine in the Early 20th Century* (forthcoming, in Hebrew). His current research is designed to lead to the publication of a book on British amphibious planning in the eastern Mediterranean prior to the First World War.

Jack Sheldon, who retired from the British Army in 2003, is a graduate of the *Bundeswehr* Command and Staff College in Hamburg and served for many years in Germany. Dr Sheldon's retirement has been devoted to researching and writing about the German Army on the Western Front 1914–1918. His published work includes eight books on the subject and he is currently preparing a ninth volume concerning the closing months of the war.

Edward Spiers was born and educated in Edinburgh, He served for forty-one years in the School of History, the University of Leeds, holding senior administrative posts in the field of Humanities Research.

Professor Spiers has written eighteen books and numerous articles and chapters on military history and strategic studies. Among his recent works are *A History of Chemical and Biological Weapons* (2010), which appeared as a Japanese edition in 2012; the co-edited *A Military History of Scotland* (2012), which was awarded the Saltire prize for the best book on Scottish history (2012) and the Templer Medal from the Society for Army Historical Research in 2012; and *Engines for Empire: The Victorian Army and its use of railways* (2014).

David Welch is Emeritus Professor of Modern History and Director of the Centre for the Study of War, Propaganda and Society, at the University of Kent. His main research interest is in twentieth-century political propaganda. His work previous to this has been in the area of late nineteenth and twentieth-century German history, focusing on the relationship between public opinion, politics and propaganda in German society. His publications include *The Third Reich: Politics and Propaganda* (Routledge, revised second edition, 2002), *Propaganda and the German Cinema, 1933-1945* (I.B. Tauris, 2001), *Propaganda and Mass Persuasion: Justifying War: Propaganda, Politics and the Modern Age* [with Jo Fox] (Palgrave, 2012), *Germany and Propaganda in World War I: Pacifism, Mobilisation and Total War* (I.B. Tauris, 2014).

In 2013, he co-curated the exhibition on propaganda and persuasion at the British Library and authored the book that accompanied the exhibition, *Propaganda. Power and Persuasion* (British Library/Chicago University Press, 2013). His latest book is *Persuading the People. British Propaganda in World War II* (British Library, 2016) and in 2017 ABC Clio will be publishing *World War II Propaganda. Analysing the Art of Persuasion during Wartime*.

Ian Whitehead is a Senior Lecturer in History and Deputy Head of Humanities at the University of Derby. His teaching interests lie in modern British history, the history of twentieth century warfare and the history of medicine. Dr Whitehead is the author of *Doctors in the Great War*, published by Pen and Sword in 1999 and has contributed chapters to Hugh Cecil's and Peter Liddle's edited *Facing Armageddon* (Pen and Sword 1996, 2016), Peter Liddle's edited *Passchendaele in Perspective* (Pen and Sword 1998) and Roger Cooter's *Medicine and Modern Warfare* (1998). He co-edited, with John Bourne and Peter Liddle, two volumes comparing the international experiences of the world wars: *The Great World War, 1914-1945: Lightning Strikes Twice* (2000) and *The Great World War, 1914-1945: Who Won? Who Lost?* (2001).

Editor
Peter Liddle for nearly fifty years has been concerned with the study of the First World War. His work in rescuing personal experience evidence of the war led to the establishment of the Liddle Collection in the Brotherton Library, University of Leeds, which documents the wartime experience of some four and a half thousand individuals by original letters, diaries, photographs, art work, artefacts and recollections.

Peter has written and edited numerous books on the Great War including volumes on Gallipoli, the Third Battle of Ypres, the Armistice and a collection of his interviews with men and women who had striking war experience. His most recent book, apart from the edited *Britain and the Widening War*, is *The 1916 Battle of the Somme Reconsidered* (Pen and Sword, 2016).

Dr Liddle was the Founder/Director of the Second World War Experience Centre in Walton near Wetherby, North Yorkshire, which documents the wartime experience of approximately 10,000 individuals. He is Life President of the Centre.

Index

The prime but not exclusive focus of this index is on locations, events, political and military leaders, people mentioned in the chapters, and issues related to 1918 and into 1919. In the main, ranks, titles, posts held, are given as for those same dates.